Positive Psychology

Third Edition

To Parrish, you fill my days with laughter and adventure.

And to Alli, you put the positive in my life.

—SJL

To my children, Ben, Cate, and Chloe,

who teach me every day about hope, optimism, and love of life.

And to Brian, for everything.

—JTP

And, as always, to the memory of C. R. Snyder (December 26, 1944–January 17, 2006),

an uncommonly good man who dedicated his life to making better lives possible for other people.

Positive Psychology

The Scientific and Practical
Explorations of Human Strengths

Third Edition

Shane J. Lopez
Gallup/Clifton Strengths School

Jennifer Teramoto Pedrotti
California Polytechnic State University, San Luis Obispo

C. R. Snyder
University of Kansas, Lawrence

Los Angeles | London | New Delhi
Singapore | Washington DC

Los Angeles | London | New Delhi
Singapore | Washington DC

FOR INFORMATION:

SAGE Publications, Inc.
2455 Teller Road
Thousand Oaks, California 91320
E-mail: order@sagepub.com

SAGE Publications Ltd.
1 Oliver's Yard
55 City Road
London EC1Y 1SP
United Kingdom

SAGE Publications India Pvt. Ltd.
B 1/I 1 Mohan Cooperative Industrial Area
Mathura Road, New Delhi 110 044
India

SAGE Publications Asia-Pacific Pte. Ltd.
3 Church Street
#10-04 Samsung Hub
Singapore 049483

Copyright © 2015 by SAGE Publications, Inc.

Printed in the United States of America

A catalog record of this book is available from the Library of Congress.

ISBN 978-1-4522-7643-4

This book is printed on acid-free paper.

Acquisitions Editor: Reid Hester
Editorial Assistant: Lucy Berbeo
Production Editor: Libby Larson
Copy Editor: Shannon Kelly
Typesetter: C&M Digitals (P) Ltd.
Proofreader: Dennis Webb
Indexer: Karen Wiley
Cover Designer: Candice Harmon
Marketing Manager: Shari Countryman

15 16 17 18 10 9 8 7 6 5 4 3 2

Brief Contents

Detailed Contents

9 Wisdom and Courage: Characteristics of the Wise and the Brave 223

10 Mindfulness, Flow, and Spirituality: In Search of Optimal Experiences   261

14   Preventing the Bad and Promoting the Good   377

Preface

For many of you, this is your first educational foray into the field of positive psychology. We are privileged to introduce you to this work. If your life is in some small way improved by reading the following pages, it will have made our efforts more than worthwhile.

In these pages, we introduce you to the growing field of positive psychology. We have borrowed from the therapy and research efforts of many outstanding psychologists, and we thank them for their pioneering contributions. So, too, do we thank our clients, our students, and our colleagues (Brian Cole, Lisa Edwards, Lindsey Hammond, Zachary Kasow, Molly Lowe, Jeana Magyar-Moe, Phil McKnight, Kristin Rasmussen, Ryan Reed, Melinda Roberts, and Brian Werter) who assisted on this project. Over the years, they have taught us as much about positive psychology as we have taught them. Much gratitude also goes to those folks who believed that college students needed a real positive psychology textbook. Our marvelous editor, Reid Hester at SAGE, and our supportive agents, Neil Salkind and Stacey Czarnowski, all thought the world would be a better place if students continued to learn about positive psychology.

We have sampled the various areas of positive psychology and have included exercises to help you to experience many of these new concepts. In Part I, titled "Looking at Psychology From a Positive Perspective," we group three chapters together. We begin with Chapter 1 ("Welcome to Positive Psychology") and introduce you to the field. In Chapter 2, we explore the Eastern and Western backgrounds of the field and ideas about blending our ME and WE styles. Next, in Chapter 3 ("Classifications and Measures of Strengths and Positive Outcomes"), we explain the attempts to categorize various topics in the field.

In Part II, titled "Positive Psychology in Context," we discuss the roles of emotions in a positive life. In Chapter 4 ("The Role of Culture in Developing Strengths and Living Well"), we examine the role of cultural factors in determining what is positive. In Chapter 5 ("Living Well at Every Stage of Life"), we trace the development of human strengths.

Part III, "Positive Emotional States and Processes," is comprised of two chapters. In Chapter 6, "The Principles of Pleasure: Understanding Positive Affect, Positive Emotions, Happiness, and Well-Being," we discuss what has been learned about emotions and happiness. And in Chapter 7, "Making the Most of Emotional Experiences: Emotion-Focused Coping, Emotional Intelligence, Socioemotional Selectivity, and Emotional Storytelling," we reveal recent findings on how emotions can contribute positively to effective coping in life.

Part IV, "Positive Cognitive States and Processes," contains three chapters. Chapter 8 ("Seeing Our Futures Through Self-Efficacy, Optimism, and Hope") covers the most powerful positive cognitive and motivational states. Then, in Chapter 9 ("Wisdom and Courage: Characteristics of the Wise and the Brave"), we introduce findings about people at their best under sometimes difficult circumstances. And in Chapter 10 ("Mindfulness, Flow, and Spirituality: In Search of Optimal Experiences"), we detail the latest findings on the power of mental processes in relation to self and higher forces.

Part V is titled "Prosocial Behavior." In this portion of the book, we examine interpersonal matters. In Chapter 11 ("Empathy and Egotism: Portals to Altruism, Gratitude, and Forgiveness") and Chapter 12 ("Attachment, Love, and Flourishing Relationships"), we show how human ties improve the quality of life.

In Part VI, "Understanding and Changing Human Behavior," we give insights into improving one's life in Chapter 13 ("Balanced Conceptualizations of Mental Health and Behavior") and Chapter 14 ("Preventing the Bad and Promoting the Good").

In Part VII, "Positive Environments," we describe how school and work (Chapter 15, "Positive Schooling and Good Work: The Psychology of Gainful Employment and the Education That Gets Us There") work together to contribute to a more productive, happier life.

Finally, in Part VIII, "The Future of Positive Psychology: A Conversation Between the Authors" we provide a conversation between the two of us to share our visions of the future direction of the field of positive psychology (Chapter 16, "The Future of Positive Psychology: A Conversation Between the Authors").

WHAT'S NEW IN THIS EDITION

- New examples and reflections on current events throughout the text make information more relevant to our current times. For example, we look at research and statistics regarding the effects of the poor economy on rates of volunteerism and new applications of resilience, optimism, and other constructs regarding dealing with job loss and coping with family members who are away at war.

- Personal Mini-Experiments and Life Enhancement Strategies have been updated in many chapters to help students broaden and enhance their inherent strengths.

Additional revisions and updates incorporated throughout the text include the following:

- Broader definition of culture explained throughout the text, with special consideration given to facets such as race, ethnicity, sexual orientation, generation, nation of origin, socioeconomic status, and gender, among others

- Discussion of culture as a contextualizing factor in the manifestation of strengths

- New research on the benefits of using emotion-focused coping in dealing with the effects of discrimination and racism

- New research suggesting that older adults may provide all age groups with more insights and strategies on how to strive for a more emotionally rich life

- New research elucidating the relationships between the concept of hope and other positive constructs in a variety of groups

- Updates on new research regarding gender differences in wisdom

- Discussion of new facets within the construct of courage, such as the inclusion of a new subcategory of the construct of courage called "civil courage"

- New applications of mindfulness in a variety of populations

Throughout the book, you will hear stories from and about Rick Snyder, often referenced as CRS. Rick (1944–2006) was the hopeful force behind the first edition of this book, and we honor his contributions by keeping his voice alive throughout the text. Thank you for honoring his memory by reading this book.

—S. J. L.
Lawrence, Kansas

—J. T. P.
San Luis Obispo, California

Remembering C. R. Snyder's Legacy of Hope

This edition of *Positive Psychology* is dedicated to C. R. "Rick" Snyder, who died on January 17, 2006. As I write this dedication, I am reminded of his memorial, held on the beautiful campus of the University of Kansas, Rick's professional home for 34 years. In fact, the hall where we gathered stood only a few thousand feet from both Rick's academic home, Fraser Hall, and his beloved family home, a beautiful white colonial where he and his wife, Becky, welcomed friends, students, and colleagues. Stories about Rick's professional and personal exploits—often downright hilarious—flowed between family, friends, students, and colleagues. We were a crowd sharing funny memories, giggling through sobs, and honoring Rick for his public and private contributions to psychology, society, and our lives.

The memorial service was moving and appropriately understated, as Rick was no fan of pomp or piety. Perhaps this is why he continually tried to teach the importance of having fun and the quiet dignity of maintaining our humility. Rick loved to say, "If you can't laugh at yourself, you have missed the biggest joke of all." He practiced what he preached; he laughed at his own gaffes just about daily. Through his own quirky behavior, Rick made it safe to say, "I don't know" and "I messed up," and, of course, he never let me take myself too seriously. Most importantly, he made me laugh, all the time. Whether Rick was dive-bombing me during a research meeting with one of the model planes in his office or breaking campus rules and a few laws by driving my wife's scooter across hallowed ground and squealing "Wheeee!" as he did it, that lovely man cracked me up.

During the memorial, colleagues remembered Rick as both King Midas and a working stiff. Both descriptions are apt. One of my favorite memories captures both facets of Rick. In 2000, Rick, along with several other leading contemporaries in positive psychology, appeared on a two-hour *Good Morning America* special dedicated to sharing the social science on the good life. Rick chose to conduct a live experiment to demonstrate hope theory in action. So, on national network television, Rick had three of the cast members—the host, the medical expert, and the weather guy—participate in the cold pressor task, dunking their right fists to the bottom of a tank of freezing water for as long as they could stand it. After a short time, the weather guy removed his hand and shook some life back into it. A battle of wills ensued between the host and the medical expert, and, as the segment was ending so the show could go to commercial, the medical expert had finally had enough. The host, seemingly oblivious to the pain, vowed to keep his hand in the freezing water through the break. Upon returning from the commercial, the host asked Rick what the cold pressor task had to do with hope. Rick calmly detailed for the audience the basics of hope theory and the connection between hope and pain tolerance. He then revealed that the cast members had taken the hope scale prior to the show and that the ranking of their scores had accurately predicted how long each would be able to withstand the numbing pain of the cold water before calling it quits. To a casual observer, his results might have been viewed as "lucky," and to Rick's friends, this might have been construed as more evidence of his Midas touch. But I believe the success of his live national demonstration was attributable to the "working stiff" mentality that Rick had for his research. His passion for his work led him to spend thousands of hours in his "Hope Lab," and his hard work resulted in a deep understanding of how hope manifested in daily life. This allowed the award-winning teacher in Rick to take a risk to show an audience of millions one of the many ways hope manifests itself in their lives.

Unfortunately, Rick had an intimate knowledge of the relationship between hope and pain tolerance beyond what he learned through his scholarly work. Unbeknownst to many colleagues and students, Rick suffered from chronic, nearly debilitating chest and abdominal pain for the last 15 years of his life. The origin of the pain was never determined, and risky surgeries and aggressive treatments did little to curb his burning, daily hurt. Nevertheless, Rick coped. And coped. And coped. Even when diagnosed with transitional cell cancer in late December 2005 (which was seemingly unrelated to his chronic illness), he coped as best he could, with Becky by his side the whole time.

Rick Snyder's scholarship demystified the concepts of excuse making, forgiveness, and hope for the world. The work he left behind shows us how to disconnect from past negative experiences through excuse making, how to free ourselves for future possibilities through forgiveness, and how to connect to positive future opportunities through hope. Along the way, Rick used his time to teach scores of us how to love and be loved, how to laugh at ourselves, how to work with passion, and how to cope. He taught me and many others how to be better people. I believe I speak for many when I say that, although I miss him terribly and every day I still wish I could talk to him, Rick's legacy in my life will be hope for our journey. His wise and loving lessons will carry me through challenges and adventures that I don't even know are coming, to the very last day of my own life. *This* is the hopeful legacy of a great teacher and a truly good man.

—S. J. L.
Lawrence, Kansas

Acknowledgments

The authors and SAGE gratefully acknowledge the contributions of the following reviewers:

Meaghan N. Altman, University of California Merced

Dana S. Dunn, Moravian College

Amy L. Baltzell, Boston University

James McGowan, Adelphi University

Thane M. Erickson, Seattle Pacific University

About the Authors

Shane J. Lopez, Ph.D., is a Gallup Senior Scientist and Research Director of the Clifton Strengths Institute. Dr. Lopez has published more than 100 articles and chapters and 10 books in addition to *Positive Psychology: The Scientific and Practical Explorations of Human Strengths*. These include *Making Hope Happen,* his first trade book; *The Oxford Handbook of Positive Psychology* (with C. R. Snyder); *Positive Psychological Assessment: A Handbook of Models and Measures* (with C. R. Snyder); *Positive Psychology: Exploring the Best in People; The Encyclopedia of Positive Psychology; and The Psychology of Courage: Modern Research on an Ancient Virtue* (with Cynthia Pury). Dr. Lopez is a Fellow of the American Psychological Association and of the International Positive Psychology Association. A professor of education for a decade, he is now professor of business at the University of Kansas.

Jennifer Teramoto Pedrotti, Ph.D., is Professor in the Department of Psychology and Child Development at California Polytechnic State University, San Luis Obispo, where she has been teaching positive psychology with a multicultural focus for over 10 years. She is the lead editor on a new volume titled *Perspectives on the Intersection of Multiculturalism and Positive Psychology* (with Lisa M. Edwards), and recently spoke on the topic of including cultural context in positive psychological discussions as a keynote speaker at the Asian Pacific Conference on Applied Positive Psychology in Hong Kong. Dr. Teramoto Pedrotti has contributed to many different volumes throughout her career such as *The Oxford Handbook of Positive Psychology, Positive Psychological Interventions, Activities for Teaching Positive Psychology,* and the *Handbook of Multicultural Counseling*. In addition, her work has appeared in multiple journals including the *Journal of Counseling Psychology, the Journal of Positive Psychology, Professional Psychology: Research and Practice,* and *Professional School Counseling*. As a Diversity and Inclusivity Faculty Mentor on her campus, she works with students daily in culturally competent ways to identify and enhance their strengths.

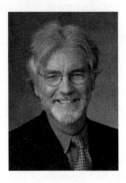 **C. R. Snyder, Ph.D.** (deceased), was the Wright Distinguished Professor of Clinical Psychology at the University of Kansas, Lawrence. Internationally known for his work at the interface of clinical, social, personality, and health psychology, his theories pertained to how people react to personal feedback, the human need for uniqueness, the ubiquitous drive to excuse transgressions and, most recently, the hope motive. He received 31 research awards and 27 teaching awards at the university, state, and national levels. In 2005, he received an honorary doctorate from Indiana Wesleyan University. Snyder appeared many times on national American television shows, and he was a regular contributor to National Public Radio. His scholarly work on the human need for uniqueness received the rare recognition of being the subject matter of an entire Sunday cartoon sequence by Garry Trudeau. All of these accomplishments were packaged in a graying and self-effacing absent-minded professor who said of himself, "If you don't laugh at yourself, you have missed the biggest joke of all!"

PART I

Looking at Psychology From a Positive Perspective

CHAPTER 1

Welcome to Positive Psychology

The gross national product does not allow for the health of our children, . . . their education, or the joy of their play. It does not include the beauty of our poetry or the strength of our marriages; the intelligence of our public debate or the integrity of our public officials. It measures neither wit nor courage; neither our wisdom nor our teaching; neither our compassion nor our devotion to our country; it measures everything, in short, except that which makes life worthwhile.

—Robert F. Kennedy, 1968

The final lines in this 1968 address delivered by Robert F. Kennedy at the University of Kansas point to the contents of this book: *the things in life that make it worthwhile.* In this regard, however, imagine that someone offered to help you understand human beings but in doing so would teach you only about their weaknesses and pathologies. As far-fetched as this sounds, a similar "What is wrong with people?" question guided the thinking of most applied psychologists (clinical, counseling, school, etc.) during the last 100 years. Given the many forms of human fallibility, this question produced an avalanche of insights into the human "dark side." As the twenty-first century unfolds, another question, "What is right about people?," seems to captivate the masses. This question is at the heart of positive psychology, which is the scientific and applied approach to uncovering people's strengths and promoting their positive functioning. (See the article "Building Human Strength," in which positive psychology pioneer Martin Seligman gives his views about the need for this new field.)

Although other subareas of psychology were not focused on human weaknesses, twentieth-century applied psychology and psychiatry typically were. For example, consider the statement attributed to Sigmund Freud that the goal of psychology should be "to replace neurotic misery with ordinary unhappiness" (cited in Simonton & Baumeister, 2005, p. 99). Thus, the applied psychology of yesteryear was mostly about mental illness and understanding and helping the people who were living such tragedies. Positive psychology, on the other hand, offers a balance to this previous weakness-oriented approach by suggesting that we also must explore people's strengths along with their weaknesses. In advocating this focus on strengths, however, in no way do we mean to lessen the importance and pain associated with human suffering.

3

Building Human Strength: Psychology's Forgotten Mission
Martin E. P. Seligman
President, American Psychological Association

Before World War II, psychology had three missions: curing mental illness, making the lives of all people more fulfilling, and identifying and nurturing high talent. After the war, two events changed the face of psychology. In 1946, the Veterans Administration was created, and practicing psychologists found they could make a living treating mental illness. In 1947, the National Institute of Mental Health was created, and academic psychologists discovered they could get grants for research on mental illness.

As a result, we have made huge strides in the understanding of and therapy for mental illness. At least 10 disorders, previously intractable, have yielded up their secrets and can now be cured or considerably relieved. Even better, millions of people have had their troubles relieved by psychologists.

Our Neglected Missions

But the downside was that the other two fundamental missions of psychology—making the lives of all people better and nurturing "genius"—were all but forgotten.

We became a victimology. Human beings were seen as passive foci: Stimuli came on and elicited "responses," or external "reinforcements" weakened or strengthened "responses," or conflicts from childhood pushed the human being around. Viewing the human being as essentially passive, psychologists treated mental illness within a theoretical framework of repairing damaged habits, damaged drives, damaged childhoods, and damaged brains.

Fifty years later, I want to remind our field that it has been sidetracked. Psychology is not just the study of weakness and damage, it is also the study of strength and virtue. Treatment is not just fixing what is broken, it is nurturing what is best within ourselves.

Bringing this to the foreground is the work of the Presidential Task Force on Prevention, headed by Suzanne Bennett Johnson and Roger Weissberg. This task force will take on a number of jobs: It will attempt to identify the "Best practices in prevention," led by Karol Kumpfer, Lizette Peterson, and Peter Muehrer; it will explore "Creating a new profession: Training in prevention and health promotion" by setting up conferences on the training of the next generation of prevention psychologists, led by Irwin Sandler, Shana Millstein, Mark Greenberg, and Norman Anderson; it will work with Henry Tomes of APA's Public Interest Directorate in the ad campaign to prevent violence in children; it will sponsor a special issue on prevention in the 21st century for the *American Psychologist*, edited by Mihaly Csikszentmihalyi; and, led by Camilla Benbow, it will ask what psychology can do to nurture highly talented children.

Building Strength, Resilience, and Health in Young People

But an underlying question remains: How can we prevent problems like depression, substance abuse, schizophrenia, AIDS, or injury in young people who are genetically vulnerable or who live in worlds that nurture these problems? What we have learned is that pathologizing does not move us closer to the prevention of serious disorders. The major strides in prevention have largely come from building a science focused on systematically promoting the competence of individuals.

We have discovered that there is a set of human strengths that are the most likely buffers against mental illness: courage, optimism, interpersonal skill, work ethic, hope, honesty, and perseverance. Much of the task of prevention will be to create a science of human strength whose mission will be to foster these virtues in young people.

Fifty years of working in a medical model of personal weakness and on the damaged brain has left the mental health professions ill equipped to do effective prevention. We need massive research on human strength and virtue. We need practitioners to recognize that much of the best work they do is amplifying the strengths rather than repairing their patients' weaknesses. We need psychologists who work with families, schools, religious communities, and corporations to emphasize their primary role of fostering strength.

The major psychological theories have changed to undergird a new science of strength and resilience. Individuals—even children—are now seen as decision makers, with choices, preferences, and the possibility of becoming masterful, efficacious, or, in malignant circumstances, helpless and hopeless. Such science and practice will prevent many of the major emotional disorders. It will also have two side effects. Given all we are learning about the effects of behavior and of mental well-being on the body, it will make our clients physically healthier. It will also re-orient psychology to its two neglected missions, making normal people stronger and more productive as well as making high human potential actual.

Source: Seligman, M., "Building human strength: Psychology's forgotten mission," in *APA Monitor,* 28(1): January 1998, p. 2. Copyright 1998 by the American Psychological Association. Reproduced with permission.

Now we are poised to study the whole human picture by exploring psychological assets and deficits within varying cultural contexts. We present this book as a guide for this journey and to welcome those of you who are new to this approach.

In this chapter, we begin by orienting you to the potential benefits of focusing on the positive in daily life and in psychological research. In this first section, we show how a positive newspaper story can shine a light on what is right in the world and how this type of storytelling can produce very favorable reactions among readers. In the second section, we discuss the importance of a balanced perspective involving the strengths and weaknesses of people. We encourage readers not to become embroiled in the debate between the strengths and weakness camps about which one best reflects the "truth." Third, we explore the attention that psychology to date has given to human strengths. In the last section, we walk you through the eight major parts of the book and give brief previews of the chapter contents.

We would like to make three final points about our approach in writing this volume. First, we believe that the greatest good can come from a positive psychology that is based on the latest and most stringent research methods. In short, an enduring positive psychology must be built on scientific principles. Therefore, in each chapter we present what we see as the best available research bases for the various topics that we explore. In using this approach, however, we describe the theories and findings of the various researchers rather than going into depth or great detail about their methods. Our rationale for this "surface over depth" approach stems from the fact that this is an introductory-level book; however, the underlying methods used to derive the various positive psychology findings represent the finest, most sophisticated designs and statistics in the field of psychology.

Second, although we do not cover in a separate chapter the physiology and neurobiology (and, occasionally, the evolutionary) underpinnings of positive psychology, we do view these perspectives as very important. Accordingly, our approach is to discuss the physiology, neurobiology, and evolutionary factors in the context of the particular topics covered in each chapter. For example, in the chapter on self-efficacy, optimism, and hope, we discuss the underlying neurobiological forces. Likewise, in the chapter on gratitude, we explore the underlying heart and brain wave patterns. Moreover, in discussing forgiveness we touch upon the evolutionary advantages of this response.

Third, we recognize and want to assert to the reader that nothing exists within a vacuum. We are all products of our environment to some extent, and as such looking at cultural context before making claims about various constructs is essential. You will notice throughout the chapters that we attempt to report on studies covering a number of different cultural groups. In our studies, we use a broad definition of the term *culture* and include race, ethnicity, generation, socioeconomic status, gender, nation of origin, and sexual orientation, among other social identity facets. As you will notice, findings are not static across these different groups, and sometimes what has been put forth as a "strength" in one cultural group does not hold this label in another. In addition, some groups have been unfairly pathologized over the years as a result of investigating constructs solely in power-holding groups and then interpreting these findings as universal. We ask the reader to be cautious in interpreting any construct as universal, as findings seem to belie the existence of this. Finally, we suggest that paying attention to worldviews other than one's own can help researchers to avoid these mistakes and harms against certain groups in the future.

GOING FROM THE NEGATIVE TO THE POSITIVE

Imagine you are a newspaper reporter and your assignment is to describe the thoughts and actions of people who are stranded one Friday evening at a large airport because of bad weather. The typical content of the newspaper story about such a situation probably would be very negative and filled with actions that portray people in a very unfavorable light. Such stories emphasize the bad side of human behavior that was the focus of many twentieth-century psychologists. But, as we shall see, not all stories about people are negative.

A Positive Newspaper Story

Juxtapose such negative newspaper stories with the following tale reported by one of the authors of this book (Snyder, 2004c, p. D4) in a local newspaper. The scene is the Philadelphia International Airport on a Friday evening as flights arrive late or are canceled.

> . . . people who were trying to make the best of difficult situations. For example, when a young Army soldier just back from Iraq noticed that he had lost his girlfriend's ring, the people working at the airport and all of us in the waiting area immediately began to search for it. In a short period of time, the ring was located, and a cheer went out in the crowd.
>
> Around 7:40 p.m., the announcer told us that there would be yet longer delays on several of the flights. To my amazement and delight, I found that my fellow travelers (and I) just coped. Some broke out supplies of food that they had stashed away in bags, and they offered their treasures to others. Decks of playing cards came out, and various games were started. The airlines people handed out snacks. There were scattered outbreaks of laughter.
>
> As if we were soldiers waiting in the trenches during a lull between battles, someone in the distance began to play a harmonica. Small boys made a baseball diamond, and as their game progressed, no one seemed to mind when one of their home runs would sail by. Although there weren't enough seats for everyone, people creatively made chairs and couches out of their luggage. The people who had computers took them out and played video games with each other. One guy even turned his computer screen into a drive-in-movie-like setup on which several people watched *The Matrix*. I used my computer to write this column.
>
> I once heard it said that grace is doing the average thing when everyone should be going crazy. When hollering and screaming, becoming angry and upset, and generally "losing it" seem to loom just over the horizon, it is wonderful instead to see the warming grace of people—similar to the rays of the sun on a cold day.

Reactions to This Positive Story

After this story appeared, Dr. Snyder (CRS) reported that he was not prepared for readers' reactions and had these words to say:

> Never have I written anything that ignited such an outpouring of heartfelt praise and gratitude. In the first week alone after this editorial appeared, I was swamped with favorable e-mails. Some recounted how it reminded them of times they had witnessed people behaving at their very best. Others wrote about how this story made them feel better for the rest of that day and even for several days afterward. Several people said they wished there were more such news stories in the paper. Not a single person among the responses I received had anything negative to say about this column.

Why would people react so uniformly and warmly to this short story about a Friday night at the Philadelphia airport? In part, people probably want to see and hear more about the good in others. Whether it is through newspaper stories such as this one or through the scientific studies and applications we present in this book, there is a hunger to know more about the good in people. It is as if the collective sentiment were, "Enough of all this negativity about people!"

In writing this book on positive psychology, we have experienced the uplifting effects of reviewing the many research and clinical applications that are appearing on the study of strengths and positive emotions in varying groups. As you read about the assets of your fellow humans from multiple cultural perspectives and hear about the many resources that promote the best in people, see whether you, too, feel good. There are many things for which we can praise people, and we will share many examples.

POSITIVE PSYCHOLOGY SEEKS A BALANCED, MORE COMPLETE VIEW OF HUMAN FUNCTIONING

Seeing only the good in one's own actions and the bad in those of others is a common human foible. Validating only the positive or negative aspects of experience is not productive. It is very tempting to focus on just the good (or the bad) in the world, *but it is not good science,* and we must not make this mistake in advancing positive psychology. Although we do not agree with the tenets of the previous pathology models, it would be inaccurate to describe their proponents as being poor scholars, poor scientists, poor practitioners, or bad people. Instead, this previous paradigm was advanced by well-meaning, bright people who were responding to the particular circumstances of their times. Likewise, it is not as if these people were wrong in their depictions of people. They developed diagnoses and measurement approaches for schizophrenia, depression, and alcoholism and validated many effective treatments for specific problems such as panic disorder and blood and injury phobia (see Seligman, *What You Can Change and What You Can't,* 1994).

Thus, those operating within the pathology model were quite accurate in their descriptions of some people at some particular times in their lives. Moreover, they were able to help certain people with select problems. Nevertheless, advocates of the pathology approach were incomplete in their portrayals of humankind. Undeniably, the negative is part of humankind, but only a part, and what is viewed as negative in one group may be positive in another. In addition, a bias toward Western culture is found, thus doubly pathologizing non-dominant goups. Positive psychology offers a look at the other side—that which is good and strong within a cultural context, along with normative ways to nurture and sustain these assets and resources.

Although we explore the positive, we emphasize that this half is no more the entire story than is the negative side. Future psychologists must develop an inclusive approach that examines both the weaknesses *and* the strengths of people in varying cultural groups, as well as the stressors *and* the resources in the environment. That approach would be the most comprehensive and valid. We have not reached that point, however, because we have yet to develop and explore fully the science and practice of positive psychology. Only when we have done such detective work on the strengths of people within their cultural contexts and the many resources of positive environments will we truly be able to understand all human beings in a more balanced fashion. Our task in these pages, therefore, is to share with you what we do know about positive psychology at this relatively early point in its development.

We look forward to that future time in the field of psychology when the positive is as likely as the negative to be used in assessing people and helping them to lead more satisfying and culturally comfortable existences. That time will probably come during the lifetimes of the readers of this book; some of you may pursue careers in psychology in which you routinely will consider people's strengths along with their weaknesses. Indeed, we feel strongly that your generation will be the one to implement a culturally competent psychology that truly balances the tenets of a positive approach with those of the previous pathology orientation. We also hope that today's parents will use positive psychology techniques to shore up families and bring out the best in their children. Likewise, we envision a time when school-age children and youth are valued as much for their major strengths as for their scores on state tests or college entrance examinations.

You, the readers, are the stewards of the eventual culturally competent and balanced positive-negative psychology. We warn you about the debate that is already in progress as to the superiority of one approach over the other. In the next section, we attempt to inoculate you against such "us versus them" thinking.

Views of Reality That Include Both the Positive and the Negative

Reality resides in people's perceptions of events and happenings in their world (Gergen, 1985), and scientific perspectives thereby depend on who defines them. Accordingly, the positive psychology and pathology "camps" may clash over how to build meaningful systems for understanding our world. On this process of **reality negotiation** (i.e., moving toward agreed-upon worldviews), Maddux, Snyder, and Lopez (2004, p. 326) have written that

> the meanings of these and other concepts are not *revealed* by the methods of science but are *negotiated* among the people and institutions of society who have an interest in their definitions. What people often call "facts" are not truths but reflect reality negotiations by those people who have an interest in using "the facts."

So, whether one is of a mind to believe the positive psychology or the pathology perspective, we must be clear that this debate involves **social constructions** about those facts. Ultimately, the prevailing views are linked to the social values of society's most powerful individuals, groups, and institutions (Becker, 1963). Likewise, because the prevailing views are social constructions that contribute to ongoing sociocultural goals and values, both the positive psychology and the pathology perspectives provide guidelines about how people should live their lives and what makes such lives worth living.

We believe that both the positive psychology view and the more traditional pathology view are useful. Accordingly, it would be a huge mistake to continue the "us versus them" debate between these two groups. Professionals in both camps want to understand and help people. To accomplish these ends, the best scientific and practical solution is to embrace both perspectives while keeping cultural context in the forefront of our minds. Therefore, although we introduce positive psychology tenets, research, and applications in this textbook, we do so in order to add the strengths approach as a complement to insights derived from the previous weakness model. Accordingly, we encourage the readers of this book—those who eventually will become the leaders in the field—to avoid being drawn into the debate aimed at proving either the positive psychology or pathology model.

WHERE WE ARE NOW AND WHAT WE WILL ASK

A notable accomplishment of the positive psychology initiative in its first decade and a half has been its success in increasing the amount of attention given to its theories and research findings.

University of Pennsylvania psychologist Martin Seligman should be singled out for having ignited the recent explosion of interest in positive psychology, as well as for having provided the label *positive psychology*. (Abraham Maslow actually coined the term *positive psychology* when he used it as a chapter title in his 1954 book, *Motivation and Personality.*) Having grown tired of the fact that psychology was not yielding enough "knowledge of what makes life worth living" (Seligman & Csikszentmihalyi, 2000, p. 5; note the similarity in this sentiment to Robert Kennedy's lament about the gross national product in this chapter's opening quotation), Seligman searched for a provocative theme when he became president of the American Psychological Association in 1998. It was during his presidency that Seligman used his bully pulpit to bring attention to the topic of positive psychology. Since that time, Seligman has worked tirelessly to initiate conferences and grant programs for research and applications of positive psychological research. Throughout his leadership of the developing positive psychology movement, Seligman has reminded psychologists that the backbone of the initiative should be good science.

Martin Seligman

Source: Courtesy of Martin Seligman.

At times, we will make mistakes in our search for human strengths. On balance, however, we firmly believe that our hunt for strengths will result in some marvelous insights about humankind. We are also aware that *humans* are incredibly diverse as a group, and so we must always look to context as well. In judging the success of positive psychology, we hold that it must be subjected to the very highest standards of logic and science. Likewise, positive psychology must undergo the analyses of skeptical yet open minds. We leave this latter important role to you.

PERSONAL MINI-EXPERIMENTS

What You Want to Experience

In this chapter, we provide numerous examples of how a focus on the positive can bring more good feelings and people into your daily life. Reorienting the focus of our thinking can help to determine whether we spend our days in pursuit of meaningful experiences or remain fearful of the bad that might happen. Too often, people act as if their thoughts were out of their control when, in fact, we are the authors of daily scripts that largely determine our daily actions. With the goal of focusing your thoughts on the positive, please go through each of these steps and follow the instructions. It is important to take your time.

- Identify three good things you would like to happen tomorrow.

- Think of one thing that you do not want to happen in the upcoming days.

- Imagine what you want not to happen as a circle that is getting smaller and smaller.

- Of the three good things you want to happen tomorrow, imagine the least important one getting smaller and smaller.

- Imagine the small circle of what you want not to happen getting so small it is hard to see.

- Let go of what you want not to happen. Say goodbye to it.

- Of the two good things you want to happen tomorrow, imagine the least important one getting smaller and smaller.

- Focus your mind on the one good thing that remains as the most important for tomorrow.

- See this good thing happening in your mind's eye.

- Think of others in your social group who might support you in this endeavor.

- Practice having this good thing happen in your mind.

- When you awaken tomorrow, focus on the good thing happening.

- Repeat to yourself during the day, "I make this positive possible."

- Repeat the phrase "I choose how to focus my thoughts."

(Continued)

(Continued)

The point of this exercise is to teach people that they have more control of their mental agendas than they often realize. Furthermore, by attending to what they want to happen, people are more likely to own their daily activities rather than to be reactive. In doing this exercise, feel free to tinker with the exact words that you may say to yourself, but try to retain the empowering message in the words we have selected. In our experiences in working with people, spending mental energies on avoiding certain unwanted outcomes tends to make people reactive to other people and events. On the other hand, thinking of what we want to happen helps to keep the negative away.

A GUIDE TO THIS BOOK

This book was written with you in mind. Throughout our collaboration, we asked each other, "Will this chapter bring positive psychology to life for the students?" These discussions helped us realize that the book needed to be an excellent summary of positive psychological science and practice *and* that it had to hook you into applying positive psychology principles in your daily lives. With that goal in mind, we have attempted to distill the most rigorous positive psychology studies and the most effective practice strategies, *and* we have constructed dozens of personal mini-experiments (try the first one, "What You Want to Experience," right now) and life enhancement strategies that promote your engagement with the positives in people and the world. Our goal is that, by the time you have finished reading this book, you will be more knowledgeable about psychology *and* will have become more skilled at capitalizing on your own strengths and generating positive emotions.

We have divided this book into eight parts. In Part I, "Looking at Psychology From a Positive Perspective," there are three chapters. Chapter 1, which you are about to complete, is introductory. Our purpose has been to give you a sense of the excitement we feel about positive psychology and to share some of the core issues driving the development of this new field. Chapter 2 is titled "Eastern and Western Perspectives on Positive Psychology: How 'ME + WE = US' Might Bridge the Gap." In the chapter, you will see that, although there are obvious positive psychology ties to Western cultures, there also are important themes from Eastern cultures, and that use of a ME-mindset (individualist) or a WE-mindset (collectivist) can both be beneficial. In addition, we encourage you here, regardless of your own mindset, to be able to view things from the different perspectives. Chapter 3, "Classifications and Measures of Strengths and Positive Outcomes," will give you a sense of how psychologists apply labels to the various types of human assets. For readers who are familiar with the more traditional pathology model, this will provide a counterpoint classification that is built on human strengths.

In Part II, "Positive Psychology in Context," we have dedicated two chapters to the factors associated with living well. In Chapter 4, "The Role of Culture in Developing Strengths and Living Well," we examine how the surrounding societal and environmental forces may contribute to a sense of well-being. Moreover, in Chapter 5, "Living Well at Every Stage of Life," we show how childhood activities can help shape a person to become adaptive in his or her later years.

Part III, "Positive Emotional States and Processes," consists of two chapters that cover topics pertaining to emotion-related processes. In Chapter 6, "The Principles of Pleasure: Understanding Positive Affect, Positive Emotions, Happiness, and Well-Being," we address the frequently asked question, "What makes a person happy?" In Chapter 7, "Making the Most of Emotional Experiences: Emotion-Focused Coping, Emotional Intelligence, Socioemotional Selectivity, and Emotional Storytelling," we introduce new findings regarding emotions as extremely important assets in meeting our goals.

In Part IV, "Positive Cognitive States and Processes," we include three chapters. Chapter 8, "Seeing Our Futures Through Self-Efficacy, Optimism, and Hope," covers the three most-researched motives for facing the future: self-efficacy, optimism, and hope. In Chapter 9, "Wisdom and Courage: Characteristics of the Wise and the Brave," we examine positive psychology topics involving the assets people bring to circumstances that stretch their skills and capacities. Likewise, in Chapter 10, "Mindfulness, Flow, and Spirituality: In Search of Optimal Experiences," we discuss how people become aware of the ongoing process of thinking and feeling, along with humans' need to believe in forces that are bigger and more powerful than they.

In Part V, "Prosocial Behavior," we describe the general positive linkages that human beings have with other people. In Chapter 11, "Empathy and Egotism: Portals to Altruism, Gratitude, and Forgiveness," we show how kindness-related processes operate to the benefit of people. And in Chapter 12, "Attachment, Love, and Flourishing Relationships," we review the importance of close human bonds for a variety of positive outcomes.

Part VI, "Understanding and Changing Human Behavior," describes how to prevent negative things from happening, as well as how to make positive things happen. Chapter 13, "Balanced Conceptualizations of Mental Health and Behavior," and Chapter 14, "Preventing the Bad and Promoting the Good," will help you to see how people can improve their life circumstances.

Part VII, "Positive Environments," looks at specific environments. In Chapter 15, "Positive Schooling and Good Work: The Psychology of Gainful Employment and the Education That Gets Us There," we describe recent findings related to positive learning outcomes for students, as well as the components of jobs that are both productive and satisfying.

The book closes with Part VIII, "A Positive Look at the Future of Psychology." This section comprises Chapter 16, "The Future of Positive Psychology: A Conversation Between the Authors" in which we present our views of the future. Moreover, we invite experts in the field to give their projections about the crucial issues for positive psychology.

Personal Mini-Experiments

In most of the chapters (including this one), we encourage you to put the ideas of leading positive psychologists to the test. In Personal Mini-Experiments, we ask you to bring positive psychology into your life by conducting the kind of experiments that positive psychology researchers might conduct in a lab or the field and that positive psychology practitioners might assign to their clients for homework. Some of these experiments take less than 30 minutes to complete, whereas some will take more than a week.

Life Enhancement Strategies

Finding the positive in daily life does not necessarily require a full-fledged experiment. In fact, we believe that a mindful approach to everyday living will reveal the power of positive emotions and strengths. Therefore, for the chapters that focus specifically on positive emotions, strengths, and healthy processes, we devised Life Enhancement Strategies, which can be implemented in a matter of minutes. We decided to develop these strategies to help you attain life's three most important outcomes: connecting with others, pursuing meaning, and experiencing some degree of pleasure or satisfaction. Specifically, love, work, and play have been referred to as the three great realms of life (Seligman, 1998e). Freud defined *normalcy* as the capacity to love, work, and play, and psychological researchers have referred to this capacity as "mental health" (Cederblad, Dahlin, Hagnell, & Hansson, 1995). Developmental researchers have described love, work, and play as normal tasks associated with human growth (Icard, 1996) and as keys to successful aging (Vaillant, 1994). Professionals interested in psychotherapy consider the ability to love, work, and play to be an aspect of the change process (Prigatano, 1992), whereas others view it as one of the primary goals of counseling (Christensen & Rosenberg, 1991). Although full engagement in pursuits of love, work, and play will not guarantee a good life, we believe it is necessary for good living. With this belief in mind, we encourage you to participate in numerous Life Enhancement Strategies that will enhance your ability to love, work, and play. We have also tried to include varying cultural perspectives in these strategies. We also think you could incorporate positive psychology into your leisure time. See the Appendix for a list of movies that bring the best in people to life.

This concludes our brief rundown of where we plan to go in the ensuing chapters and of our many hopes for you. If you become fully engaged with the material and the exercises in this book, you will gain knowledge and skills that may help you lead a better life.

THE BIG PICTURE

Despite the horror and uncertainty of terrorism and natural disasters, the United States of the twenty-first century is prosperous, stable, and poised for peace. At such a positive point in its evolution, a culture can focus on such issues as virtues, creativity, and hope. Three earlier cultures faced similar positive eras. In the fifth century BC, Athens used its resources to explore human virtues—good character and actions. Democracy was formed during this period. In fifteenth-century Florence, riches and talents were spent to advance beauty. And Victorian England used its assets to pursue the human virtues of duty, honor, and discipline.

Like the gifts emanating from these three previous eras, perhaps the contribution of the United States in the twenty-first century lies in adopting and exploring the tenets of positive psychology—the study and application of that which is good in people (Seligman & Csikszentmihalyi, 2000). Certainly, never in our careers have we witnessed such a potentially important new development in the field of psychology. But we are getting ahead of ourselves because the real test will come when new students are drawn to this area. For now, we welcome you to positive psychology.

APPENDIX: MOVIES FOR REVIEW

1. Wisdom & Knowledge—Cognitive strengths that entail the acquisition and use of knowledge.

   Creativity: Thinking of novel and productive ways to do things

Amadeus (1984)

Shine (1996)

The Pianist (2002)

Curiosity: Taking an interest in all of ongoing experience

October Sky (1999)

Amélie (2001, French)

In America (2003)

Open-Mindedness: Thinking things through and examining them from all sides

No Man's Land (2001, Bosnian)

Love of Learning: Mastering new skills, topics, and bodies of knowledge

Billy Elliott (2000)

A Beautiful Mind (2001)

Perspective (Wisdom): Being able to provide wise counsel to others

The Devil's Advocate (1997)

American Beauty (1999)

2. Courage—Emotional strengths that involve the exercise of will to accomplish goals in the face of opposition, external or internal

Bravery: Not shrinking from threat, challenge, difficulty, or pain

Schindler's List (1993)

Life as a House (2001)

The Kite Runner (2007)

Gravity (2013)

Persistence (Perseverance): Finishing what one starts; persisting in a course of action despite obstacles

The Piano (1993)

The Legend of Bagger Vance (2000)

The Blind Side (2009)

The King's Speech (2010)

Twelve Years a Slave (2013)

Integrity (Authenticity, Honesty): Speaking the truth and presenting oneself in a genuine way

A Few Good Men (1992)

Erin Brockovich (2000)

Lincoln (2013)

3. Humanity—Interpersonal strengths that involve tending and befriending others

   Love: Valuing close relations with others, in particular those in which sharing and caring are reciprocated; being close to people

   > *My Fair Lady* (1964)
   >
   > *Doctor Zhivago* (1965)
   >
   > *Sophie's Choice* (1982)
   >
   > *The Bridges of Madison County* (1995)
   >
   > *The English Patient* (1996)
   >
   > *Iris* (2001)
   >
   > *Brokeback Mountain* (2005)
   >
   > *Frozen* (2013)

   Kindness (Generosity, Nurturance, Care, Compassion, Altruistic Love): Doing favors and good deeds for others; helping them; taking care of them

   > *Promise* (1986)
   >
   > *As Good as It Gets* (1997)
   >
   > *Children of Heaven* (1997)
   >
   > *Cider House Rules* (1999)
   >
   > *The Secret Life of Bees* (2008)

   Social Intelligence (Emotional Intelligence, Personal Intelligence): Being aware of the motives and feelings of self and others; knowing what to do to fit into different social situations; knowing what makes other people tick

   > *Driving Miss Daisy* (1989)
   >
   > *Children of a Lesser God* (1986)
   >
   > *K-Pax* (2001)
   >
   > *The Five Senses* (2001, Canadian)
   >
   > *I Am Sam* (2002)

4. Justice—Civic strengths that underlie healthy community life

   Citizenship (Social Responsibility, Loyalty, Teamwork): Working well as a member of a group or team; being loyal to the group; doing one's share.

   > *Awakenings* (1990)
   >
   > *L.A. Confidential* (1997)
   >
   > *Finding Forrester* (2001)
   >
   > *A Mighty Heart* (2007)

   Fairness: Treating all people the same according to notions of fairness and justice; not letting personal feelings bias decisions about others; giving everyone a fair chance

Philadelphia (1993)

The Emperor's Club (2002)

Leadership: Encouraging a group of which one is a member to get things done and at the same time maintaining good relations within the group; organizing group activities and seeing that they happen

Lawrence of Arabia (1962)

Dances With Wolves (1990)

5. Temperance—Strengths that protect against excess

Forgiveness and Mercy: Forgiving those who have done wrong; accepting the shortcomings of others; giving people a second chance; not being vengeful

Ordinary People (1980)

Terms of Endearment (1983)

Dead Man Walking (1995)

Pay It Forward (2000)

Humility/Modesty: Letting one's accomplishments speak for themselves; not seeking the spotlight; not regarding oneself as more special than one is

Gandhi (1982)

Little Buddha (1994)

Prudence: Being careful about one's choices; not taking undue risks; not saying or doing things that might later be regretted

Sense and Sensibility (1995)

Self-Regulation (Self-Control): Regulating what one feels and does; being disciplined; controlling one's appetites and emotions

Forrest Gump (1994)

6. Transcendence—Strengths that forge connections to the larger universe and provide meaning

Appreciation of Beauty and Excellence (Awe, Wonder, Elevation): Noticing and appreciating beauty, excellence, and skilled performance in all domains of life, from nature to arts to mathematics to science to everyday experience

Out of Africa (1985)

Colors of Paradise (2000, Iranian)

An Inconvenient Truth (2006)

Gratitude: Being aware of and thankful for the good things that happen; taking time to express thanks

Fried Green Tomatoes (1991)

Sunshine (2000)

Hope (Optimism, Future-Mindedness, Future Orientation): Expecting the best in the future and working to achieve it; believing that a good future is something that can be brought about

> *Gone With the Wind* (1939)
>
> *Good Will Hunting* (1997)
>
> *Life Is Beautiful* (1998, Italian)
>
> *Cinderella Man* (2005)

Humor (Playfulness): Liking to laugh and tease; bringing smiles to other people; seeing the light side; making (not necessarily telling) jokes

> *Patch Adams* (1999)

Spirituality (Religiousness, Faith, Purpose): Knowing where one fits within the larger scheme; having coherent beliefs about the higher purpose and meaning of life that shape conduct and provide comfort

> *Contact* (1997)
>
> *Apostle* (1997)
>
> *Priest* (1994)
>
> *What the Bleep Do We Know!?* (2004)

Vitality (Zest, Enthusiasm, Energy): Approaching life with excitement and energy; not doing things halfway or halfheartedly; living life as an adventure; feeling alive and activated

> *One Flew Over the Cuckoo's Nest* (1975)
>
> *Cinema Paradiso* (1988, Italian)
>
> *My Left Foot* (1993)

Appendix Note: These movies and classification are largely taken from Rashid (2006), with one alteration: *Vitality* has been moved to the *Transcendence* category. Reprinted with permission of Tayyab Rashid. We have also added a few more recent films to the list.

KEY TERMS

Mental illness: Within the pathology psychological approach, refers to a variety of problems that people may have. A catch-all term for someone having severe psychological problems, as in "he is suffering from mental illness."

Positive psychology: The science and applications related to the study of psychological strengths and positive emotions.

Reality negotiation: The ongoing processes by which people arrive at agreed-upon worldviews or definitions.

Social constructions: Perspectives or definitions that are agreed upon by many people to constitute reality (rather than some objectively defined "truth" that resides in objects, situations, and people).

Eastern and Western Perspectives on Positive Psychology

How "ME + WE = US" Might Bridge the Gap

Contributions From Phil McKnight Included

A MATTER OF PERSPECTIVE

Positive psychology scholars aim to define specific strengths and highlight the many paths that lead to better lives (Aspinwall & Staudinger, 2002; Keyes & Haidt, 2003; Lopez & Snyder, 2003; Lopez & Snyder, 2009; Peterson & Seligman, 2004). As Western civilization and European events and values shaped the field of psychology as we know it today in the United States, it is not surprising that the origins of positive psychology have focused more on the values and experiences of Westerners. Constructs such as hope, optimism, and personal self-efficacy, among others, are particularly valued in these cultures and have been prominent throughout Western history. Increasingly, however, scholars are taking the broader historical and cultural contexts into account to understand strengths and the practices associated with living well (see, e.g., Leong & Wong, 2003; Schimmel, 2000; Sue & Constantine, 2003). Today, the previously neglected wisdoms of the Eastern traditions are being consulted in addition to those originating in the West, with the goal of adding different viewpoints about human strengths.

"A good fortune may forebode a bad luck, which may in turn disguise a good fortune." This Chinese proverb exemplifies the Eastern perspective that the world and its inhabitants are in a perpetual state of flux. Thus, just as surely as good times occur, so, too, will bad times visit us. This expectation of and desire for balance distinguishes Easterners' views of optimal functioning from the more linear path taken by Westerners to resolve problems and monitor progress. Ever adaptive and mindful, Easterners move with the cycle of life until the change process becomes natural and enlightenment (i.e., being able to see things clearly for what they are) is achieved. While Westerners might search for rewards in the physical plane, Easterners seek to transcend the human plane and rise to the spiritual one.

In this chapter, we discuss and contrast both Western and Eastern historical and philosophical traditions that demonstrate how these different groups characterize important strengths and life outcomes. Next, we discuss some of the inherent and fundamental differences between Eastern and Western value systems, thought processes, and life outcomes sought. We also articulate the idea of the "good life" from both perspectives and discuss the associated strengths that assist each group in attaining positive life outcomes. We then delve into a discussion of some specific concepts that are deemed to be necessary qualities for achieving the "good life" in each group. It is important to note that what is viewed as the "good life" may be different in each cultural group. Though we will not always enclose this term in quotation marks as we do here, please note that it is always culturally bound. In closing we talk about the ME perspective and the WE perspective and give our thoughts on trying to see things from more than one perspective.

HISTORICAL AND PHILOSOPHICAL TRADITIONS

To summarize thousands of years of Western and Eastern ideology and traditions is obviously beyond the scope of this chapter. Therefore, we highlight the basic tenets of three influential Western traditions: (1) Athenian, (2) Judeo-Christian, and (3) Islam, as well as four influential Eastern disciplines: (1) Confucianism, (2) Taoism (these two traditions are generally associated with China), (3) Buddhism (associated with Japan), and (4) Hinduism (rooted in traditions of Southeast Asia). Within both Western and Eastern historical contexts, the concept of the "good life" has existed for many centuries. While Western cultures emphasize optimal functioning as it occurs intrapsychically, Eastern cultures hold that an optimal life experience is a spiritual journey involving others and resulting in transcendence and enlightenment. The Eastern search for spiritual transcendence parallels the Westerner's hopeful pursuits for a better life on Earth.

Aristotle

Source: Photos.com/Thinkstock.

WESTERN INFLUENCES: ATHENIAN, JUDEO-CHRISTIAN, AND ISLAMIC TRADITIONS

Athenian Views

Discussion of virtue and human strength is something on which both Plato and Aristotle focused heavily in their teachings in Ancient Greece. Aristotle, after expanding on Plato's ideas regarding virtue, detailed 11 moral virtues: *courage, moderation, generosity, munificence* (this relates to money spending at an appropriate level), *magnificence* (described as "greatness of soul"), *even temper, friendliness, truthfulness, wit* (describing an ability to laugh and have fun at an appropriate level), *justice,* and *friendship* (Solomon,

2006). In addition to these moral virtues, Aristotle described intellectual virtues (mainly associated with ideas regarding wisdom) and believed that "strength of character, as inculcated by the political community, would lead to enduring human excellence" (Solomon, 2006, p. 9).

Aristotle and Plato also emphasized the influence the political community, termed *polis,* has on the development and maintenance of these virtues (Euben, Wallach, & Ober, 1994; Solomon, 2006). Aristotle discussed this community as being a necessity in helping the average individual to self-actualize with regard to virtue; he stated it was only within a life of order and sanction that one could rise above hedonistic desire and become truly virtuous (Peterson & Seligman, 2004; Solomon, 2006). In this view, people with good human virtue create such a community and then can provide a good model for others so that the masses also develop such human excellence. In addition, Aristotle believed that government should be charged with the development of virtue in a particular society via early education (i.e., in childhood) and training (Solomon, 2006).

Judeo-Christianity

In thinking about virtue in general, the religious teachings of Judaism and Christianity often come directly to mind. The Bible contains discussions of virtues in many chapters and verses. In the Old Testament, the virtues of *faith, hope,* and *charity* are highlighted and encouraged and were later discussed as part of the "Seven Heavenly Virtues" by Thomas Aquinas (Williams & Houck, 1982). According to historians, Aquinas lists these virtues as *fortitude* (courage), *justice, temperance, wisdom* (these four are often called the cardinal virtues; Peterson & Seligman, 2004), *faith, hope,* and *charity* (Williams & Houck, 1982). Other scholars cite the Ten Commandments given by Moses in the Old Testament as directives toward cultivating certain strengths within the Jewish tradition. Peterson and Seligman (2004) interpret the acts that the commandments prohibit as falling under the category of particular cardinal virtues: "Justice is implied in prohibitions against murder, theft, and lying; temperance in those against adultery and covetousness; and transcendence generally within the divine origin of the commands" (p. 48).

Other mentions are made of various gifts and strengths throughout the New Testament. For example, the Book of Romans describes the "gifts" that are valued by God and includes strengths such as leadership, faith, mercy, love, joy, hope, patience, hospitality, and others (12:3–21). In addition, the Book of Proverbs has many affirmations of specific virtuous behaviors (Peterson & Seligman, 2004). In the prologue of this book of the Bible, the following words are given as the purpose and theme of Proverbs:

1 *The proverbs of Solomon, son of David, king of Israel:*

2 *for attaining wisdom and discipline; for understanding words of insight;*

3 *for acquiring a disciplined and prudent life, doing what is right and just and fair;*

4 *for giving prudence to the simple, knowledge and discretion to the young-*

5 *let the wise listen and add to their learning, and let the discerning get guidance-*

6 *for understanding proverbs and parables, the sayings and riddles of the wise.*

7 *The fear of the LORD is the beginning of knowledge, but fools despise wisdom and discipline.*

(Proverbs 1: 1–7)

These words caution followers to live virtuous lives, giving particular weight to the virtue of wisdom. Finally, the Beatitudes discussed in the Book of Matthew give a series of virtuous traits (e.g., meekness, being a "peacemaker," mercy, righteousness, etc.) that are said to be pleasing to God (Matthew 5: 1–11).

The Talmud also provides instructions about living a virtuous life. In the Pirke Avot, or *Ethics of the Fathers*, directives are given on how to live life as an ethical follower of Judaism (N. Mendel, personal communication, February 3, 2010). The lessons here include being a hospitable host, particularly to the poor, being fair in decision-making and judgments, and seeking peace in everyday life (Bokser, 1989). In addition, the Talmud states, "You shall administer truth, justice and peace within your gates" (Zech 8:16), showing similar value to other religious traditions for these specific virtues (Bokser, 1989).

Islam

Though we have added Islam to the "Western" heading in this section as is commonly done in texts that discuss both Western and Eastern religions, it is important to note that scholars disagree as to whether Islam should be considered a Western or an Eastern religion (S. Lloyd-Moffet, personal communication, November 21, 2013). Islam is practiced by both Western and Eastern individuals and groups, and thus its virtues and practices may be influenced by more than one context.

Allah

Source: Nevit Dilmen / CC BY-SA 3.0

Islam incorporates many virtues recognizable in other philosophical traditions and categorizes them as moral obligations. Among others, *gratitude* (e.g., to Allah for His benevolence), *love* (of Allah because of His forgiveness), *kindness* (especially toward parents), *justice* (emphasizing fraternity and equality of all), and *courage* (acts of bravery) are valued (Farah, 1968). In addition, there is a strong component of looking out for one's brother, particularly if one has more than one needs. This emphasis is especially directed toward the wealthy in terms of their support of the poor as "[the wealthy] are obligated . . . to aid the poor as a duty, not a privilege" (Farah, 1968, p. 127). Giving to the poor is a requirement in the Islamic faith reflected in the third pillar, *zakat* (alms), and it is something that is to be done secretly as opposed to directly if possible so that the giver maintains his or her humility and the recipient is not embarrassed by having to accept the gift (Ahmed, 1999). Abiding by these moral obligations and pillars assists the faithful in pleasing Allah in this tradition.

EASTERN INFLUENCES:
CONFUCIANISM, TAOISM, BUDDHISM, AND HINDUISM

Confucianism

Confucius, or the Sage, as he is sometimes called, held that leadership and education are central to morality. Born during a time when his Chinese homeland was fraught with strife, Confucius emphasized morality as a potential cure for the evils of that time (Soothill, 1968), and the tenets of Confucianism are laden with quotations that encourage looking out for others. In fact, one of Confucius's most famous sayings is a precursor of the Golden Rule and can be translated as, "You would like others to do for you what you would indeed like for yourself" (Ross, 2003; *Analects* 6:28). In some ways, these teachings are parallel to thoughts put forth by Aristotle and Plato regarding the responsibility of leaders to take *charge* of the group, though there is less emphasis in Western writings on the collectivist ideal of taking *care* of others in the group.

CONFUCIUS.

Confucius

Source: © iStockphoto.com/duncan1890

The attainment of virtue is at the core of Confucian teachings. The five virtues deemed central to living a moral existence are *jen* (humanity, the virtue most exalted by Confucius and said to encompass the other four virtues); *yi* (duty to treat others well); *li* (etiquette and sensitivity for others' feelings); *zhi* (wisdom), and *xin* (truthfulness). Confucian followers must strive to make wise decisions based on these five virtues; this continual striving leads the Confucian follower to enlightenment, or the good life.

Taoism

Ancient Taoist beliefs are difficult to discuss with Western audiences partly because of the untranslatable nature of some key concepts in the tradition of Taoism. Lao-Tzu (the creator of the Taoist tradition) states in his works that his followers must live according to the Tao (pronounced "dow" and roughly translated as "the Way"). The Chinese character portraying the concept of the Way is a moving head and "refers simultaneously to direction, movement, method, and thought" (Peterson & Seligman, 2004, p. 42; Ross, 2003); Tao is the energy that surrounds everyone and is a power that "envelops, surrounds, and flows through all

The Way

things" (*Western Reform Taoism*, 2003, p. 1). In this regard, Lao-Tzu (1994) described the Way in the following lines:

The Way can be spoken of,

But it will not be the constant way;

The name can be named,

But it will not be the constant name.

The nameless was the beginning of the myriad creatures;

The named was the mother of the myriad creatures.

Hence constantly rid yourself of desires in order to observe its subtlety;

But constantly allow yourself to have desires in order to observe what it is after.

These two have the same origin but differ in name.

They are both called dark,

Darkness upon darkness

The gateway to all is subtle. (p. 47)

Lao-Tzu

Source: E. T. C. Werner, Myths and Legends of China, 1922, PD.

According to Taoist traditions, the difficulty in understanding the Way stems from the fact that one cannot teach another about it. Instead, understanding flows from experiencing the Way for oneself by fully participating in life. In this process, both good and bad experiences can contribute to a greater understanding of the Way. Achieving naturalness and spontaneity in life is the most important goal in Taoist philosophy. Thus, the virtues of *humanity, justice, temperance,* and *propriety* must be practiced by the virtuous individual without effort (Cheng, 2000). One who has achieved transcendence within this philosophy does not have to think about optimal functioning but behaves virtuously naturally.

Buddhism

Seeking the good of others is woven throughout the teachings of "the Master" or "the Enlightened One" (i.e., the Buddha). In one passage, the Buddha is quoted as saying, "Wander for the gain of the many, for the happiness of the many, out of compassion for the world" (Sangharakshita, 1991, p. 17). At the same time, the Buddha teaches that suffering is a part of being and that this suffering is brought on by the human emotion of desire. In the Buddhist philosophy, Nirvana is a state in which the self is freed from desire for anything (Schumann, 1974). It should be noted that both premortal and postmortal nirvana states are proposed as possible for the individual. More specifically, the premortal nirvana may be likened to the idea of the ultimate good life in this philosophy. Postmortal nirvana may be similar to the Christian idea of heaven.

Like the other Eastern philosophies, Buddhism gives an important place to virtue, which is described in several catalogs of personal qualities. Buddhists speak of the *Brahma Viharas,* those virtues that are above all others in importance, described by Peterson and Seligman as "universal virtues" (2004, p. 44). These virtues include love (*maitri*), compassion (*karuna*), joy (*mudita*), and equanimity (*upeksa*) (Sangharakshita, 1991). The paths to achieving these virtues within Buddhism require humans to divorce themselves from the human emotion of desire to put an end to suffering.

Buddha

Source: ©iStockphoto.com/pixonaut

Hinduism

The Hindu tradition differs somewhat from the other three philosophies discussed previously in that it does not appear to have a specific founder, and it is not clear when this tradition began in history (Stevenson & Haberman, 1998). The main teachings of the Hindu tradition emphasize the interconnectedness of all things. The idea of a harmonious union among all individuals is woven throughout the teachings of Hinduism, which refer to a "single, unifying principle underlying all of Earth" (Stevenson & Haberman, 1998, p. 46).

One's goal within this tradition would be to live life so fully and so correctly that one would go directly to the afterlife without having to repeat life's lessons in a reincarnated form (Stevenson & Haberman, 1998). Hindu teachings are very clear about the qualities one must embody to avoid reincarnation: "To return to this world is an indication of one's failure to achieve ultimate knowledge of one's self" (Stevenson & Haberman, 1998, p. 53). Thus, the quest of one's life is to attain ultimate self-knowledge and to strive for ultimate self-betterment (notably also a Western concept). Individuals are encouraged to be good to others as well as to improve themselves; the *Upanishads* state, "A man turns into something good by good action and something bad by bad action" (Stevenson & Haberman, 1998, p. 54). "Good action" is also encouraged in the sense that, if one does not reach ultimate self-knowledge in one's life and thus does have to return to Earth via reincarnation after death, the previous life's good actions correlate directly with better placement in the world in the subsequent life (Stevenson & Haberman, 1998). This process is known as *karma*. The good life in the Hindu tradition, therefore, encompasses individuals who are continually achieving knowledge and continually working toward good actions (Dahlsgaard, Peterson, & Seligman, 2005; Peterson & Seligman, 2004; Stevenson & Haberman, 1998).

Summary of Eastern and Western Philosophies

Each of the philosophies discussed here incorporates ideas about the importance of virtue, along with human strengths, as people move toward the good life. Similarities also can be drawn among the different ideologies, especially in the types of human qualities and experiences that are valued, though there are also differences in terms of which traits are particularly valued. Thus, it is important to contrast these Eastern beliefs with Western ideology to understand the differences in positive psychology viewed from each perspective.

EAST MEETS WEST

Eastern and Western ideologies stem from very different historical events and traditions. We begin this section with a thorough discussion of these different value systems (individualism and collectivism). Next, we explore ways in which differences can be seen explicitly in each cultural approach with regard to orientations toward time, and their respective thought processes. Finally, we discuss various constructs that may be viewed as exemplars of the values held as strengths in these very different traditions. These cultural differences give more information about strengths identified in each culture and ways in which positive life outcomes are pursued and achieved.

INDIVIDUALISM: THE PSYCHOLOGY OF ME

In this section, we touch on the United States' history of rugged individualism, along with the core and secondary emphases that define a person as individualistic. We then discuss two constructs related to individualism—hope and the need for uniqueness—and show how these constructs may be manifested in a variety of activities.

Alexis de Tocqueville

Source: © adoc-photos/Corbis

A Brief History of American Individualism

Since the publication of Alexis de Tocqueville's (1835/2003) *Democracy in America,* the United States has been known as the land of the "rugged individualist." The essence of this view is that any person with a good idea can succeed in the pursuit of personal goals through hard work. In the words of de Tocqueville, people in the United States "form the habit of thinking of themselves in isolation and imagine that their whole destiny is in their own hands" (p. 508). Such individualism was linked to the emphases on equal rights and freedom found in the United States (Lukes, 1973), as well as to the country's capitalistic economy and open frontiers (Curry & Valois, 1991). Since the establishment of American independence in 1776, this rugged individualism has metamorphosed into the "me generation" that held sway from the 1960s through the early 1990s (Myers, 2004).

Emphases in Individualism

When concern for the individual is greater than concern for the group, then the culture is said to be individualistic; however, when each person is very concerned about the group, then the society is collectivistic. As shown in Figure 2.1, when the average person in a society is disposed toward individual independence, that society is deemed individualistic (see the bell-shaped curve drawn with the dotted line).

Core Emphases

The three core emphases within individualism involve a sense of independence, a desire to stand out relative to others (a need for uniqueness), and the use of the self or the individual as the unit of analysis in thinking about life. In individualistic societies such as the United States, social patterns resemble a loosely interwoven fabric, and it is the norm for each person to see themselves as independent of the surrounding group of people (Triandis, 1995). On this point, research involving many studies supports the conclusion that individualism in the United States reflects a sense of independence rather than dependence (see Oyserman, Coon, & Kemmelmeier, 2002).

A second core emphasis within individualism is that the person wants to stand out relative to the population as a whole. Within individualistic societies, therefore, people follow their own motives and preferences instead of adjusting their desires to accommodate those of the group (this sometimes is called *conforming*). The individualistic person thus sets personal goals that may not match those of the groups to which he or she belongs (Schwartz, 1994; Triandis, 1988, 1990). Because of the individualistic propensity to manifest one's specialness, coupled with societal support for actions that show such individuality, it follows that the citizens of individualistic societies such as the United States will have a high need for uniqueness. We explore this fascinating motive in greater detail later in this section.

A third core emphasis of individualism is that the self or person is the unit of analysis in understanding how people think and act in a society. That is, explanations of events are likely to involve

Figure 2.1   Norms and Individual Differences for Individualistic and Collectivistic Societies

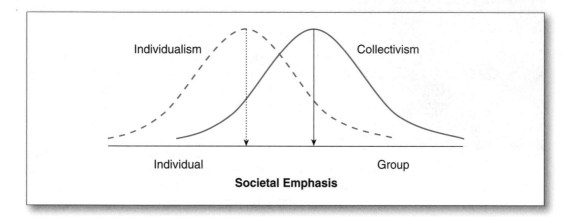

the person rather than the group. Therefore, the various definitions of individualism draw upon worldviews in which personal factors are emphasized over social forces (Bellah, Madsen, Sullivan, Swidler, & Tipton, 1985; Kagitcibasi, 1994; Triandis, 1995).

Secondary Emphases

Several secondary emphases flow from the individualistic focus upon the self rather than the group. Goals set by citizens of an individualistic society typically are for the self; moreover, success and related satisfactions also operate at the level of the self. Simply put, the payoffs are at the personal level rather than the group level. The individualistic person pursues what is enjoyable to him or her, in contrast to collectivistic people, who derive their pleasures from things that promote the welfare of the group. Of course, the individualist at times may follow group norms, but this usually happens when she or he has deduced that it is personally advantageous to do so.

As may be obvious by now, individualists are focused upon pleasure and their own self-esteem in interpersonal relationships and beyond. Individualists also weigh the disadvantages and advantages of relationships before deciding whether to pursue them (Kim, Sharkey, & Singelis, 1994). Thus, individualistic persons engage in benefit analyses to determine what may profit them, whereas collectivists are more likely to give their unconditional support to their group and think first and foremost in terms of their duties to the group. Individualists tend to be rather short term in their thinking, whereas collectivists are more long term in their thought patterns. Last, people in individualistic societies often are somewhat informal in their interactions with others, whereas people in collectivistic societies are more formal in their interactions, as they attend to the expected and important norms that determine such behaviors. (For a thorough discussion of all these secondary emphases, we recommend the review articles by Oyserman et al., 2002, and Vargas & Kemmelmeier, 2013.)

Roy F. Baumeister

Source: Reprinted with permission of Roy F. Baumeister.

COLLECTIVISM: THE PSYCHOLOGY OF WE

In this section, we comment on the history of collectivism and then describe its core and secondary emphases.

A Historical Comment on Collectivism: We Came Together Out of Necessity

Thousands of years ago, our hunter–gatherer ancestors realized that there were survival advantages to be derived from banding together into groups with shared goals and interests (Chency, Seyforth, & Smuts, 1986; Panter-Brick, Rowley-Conwy, & Layton, 2001). These groups contributed to a sense of belonging, fostered personal identities and roles for their members (McMillan & Chavis, 1986), and offered shared emotional bonds (Bess, Fisher, Sonn, & Bishop, 2002). Moreover, the resources of the people in groups helped them fend off threats from other humans and animals.

Simply stated, groups offered power to their members (Heller, 1989). The people in such groups protected and cared for each other, and they formed social units that were effective contexts for the propagation and raising of offspring. Gathered into groups, humans reaped the benefits of community (Sarason, 1974).

By today's standards, our hunter–gatherer relatives were more primitive in their needs and aspirations. But were they really that much different from people today in the satisfactions and benefits they derived from their group memberships? We think not, because human beings always have had the shared characteristics of what social psychologist Elliot Aronson (2003) has called "social animals." In this regard, one of our strongest human motives is to belong—to feel as if we are connected in meaningful ways with other people (Baumeister & Leary, 1995). Social psychologists Roy Baumeister and Mark Leary (1995) and Donelson Forsyth (1999; Forsyth & Corazzini, 2000) have argued that people prosper when they join together into social units to pursue shared goals.

Mark Leary

Source: Reprinted with permission of Mark Leary.

Emphases in Collectivism

Now, let's return to Figure 2.1 on p. 27. As shown there, when the average person in a society is disposed toward group interdependence, then that society is labeled collectivist (see the bell-shaped curve drawn with the solid line). At this point, you may be curious as to which country most markedly adheres to collectivistic values. In response to this question, research suggests that China is the most collectivistic of the various nations around the globe (see Oyserman et al., 2002).

Core Emphases

The three core emphases of collectivism are dependence; conformity, or the desire to fit in; and perception of the group as the fundamental unit of analysis. First, the dependency within collectivism reflects a genuine tendency to draw one's very meaning and existence from being part of an important group of people. In collectiv-

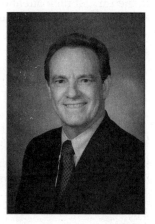

Donelson Forsyth

Source: Reprinted with permission of Donelson Forsyth.

ism, the person goes along with the expectations of the group, is highly concerned about the welfare of the group, and is very dependent upon the other members of the group to which he or she belongs (Markus & Kitayama, 1991; Reykowski, 1994).

Regarding the desire to fit in, Oyserman et al. (2002, p. 5) wrote, "The core element of collectivism is the assumption that groups bind and mutually obligate individuals." As such, collectivism is an inherently social approach in which the movement is toward in-groups and away from out-groups.

Turning to the third core emphasis, the group as the perceived unit of analysis, the social patterns in collectivist societies reflect close linkages in which people see themselves as part of a larger, more important whole. In brief, the collectivist concern is for the group as a whole rather than its constituents (Hofstede, 1980).

Secondary Emphases

The collectivist is defined in terms of the characteristics of the groups to which he or she belongs. Thus, collectivist-oriented people pay close attention to the rules and goals of the group and often may subjugate their personal needs to those of the group. Moreover, success and satisfaction stem from the group's reaching its desired goals and from feeling that one has fulfilled the socially prescribed duties as a member of that effective, goal-directed, group effort (Kim, 1994).

Collectivist people obviously become very involved in the ongoing activities and goals of their group, and they think carefully about the obligations and duties of the groups to which they belong (Davidson, Jaccard, Triandis, Morales, & Diaz-Guerrero, 1976; Miller, 1994). Furthermore, the interchanges between people within the collectivist perspective are characterized by mutual generosity and equity (Sayle, 1998). For such people, interpersonal relationships may be pursued even when there are no obvious benefits to be attained (see Triandis, 1995). In fact, given the great emphasis that collectivists place on relationships, they may pursue such relationships even when such interactions are counterproductive.

Because of their attentions to the guidelines as defined by the group, the individual members with a collectivist perspective may be rather formal in their interactions. That is, there are carefully followed, role-defined ways of behaving. Additionally, the person within the collectivistic perspective monitors the social context carefully to form impressions of others and to make decisions (Morris & Peng, 1994).

Recall our earlier discussion of the need for uniqueness as reflecting individualism. In this regard, Kim and Markus (1999) have reasoned that advertisements in Korea should accentuate collectivist themes related to conformity, whereas ads in the United States should be based more on themes of uniqueness. Consistent with this proposal, Kim and Markus's research shows that the need for uniqueness is lower in collectivistic societies than in individualistic ones (Yamaguchi, Kuhlman, & Sugimori, 1995).

Collectivist societies appear to have core elements of dependency, conformity (low need for uniqueness), and definition of existence in terms of the important group to which one belongs. The research also corroborates the fact that collectivism rests on a core sense of dependency, as well as an obligation or duty to the in-group and a desire to maintain harmony between people (Oyserman et al., 2002). Before leaving this section, we salute Daphne Oyserman and her colleagues at the University of Michigan Institute for Social Research for their seminal scholarly review of the characteristics of individualism and collectivism.

Demographics Related to Collectivism

Positive psychologists must consider what the future will bring in regard to collectivism. For example, related research suggests that the gulf between the wealthy and the poor in societies throughout the world is widening as we move farther into the twenty-first century (see Ceci & Papierno, 2005). Research reveals that people in the lower social classes, as compared to the upper ones, are more likely to be collectivist in their perspectives (Daab, 1991; Kohn, 1969; Marjoribanks, 1991). Turning to the role of aging as yet another demographic issue pertaining to collectivism, it appears that people become more collectivist as they grow older (Gudykunst, 1993; Noricks et al., 1987).

The Stories We Tell

Cultural value systems have significant effects on the determination of strengths versus weaknesses (Pedrotti & Edwards, 2014; Pedrotti, Edwards, & Lopez, 2009). Whereas most Western cultures have *individualist* perspectives, most Eastern cultures are guided by *collectivist* viewpoints. Commonly told stories often give examples of valued traits, and so we would like to share some for with you here. The Japanese story "*Momotaro*" ("Peach Boy," Sakade, 1958) gives an excellent example of the cultural importance of the traits of interdependence, the ability to avoid conflict, and duty to the group within Eastern traditions. The story begins with an elderly couple who have always wished for a child, although they are not able to conceive. One day, as the woman is washing her clothes in a stream, a giant peach floats to where she is standing and, upon reaching the woman, splits open to reveal a baby! The woman takes Momotaro home, and she and her husband raise him. At the age of 15, to the great pride of his parents, he decides to go to fight the ogres who have been tormenting the village and to bring back their treasure to his community. Along the way, Momotaro befriends many animals one by one. The animals want to fight each new animal they meet, but at Momotaro's urging, "The spotted dog and the monkey and the pheasant, who usually hated each other, all became good friends and followed Momotaro faithfully" (Sakade, 1958, p. 6). At the end of the story, Momotaro and his animal friends defeat the ogres by working together and bring the treasure back to the village, where all who live there share in the bounty. As the hero, Momotaro portrays the strengths valued in Japanese and other Asian cultures: (1) He sets out for the good of the group, although in doing so risks individual harm (collectivism); (2) along the way, he stops others from petty squabbling (promoting harmony); (3) he works with these others to achieve his goal (interdependence and collaboration); and (4) he brings back a treasure to share with the group (interdependence and sharing).

This story highlights important Eastern values and differs sharply from common Western stories. First, in most Western fairy tales the hero is fighting alone and takes dangers on single-handedly, as is the case with the princes in *Sleeping Beauty* and *Rapunzel* and the title character in *The Valiant Little Tailor* (Grimm & Grimm, as cited in Tatar, 2002), showing that individual independence is often valued over needing others' assistance. In instances where the hero does accept help from another, there is often a price involved where the "helper" makes sure that he or she also personally benefits from the transaction. Such examples can be found in the classic Western tale of *Rumplestiltskin* (Grimm & Grimm), where the title character offers to help the maiden only if he can be promised her firstborn in return, or *The Little Mermaid* (Andersen, as cited in Tatar), where the Sea Witch will only help the Little Mermaid to gain legs to meet her love if she surrenders her beautiful voice to the witch. This more closely follows the Western value on personal gain despite potential loss to another. Finally, many stories emphasize seeking personal fortune (or payment for service in the form of a bride or kingdom), but few discuss seeking fortune for the community (without any payment) as occurs in many Eastern stories.

A discussion of fairy tales is not often included in a scholarly publication such as this; however, these stories tell the tale of our cultural values, and they have been used throughout the ages to promote some behaviors and to decry others. Here it is clear that cultural orientation determines which characteristics are transmitted as the valued strengths to its members.

Orientation to Time

Differences also exist between East and West in terms of their orientations to time. In Western cultures such as the United States, individuals (particularly within the majority culture) often look to the future. Indeed, some of the strengths that are valued most (e.g., hope, optimism, self-efficacy; see Chapter 8) reflect future-oriented thinking. In Eastern cultures, however, there is a greater focus on and respect for the past. This past-oriented focus is revealed in the ancient Chinese proverb, "To know the road ahead, ask those coming back." Thus, Eastern cultures value the strength of "looking backward" and recognizing the wisdom of their elders, whereas Western cultures are more firmly focused on the future.

Thought Processes

When considering the unique aspects of Western and Eastern thought, we often focus on the nature of specific ideas, but we do not as commonly reflect on the process of linking and integrating ideas. Indeed, as researchers (e.g., Nisbett, 2003) have noted, stark differences exist in the very thought processes used by Westerners and Easterners, and this results in markedly divergent worldviews and approaches to meaning making. Richard Nisbett, a professor at the University of Michigan who studies social psychology and cognition and who comes from a Western cultural background, illustrates how he became aware of some of these differences in thinking during a conversation he had with a student from China. Nisbett recalls,

> A few years back, a brilliant student from China began to work with me on questions of social psychology and reasoning. One day early in our acquaintance, he said, "You know, the difference between you and me is that I think the world is a circle, and you think it is a line." The Chinese believe in constant change, but with things always moving back to some prior state. They pay attention to a wide range of events; they search for relationships between things; and they think you can't understand the part without understanding the whole. Westerners live in a simpler, more deterministic world; they focus on salient objects or people instead of the larger pictures; and they think they can control events because they know the rules that govern the behavior of objects. (p. xiii)

As Nisbett's story shows, the thinking style used by the Chinese student, and not just the ideas themselves, was vastly different from Nisbett's. This more circular thinking style is best exemplified by the Taoist figure of the *yin* and the *yang*. Most people are familiar with the *yin* and *yang* symbol. This figure represents the circular, constantly changing nature of the world as viewed by Eastern thought. The dark part of the symbol represents the feminine and passive, and the light side represents the masculine and active. Each part exists because of the other, and neither could exist alone, according to Taoist beliefs. As one state is experienced, the other is not far to follow; if hard times are occurring, easier times are on the way. This more circular thinking pattern affects the way in which the Eastern thinker maps out his or her life and therefore may influence the decisions a person makes in the search for peace.

An example of the effects of such different ways of thinking may be found in the life pursuits of the Westerner as compared with those of the Easterner. Whereas in the United States we give high priority to the right to "life, liberty, and the pursuit of happiness," the goals of the Easterner might have a different focus. Take, for instance, the positive psychological construct of happiness (see Chapter 6). Researchers have posited that happiness (whether group or individual) is a state commonly sought by Easterners and Westerners alike (Diener & Diener, 1995). The difference in the philosophical approaches to life, however, may make the searches look very different. For example, a Westerner whose goal is happiness draws a straight line to that goal, looking carefully for obstacles and finding possible ways around them. His or her goal is to achieve this eternal happiness and the strength of hope is used to achieve this. For the Easterner who follows the *yin* and the *yang,* however, this goal of happiness may not make sense. If one were to seek happiness and then achieve it, in the Eastern way of

Yin Yang

thinking, this would only mean that unhappiness was close on its heels. Instead, the Easterner might have the goal of balance (perhaps based more on using the strength of endurance), trusting in the fact that, although great unhappiness or suffering may occur in one's life, it would be equally balanced by great happiness. These two different types of thinking obviously create very different ways of forming goals to achieve the good life.

East and West: Is One Best?

There are substantial differences in the types of ideas and the ways in which those ideas are put together that emerge from Eastern and Western traditions. It is important to remember, however, that neither is "better" than the other. This is especially relevant for discussions regarding strengths. Therefore, we must use culture as a lens for evaluating whether a particular characteristic might be considered a strength or a weakness within a particular group.

PERSONAL MINI-EXPERIMENTS

Getting and Giving Help

In this chapter, we explore how the sense of community can promote optimal human functioning. The following exercises encourage you to think about how your relationships to others and the broader community can make a positive difference in your life.

Asking for Help. A primary way in which individualists and collectivists differ is in the cultural messages they receive regarding asking for help. If you are more on the individualist side, and thus a person who finds it difficult to ask for the help of another, this exercise

(Continued)

(Continued)

offers you a chance to break that habit. Select some activity for which you are especially unlikely to ask for help, and the next time you are in this situation, instead of trying to struggle through it by yourself, go ahead and ask another person for a hand. Here are some questions to ask yourself about a recent situation in which you could have asked for help:

1. Describe the circumstance, including all your thoughts and feelings. What did you imagine people would say if you asked for help? What would you have thought about yourself if you had asked for help?

2. Did you ask for help? If not, why not? If so, how did you overcome your rule of not asking for help?

3. How did the situation turn out when you did ask for help? What were the reactions of the person you asked for help? Did you get the needed help? If you did, how did you feel? Do you think you could ask for help in a future, similar situation?

Part of being in a community is being able to call upon the people in that community for assistance. Contrary to what you have been taught about not asking for help, it is not a weakness to ask for help. Indeed, it is a strength. You are human. You do need other people to get things accomplished. This is not a bad thing, but a wonderful reality that is part of being a member of a community. As we have suggested in this exercise, give it a try. Once people do, they rarely turn back.

Volunteering Your Help. Remember the last time you offered your assistance to someone else? It probably took very little of your time, and you made a small improvement in your community. The other beautiful aspect of offering help is that it feels absolutely wonderful. (See the Personal Mini-Experiments in Chapter 11, pp. 296–297.) Helping thus provides two benefits: one to the recipient and one to the giver. To implement this exercise, just look around your local community and watch your neighbors. Part of this may be a simple wave or greeting. At other times, it may be obvious that someone really could use a helping hand. There are many flat tires needing to be fixed, people who need assistance carrying packages, tourists needing directions, and so on. To see how you have fared in this exercise, answer the following questions:

1. Describe the last circumstance in which you noticed that a person needed help, and include all your thoughts and feelings. What did you imagine people would say if you offered help? What did you think about yourself after offering help?

2. Did you offer help? If not, why not? If you did, how were you able to overcome any rule to the contrary (such as "Don't bother others")?

3. How did the situation turn out when you offered help? How did the person to whom you offered help react? Did you give the needed help? If you did, how did you feel? Do you think you could do this again in a future, similar situation?

Being Alone or With Others. To complete this exercise, merely think about the goal-related activity listed in the left column and place a check mark in the column to the right that reflects your preferences about doing this alone or with others. Under each general life category, briefly write your desired goal. If you have more than one goal under each category, write each of these goals. Likewise, if you do not have a goal in a given category, then ignore it. Go through each of the goal categories and write a goal (or goals) on the blank line below each one. Then, go back to each goal category and, if you would prefer to seek the goal totally alone, place a check mark under the "Alone" column. If you would prefer to seek the goal with another person, place a check mark under the "Another" column. Finally, if you would prefer to seek the goal with two or more other people, place a check mark under the "Others" column.

Goal Category	Alone	Another	Others
Religious/Spiritual goal(s)			
_____	_____	_____	_____
Sport goal(s)			
_____	_____	_____	_____
Academic goal(s)			
_____	_____	_____	_____
Physical health goal(s)			
_____	_____	_____	_____
Psychological health goal(s)			
_____	_____	_____	_____
Work goal(s)			
_____	_____	_____	_____

(Continued)

(Continued)

Now that you have completed this inventory, simply count the life goals you want to pursue alone, those you want to do with another person, and those you want to do with two or more other people. Are you a person who wants to go it alone? If so, you truly may be prone to the individualistic perspective. Did you find that most of your goals involved one or more other people? If so, you probably have a more collectivistic perspective. This should give you a rough idea of the importance of other people to you as you seek the major goals in your life.

For some of your goals, you may prefer going it alone, whereas for other goals, you may want to be with one or more others. This is useful information, and it is part of our general belief that a balanced life entails some things done alone and others done in concert. Stated another way, you can determine the areas of your life in which you are an individualist and those in which you are a collectivist.

DIFFERENT WAYS TO POSITIVE OUTCOMES

So far, we have discussed how thinking styles influence the development of goals in the lives of both Westerners and Easterners. Differences also exist, however, in the routes that each group uses to move toward its goals. Western-oriented thinking focuses on the individual's goal, whereas Eastern philosophers suggest a different focus, one in which the group is highlighted. Here, we detail constructs that may have particular value to the different groups. For Western cultures, the construct of hope is a key component mentioned throughout time. For Eastern cultures, the constructs of compassion and harmony are highly valued.

The "Rugged Individualist," the Construct of Hope, and the Need for Uniqueness

Hope has been a powerful underlying force in Western civilization. Indeed, looking back through the recorded history of Western civilization and religion, hope—the agentic, goal-focused thinking that gets one from here to there—has been so interwoven into the fabric of our civilization's eras and events that it can be hard to detect. In this regard, the belief in a positive future is reflected in many of our everyday ideas and words.

During the Dark Ages, intellectual and social immobility pervaded and a paralysis of curiosity and initiative existed. From the years of the Middle Ages (500–1500), such paralysis precluded the purposeful, sustained planning and action required by a hopeful, advancing society. The fires of advancement were reduced to embers during this dark millennium and kept glowing only by a few institutions such as the monasteries and their schools. Eventually, as the Dark Ages were ended by the brightness of the Renaissance and its economic growth and prosperity, hope was seen as more relevant to present life on Earth than to the afterlife (i.e., a better life on Earth became possible, even probable).

With the advent of the Renaissance, these active and hopeful thoughts began to be coupled with goal-directed actions. The period following the Renaissance, from approximately 1700 to the late 1700s, is known as the Age of Enlightenment. In a cultural atmosphere conducive to exploration and change, the Enlightenment reflected the nature of hope because of its emphases on rational agencies and rational abilities. These qualities were interwoven in the dominant belief of the age, that reason brought to life with the scientific method led to the achievements in science and philosophy. These latter perspectives are in direct contrast to the prevalence of ignorance, superstition, and the acceptance of authority that characterized the Middle Ages. Education, free speech, and the acceptance of new ideas burgeoned during the Enlightenment. Indeed, the consequences of such enlightened thinking were long lasting and reflective of the power of hope.

Beginning approximately in the late 1700s and continuing to the end of the 1800s was the period known as the Industrial Revolution (or the Age of Industrialization). The movement of production from homes and small workshops to large factories vastly increased material benefits for individual citizens and made hope for the future seem more attainable.

Western civilization has been defined by its critical mass of hopeful events and beliefs. Before the Renaissance, the Enlightenment, and the Industrial Revolution, and even during the Middle Ages, hopeful thinking was a critical part of humankind's belief system. If some historical eras do not reveal major signs, there nonetheless have been implicit markers of hope. The idea of hope has served as an underpinning for thinking in Western civilization. Personal and individual goals, as exemplified by the construct of hope, seem to be the primary tool of the "rugged individualist" (i.e., Westerner) in moving toward the good life.

The Need for Uniqueness

Let's take another look at Figure 2.1. Although it is true that the norms in individualistic societies emphasize the person (see the dotted line with an arrow at the bottom), you will notice that some people belong toward the group end of the continuum and others toward the individual end. In this latter regard, we now explore the desire to manifest specialness relative to other people.

The pursuit of individualistic goals to produce a sense of specialness has been termed the need for uniqueness (see Lynn & Snyder, 2002; Snyder & Fromkin, 1977, 1980; Vignoles, 2009). This need is posited to have a strong appeal to many, as people often seek to maintain some degree of difference from others (as well as to maintain a bond to other people). In the 1970s, researchers Howard Fromkin and C. R. Snyder (see Snyder & Fromkin, 1977, 1980) embarked on a program of research based on the premise that most people have some desire to be special relative to others. They called this human motive the *need for uniqueness*; others have termed it the *motive for distinctiveness* (Vignoles). Beyond establishing that some specialness was desirable for most of the people in their samples from the United States, these researchers also reasoned that some people have a very high need for uniqueness, or distinctiveness, whereas others have a very low need for uniqueness.

Encoding of Similarity Information

People define themselves along a variety of identity dimensions. An identity dimension is defined as "a set of person attributes which have a common core of meaning" (Miller, 1963, p. 676). In their theory of uniqueness, Snyder and Fromkin (1980) proposed that people think about their perceived similarity to others and use a dimension (in their minds) on which they evaluate how correct any given feedback seems about their degree of similarity to other people (technically, this is encoded on a uniqueness identity schema). In brief, people evaluate the acceptability of their having varying degrees of similarity to other people. These hypothetical encodings on the uniqueness identity dimension are shown in Figure 2.2.

As can be seen in Figure 2.2, the similarity information is encoded as increasingly higher in acceptability, from very slight, to slight, to moderate, to high levels of perceived similarity to others, with a drop to low acceptability for very high similarity. Thus, the moderate-to-high sense of similarity is rated as the most comfortable, most accurate one for people—the reasons being that people realize that most others are somewhat similar to them (see Brown, 1991) and that people desire some specialness. In other words, in terms of *reality as people actually have perceived it* and *how they want it to be,* people prefer the moderate-to-high range of similarity (points C and D in Figure 2.2). Finally, people are not comfortable with either of the extremes of low similarity (point A in Figure 2.2) or high similarity (point E in Figure 2.2).

Emotional and Behavioral Reactions to Similarity Information

When confronted with the varying degrees of perceived similarity that produce the acceptability encodings of Figure 2.2, people then should have the most positive emotional reactions when they perceive that they are highly similar to others (point D in Figure 2.2). Consistent with this hypothesis, people's emotional reactions become more positive as levels of similarity increase from the very slight, to slight, to moderate, to high, becoming negative as the level of similarity enters the

Figure 2.2   Acceptability Encoding as a Function of Perceived Similarity to Other People

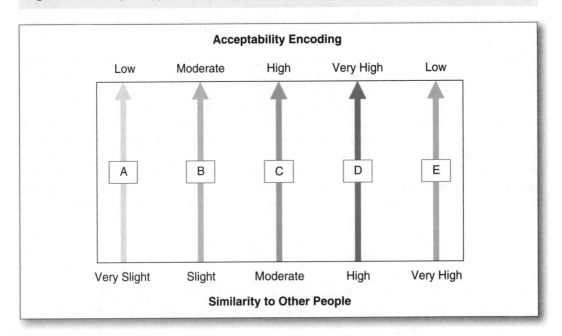

Figure 2.3   Emotional Reactions as a Function of Perceived Similarity to Other People

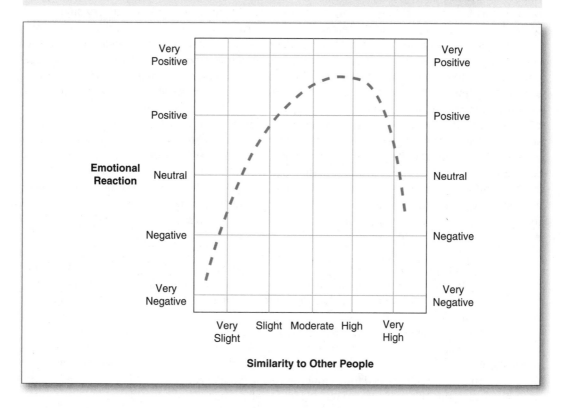

very high range (Figure 2.3). Note that the very highest positive emotional reactions occur when people perceive that they have a relatively moderate to high degree of similarity, thereby showing the maximal pleasure derived from human bonds.

It may help here to give an example of how moderate similarity to another person is emotionally satisfying. I (JTP) reflect upon my initial reaction at moving from California to the Midwest for graduate school as a good example of the desire for moderate similarity. At first, I was a bit taken aback at being one of very few individuals of racial minority background on my new campus. Feeling very different was a challenge at first, and looking for some similarity in fellow students became a goal of mine. It was a stroke of good luck that another student in my cohort shared this circumstance and was having a similar experience. We soon discovered that we were also both of biracial descent, though of different racial groups. This moderate similarity provided us with some shared experiences and understandings, while still allowing for our own individual differences. Our friendship has now lasted more than 15 years, and, as we have moved through other experiences in life (parenthood, professional development, etc.), we continue to enjoy the emotional satisfaction that comes from having these moderate similarities.

The acceptability reactions that result from a degree of perceived similarity to others (see Figure 2.2) also can cause people to change their actual behaviors to become more or less similar to another person. More specifically, the most positive acceptability (i.e., high similarity) not only produces the highest positive emotional reactions, but it also should result in no need to make any behavioral changes relative to other people. On the other hand, a very slight level of similarity to others yields low acceptability; therefore, people should change to become more similar to others. Moreover, a very high level of similarity to other people is low in acceptability, and therefore people should change to become less similar to others. In this latter sense, because people's need for uniqueness is not being satisfied, they should strive to reestablish their differences. Consistent with these predicted behavioral reactions, the results of several studies (see Figure 2.4) have supported this proposed pattern (Snyder & Fromkin, 1980).

To illustrate how people actually may change because of feedback that they are extremely similar to others, consider the reactions of a young woman named Shandra. After joining a sorority at the beginning of college, she was required to wear the same outfits as her sorority sisters whenever they went on group trips. From the beginning, Shandra reacted negatively to what she saw as "uniform requirements" that were being placed on her. In a bold attempt to break away and assert her uniqueness, Shandra started wearing outfits that differed from those of her sorority sisters. Her "sisters" tried to get her to conform, but Shandra stood fast in her desire to dress differently. In fact, she later resigned from this sorority because of their reaction to her desire to be unique.

Taken together, these findings suggest that people are drawn to moderate-to-high levels of perceived similarity to their fellow humans but that there are upper limits to this desire for the human bond. Furthermore, there appears to be a desire for balance in this area, such that people are motivated by a need for uniqueness when they feel too much similarity and that they will strive for similarity when they feel too different. Based on the previously discussed theoretical predictions and findings on uniqueness-related behaviors, Snyder and Fromkin (1977) proposed that there should be individual differences in self-reported need for uniqueness. Accordingly, they developed and validated the Need for Uniqueness Scale (Snyder & Fromkin, 1977). This self-report scale appears in the Appendix. If you would like to get a sense of your own desire for specialness by completing the scale, refer to this Appendix.

Uniqueness Attributes

Having explored the personal need for uniqueness, at this point we describe the acceptable societal processes by which our uniqueness needs are met. People are punished when they deviate from normal or expected behaviors in a society (Goffman, 1963; Schachter, 1951). Thus, unusual behaviors quickly may elicit societal disapprovals and rejections (see Becker, 1963; Freedman & Doob, 1968; Goffman, 1963; Palmer, 1970; Schur, 1969). On the other hand, the following of rules (normal behaviors) typically does not elicit much reaction from other people.

How, then, are people to show their specialness? Fortunately, each society has some acceptable attributes whereby its citizens can show their differences, and these are called *uniqueness attributes*. On this point, Snyder and Fromkin (1980, p. 107) have written, "There are a number of attributes (physical, material, informational, experiential, etc.) that are valued because they define the person as different from members of his or her reference group and that, at the same time, will not call down the forces of rejection and isolation for deviancy."

One example may be found in the attractiveness to "scarce commodities" in our society. Salespeople know this is a desire and often use a "Hurry on down while the supply lasts" pitch

Figure 2.4   Direction and Amount of Change as a Function of Perceived Similarity to Other People

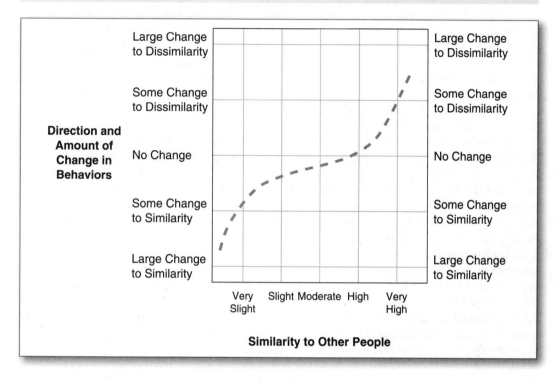

to draw in potential buyers. In what has been called a "catch-22 carousel" (Snyder, 1992), advertisers use uniqueness appeals to persuade people to buy products, and then, by making yearly changes in their products (styles of clothes, cars, etc.), motivate customers to purchase the latest version. The irony is that, after the latest uniqueness-based advertisement has persuaded people to buy, they notice that what they have bought is now quite common—many other people also have it. Of course, the yearly change of styles keeps people on the consumer "catch-22 carousel."

We have reviewed the theory and measurement of hope and the need for uniqueness, which are perhaps two of the quintessential Western constructs. We now turn to the Eastern side, for a closer look at two more collectivist constructs: compassion and harmony.

Eastern Values: Compassion and Harmony

In the main Eastern philosophical branches of learning (Confucianism, Taoism, Buddhism, and Hinduism), repeated mention is made of the two constructs of compassion for others and the search for harmony or life balance. Thus, each has a clear place in the study of positive psychology from an Eastern perspective.

The idea of compassion has origins in both Western and Eastern philosophies. Within the Western tradition, Aristotle often is noted for early writings on the concept of compassion. Likewise, compassion can be traced in the Eastern traditions of Confucianism, Taoism, Buddhism, and Hinduism. In Confucian teachings, compassion is discussed within the concept of *jen* (humanity) and is said to encapsulate all other virtues. Within the Taoist belief system, humanity also reflects behaviors that must occur naturally, without premeditation. Finally, the Buddha often is described as "perfectly enlightened, and boundlessly compassionate" (Sangharakshita, 1991, p. 3). As such, the idea of compassion, or *karuna,* also is woven throughout Buddhism as a virtue on the path toward transcendence. Finally, within the Hindu tradition, compassion is called for in good actions toward others, which will direct followers upon the path that will not require them to return to Earth after death.

In recent writings in positive psychology, physician Eric Cassell (2009) proposes the three following requirements for compassion: (1) the difficulties of the recipient must be serious, (2) the recipient's difficulties cannot be self-inflicted, and (3) we, as observers, must be able to identify with the recipient's suffering. Compassion is described as a "unilateral emotion" (Cassell, p. 394) that is directed outward from oneself. In Buddhist teachings, the attainment of compassion means being able to "transcend preoccupation with the centrality of self" (Cassell, p. 397)—to focus on others rather than merely on ourselves. The ability to possess feelings for something completely separate from our own suffering allows us to transcend the self and, in this way, to be closer to the achievement of the "good life." In fact, transcendental compassion is said to be the most significant of the four universal virtues, and it often is called Great Compassion (*mahakaruna*) to distinguish it from the more applied *karuna* (Sangharakshita, 1991). Similarly, although discussed in somewhat different ways as Confucian, Taoist, and Hindu principles, the capacities to feel and to do for others are central to achieving the "good life" for each of these traditions as well.

Possessing compassion helps the person to succeed in life and is viewed as a major strength within the Eastern tradition. Feeling for fellow group members may allow identification with others and development of group cohesion. Furthermore, acting compassionately fosters group, rather than personal, happiness.

Compassion also may come more naturally to a person from a collectivist culture than to someone from an individualist culture. On this point, researchers have argued that a collectivist culture may breed a sense of compassion in the form of its members' prosocial behaviors (Batson, 1991; Batson, Ahmad, & Lishner, 2009). When a group identity has been formed, therefore, the natural choice may be group benefits over individual ones. More information from qualitative and quantitative studies in this area would be helpful in defining the mechanisms used to foster such compassion.

Within Eastern traditions, in particular, it is taught that the ability to feel for others is a necessary part of the search for the good life. Compassion, an aspect of humanity, involves looking outside ourselves and thinking about others as we care for and identify with them. This other-than-self focus is needed to transcend one's physical body, according to Eastern traditions. Thus, nirvana can be attained only when one's independent identity and the self-motivated desires that accompany it are eradicated completely.

In moving toward the good life, therefore, compassion is essential for dealing with daily life tasks. As one walks along the path toward this good life, the continual goal is to transcend the human plane and to become enlightened through experiences with others and the world. Compassion asks people to think outside themselves and to connect with others. Additionally, as the person comes to understand others, she or he comes closer to self-understanding. This is yet another key component in attaining transcendence.

In Western history, the Greeks are said to have viewed happiness as the ability "to exercise powers in pursuit of excellence in a life free from constraints" (Nisbett, 2003, pp. 2–3). Thus, the good life was viewed as a life with no ties to duty and the freedom to pursue individual goals. There are clear distinctions in comparing this idea of happiness to Confucian teachings, for example, in which duty (*yi*) is a primary virtue. In Eastern philosophy, happiness is described as having the "satisfactions of a plain country life, shared within a *harmonious* social network" (Nisbett, pp. 5–6, emphasis added). In this tradition, harmony is viewed as central to achieving happiness.

In Buddhist teachings, when people reach a state of nirvana, they have reached a peacefulness entailing "complete harmony, balance, and equilibrium" (Sangharakshita, 1991, p. 135). Similarly, in Confucian teachings, harmony is viewed as crucial for happiness. Confucius had high praise for individuals who were able to harmonize; he compared this capacity to "a good cook blending the flavors and creat[ing] something harmonious and delicious" (Nisbett, 2003, p. 7). Getting along with others allows the person to be freed from individual pursuits and, in so doing, to gain "collective agency" (Nisbett, 2003, p. 6) in working out what is good for the group. Thus, the harmonizing principle is a central tenet of the Eastern way of life. The balance and harmony that one achieves as part of an enlightened life often are thought to represent the ultimate end of the good life. In Hindu teachings, one also can see that, as all humans are interconnected by a "single unifying principle" (Stevenson & Haberman, 1998, p. 46), harmony must be pursued. If an individual walks through life without thought of others as connected to him or her, the effects may be far-reaching for both the individual and the group (Stevenson & Haberman, 1998).

The concept of harmony has received minimal attention in the field of positive psychology to date, although some attention has been given to the idea of appreciating balance in one's life in reference to certain other constructs (e.g., wisdom; see Baltes & Staudinger, 2000, and Chapter 9). Moreover, Clifton and colleagues (Buckingham & Clifton, 2001; Lopez, Hodges, & Harter, 2005) include a harmony theme in the Clifton StrengthsFinder (see Chapter 3); they describe this construct as a desire to find consensus among the group, as opposed to putting forth conflicting ideas. Little more scholarly attention has been paid to harmony in American psychological literature. Given the central role of harmony as a strength in Eastern cultures, more research may be warranted on this topic in the future. First, the concept of harmony often is mistakenly equated with the notion of conformity. Studies to ferret out the differences between these two constructs could be beneficial in defining each more clearly. Because the term *conformity* has somewhat negative connotations in our independence-oriented culture, it is possible that some of these same negative characterizations have been extended to the concept of harmony.

Second, qualitative research methods could be used to develop a better definition of harmony. At present, the concept of harmony is reflected in the virtue of justice as discussed by Peterson and Seligman (2004) in their classification of strengths. These authors note that the ability to "work well as a member of a group or team; being loyal to the group; doing one's share" (p. 30) may be a subset of the idea of civic strength. Although this may be one way to classify this strength, it might be argued that the idea of harmony is broader than this particular definition and may be thought of separately from loyalty and "pitching in." Furthermore, the phenomenon of harmony may be both an interpersonal strength (as described in the previous paragraphs) and an intrapersonal strength.

Finally, after more conceptual work is completed, positive psychology scholars interested in harmony would benefit greatly from the development of reliable and valid measuring devices. Such tools would help researchers to uncover the primary contributors and correlates of harmony.

WHERE WE ARE GOING: FROM ME TO WE TO US

In this chapter, we have discussed two important human frameworks—individualist and collectivist—and the historical traditions derived from them that are relevant to positive psychology. In closing this chapter, we propose that being able to utilize a blend of the one and the many—the WE/ME, or, more simply, US—may enhance our ability to interact with a variety of others and spur our multicultural competence. This approach represents an intermingling in which both the individual and the group are able to be considered for satisfying and productive lives. As we see it, the US perspective reflects a viable positive psychology resolution for a more multiculturally competent world.

ME/WE BALANCE: THE POSITIVE PSYCHOLOGY OF US

Both the Individualistic and the Collectivistic Perspectives Are Viable

Social scientists often have conceptualized individualism and collectivism as opposites (Hui, 1988; Oyserman et al., 2002), and this polarity typically has been applied when contrasting the individualism of European Americans with the collectivism of East Asians (Chan, 1994; Kitayama, Markus, Matsumoto, & Norasakkunkit, 1997). This polarity approach strikes us as being neither good science nor necessarily a productive strategy for fostering healthy interactions among people from varying ethnicities within and across societies.

Viewing individualism and collectivism as opposites also has the potential to provoke disputes in which the members of each camp attempt to demonstrate the superiority of their approach. Such acrimony between these two perspectives seems especially problematic given that the distinctions between individualism and collectivism have not been found to be clear cut. For example, Vandello and Cohen (1999) found that, even within individualistic societies such as the United States, the form of the individualism differs in the Northeast, the Midwest, the Deep South, and the West. Moreover, cultures are extremely diverse; each has dynamic and changing social systems that are far from the monolithic simplicities suggested by the labels "individualist" and "collectivist" (Bandura, 2000; Vargas & Kemmelmeier, 2013). Likewise, there may be generational differences in the degree to which individualism and collectivism are manifested (e.g., Matsumoto, Kudoh, & Takeuchi, 1996). And when different reference groups become more salient, propensities toward individualism and collectivism vary (Freeman & Bordia, 2001). Furthermore, a seemingly individualistic propensity in actuality may contribute to collectivism; for example, consider the fact that a robust personal sense of efficacy may contribute to the collective efficacy of a society (Fernandez-Ballesteros, Diez-Nicolas, Caprara, Barbaranelli, & Bandura, 2002).

The United States has always been thought of as a very individualistic nation. Current reports, however, suggest that this may have had more to do with the fact that the majority of individuals living in the United States were originally of European (Western) origin. Interestingly, today, as more and more non-Europeans reside in the United States, changes are beginning to emerge with regard to the individualist orientation of the country as a whole (Vargas & Kemmelmeier, 2013). Today, there is preliminary "evidence of convergence of cultural orientations" (Vargas & Kemmelmeier, 2013, p. 195). In this way, perhaps due to its unique diversity of cultural influences, the United States is becoming more of an "US" nation. That said, there are still verifiable differences between cultural groups (e.g., African American, Latino, Asian American, and Caucasian) that appear to be related to systematic socioeconomic differences between these groups (Vargas & Kemmelmeier, 2013). These distinct differences are most marked between European Americans/Asian Americans versus their African American/Latino counterparts. The fact that these economically disadvantaged groups are lower in competitiveness is a finding that might suggest a sense of hopelessness at being able to compete in the first place due to their disadvantages. It is also a possibility that cooperation is more necessary at a lower socioeconomic status. If our goal is to see more of an understanding of both individualistic and collectivistic mindsets, and a potential convergence toward each other to some extent, we may need to work harder to extend economic equality across cultural groups.

Based on findings such as these and others, researchers in the field have suggested that we should move beyond the rather static view of individualism and collectivism as separate categories and instead take more dynamic approaches to culture to find when, where, and why these mental sets operate (Oyserman et al, 2002; Vargas & Kemmelmeier, 2013). They argue for an understanding of how individualism and collectivism can operate together to benefit people. We, too, believe that both the individualist and collectivistic perspectives have advantages for people and that the best resolution is to learn to embrace aspects of each.

One characteristic of a happy and productive life is a sense of balance in one's views and actions. We believe that a positive psychology approach to this issue would equate the ME and the WE emphases. As shown in Figure 2.5, the ME/WE perspective allows a person to attend to both the person and the group. Indeed, this is what has been found to characterize the perspectives of high-hope people about their lives and their interactions with others (Snyder, 1994/2000, 2000b).

Figure 2.5   The Balanced Perspective: ME/WE

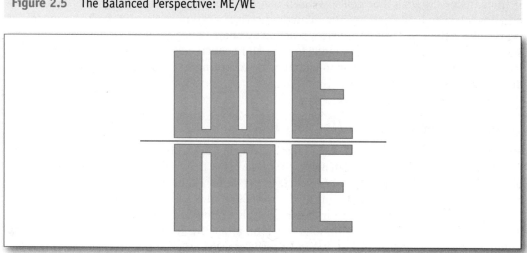

That is to say, in their upbringings, the high-hope children learned about the importance of other people and their perspectives and the role that consideration for others plays in the effective pursuit of personal goals. Just as the high-hopers think of ME goals, then, they simultaneously can envision the WE goals of other people. Thus, ME and WE become reflections of each other (see Figure 2.5). The high-hope people thereby think automatically of both the ME goals and the WE goals. Remember, too, that it is the high-hopers who seem to reap the greatest rewards in terms of successful performances and life satisfactions. In addition, being able to see things from a ME perspective and a WE perspective allows us all to interact with a larger group of individuals, even those who come from different perspectives than our own: "As the heterogeneity of American culture continues to expand, more opportunities for meaningful interaction between differing ethnic/racial groups have emerged than ever before" (Vargas & Kemmelmeier, 2013, p. 198). Being rigidly ME or WE may be problematic for these types of interactions.

Thinking About Your Own Life

Now that you have explored various issues related to the individualist and collectivist perspectives, it also may be informative to take a closer look at your own life. Have you ever thought about all the activities you undertake with an eye toward whether you would prefer to do them alone or with other people? We sometimes go about our lives on "automatic pilot" and do not give much thought to how we want to spend our time. Our point here is to help you get a better sense of your preferences for doing things alone or with others. Accordingly, we have developed a short exercise to help you to gain insights about your own desires to pursue goals alone or with others. If you have not done so already, complete the exercise "Being Alone or With Others" in the Personal Mini-Experiments (pp. 35–36).

Most people who have undertaken this exercise have been somewhat surprised at how important other people are to them as they try to reach desired goals. In fact, other people may be quite helpful when it comes to the goals we deem most important. Many of us, especially if we are individualists, see ourselves as being fairly independent as we go about our lives. But is this really so? As we pursue our goals, we also may be explicitly and implicitly intertwined with other people who help us reach them. Thus, our collectivist tendencies may be far stronger than we may have thought. A typical insight reached by people after completing this Personal Mini-Experiment is that they are *both* individualists and collectivists. Likewise, such individualistic and collectivistic thoughts and actions may vary according to the surrounding circumstances and people.

Suggestions for ME People (Individualists)

You now should have better ideas about your individualist and collectivist tendencies. In this section and the next, therefore, we offer some suggestions to help you navigate more effectively in environments in which people hold perspectives that differ from the individualistic or collectivistic ones that you typically hold. In this section, we offer advice for collectivists who will at times interact with individualists. (For an in-depth analysis of how individualists and collectivists can interact more effectively, we recommend the 1988 article by Triandis, Brislin, and Hui, "Cross-Cultural Training Across the Individualism-Collectivism Divide.")

To begin, individualists often perceive collectivists as being far too "laid back" and lacking in competitiveness. In this regard, it helps to realize that collectivists derive their sense of status from their group memberships and not from their personal accomplishments.

Individualists must take into account the collectivist norms in conducting business. That is to say, whereas the individualist may want to immediately get down to business when negotiating, the collectivists often expect some initial warm-up banter to set the stage. In this regard, collectivists want respect and patience between people (Cohen, 1991). When problem solving is needed, collectivists prefer that it be done at the group level, whereas individualists desire more one-on-one negotiating. Obviously, there are subtle differences, including important nonverbal gestures and cues, that must be honored when individualists and collectivists interact. Diversity can assist in productivity in a business due to the increase of ideas and thinking strategies (Cunningham, 2009), but if leaders are not cognizant of the differences in how collectivists and individualists interact, this gain could be lost.

Individualists should understand that collectivists want interpersonal harmony and therefore try very hard to avoid situations involving conflict (Ting-Toomey, 1994). In such circumstances, the individualists may view conflicts as a useful means of clearing the air so that people can move on to other matters, but they should realize that collectivists are quite concerned with saving face after such conflicts. Thus, individualists can help by solving problems before they escalate into huge confrontations. Similarly, the individualist should not push the collectivist into a corner by repeatedly asking confrontational "Why?" questions in response to which the collectivist must defend his or her position. Moreover, if conflict is necessary, the individualist should try, whenever possible, to help the collectivist maintain his or her pride (what sociologists call *face*).

Suggestions for WE People (Collectivists)

In this section, we offer advice for collectivists to interact more effectively with individualists. Collectivists often see individualists as too competitive. One useful lesson here is to understand that individualists see their status as based on their personal accomplishments rather than on their memberships in groups. Moreover, the more recent the accomplishments, the more power they wield in terms of status. Thus, collectivists should not be shocked when individualists do not seem impressed with group successes that are based in large part on lineage, family name, age, or gender (males may have more status in some collectivistic societies). It may help the collectivist to use recent accomplishments to attain status in the eyes of individualists with whom they interact.

Collectivists' dependence on cooperative solutions to dilemmas may not work when they are dealing with individualists. Instead, the collectivist must be able to take into account the "What's in it for me" perspective of the individualist in order to understand the latter's reactions during negotiations. Likewise, the normal arguing of individualists should not be interpreted by collectivists as intentionally hurtful behavior; this is just how the individualist conducts business. Thus, whereas a collectivist interacting with another collectivist may interpret "Let's have lunch" as a genuine invitation, it is often merely social talk when uttered by the individualist. Recognizing these cultural differences may help to diminish hurt feelings and misunderstandings, both of which can be detrimental to meaningful interactions between groups.

FINAL THOUGHTS

It is important to recognize that, in discussing Western and Eastern thoughts in this chapter, a central tenet of Eastern ways of life is broken in the decidedly Western, didactic teaching method used to bring this information to students of positive psychology. The traditional Easterner would object to the notion that the concepts here could be learned from mere words and would argue that only life experience would suffice. As part of Eastern teachings, self-exploration and actual hands-on experience are essential for true understanding of the concepts that are presented in only an introductory fashion in this chapter. Thus, we encourage students to seek out more experience of these ideas in everyday life and to attempt to discover the relevance of strengths such as hope, compassion, and harmony in your own lives, regardless of your cultural background. Ideas that stem from Eastern ideology can be relevant for Westerners who want to discover new ways of thinking about human functioning, and vice versa. Challenge yourself to be open minded about the types of characteristics to which you assign the label "strength" and about different perspectives, and remember that different traditions bring with them different values.

Stepping back and taking a "big-picture" view of how the people from various parts of our planet get along with each other, it is obvious that we do not have a very good record. Think of the irony in the fact that historians tend to view peace as anomalous periods between major conflicts of cultures. We wonder to what degree the previous warring of nations has reflected the difficulties of individualists and collectivists in understanding and getting along with each other (see Huntington, 1993).

There is an exceedingly important lesson here for individuals residing in the United States. Namely, those with individualist perspectives must realize that their views are not widely shared around the world. It has been estimated that 70% of the present 6 and a half billion or so people on Earth take a collectivist view of people and their interactions (Triandis, 1995). Let's do the math here: *That is about 4 and a half billion collectivists and 2 billion individualists.* As cherished as the individualist perspective held by many United States citizens may be, *individualists are the minority in a world populated by collectivists.*

The realization that all people are part of a larger whole may grow in the twenty-first century. We are becoming increasingly interdependent, and nowhere is this more obvious than in the operation of global markets that influence many countries (Keohane, 1993). The rapid change in our telecommunication technologies also has led to a globalization that has raised our consciousness about other peoples around the globe (Friedman, 2005; Holton, 2000; Robey, Khoo, & Powers, 2000).

In thinking about our relationships with each other, our futures will rest upon a willingness to cooperate and come together. Although the pursuit of specialness certainly can and has produced benefits for humankind, if too many people act in pursuit of their own individuality, we will miss our chance to work together to build shared cultures.

Considering the increased global access we have to one another as technology shrinks the distance between us, and the ever-increasing diversity occurring in the United States in particular, we are poised on the cusp of a major change in the balancing of individualism and collectivism—the needs of the "one" and the "many" (Newbrough, 1995; Snyder & Feldman, 2000). As such, the positive psychology of US may be just around the corner.

APPENDIX: THE NEED FOR UNIQUENESS SCALE

Directions: The following statements concern your perceptions about yourself in several situations. Rate your agreement with each statement by using a scale in which 1 denotes strong disagreement, 5 denotes strong agreement, and 2, 3, and 4 represent intermediate judgments. In the blanks before each statement, place a number from 1 to 5 from the following scale:

1	2	3	4	5
Strongest Disagreement				**Strongest Agreement**

There are no right or wrong answers, so select the number that most closely reflects you on each statement. Take your time, and consider each statement carefully.

_____ 1. When I am in a group of strangers, I am not reluctant to express my opinion publicly.

_____ 2. I find that criticism affects my self-esteem.

_____ 3. I sometimes hesitate to use my own ideas for fear that they might be impractical.

_____ 4. I think society should let reason lead it to new customs and throw aside old habits or mere traditions.

_____ 5. People frequently succeed in changing my mind.

_____ 6. I find it sometimes amusing to upset the dignity of teachers, judges, and "cultured" people.

_____ 7. I like wearing a uniform because it makes me proud to be a member of the organization it represents.

_____ 8. People have sometimes called me "stuck-up."

_____ 9. Others' disagreements make me uncomfortable.

_____10. I do not always need to live by the rules and standards of society.

_____11. I am unable to express my feelings if they result in undesirable consequences.

_____12. Being a success in one's career means making a contribution that no one else has made.

_____13. It bothers me if people think I am being too unconventional.

_____14. I always try to follow rules.

_____15. If I disagree with a superior on his or her views, I usually do not keep it to myself.

_____16. I speak up in meetings in order to oppose those whom I feel are wrong.

_____17. Feeling "different" in a crowd of people makes me feel uncomfortable.

_____18. If I must die, let it be an unusual death rather than an ordinary death in bed.

1	2	3	4	5
Strongest Disagreement				**Strongest Agreement**

_____19. I would rather be just like everyone else than be called a "freak."

_____20. I must admit I find it hard to work under strict rules and regulations.

_____21. I would rather be known for always trying new ideas than for employing well-trusted methods.

_____22. It is better to agree with the opinions of others than to be considered a disagreeable person.

_____23. I do not like to say unusual things to people.

_____24. I tend to express my opinions publicly, regardless of what others say.

_____25. As a rule, I strongly defend my own opinions.

_____26. I do not like to go my own way.

_____27. When I am with a group of people, I agree with their ideas so that no arguments will arise.

_____28. I tend to keep quiet in the presence of persons of higher ranks, experience, etc.

_____29. I have been quite independent and free from family rule.

_____30. Whenever I take part in group activities, I am somewhat of a nonconformist.

_____31. In most things in life, I believe in playing it safe rather than taking a gamble.

_____32. It is better to break rules than always to conform with an impersonal society.

To calculate the total Need for Uniqueness Scale score, first reverse each of the scores on items 2, 3, 5, 7, 9, 11, 13, 14, 17, 19, 22, 23, 26, 27, 28, and 31. That is, on these items only, perform the following reversals: 1—> 5; 2—> 4; 3—> 3; 4—> 2; 5—> 1. Then, add the scores on all 32 items, using the reversed scores for the aforementioned items. Higher scores reflect a higher need for uniqueness.

KEY TERMS

Athenian tradition: Western philosophical tradition focused on the writings and teachings of Plato and Aristotle.

Buddhism: A philosophical and religious system based on the teachings of Buddha: Life is dominated by suffering caused by desire; suffering ends when we end desire; and enlightenment obtained through right conduct, wisdom, and meditation releases one from desire, suffering, and rebirth.

Collectivism: A cultural value that prizes the concepts of sharing, cooperation, interdependence, and duty to the group.

A perspective in which the needs of the group are placed above the needs of the individual.

Compassion: An aspect of humanity that involves looking outside oneself and thinking about others as we care for and identify with them. In positive psychology, compassion requires (1) that the difficulty of the recipient be serious; (2) that the recipient's difficulties are not self-inflicted; and (3) that we, as observers, are able to identify with the recipient's suffering.

Confucianism: A philosophical and religious system developed from the teachings of Confucius. Confucianism values love for humanity, duty, etiquette, and truthfulness. Devotion to family, including ancestors, is also emphasized.

Enlightenment: A human's capacity to transcend desire and suffering and to see things clearly for what they are.

Harmony: A state of consensus or balance. Eastern traditions view harmony as essential to happiness.

Hinduism: A diverse body of religion, philosophy, and cultural practice native to and predominant in India. Hinduism is characterized by a belief in the interconnectedness of all things and emphasizes personal improvement with the goal of transcending the cycle of reincarnation.

Hope: As defined by Snyder, goal-directed thinking in which a person has the perceived capacity to find routes to desired goals (pathway thinking) and the requisite motivations to use those routes (agency thinking). Snyder believes that hope is not genetically based but an entirely learned and deliberate way of thinking. (See Chapter 8.)

Individualism: A cultural value that emphasizes individual achievement, competition, personal freedom, and autonomy. A perspective in which the needs of the individual are placed above the needs of the group.

Islam: A philosophical and religious tradition based on the teachings of Muhammad that emphasizes duty to one's fellow man. Followers believe in Allah as the creator and benefactor in all things.

Judeo-Christian tradition: Western religious tradition emphasizing Christianity and Judaism.

Need for uniqueness: The pursuit of individualistic goals to produce a sense of specialness.

Nirvana: A state in which the self is freed from desire. This is the final destination in the Buddhist philosophy.

Taoism: A philosophical and religious system developed by Lao-Tzu that advocates a simple, honest life and noninterference in the course of natural events.

CHAPTER 3

Classifications and Measures of Strengths and Positive Outcomes

Let us imagine that one could set up a kind of scale or yardstick to measure the success of life—the satisfactoriness to the individual and the environment in their mutual attempts to adapt themselves to each other. Toward the end of such a yardstick, positive adjectives like "peaceful," "constructive," "productive," might appear, and at the other end such words as "confused," "destructive," "chaotic." These would describe the situation in general. For the individual himself there might be at one end of the yardstick such terms as "healthy," "happy," "creative," and at the other end "miserable," "criminal," "delirious."

—Menninger, Mayman, & Pruyser (1963, p. 2)

Karl Menninger, one of the brothers who helped build the world-renowned Menninger Clinic, attempted to change the way that health care professionals viewed the diagnosis, prevention, and treatment of mental illness. As part of his mission, he encouraged clinicians and researchers to dispense with the old, confusing labels of sickness. Then, he called for the development of a simple diagnostic system that described the life *process* rather than *states* or *conditions*. Finally, he reminded us of the power of the "sublime expressions of the life instinct" (Menninger et al., 1963, p. 357), specifically hope, faith, and love. Over the last 50 years, psychology and psychiatry have busied themselves with the confused and miserable aspects of human nature, and, as a result of maintaining the pathology focus, health care providers have helped millions of people relieve their suffering. Unfortunately, too few professionals have engaged in the entire thought experiment described previously, and this has resulted in the unmet needs of millions more people. We continue to add complexity to an ever-growing diagnostic system (American Psychiatric Association, 2013); we know little about the process of living; and we spend far too little time and energy making sense of the intangibles of good living—hope, faith, and love. If Menninger were alive, we think he would consider our professional acumen and knowledge lacking in utility and out of balance.

Karl Menninger

Source: Reprinted with permission of the Menninger Clinic.

Most important, he probably would ask, "What about the productive and healthy aspects of personal functioning?"

Although the missions of many positive psychologists bear similarities to Dr. Menninger's ideas, there is a long way to go in measuring human strengths. (We subscribe to Linley and Harrington's [2006] definition of strength as a capacity for feeling, thinking, and behaving in a way that allows optimal functioning in the pursuit of valued outcomes.) In this regard, the argument can be made that work on the classification of illnesses had a 2,000-year head start on the more recent efforts to classify strengths and positive outcomes. Therefore, it is easy to understand why we have better understandings of weaknesses than we do of strengths. In the Menninger et al. (1963) review of the history of classifying disorders, it is noted that the Sumerians and the Egyptians drew distinctions between hysteria and melancholia as early as 2600 BC. The earliest attempt to define a set of virtues is contained in Confucian teachings dating to 500 BC, where Confucius systematically addressed *jen* (humanity or benevolence), *li* (observance of rituals and customs), *xin* (truthfulness), *yi* (duty or justice), and *zhi* (wisdom) (Cleary, 1992; Haberman, 1998; see Chapter 2 for a discussion of Confucian philosophy and other Eastern perspectives on positive psychology).

In the twenty-first century, two classifications of illness have attained worldwide acceptance. First, the World Health Organization's (1992) *International Classifications of Diseases (ICD)* is in its 10th edition and continues to evolve (the 11th edition is set for publication in 2015). Second, the American Psychiatric Association's (2013) *Diagnostic and Statistical Manual (DSM)* now is in its 7th iteration as the *DSM-5*. The *ICD* is broader in scope than the *DSM* in that it classifies all diseases, whereas the *DSM* describes only the mental disorders. Currently, no classification of strengths or positive outcomes has achieved worldwide use or acceptance. Some classifications and measures, however, have been created, refined, and broadly disseminated in the last decade. In this chapter, we discuss the following three classification systems:

1. The Gallup Themes of Talent (Buckingham & Clifton, 2001; Rath, 2007) as measured by the Clifton StrengthsFinder and the Clifton Youth StrengthsExplorer

2. The Values in Action (VIA) Classification of Strengths (Peterson & Seligman, 2004) as measured by the adult and youth versions of the VIA Inventory of Strengths

3. The Search Institute's 40 Developmental Assets (Benson, Leffert, Scales, & Blyth, 1998) as measured by the Search Institute Profiles of Student Life: Attitudes and Behaviors

Then, we explore the dimensions of well-being commonly used to describe mental health. Next, we call for greater attention to the development of broader descriptions and more sensitive measures of positive outcomes. Finally, we emphasize the need for a comprehensive and culturally competent classification of behavior.

CLASSIFICATIONS AND MEASURES OF STRENGTHS

Whether for positive traits and behaviors or for negative ones, the development of classification systems and measures is influenced by the values of culture and society and the professionals who create these values. As cultures change over time, it is important that these tools be revised regularly to remain applicable to their targeted groups. We now discuss the present three frameworks, along with measures of strengths and their psychometric properties (the measurement characteristics of the tools). Specifically, we comment on the reliability (the extent to which a scale is consistent or stable) and the validity (the extent to which a scale measures what it purports to measure) of these recently designed tools.

Gallup's Clifton StrengthsFinder

Over his 50-year career at the University of Nebraska, Selection Research Incorporated, and Gallup, Donald Clifton[1] studied success across a wide variety of business and education domains (Buckingham & Clifton, 2001; Clifton & Anderson, 2002; Clifton & Nelson, 1992, Rath, 2007). He based his analysis of success on a simple question: "What would happen if we studied what is right with people?" Furthermore, he focused on straightforward notions that stood the test of time and empirical scrutiny. First, Clifton believed that talents could be operationalized, studied, and accentuated in work and academic settings. Specifically, he defined talent as "naturally recurring patterns of thought, feeling, or behavior that can be productively applied" (Hodges & Clifton, 2004, p. 257) and manifested in life experiences characterized by yearnings, rapid learning, satisfaction, and timelessness. He considered these trait-like "raw materials" to be the products of normal, healthy development and successful childhood and adolescence experiences. Likewise, Clifton viewed strengths as extensions of talent. More precisely, the strength construct combines talent with associated knowledge and skills and is defined as the ability to provide consistent, near-perfect performance in a specific task.

Donald Clifton

Source: Reprinted with permission.

Second, Clifton considered success to be closely allied with personal talents, strengths, and analytical intelligence. Based on these beliefs, he identified hundreds of personal talents that predicted success in work and academics. Moreover, he constructed **empirically based** (grounded in theory and research findings), semistructured interviews for identifying these talents. When developing these interviews, Clifton and his colleagues examined the prescribed roles of a person (e.g., student, salesperson, administrator), visited the job site or academic setting, identified outstanding performers in these roles and settings, and determined the long-standing thoughts, feelings, and behaviors associated with situational success. These interviews also were useful in predicting positive outcomes (Schmidt & Rader, 1999) and subsequently were administered to more than 2 million people for the purposes of personal enrichment and employee selection. When considering the creation of an objective measure of talent in the mid-1990s, Clifton and his colleagues systematically reviewed the data in these interviews and identified about three dozen themes of talent involving enduring, positive personal qualities. (See Table 3.1 for a listing and description of the 34 themes in the Gallup classification system.)

Table 3.1   The 34 Clifton StrengthsFinder Themes

Achiever: People strong in the Achiever theme have a great deal of stamina and work hard. They take great satisfaction from being busy and productive.

Activator: People strong in the Activator theme can make things happen by turning thoughts into action. They are often impatient.

Adaptability: People strong in the Adaptability theme prefer to "go with the flow." They tend to be "now" people who take things as they come and discover the future one day at a time.

Analytical: People strong in the Analytical theme search for reasons and causes. They have the ability to think about all the factors that might affect a situation.

Arranger: People strong in the Arranger theme can organize, but they also have a flexibility that complements that ability. They like to figure out how all of the pieces and resources can be arranged for maximum productivity.

Belief: People strong in the Belief theme have certain core values that are unchanging. Out of those values emerges a defined purpose for their life.

Command: People strong in the Command theme have presence. They can take control of a situation and make decisions.

Communication: People strong in the Communication theme generally find it easy to put their thoughts into words. They are good conversationalists and presenters.

Competition: People strong in the Competition theme measure their progress against the performance of others. They strive to win first place and revel in contests.

Connectedness: People strong in the Connectedness theme have faith in links between all things. They believe there are few coincidences and that almost every event has a reason.

Consistency: People strong in the Consistency theme are keenly aware of the need to treat people the same. They try to treat everyone in the world with consistency by setting up clear rules and adhering to them.

Context: People strong in the Context theme enjoy thinking about the past. They understand the present by researching its history.

Deliberative: People strong in the Deliberative theme are best characterized by the serious care they take in making decisions or choices. They anticipate the obstacles.

Developer: People strong in the Developer theme recognize and cultivate the potential in others. They spot the signs of each small improvement and derive satisfaction from those improvements.

Discipline: People strong in the Discipline theme enjoy routine and structure. Their world is best described by the order they create.

Empathy: People strong in the Empathy theme can sense the feelings of other people by imagining themselves in others' lives and in others' situations.

Focus: People strong in the Focus theme can take a direction, follow through, and make the corrections necessary to stay on track.

Futuristic: People strong in the Futuristic theme are inspired by the future and what could be. They inspire others with their vision of the future.

Harmony: People strong in the Harmony theme look for consensus. They don't enjoy conflict; rather, they seek areas of agreement.

Ideation: People strong in the Ideation theme are fascinated by ideas. They are able to find connections between seemingly disparate phenomena.

Includer: People strong in the Includer theme are accepting of others. They show awareness of those who feel left out and make efforts to include them.

Individualization: People strong in the Individualization theme are intrigued with the unique qualities of each person. They have a gift for figuring out how people who are different can work together productively.

Input: People strong in the Input theme have a craving to know more. Often they like to collect and archive all kinds of information.

Intellection: People strong in the Intellection theme are characterized by their intellectual activity. They are introspective and appreciate intellectual discussions.

Learner: People strong in the Learner theme have a great desire to learn and want to improve continuously.

Maximizer: People strong in the Maximizer theme focus on strengths as a way to stimulate professional and group excellence. They seek to transform strengths into something superb.

(Continued)

Table 3.1 (Continued)

Positivity: People strong in the Positivity theme have an enthusiasm that is contagious. They are upbeat and can get others excited about what they are going to do.

Relator: People who are strong in the Relator theme enjoy close relationships with others. They find deep satisfaction in working hard with friends to achieve a goal.

Responsibility: People strong in the Responsibility theme take psychological ownership of what they say they will do. They are committed to stable values such as honesty and loyalty.

Restorative: People strong in the Restorative theme are adept at dealing with problems. They are good at figuring out what is wrong and resolving it.

Self-Assurance: People strong in the Self-Assurance theme feel confident in their ability to manage their own lives. They possess an inner compass that gives them confidence that their decisions are right.

Significance: People strong in the Significance theme want to be very important in the eyes of others. They are independent and want to be recognized.

Strategic: People strong in the Strategic theme create alternative ways to proceed. Faced with any given scenario, they can quickly spot the relevant patterns and issues.

WOO: WOO stands for "winning others over." People strong in the WOO theme love the challenge of meeting new people and winning them over. They derive satisfaction from breaking the ice and making a connection with another person.

Source: Reprinted with permission. Gallup®, StrengthsFinder®, Clifton StrengthsFinder™, and each of the 34 Clifton Strengths Finder theme names are trademarks of the Gallup Organization, Princeton, NJ.

The first step in developing the Clifton StrengthsFinder (see www.strengthsfinder.com) as an online measure was to construct a pool of more than 5,000 items. Selection of items was based on traditional construct, content, and criterion validity evidence, suggesting that the tool tapped underlying attributes, the full depth and breadth of content, and the shared relationships and predictive powers, respectively. A smaller pool was derived subsequently on the basis of item functioning. More specifically, the evidence used to evaluate the item pairs was taken from a database of more than 100 predictive validity studies (Schmidt & Rader, 1999). Factor and reliability analyses were conducted in multiple samples to produce maximal theme information in an instrument of minimal length. Many sets of items were pilot tested, and those with the strongest psychometric properties were retained.

In 1999, an online version of the Clifton StrengthsFinder was launched. That version had 35 themes. After several months of collecting data, the researchers decided on the 180 item pairs (360 items, 256 of which are scored) and the 34-theme version currently available. Although some theme names have changed since 1999, the theme definitions have not been altered. See Figure 3.1 for a

Figure 3.1 Clifton StrengthsFinder Signature Themes for Shane Lopez

Your Signature Themes

Many years of research conducted by The Gallup Organization suggest that the most effective people are those who understand their strengths and behaviors. These people are best able to develop strategies to meet and exceed the demands of their daily lives, their careers, and their families.

A review of the knowledge and skills you have acquired can provide a basic sense of your abilities, but an awareness and understanding of your natural talents will provide true insight into the core reasons behind your consistent successes.

Your Signature Themes report presents your five most dominant themes of talent, in the rank order revealed by your responses to StrengthsFinder. Of the 34 themes measured, these are your "top five."

Your Signature Themes are very important in maximizing the talents that lead to your successes. By focusing on your Signature Themes, separately and in combination, you can identify your talents, build them into strengths, and enjoy personal and career success through consistent, near-perfect performance.

Futuristic

"Wouldn't it be great if. . . ." You are the kind of person who loves to peer over the horizon. The future fascinates you. As if it were projected on the wall, you see in detail what the future might hold, and this detailed picture keeps pulling you forward, into tomorrow. While the exact content of the picture will depend on your other strengths and interests—a better product, a better team, a better life, or a better world—it will always be inspirational to you. You are a dreamer who sees visions of what could be and who cherishes those visions. When the present proves too frustrating and the people around you too pragmatic, you conjure up your visions of the future, and they energize you. They can energize others, too. In fact, very often people look to you to describe your visions of the future. They want a picture that can raise their sights and thereby their spirits. You can paint it for them. Practice. Choose your words carefully. Make the picture as vivid as possible. People will want to latch on to the hope you bring.

Maximizer

Excellence, not average, is your measure. Taking something from below average to slightly above average takes a great deal of effort and in your opinion is not very rewarding. Transforming something strong into something superb takes just as much effort but is much more thrilling. Strengths, whether yours or someone else's, fascinate you. Like a diver after pearls, you search them out, watching for the telltale signs of a strength. A glimpse of untutored excellence, rapid learning, a skill mastered without recourse to steps—all these are clues that a strength may be in play. And having found a strength, you feel compelled to nurture it, refine it, and stretch it toward excellence. You polish the pearl until it shines. This natural sorting of strengths means that others see you as discriminating. You choose to spend time with people

(Continued)

Figure 3.1 (Continued)

who appreciate your particular strengths. Likewise, you are attracted to others who seem to have found and cultivated their own strengths. You tend to avoid those who want to fix you and make you well rounded. You don't want to spend your life bemoaning what you lack. Rather, you want to capitalize on the gifts with which you are blessed. It's more fun. It's more productive. And, counterintuitively, it is more demanding.

Arranger

You are a conductor. When faced with a complex situation involving many factors, you enjoy managing all the variables, aligning and realigning them until you are sure you have arranged them in the most productive configuration possible. In your mind, there is nothing special about what you are doing. You are simply trying to figure out the best way to get things done. But others, lacking this theme, will be in awe of your ability. "How can you keep so many things in your head at once?" they will ask. "How can you stay so flexible, so willing to shelve well-laid plans in favor of some brand-new configuration that has just occurred to you?" But you cannot imagine behaving in any other way. You are a shining example of effective flexibility, whether you are changing travel schedules at the last minute because a better fare has popped up or mulling over just the right combination of people and resources to accomplish a new project. From the mundane to the complex, you are always looking for the perfect configuration. Of course, you are at your best in dynamic situations. Confronted with the unexpected, some complain that plans devised with such care cannot be changed, while others take refuge in the existing rules or procedures. You don't do either. Instead, you jump into the confusion, devising new options, hunting for new paths of least resistance, and figuring out new partnerships— because, after all, there might just be a better way.

Ideation

You are fascinated by ideas. What is an idea? An idea is a concept, the best explanation of the most events. You are delighted when you discover beneath the complex surface an elegantly simple concept to explain why things are the way they are. An idea is a connection. Yours is the kind of mind that is always looking for connections, and so you are intrigued when seemingly disparate phenomena can be linked by an obscure connection. An idea is a new perspective on familiar challenges. You revel in taking the world we all know and turning it around so we can view it from a strange but strangely enlightening angle. You love all these ideas because they are profound, because they are novel, because they are clarifying, because they are contrary, because they are bizarre. For all these reasons, you derive a jolt of energy whenever a new idea occurs to you. Others may label you creative or original or conceptual or even smart. Perhaps you are all of these. Who can be sure? What you are sure of is that ideas are thrilling. And on most days this is enough.

Strategic

The Strategic theme enables you to sort through the clutter and find the best route. It is not a skill that can be taught. It is a distinct way of thinking, a special perspective on the world at large. This perspective allows you to see patterns where others simply see complexity. Mindful of these patterns, you play out alternative scenarios, always asking, "What if this happened? Okay, well what if this happened?" This recurring question helps you see around the next corner. There you can evaluate accurately the potential obstacles. Guided by where you see each path leading, you start to make selections. You discard the paths that lead nowhere. You discard the paths that lead straight into resistance. You discard the paths that lead into a fog of confusion. You cull and make selections until you arrive at the chosen path—your strategy. Armed with your strategy, you strike forward. This is your Strategic theme at work: "What if?" Select. Strike.

Source: Reprinted with permission. Gallup®, StrengthsFinder 2.0®, Clifton StrengthsFinder 2.0™, and each of the 34 Clifton StrengthsFinder 2.0 theme names are trademarks of the Gallup Organization, Princeton, NJ.

summary of the signature themes of one of this textbook's authors (SJL). To learn your own Top 5, go to www.gallupstrengthscenter.com.

In the last decade, extensive psychometric research on the Clifton StrengthsFinder was conducted by Gallup researchers (and summarized in a technical report by Lopez, Hodges, & Harter, 2005, and Asplund, Agrawal, Hodges, Harter, & Lopez, 2014), which resulted in the revised 178-item StrengthsFinder 2.0, released in 2007 (Rath, 2007). Across samples, most scales (i.e., themes) on StrengthsFinder 2.0 have been found to be internally consistent (despite containing as few as four items) and stable over periods ranging from 1 week to 6 months. Specifically, the coefficient alphas have ranged from .52 to .79 (.70 or above is a desirable psychometric standard), with WOO having the highest internal consistency (.79) and Individualization, Input, and Relator having the lowest (all below .60). Regarding the stability of scales, most test–retest correlations were above .70 (considered appropriate for a measure of a personal trait).

Regarding construct validity, the theme score intercorrelations support the relative independence of themes, thereby showing that the 34 themes provide unique information. Finally, a study correlating Clifton StrengthsFinder themes with the Big 5 personality constructs (openness, conscientiousness, extroversion, agreeableness, and neuroticism; McCrae & Costa, 1987) provided initial evidence for the measures' convergent validity (i.e., they were correlated, but not at such a high level as to suggest redundancy). To date, there are no published studies examining the intercorrelations between the 34 theme scores and personality measures other than the Big 5 measure.

Today, the Clifton StrengthsFinder is available in 17 languages, and it is modifiable for individuals with disabilities. It is appropriate for administration to adolescents and adults with reading levels at 10th grade or higher. Although it is used to identify personal talents, the related supporting materials (e.g., Buckingham & Clifton, 2001; Clifton & Anderson, 2002; Clifton & Nelson, 1992; Rath, 2007) can help individuals discover how to build on their talents to develop strengths within their particular life roles. It should be noted, however, that this instrument is not designed or validated for use in employee selection or mental health screening. Another caveat also is warranted: namely, given that Clifton StrengthsFinder feedback (presented as your "Five Signature Themes") is provided to foster intrapersonal development, using it for comparisons of individuals' profiles is discouraged. (A respondent's top five themes, in order of potency, are included in the feedback. Remaining themes are not rank ordered and shared with respondents. This is also the case with the strengths feedback that results from the Values in Action measure, to be discussed subsequently.) Furthermore, the Clifton StrengthsFinder is not sensitive to change and, as such, it should not be used as a pre–post measure of growth.

Gallup developed a new talent classification system and a measure that is appropriate for children and youth (ages 10 to 14). This is called the Clifton Youth StrengthsExplorer and was released in 2006. StrengthsExplorer developers believe that knowledge about young people's strengths will help in directing their energies to maximize their potentials (P. Juszkiewicz, personal communication, November 7, 2005). The version of the StrengthsExplorer tested in the summer of 2005 taps 10 themes (Achieving, Caring, Competing, Confidence, Dependability, Discoverer, Future Thinker, Organizing, Presence, and Relating). When respondents complete the measure, they receive the Youth Workbook summarizing their top three themes and including action items and exercises that, if completed, could help youth capitalize on their strengths. Parent and educator guides also are available so that caregivers can help youth in developing their positive characteristics. (The psychometric report details the reliability and validity of the measure. See Lopez, Harter, Juszkiewicz, & Carr, 2007.)

The VIA Classification of Strengths

The VIA (Peterson & Seligman, 2004) Classification of Strengths serves as the antithesis of the *DSM,* and it holds promise for fostering our understanding of psychological strengths. Peterson and Seligman make the point that we currently have a shared language for speaking about the negative side of psychology, but we have no such equivalent terminology for describing human strengths. The VIA Classification of Strengths provides such a common language, and it encourages a more strength-based approach to diagnosis and treatment (treatment manuals focused on enhancing strengths may one day accompany the diagnostic manual). As these pioneering positive psychologists write, "We . . . rely on the 'new' psychology of traits that recognizes individual differences . . . that are stable and general but also shaped by the individual's setting and thus capable of change" (Peterson & Seligman, 2004, p. 5).

Christopher Peterson

Source: Reprinted with permission.

The VIA classification system, originally commissioned by the Mayerson Foundation, was generated in response to two basic questions: "(1) How can one define the concepts of 'strength' and 'highest potential,' and (2) how can one tell that a positive youth development program has succeeded in meeting its goals?" (Peterson & Seligman, 2004, p. v). These questions led to more philosophical and practical questions about character. Ultimately, Peterson and Seligman and many colleagues decided that components of character included virtues (core characteristics valued by some moral philosophers, religious thinkers, and everyday folk), character strengths (psychological processes and mechanisms that define virtues), and situational themes (specific habits that lead people to manifest strengths in particular situations).

The generation of entries for the classification system first was attempted by a small group of psychologists and psychiatrists after dozens of inventories of virtues and strengths and perspectives of character were reviewed. Upon applying 10 criteria for strength (e.g., a strength is morally valued in its own right; a person's display of a strength does not diminish other people) to a long list of potential constructs, 24 strengths were identified and then organized under 6 overarching virtues (wisdom and knowledge, courage, humanity, justice, temperance, and transcendence) thought to "emerge consensually across cultures and throughout time" (Peterson & Seligman, 2004, p. 29). Table 3.2 lists and describes the 6 virtues and 24 strengths. Peterson and Seligman state that their classification approach is sensitive to the developmental differences in which character strengths are displayed and deployed.

Table 3.2 The VIA Classification of Virtues and Strengths

Wisdom and Knowledge—Cognitive strengths that entail the acquisition and use of knowledge

  Creativity: Thinking of novel and productive ways to conceptualize and do things

  Curiosity: Taking an interest in ongoing experience for its own sake

  Open-mindedness: Thinking things through and examining them from all sides

  Love of learning: Mastering new skills, topics, and bodies of knowledge

  Perspective: Being able to provide wise counsel to others

Courage—Emotional strengths that involve the exercise of will to accomplish goals in the face of opposition, external and internal

  Bravery: Not shrinking from threat, challenge, difficulty, or pain

  Persistence: Finishing what one starts; persisting in a course of action in spite of obstacles

  Integrity: Speaking the truth but more broadly presenting oneself in a genuine way

  Vitality: Approaching life with excitement and energy; not doing anything halfheartedly

Humanity—Interpersonal strengths that involve tending and befriending others

  Love: Valuing close relations with others, in particular those in which caring is reciprocated

  Kindness: Doing favors and good deeds for others; helping them; taking care of them

  Social intelligence: Being aware of the motives and feelings of other people and oneself

Justice—Civic strengths that underlie healthy community life

  Citizenship: Working well as a member of a group or team; being loyal to a group

  Fairness: Treating all people the same according to the notions of fairness and justice

  Leadership: Encouraging a group of which one is a member to get things done

(Continued)

Table 3.2 (Continued)

Temperance—Strengths that protect against excess

Forgiveness and mercy: Forgiving those who have done wrong; accepting others' faults

Humility/Modesty: Letting one's accomplishments speak for themselves

Prudence: Being careful about one's choices; not taking undue risks

Self-regulation: Regulating what one feels and does; being disciplined

Transcendence—Strengths that forge connections to the larger universe and provide meaning

Appreciation of beauty and excellence: Noticing and appreciating beauty, excellence, and/or skilled performance in various domains of life

Gratitude: Being aware of and thankful for the good things that happen

Hope: Expecting the best in the future and working to achieve it

Humor: Liking to laugh and tease; bringing smiles to other people

Spirituality: Having coherent beliefs about the higher purpose and meaning of the universe

Source: From Peterson, C., & Seligman, M. E. P., *Character strengths and virtues: A handbook and classification*, Table 1.1: Classification of Character Strengths. Copyright © 2004 by Values in Action Institute. Used with permission of Oxford University Press, Inc.

The measure of this system of virtues and strengths, the Values in Action Inventory of Strengths (VIA-IS), was designed to describe the individual differences of character strengths on continua and not as distinct categories. The development of the measure was influenced by a tool once known as the "wellsprings" measure (Lutz, 2000), and it "took inspiration from the Gallup's Strengths-Finder measure . . . by wording items in extreme fashion ('I always . . .') and by providing feedback to respondents concerning their top—not bottom—strengths of character" (Peterson & Seligman, 2004, p. 628).

To date, the VIA-IS has been refined several times, and the current version appears reliable and valid for the purposes of identifying strengths in adults (based on summary information presented in Peterson & Seligman [2004], which is referenced heavily in this paragraph). Regarding the reliability of the measure, all scales have satisfactory consistency and stability across a 4-month period. Correlations among scales are higher than expected given that the inventory was designed to measure 24 unique constructs. Women score higher on humanity strengths than men, and African Americans score higher than members of other racial and ethnic groups on the scale of the spirituality strength. Evidence of the measure's validity includes the following three sets of findings:

1. Nominations of strengths by friends and family correlate at about a .50 level with matching scales' scores for most of the 24 strengths.

2. The majority of the scales correlate positively with scores on measures of life satisfaction.

3. Factor analyses provide some support for the existence of six virtues.

The results from the factor analysis conducted on existing data, however, actually suggest five factors (strengths of restraint, intellectual strengths, interpersonal strengths, emotional strengths, theological strengths) instead of the six proposed virtues. Peterson and Seligman (2004) described studies comparing strengths across groups of people, and they reason that the VIA-IS is an outcome measure that is sensitive to change. The researchers at the VIA Institute plan additional examinations of the psychometric properties of the measure.

The current iteration of the VIA-IS is available as an online (www.viame.org) and paper-and-pencil measure in English and several other languages. The 240 items, answered with a 5-point Likert scale, can be completed in about 30 minutes. The feedback report consists of the top five strengths, which are called signature strengths. See Figure 3.2 for the summary of this textbook's author's (JTP) report from the VIA-IS.

An adolescent version of this measure, referred to as the Values in Action Inventory of Strengths for Youth (VIA-Youth; for ages 10 to 17), has been developed. Preliminary validation of the VIA-Youth, which contains 96 items (also using a 5-point Likert scale), suggested that internal consistency of the scales is adequate for most and that the basic structure of the measure may be best described by four factors rather than six (Peterson & Park, 2003). Child and youth versions of a strengths cardsort (Lopez, Janowski, & Quinn, 2004; Quinn, 2004;), based on the 24 VIA strengths, have been developed, initially validated, and widely used by practitioners.

The Search Institute's 40 Developmental Assets

The Search Institute's Developmental Assets (Benson et al., 1998), which originally were conceptualized in the 1980s in response to the question, "What protects children from today's problems?" considers internal and external variables that contribute to a child's thriving. The Search Institute researchers, headed by Peter Benson, conducted numerous research projects and also held informal

---

Figure 3.2   VIA-IS Signature Strengths for Jennifer Teramoto Pedrotti

> **VIA Character Strengths Profile (English, United States)**
>
> Character Strength #1
>
> *Love*
>
> You value close relations with others, in particular those in which sharing and caring are reciprocated. The people to whom you feel most close are the same people who feel most close to you.

(Continued)

Figure 3.2 (Continued)

Character Strength #2

Bravery

You are a courageous person who does not shrink from threat, challenge, difficulty, or pain. You speak up for what is right even if there is opposition. You act on your convictions.

Character Strength #3

Hope

You expect the best in the future, and you work to achieve it. You believe that the future is something that you can control.

Character Strength #4

Social intelligence

You are aware of the motives and feelings of other people. You know what to do to fit in to different social situations, and you know what to do to put others at ease.

Character Strength #5

Fairness

Treating all people fairly is one of your abiding principles. You do not let your personal feelings bias your decisions about other people. You give everyone a chance.

Source: VIA Institute on Character, 2011.

discussions and focus groups to ensure that the developmental assets included in their framework were applicable to all people, cultures, and settings in America.

The Search Institute's 40 Developmental Assets are considered commonsense, positive experiences and qualities and are identified as reflecting primary contributors to the thriving of young people. The Developmental Assets framework categorizes assets according to external and internal groups of 20 assets each. The 20 external assets are the positive experiences that children and youth gain through interactions with people and institutions; the 20 internal assets are those personal characteristics and behaviors that stimulate the positive development of young people. (See Table 3.3.)

The 156-item survey, Search Institute Profiles of Student Life: Attitudes and Behaviors, was developed in 1989 and revised in 1996 (see Benson et al., 1998, for a review). The measure (appropriate for children and youth) describes the respondent's 40 Developmental Assets, along with 8 thriving indicators, 5 developmental deficits, and 24 risk-taking behaviors. Unfortunately, there is little information in the public domain about its psychometric properties.

Additional lists of developmental assets (for infants, toddlers, preschoolers, etc.) have been created by Dr. Benson and the Search Institute researchers. Parents and other caregivers are directed to observe the assets manifested by children and available in the environment.

Table 3.3   The Search Institute's 40 Developmental Assets

External Assets	
Support	
Family support	Family life provides high levels of love and support.
Positive family communication	Young person and her or his parent(s) communicate positively, and young person is willing to seek advice and counsel from parent(s).
Other adult relationships	Young person receives support from three or more nonparent adults.
Caring neighborhood	Young person experiences caring neighbors.
Caring school climate	School provides a caring, encouraging environment.
Parent involvement in schooling	Parent(s) are actively involved in helping young person succeed in school.
Empowerment	
Community values youth	Young person perceives that adults in the community value youth.
Youth as resources	Young people are given useful roles in the community.
Service to others	Young person serves in the community one hour or more per week.
Safety	Young person feels safe at home, at school, and in the neighborhood.
Boundaries and Expectations	
Family boundaries	Family has clear rules and consequences and monitors the young person's whereabouts.
School boundaries	School provides clear rules and consequences.
Neighborhood boundaries	Neighbors take responsibility for monitoring young people's behavior.
Adult role models	Parent(s) and other adults model positive, responsible behavior.
Positive peer influence	Young person's best friends model responsible behavior.
High expectations	Both parent(s) and teachers encourage the young person to do well.
Constructive Use of Time	
Creative activities	Young person spends three or more hours per week in lessons or practice in music, theater, or other arts.
Youth programs	Young person spends three or more hours per week in sports, clubs, or organizations at school and/or in community organizations.
Religious community	Young person spends one hour or more per week in activities in a religious institution.
Time at home	Young person is out with friends "with nothing special to do" two or fewer nights per week.

(Continued)

Table 3.3 (Continued)

Internal Assets	
Commitment to Learning	
Achievement motivation	Young person is motivated to do well in school.
School engagement	Young person is actively engaged in learning.
Homework	Young person reports doing at least one hour of homework every school day.
Bonding to school	Young person cares about her or his school.
Reading for pleasure	Young person reads for pleasure three or more hours per week.
Positive Values	
Caring	Young person places high value on helping other people.
Equality and social justice	Young person places high value on promoting equality and reducing hunger and poverty.
Integrity	Young person acts on convictions and stands up for her or his beliefs.
Honesty	Young person tells the truth even when it is not easy.
Responsibility	Young person accepts and takes personal responsibility.
Restraint	Young person believes it is important not to be sexually active or to use alcohol or other drugs.
Social Competencies	
Planning and decision making	Young person knows how to plan ahead and make choices.
Interpersonal competence	Young person has empathy, sensitivity, and friendship skills.
Cultural competence	Young person has knowledge of and comfort with people of different cultural/racial/ethnic backgrounds.
Resistance skills	Young person can resist negative peer pressure and dangerous situations.
Peaceful conflict resolution	Young person seeks to resolve conflict nonviolently.
Positive Identity	
Personal power	Young person feels he or she has control over "things that happen to me."
Self-esteem	Young person reports having high self-esteem.
Sense of purpose	Young person reports that "my life has a purpose."
Positive view of personal future	Young person is optimistic about her or his personal future.

Source: The 40 Developmental Assets™ are used with permission from Search Institute, Minneapolis, MN. More information is available at www.search-institute.org.

Distinguishing Among the Measures of Psychological Strength

Although the Clifton StrengthsFinder, the VIA-IS, and the Search Institute Profiles of Student Life were created for different reasons, they currently are used for similar purposes. Namely, they identify a person's primary strengths. Table 3.4 illustrates some of the similarities and differences among the measures. This information may help in the selection of the correct instrument for specific purposes, but more data should be solicited from the developers of the measures before making the final choice. The information below, regarding cultural equivalence, however, must be taken into consideration as well when using any of these measures.

Issues of Equivalence in Using Measures of Psychological Strength

It should be noted that each of these scales of measurement has been created within a Western framework. As such, different cultural groups may not define these concepts in the same way and may not respond to questions about the various constructs using the same signifiers. For example, the construct of Courage is defined by the VIA-IS as containing, in part, the factor of *Integrity*, which is defined by the authors as "speaking the truth but more broadly, presenting oneself in a genuine way." While this definitely fits for majority culture in the United States, it may not for other cultural groups. Collectivist groups, such as Asian cultures, may advocate integrity as going with the grain and not causing conflict, as well as preserving social order as opposed to always speaking the truth. In this way, an Asian individual may not endorse these items as similar to himself or herself, and as such end up with a profile that does not list courage as a strength. In an Asian culture, however, maintaining harmony regardless of personal feelings may certainly be viewed as being integrity-filled as well as courageous. Cross-cultural research has begun to be conducted with the VIA-IS (Park, Peterson, & Seligman, 2006), but data on race and ethnicity within the U.S. sample have not often been collected. This type of information regarding status within the country of origin is important, as it could be that these data are comparing majority groups across countries (e.g., majority groups in Japan or China to majority groups within the United States [i.e., White Americans]) and these profiles of groups who enjoy privilege within a country could be different from groups who have racial or ethnic minority status. Descriptions thus far may not provide the most complete picture of the within-group heterogeneity that may exist. This research gives us an important starting place for more culturally competent understandings of strengths, but the types of measurement issues mentioned here must be addressed, perhaps via qualitative research and studies that specifically sample various racial and ethnic minority groups.

In addition, these measures do not address manifestation or definition of these various traits, and thus more research in the areas of *cultural equivalence* must be conducted (Pedrotti, Edwards, & Lopez, 2009). In attempting to measure various strengths, it is often the case that researchers use measures that reflect their culturally normative understanding of a particular construct. This is problematic at times because there may be differences in terms of the way that this trait is defined in the two cultures, i.e., the two cultures do not have construct equivalence. For example, research shows that the concept of wisdom is defined differently in different cultural groups. In a study measuring wisdom in United States college students and Slovak college students, the first group viewed wisdom as a cognitive trait, while the second emphasized more affective components (Benedikovičová & Ardelt, 2008, see Chapter 9 for more details on this and other cultural studies of wisdom). If, for example, a researcher is from a Western context and develops a measure of wisdom that doesn't ask questions about the affective components of wisdom emphasized by the Slovak culture, he or she may miss crucial information about this construct if studying Slovak individuals. At best, this means that we have a dearth of information about particular cultural groups. At worst, however, this means that as a field we are setting up deficit models in which certain groups are thought not to possess a strength such as wisdom, purely because of a measurement error such as this.

In addition, other types of measurement equivalence can mask our true understanding of cultural similarities and differences (Ho et al., 2014). Linguistic equivalence, for example, must be established when measures for these positive traits are translated into languages other than the one in which they were originally developed (Mio, Barker, & Tumambing, 2009). Idioms, common phrases, and vocabulary may not translate well depending on the phraseology used in the scale, and as such appropriate procedures of translation and back-translation must be taken into consideration. Finally, metric equivalence must be considered, i.e., the same metric must be utilized in measuring a construct in one culture and comparing it to results found in another cultural group. When using a Likert scale, one may feel comfortable that the same metric is being used if the number of choices is equal on both scales. Some cultural groups, however, may be more or less adverse toward exhibiting extreme declarations, and as such even the commonly used Likert scale can have different meanings to different cultural groups (Mio et al.). If a 10-point scale is used, for example, with 1 denoting a low level of a particular trait and 10 denoting a high level of that same trait, these two numbers (1 and 10) are to be the outside markers of the measurement of this trait. Mio and colleagues state that some cultures may be more cautious about making extreme statements regarding their views and, as such, the ends of the continuum (i.e., 1 and 10) may never be used by members of this type of culture. In this case, the markers of 2 and 9 may be as low or high as members of these cultures are willing to go. This creates issues in metric equivalence for use of these scales with risk-adverse cultures. As such, researchers must take care to note these cultural factors before making comparisons between groups.

Often researchers tout the linguistic equivalence of their measure. "Offered in 12 different languages!" is often a comforting endorsement to the layperson and even the psychologist not well-versed in cultural equivalence issues. "It *must* be culturally competent," we think to ourselves, because such care was given as to translate this measure. It is very important to note that *linguistic* equivalence does not necessarily mean that a measure has conceptual equivalence. In some studies, similarities between cultures have been found (e.g., the German versus English version of the VIA-IS; Ruch et al., 2010). Very recently however, Choubisa and Singh (2011) analyzed the factor structure of the VIA-IS in past studies in different cultural groups and languages (i.e., the English version with an Indian sample, the Hindi version with an Indian sample, the English version with an Australian sample, the Croatian version with a Croatian sample, and the English version in a mixed sample). Researchers found that in comparing the use of the various versions of the VIA-IS in these studies, there was not a single consistent factor structure. Instead, different factor solutions were found for the different populations, ranging from a one-factor solution found in the Indian adaptation of the Hindi version of the VIA-IS (i.e., the various virtues could not be distinguished from one another statistically) to different five-factor structures found in studies using the English version in an Indian population and in a mixed population (Choubisa & Singh, 2011; Singh & Choubisa, 2010). The main finding we might take from this research is that it "suggests that culture may play a substantial role in the preferential

Table 3.4   Characteristics of Measures of Human Strengths

Measure	Cost $	Available Online	Completed in < 45 Minutes	Multiple Age-Specific Versions	Direct Focus on Environment
Gallup's Clifton StrengthsFinder	Yes	Yes	Yes	Yes	No
Values in Action Inventory of Strengths	No	Yes	Yes	Yes	No
Search Institute Profiles of Student Life	Yes	No	Yes	Yes	Yes

treatment, expression and usage of the character strengths" (Choubisa & Singh, 2011, p. 328). As such, it is important not to interpret linguistic equivalence as actual conceptual equivalence; just because a measure is offered in another language does not mean it is measuring the same thing in both cultures (see Chapter 4 of this volume for further discussion).

Identifying Your Personal Strengths

Over the years, we have asked hundreds of clients and students about their weaknesses and strengths. Almost without exception, people are much quicker to respond about weaknesses than strengths. (See the Personal Mini-Experiments to examine this issue and to explore your strengths by taking the measures discussed in this chapter.) We also have observed that people struggle for words when describing strengths, whereas they have no shortage of words or stories that bring their weaknesses to life.

PERSONAL MINI-EXPERIMENTS

Discovering and Capitalizing on Your Strengths

In this chapter, we have discussed classifications and measures of strengths. We encourage you to learn more about your personal strengths as they exist within your own cultural framework and to share them with friends, family, teachers, and coworkers.

(Continued)

(Continued)

Getting to Know Your Friend's Weaknesses and Strengths: Ask a friend (or several friends), "What are your weaknesses?" and note how quickly they respond to the question, how many weaknesses they identify, and how descriptive they are when telling the story of weaknesses. Then, ask that friend (or friends), "What are your strengths?" Make similar mental notes about reaction time, number of strengths, and descriptiveness. If you are asking these questions of more than one friend, alternate between asking the weaknesses question first and the strengths question first. In turn, share your thoughts about your strengths (before or after you complete the measures presented in this chapter), and ask for your friend's feedback on your self-assessment.

Discovering Your Strengths: In just over an hour, you can identify 10 of your personal strengths by completing the Clifton StrengthsFinder (www.gallupstrengthscenter.com) and the Values in Action Inventory of Strengths (www.positivepsychology.org). We encourage you to take both inventories and share the results with people close to you.

Capitalizing on Your Strengths: There are numerous strategies for capitalizing on your strengths (see www.strengthsquest.com and/or www.happier.com). For now, we would like you to capitalize on one strength. Pick 1 of your 10 strengths and try to use that strength 5 times a day for 5 days. Your 25 attempts to capitalize on that strength have the potential to bolster it and create a habit of using that strength more each day.

Viewing Your Strengths Within Your Personal Context: As stated above and in subsequent chapters in this text, strengths must be viewed within a cultural context. They can also be derived from your personal cultural facets (e.g., gender, race, nation of origin, etc.). For example, a Latina individual's heritage of collectivism might imbue her with natural strength in caring for others, and any individual born in the United States might find that the nation's ideal of possessing a "can-do" attitude has helped him or her to develop the strengths of perseverance and determination. What strengths might your cultural facets provide for you?

We hope that readers take advantage of the opportunity to discover their strengths and that in several decades people will have as much to say about their strengths as they do about their weaknesses. Our observations of people upon the completion of a strengths measure suggest that the new or validated information about your personal strengths will give you a slight, temporary boost in positive emotions and confidence. Also, you will want to share the results with people around you. In addition, a growing body of research points to the idea that using one's strengths is a source of, and sometimes a precursor to, increases in well-being. Researchers have found that use of strengths is able to predict changes and variance in subjective well-being within the individual (Govindji & Linley, 2007; Proctor, Maltby, & Linley, 2011). It follows logically that in knowing about our strengths we might more readily think of using them in our daily lives, and this can have an overall positive effect upon our personal well-being.

The Case of Shane

As positive psychologists, we have committed ourselves to the development of the positive in others and, of course, we try to practice what we preach. We both have identified our strengths through formal and informal assessment, and we try to capitalize on our strengths every day. Here is a brief account of how one of us (SJL) uses his strengths in daily life.

> When I received the results of the Clifton StrengthsFinder (see Figure 3.1) and the VIA-IS, I reflected on the findings and tried to figure out how I could put them to immediate use. Then, I realized that I have been using these strengths every day. . . that is why they are my strengths! Nevertheless, I decided to be more intentional in my efforts to make my strengths come alive. That goal of intentionality addressed *how* I would capitalize on my strengths, but I hadn't addressed *why*. It turns out, however, that it was pretty simple—I wanted to make my good life even better. That was the outcome I desired, and I thought that these "new" strengths would provide pathways to that goal.
>
> Admittedly, my initial efforts to intentionally use my strengths every day were not that successful. Although I thought the findings were accurate, and I was excited to receive the strengths feedback, I was overwhelmed by the idea of refining my use of 5 or 10 strengths at the same time. For that reason, I decided to capitalize on the strengths that I thought would help me the most in making my life better. I chose the top two themes (Futuristic and Maximizer) from the Gallup feedback and the top strength (Gratitude) from the VIA results. Right away, focusing on three strengths seemed doable.
>
> With those "three strengths that matter most" (as I began to refer to them) in hand, I consulted the action items (shared in a printable form as a supplement to the Signature Themes presented in Figure 3.1) associated with my Futuristic and Maximizer themes. For Futuristic, I settled on one daily activity that might spark my tendency to project into the future: Take time to think about the future. Pretty straightforward, but reading this action item made me realize that I would go for a considerable time without thinking about the future, and this led to dissatisfaction with how my life was going. Putting this guidance into action has involved taking daily walks dedicated to thinking about the future. Often, I walk in the evening, and I chat with my wife about the future of our work and our family. At other times, I leave the office around midday and walk through the campus reflecting on some of my aspirations. These walks have turned into a cherished time that yields exciting ideas and considerable satisfaction.
>
> Regarding my Maximizer theme, I believe this talent of making good ideas, projects, and relationships better contributes greatly to my success at work. Through examining my

habits at home and work, I realized I was doing a fairly good job of systematically using this strength. This left me feeling unsure about how to proceed in my efforts to capitalize on this strength. Then, one day I encountered a person who prided herself on playing "the devil's advocate" every time an idea was presented during a meeting. I thought about the many devil's advocates whom I have encountered over the years, and I concluded that these people were not necessarily providing constructive feedback that made a good idea better. They also were not offering alternative ideas that would work better. In my opinion, all they were doing was undercutting my creativity and enthusiasm (or that of other people). To maximize, I realized that I had to surround myself with people who knew how to make good ideas better. That criterion has become a critical one when I select friends, colleagues, and students, and I believe it has boosted my creativity and the quality of my work.

I have used Futuristic and Maximizing themes both at work and at home, and I think my efforts have helped me in both domains. I believe that capitalizing on these strengths has led to more creativity and productivity at work and greater sense of purpose for my family and me. Using gratitude (my third "strength that matters most") with more intentionality has not generated more productivity or greater clarity in my personal mission, but it has been rewarding in that it brings joy and a sense of closeness to people. To make the most of my gratitude, I decided to spend part of most Friday afternoons writing thank-you notes (handwritten and mailed the old-fashioned way) to people who have touched my life that week, and at other times I thank people who have done something nice for me that week. Occasionally, I write to a person who did a good deed for me years ago (and whom I had never thanked or whom I wanted to thank again). Finally, I also write to people who have done good works (I may or may not know them personally) to express my gratitude for their efforts. This practice has enriched my emotional life, and it has strengthened many of my relationships.

By focusing on three of my strengths, I have been successful at making an already good life even better. Over time, I have become more facile at capitalizing on other strengths, particularly ideation, hope, and wisdom. Living my strengths has become a way of life for me, and I look forward to finding out how this will influence the futures of my loved ones and me.

POSITIVE OUTCOMES FOR ALL

Dimensions of Well-Being

The pursuit of happiness has been the topic of discussion in religious writings, philosophical texts, and proclamations of the United States forefathers. Most recently, magazine articles and trade books have positioned happiness as the de facto central outcome of positive psychology research and practice. Yet, as described in this text, the pursuit of happiness is only one aspect of positive psychology. As positive psychology researchers and practitioners, we certainly want our participants and clients to be happy, but we also are interested in whether they are realizing their potentials, pursuing their interests, nurturing others, and leading authentic lives. To date, however, happiness (spontaneous reflections of pleasant and unpleasant feelings in one's immediate experience) and life satisfaction (a sense of contentment and peace stemming from small gaps between wants and needs) are of major interest in the positive psychology field. In this section of the chapter, we discuss happiness and life satisfaction as components of emotional well-being but not as the single or most important outcome in positive psychology. (This chapter provides a basic description of happiness as a meaningful life outcome. The basic research on happiness is discussed in Chapter 6. It is also important to consider that happiness is not necessarily a major goal, nor manifested or defined similarly, for individuals from all cultural backgrounds; see discussion of this in Chapter 4).

Theories of *subjective* well-being (also referred to as emotional well-being and happiness), such as the emotional model posited by Diener and others (Diener, 1984; Diener, Suh, Lucas, & Smith, 1999), suggest that individuals' appraisals of their own lives capture the essence of well-being. *Objective* approaches to understanding psychological well-being and social well-being have been proposed by Ryff (1989) and Keyes (1998), respectively. Our view is that psychological and social well-being provide useful frameworks for conceptualizing positive functioning, especially when viewed through a culturally appropriate lens. Taken together, subjective descriptions of emotional well-being (i.e., happiness) and objective descriptions of psychological and social well-being constitute a more complete portrayal of mental health (Keyes, 2009; Keyes & Lopez, 2002). Table 3.5 presents the descriptions of the three types of well-being and sample items that tap these components of positive functioning.

Emotional well-being consists of perceptions of avowed happiness and satisfaction with life, along with the balance of positive and negative affects. This threefold structure of emotional well-being consists of life satisfaction, positive affect, and the absence of negative affect, and it has been confirmed in numerous studies (e.g., Bryant & Veroff, 1982; Lucas, Diener, & Suh, 1996; Shmotkin, 1998). Indeed, the coupling of satisfaction and affect serves as a meaningful and measurable conceptualization of emotional well-being.

Ryff (1989) posits that some of the favorable outcomes described by positive psychologists can be integrated into a model of psychological well-being (see Table 3.5). Self-acceptance, personal growth, purpose in life, environmental mastery, autonomy, and positive relations with others are the six components of Ryff's conceptualization of positive functioning. This model of well-being has been investigated in numerous studies, and the findings reveal that the six dimensions are independent, though correlated, constructs of well-being. Specifically, Ryff and Keyes (1995) conducted an analysis of the six-part well-being model and found that the multidimensional model was a superior fit over a single-factor model of well-being.

Carol Ryff

Source: Reprinted with permission of Carol Ryff.

Table 3.5 Elements of Psychological, Social, and Emotional Well-Being

Psychological Well-Being	Social Well-Being	Emotional Well-Being
Self-acceptance: Possess positive attitude toward the self; acknowledge and accept multiple aspects of self; feel positive about past life.	**Social acceptance:** Have positive attitudes toward people; acknowledge others and generally accept people despite others' sometimes complex and perplexing behavior.	**Positive affect:** Experience symptoms that suggest enthusiasm, joy, and happiness for life.
• *I like most parts of my personality.* • *When I look at the story of my life, I am pleased with how things have turned out so far.* • *In many ways, I feel disappointed about my achievements in life. (-)*	• *People who do a favor expect nothing in return.* • *People do not care about other people's problems. (-)* • *I believe that people are kind.*	• *During the last 30 days, how much of the time did you feel cheerful; in good spirits; extremely happy; calm and peaceful; satisfied; and full of life?* **
Personal growth: Have feelings of continued development and potential and are open to new experience; feel increasingly knowledgeable and effective.	**Social actualization:** Care about and believe society is evolving positively; think society has potential to grow positively; think self/society is realizing potential.	**Negative affect:** Absence of symptoms that suggest that life is undesirable and unpleasant.
• *For me, life has been a continuous process of learning, changing, and growth.* • *I think it is important to have new experiences that challenge how I think about myself and the world.* • *I gave up trying to make big improvements/changes in my life a long time ago. (-)*	• *The world is becoming a better place for everyone.* • *Society has stopped making progress. (-)* • *Society hasn't improved for people like me. (-)*	• *During the last 30 days, how much of the time did you feel so sad nothing could cheer you up; nervous; restless or fidgety; hopeless; that everything was an effort; worthless?* **
Purpose in life: Have goals and a sense of direction in life; past life is meaningful; hold beliefs that give purpose to life.	**Social contribution:** Feel they have something valuable to give to the present and to society; think their daily activities are valued by their community.	**Life satisfaction:** A sense of contentment, peace, and satisfaction from small discrepancies between wants and needs with accomplishments and attainments.

Psychological Well-Being	Social Well-Being	Emotional Well-Being
• *Some people wander aimlessly through life, but I am not one of them.* • *I live life one day at a time and don't really think about the future. (-)* • *I sometimes feel as if I've done all there is to do in life. (-)*	• *I have something valuable to give to the world.* • *My daily activities do not create anything worthwhile for my community. (-)* • *I have nothing important to contribute to society. (-)*	• *During the past 30 days, how much of the time did you feel satisfied; full of life?*** • *Overall these days, how satisfied are you with your life? (0–10, where 0 = terrible and 10 = delighted)* • *Satisfaction may be measured in life domains such as work, home, neighborhood, health, intimacy, finances, and parenting, or it is measured globally. (see the Satisfaction With Life Scale, Diener et al., 1985).*
Environmental mastery: Feel competent and able to manage a complex environment; choose or create personally suitable community.	**Social integration:** Feel part of community; think they belong, feel supported, and share commonalities with community.	**Happiness:** Having a general feeling and experience of pleasure, contentment, and joy.
• *The demands of everyday life often get me down. (-)* • *In general, I feel I am in charge of the situation in which I live.* • *I am good at managing the responsibilities of daily life.*	• *I don't feel I belong to anything I'd call a community. (-)* • *I feel close to other people in my community.* • *My community is a source of comfort.*	• *Overall these days, how happy are you with your life?**** • *How frequently have you felt (joy, pleasure, happiness) in the past week, month, or year?*
Autonomy: Are self-determining, independent, and regulated internally; resist social pressures to think and act in certain ways; evaluate self by personal standards.		
• *I tend to be influenced by people with strong opinions. (-)* • *I have confidence in my own opinions even if they are different from the way most other people think.*		

(Continued)

Table 3.5 (Continued)

Psychological Well-Being	Social Well-Being	Emotional Well-Being
• I judge myself by what I think is important, not by the values of what others think is important.		
Positive relations with others: Have warm, satisfying, trusting relationships; are concerned about others' welfare; capable of strong empathy, affection, and intimacy; understand give-and-take of human relationships.		
• Maintaining close relationships has been difficult and frustrating for me. (-) • People would describe me as a giving person, willing to share my time with others. • I have not experienced many warm and trusting relationships with others. (-)		

Note: A negative sign in parenthesis indicates that the item is reverse scored. Response options range from strongly disagree (1), moderately disagree (2), or slightly disagree (3) to neither agree nor disagree (4), slightly agree (5), moderately agree (6), or strongly agree (7).

** Indicates response range from all the time (1), most of the time (2), some of the time (3), a little of the time (4), none of the time (5).

*** Indicates response range from worst possible situation (0) to best possible situation (10).

Keyes (1998) suggests that just as clinicians categorize the social challenges that are evident in an individual's life, so should they assess the social dimensions of well-being. On this point, he proposes that the dimensions of coherence, integration, actualization, contribution, and acceptance are the critical components of social well-being. Keyes (2009; Keyes & Lopez, 2002) also suggests that complete mental health can be conceptualized via combinations of high levels of emotional well-being, psychological well-being, and social well-being. Individuals with these high levels are described as flourishing (see the criteria in Table 3.6). Accordingly, individuals who have no mental illness but who have low levels of well-being are described as languishing. (We have found that informal assessment of levels of well-being provides valuable information about the range of functioning between flourishing and languishing.) This conceptualization of mental health describes a syndrome of symptoms that might be amenable to intervention techniques aimed at increasing levels of emotional, social, and psychological well-being. Conceptualization and treatment are well connected in this model.

A new, integrative theoretical perspective on well-being may provide additional assistance in bridging the gap between our research-based understanding of living well and the ability to promote it (Lent, 2004). By describing one model that explains our capacity for positive functioning during normative life conditions and one that provides direction for restoring well-being during difficult life circumstances, Lent highlights numerous treatment alternatives (e.g., setting goals, enhancing efficacy, building social support) that promote this much-prized life outcome.

Ong and Zautra (2009) discuss ways that well-being might be evaluated using empirical methods drawing upon a variety of research and analysis techniques. Longitudinal methodology may be a particularly important avenue toward getting a more accurate view of well-being in its complex manifestation in everyday life. Ong and colleagues (Ong & van Dulmen, 2007; Ong & Zautra, 2009) note that researchers must make use of techniques that explicate *nomothetic* (between-person) and *idiographic* (within-person) differences so as to avoid extra sources of error.

Toward a Better Understanding of Positive Outcomes

As discussed in this chapter and suggested elsewhere throughout this book, we believe that character strengths are the active ingredients of positive living. This belief can be tested empirically in everyday life and in research studies if, and only if, the definitions and measures of strengths capture the true essence of the best in people and do so within the cultural contexts in which they live. Therefore, we submit information in this chapter about three classifications of strengths and their respective measures for your critical evaluation.

Most of the remaining chapters of this text focus on the science of strengths (some of these strengths are not listed in the classification systems) that is being developed by clinical, counseling, developmental, health, evolutionary, personality, school, and social psychologists. Numerous chapters address the practice of leading a good life and how you and your friends and family capitalize on strengths and build on positive emotions to attain positive life outcomes. Notice that we do not address the "science of good living." Positive psychology research initiatives have done little to describe and measure outcomes other than those associated with happiness and life satisfaction, or "the pleasant life" (Seligman, 2002). Although we encourage a focus on objective aspects of well-being, we contend that a more expanded conceptualization of living well is needed to guide our efforts at change and positive growth. Here, in the remaining portion of this chapter, we dream a little about the future of positive psychology, one where romantic and agapic love; rewarding school, work, and civic contributions; and resource-producing play share the spotlight with happiness.

Positive Outcomes Associated With Love

Agape is a spiritual love that reflects selflessness and altruism. This type of love involves concern for another's welfare and being relatively undemanding for oneself. Although this is not the most celebrated form of love, it may be the most beneficial. Our view is that we could use our strengths to be more giving and to build relationships founded on selflessness.

Romantic love, especially passionate romantic love (described further in Chapter 12), is much desired and talked about by people of all ages. There is little celebration, however, of *resilient*

Table 3.6 Diagnostic Criteria for Flourishing

Flourishing in Life

A. Individual must have had no episodes of major depression in the past year.

B. Individual must possess a high level of well-being as indicated by the individual's meeting all three of the following criteria:

1. High emotional well-being, defined by 2 of 3 scale scores on appropriate measures falling in the upper tertile.

   a. Positive affect
   b. Negative affect (low)
   c. Life satisfaction

2. High psychological well-being, defined by 4 of 6 scale scores on appropriate measures falling in the upper tertile.

   a. Self-acceptance
   b. Personal growth
   c. Purpose in life
   d. Environmental mastery
   e. Autonomy
   f. Positive relations with others

3. High social well-being, defined by 3 of 5 scale scores on appropriate measures falling in the upper tertile.

   a. Social acceptance
   b. Social actualization
   c. Social contribution
   d. Social coherence
   e. Social integration

romantic love or *sustained* romantic love. What strengths does it take to make a relationship work despite hard times and thereafter flourish for 10 years, 30 years, and 50 years? We could determine this through more systematic study of couples who report high levels of romantic love many years into their relationships.

Positive Outcomes Associated With School, Work, and Civic Contributions

Schools are becoming more accountable for the educational outcomes of their students, and businesses continue to keep a close eye on the bottom line. Although desired outcomes for students and employees are fairly well articulated as learning and productivity, respectively, there must be other positive outcomes associated with these important activities that occupy us for our entire lives.

Certainly the meaningfulness of academic pursuits and work can be described. But could we measure the extent to which positive schooling and gainful employment (see Chapter 15) stimulate psychological growth? And what about distal outcome measures of school and work? Civic contributions of students and employees could be linked to developmental gains attained early during important periods in school or work. Perhaps one of the most influential societal contributions might be to teach our children to be broad-minded in their understanding of themselves and their place in the world. Teaching children how to be multiculturally competent at an early age sets the scene for more effective diverse work relationships and potentially better global involvement. As our globe becomes more connected with technology, we must remember to look outside our own worldviews and help students and employees to do the same.

Positive Outcomes Associated With Play

Play introduces us to the social, emotional, and physical skills needed to make the most out of life. Indeed, play is regarded as a "form of practice, or proximal growth, or mastery of skills" (Lutz, 2000, p. 33). The positive outcomes of childhood play are undeniable . . . yet we do not value the role of play in adulthood. In addition, play may currently be only accessible to certain socioeconomic and social classes (e.g., those who have the time to engage in such). The benefits of competitive and noncompetitive adult play have not been delineated, and this topic is ripe for more research.

IDENTIFYING STRENGTHS AND MOVING TOWARD A VITAL BALANCE

The staid view of mental illness as progressive and refractory was challenged by the noted psychiatrist Karl Menninger (Menninger et al., 1963). He called for psychiatrists to view mental illness as amenable to change. Thus, this new view of mental illness would bring the old view into balance. Positive psychologists now call for a different type of balance—a view of human life that gives attention both to weaknesses and to strengths but that is presented with consideration of cultural context. Although there is no question that we presently know much more about fallibilities than about assets, a strong culturally competent science and robust applications aimed at strengths will yield not only a more thorough but also a more accurate view of the condition of our world's inhabitants.

NOTE

1. In January 2003, Dr. Clifton was awarded an American Psychological Association presidential commendation in recognition of his pioneering role in strengths-based psychology. The commendation states, "Whereas, living out the vision that life and work could be about building what is best and highest, not just about correcting weaknesses, [Clifton] became the father of Strengths-Based Psychology and the grandfather of Positive Psychology."

KEY TERMS

Agape: A spiritual love that reflects selflessness and altruism.

Construct validity: The extent to which a scale measures the underlying attributes it intends to measure. Construct validity can be achieved by comparing your measure to other measures that assess a similar construct.

Construct equivalence: The extent to which a particular construct or concept has the same definition in two different cultures.

Criterion validity: The extent to which scores on a scale can predict actual behavior or performance on another, related measure.

Emotional well-being: A type of well-being consisting of perceptions of affirmed happiness and satisfaction with life, along with a balance of positive and negative affect.

Empirically based: Developed using available research knowledge.

Flourishing: A term pertaining to individuals who have simultaneously high levels of social, emotional, and psychological well-being.

Languishing: A term pertaining to individuals who do not have a mental illness but who are low in social, emotional, and psychological well-being.

Life satisfaction: A sense of contentment and peace stemming from small gaps between wants and needs.

Linguistic equivalence: The extent to which a measure has been appropriately translated from its original language into another; items on the measure must have the same linguistic meaning in both languages, meaning that various idioms, vocabulary, etc. must be examined carefully.

Metric equivalence: The extent to which scales of measurement used on various tests are equivalent; one issue with this type of equivalence is even if two scales contain the same metrics visually, different cultures may not use them in an equivalent manner.

Psychological well-being: A type of well-being that consists of six elements: self-acceptance, personal growth, purpose in life, environmental mastery, autonomy, and positive relations with others.

Psychometric properties: The measurement characteristics of a scale that include its reliability, validity, and statistics on items of the measure.

Reliability: The ability of a scale to produce consistent and reliable results over a number of administrations or after the passage of time.

Social well-being: A type of well-being that consists of coherence, integration, actualization, contribution, and acceptance by others.

Strength: A capacity for feeling, thinking, and behaving in a way that allows optimal functioning in the pursuit of valued outcomes (Linley & Harrington, 2006).

Talent: Naturally recurring patterns of thought, feeling, or behavior that can be productively applied and manifested in life experiences characterized by yearnings, rapid learning, satisfaction, and timelessness.

Validity: The ability of a scale to measure what it is intended to measure.

PART II

Positive Psychology in Context

CHAPTER 4

The Role of Culture in Developing Strengths and Living Well

CULTURE AND PSYCHOLOGY

David Satcher, the 16th surgeon general of the United States, who served from 1998 to 2002, sat on a dimly lit stage in the overflowing convention hall. He clutched a copy of a thick document, the report titled *Mental Health: Culture, Race, Ethnicity* (U.S. Department of Health and Human Services [DHHS], 2001), which was being officially released that same day. Psychologists poured into the meeting room to hear Dr. Satcher's summary of this report, which had been years in the making. To a packed house, Satcher spoke on the crucial influences of culture on mental health. This excerpt from the report summarizes some of the surgeon general's comments:

> Culture is broadly defined as a common heritage or set of beliefs, norms, and values (U.S. DHHS, 1999). It refers to the shared attributes of one group. . . . [C]ulture bears upon whether people even seek help in the first place, what types of help they seek, what coping styles and social supports they have, and how much stigma they attach to mental illness. All cultures also feature strengths, such as resilience and adaptive ways of coping, which may buffer some people from developing certain disorders. Consumers of mental health services naturally carry this cultural diversity directly into the treatment setting. . . . The culture of the clinician and the larger health care system govern the societal response to a patient with mental illness. They influence many aspects of the delivery of care, including diagnosis, treatment, and the organization and reimbursement of services. Clinicians and service systems have been ill equipped to meet the needs of patients from different backgrounds and, in some cases, have displayed bias in the delivery of care. (U.S. DHHS, 2001; see the complete executive summary of the report below)

There were two take-home messages from Dr. Satcher's summary. First, "culture counts" in the consideration of the etiology (the cause of something, such as an illness), effects, and treatment of educational and psychological problems. Second, psychologists need to incorporate cultural issues into their conceptualizations of psychological problems and treatments.

Main Message: Culture Counts
David Satcher
Surgeon General of the United States

Culture and society play pivotal roles in mental health, mental illness, and mental health services. Understanding the wide-ranging roles of culture and society enables the mental health field to design and deliver services that are more responsive to the needs of racial and ethnic minorities.

Culture is broadly defined as a common heritage or set of beliefs, norms, and values (DHHS, 1999). It refers to the shared attributes of one group. Anthropologists often describe culture as a system of shared meanings. The term *culture* is as applicable to whites as it is to racial and ethnic minorities. The dominant culture for much of United States history focused on the beliefs, norms, and values of European Americans. But today's America is unmistakably multicultural. And because there are a variety of ways to define a cultural group (e.g., by ethnicity, religion, geographic region, age group, sexual orientation, or profession), many people consider themselves as having multiple cultural identities.

David Satcher

Source: National Institutes of Health.

With a seemingly endless range of cultural subgroups and individual variations, culture is important because it bears upon what *all* people bring to the clinical setting. It can account for variations in how consumers communicate their symptoms and which ones they report. Some aspects of culture may also underlie culture-bound syndromes sets of symptoms much more common in some societies than in others. More often, culture bears upon whether people even seek help in the first place, what types of help they seek, what coping styles and social supports they have, and how much stigma they attach to mental illness. All cultures also feature strengths, such as resilience and adaptive ways of coping, which may buffer some people from developing certain disorders. Consumers of mental health services naturally carry this cultural diversity directly into the treatment setting.

Culture is a concept not limited to patients. It also applies to the professionals who treat them. Every group of professionals embodies a "culture" in the sense that they too have a shared set of beliefs, norms, and values. This is as true for health professionals as it is for other professional groups such as engineers and teachers. Any professional group's culture can be gleaned from the jargon they use, the orientation and emphasis in their textbooks, and from their mindset or way of looking at the world.

Health professionals in the United States and the institutions in which they train and practice are rooted in Western medicine, which emphasizes the primacy of the human body in disease and the acquisition of knowledge through scientific and empirical methods. Through objective methods, Western medicine strives to uncover universal truths about disease: its causation, diagnosis, and treatment. Its achievements have become the cornerstone of medicine worldwide.

To say that physicians or mental health professionals have their own culture does not detract from the universal truths discovered by their fields. Rather, it means that most clinicians share a worldview about the interrelationship between body, mind, and environment informed by knowledge acquired through the scientific method. It also means that clinicians view symptoms, diagnoses, and treatments in ways that sometimes diverge from their clients' views, especially when the cultural backgrounds of the consumer and provider are dissimilar. This divergence of viewpoints can create barriers to effective care.

The culture of the clinician and the larger health care system govern the societal response to a patient with mental illness. They influence many aspects of the delivery of care, including diagnosis, treatments, and the organization and reimbursement of services. Clinicians and service systems, naturally immersed in their own cultures, have been ill equipped to meet the needs of patients from different backgrounds and, in some cases, have displayed bias in the delivery of care.

The main message of this Supplement is that "culture counts." The cultures that patients come from shape their mental health and affect the types of mental health services they use. Likewise, the cultures of the clinician and the service system affect diagnosis, treatment, and the organization and financing of services. Cultural and social influences are not the only influences on mental health and service delivery, but they have been historically underestimated—*and they do count.* Cultural differences must be *accounted for* to ensure that racial and ethnic minorities, like all Americans, receive mental health care tailored to their needs.

Source: U.S. Department of Health and Human Services, *Executive summary: Mental health: Culture, race, ethnicity.* Retrieved from http://www.ct.gov/dmhas/lib/dmhas/publications/mhethnicity.pdf

The need to acknowledge cultural influences also applies to our efforts to understand educational successes, psychological strengths, and the very nature of the good life. This need, however, has gone unmet according to the critics of the positive psychology initiative. These critics have observed that most strength-focused scholarship fails to address cultural influences in our research plans, service delivery, and program evaluations (Ahuvia, 2001; Christopher & Hickinbottom, 2008; Leong & Wong, 2003; Sue & Constantine, 2003). Furthermore, critics call for more discussion about how "culture counts" in positive psychology research and practice activities. Finally, as Satcher mentions, culture must be viewed in a broad sense as including facets such as race, ethnicity, gender, sexual orientation, socioeconomic status, religion, disability, and nation of origin (Hays, 2008). Each of these facets may have different meaning, relevance, and salience in the lives of unique individuals, and all may affect what is decided to be a "positive" behavior or trait within a particular cultural context.

We exhort any future positive psychologists who are reading this chapter to count culture as a major influence on the development and manifestation of human strengths and good living. This goal is challenging because psychology as a discipline has been ineffective in including cultural variables in the study of mental health and illness. This is doubly problematic when considering the impact on minority groups in various settings. As psychology as a whole has focused almost singularly on weakness, without attention to strength (Seligman & Csikzentmihalyi, 2000), and within this framework has often pathologized those who do not adhere to Western norms via deficit models, people of color, women, sexual minorities, and other underrepresented groups have been subjected to a sort of "double jeopardy" (Pedrotti, Edwards, & Lopez, 2009). In this way they are "branded as pathological in comparison to the majority group, and within a system that only acknowledges weakness and leaves no room for a balanced description of behavior" (Pedrotti & Edwards, 2010, p. 166). For positive psychology to remain viable, we must open our minds in terms of understanding that "healthy functioning" or "positive trait" are subjective phrases influenced heavily by cultural worldview (Pedrotti, 2014; Pedrotti & Edwards, 2014).

In this chapter, we describe (1) psychologists' historical stances regarding the roles of culture on positive and negative behaviors, (2) positive psychologists' approaches to incorporating cultural perspectives into their work, and (3) the role of cultural influences in our future explorations of strengths and positive functioning. We first address the field's historical (and often flawed) attempts to understand the roles of cultural forces in determining our psychological makeups. Second, we examine the assertions that positive psychology is culture free or culturally embedded. Third and finally, we discuss the steps that need to be taken in order to position positive psychology in the cultural context. At the end of this chapter, we may have raised more questions than we have answered. Obviously, we view these questions as central to the future of positive psychology, and most of the readers of this text will likely be called upon to address these issues in their careers.

UNDERSTANDING CULTURE: A MATTER OF PERSPECTIVE

Psychology in the twentieth century grappled with the topic of individual differences. Many of these discussions of individual differences pertained to culture. Over the last 100 years, for example, psychology moved from identifying differences associated with culture to the identification and appreciation of individual uniqueness.

In the late 1800s and early 1900s, anthropologists and psychologists often referred to race and culture as determinants of positive and negative personal characteristics and behaviors. Research paradigms, influenced by the sociopolitical forces of the times, produced findings that were generally consistent with the belief that the dominant race or culture (i.e., of European ancestry) was superior to all other racial or ethnic minority groups within the United States. These approaches to highlighting the inferiority of certain racial and cultural groups have been referred to as the genetically deficient perspective and the culturally deficient perspective on human diversity, whereas the culturally different perspective recognizes the potential of each culture to engender unique strengths (Sue & Sue, 2003). Psychologists who subscribed to the genetically deficient model hypothesized that biological differences explained perceived gaps in intellectual capabilities between racial groups. Moreover, the proponents of the genetically deficient model argued that people who possessed "inferior intelligence" could not benefit from growth opportunities and, as such, did not contribute to the advancement of society.

Pseudoscience was used to demonstrate the presumed genetic basis of intelligence and to emphasize the "finding" of intellectual superiority of Europeans and European Americans. For example, craniometry, which is the study of the relationship between skull characteristics and intelligence (sometimes measuring the amount of pepper seeds that filled the brain pan in dried skulls), was a pseudoscientific approach intended to demonstrate the relative superiority of one group over another group.

These notions of genetic inferiority were a prominent focus of eugenics (the study of methods of reducing "genetic inferiority" by selective breeding) research led by American psychologists such as G. Stanley Hall and Henry Goddard. Hall "was a firm believer in 'higher' and 'lower' human races" (Hothersall, 1995, p. 360). Goddard held similar views about race and intelligence, and in the early 1900s he established screening procedures (using formal intelligence tests similar to those used today) at Ellis Island to increase the deportation rates of the "feebleminded" (Hothersall, 1995). In this regard, people from around the world were given complex intelligence tests—typically in a language other than their native tongue—the same day that they completed a long, overseas voyage. Not surprisingly, these test results generally were a poor estimate of the immigrants' intellectual functioning.

By the middle of the twentieth century, most psychologists had abandoned the belief that race predetermined cognitive capacities and life outcomes. Indeed, the focus shifted from race to culture, or, more specifically, the "cultural deficiencies" evidenced in the daily lives of some people. In the culturally deficient approach to understanding differences among people, psychologists (e.g., Kardiner & Ovesey, 1951) identified a host of environmental, nutritional, linguistic, and interpersonal factors that supposedly explained the stunted physical and psychological growth of members of selected groups. It was hypothesized that people were lacking in certain psychological resources because they had limited exposure to the prevailing values and customs of the day, namely, those of European Americans (see the discussion of cultural deprivation in Parham, White, & Ajamu, 1999). Many researchers and practitioners attempted to explain problems and struggles of people by carefully examining the juxtaposition of cultures, specifically those cultures that were viewed as somewhat marginal as compared to those considered mainstream (middle-class, suburban, socially conservative). Deviations from the normative culture were considered "deficient" and cause for concern. Although this model focused greater attention on the effects of external variables than the earlier genetically deficient model, it nevertheless continued to apply a biased, negative, and oversimplified framework for appraising the cognitive capacities of racial or ethnic minority group members (Kaplan & Sue, 1997).

After decades in which some psychologists argued that specified races and cultures were better than others (i.e., that European Americans were superior to non-Whites), many professionals began to subscribe to the culturally different perspective, in which the uniqueness and strengths of all cultures were recognized. Recently, researchers and practitioners have begun to consider culturally pluralistic (i.e., recognizing distinct cultural entities and adopting some values of the majority group) and culturally relativistic (i.e., interpreting behaviors within the context of the culture) explanations of the diversities inherent in positive and negative human behaviors. Although pluralistic and relativistic explanations are broadly accepted, there is debate about whether positive psychology research and practice is culture free or culturally embedded. This debate is framed and discussed in the next section.

POSITIVE PSYCHOLOGY: CULTURE IS EVERYWHERE

Positive psychology scientists and practitioners are committed to studying and promoting optimal functioning. Although we share this common goal, we pursue it along many different routes. Outside observers might conclude that all positive psychology researchers ask similar questions and use similar methods. Such observers also may note that all positive psychology practitioners focus on clients' strengths and help move people toward positive life outcomes. Our educational specialties (e.g., social, health, personality, developmental, counseling, and clinical psychology), however, may determine particular aspects of the questions examined and research tools used. Likewise, our theoretical orientations to counseling (e.g., humanistic, cognitive–behavioral, solution-focused) may influence our efforts to help people to function more optimally. Along these same lines, our cultural facets, including race, socioeconomic status, nation or origin, gender and others, may shape our foci, our hypotheses, and our methods.

In years past, the debate about cultural influences on psychology research and practice in general has been conducted formally at conventions and informally on listservs and in classrooms. Most professionals probably have confidence in the objectivity of their methods. They also are likely to acknowledge the need to make sense of the amazing diversity in human existence. Three recurring issues appear to involve (1) the effects of professionals' cultural values on their research and practices, (2) the universality of human strengths, and (3) the universality of the pursuit of happiness.

PERSONAL MINI-EXPERIMENTS

Culturally Embedded Daily Practice

In this chapter, we have discussed the extent to which you "count culture" in your daily work as a positive psychologist or student. These examples of culture's role in positive psychology come to life when applied to a real professional situation.

Imagine that you join a professor's lab that is committed to the study of positive functioning of first-generation college students. During your initial discussion with the faculty member, you learn that the project you will be working on involves developing and evaluating a mentoring program for a culturally diverse group of students, some of whom first moved to the United States only years ago when their families were providing seasonal labor to regional farmers. At the first meeting of the research group, you, fellow students, and the faculty member brainstorm ideas about the content and process of the mentoring sessions and about the salient outcome measures. As these topics are discussed, the professor interjects the following questions:

- Which of the students' strengths are most likely to aid them in school and in life?

- Should we measure happiness as a desired outcome in addition to academic self-efficacy, performance, and retention?

- What cautions should we take with regard to the measures we choose?

- What about family-of-origin influence on a student's academic behaviors? Should we account for that?

- How might our own values affect the mentoring process or research (e.g., hypothesis formation)?

Please share your response with fellow students and attempt to determine the extent to which you account for the role of culture in your responses. Remember to use a broad definition of culture in your considerations (e.g., does your gender influence what you value? Your race or ethnicity? Your religion?)

Culturally Embedded Positive Psychology Research and Practice

The culturally embedded perspective on positive psychology is closely associated with ongoing efforts to contextualize all research and practice efforts. Specifically, culture-sensitive recommendations for research, practice, and policymaking (APA, 2003) encourage professionals to develop specific competencies to help account for cultural influences on psychology. Accordingly, subscribers to the culturally embedded position would agree that research and practice are conducted at the intersections of the professionals' cultures and the research participants' or clients' cultures and argue that cultural values of the researcher and practitioner influence their work.

Many researchers in times past have asserted that certain characteristics or virtues are present as positive facets across many cultures, and for this reason we should assume some strengths to be *universal*. Although professionals who study the culturally embedded nature of strengths concede that a core group of positive traits and processes might exist across cultures, they nevertheless hold that most positive traits and processes manifest themselves in very different ways for different purposes in different cultures. Sandage, Hill, and Vang (2003) provide a good example of how forgiveness (one of the 24 VIA-IS strengths; see Chapter 3) is valued cross-culturally and yet operates very differently within cultures. In their examination of the forgiveness process of Hmong Americans, Sandage and colleagues discovered that forgiveness focuses on the restoration of respect and relational repair, emphasizes a spiritual component, and is facilitated by a third party. Although other conceptualizations of forgiveness also emphasize relationship repair, the spiritual components and the need for third-party facilitation appear to be rare. Thus, in this example, the manifestation of forgiveness is different due to cultural values.

On the notion of happiness as a universally desired human state, psychologists (e.g., Constantine & Sue, 2006; Leong & Wong, 2003; Sue & Constantine, 2003) have noted that suffering and transcendence are the goals for some individuals who adopt an Eastern perspective on positive psychology (see Chapter 2). Thus, happiness may be simply a by-product of the life process. Ahuvia (2001) recounted his experiences with people who did not share the "universal" desire to be happy.

> Some years ago, an Indian doctoral student of mine saw the back cover of Myers's (1993) book, which read, "We all want to be happy. . . ." The student remarked simply, "I don't." I recall another conversation, this with a young Singaporean man, who confided to me that he was going to marry his fiancée because it was socially expected of him, not because he thought he would be happy in the marriage. . . . Similarly, I exchanged lengthy e-mails with a Korean student who was very explicit about choosing a career to be rich, not to be happy, so that he could bring face to his parents by buying them a new Mercedes. (p. 77)

An additional point is that definitions of strengths may vary across different cultural groups, and thus what is meant by words such as *hope* or *courage* in one culture may not be the same in others. Those who believe that strengths are culturally embedded contend that studies that include diverse groups of individuals must first establish that the construct of interest is defined in a way that makes sense for that particular cultural group. When asked questions about their own happiness, Western individuals, such as those from majority culture in the United States, usually mention personal achievement and other individual-related contributing factors. In contrast, Eastern individuals, such as those from China or Japan, more commonly reference harmony and aspects related to their social spheres as contributing heavily to their happiness (Uchida, Norasakkunkit, & Kitayama, 2004). As another example, people from different cultural groups also define wisdom differently. While individuals from the majority culture in the United States define wisdom as more of a cognitive construct, other groups define it as both affective and cognitive (Benedikovičová & Ardelt, 2008; Yang, 2008). Additionally, researchers have often found differences in how various constructs relate to others in different cultural groups. Hope, for example, correlates strongly with life satisfaction, optimism, and other traits and states that those in the United States find to be beneficial (Snyder et al., 1991). These links, however, are not found in the same strength, direction, or significance in other groups. Hope, as an example, has different significant predictors depending on which cultural group one is studying (Chang & Banks, 2007; See Chapter 8 for a more thorough description of this work). Thus, relationships between constructs may be different as a function of culture.

As attention to culture becomes more and more necessary in our diverse society, it seems clear that a decision regarding what types of characteristics and actions are deemed positive for a particular individual will be guided and influenced by the cultural environment and the salience of various cultural values in this individual's life (Christopher & Hickinbottom, 2008; Pedrotti, 2012;

Pedrotti & Edwards, 2009; Pedrotti, Edwards, & Lopez, 2009; Sue & Constantine, 2003). John Chambers Christopher (2005) of the University of Montana contends that "positive psychology requires a philosophy of social science that is robust enough to handle ontological, epistemological, and ethical/moral issues and move beyond both objectivism and relativism" (pp. 3–4). The full text of Christopher's article, reprinted here, details his suggestions for undergirding positive psychology with a stronger conceptual framework.

Situating Positive Psychology
John Chambers Christopher

To post-modern thinkers of a variety of stripes, ontological and moral commitments are increasingly recognized to be inescapable in the social sciences. This poses problems for positive psychology if it is pursued as if it were a "descriptive" or objective science that can "transcend particular cultures and politics and approach universality" (Seligman & Csikszentmihalyi, 2000, p. 5). Prior initiatives in the field of psychology that claimed to be objective, value free, culture free, ahistorical, and universal were shown by critical psychologists to presuppose individualistic cultural values and assumptions. Preliminary inquiry suggests that theory and research in positive psychology is likewise influenced by Western cultural outlooks (Christopher, 1999, 2003; Guignon, 2002; Woolfolk, 2002). One implication is that positive psychology requires a philosophy of social science that is robust enough to handle ontological, epistemological, and ethical/moral issues and move beyond both objectivism and relativism.

I believe conceptual resources for positive psychology can be found in the philosophical hermeneutics of Charles Taylor and Martin Heidegger and in Mark Bickhard's interactivism. These metatheories provide (a) conceptual tools for critiquing how cultural values and assumptions shape psychological theory, research, and practice, (b) an alternative non-individualistic and non-dualistic metatheory regarding the nature of the self and how the self is related to culture, and (c) ways of thinking interpretively about cultural meanings and discerning their specific manifestations (Campbell, Christopher, & Bickhard, 2002; Christopher, 2001; Christopher, 2004). A useful way of thinking about culture comes from considering how human beings always and necessarily exist within *moral visions.* Moral visions entail a set of ontological presuppositions about the nature of the person or self and a set of moral or ethical assumptions about what the person should be or become. I believe that any positive psychology, whether in the current movement or in the indigenous psychologies of other cultures, is based on moral visions.

From this moral visions framework, positive psychology will need to be able to address how the self varies across culture. To promote subjective well-being, psychological well-being, or character, we need to have a clear understanding of the self that is at stake. Failing to do this can potentially pathologize individuals whose sense of self is not the "bounded, masterful self" of Western psychology (Cushman, 1990). In addition, positive psychology will need to address what role the various

(Continued)

(Continued)

configurations of the self have for positive psychology. For example, positive psychology encourages the development and enhancement of the self. Yet for many non-Western indigenous psychologies such as Buddhism and classical yoga, identification with this notion of the self is the source of suffering and the true stumbling block to growth. Or as Alfred Adler suggested, mental health and well-being may in part require a sense of identification with the larger communities of which one is a part. Dialogue and debate regarding these types of underlying assumptions will be essential to help positive psychology not become culture-bound.

The second aspect of moral visions that positive psychology will need to contend with are those assumptions regarding how we should be or become (or what the good person and the good life are). Psychology tends to define its virtues, like autonomy, relatedness, and personal growth, in abstract and decontextualized ways that tend to obscure the local and specific interpretations with which these virtues are actually lived out (Campbell & Christopher, 1996b; Christopher, 1999; Christopher, Nelson, & Nelson, 2004). This is a point that applies to various aspects of positive psychology, including Peterson and Seligman's (2004) VIA project, character education, and well-being (Christopher et al., 2004). I contend that positive psychology will need to more fully consider how interpretation plays a central role in understanding those characteristics and qualities that define the good person and the good life. To the extent that certain virtues can be found to be present across most cultures, there are huge and generally unexplored ways that the meaning of these virtues can be radically different for those who hold them. The virtue of caring, for instance, is generally interpreted within Western cultures to mean caring about other people—yet there are traditions for whom caring about the environment and about the self are also moral imperatives (Campbell & Christopher, 1996b). Moreover, even when there is consensus about the object or domain of caring, there are frequently considerable differences across and within cultures around what it means to care in a particular situation, such as with the elderly. A hasty attempt to declare that certain virtues are universally endorsed can obscure how these common virtues are often prioritized in very different ways. Respect, for example, is an important virtue in most cultures. Yet, while Turkish and Micronesian college students consider respect the most important attribute of the good person, American students ranked it 35th (Smith, Türk-Smith, & Christopher, 1998).

Comprehending how culture shapes peoples' understanding of virtues, values, and well-being will indeed complicate research endeavors. Our commitment to cultural pluralism demands more of us than the inclusion of other countries in standard research relying on self-report measures. One implication of the moral visions perspective is that people already live out positive folk psychologies: The structure of their lives provides an answer to the question of the good person and good life. These implicit and embodied outlooks need to be juxtaposed with notions of the good that are consciously accessible and espoused by lay persons, as well as with indigenous professional theories of well-being. To fully address how positive psychologies exist at a variety of levels of awareness requires the addition of interpretive methods. This will initially result in a kind of messiness, as some moral development theorists now acknowledge is necessary (Campbell & Christopher, 1996a; Walker & Hennig,

2004; Walker & Pitts, 1998), but this is offset by the potential to capture more of the richness and diversity of human experience.

Positive psychology is critical to the well-being of 21st-century psychology. It will require vigilance to ensure that positive psychology does not become yet another form of a disguised individualistic ideology that perpetuates the sociopolitical status quo and fails to do justice to the moral visions of those outside the reigning outlook. I believe that by paying attention to our underlying moral visions, learning about the moral visions of those across cultures and across time, and learning to think culturally, we can avoid prematurely rushing to ethnocentric conclusions that fail to take full measure of the wisdom of non-Western cultural traditions.

Source: Christopher (2005). Reprinted with permission of the author.

Note: Citations for Dr. Christopher's article are presented in the References section at the back of this book.

PUTTING POSITIVE PSYCHOLOGY IN A CULTURAL CONTEXT

Psychology's past perspectives on culture tell of the pitfalls and progress associated with professional attempts to understand the influence of culture on positive psychology research and practice. Here we provide recommendations to help make sense of culture's role in positive psychology.

Examining the Equivalence of the "Positives" to Determine What Works

Establishing cross-cultural or multicultural applicability of positive constructs and processes goes beyond determining whether strengths and coping mechanisms exist and are valued by members of different cultural groups. It requires an understanding of the indigenous psychology of the group (Sandage et al., 2003) that tells the story of how and when the strength or process became valued within the culture and how it currently functions positively. Studies must be conducted *across* nations (cross-culturally) but must also investigate potential differences between cultural groups *within* diverse nations (multiculturally) such as the United States in order to fully appreciate within-group heterogeneity. Qualitative study of a people's development of particular strengths or use of them in their daily lives could enhance our understanding of how culture counts in the development and manifestation of that strength, and rigorous, quantitative, cross-cultural, and multicultural studies could reveal additional information about how a strength leads to or is associated with a particular outcome in one culture but a different outcome in another.

Another means of uncovering the cultural nuances associated with a positive construct or process is to ask people how a particular strength became potent in their daily lives. For example, the "Head, Heart, Holy Test of Hope" has proven to be an effective means of starting discussions (in and out of counseling sessions) and lectures on hope because it allows people to reflect on their story of how hope came to be meaningful in their lives and to be part of their culture. Here is how we (Lopez, 2005) introduce it:

> Today, we will talk about the power of hope in your lives. Before I get started, I need to know how you understand this thing called hope. Here is what we are going to do, raise both hands (facilitator raises both hands). And on the count of three, I want you to point to where YOUR hope comes from. Given your background and all of your life experiences, where do you think your hope originates . . . in your head (facilitator points to head)—that thinking part of you, in your heart (facilitator points to heart)—from the love you have for others and they have for you, or from the holy (facilitator points up and all around)—your spiritual life? Now, you can use both hands to point to one place if you think all of your hope comes from that place, or you can use one hand to point to one place and the other hand to point to another (facilitator demonstrates.) Any questions? So, on three, point to where your hope comes from . . . 1, 2, 3. (p. 1)

Inevitably, there is a diversity of gestures capturing people's beliefs about their hope. As participants look around the room, they start asking questions of one another and sometimes launch into stories. Some of these stories about hope are shared with the larger group, and the cultural base of each person's hope becomes more evident. Hope, as laypeople understand it, is clearly grounded in beliefs, values, and experiences.

Chang (1996a, 1996b), in a series of quantitative studies on optimism in Asian Americans and Caucasians, highlighted the importance of understanding the equivalence of constructs across cultural groups. In one study, Chang (1996a) examined the utility of optimism and pessimism in predicting problem-solving behaviors, depressive symptoms, general psychological symptoms, and physical symptoms. In general, the results of this study revealed that Asian Americans were significantly more pessimistic than Caucasians (according to the Extended Life Orientation Test; Chang, Maydeu-Olivares, & D'Zurilla, 1997) but not significantly different from Caucasians in their level of optimism. These findings were corroborated when data from an independent sample were examined (Chang, 1996b). Chang points out that his findings might suggest that Asian Americans are generally more negative in their affectivity than Caucasian Americans, *except for the fact that he found no significant differences in reported depressive symptoms between the two groups. In fact, optimism was negatively correlated with both general psychological symptoms and physical symptoms for Asian Americans but not for Caucasians.* Also, problem solving was found to be negatively correlated with depressive symptoms for Asian Americans but unrelated for Caucasians. Finally, it was revealed that, whereas pessimism was negatively correlated with problem-solving behaviors for Caucasians, it was positively correlated for Asian Americans (See Chapter 8 for a more thorough discussion of this study).

Similarly, one may gain insight as to how a strength plays out in one's life by thinking about how the salience of various cultural identities may provide sources of strength for different individuals. This exercise was developed as a class activity by one of this textbook's authors (JTP) and is introduced by asking people to identify three cultural facets (such as race, gender, religion, etc.) and to then think about which personal strengths might be derived from membership in these various groups. In the ensuing discussion, it is easy to see that cultural facets can provide many sources of strength for individuals (Pedrotti, 2013b). For example, one may say that coming from a low socioeconomic status has forced them to come up with creative solutions to various problems. Others may feel that being a member of a collectivist group (such as Asian or Latino cultures) may have helped them to develop strong networking skills in their lives. An individual who holds religion to be a salient factor in his or her life may feel that he or she has more opportunities to cultivate strengths such as altruism or gratitude. In exercises such as these, it seems that identification with various cultural facets can influence the recognition, development, and enhancement of personal strengths.

Utsey, Hook, Fischer, and Belvet (2008) make this point clear in their investigation of the roles of optimism, cultural orientation, and ego resilience in predicting levels of subjective well-being in African American populations. Utsey and colleagues found that adherence to a traditional African American worldview (such as valuing the importance of religion) and pride in racial heritage predicted higher well-being and positive psychological functioning. Participants who reported higher levels of racial pride also showed higher levels of resilience; thus findings such as these support the idea that salience of particular cultural factors may elicit various strengths.

Even in cases where common strategies are used in similar ways by people of different backgrounds, the benefits of those strategies often are not shared. Hence, we should be cautious when prescribing particular coping strategies that, on the surface, seem universally beneficial. Consider another example. Shaw et al. (1997) found that the use of four coping strategies seemed to transcend culture (or were equally valued in cultures) for family caregivers (participants were from Shanghai, China, and San Diego, California) aiding a loved one grappling with Alzheimer's disease. These four strategies involved (1) taking action, (2) utilizing social support, (3) cognitively reappraising life situations, and (4) denying the health problem and demands or avoiding thinking about it. The benefits, however, of these four strategies were not shared across the cultural groups. These results are consistent with other research indicating that common coping strategies have unique effects across cultures (Liu, 1986).

Discussions with clients, along with well-designed quantitative and qualitative studies with research participants, can provide good data on the equivalence of positive constructs and processes across cultures. With these data in hand, we will be better able to assess what strengths benefit whom (in what situations) and what positive interventions might help people create better lives for themselves (Pedrotti, 2014). As professionals attempt to enhance strengths in culturally diverse groups of people (see Chapter 14 of this text, along with Linley and Joseph [in press] and Magyar-Moe [2014], for discussions of positive psychology in practice), we must ask and answer the question, "What works for whom?"

Determining the Foundations of the Good Life

As suggested in the previous section, people's cultural beliefs about forgiveness, hope, optimism, coping, independence, collectivism, spirituality, religion, and many other topics may bear on how particular strengths work in their lives, how they respond to efforts to enhance personal strengths, and which life outcomes they value. Our version of a common story, which we have titled "The Wise Man of the Gulf," brings some of these issues to life.

The Wise Man of the Gulf

An American businessman, Woody, was at the pier of a small Mexican village when a boat with just one fisherman docked. Inside the boat were many pounds of large gulf shrimp.

The American complimented the Mexican on the quality of his catch and asked about the mesh of his cast net, "Why is the mesh so large? Couldn't you catch more with a tighter weave?" Hector, the fisherman, replied, "I catch what I need, *Señor*. And the net, the net is a fine net. I was taught how to weave this net by my father, who was taught by his father. I work on the net every day to keep it strong."

Woody then asked how long it took to seine for his catch. Hector replied, "Only a little while." The American questioned, "So what do you do with the rest of your time?" The Mexican fisherman said, "I sleep late, I pray, go shrimping for a while, play with my children, take *siesta* with my wife, Maria, examine and repair the net, stroll into the village each evening, where I sip wine and play guitar with my *amigos*. On Sundays, I go to mass and spend the rest of the day with *la familia*. I have a full and busy life, *Señor*. I am very happy."

After hearing the fisherman's account of his week, Woody scoffed, "I am a Harvard MBA and could help you be more successful. You should use a net with a smaller weave and spend more time fishing and, with the proceeds, buy a bigger boat with a larger net you could troll for many miles. With the profits from the bigger boat, you could buy several boats; eventually, you would have a fleet of boats. Instead of selling your catch to a middleman, you would sell directly to the processor and then open your own plant. You would control the product, processing, and distribution. You would need to leave the small coastal fishing village and move to Mexico City, then Houston, and then Los Angeles. There, you will run your expanding enterprise."

Hector was somewhat taken aback by the complicated plan and asked, "But, *Señor*, how long will all this take?" Woody replied, "Fifteen to 20 years." "But what then, *Señor?*" The American laughed and said, "That's the best part. When the time is right, you would sell your company stock to the public and become very rich; you would make millions." "Millions, *Señor?* Then what?" Hector questioned. The American said, "Then you would retire, move to a small coastal fishing village, where you would sleep late, pray, fish a little, play with your grandkids, take a *siesta* with your wife, stroll in the village in the evenings, where you could sip wine and spend time with *la familia*."

Source: Lopez, et. al. *The Handbook of Positive Psychology* (pp. 700–714). NY: Oxford University Press, 2002.

Views of the good life are personally constructed over our lifetimes. At the beginning of life, we have natural urges that persist, such as eating and sleeping, and, as we become more cognizant of our surroundings, we link our natural urges to cultural ones, such as eating certain foods and adopting sleep rituals. This link of our natural needs to our cultural influences defines the contours of our daily lives (Baumeister & Vohs, 2002). From the experiences of our daily lives, we construe personal views of what life is all about, and we form worldviews (Koltko-Rivera, 2004), or "way[s] of describing the universe and life within it, both in terms of what is and what ought to be" (p. 4). Theoretically, our personal view of the world defines what motivations and behaviors are desirable and undesirable and, ultimately, what life goals should be sought (Koltko-Rivera). Given that our cultural experiences may be inextricably linked to what we consider to be the foundations of the good life, is it reasonable to believe that all people (in the world) desire happiness (as positive psychologists from majority cultures in the West define it; see Chapter 6)? Or are there life outcomes that are just as valued and as valuable as happiness? These are questions that can be explored in a casual debate among friends (and we encourage you to do this), but they also must be examined empirically. Other cultural facets, such as socioeconomic status, may determine what the good life looks like. To an individual who can barely make ends meet, the good life may include having consistent shelter in the winter or having enough food to feed one's entire family. To an individual at a higher end of the socioeconomic spectrum, the good life may include the feeling of accomplishment at being able to afford to travel or to send one's children to a good college. The value of these material objects and events are influenced by what we consider to mean that we are actually flourishing as opposed to just surviving. Future positive psychology clinical work and research also must consider the possibility that cultural forces influence what individuals consider to be the basic foundations of the good life.

Using Caution in Measuring "Universal" Strengths

Throughout this chapter, we have provided examples of how various cultures may use the same word (e.g., *happiness*, *wisdom*) to talk about traits or characteristics that are defined differently in different cultures. These definitional differences are very important when conducting multicultural and cross-cultural research, particularly with regard to how we interpret our results. If a Western psychologist, for example, decides to measure "life satisfaction" as defined by a Western definition in a non-Western population, he or she may find that this construct exists and is at similar or different levels in comparison to what has been found in the United States. We must look deeper than this more superficial analysis, however. For example, many researchers discuss their findings of "happiness," "hope," or "courage" in a variety of cultures and sometimes use this as evidence of the universality of these constructs. This may not be the case, however, as much research shows that there are differences between cultural groups in definitions, manifestations, and values placed on various constructs (Pedrotti, 2014). Instead we may just be measuring *our* version of whatever characteristic we are studying. Linguistic equivalence of a measure is not a substitute for conceptual equivalence (Ho et al., 2014; see Chapter 3 for more detail on these concepts). Our own cultural facets determine our operationalizing of various traits, and even our hypotheses are based on our culturally biased views of what is good and what is not.

Multicultural Mindset as a Strength

Ponterotto and others have proposed that a person's ability to navigate and adapt to the ever-increasingly diverse context of our world may be a strength in and of itself, and they define this multicultural personality as "a strength-based cluster of personality dispositions or traits that . . . is hypothesized to predict cultural adjustment and quality of life outcomes in culturally heterogeneous societies" (Ponterotto, Mendelowitz, & Collabolletta, 2008, p. 95). Van der Zee and Van Oudenhoven (2000) developed the Multicultural Personality Questionnaire (MPQ) and have identified five factors that describe the personality style: cultural empathy, open-mindedness, emotional stability, initiative, and flexibility. Several studies have found correlations between a multicultural personality orientation and well-being (Brummett, Wade, Ponterotto, Thombs, & Lewis, 2007; Ponterotto et al., 2007), thus suggesting that cultivating this personality style could lead to further benefits. As such, it may be that in broadening our field of study to include perspectives from multiple origins, we, as researchers, teachers, and practitioners, have the opportunity to develop strengths of our own!

FINAL THOUGHTS ON THE COMPLEXITY OF CULTURAL INFLUENCES

John Chambers Christopher and Katie Howe (2014) state, "A multiculturally inclusive positive psychology requires not only extending positive psychology to groups that have been ignored or marginalized. It also requires critically examining the values and assumptions that underlie the field of positive psychology to prevent perpetuating the socioeconomic and political status quo" (para. 1). This is our charge as positive psychologists. Psychology and future positive psychologists must continue to work to understand the complexity of cultural influences on the development and manifestation of positive personal characteristics and desirable life outcomes. The increasing cultural diversity in the United States, along with rapid technological advances that facilitate our interaction with people from around the world (Friedman, 2005), will outpace our discoveries of the specific roles that cultural backgrounds play in psychology. Given that we cannot be certain about issues such as the universality of particular strengths or the extent to which culture modifies how a strength is manifested, we must do our best to determine if and how "culture counts" in each interaction with a client or research participant.

It has been suggested by others that "many conceptualizations of optimal psychological functioning and well-being are of limited applicability to people of color" (Utsey, Hook, Fischer, & Belvet, 2008, p. 207). In addition, researchers have posited that discussions of strengths may be particularly necessary when investigating non-European American individuals and their experiences due to the damage done by the early pseudoscience discussed earlier in this chapter (Constantine & Sue, 2006; Pedrotti & Edwards, 2009). In fact, people in non-dominant cultural groups across the world have often been pathologized for failing to assimilate fully into dominant cultural groups and may experience negative phenomena as a result (e.g., stereotype threat; Aronson & Rogers, 2008). As such, it becomes particularly important to broaden our efforts toward investigation of strengths in traditionally marginalized groups such as women, racial and ethnic minorities, sexual minorities, and other similar groups. In addition, research must be expanded beyond the constructs most often studied today. In a quick PsycINFO search completed at press time of articles published in the *Journal of Positive Psychology* (2006–2014) and the *Journal of Happiness Studies* (2000–2014), the keyword of *happiness* yields 76 and 607 hits, respectively, in the two journals, *hope* is listed 36 and 25 times, respectively, and *optimism* 26 and 17 times, respectively. These are all very Western-oriented constructs, as discussed in Chapter 2 in this volume. In contrast, we find only 7 total articles on *altruism* in the two journals combined, 11 on *compassion* (3 of which are focused on the more Western construct of *self-compassion*, and 1 of which is one of the articles above on the topic of altruism), and 3 on *harmony* (0 articles in the *Journal of Positive Psychology*); all of these are constructs that may be more relevant to Eastern groups. We believe broadening our areas of study as a field and publishing results about a diverse array of individuals both within and outside the United States would be beneficial to all groups in that it may lead to greater understanding of strengths in a wider range of people.

Progress toward the goal of counting culture as a primary influence on the development and manifestation of human strengths and good living in your research and practice may be best facilitated when you become aware of what you believe about the interplay between cultural and psychological phenomena. Through our personal and professional experiences, we have made some progress toward putting the positive in a cultural context. The authors of this text have different levels of power and privilege based on our various cultural facets as well, and this makes our understandings of how and when culture plays a role in our lives different from one another, even in talking amongst ourselves. We have come to some general agreement, however, on the following issues. First, psychological strength is universal. Across time, place, and culture, most people have developed and refined extraordinary qualities that promote adaptation and the pursuit of a better life. Second, there are no universal strengths. Although most people manifest strengths, the nature of the manifestation differs subtly and not so subtly across time, place, and culture. Third, life's contexts affect how strengths are developed, defined, manifested, and enhanced, and our understanding of these contexts contributes to diverse presentation of human capacity. History, passage of time, culture, situations and settings, professional perspectives, and human potentialities are reciprocally determined. Fourth, culture is a reflection of and a determinant of the life goals that we value and pursue. More research must be conducted on constructs that are central to non-Western groups as well. Finally, we must be willing to look beyond our own worldview to truly be able to see strengths in all individuals. The good life is in the mind of the beholder, and the vision of what is meaningful will drive our life pursuits.

In honor of this last statement, we encourage you to look at the field of positive psychology from both your cultural perspective and from the perspective of others. Some of you may find that you are drawn to constructs such as happiness, hope, and optimism. Others of you may find that constructs such as compassion, altruism, and harmony make more sense in your lives. All of these constructs are viable and cannot be ranked except for in our own minds and from our own perspectives. Be cautious of statements regarding "the most important" strength or "universal strengths" and instead learn to view all constructs through the lens of culture. In doing this, *you* become the viable future of the field!

KEY TERMS

Culturally deficient perspective: A view that identifies a host of environmental, nutritional, linguistic, and interpersonal factors (namely, those factors that differ most from European American values) that supposedly explain the physical and psychological growth of members of selected groups.

Culturally different perspective: A view of human diversity that recognizes the potential of each culture to engender unique strengths.

Culturally pluralistic: Explanations that recognize distinct cultural entities and adopt some values of the majority group.

Culturally relativistic: Explanations that interpret behaviors within the context of cultures.

Culture: A common heritage or set of beliefs, norms, and values.

Culture-bound syndromes: Sets of symptoms much more common in some societies than in others.

Etiology: The cause, origin, or a reason for something.

Eugenics: The study of methods of reducing "genetic inferiority" by selective breeding, especially as applied to human reproduction.

Genetically deficient perspective: A view of human diversity that suggests that biological difference explains perceived gaps in intellectual capabilities among racial groups. Proponents of this perspective believe that those of inferior intelligence cannot benefit from growth opportunities and do not contribute to the advancement of society.

Multicultural personality: "A strength-based cluster of personality dispositions that . . . is hypothesized to predict cultural adjustment and quality of life outcomes in culturally heterogenous societies" (Ponterotto, Mendelowitz, & Collabolletta, 2008, p. 95).

Worldview: "Ways of describing the universe and life within it, both in terms of what is and what ought to be" (Koltko-Rivera, 2004, p. 4).

CHAPTER 5

Living Well at Every Stage of Life

"Psychologists have abandoned the missions of identifying and nurturing talent."

"Psychology is half baked! We know very little about optimal human functioning."

With each presenter's statements about psychology's neglect of the positive side of human functioning, Dr. Paul Baltes squirmed a little more in his seat. Finally, it was his opportunity to share his research on wisdom (see Chapter 9). By now, however, he had something else on his mind. He politely reminded the group of psychologists, most of whom were trained in social, personality, and clinical specialties, that one branch of psychology had never wavered in its commitment to studying adaptability and positive functioning. That branch was developmental psychology. Indeed, developmental psychologists typically had approached their research with questions about what was working instead of what was not working. The efforts of developmental psychologists and other developmentalists (social scientists who maintain life-span perspectives) produced findings that often transcended historical, geographical, ethnic, and class boundaries to focus on people's self-correcting tendencies.

In this chapter, we review developmental researchers' discoveries about "what works" across the life span. For our purposes, the life span is described across childhood (birth to age 11), youth (ages 12 to 25), adulthood (ages 26 to 59), and older adulthood (age 60 to death). We assume that your basic knowledge of prominent development theories (see Table 5.1) will provide a backdrop for the discussions of resilience in childhood, positive youth development, living well as an adult, and successful aging.

Resilience researchers and positive youth development scholars have shared interests in the positive traits and outcomes of young people. As discussed subsequently, professionals who study resilience identify the "naturally occurring" personal and environmental resources that help children and adolescents to overcome life's many challenges. Positive youth developmentalists put the findings of resilience researchers and other positive psychologists into action and give growth a nudge by designing and conducting programs that help youth capitalize on their personal assets and environmental resources.

Table 5.1 An Overview of Major Theories of Development

	Maturational and Biological	Psychoanalytic	Behavioral	Cognitive Developmental
What are the basic assumptions of the theory?	The sequence and content of development are determined mostly by biological factors and the evolutionary history of the species	Humans are conflicted beings, and individual differences as well as normal growth result from the resolution of those conflicts	Development is a function of the laws of learning, and the environment has an important influence on growth and development	Development is the result of the individual's active participation in the developmental process in interaction with important environmental influences
What is the philosophical rationale for the theory?	Recapitulation theory, preformationism, and predeterminism	Embryological	Tabula rasa ("blank slate")	Predeterminist
What are the important variables most often studied?	Growth of biological systems	Effects of instincts on needs and the way instincts are satisfied	Frequency of behaviors	Stage-related transformations and qualitative changes from one stage to another
In what areas has the theory had its greatest impact?	Child rearing, the importance of biological determinants, aspects of cultural and historical development	Personality development and the relationship between culture and behavior	Systematic analysis and treatment of behavior, and educational applications	Understanding how thinking and cognition develop in light of cultural conditions and demands

Source: From Salkind, N., *An introduction to theories of human development.* Copyright © 2004 by SAGE Publications.

In the first half of this chapter, we highlight what developmental researchers have discovered about healthy growth. Moreover, we address some of the limitations in this line of research. Scholars who study adult development typically are able to provide prospective information about the gradual unfolding of people's lives. Their in-depth knowledge of the past and the present helps them predict the future. Rather than taking snapshots of life, the developmentalists who study adults use a methodology akin to time-lapse photography—thousands of still pictures of life (or interviews of people) are linked together to tell a compelling story of individual development.

In the second half of the chapter, we explore the life tasks associated with adulthood and the characteristics of people who have aged successfully. Additionally, we discuss many of the gaps in our knowledge about adulthood. Throughout this chapter, we encourage the reader to consider the developmental factors associated with adaptation and good living.

RESILIENCE IN CHILDHOOD

In the 1970s, a core group of developmental scientists began to study children who succeeded in life despite severe challenges. These children who triumphed in the face of adversity were referred to as "resilient," and their stories captivated the interests of clinicians, researchers, and laypeople. Society within the United States is currently dealing with many issues that call for children to be resilient, including mothers and fathers who have gone off to war, shaky economic times that have led to job or home loss for many families, and natural disasters such as Hurricanes Katrina and Sandy that have decimated whole communities. Fostering resilience and helping children to "bounce back" during these difficult times is a natural and important goal. In the present section on resilient children, we begin by presenting a brief case history. Then, we define *resilience* and the related issues about which scholars have differed. Next, we describe the work of Emmy Werner and other resilience scholars (e.g., Garmezy and Rutter). Finally, we discuss the internal (personal) and external (environmental) resources that protect children from developmental insults, along with the problems in such resilience research.

The Case of Jackson

We have met many resilient children in our work as teachers and clinicians. The story of Jackson's struggles and triumphs is one that stands out. Jackson, by all accounts, was charming from birth. His giggles made people laugh. People were naturally drawn to him. And he seemed comfortable with and trusting of all family and friends.

When he entered school, he thrived socially and academically. He seemed to be growing up healthy and strong. Unfortunately, when Jackson was 8 years old, a family member sexually abused him. Jackson quickly learned to protect himself from the perpetrator, and the abuse was limited to one incident. The effects of the abuse, however, were significant. Jackson's trust in people became shaky. Within weeks of the abuse, he became withdrawn, severely anxious, and developed constant stomach pains and headaches. His psychological and physical problems led to school absences and poor academic performance. Once a confident child with an eye toward the future, he now seemed scared, and the look in his eyes suggested that he was lost in the past.

In time, some caring adults in Jackson's life realized that he was struggling. The teachers at his small school realized that he was not the child he used to be. Two of these teachers reached out, one saying, "We don't know what is bothering you, but whatever it is, we are here to help you." Although he would not talk about the abuse incident until 20 years later, Jackson was able to get the support he needed from his teachers. He showed up at school a little early each morning and sat quietly in one teacher's class. Not much talking took place, but the quiet smiles they shared communicated volumes.

The two elementary teachers gave Jackson a safe place to sit and heal. The quiet support helped him to let go of his fears. Over time, he began to interact more comfortably with adults. Within a year, his anxiety had subsided and his grades had improved. He returned to his old, charming ways and built a large circle of friends and mentors throughout his youth. Today, he is happily married and employed in a job he loves. Jackson, as is the case with many other resilient children, is a survivor.

What Is Resilience?

Perhaps the most parsimonious definition of resilience is "bouncing back." The following comments on resilience from Masten, Cutuli, Herbers, and Reed (2009) illustrate this positive process. Specifically, resilience refers to

> a class of phenomena characterized by patterns of positive adaptation in the context of significant adversity or risk. Resilience is an inferential concept, in that two major judgments must be rendered to diagnose resilience. First, there is a judgment that individuals are at least "doing OK" with respect to a set of expectations for behavior. Second, there must be significant exposure to risk or adversity that has posed a serious threat to good outcomes. Thus, the study of resilience phenomena requires that investigators define (a) the criteria or method for identifying positive adaptation or development, and (b) the past or current presence of conditions that threaten to disrupt positive adaptation or harm development. (p. 118)

This broad definition is widely accepted; scholars agree that risk or adversity must be present for a person to be considered resilient. Despite this consensus, however, there is considerable debate regarding the universality of protective factors (Harvey & Delfabbro, 2004) and the extent to which children are doing "OK" according to the criteria of good adaptation (Luthar, Cicchetti, & Becker, 2000; Masten, 1999; Wang & Gordon, 1994). Thus, although a long list of protective factors has been identified (see the discussion later in this chapter), there are notable differences in the extent to which these factors "protect" (i.e., how well these factors yield positive outcomes), along with variability in how and when people call upon particular resources when facing risks and disadvantages (Harvey & Delfabbro, 2004). Indeed, given the state of resilience research, scholars can suggest what might work, but they cannot describe a formula for the operation of resilience.

Researchers often disagree on the answer to the question, "Bounced back to what?" When determining a resilient child's level of post-threat functioning, observers are looking for a return to normal functioning (i.e., attainment of developmental milestones) and/or for evidence of excellence (functioning that is above and beyond that expected of a child of a similar age). Most investigators, however, "have set the bar at the level of the normal range, no doubt because their goal is to understand how individuals maintain or regain normative levels of functioning and avoid significant problems in spite of adversity—a goal shared by many parents and societies" (Masten et al., 2009, p. 119). Certainly, the most celebrated cases of resilience often are depictions of individuals overcoming overwhelming odds to become stronger. (For example, Mattie Stepanek, a child poet and advocate, seemingly became more prolific as the neuromuscular disease he battled became more difficult to manage.)

One major consideration that may be ignored in the conceptualization of resilience outcomes is culture (Rigsby, 1994; see Chapter 4 for a related discussion). "Bounced back to what?" must be answered within the context of the values of the culture and the expectations of the community for its youth. Cultural forces dictate whether researchers examine positive educational outcomes, healthy within-family functioning, or psychological well-being—or perhaps all three. Due to unexamined personal bias, sometimes researchers may not be asking the types of questions that help to obtain an accurate picture of some groups, particularly when dealing with participants from racial and ethnic backgrounds who have been historically pathologized. Clauss-Ehlers (2008) suggests that often researchers are unintentionally biased in the types of topics they examine; e.g., looking at reasons for *poor* school achievement in Latino youth with the goal of being able to change this negative outcome. Though this approach may yield some helpful information, Clauss-Ehlers applauds researchers such as Cabrera and Padilla (2004), who instead studied Latino adolescents with *high* academic achievement and centered their work around the question of what types of resilience factors *promoted* this school success. Unconscious or conscious stereotypes about certain groups can lead us away from asking questions that allow for members of traditionally marginalized groups to show their true strengths.

Second, it may be that having "positive feelings about the self, one's culture, and one's ethnic group promote resiliency and are linked to positive behaviors" (Belgrave, Chase-Vaughn, Gray, Addison, & Cherry, 2000, p. 143). In a study investigating resilience in American Indian adolescents, researchers found that enculturation (i.e., strong ties to their American Indian heritage) was significantly linked to resilience (Stumblingbear-Riddle & Romans, 2012). Thus, encouraging children to develop positive connections with cultural communities may increase resiliency toward negative factors in life, which may include reactions to discrimination, racism, and prejudice. Teachers, parents, and counselors can assist with this outcome by working to decrease negative (and increase positive) associations and bias toward various cultural groups within their personal belief systems and within their organizations as a whole.

Regarding "good adaptation," resilience researchers agree that external adaptation (meeting the social, educational, cultural, and occupational expectations of society) is necessary in order to determine who is resilient. The network of researchers is split, however, on whether a determination of internal adaptation (positive psychological well-being) is necessary as well. This debate creates confusion because some people see bouncing back as inexorably linked to emotional and intrapsychic adaptation.

The Roots of Resilience Research

Case studies have long been used to tell the stories of amazing people and their triumphs. Stories about youth who transcended terrible life circumstances have compelled people to find out more about these resilient people and the resilience process. Some researchers (e.g., Garmezy, 1993; Garmezy, Masten, & Tellegen, 1984) approach their work by focusing on the building blocks of resilience and then identifying how these blocks stack up in a large group of people who are at risk due to a stressor. Other researchers (e.g., Werner & Smith, 1982) identify subsamples of larger groups of people who are functioning well or thriving despite having experienced a recent stressor. Then, these latter researchers study the resilient people in depth to determine what similarities they share with each other and with members of less resilient groups and to identify what distinguishes them from the people who fail to bounce back.

Emmy Werner, sometimes called the "mother of resiliency," is a person-focused resilience researcher. She identified resilient people and then got to know them really well over time. Given her prominence in this area of positive psychology, we discuss her work as an exemplar of informative resilience research. Werner collaborated with her colleague, Ruth Smith (Werner & Smith, 1982, 1992), in a study involving a cohort of 700 children born on the Hawaiian island of Kauai from 1955 to 1995. From birth on, psychological data were collected from the children and adult caregivers, many of whom worked in jobs associated with the sugarcane plantations that used to dominate the island. At birth, one-third of these children were considered at high risk for academic and social problems because of their deficits in family support and home environments (e.g., poverty, parental alcoholism, and domestic violence).

Of the at-risk students, one-third appeared to be invulnerable to the undermining risk factors. Two primary characteristics accounted for the resiliency of these children: (1) They were born with outgoing dispositions, and (2) they were able to engage several sources of support. (Better care during infancy, intelligence, and perceptions of self-worth also contributed to positive outcomes.) The other two-thirds of the children in the high-risk group did develop significant life problems in childhood or adolescence. By their mid-30s, however, most research participants in the Kauai study reported (and psychological tests and community reports corroborated) that they had "bounced back" from the challenges faced earlier in their lives. Over time, more than 80% of the original high-risk group had bounced back. In retrospect, many of those who were resilient attributed their buoyancy to the support of one caring adult (e.g., a family member, neighbor, teacher, mentor).

Given these findings, resilience researchers over the last three decades have examined the dispositions of at-risk children, along with the physical and social resources of the youngsters who faced these disadvantages. In this regard, the finding that many children who did not possess protective factors ultimately (by their fourth decade of life) bounced back has not been adequately explained.

Resilience Resources

According to Masten et al. (2009), findings from case studies, qualitative research, and large-scale quantitative projects "converge with striking regularity on a set of individual and environmental attributes associated with good adjustment and development under a variety of life-course-threatening conditions across cultural contexts" (p. 82). These potent protective factors in development were identified in research and reviews in the 1970s and 1980s (Garmezy, 1985; Masten, 1999; Masten & Garmezy, 1985; Rutter, 1985; Werner & Smith, 1982), and some protective factors continue to be borne out in ongoing studies. Indeed, this broad list has held up reasonably well over time and across groups (see Table 5.2). (These factors are addressed elsewhere in this volume. For example, self-efficacy and a positive outlook on life are discussed in Chapter 8.)

Although we agree that most of these resilience resources are positive for most people in many situations, there are few universal truths in the resilience literature (with the possible exception that a caring adult can help a child or young person adapt). For example, D'Imperio, Dubow, and Ippolito (2000) found that a multitude of previously identified protective factors failed to distinguish between youth who coped well with adversity and those who did not. Culture and other factors (e.g., past experiences with adversity) undoubtedly influence how young people bounce back from adversity.

The resilience resources listed in Table 5.2 have been translated into strategies for fostering resilience. (Note the overlap between some of these recommendations and those discussed in the next section on positive youth development; some of these strategies may simultaneously prevent the "bad" and promote the "good" in people.) By using these strategies, developmentalists have developed thousands of programs that can help young people overcome adversities and build competencies. Some scholars (e.g., Doll & Lyon, 1998; Gaylord-Harden, 2008; Miller, Nickerson, & Jimerson, 2009) argue that the proliferation of resilience programs has occurred in the absence of rigorous research examining the construct of resilience and the effectiveness of the programs that supposedly foster it. Furthermore, Doll and Lyon note that many resilience programs teach young people life skills that are not reinforced in the cultures in which they live. Given these concerns about programming, policy makers and people who develop promotion efforts should attempt to adopt existing programs that have effectively served similar youth (i.e., promoted resilience-related competencies) or evaluate the effectiveness of programs with small, focused samples rather than large community groups. (See Table 5.3.)

Table 5.2   Protective Factors for Psychosocial Resilience in Children and Youth

In the child

  Problem-solving skills

  Self-regulation skills for self-control of attention, arousal, and impulses

  Easy temperament in infancy; adaptable personality later in development

  Positive self-perceptions; self-efficacy

  Faith and a sense of meaning in life

  A positive outlook on life

  Talents valued by self and society

  General appealingness or attractiveness to others

In the family and close relationships

  Positive attachment relationships

  Close relationships to competent, prosocial, and supportive adults

  Authoritative parenting (high on warmth, structure/monitoring, and expectations)

  Positive family climate with low discord between parents

  Organized home environment

  Postsecondary education of parents

  Parents with qualities listed as protective factors with the child (above)

(Continued)

Table 5.2 (Continued)

Parents involved in child's education

Socioeconomic advantages

Connections to prosocial and rule-abiding peers

Romantic relationships with prosocial and well-adjusted partners

In the community and relationships with organizations

Effective schools

Ties to prosocial organizations, (such as schools, clubs, scouting)

Neighborhoods with high "collective efficacy"

High levels of public safety

Good emergency social services (such as 911 or crisis nursery services)

Good public health and health care availability

Source: Masten, Cutuli, Herbers, and Reed (2009). *Oxford Handbook of Positive Psychology* 2nd Edition (pp. 117–131). NY: Oxford University Press.

Table 5.3 Strategies for Promoting Resilience in Children and Youth

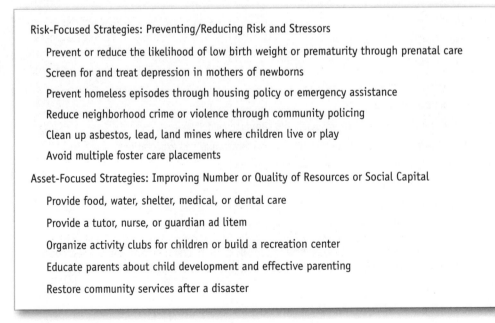

Risk-Focused Strategies: Preventing/Reducing Risk and Stressors

Prevent or reduce the likelihood of low birth weight or prematurity through prenatal care

Screen for and treat depression in mothers of newborns

Prevent homeless episodes through housing policy or emergency assistance

Reduce neighborhood crime or violence through community policing

Clean up asbestos, lead, land mines where children live or play

Avoid multiple foster care placements

Asset-Focused Strategies: Improving Number or Quality of Resources or Social Capital

Provide food, water, shelter, medical, or dental care

Provide a tutor, nurse, or guardian ad litem

Organize activity clubs for children or build a recreation center

Educate parents about child development and effective parenting

Restore community services after a disaster

Train care providers, corrections staff, or police in child development

Educate teachers about child development and effective teaching

Process-Focused Strategies: Mobilizing the Power of Human Adaptation Systems

Foster secure attachment relationships between infants and parents through parental-sensitivity training or home-visiting programs for new parents and their infants

Nurture healthy brain development through high-quality nutrition and early childhood programs

Nurture mentoring relationships for children through a program to match children with potential mentors

Build self-efficacy through graduated success model of teaching

Encourage friendships of children with prosocial peers in healthy activities, such as extracurricular activities

Support cultural traditions that provide children with adaptive rituals and opportunities for bonds with prosocial adults, such as religious education or classes for children where elders teach ethnic traditions of dance, meditation, etc.

Source: Masten, Cutuli, Herbers, and Reed (2009). *Oxford Handbook of Positive Psychology* 2nd Edition (pp. 117–131). NY: Oxford University Press.

An Excerpt From *Finding Strength: How to Overcome Anything*
Deborah Blum

Resilience research is often not bright and shiny at all. If you're going to study people climbing upward, you have to start at the very rocky bottom. "I decided to look at adults who'd had traumatic childhoods because I knew some very neat people who had come from that background," said John DeFrain, PhD, a professor of family studies at the University of Nebraska. "I thought it would be all warm and fuzzy-feeling. But these were people who were sometimes just barely hanging on. They were surviving as children, but just."

He found that it was in adulthood that people really began to transcend the difficulties of childhood and to rebuild. One man, beaten as a child by his father with belts, razor strops, and tree branches, reached a point in his mid-twenties when he decided to die. He wrote a suicide note, put the gun to his head, and then suddenly thought, "I'm not going to die because of what someone else did to me." That day, for the first time, he called a psychologist and went into counseling.

That dramatically emphasizes one of several key aspects of resilience research:

- There is no timeline, no set period, for finding strength, resilient behaviors, and coping skills. People do best if they develop strong coping skills as children, and some researchers suggest the first 10 years are optimum. But the ability to turn around is always there.

(Continued)

(Continued)

- About one-third of poor, neglected, abused children are capably building better lives by the time they are teenagers, according to all resilience studies. They are doing well in school, working toward careers, often helping to support their siblings.

- Faith—be it in the future, the world at the end of the power lines, or in a higher power—is an essential ingredient. Ability to perceive bad times as temporary times gets great emphasis from Seligman [see Chapter 1] as an essential strength.

- Most resilient people don't do it alone—in fact, they don't even try. One of the standout findings of resilience research is that people who cope well with adversity, if they don't have a strong family support system, are able to ask for help or recruit others to help them. This is true for children and adults; resilient adults, for instance, are far more likely to talk to friends and even coworkers about events in their lives.

- Setting goals and planning for the future [are] strong factor[s] in dealing with adversity. In fact, as University of California–Davis psychologist Emmy Werner, PhD, points out, it may minimize the adversity itself. For instance, Werner found that, when Hurricane Iniki battered Hawaii in 1993, islanders who were previously identified as resilient reported less property damage than others in the study. Why? They'd prepared more, boarded up windows, invested in good insurance.

- Believing in oneself and recognizing one's strengths is important. University of Alabama psychologist Ernestine Brown, PhD, discovered that, when children of depressed, barely functioning mothers took pride in helping take care of the family, they didn't feel as trapped. "You pick yourself up, give yourself value," Brown says. "If you can't change a bad situation, you can at least nurture yourself. Make yourself a place for intelligence and competence, surround yourself with things that help you stabilize, and remember what you're trying to do."

- And it's equally important to actually recognize one's own strengths. Many people don't. Teaching them such self-recognition is a major part of the approach that the Wolins [resilience researchers and developers of Project Resilience] try when helping adults build a newly resilient approach to life. They are among a small group of professionals testing the idea that resilience can be taught, perhaps by training counselors and psychologists to focus on building strengths in their clients.

Source: An excerpt from Blum, D., *Finding strength: How to overcome anything*. Reprinted with permission from *Psychology Today.* Copyright © 1998 Sussex Publishers, LLC.

POSITIVE YOUTH DEVELOPMENT

In this section, we define positive youth development and the socially valued, positive outcomes that have been identified by youth advocates and researchers. Additionally, we identify youth development programs that work.

What Is Positive Youth Development?

The teachers, counselors, and psychologists who are committed to positive youth development recognize the good in our youth and focus on each child's strengths and potential (Damon, 2004). Building on Pittman and Fleming's definition (1991), Lopez and McKnight (2002) articulate how components of development interact over time to yield healthy adults:

> [Positive youth development] should be seen as an ongoing process in which all youth are engaged and invested. Youth interact with their environment and positive agents (e.g., youth and adults who support healthy development, institutions that create climates conducive to growth, programs that foster change) to meet their basic needs and cultivate assets. Through [their] initiative (sometimes combined with the support of positive agents), momentum builds, and youth who are capable of meeting basic needs challenge themselves to attain other goals; youth use assets to build additional psychological resources that facilitate growth. Ideally, PYD generates physical and psychological competencies that serve to facilitate the transition into an adulthood characterized by striving for continued growth. (pp. 2–3)

Through the benefits provided to youth via the intentional combination of these environmental resources and caring supporters in the context of PYD programs, youth are able to thrive. This healthy development is marked by the attainment of some of the following nine positive outcomes (Catalano, Berglund, Ryan, Lonczak, & Hawkins, 1998; Catalano, Berglund, Ryan, Lonczak, & Hawkins, 2002) targeted by positive programs (all of these positive outcomes are addressed elsewhere in this book):

1. Rewarding bonding

2. Promoting social, emotional, cognitive, behavioral, and moral competencies

3. Encouraging self-determination

4. Fostering spirituality

5. Nurturing a clear and positive **identity**

6. Building beliefs in the future

7. Recognizing positive behavior

8. Providing opportunities for prosocial development

9. Establishing prosocial norms

Many authors call for a more complex understanding of what it means to study positive youth development with the conclusion that positive behaviors can only be promoted once one understands the types of pitfalls and difficulties that exist for youth today (Lewis, 2011; Pittman, 1991). Others counter by saying that focus on decreasing problems has overshadowed efforts to instead bolster positive growth (Lerner, von Eye, Lerner, Lewin-Bizan, & Bowers, 2010). To our understanding, this places researchers of positive psychology, with their commitment to balance both positive and negative sides, in an excellent position to study more about this important area. In addition, exploring both positive and stressful situations for youth in many different social identity circles is very important. It may be, for example, that different developmental assets exist for different populations (Holtz & Martinez, 2014). In some groups, such as African American youth, research has pointed to the fact that strong ethnic identity is related to positive characteristics such as higher self-esteem (Negy, Shreve, Jensen, & Uddin, 2003; Sellers, Copeland-Linder, Martin, & Lewis, 2006). In addition, Mexican immigrant children who have stronger ethnic identity have greater academic performance, particularly at schools that are predominantly White (Spears-Brown & Chu, 2012). These links do not appear to be found in White populations in some studies, however (Worrell, 2007). Thus, exploring a broader and more diverse group may add information about how to enrich the development of children and adolescents in different racial and ethnic groups.

Some of this work might look individually at different social identity groups without making comparisons with a majority group. Kenyon and Hanson (2012), for example, investigated programs that were particularly helpful for American Indian and Alaska Native (AI/AN) youth. These researchers highlight the PYD program Project Venture, which is specifically designed for AI/AN youth and uses traditional American Indian approaches and values to help youth to develop many positive characteristics (you can read more about this impressive program below).

In addition, some researchers have noted that programs aimed at positive youth development may not be equally accessible to all youth for various reasons. For example, Fredricks and Simpkins (2012) note that African American and Latino youth do not participate in after-school activities (which can fulfill the function of positive youth development) as often as White youth. There may be many reasons for this finding, such as differences in cultural orientation, variations in feelings of belongingness, and/or combined effects of race and other social facets (e.g., socioeconomic status).

In addition, Evans and colleagues (2012) talk about the fact that studies on African American youth more often investigate deficits and negative outcomes, whereas articles on Asian American and European youth in these same journals tend to focus on positive development or standard outcomes. An example might be studying predictors of well-being in the lives of successful American Indian adolescents *in addition* to protection against suicide attempts in these same youth. Though articles like this often have good intentions, including attempting to help populations that are struggling, they have the additional affect of stigmatizing and/or creating deficit models from which it is difficult for these groups to recover (Reyes & Elias, 2011). Making sure to include underrepresented groups in positive youth development research may balance some of the more negatively focused research about these groups.

As the idea of positive youth development becomes more popular in today's literature, researchers Peter Benson and Peter Scales (2009) note that the related concept of "thriving" has not been studied as much as may be warranted. They define thriving as "a specific expression of positive youth development" (p. 90) and discuss it as a process between self and environment that develops over time. Thriving youth are doing more than just "surviving" or "getting by;" they are achieving their potential and living a rich life that involves giving back to their communities and that brings them personal high levels of personal well-being. Thriving is thought to be set in motion by the presence of "spark," which the researchers conceptualize as "a passion for, and the exercise of action to nurture, a self-identified interest, skill, or capacity" (Benson & Scales, 2009, p. 91).

In comparing youth who had spark with those who didn't, those in the first group were significantly more advantaged on many developmental outcomes (Benson & Scales, 2009). Thus, assisting youth with development of spark and then facilitating the thriving construct as it develops is a worthwhile area of study in resilience research. Determining the origins of this spark, including examining potential factors such as environment, culture, personal strengths, and presence of role models, may result in increased positive youth development overall.

The impact of strong relationships, either with parents or other stable and consistent adults, appears to be greatly desirable in producing positive youth development. In one study, researchers measured adolescents' perceptions of their parents' success at several variables to determine whether or not the presence of certain parental behaviors appeared to be related to positive development in their children (Napolitano et al., 2011). Results showed that adolescents who had parents who were higher on maternal warmth (e.g., "My mother speaks to me in a warm and friendly manner"); parental monitoring (e.g., "My parents know who my friends are"); and involvement in their school (e.g., "How often does one of your parents ask about your homework?") were likely to have developed certain other positive behaviors. This highlights the important role that parents play in their children's well-being. This said, other research shows that it does not always have to be an actual parent who assists a child in developing these good traits. Bowers and colleagues (2012) found that non-parental adults were still very influential on the development of positive behaviors and traits. Thus, it seems that even children who do not have parents who assist them in these ways can still thrive with the help from others outside their family. In looking at individuals we have each worked with over the years, we have heard many stories of teachers, camp counselors, coaches, and family friends who have gone above and beyond their duties to provide positive mentoring and caring for children who were not biologically their own. This research shows evidence of the potential of their positive impact.

Positive Youth Development Programs That Work

The report on positive youth development (Catalano et al., 1998; Catalano et al., 2002) is a valuable resource for the people who believe that "problem free does not mean fully prepared" (Pittman & Fleming, 1991, p. 3). Indeed, some developmentalists focus their helpful efforts on youth who are not struggling with major life problems but who also do not possess the personal assets or environmental resources needed to reach many of their goals as they transition into adulthood. As such, the challenge in helping those who might fall through the cracks is to build the confidences and competencies in young people.

Positive youth development programs come in many forms (Benson & Saito, 2000), including structured or semistructured activities (e.g., Big Brothers and Big Sisters); organizations providing activities and positive relationships (e.g., Boy's Club, YMCA, YWCA); socializing systems promoting growth (e.g., day care centers, school, libraries, museums); and communities facilitating the coexistence of programs, organizations, and communities. The soundness of these programs is determined by the extent to which they promote the "good" and prevent the "bad" in today's youth.

Programs that work help youth move toward competencies that make their lives more productive and meaningful. A brief listing of more than a dozen effective programs was developed after

(Text continues on page 118)

Project Venture

Proven Results*

- 2001 program participants demonstrated a 32% decrease in past 30-day alcohol use (p<.05), pre- to posttest.

- 2003 program participants did not significantly (p<.05) increase alcohol or marijuana use, pre- to posttest, compared to control group youth, who increased use by 16% and 14%, respectively.

Project Venture (PV) is an outdoors experiential youth development program designed for high-risk American Indian youth. NREPP* has reviewed outcome data from program evaluation surveys conducted with middle school-aged American Indian youth and youth from other ethnic groups. Project Venture aims to prevent substance use and related problems through:

- Classroom-based problem-solving and skill-building activities
- Outdoor adventure-based experiential activities
- Adventure camps and treks
- Community-oriented service learning

The program relies on American Indian traditional values to help youth develop positive self-concept, effective social skills, a community service ethic, internal locus of control, and increased decisionmaking and problem-solving skills.

INTENDED POPULATION

Project Venture was designed for and tested with early adolescents in grades 5 through 9 in American Indian school and community settings (approximately 75 percent American Indian) in rural and low socio-economic areas. NREPP* has reviewed program evaluations conducted within these settings and populations. PV also has been replicated in rural Alaska Native, Hispanic/Latino, and Native Hawaiian settings and in urban American Indian settings. PV also has been implemented with youth in grades 4 and 10 through 12, but was not studied systematically with these populations. PV can be adapted for all cultural/ethnic and socioeconomic groups.

HOW IT WORKS

Project Venture typically consists of 20 to 30 hourly classroom sessions delivered over the course of a school year during which youth also engage in experiential games and initiatives facilitated by a PV staff member. Through these classroom-based sessions, a smaller number of youth are recruited and enrolled into the program's community-based activities that include increasingly challenging outdoor activities such as team- and trust-building, hiking, bicycling, climbing, and rappelling. During these activities, delivered to groups of 7 to 15 youth per staff member, PV staff work with youth to plan, implement, and debrief in specific ways that use the experiences as metaphors for life. The community-based component also includes four service-learning projects per year, which are designed to facilitate service leadership. School vacations and summertime include a weeklong camp and/or wilderness trek for participants. Older high school-age youth are selected and trained as service staff, where they become peer role models during Project

U.S. DEPARTMENT OF HEALTH AND HUMAN SERVICES
Substance Abuse and Mental Health Services Administration
Center for Substance Abuse Prevention
www.samhsa.gov

Effective Substance Abuse and Mental Health Programs for Every Community

OUTCOMES

A repeated measures ANCOVA design tested the effects of Project Venture on treatment and control youth from baseline to 15 months (Wave 2) and 21 months (Wave 3) after program exit. Results indicate that Project Venture participants were less likely to be current users of alcohol ($p<.05$) at Waves 2 and 3 than those in the control group. Program effect sizes (Eta2) were calculated for past 30-day alcohol use at .20. Additionally, there were more modest effect sizes for past 30-day cigarette smoking (.11) and marijuana use (.13).

The National Study of High Risk Youth found that 2 years after program enrollment, Project Venture participants had a 25% increase in past 30-day alcohol use ($p<.05$), compared to a 64% ($p<.05$) increase seen in control group youth.

CONTACT INFORMATION

McClellan Hall, Executive Director
National Indian Youth Leadership Project
205 Sunde Street
Gallup, NM 87301
Phone: (505) 722–9176
Fax: (505) 722–9794
E-mail: machall@niylp.org
Web site: www.niylp.org

Venture's year-long community-based components. The community component can include 150 hours or more of program services.

In addition, four potluck dinners or other community events for families, such as "family fun days," are conducted throughout the year. The program's youth facilitate a portion of the activities, providing opportunities for parents to see their children as capable and skilled.

IMPLEMENTATION ESSENTIALS

Project Venture is a relatively complex model, so an initial orientation session between the developer and potential replication team (on- or offsite or by phone) is recommended to determine the site's readiness and capacity. The developer can provide guidance regarding staffing, connecting with schools, and related issues. Key direct service and support staff are required to enroll in a 2-day (minimum) basic onsite training in order to purchase *Project Venture Replication Guide*.

Implementers are required to contact the developer to obtain implementation and evaluation support at least quarterly during the program's first year, and at least semiannually during subsequent program years. PV implementers are encouraged to obtain a formal agreement with participating schools, to use community/cultural resources, and to access recreational space and equipment. Project Venture recommends a minimum of 1 staff per 25 youth in the classroom component and 1 staff for 7 to15 youth in the community-based component.

PROGRAM DEVELOPERS

Project Venture was developed by the National Indian Youth Leadership Project (NIYLP), an American Indian-owned and -operated, community-based, nonprofit organization with nearly 20 years of experience in youth development. NIYLP has conducted summer youth leadership camps since 1986, from which grew the year-round Project Venture model. In 1990, NIYLP received its first SAMHSA/CSAP grant to implement Project Venture. The program has operated continuously since that time in Native and other communities, regionally, and nationally, with nearly 30 implementations in 11 States.

* National Registry of Effective Programs and Practices

Program detail and citations can be obtained at http://modelprograms.samhsa.gov

(Continued from page 115)

a critical review of published and unpublished program evaluations that included, at a minimum, the following (Catalano et al., 1998; Jamieson, 2005):

- Adequate design and outcome measures
- Adequate description of research methodologies
- Description of the population served
- Description of the intervention and fidelity of implementation
- Effects demonstrated on behavioral outcomes

Regarding effectiveness, Catalano et al. (1998) wrote, "Programs were included if they demonstrated behavioral outcomes at any point, even if these results decayed over time. Programs were also included if they demonstrated effects on part of the population studied" (p. 26). These effective programs include some that are well known and others that are less known. For the purpose of illustrating how some of these effective programs engage youth and cultivate personal resources, we describe the basic operations and effects of Big Brothers and Big Sisters and the Penn Resiliency Program. We also describe some of the developmental tasks associated with a positive college experience.

Big Brothers and Big Sisters is a community-based mentoring program (3–5 contact hours per week) initiated in 1905. For no fee, the program matches low-income children and adolescents with adult volunteers who are committed to providing caring and supportive relationships. Typically, mentors are screened carefully and then provided with some training and guidelines for positively influencing youth. Mentoring activities are unstructured or semistructured, and they typically take place in the community. Regarding the effectiveness of the program, Tierney and Grossman (2000) found that this mentoring program did promote the good (academic achievement, parental trust) and prevent the bad (violence, alcohol and drug use, truancy).

The Penn Resiliency Program (Gillham & Reivich, 2004) is a highly structured life-skills development program that is offered to schoolchildren for a fee (or as part of a research study). A highly trained facilitator conducts the scripted sessions in the classroom. The 12 sessions focus on awareness of thought patterns and on modifying the explanatory style of students to change the attributions for events so that they are more flexible and accurate. Extensive evaluation of the program demonstrated its effectiveness at preventing the bad (the onset and severity of depressive symptoms) and promoting optimism and better physical health.

The Changing Lives Program (CLP; Eichas et al., 2010) is a positive youth development program that is community based and supported and has aims to be inclusive of both gender and ethnicity. In this program, facilitators work with a two-pronged approach, attempting to decrease problem behaviors while at the same time promote positive development. This program works to enhance positive identity development while "facilitating mastery experiences" (Eichas et al., 2010, p. 213). Research has shown that this program achieves both of these goals in a diverse sample, though these researchers allowed that some of the findings may be differential at times as a result of race or gender. More research is needed with non-majority groups in order to more fully understand the impact of race, ethnicity, and gender on the applicability and design of these and future programs (Eichas et al., 2010).

Specific programs such as those just discussed are of course valuable options, but they may not be available to all schools and thus all youth depending on multiple factors. Bundick (2011), however, asserts that other more general extracurricular activities may also promote positive youth development. In his comprehensive analysis of a number of different types of clubs and activities, Bundick found that, in particular, leadership activities and volunteering in a prosocial way predicted positive variables. Participation in leadership activities seemed to promote a development of purpose in life and a sense of a hopeful future; participation in volunteering appeared instead to contribute to overall positive development, particularly greater life satisfaction (Bundick, 2011). These findings show that these potentially more accessible activities can also make a difference in developing positive attributes.

Foster youth systems are another group that has a vested interest in assisting positive youth development. In a study conducted by Hass and Graydon (2009), surveys were administered to individuals who had been removed from their biological parents as children but were able to "beat the odds" by completing a higher level of education than most foster youth. Results showed that several protective factors existed in the lives of these individuals as children and adolescents including social support, involvement in community service, a sense of competence, and the possession of future goals (Hass & Graydon, 2009). Foster youth programs that work to create and enhance relationships of support with caring adults, as well as to provide experiences for youth to give back to their communities, may see increases in resilience in this often marginalized population.

Colleges and universities, as socializing systems, also can promote positive youth development. Chickering's work on education and identity (1969; Chickering & Reisser, 1993) provides a set of developmental tasks that is the joint focus of college students and positive agents (student peers, faculty, and staff). Within the Chickering model, development of competence is identified as a primary developmental direction or goal for college students during their educational experiences. With increased confidence in their resourcefulness, students then begin working on the developmental tasks of managing emotions, moving through autonomy toward interdependence, developing mature interpersonal relationships, establishing identity, developing purpose, and developing integrity. Progress toward each of these goals equips students to succeed in school, work, and life in general. More intentional focus on developing colleges and universities into positive socializing systems could enhance the value of a college education for the students and society at large. Integrating strengths development programming into the college experience also could enhance the positive effects of higher education (Lopez, Janowski, & Wells, 2005).

THE LIFE TASKS OF ADULTHOOD

Some longitudinal studies (e.g., Werner & Smith, 1982) started because of a researcher's interest in childhood experiences yet went on (for decades) to reveal a great deal about adult experiences. In this section, we describe two such prospective studies (Terman's Life Cycle Study of gifted children and the Harvard study of the "best of the best" known as the Study of Adult Development). It should be noted that many aspects of adult development are addressed in this section and in prominent developmental theories (see Table 5.1), but a great deal is still unknown about how people grow and change between ages 26 and 59.

The Trajectories of Precocious Children

Lewis Terman (Terman & Oden, 1947) spent most of his life studying intelligence, which he viewed as an adaptive quality that would lead directly to life success and, more specifically, to national leadership. In the 1920s, Terman began an ambitious study of 1,500 intellectually gifted children (IQ > 140) who were nominated by teachers in California schools; the study participants nicknamed themselves the "Termites."

These participants were physically hardy during childhood and typically were healthier than their peers. Most of the children graduated from college and secured professional jobs. Although many of the Termites were productive in their jobs, few went on to be national leaders as Terman had hypothesized. It should be emphasized, therefore, that elevated childhood IQs did not guarantee adult successes and better mental health.

Lewis Terman

Source: Courtesy of Stanford University Archives.

Although Terman's predictions regarding the adult prowess of bright children were not borne out, his sample revealed information about adult development. On the negative side of human functioning, Peterson, Seligman, Yurko, Martin, and Friedman (1998) studied the Termites' childhood responses to open-ended questions and found that an explanatory style that was characterized as *catastrophizing* (explaining bad events with global causes) predicted risks of mortality in this sample of healthy children. This link between explanatory style and longevity/mortality is probably meditated by lifestyle choices. Given these findings, it would seem that genius-level IQ and good health in childhood do not protect individuals from making bad choices that lead to poor health and premature death.

George Vaillant

Source: Reprinted with permission of George Vaillant.

What Are the Primary Tasks of Adulthood?

A subset of the Terman sample data was reviewed by George Vaillant, the keeper of decades of data from the Harvard study (described in more detail subsequently). Specifically, 90 women in the Terman sample were interviewed by Vaillant to examine the generalizability of his findings on adult development from his all-male sample. Consideration of the Terman data and review of data from the Study of Adult Development helped Vaillant build on existing developmental theories and identify the life tasks associated with adulthood.

Guided by Erik Erikson's (1950) stage theory of development, Vaillant mapped out (1977) and refined (2002) six tasks of adult development: identity, intimacy, career consolidation, generativity, keeper of meaning, and integrity. Identity is typically developed during adolescence or early adulthood, when people's views, values, and interests begin to become their own rather than a reflection of their caregivers' beliefs. (Failure to develop a personal identity can preclude meaningful engagement with people and work.) With the development of identity, a person is more likely to seek an interdependent, committed relationship with another person and thereby achieve intimacy. Many of the women in the original Terman sample identified close female friendships as their most intimate relationships, whereas the men in the Harvard study invariably identified their relationships with their wives as the most intimate connections. A related conclusion reached by Vaillant (2002, p. 13) was, "It is not the bad things that happen to us that doom us; it is the good people who happen to us at any age that facilitate enjoyable old age."

Career consolidation is a life task that requires the development of a social identity. Engagement with a career is characterized by contentment, compensation, competence, and commitment. For many people, career consolidation, like the other tasks, is "worked on" rather than achieved. That is, people may consolidate their career for decades, even as they move toward and into retirement. In today's workforce, consolidation often is compromised by the need to transition into a new job. As a result, career adaptability (Ebberwein, Krieshok, Ulven, & Prosser, 2004; Super & Knasel, 1981) has emerged as a prerequisite of career consolidation. The level of adaptability required may be more marked in today's difficult economic times. Ability to adjust to layoffs, loss of income, and lack of new job opportunities may be new markers of this type of resilience.

Regarding tasks associated with generativity, people become involved in the building of a broader social circle through a "giving away" of self. As mastery of the first three tasks is achieved, adults may possess the competence and altruism needed to directly mentor the next generation of adults. Indeed, as people age, social goals become more meaningful than achievement-oriented goals (Carstensen & Charles, 1998; Carstensen, Pasupathi, Mayr, & Nesselroade, 2000). In recent studies generativity has been shown to contribute to longer life and less impairment in daily living activities (Gruenewald, Liao, & Seeman, 2012). The way in which this works may differ depending on racial group, however (Versey & Newton, 2013).

In the context of a larger social circle, some people take on the task of becoming keepers of meaning. The keeper of meaning has perspective on the workings of the world and of people, and this person is willing to share that wisdom with others. The keeper protects traditions and rituals that may facilitate the development of younger people. In essence, the keeper links the past to the future.

Finally, achieving the task of developing integrity brings peace to a person's life. In this stage, increased spirituality often accompanies a greater sense of contentment with life.

Mastery of these tasks is the object of adulthood. Intentional work on each of these tasks leads sequentially to work on the next task, and the mastery of all tasks is the essence of successful aging.

The Case of Keyonna

The ability to anticipate changes at work, plan for future opportunities, develop new skills, and create a social network that would facilitate a transition at work has been displayed by dozens of our clients over the years, but Keyonna's story is notable because she anticipated the need for such flexibility in her sixth decade of life. This is a time when many would say she had achieved career consolidation.

Keyonna had been working in the same job for the same company for 33 years. As a graphic designer for a national greeting card company, she knew her position was a cherished one, and she also realized that computer software and high-quality printers were replacing her traditional pencil-and-ink methods. She mastered new computerized design skills, yet she did not experience the same creative satisfaction from this new way of working. How could she continue to feel creative so as to derive pleasure from her work? First, she had to identify exactly what she liked about the creative process. After weeks of pondering, she came to the insight that she enjoyed thinking about the design more than she enjoyed the actual design process, whether that process involved a notepad or a computer screen. Could she convince her team leader to pay her to "think about design" rather than to produce designs? At the beginning of one workday, when she was feeling particularly gutsy, Keyonna floated the idea to her team leader, who looked intrigued and relieved. It turned out that the team leader was trying to figure out how to let Keyonna know that some of the technical aspects of the design work were going to be completed by people from another group (who were much cheaper by the hour) and that the small cadre of current designers was going to be asked to produce concepts for the young computer-based artists. So, for the last 10 years of her career, Keyonna envisions that she will be paid for her ideas rather than her artwork. She also has the pleasure of visiting with young graphic artists from around the world. Although fairly confident of her career future, she continues to anticipate changes in the greeting card industry that might shape her work and her life.

SUCCESSFUL AGING

With the baby boomers joining the older adult group of Americans, stories of successful aging are becoming more prominent in today's media. The stories of older adults provide valuable lessons to all of us. This was definitely the case in the life of Morrie Schwartz (the focus of Mitch Albom's 2002 book, *Tuesdays with Morrie*), who lived life to its fullest and found great meaning during the physical decline before his death.

The study of the positive aspects of aging (referred to as *positive aging, healthy aging, successful aging,* and *aging well*) is only several decades old. It will become a primary focus of psychological science, however, given the trends in American demography that will demand the attentions of scientists and the general public. Our goal for this section is to describe successful aging based on the MacArthur Study of Successful Aging and the prospective study by Vaillant (2002).

What Is Successful Aging?

The term *successful aging* was popularized by Robert Havighurst (1961) when he wrote about "adding life to years" (p. 8) in the first issue of *The Gerontologist*. Havighurst also primed scholarly interest in healthy aspects of getting older. Rowe and Kahn (1998), summarizing the findings from the MacArthur Study of Successful Aging, proposed three components of successful aging: (1) avoiding disease, (2) engagement with life, and (3) maintaining high cognitive and physical functioning.

These three components are aspects of "maintaining a lifestyle that involves normal, valued, and beneficial activities" (Williamson & Christie, 2009, p. 168). Vaillant (2002) simplifies the definition further by characterizing successful aging as joy, love, and learning. These descriptions, though not detailed, provide an adequate image of successful aging. Notice that this description leaves much room for cultural interpretation as well, which strengthens its continued utility with multiple groups. While for one person some of these components may be fulfilled in the home and with family, others may find them in the workplace (particularly since retirement does not always occur at age 65 these days). Different genders, racial and ethnic groups, and other social identity groups may achieve successful aging in different ways.

The Case of Tony

Tony had worked as a microbiologist since achieving his doctoral degree in 1974 and was now newly retired. Tony had recently moved with his wife of 41 years to a town close to his eldest daughter and her family. While getting settled in the new home, Tony found contentment in taking on small projects around the house and allowing himself to enjoy his newfound freedom. When this work was done, however, he began to feel a bit restless. Upon talking with his daughter one day, she mentioned that she had spoken to her son's kindergarten teacher about how impressed the entire family was with the school's science program. The teacher had further inquired about the family, and the fact that Tony had been a microbiologist came up in the conversation. The excited teacher asked if Tony might be interested in volunteering at the school with another grandfather who had been a physicist before he retired. Tony decided to help out, and over the course of the next year he developed several experiments for various classrooms at the elementary school. His enthusiasm for devising lesson plans for interesting activities across the age groups, and his clear love of teaching children about the wonders of science, are evident when one asks him about his involvement at the school. Today, "Dr. T." is a beloved member of the school community, still doing what he loves, though in a different and more relaxed way than his working life. The generativity he spreads in reaching out to youth, the cognitive stimulation of continuing in his field in a different role, and his engagement in this new community are all factors in his very successful aging process.

The MacArthur Foundation Study of Successful Aging

The MacArthur Foundation Study of Successful Aging (which ran from 1988 to 1996) was conducted by John Rowe and a multidisciplinary group of colleagues. They investigated physical, social, and psychological factors related to abilities, health, and well-being. Using physical and cognitive criteria, a sample of 1,189 healthy adult volunteers between the ages of 70 and 79 was selected from a pool of 4,030 potential participants. These high-functioning adults participated in a 90-minute personal interview and then were followed for an average of 7 years, during which time they completed periodic interviews.

As mentioned previously, the MacArthur study revealed that the three components of successful aging were avoiding disease, engaging with life, and maintaining physical and cognitive functioning (Rowe & Kahn, 1998). We will focus on life engagement because it is the component of successful aging that positive psychologists are most likely to address in their research and practice. Indeed, the two components of life engagement—social support and productivity (Rowe & Kahn, 1998)—parallel the life pursuits of love, work, and play that we address in many of the chapters in this book.

Social support is most potent when it is mutual; the support given is balanced by support received. Two kinds of support are important for successful aging: socioemotional support (liking and loving) and instrumental support (assistance when someone is in need). Further examination of the MacArthur data revealed that support increased over time (Gurung, Taylor, & Seeman, 2003). Moreover, the respondents with more social ties showed less decline in functioning over time (Unger, McAvay, Bruce, Berkman, & Seeman, 1999). The positive effects of social ties were shown to vary according to the individual's gender and baseline physical capabilities (Unger et al.). Gender also influenced how married participants (a 439-person subset of the total sample) received social support: "Men received emotional support primarily from their spouses, whereas women drew more heavily on their friends and relatives and children for emotional support" (Gurung et al., p. 487).

Regarding productive activity in later adulthood, Glass, Seeman, Herzog, Kahn, & Berkman, (1995) examined patterns of change in the activities of a highly functioning sample of 70-to-79-year-olds and in a group of 162 moderate-to-low-functioning 70-to-79-year-olds over a 3-year period. The highest-functioning cohort was found to be significantly more productive than the comparison group. Changes in productivity over time were associated with more hospital admissions and strokes, whereas age, marriage, and increased mastery of certain skills were related to greater protection against declines. These findings are consistent with the work of Williamson and Christie (2009), who suggest that sustained physical activity (an aspect of productive activity) helps to maintain healthy functioning. Accordingly, interruptions of physical activity regimens often precipitate declines in overall well-being.

The Adult Development Study

Vaillant (2002) acknowledges that subjective evaluation of functioning is not the most rigorous approach to identifying those who age successfully. He has relied on a system of independent evaluations of the functioning (e.g., physical, psychological, occupational) of the participants in the Study of Adult Development. The original 256 Caucasian, socially advantaged participants were identified in the late 1930s by the deans at Harvard (who viewed the students as sound in all regards). For the past 80 years, these participants have been studied via physical examinations, personal interviews, and surveys. More than 80% of the study participants lived past their 80th birthdays, whereas only 30% of their contemporaries lived to that age. Vaillant's extensive study of these older adults (and members of two other prospective studies) identified the following lifestyle predictors of healthy aging: not smoking, or stopping smoking while young; coping adaptively, with mature defenses; not abusing alcohol; maintaining a healthy weight, a stable marriage, and some exercise; and being educated. These variables distinguished people on the ends of the health spectrum: the happy–well (62 individuals who experienced good health objectively and subjectively, biologically and psychologically) and the sad–sick (40 individuals who were classified as unhappy in at least one of three dimensions: mental health, social support, or life satisfaction). The most robust predictor of membership in the happy–well group versus the sad–sick group was the extent to which people used mature psychological coping styles (e.g., altruism, humor) in everyday life.

One Man's View of Aging

Contrary to all expectations, I seem to grow happier as I grow older. I think that America has been sold on that theory that youth is marvelous but old age is terror. On the contrary, it's taken me 60 years to learn how to live reasonably well, to do my work and cope with my inadequacies.

For me, youth was a woeful time—sick parents, war, relative poverty, the miseries of learning a profession, a mistake of a marriage, self-doubts, booze, and blundering around. Old age is knowing what I am doing, the respect of others, a relatively sane financial base, a loving wife, and the realization that what I can't beat, I can endure.

Source: Vaillant (2002, p. 14).

Nuns

Source: Digital Vision/Thinkstock

Perhaps prediction of successful aging is not as complex as the MacArthur studies and Vaillant make it out to be. What if successful aging, or at the very least longevity, boils down to experiencing positive emotions in early life? Danner, Snowdon, and Friesen (2001), in their study of the autobiographies of 180 Catholic nuns written in the early 20th century, demonstrated that positive emotional content in the writings was inversely correlated with risk of mortality 60 years later. These nuns, who had seemingly had a lifestyle conducive to successful aging, were more likely to live past their 70th and 80th birthdays if they had told stories of their lives that were laden with positive emotions many decades before. Others have found that resilience, as a construct, may look different in older adults as compared to children and younger adults. Lamond and colleagues (2009) found that resilience was related more strongly to the ability to accept and tolerate negative affect in older adults, as compared to usual correlations found between resilience and more active coping styles in younger adults (Campbell-Sills, Cohan, & Stein, 2006). Thus the statement "what I can't beat, I can endure" may hold much truth for this portion of the population.

The body of research on successful aging is growing quickly, and the findings suggest that people have more control over the quality of their lives during the aging process than we once believed. Furthermore, across studies, social support is one of the psychological factors that promotes successful aging. Despite this communality, as more cross-cultural and multicultural research is conducted and published, it appears that aging and successful aging may vary depending on the particular groups studied. Therefore, successful aging should not be measured against a universal standard (Baltes & Carstensen, 1996). This suggests that future work should consider the cultural aspects of adaptive aging in pursuing clues to the good life in the later years.

A MORE DEVELOPMENTAL FOCUS IN POSITIVE PSYCHOLOGY

We all face daily hassles and adversities. This is true during childhood, adolescence, adulthood, and older adulthood. Hopefully, as we age, we become more resourceful and adaptable. This appears to be the case because there are numerous positive developmental factors that help children and adults to bounce back. The findings discussed in this chapter also suggest that positive psychology is well on its way to identifying and sharing meaningful information about how to live a better life. Try the Personal Mini-Experiments to bring some of these findings to life.

Although much is known about how to thrive during each decade of our lives, the next generation of positive psychologists (you and your peers) has many questions to answer regarding topics such as positive adult development and making successful aging possible for more people. Furthermore, more theory and research are needed to help us understand how each human strength is manifested and to describe how culture shapes a given strength and its potency over time. If positive psychology is to grow as a field, we believe that it is crucial to understand the unfolding developmental processes from childhood to older age.

PERSONAL MINI-EXPERIMENTS

Finding Amazing People of All Ages

In this chapter, we discuss many of the factors that promote healthy development over the life span. Here are a few ideas that might help you discover the positive in people of all ages.

Testing the Effectiveness of Your Mentorship. According to resilience research, a warm relationship with one caring adult can bring out the positive in children and youth. The effectiveness of your own mentorship can be tested through your ongoing work with Big Brothers and Big Sisters or another community-based mentoring program. A true test would involve giving 3 to 4 hours a week to one child and tracking the child's development over time by considering the enhancement of resources listed in Table 5.2.

Building a Stronger Social Circle. Several of the life tasks of adults are related to developing a stronger social network. Consider the state of your own social network. Draw four concentric circles. In the middle circle, write "Me," and then fill in the remaining circles with the names of the people to whom you give your time and talents on a regular basis; the closer the names are to the center circle, the closer these people are to you. Consider how you can maintain the people in the circles closest to you and bring the other folks closer to you. In particular, look to make new connections to those who may be from a different background than yourself. When you have identified a few strategies, end the exercise by acting on one of your thoughts and giving your time or talent to someone close to you.

Collecting Stories of Aging Well. Every day you encounter people 60 and older. Some of these folks are exuberant; they could be members of Vaillant's happy–well group. Approach five of these people and ask them if they would be willing to participate in a brief interview. (Tell them that you have just learned about successful aging and you would like to develop a better understanding of how people live well as they age.) Here are some questions you can ask (derived from Dr. Vaillant's Scale of Objective Mental Health, 2002, p. 342):

- How well are you enjoying your career/retirement?
- How would you describe your last vacation?
- What personal relationships have been important to you since you turned 50? Please describe the most important one.

Log your responses to these questions and attempt to draw conclusions about successful aging in your community from these five interviews.

KEY TERMS

Career consolidation: A life task that requires the development of a social identity and engagement in a career characterized by contentment, compensation, competence, and commitment.

External adaptation: A person's ability to meet the social, education, and occupational expectations of society.

Generativity: A life task that requires one to "give the self away" and expand one's social circle. This may include mentoring the next generation of adults.

Identity: A life task that requires one to develop one's own views, values, and interests instead of simply reflecting the beliefs of one's parents or others.

Instrumental support: Support that involves giving assistance or help when needed.

Integrity: A life task that requires one to cultivate contentment with life and a sense of peace. Often accompanied by increased spirituality.

Internal adaptation: A person's ability to achieve emotional and psychological well-being.

Intimacy: A life task that requires one to develop an interdependent, committed, and close relationship with another person.

Keeper of meaning: A life task that engenders perspective on the workings of the world and of people and that is characterized by a willingness to share this wisdom with others. The keeper of meaning is seen as linking the present and the past by protecting traditions and rituals and passing them on to the next generation.

Positive youth development (PYD): Positive, healthy youth development is marked by the attainment of nine outcomes: (1) bonding; (2) social, emotional, cognitive, behavioral, and moral competencies; (3) self-determination; (4) spirituality; (5) clear and positive identity; (6) belief in the future; (7) positive behavior; (8) prosocial development; (9) prosocial norms.

Positive youth developmentalists: Professionals who put the findings of resilience researchers and other positive psychologists into action and create opportunities for growth by developing and conducting programs that help youth capitalize on their personal assets and environmental resources.

Resilience: The ability to bounce back or positively adapt in the face of significant adversity or risk.

Resilience researchers: Professionals who study resilience and identify the naturally occurring personal and environmental resources that help children and adolescents overcome life challenges.

Socioemotional support: Support that involves providing friendship, kindness, and love for others.

Successful aging: A lifestyle defined by avoiding disease, engaging in life, and maintaining high cognitive and physical functioning in one's later years.

PART III

Positive Emotional States and Processes

CHAPTER 6

The Principles of Pleasure

Understanding Positive Affect, Positive Emotions, Happiness, and Well-Being

Standing at the front of a small lecture hall, Ed Diener, University of Illinois psychologist and world-renowned happiness researcher, held up a real brain in a jar with a blue liquid, which he called "joy juice," trickling into it from a small plastic pouch held above. He asked the audience to pretend that their brains could be treated with a hormone (i.e., joy juice) that would make them ecstatically happy and that they could be happy *all the time*. Then he asked the crucial question, "How many people in this room would want to do this?" Of the 60 audience members, only 2 raised their hands to signify their desires for perpetual happiness.

Given that I (SJL) had had little exposure to philosophy coursework and that my undergraduate and graduate training in psychology had not exposed me to the science of happiness, I hadn't thought much about happiness in its many forms. Dr. Diener's question intrigued me, and since attending his lecture in 1999, I have attempted to develop a better understanding of the positive side of the emotional experience; this has led me to the solid research I summarize here.

In this chapter, we attempt to add to what you know about pleasure by going far beyond Freud's (1936) pleasure principle (the demand that an instinctive need be gratified regardless of the consequences) and by fostering an understanding of the many principles of pleasure that have been linked to good living. In this process, we present what we know about that which makes modern life pleasurable. We also summarize research that examines the distinctions between positive and negative affect. Likewise, we highlight positive emotions and their pleasure-expanding benefits, and we explore the many definitions of happiness and well-being, qualities of pleasurable living. To begin, we clarify the numerous terms and concepts used in this chapter.

DEFINING EMOTIONAL TERMS

The terms *affect* and *emotion* often are used interchangeably in scholarly and popular literatures. Furthermore, *well-being* and *happiness* appear to be synonymous in psychology articles.

Ed Diener

Source: Reprinted with permission of Ed Diener.

Unfortunately, however, the interchangeable use of these terms is very confusing. Although we try to clarify the distinctions among these closely related ideas, we acknowledge the overlap that exists. We begin by suggesting that affect is a component of emotion, and emotion is a more specific version of mood.

Affect

Affect is a person's immediate, physiological response to a stimulus, and it is typically based on an underlying sense of arousal. Specifically, Professor Nico Frijda (1999) reasoned that affect involves the appraisal of an event as painful or pleasurable—that is, its valence—and the experience of autonomic arousal.

Emotion

Parsimonious definitions of emotion are hard to find, but this one seems to describe the phenomenon succinctly: "Emotions, I shall argue, involve judgments about important things, judgments in which, appraising an external object as salient for our own well-being, we acknowledge our own neediness and incompleteness before parts of the world that we do not fully control" (Nussbaum, 2001, p. 19). These emotional responses occur as we become aware of painful or pleasurable experiences and associated autonomic arousal (i.e., affect; Frijda, 1999) and evaluate the situation. An emotion has a specific and "sharpened" quality, as it always has an object (Cohn & Fredrickson, 2009), and it is associated with progress in goal pursuit (Snyder et al., 1991; Snyder, 1994). In contrast, a mood is objectless, free floating, and long lasting.

Happiness

Happiness is a positive emotional state that is subjectively defined by each person. The term is rarely used in scientific studies because there is little consensus on its meaning. In this chapter, we use this term only when it is clarified by additional information.

Subjective Well-Being

Subjective well-being involves the subjective evaluation of one's current status in the world. More specifically, Diener (1984, 2000, 2013; Diener, Oishi, & Lucas, 2009) defines subjective well-being as a combination of positive affect (in the absence of negative affect) and general life satisfaction (i.e., subjective appreciation of life's rewards). The term *subjective well-being* often is used as a synonym for *happiness* in the psychology literature. Almost without exception, the more accessible word *happiness* is used in the popular press in lieu of the term *subjective well-being.*

DISTINGUISHING THE POSITIVE AND THE NEGATIVE

Hans Selye (1936) is known for his research on the effects of prolonged exposure to fear and anger. Consistently, he found that physiological stress harmed the body yet had survival value for humans. Indeed, the evolutionary functions of fear and anger have intrigued both researchers and laypeople. Given the historical tradition and scientific findings pertaining to the negative affects, their importance in our lives has not been questioned over the last century.

Historically, positive affects have received scant attention over the last century because few scholars hypothesized that the rewards of joy and contentment went beyond hedonic (pleasure-based) values and had possible evolutionary significance. The potentialities of positive affect have become more obvious over the last 20 years (Cohn & Fredrickson, 2009) as research has drawn distinctions between the positive and negative affects.

David Watson (1988) of the University of Iowa conducted research on the approach-oriented motivations of pleasurable affects—including rigorous studies of *both* negative and positive affects. To facilitate their research on the two dimensions of emotional experience, Watson and his collaborator Lee Anna Clark (1994) developed and validated the Expanded Form of the Positive and Negative Affect Schedule (PANAS-X), which has become a commonly used measure in this area. This 20-item scale has been used in hundreds of studies to quantify two dimensions of affect: valence and content. More specifically, the PANAS-X taps both "negative" (unpleasant) and "positive" (pleasant) valence. The content of negative affective states can be described best as general distress, whereas positive affect includes joviality, self-assurance, and attentiveness. (See the PANAS, a predecessor of the PANAS-X, which is brief and valid for most clinical and research purposes.)

David Watson

Source: Reprinted with permission of David Watson.

Using the PANAS and other measures of affect, researchers systematically have addressed a basic question: "Can we experience negative affect and positive affect at the same time?" (See Diener & Emmons, 1984; Green, Salovey, & Truax, 1999.) For example, could we go to an engaging movie and come out feeling both pleasure and fear? Although negative and positive affects once were thought to be polar opposites, Bradburn (1969) demonstrated that unpleasant and pleasant affects are independent and have different correlates. Psychologists such as Watson (2002; Watson & Naragon, 2009) continue to examine this issue of independence in their research. In a recent study, Watson found that negative affect correlated with joviality, self-assurance, and attentiveness at only –.21, –.14, and –.17, respectively. The small magnitudes of these negative correlations suggest that, while negative and positive affect are inversely correlated in some groups as expected, the relationships are quite weak and indicative of independence of the two types of affect. The size of these relationships, however, may increase when people are taxed by daily stressors (Keyes & Ryff, 2000; Zautra, Potter, & Reich, 1997). This said, positive as opposed

The Positive and Negative Affect Schedule

This scale consists of a number of words that describe different feelings and emotions. Read each item and then mark the appropriate answer on the line provided. **Indicate to what extent you feel this emotion right now.** Use the following scale as you record your answers.

	Feeling or Emotion	Very Slightly or Not at All	A Little	Moderately	Quite a Bit	Extremely
1.	interested	1	2	3	4	5
2.	distressed	1	2	3	4	5
3.	excited	1	2	3	4	5
4.	upset	1	2	3	4	5
5.	strong	1	2	3	4	5
6.	guilty	1	2	3	4	5
7.	scared	1	2	3	4	5
8.	hostile	1	2	3	4	5
9.	enthusiastic	1	2	3	4	5
10.	proud	1	2	3	4	5
11.	irritable	1	2	3	4	5
12.	alert	1	2	3	4	5
13.	ashamed	1	2	3	4	5
14.	inspired	1	2	3	4	5
15.	nervous	1	2	3	4	5
16.	determined	1	2	3	4	5
17.	attentive	1	2	3	4	5
18.	jittery	1	2	3	4	5
19.	active	1	2	3	4	5
20.	afraid	1	2	3	4	5

to inverse correlations are found between positive and negative affect in many Eastern groups, namely in Asian samples (Spencer-Rodgers, Peng, & Wang, 2010). This ability to feel and think dialectically (i.e., in more than one direction, or from more than one point of view) about events in one's life can be labeled a strength in Asian cultures. It may be that this emotional complexity allows Asians to have a greater level of social intelligence, which is of course beneficial in a collectivist society (Spencer-Rodgers et al., 2010).

POSITIVE EMOTIONS: EXPANDING THE REPERTOIRE OF PLEASURE

As some psychologists refine the distinction between the positive and negative sides of the emotional experience through basic research and measurement, other scholars (e.g., Isen, Fredrickson) have begun to explore questions about the potency and potentialities of positive emotions. (Here we use the term *emotion* rather than *affect* because we are addressing the specific response tendencies that flow from affective experience.) Cornell University psychologist Alice Isen is a pioneer in the examination of positive emotions. Dr. Isen found that, when experiencing mild positive emotions, we are more likely (1) to help other people (Isen, 1987); (2) to be flexible in our thinking (Ashby, Isen, & Turken, 1999); (3) to come up with solutions to our problems (Isen, Daubman, & Nowicki, 1987); and (4) to be more willing to exhibit self-control (Pyone & Isen, 2011). In classic research related to these points, Isen (1970; Isen & Levin, 1972) performed an experimental manipulation in which the research participants either did or did not find coins (placed there by the researcher) in the change slot of a public pay phone. Compared to those who did not find a coin, those who did were more likely to help another person carry a load of books or to help pick up another's dropped papers. Therefore, the finding of a coin and the associated positive emotion made people behave more altruistically.

Alice Isen

Source: Reprinted with permission of Alice Isen.

Feeling positive emotion also can help in seeing problem-solving options and finding cues for good decision making (Estrada, Isen, & Young, 1997). In one study related to these latter points, the researchers randomly assigned physicians to an experimental condition in which the doctor either was or was not given a small bag that contained 6 hard candies and 4 miniature chocolates (the doctors were not allowed to eat the candy during the experiment). Those physicians who had, rather than had not, been given the gift of candy displayed superior reasoning and decision making relative to the physicians who did not receive the candy. Specifically, the doctors in the positive emotion condition did not jump to conclusions; they were cautious even though they arrived at the diagnosis sooner than the doctors in the other condition (A. Isen, personal communication, December 13, 2005). Perhaps, therefore, we should give our doctor some candy next time we see him or her!

Here is a more detailed description of that study that led us to this lighthearted suggestion. (Although Dr. Isen uses the term *affect,* we believe *emotion* would be more appropriate here.)

Forty-four physicians were randomly assigned to 1 of 3 groups: a control group, an affect-induction group (these participants received a small package of candy), or a group that asked participants to read humanistic statements regarding the practice of medicine. Physicians in all three groups were asked to "think aloud" while they solved a case of a patient with liver disease. Transcripts of the physicians' comments were typed, and two raters reviewed the transcripts to determine how soon the diagnosis of liver disease was considered and established, and the extent to which thinking was distorted or inflexible. The affect group initially considered the diagnosis of liver disease significantly earlier in the experiment and showed significantly less inflexible thinking than did controls. The affect and control groups established the diagnosis at similar points in the experiment. So positive affect led to the earlier integration of information (considered liver disease sooner) and resulted in little premature foreclosure on the diagnosis.

Risk-taking may also be influenced by positive affect when the return on the risk is anticipated to be high (Xing & Sun, 2013). In another study, happier participants showed greater willingness to take greater financial risks for high returns. This process appears to be related to links between positive affect and the psychological resilience that high levels of this type of affect may build over time (Xing & Sun, 2013). Thus, it may be that the link between happiness and psychological resilience allows individuals who are high in both of these areas to be able to feel more comfortable taking risks in general. Risk-taking could, of course, lead to either a positive and negative outcome (e.g., one could lose money or gain money with a risky financial investment). That said, however, taking opportunities as they come could provide more benefits in the long term. In addition, even when crises occur, an individual with psychological resilience (as developed by increased positive affect experiences) may be better able to handle this type of circumstance (Xing & Sun, 2013).

PERSONAL MINI-EXPERIMENTS

In Search of Joy and Lasting Happiness

In this chapter, we discuss positive emotion and happiness. Our review suggests that pleasant emotional experiences can be induced via brief mini-experiments. Here are a few ideas for experiments aimed at boosts in joy and happiness.

The Cartoon/Comedy Pretest–Posttest. Respond to the PANAS (see p. 134) based on how you feel at the moment, then watch an episode (5 to 20 minutes without commercials, if possible) of your favorite cartoon or situation comedy that showcases good-natured humor (not sarcastic or sardonic humor). Complete a second PANAS immediately after viewing the show. Then, note the changes that have occurred in your positive and negative affect.

The "Movie, Then What?" Experiment. This experiment requires careful selection of two movies: one that has sad themes and a sanguine ending (a "feel-bad" film), and one that emphasizes joy and triumph (a "feel-good" film). Across two occasions, invite the same group of friends for movie watching at home or in the theater. After the movies, ask your friends, "Hey, if you could do anything at all right now, what would you do? What else?" Make mental notes of how many future activities are mentioned and the exuberance with which your friends discuss these activities. Identify the differences in the thought–action repertoires across the conditions of the "feel-bad" movie and the "feel-good" movie.

Commonsense Definitions of Happiness. Have you ever asked someone about his or her views on happiness? We encourage you to ask friends and acquaintances of various ages and backgrounds, "How do you define happiness in your life? What are some benchmarks or signs of your happiness?" You will be surprised by the diversity of answers and refreshed and entertained by the many stories accompanying people's responses. In listening, pay attention to the cultural contexts that often shape these definitions.

Building on Isen's work, Fredrickson (2000) has developed a new theoretical framework, the **broaden-and-build model of positive emotions**, which may provide some explanations for the robust social and cognitive effects of positive emotional experiences. In Fredrickson's review of models of emotions (Smith, 1991), she found that responses to positive emotions have not been extensively studied and that, when researched, they were examined in a vague and underspecified manner. Furthermore, action tendencies generally have been associated with physical reactions to negative emotions (imagine "fight or flight"), whereas human reactions to positive emotions often are more cognitive than physical. For these reasons, she proposes discarding the **specific action tendency** concept (which suggests a restricted range of possible behavioral options) in favor of a newer, more inclusive term, *momentary thought–action repertoires* (which suggest a broad range of behavioral options; imagine "taking off blinders" and seeing available opportunities).

Barbara Fredrickson

Source: Reprinted with permission of Jeff Chapell.

To illustrate the difference in that which follows positive and negative emotions, consider the childhood experience of one of the authors (SJL). Notice how positive emotions (e.g., excitement and glee) lead to cognitive flexibility and creativity, whereas negative emotions (e.g., fear and anxiety) are linked to a fleeing response and termination of activities.

During a Saturday visit to my grandmother's home, I had the time of my life playing a marathon game of hide-and-seek with my brother and four cousins. The hours of play led to excitement and giggling . . . and the creation of new game rules and obstacles. The unbridled joy we experienced that afternoon made us feel free; we felt like that day would go on forever. Unfortunately, the fun was interrupted. The abrupt end to the game came when my cousin Bubby spotted me hiding behind the tall grasses on the back of my grandmother's property. I darted out of my hiding place to escape from him. As I ran around the house, I veered off into the vacant lot next door. Laughing with *glee,* I ran as hard as I could. Suddenly, there was an obstacle in my path. I leaped over it as Bub screamed uncontrollably. As I turned around, I realized I had jumped over a four-foot water moccasin, a highly poisonous snake. As my cousin's screaming continued, I grew increasingly jittery. Without thinking, we backed away from the snake . . . and then ran for our lives. When we finally stopped running, we could not catch our breaths. No one was hurt, but our fear and anxiety had taken the fun out of our day.

In testing her model of positive emotions, Fredrickson (2000) demonstrated that the experience of joy expands the realm of what a person feels like doing at the time; this is referred to as the *broadening* of an individual's momentary thought-action repertoire. Following an emotion-eliciting film clip (the clips induced one of five emotions: joy, contentment, anger, fear, or a neutral condition), research participants were asked to list everything they would like to do at that moment (see the results in Figure 6.1). Those participants who experienced joy or contentment listed significantly more desired possibilities than did the people in the neutral or negative conditions. In turn, those expanded possibilities for future activities should lead the joyful individuals to initiate subsequent actions. Those who expressed more negative emotions, on the other hand, tended to shut down their thinking about subsequent possible activities. Simply put, joy appears to open us up to many new thoughts and behaviors, whereas negative emotions dampen our ideas and actions.

Joy also increases our likelihood of behaving positively toward other people, along with aiding in developing more positive relationships. Furthermore, joy induces playfulness (Frijda, 1994),

Figure 6.1   The Broadening Effects of Positive Emotions

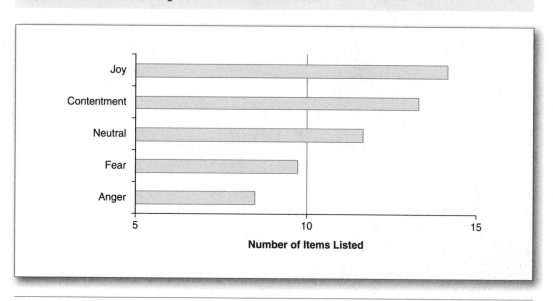

Source: Fredrickson (2002). Used with permission of Oxford University Press, Inc.

which is quite important because such behaviors are evolutionarily adaptive in acquisition of necessary resources. Juvenile play builds (1) enduring social and intellectual resources by encouraging
attachment, (2) higher levels of creativity, and (3) brain development (Cohn & Fredrickson, 2009;
Fredrickson, 2002). Playfulness is now also being studied in adults with more positive results. Young
adults who are more playful have less perceived stress and are found to cope better with various
stressors in their lives (Magnuson & Barnett, 2013). Other research has found that playfulness
can be linked to greater life satisfaction (Proyer, 2012) and other positive attributes (Proyer &
Ruch, 2011).

It appears that, through the effects of broadening processes, positive emotions also can help
build resources. In 2002, Fredrickson and her colleague, Thomas Joiner, demonstrated this building phenomenon by assessing people's positive and negative emotions and broad-minded coping
(solving problems with creative means) on two occasions 5 weeks apart. The researchers found
that initial levels of positive emotions predicted overall increases in creative problem solving.
These changes in coping also predicted further increases in positive emotions (see Figure 6.2).
Similarly, controlling for initial levels of positive emotion, initial levels of coping predicted
increases in positive emotions, which in turn predicted increases in coping. These results held
true only for positive emotions, *not* for negative emotions. Therefore, positive emotions such as
joy may help generate resources; maintain a sense of vital energy (i.e., more positive emotions);
and create even more resources. Cohn and Fredrickson (2009) referred to this positive sequence
as the "upward spiral" of positive emotions (see Figure 6.3).

Figure 6.2 The Building Effects of Positive Emotions

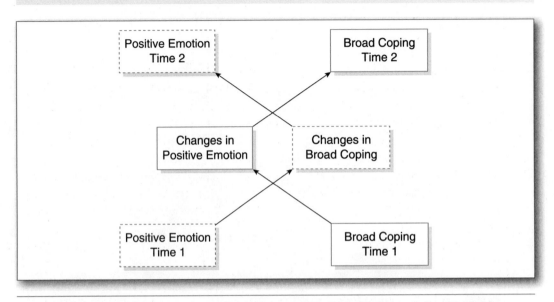

Source: From Mayne, T. J., & Bonanno, G. A., *Emotions.* Copyright © 2001. Reprinted with permission of Guilford Press.

Figure 6.3 The Upward Spiral of Positive Emotions

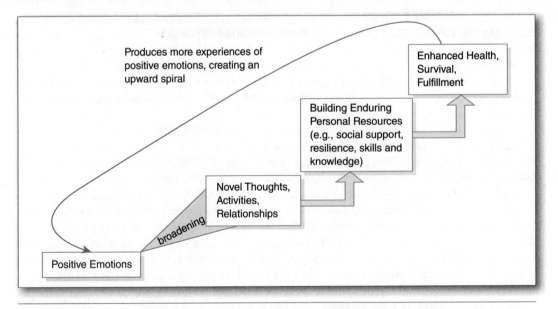

Source: From Cohn, M. A., & Fredrickson, B. L., Positive emotions, in S. J. Lopez & C. R. Snyder (Eds.), *Oxford handbook of positive psychology* (pp. 13–24). Copyright © 2009. Reprinted with permission of Oxford University Press.

Positive Emotion Styles Linked to the Common Cold
A. Palmer

Positive emotions may increase resistance to the common cold, according to a recent study in *Psychosomatic Medicine* (Vol. 65, No. 1). The research by Sheldon Cohen, PhD, of Carnegie Mellon University, and colleagues adds to a body of literature that suggests that emotional styles influence health. The researchers interviewed 334 healthy volunteers by phone for 7 evenings over 3 weeks to assess their emotional states. Participants described how they felt throughout the day in three positive-emotion areas of vigor, well-being, and calm and three negative-emotion areas of depression, anxiety, and hostility by rating their emotions on a scale of 0 to 4.

After this initial evaluation, researchers administered a shot of a rhinovirus, the germ that causes colds, into each participant's nose. Afterward, participants were observed for 5 days to see if they became sick and in what ways cold symptoms manifested. The volunteers were considered to have a clinical cold if they were both infected and met illness criteria.

"People who scored low on positive emotional style were three times more likely to get sick than those with high positive emotional styles," Cohen says.

The researchers then measured how emotional style affected all sick participants' reporting of cold symptoms. Each day of the quarantine, researchers asked them to report the severity of such cold symptoms as a runny nose, cough, and headaches on a 4-point scale.

While negative emotional style did not affect whether people developed colds, the study found that people with higher negative emotional styles reported more symptoms than expected from objective health markers, Cohen says. Those with lower positive emotions reported fewer symptoms of illness than expected.

Positive emotional style was also associated with better health practices and lower levels of epinephrine, norepinephrine, and cortisol, three stress-related hormones, but the researchers found that this did not account for the link between positive emotional style and illness.

Considering the average adult catches 2 to 5 colds per year and children average 7 to 10 colds per year, developing psychological risk profiles and considering ways to enhance positive emotions might reduce the risk of colds, says Cohen.

Cohen adds that future research should focus on the unique biological role that emotions play in health.

Extending her model of positive emotions, Fredrickson and colleagues examined the "undoing" potential of positive emotions (Fredrickson, Mancuso, Branigan, & Tugade, 2000) and the ratio of positive to negative emotional experiences that is associated with human flourishing

(Fredrickson & Losada, 2005). Fredrickson et al. (2000) hypothesized that, given the broadening and building effects of positive emotions, joy and contentment might function as antidotes to negative emotions. To test this hypothesis, the researchers exposed all participants in their study to a situation that aroused negative emotion and immediately randomly assigned people to emotion conditions (sparked by evocative video clips) ranging from mild joy to sadness. Cardiovascular recovery represented the undoing process and was operationalized as the time that elapsed from the start of the randomly assigned video until the physiological reactions induced by the initial negative emotion returned to baseline. The undoing hypothesis was supported, as participants in the joy and contentment conditions were able to undo the effects of the negative emotions more quickly than the people in the other conditions. These findings suggest that there is an incompatibility between positive and negative emotions and that the potential effects of negative experiences can be offset by positive emotions such as joy and contentment.

Given that positive emotions help people build enduring resources and recover from negative experiences, Fredrickson and Losada (2005) hypothesized that positive emotions might be associated with optimal mental health or flourishing (i.e., positive psychological and social well-being; see the complete mental health model on p. 140). By subjecting data on undergraduate participants' mental health (from a flourishing measure) and their emotional experience (students rated the extent to which they experienced 20 emotions each day for 28 days) to mathematical analysis, the researchers found that a mean ratio of 2:9 positive to negative emotions predicts human flourishing. Unfortunately, it was recently discovered that the math used to attain this ratio had many flaws. Nicholas Brown, a graduate student at the University of East London, discovered the math mistakes and submitted a paper (Brown, Sokal, & Friedman, 2013) questioning the assertion that a critical point between flourishing and languishing could actually be quantified. Fredrickson (2013) responded to the critique, noting computation errors and acknowledging the absence of such a tipping point between languishing and flourishing, but she defended the merit of the body of research on positive emotions. Fredrickson states that, regardless of an actual number existing to represent this point, it still appears that the data reflect the effect of a higher number of positive events in comparison to negative events and that this effect is a beneficial one. Individuals in the original study who were flourishing did have ratios that reflected this balance (Fredrickson, 2013; Fredrickson & Losada, 2005). Brown and his colleagues reject this response as being valid to the argument.

In the end, we are left with more questions in this area, and it is clear that more research may provide us with answers. All in all, perhaps it was the act of trying to assign a number to the human condition that began the argument. It may be that it is more beneficial for us to think both *qualitatively* and *quantitatively* about positive experiences. In daily life, looking for the positive more often than the negative still seems to be a worthwhile pursuit.

Positive affect may have other benefits as well. Sonja Lyubomirsky, Laura King, and Ed Diener (2005) conducted an extensive review of 225 papers across three classes of studies (longitudinal, cross-sectional, and experimental) to investigate the complicated links between happiness and other positive outcomes, such as success. Though many studies in the past have found correlational links between these constructs, Lyubomirsky and colleagues posit that "positive affect—the hallmark of well-being—may be the cause of many of the desirable characteristics, resources, and successes correlated with happiness" (p. 803). These researchers found that preliminary evidence exists to suggest that success and other beneficial outcomes may be caused by the presence of happiness in a person's life. Though more research in this area must be done, these initial findings lay the groundwork for future studies to determine more information about the causal links between happiness and other related constructs.

HAPPINESS AND SUBJECTIVE WELL-BEING: LIVING A PLEASURABLE LIFE

Age-Old Definitions of Happiness

Buddha left home in search of a more meaningful existence and ultimately found enlightenment, a sense of peace, and happiness. Aristotle believed that *eudaimonia* (human flourishing associated with living a life of virtue), or happiness based on a lifelong pursuit of meaningful, developmental goals (i.e., "doing what is worth doing"), was the key to the good life (Waterman, 1993). America's founders reasoned that the pursuit of happiness was just as important as our inalienable rights of life and liberty. These age-old definitions of happiness, along with many other conceptualizations of emotional well-being, have had clear influences on the views of twentieth- and twenty-first-century scholars, but more recent psychological theory and genetic research have helped us to clarify happiness and its correlates.

Theories of happiness have been divided into three types: (1) need/goal satisfaction theories, (2) process/activity theories, and (3) genetic/personality predisposition theories (Diener et al., 2009). (Explore folk definitions of happiness by completing the third exercise in the Personal Mini-Experiments earlier in this chapter.)

In regard to need/goal satisfaction theories, the leaders of particular schools of psychotherapy proffered various ideas about happiness. For example, psychoanalytic and humanistic theorists (Sigmund Freud and Abraham Maslow, respectively) suggested that the reduction of tension or the satisfaction of needs lead to happiness. In short, it was theorized that we are happy because we have reached our goals. Such "happiness as satisfaction" makes happiness a target of our psychological pursuits.

In the process/activity camp, theorists posit that engaging in particular life activities generates happiness. For example, Mike Csikszentmihalyi, who was one of the first twentieth-century theorists to examine process/activity conceptualizations of happiness, proposed that people who experience flow (engagement in interesting activities that match or challenge task-related skills) in daily life tend to be very happy. Indeed, Csikszentmihalyi's (1975/2000, 1990) work suggests that engagement in activity *produces* happiness. Other process/activity theorists (e.g., Emmons, 1986; Snyder, 1994) have emphasized how the *process* of pursuing goals generates energy and happiness. This pursuit-of-happiness perspective mirrors the United States' founders' promise of "life, liberty, and the pursuit of happiness." Activities such as the practice of gratitude and kindness may also provide boosts in well-being for some groups. Empirical evidence exists for the fact that regular engagement in these types of positive acts can help individuals to improve their happiness over time by prescriptive use of tasks such as the writing of gratitude letters and purposeful acts of kindness (Sin & Lyubomirsky, 2009), or strategic use of optimism (Lyubomirsky, Dickerhoof, Boehm, & Sheldon, 2011).

Interestingly, however, well-being is not always improved by the same activities in different cultural groups. In a comparison of participants from the United States and those from South

Korea, it was found that while expressing gratitude benefited the U.S. participants with spikes in well-being, this activity was significantly less helpful for South Korean participants, resulting in decreases in well-being (Layous, Lee, Choi, & Lyubomirsky, 2013). This same study found that acts of kindness had the same effect in both groups, however. The authors of this study suggest that a construct such as gratitude may have different cultural meanings for the two groups. In South Korea, feelings of gratitude may be more closely linked with feelings of indebtedness, showing the dialectical pattern that is often found between positive and negative affect in Asian groups. In United States samples, gratitude may not be linked to negative feelings in quite the same way. Other research has shown that even when the same construct boosts well-being in multiple cultures, there may be significant differences in the amounts of increases seen in different groups (Boehm, Lyubomirsky, & Sheldon, 2011). Thus, we must consider which types of processes and activities are valued and deemed positive by a particular cultural group before deciding which may have the desired effects on well-being. Lyubomirsky and Layous (2013) suggest a model for determining whether certain activities will provide the desired increases in well-being. Their parameters include looking closely at the types of activities and their "dosage" (p. 57), the effort and agency of the participant toward the activity, and the fit between person and activity. This last criterion can be attained by taking care to devise interventions and activities that have cultural relevance for the group one is studying.

Those who emphasize the genetic and personality predisposition theories of happiness (Diener & Larsen, 1984; Watson, 2000) tend to see happiness as stable, whereas theorists in the happiness-as-satisfaction and process/activity camps view it as changing with life conditions. On this latter point, Costa and McCrae (1988) found that happiness changed little over a 6-year period, thereby lending credence to theories of personality-based or biologically determined happiness. More recent research, however, found evidence that the links between personality and happiness may be more idiographic than previously thought (e.g., personal set points for happiness may not be neutral and may be more dependent on temperament, or individuals may vary in the type of adaptation to positive or negative external experiences; Diener, Lucas, & Scollon, 2006). In addition, these researchers believe that multiple set points for positive emotion may exist for any one individual, and these set points may be able to be changed under some conditions. More work is needed in this area to determine the nuances of these complex relationships between happiness and personality.

Further elucidating the link between happiness and personality, Lucas and Fujita (2000) showed that extroversion and neuroticism, two of the Big 5 factors of personality (openness, conscientiousness, extroversion, agreeableness, neuroticism), were closely related to the characteristics of happiness. Shiota, Keltner, and John (2006) found similar results with regard to these Big 5 personality factors and also link positive affect to adult attachment styles. The link between personality and life satisfaction has been found to occur in many cultures; however, the strength of influence of personality on well-being has been shown to be moderated by culture (Pavot & Diener, 2008). Thus, culture also plays a role in the determinants of the strength of this relationship.

Studies of the biological or genetic determinants of happiness have found that up to 40% of positive emotionality and 55% of negative emotionality are genetically based (Tellegen et al., 1988). Obviously, this leaves about 50% of the variance in happiness that is not explained by biological components. Overall, therefore, a thorough understanding of happiness necessitates an examination of genetic factors *and* the variables suggested by need/goal satisfaction and the activity/process theorists.

Subjective Well-Being as a Synonym for Happiness

Building on a utilitarian tradition and the tenets of hedonic psychology (which emphasizes the study of pleasure and life satisfaction), Diener (1984; 2000; Diener et al., 2009) considers well-being to be the subjective evaluation of one's current status in the world. More specifically, well-being involves our experience of pleasure and our appreciation of life's rewards. Given this view, Diener defines subjective well-being as a combination of positive affect (in the absence of negative affect) and general life satisfaction. Furthermore, he uses the term *subjective well-being* as a synonym for *happiness*. (The satisfaction component often is measured with the Satisfaction With Life Scale; Diener, Emmons, Larsen, & Griffin, 1985).

The Satisfaction With Life Scale

Instructions: Please use one of the following numbers from 1 to 7 to indicate how much you agree or disagree with the following statements.

1	2	3	4	5	6	7
Strongly Disagree	Disagree	Slightly Disagree	Neither Agree nor Disagree	Slightly Agree	Agree	Strongly Agree

1.	_____ In most ways, my life is close to my ideal.
2.	_____ The conditions of my life are excellent.
3.	_____ I am satisfied with my life.
4.	_____ So far, I have gotten the important things I want in my life.
5.	_____ If I could live my life over, I would change almost nothing.

Note: Scores for all items are summed to calculate a total score.

Subjective well-being emphasizes peoples' reports of their life experiences. Accordingly, the subjective report is taken at face value. This subjective approach to happiness assumes that people from many cultures are comfortable focusing on individualistic assessments of their affects and satisfaction and that people will be forthright in such personal analyses (Diener et al., 2009). These assumptions guide the researchers' attempts to understand a person's subjective experiences in light of his or her objective circumstances.

Determinants of Subjective Well-Being

When examining satisfaction in various life domains of college students from 31 nations, financial status was more highly correlated with satisfaction for students in poor nations than for those in wealthy nations (Diener & Diener, 1995). Moreover, the students in wealthy nations generally were happier than those in impoverished nations. Within-nation examination of this link between income and well-being reveals that, once household income rises above the poverty line, additional bumps in income are not necessarily associated with increases in well-being. When well-being data are divided further by categories of economic status (very poor versus very wealthy), it appears that there is a strong relationship between income and well-being among the impoverished but an insignificant relationship between the two variables among the affluent (Diener, Diener, & Diener, 1995). Other analyses have shown that the link between wealth and happiness may be strongest when "wealth" is defined as economic status (as opposed to flow of income) and when measures of life satisfaction are used (as opposed to measures of happiness) to determine subjective well-being (Howell & Howell, 2008). While some may feel that their road to happiness is by spending some of this wealth, studies show that thrift is actually much more closely related to *hedonic* happiness. Though the idea that thrift (as opposed to spending) could be a hedonic pleasure sounds like an oxymoron, Chancellor and Lyubomirsky (2011) found that hedonic happiness can be derived from refraining from spending with the goal of eliminating debt and savoring what one has as opposed to replacing those materials. As over-consumption, materialism, and greed are all detractors from a healthy society, these data bode well for our future.

Data specific to Western samples indicate that married men and women alike report more happiness than those who are not married (never married, divorced, or separated; Lee, Seccombe, & Shehan, 1991). The link between subjective well-being and being married is different for people of all ages, incomes, and educational levels, and it also varies across racial and ethnic backgrounds (Argyle, 1987). Same-sex couples who have legalized unions (i.e., marriages and/or civil unions) also report greater levels of well-being (Rothblum, Balsam, & Solomon, 2011). Not surprisingly, marital quality also is positively associated with personal well-being (Sternberg & Hojjat, 1997). Though some believe that a dimming of passion and happiness is a natural by-product of being in a long-term relationship, this is not always (or even often) the case. Couples who practice certain behaviors in their relationships may have an even better chance at avoiding this decrease. Bao and Lyubomirsky (2013) have created a list of ways to combat this "hedonic adaptation"—that is, the tendency for people to adjust back to their baseline happiness after a positive event such as the start of a relationship. Their specific strategies are presented in Table 6.1 below (see also Chapter 12 in this volume on love and relationships).

Table 6.1   Strategies to Combat Hedonic Adaptation in Long-Term Relationships

Strategy	Explanation
Experience more positive events and feel more positive emotions	The more positive events and emotions one experiences, the more slowly one adapts.
Variety is the spice of relationships	Increasing variety in a relationship may help increase well-being and decelerate adaptation.
Maintain reasonable aspirations	Couples might benefit from remaining mindful of their aspirations about the relationship and their partner, and trying to avoid ever-increasing aspirations.
Cultivate appreciation	Appreciation draws an individual's attention back to the positive change in her life (e.g., getting married or promoted), allowing her to continue to experience that positive change and the events and emotions that accompany it.

Data from Bao, K. J., & Lyubomirsky, S. (2013). Making it last: Combating hedonic adaptation in romantic relationships. *The Journal of Positive Psychology, 8,* 196–206.

In a study of the happiest 10% of U.S. college students, Diener and Seligman (2002) found that the qualities of good mental health and good social relationships consistently emerged in the lives in the sample of happiest young adults. Upon closer inspection of their data, analyses revealed that good social functioning among the happiest subset of students was a necessary but not sufficient cause of happiness.

Happiness + Meaning = Well-Being

Psychologists who support the hedonic perspective view subjective well-being and happiness as synonymous. Alternatively, the scholars whose ideas about well-being are more consistent with Aristotle's views on *eudaimonia* believe that happiness and well-being are not synonymous. In this latter perspective, *eudaimonia* is comprised of happiness and meaning. Stated in a simple formula, well-being = happiness + meaning. In order to subscribe to this view of well-being, one must understand virtue and the social implications of daily behavior. Furthermore, this view requires that those who seek well-being be authentic and live according to their real needs and desired goals (Waterman, 1993). Thus, living a eudaimonic life goes beyond experiencing "things pleasurable," and it embraces flourishing as the goal in all our actions. Both hedonistic and eudaimonic versions of happiness have influenced the twenty-first-century definitions.

Twenty-First-Century Definitions of Happiness

Modern Western psychology has focused primarily on a postmaterialistic view of happiness (Diener et al., 2002, 2009) that emphasizes pleasure, satisfaction, *and* life meaning. Indeed, the type of happiness addressed in much of today's popular literature emphasizes hedonics, meaning, and authenticity. For example, Seligman (2002) suggests that a pleasant and meaningful life can be built on the happiness that results from using our psychological strengths.

Excerpts From *Authentic Happiness*
Martin E. P. Seligman

When well-being comes from engaging our strengths and virtues, our lives are imbued with authenticity. Feelings are states, momentary occurrences that need not be recurring features of personality. Traits, in contrast to states, are either negative or positive characteristics that bring about good feeling and gratification. Traits are abiding dispositions whose exercise makes momentary feelings more likely. The negative trait of paranoia makes the momentary state of jealousy more likely, just as the positive trait of being humorous makes the state of laughing more likely. (p. 9)

The well-being that using your signature strengths engenders is anchored in authenticity. But just as well-being needs to be anchored in strengths and virtues, these in turn must be anchored in something larger. Just as the good life is something beyond the pleasant life, the meaningful life is beyond the good life. (p. 14)

Source: Seligman (2002).

Beach Man Named Nation's Happiest
Jason Skog

VIRGINIA BEACH—Who's the happiest man in America?

He's not rich or powerful, so scratch Bill Gates and President Bush. And he's not a famous movie or rock star, so forget Tom Cruise and Bruce Springsteen.

According to the March 7–9 cover story of *USA Weekend* magazine, a Sunday supplement in almost 600 newspapers, the nation's happiest guy is a 45-year-old Virginia Beach stockbroker, J. P. "Gus" Godsey.

Godsey will be introduced early today on ABC's *Good Morning, America,* and he's, well, happy.

"It's real cool," Godsey said. "I didn't realize how big this was going to be."

Since word of the recognition leaked, he's had inquiries for national TV interviews. And there's been talk of appearances with Regis, Oprah, and Letterman.

Godsey's grin is nearly as broad as his shoulders. When he speaks, words tumble out in rambling, overflowing tones that are full, raspy, and fast. He can hardly contain himself.

"I'm not going to believe all the hype," Godsey said, "but I do know, if there are happier people, I haven't met many of them."

Godsey earned the distinction based on studies that suggest that volunteer work and civic involvement contribute to a person's happiness. Virginia Beach's quality of life also helped the magazine pick Godsey.

"It was a combination of science, sleuthing, and surveys," the *USA Weekend* story reads.

The magazine set out to find the happiest man in Virginia Beach, and Godsey's name continued to come up. After some initial interviews, he was subjected to a battery of psychological and emotional tests—five in all—measuring his level of contentment.

Dr. Martin E. P. Seligman, author of *Authentic Happiness* and a University of Pennsylvania professor, spent a day in Virginia Beach administering some of the tests.

Seligman divides happiness into three types: the pleasant life, the good life, and the meaningful life.

"He did great in all three and actually was off the scale in the second one. He's real unusual," Seligman said.

Godsey is a member of the city's Human Rights Commission, founder of local Thanksgiving and holiday food and toy drives, past chairman of the Republican Party of Virginia Beach, and a coordinator of benefit concerts.

He and his wife, Judi, have a son, Jeremy, 23, and a daughter, Jessica, 20. The couple lives on a 1¼-acre lot along the Lynnhaven Inlet in the Wolfsnare Plantation neighborhood.

"Not only is Mr. Godsey a very amiable, pleasant person," said Mayor Meyera E. Oberndorf, "he is a perfect example of the young people we want to return to our city to establish their lives and families and their careers."

Lynda Filipiak-Wilchynski, Godsey's sales assistant at Ferris, Baker, Watts Inc., a regional brokerage house based in Washington, said her boss's good humor is contagious.

"Everything is cool, everything is smooth with J.P.," she said.

Godsey said the key to happiness is simple.

"We wake up every morning full of choices," he said. "And your state of happiness is something you can do every single day. How are you going to make your day this morning? And we only have today. God never promised us tomorrow."

Do the faltering economy, threats of terrorism, and a looming war make this a difficult time to be happy?

"No. Absolutely not," he said. "Because I cannot control those things. . . . Why focus on something I can't control or that will bring me down?"

Reach Jason Skog at jskog@pilotonline.com or 757-222-5113.

Source: From Skog, J., Beach man named nation's happiest, *The Virginian-Pilot*, March 3, 2003, p. A1. Reprinted with permission of *The Virginian-Pilot*.

Describing a new model of happiness, Lyubomirsky, Sheldon, and Schkade (2005) propose that "[a] person's chronic happiness level is governed by three major factors: a genetically determined set point for happiness, happiness-relevant circumstantial factors, and happiness-relevant activities and practices" (p. 111). Lyubomirsky and colleagues' "architecture of sustainable happiness" (p. 114) incorporates what is known about the genetic components of happiness, the circumstantial/demographic determinants of happiness, and the complex process of intentional human change. Based on past research, which they summarize, Lyubomirsky et al. propose that genetics accounts for 50% of population variance for happiness, whereas life circumstances (both good and bad) and intentional activity (attempts at healthy living and positive change) account for 10% and 40% of the population variance for happiness, respectively. This model of happiness acknowledges the components of happiness that can't be changed, but it also leaves room for volition and the self-generated goals that lead to the attainment of pleasure, meaning, and good health.

Publications on the topic of cultural differences and well-being have grown substantially in the past two decades (Suh & Koo, 2008). Past research has found that the extent to which a nation is more collectivist (i.e., cooperative and group-oriented) in orientation versus individualistic (i.e., competitive and individual focused) is one of the strongest predictors of differences in subjective well-being across nations, even when national income level was held constant (Diener, Diener, & Diener, 1995). In addition, different relationships have been found between subjective well-being and variables such as self-esteem when studying different cultural groups; this relationship, which is very strong in individualist nations, was weaker in collectivist nations (Diener & Diener, 1995). Something that must be considered in analyzing the results from the above studies is the fact that

Western measures of well-being were used in these cases. Though translated appropriately, and thus linguistically equivalent measures, this does not account for the differences in *conceptual* equivalence with regard to definitions and culturally normative manifestations of happiness that are found in other studies. For example, in another study, Lu and Gilmour (2004) analyzed essays entitled "What is Happiness?" from Chinese students and compared them with those of students in the United States, and differences were found in the way in which these two groups described the construct. The Chinese students "emphasized spiritual cultivation and transcendence of the present," whereas their U.S. counterparts "emphasized the enjoyment of present life" (Suh & Koo, 2008, p. 416). Other researchers have found similar differences between Western and Eastern individuals with predictors of happiness varying from independence, autonomy, and agency (West) to interconnectedness of self and closeness to others (East) (Kitayama & Markus, 2000; Uchida, Norasakkunkit, & Kitayama, 2004). Other findings point to the fact that different racial and ethnic groups may also obtain happiness by different methods (Le, Lai, & Wallen, 2009). More research must be done in these areas; however, these findings remind us that we must view constructs through the appropriate cultural lens in order to have a fuller understanding of them. In addition, we must be careful to be culturally competent in interpreting studies that are conducted from Western perspectives on non-Western samples, or vice versa. In the study above regarding lower well-being found in collectivist nations, for example, one might falsely draw the conclusion that, due to the differences found, collectivism is problematic for well-being; this may in turn accidentally set up a deficit model that favors the West. It is not likely the case that collectivism leads to lower well-being, and these results may instead be a function of lack of equivalence in constructs in the two cultural groups. But without consideration of potential lack of conceptual equivalence, we may make mistakes such as this in interpreting. On this topic, based on empirical findings, Sheu (2014) cautions that it may be inappropriate to compare life satisfaction or other well-being means among various cultural groups. Careful consideration of cultural, linguistic, functional, and metric equivalence is necessary in any cross-cultural or multicultural research (see Chapter 3 for a more thorough description of equivalence).

Twenty-first-century scholars will undoubtedly produce many more refined views of happiness. Our prediction is that the pursuit of happiness through positive psychological science and practice ultimately will develop a better sense of the genetic (summarized in Lyubomirsky, Sheldon, & Schkade, 2005); neural (Urry et al., 2004); and neurobiological correlates and underpinnings of happiness and will embrace the contentment, peace, and happiness of Eastern philosophy along with the folk wisdom of the Western world. So imagine a science of happiness that is grounded in what is known about the genetic and biological bases of happiness and that examines the rigor and relevance of Buddha's teachings alongside Benjamin Franklin's recommendations for virtuous living (see Figure 6.4). Through good biological and psychological science and an appreciation of philosophical stances on happiness, we can increase the international relevance of our scholarship in positive psychology.

Complete Mental Health: Emotional, Social, and Psychological Well-Being

Ryff and Keyes (1995; Keyes, 2009; Keyes & Lopez, 2002; Keyes & Magyar-Moe, 2003) combine many principles of pleasure to define complete mental health. Specifically, they view optimal functioning as the combination of emotional well-being (as they refer to subjective well-being; defined as the presence of positive affect and satisfaction with life and the absence of negative affect); social well-being (incorporating acceptance, actualization, contribution, coherence, and integration); and psychological well-being (combining self-acceptance, personal growth, purpose in life, environmental mastery, autonomy, positive relations with others). Taking the symptoms of mental illness into consideration, they define "complete mental health" as the combination of "high levels of symptoms of emotional well-being, psychological well-being, and social well-being, as well as the absence of recent mental illness" (Keyes & Lopez, 2002, p. 49). This view of mental health combines all facets of well-being into a model that is both dimensional (because extremes of mental health and illness symptomatology are reflected) and categorical (because assignment to distinct diagnostic categories is possible). This complete state model (Keyes & Lopez, p. 49; see Figure 6.5) suggests that combined mental health and mental illness symptoms may be always changing, resulting in fluctuations in states of overall well-being ranging from complete mental illness to complete mental health.

Figure 6.4   East Meets West in the Discussion of Happiness

Source: Malcolm Tarlofsky. Reprinted with permission.

Increasing Happiness in Your Life

Although there are numerous theories of happiness and countless definitions of it, researchers (e.g., Sheldon & Lyubomirsky, 2004) have begun to build on past work (Fordyce, 1977, 1983) in their attempts to answer the question many of our clients ask: "Can I learn how to be happier?" David Myers (1993), an expert on the subject and the author of *The Pursuit of Happiness,* provides general strategies for increasing the happiness in daily life (see Figure 6.6). We provide additional Life Enhancement Strategies for boosting happiness in specific domains of your life. When looking at the suggestions below, we would ask the reader to consider that not all suggestions necessarily work for all cultural groups. Use a discerning eye while reading, and this may help you determine what seems plausible and culturally valid in your own life.

Figure 6.5   A Model of Complete Mental Health

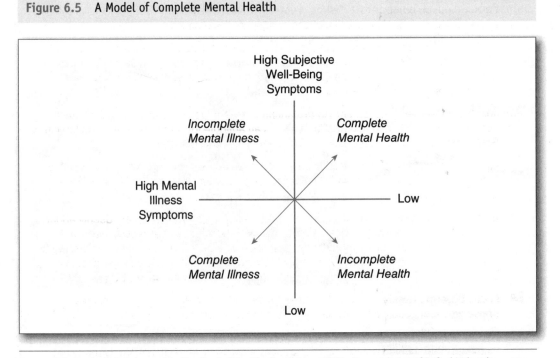

Source: C. R. Snyder & S. J. Lopez. *The Handbook of Positive Psychology* - 2002. By permission of Oxford University Press, Inc.

Figure 6.6   David Myers's Suggestions for a Happier Life

1. Realize that enduring happiness doesn't come from success. People adapt to changing circumstances—even to wealth or a disability. Thus wealth is like health: its utter absence breeds misery, but having it (or any circumstance we long for) doesn't guarantee happiness.

2. Take control of your time. Happy people feel in control of their lives, often aided by mastering their use of time. It helps to set goals and break them into daily aims. Although we often overestimate how much we will accomplish in any given day (leaving us frustrated), we generally underestimate how much we can accomplish in a year, given just a little progress every day.

3. Act happy. We can sometimes act ourselves into a frame of mind. Manipulated into a smiling expression, people feel better; when they scowl, the whole world seems to scowl

back. So put on a happy face. Talk as if you feel positive self-esteem, are optimistic, and are outgoing. Going through the motions can trigger the emotions.

4. Seek work and leisure that engages your skills. Happy people often are in a zone called "flow"—absorbed in a task that challenges them without overwhelming them. The most expensive forms of leisure (sitting on a yacht) often provide less flow experience than gardening, socializing, or craft work.

5. Join the "movement" movement. An avalanche of research reveals that aerobic exercise not only promotes health and energy, it also is an antidote for mild depression and anxiety. Sound minds reside in sound bodies. Off your duffs, couch potatoes.

6. Give your body the sleep it wants. Happy people live active, vigorous lives yet reserve time for renewing sleep and solitude. Many people suffer from a sleep debt, with resulting fatigue, diminished alertness, and gloomy moods.

7. Give priority to close relationships. Intimate friendships with those who care deeply about you can help you weather difficult times. Confiding is good for soul and body. Resolve to nurture your closest relationships, to not take those closest to you for granted, to display to them the sort of kindness that you display to others, to affirm them, to play together and share together. To rejuvenate your affections, resolve in such ways to act lovingly.

8. Focus beyond the self. Reach out to those in need. Happiness increases helpfulness (those who feel good do good). But doing good also makes one feel good.

9. Keep a gratitude journal. Those who pause each day to reflect on some positive aspect of their lives (their health, friends, family, freedom, education, senses, natural surroundings, and so on) experience heightened well-being.

10. Nurture your spiritual self. For many people, faith provides a support community, a reason to focus beyond self, and a sense of purpose and hope. Study after study finds that actively religious people are happier and that they cope better with crises.

Source: Adapted from Myers, D., *The pursuit of happiness.* Copyright © 1993. Reprinted with permission of the author.

Life Enhancement Strategies

Following is a list of additional tips for increasing pleasant emotional experiences, happiness, and well-being in your life. Although we categorize these suggestions within life's important domains, as we do in most chapters, we do not mean to suggest that all aspects of positive affect, emotions, and happiness are domain specific. We do believe, however, that some aspects of both the pleasant life and the meaningful life can be found in each of life's domains.

(Continued)

(Continued)

Love

- Be kind to those you love and those you have just met! Research shows that engaging in kind acts on a regular basis increases well-being in many different types of people.

- Tell those close to you that you love them. Your sincere expression of love will bolster your relationship and induce positive affect in others.

Work

- Start a meeting with positive comments about peers' contributions. This may raise positive affect that generates creativity and good decision making.

- Bring homemade treats to work or class. This may generate productive interactions.

Play

- Help others to find time to play! Take a moment to think of someone in your life who may need some play time but has responsibilities that make it difficult to take that time. Offer to babysit for new parents, take a larger share of a project for someone who is overloaded at work, or bring dinner and a board game to a single parent and stay to play yourself!

- Participate in brief relaxation activities to break up your day. Relaxation can make your mind and body more sensitive to the pleasurable daily moments.

MOVING TOWARD THE POSITIVE

It is very easy to find the unpleasant, negative aspects of emotions and dysfunctions in life (Baumeister, Bratslavsky, Finkenhaur, & Vohs, 2001). All you have to do is read the morning newspaper or watch the nightly news. Our human need to understand the negative is great, given the suffering and loss associated with anger and fear, as well as the evolutionary functions of avoidance strategies. Although the positive aspects of emotional experiences rarely capture the attention of media or science, things are beginning to change. It was only three decades ago, for example, that a few brave social scientists (e.g., Bradburn, 1969; Meehl, 1975) shared their thoughts about the lighter side of life. Today, we know that the flow of "joy-juice" (Paul Meehl's flippant term for that which induces pleasant emotional experiences) and biological factors are important, but they do not define our entire emotional experience. In addition, we must shift our lens to look at things from perspectives other than our own or risk missing the emotional experiences of those who are different from us. By doing this, we can also contribute to the happiness of others in ways that feel culturally relevant for them; this might also open our minds to new perspectives that can lead to more happiness experiences of our own. In the words of Diener et al. (2002, p. 68), "It appears that the way people perceive the world is much more important to happiness than objective circumstances."

It seems evident that cultural differences exist between the origins, determinants, and moderators of well-being (Layous et al., 2013; Layous & Lyubomirksy, 2013, Lu & Gilmour, 2004; Suh & Koo, 2008; Uchida et al., 2004), and different rankings may be applied by different cultures as to how important personal happiness is for the individual (Lu & Gilmour, 2004). This said, it must be made clear that well-being is still a desired goal across cultural groups *especially when it is experienced in culturally normative ways* (Diener, 2013). Ed Diener has spoken for several years about the need for our nations to develop "National Accounts" of subjective well-being alongside the economic accounts they regularly determine. These accounts of how our various nations are doing with regard to well-being overall could be helpful for many reasons. For example, national policies could be set to authorize funding in ways that could benefit large portions of a nation. Today, policy makers are starting to heed Diener's suggestions and some are beginning to collect these data. Specifically, the prime minister of the United Kingdom pledged to collect data on subjective well-being starting in 2010, and the Organization of Economic Cooperation has very recently provided guidelines to leaders who would like to create these types of national accounts of subjective well-being in their respective countries (Diener, 2013). Knowing more about well-being on a more global scale can only be beneficial for our continued health across the world. In Diener's words, "Although exciting gains have been made in our understanding of subjective well-being, there is much more yet to be discovered" (p. 665).

KEY TERMS

Affect: A person's instinctive response to a stimulus; characterized by a sense of arousal. Affect is considered the most basic element of feeling and often involves evaluation of a stimulus as good or bad.

Broaden-and-build model of positive emotions: Model developed by Fredrickson (2000) that suggests positive emotions expand what an individual feels like doing at any given time. Fredrickson calls this expansion *broadening of an individual's momentary thought–action repertoire*. Positive emotions also allow people to build resources through the increasing of creative problem solving and recognition of personal resources.

Complete state model: Model developed by Keyes and Lopez (2002) in which mental health is defined as high levels of emotional, psychological, and social well-being and the absence of mental illness symptoms; the model acknowledges that well-being and mental illness symptomatology change over time.

Emotion: A feeling state resulting from the appraisal of an external object as salient to our own well-being. An emotion has a specific, "sharpened" quality, as it always has an object.

Eudaimonia: Human flourishing, or happiness associated with living a life of virtue.

Flow: According to Csikszentmihalyi (1990), the pleasurable experience resulting from engagement in an interesting activity that properly matches or challenges a person's skills and abilities.

Genetic/personality predisposition theories: Theories of happiness suggesting that happiness may be a more stable personality trait or a characteristic that is genetically based.

Momentary thought–action repertoire: Suggested by Fredrickson (2000), the broadening of a specific action tendency to include cognitive as well as physical responses to an emotion. Fredrickson suggests that specific action tendencies associated with negative emotions fail to consider responses to positive emotions, which often are more cognitive than physical. See also *specific action tendency*.

Mood: General, free-floating feelings that last longer than an emotion. Mood is thought to be tied to expectations of future positive or negative affect.

Need/goal satisfaction theories: Theories of happiness suggesting that happiness lies in the reduction of tension though the satisfaction of goals and needs.

Pleasure principle: Freud's idea that humans seek to reduce tension by gratifying instinctive needs. He believed that well-being was the result of satisfied biological and psychological needs and that humans will seek gratification regardless of the consequences.

Process/activity theories: Theories of happiness suggesting that happiness is produced by engaging in certain activities or working toward a goal.

Specific action tendency: Suggested by most models of emotion, the tendency to act in a specific manner that follows an emotion. The most famous specific action tendency is the "fight or flight" response, the theory of which suggests that, when confronted with a situation that elicits a negative emotion, humans and animals will act either by approaching (fight) or by retreating (flight) from the situation.

Subjective well-being: A person's individual judgment about his or her current status in the world. Often used synonymously with happiness.

Valence: The direction of affect: positive (pleasant) or negative (unpleasant).

CHAPTER 7

Making the Most of Emotional Experiences

Emotion-Focused Coping, Emotional Intelligence, Socioemotional Selectivity, and Emotional Storytelling

At times during the twentieth century, psychology research and practice sullied the reputation of emotions. At worst, helping professionals and the public at large characterized emotions as toxic to our lives or detrimental to rational decision making. At best, emotions were portrayed as reflections of life satisfaction or signals of specific daily actions that needed to be taken. Research popularized in the twenty-first century (reviewed in Chapter 6 and in this chapter) demonstrates that both positive and negative emotions may determine how adaptive we are in our daily lives and contexts (see Chapter 6 to review Nussbaum's [2001] definition of *emotion*). The purpose of this chapter is to introduce you to how people make the most of their emotional experiences—that is, how they generally handle positive and negative emotions in a manner that leads to a positive outcome—by discussing theory and research associated with emotion-focused coping, emotional intelligence, socioemotional selectivity, and emotional storytelling. We discuss how we *benefit* from engaging our emotions, how we can *learn* to process and use emotion-laden material competently, and how we more efficiently *sort* the good from the bad emotional content of life as we age. Finally, we describe how sharing stories of emotional upheaval helps us *overcome* traumatic stress and pain. All of this, of course, is influenced by the cultural context of the individual.

EMOTION-FOCUSED COPING: DISCOVERING THE ADAPTIVE POTENTIAL OF EMOTIONAL APPROACH

The power of emotions traditionally was described in such negative terms as "the beast within" (Averill, 1990). Intense emotions were seen as dysfunctional and opposed to rationality. Research in the twentieth century often supported this view of emotional experiences by linking them with maladaptive outcomes in life. But when Annette Stanton, a positive psychologist at the University of

Annette Stanton

Source: Reprinted with permission of Annette Stanton.

California at Los Angeles, considered the adaptive potential of emotion-focused coping (i.e., regulating the emotions surrounding a stressful encounter), she found that there was a problem in how emotions were defined and measured in some of the research. Indeed, wide disparity was apparent in the items used to measure the emotion-focused coping phenomenon, and this led to unclear associations between what was referred to as "emotion-focused coping" and psychological adjustment. Stanton, Danoff-Burg, Cameron, and Ellis (1994) found that scales assessing emotion-focused coping contained items in which the respondent had to engage in self-deprecation or admit to experiencing distress or psychopathology whenever he or she acknowledged experiencing intense emotion. Responses to items such as "I blame myself for becoming too emotional" (Scheier, Weintraub, & Carver, 1986) and "I get upset and let my emotions out" (Carver, Scheier, & Weintraub, 1989) most probably would have been positively correlated with responses to items about a negative view of self or about general distress. When questions that framed emotional regulation in such a confounding manner were removed from research protocols, the frequently cited relationship between greater emotion-focused coping and poorer life outcomes was deemed invalid.

Stanton and her colleagues have spent the last decade working to clarify what "emotion-focused coping" means. Specifically, Stanton, Parsa, and Austenfeld (2002, p. 150) stated that "coping through emotional approach might be said to carry adaptive potential, the realization of which may depend on . . . the situational context, the interpersonal milieu, and attributes of the individual." What they call emotional approach involves active movement *toward, rather than away from,* a stressful encounter. This distinction between emotional approach and emotional avoidance is supported by the existence of two neurobiological systems that govern approach (i.e., appetitive) and avoidance behavior. The *behavioral activation system* regulates our appetitive motivation, which helps us realize emotional or behavioral rewards, whereas the *behavioral inhibition system* functions to help us avoid negative events and punishment (Depue, 1996).

Stanton, Kirk, Cameron, and Danoff-Burg (2000) identified two related but distinct processes involved in approach-oriented emotion-focused coping. One involves emotional processing, or attempts to understand emotions, and a second reflects emotional expression, or free and intentional displays of feeling. The researchers then created scales to tap these two approaches of emotional processing and emotional expression (see Table 7.1 for a list of components of the two processes).

With emotion-focused coping defined and measured more clearly and objectively, Stanton and colleagues (Stanton et al., 2000; Stanton, Danoff-Burg, & Huggins, 2002) were able to illuminate the functions of emotional approach. Using their revised measures, Stanton et al. (2000) studied the impact of emotion-focused coping on women's adjustment to breast cancer. Over a 3-month period, women who used emotion-focused coping perceived their health status as better, had lower psychological distress, and had fewer medical appointments for cancer-related pain and ailments, as compared to those who did not.

Working with an undergraduate population, Stanton and colleagues (2000) found that students who were dealing with a parent's psychological or physical illness coped better with their stressors

Table 7.1 Measures of Emotion-Focused Coping

Emotional Processing

> I realize that my feelings are valid and important.
>
> I take time to figure out what I am really feeling.
>
> I delve into my feelings to get a thorough understanding of them.
>
> I acknowledge my emotions.

Emotional Expression

> I feel free to express my emotions.
>
> I take time to express my emotions.
>
> I allow myself to express my emotions.
>
> I let my feelings come out freely.

Source: From Stanton, A. L., Kirk, S. B., Cameron, C. L., & Danoff-Burg, S., Coping through emotional approach: Scale construction and validation, *Journal of Personality and Social Psychology, 78*(6), pp. 1150–1169. Copyright © 2000 by the American Psychological Association. Adapted with permission. No further reproduction or distribution is permitted without written permission from the American Psychological Association.

if they were assigned to sessions that matched their emotional approach tendencies. That is to say, people who previously had reported a preference for expressing emotions when under duress did better when attending sessions that allowed them to vent emotions rather than receive facts. On the other hand, those participants who did not report a preference for expressing emotions when dealing with stress did better when placed in the information condition rather than the emotion-focused coping condition. These findings suggest that emotional preferences related to coping may interact with environmental contingencies to determine psychological outcomes.

Emotion-focused coping may be a key component related to medical issues such as cardiac stress. In a study examining different types of coping as predictors of disease severity of acute coronary syndrome, patients who used emotion-focused coping had less severity overall. The researchers hypothesize that emotion-focused coping may moderate certain physiological responses to a stressful event such that the heart has reduced reactivity to stress (Chiavarino et al., 2012). This research has great implications for creating psychological interventions in those who show symptoms of diseases related to stress reactions.

The benefits of emotion-focused coping styles may have mediating qualities as well. Other researchers have found that, when dealing with the stress of chronic racism, racial and ethnic minority individuals' positive appraisal of emotion-focused coping options may intervene in the relationship between self-esteem, life satisfaction, and racial identity development (Outten, Schmitt, Garcia, & Branscombe, 2009; Peters, 2006). Specifically, when individuals of racial and ethnic minority groups feel that they have ways of coping emotionally with experiences of discrimination, greater self-esteem and greater life satisfaction were more closely linked with a strong identification with their racial group (Outten et al., 2009). It may be that when a victim of racism feels the negative effects of being associated with a group that is seen to be at a disadvantage, being able to use positive reframing helps the individual to retain good feelings about himself or herself and the groups to which he or she belongs. One way of coping utilized in cases of discrimination is a strong identification with others in one's own ethnic group. This type of identification, used as a form of coping, has been found to foster psychological well-being (Giamo, Schmitt, & Outten, 2012). In other research, Peters (2006) found that in an African American sample, emotion-focused coping was negatively correlated with the experience of chronic stress emotions as brought on by exposure to racism. These results point to the conclusion that use of emotion-focused styles of coping to deal with stressors related to personal racism, or as part of a racial group, may increase well-being and/or decrease stress for individuals experiencing these types of stressors in their environments (Outten et al.).

Work on emotion-focused coping, summarized in a review by Austenfeld and Stanton (2004), highlights the adaptive potential of emotional expression and processing when coping with infertility, cancer, and chronic pain. Anecdotal evidence collected from the reports of our clients and friends suggests that the adaptive potential of emotional approach also is realized in normal life circumstances. For instance, each day we are challenged by minor stresses (junk mail, schedule changes, traffic) and real problems (shortages of money, minor illnesses, subtle prejudices) that stir up emotions that we can approach or avoid. Many people within a Western context seem to benefit, at least in the short run, from expressing their emotions in a meaningful way. Further, emotional processing seems to become more adaptive as people learn more about what they feel and why they feel it (Stanton, Sullivan, & Austenfeld, 2009).

This is not always the case, however. Specifically, many Asian cultures encourage suppression of emotions, as opposed to expression, with the goal of preserving harmony in the group (Chiang, 2012; Lee, 2013; Murata, Moser, & Kitayama, 2013). Recent studies show that even today emotional suppression is common in Chinese individuals and is not necessarily associated with the same negative correlates found in Western studies (Chiang, 2012). This said, there may be some circumstances, such as within close personal relationships, where emotional expression is considered by Asians to be appropriate and healthy. Contemporary Asian individuals may use a mixture of emotion suppression (culturally normative in traditional Asian culture) and emotional expression (culturally normative in more contemporary Asian culture, which is influenced by Western values). In situations where Asians are expected to emote expressively, they may feel stress at not wanting to do this. On the other hand, they may also feel stress in contexts where they should suppress but have a desire to emote. In this way, "This cultural complexity may result in value conflict whereby some Asians may become emotionally ambivalent when their expressive styles clash with different sociocultural norms" (Lee, 2013, p. 171). Different coping strategies may be used in these cultural groups to combat this stress.

Given the robust findings linking emotion-focused coping and adaptive outcomes under particular circumstances, it is important to understand how emotional approach works to our benefit. Of course, if we turned our attentions away from unpleasant feelings each time we experienced them, we would learn very little about how these feelings influence us and our friends (Salovey, Mayer, & Caruso, 2002). This approach to coping may foster a better understanding of our experiences and direct our attention to central concerns (Frijda, 1994). Furthermore, over time we may develop the tendency to face our stressors directly and repeatedly (instead of avoiding them on occasion) and thereby habituate to certain predictable negative experiences. We learn that emotional pain does subside, and time heals both psychological and physical wounds. As we discuss later in this chapter, understanding our emotional experience can help us select optimal relationships and environments (Carstensen, 1998), particularly when we consider the norms in our own cultural context. On a neurobiological level, Depue (1996) points to the involvement of the behavioral activation system, and LeDoux (1996) reveals that a particular brain structure, the amygdala, plays a significant role in processing matters of emotional significance. Specifically, LeDoux suggests that, under stress-free life circumstances, our thinking is governed by the hippocampus, but, during more stressful times, our thought processes—and hence aspects of our coping—are ruled by the amygdala. Interestingly, culture may even affect individuals at the neurological level to some extent. In comparing Asian individuals to European American individuals a study found that Asians seem to be "culturally trained to down-regulate emotional processing when required to suppress emotion" (Murata et al., 2013, p. 595). Researchers in this study measured levels of emotional processing at a neurological level and found that when asked to suppress their reactions to negative pictures, Asians were able to decrease their neurological reaction to such a picture. European Americans in comparison did not seem to be able to control this in the same way. This provides intriguing information for potential environmental control on neurological response. Future examination of the neurobiology of emotion-focused coping and emotional processing may further demystify the potential benefits of approaching or avoiding emotions and the related workings of brain structures such as the amygdala.

The Case of a Hurricane Survivor

While standing in a line for hurricane relief with dozens of survivors, I (SJL) witnessed people who were avoiding all emotions, some who were approaching their emotions productively, and some who were frankly overwhelmed by what they were experiencing. My guess is that those who were approaching their emotions productively are doing better today than those who did not. I was a visitor to the disaster area; my mother's home was damaged, but she was safe and sound. She and I chatted with many of her neighbors who had lost their homes and were trying to pull their lives together.

I struck up a conversation with a fellow about my age that I thought I recognized from high school. It turned out that Ted was from the New Orleans area, about 150 miles away. He and his family had survived Hurricane Katrina, but his home was uninhabitable. He moved to New Iberia to find a home for his family, and then Hurricane Rita hit that town. Ted told me the whole story. He heard that Katrina had pushed five feet of water into his family's New Orleans home, but he was not allowed to go back and see it because of the unsafe conditions. He found his way to New Iberia and rented an apartment for his wife and two boys. Then, Ted said, "Rita hit and scared the hell out of my family." He told me that he felt frightened because he might never be able to keep his wife and boys safe again. Ted *expressed his emotions* in simple, honest language that communicated the depths of his fear and sadness.

Ted and I chatted some more, and it was clear that he had spent a great deal of time with his wife, *processing their emotions*. I asked him about how his boys were coping. He laughed, "Kids are amazing!" He said that they didn't understand the need for all the changes in their lives, but they had coped well with the ups and downs. At that time, he told me, "Yesterday, we bought the boys bunk beds, and I put them up last night. I placed my son in the top bunk, and then, well, you know what he said? 'Daddy, it is starting to feel like we have a home again.'" Ted teared up and said, "I hope this line starts moving."

EMOTIONAL INTELLIGENCE: LEARNING THE SKILLS THAT MAKE A DIFFERENCE

Daniel Goleman, once a science writer for numerous periodicals and newspapers, popularized the concept of *emotional intelligence* in the 1990s. His 1995 book, *Emotional Intelligence: Why It Can Matter More Than IQ,* introduced the general public to the emotional concepts that had been discussed by psychologists and knowledgeable laypeople for decades. Professionals of all types built on this "next big thing" and shared their views on emotional intelligence in the popular press or in what has been referred to as the "organizational development industry" (which primarily involves training programs designed to help employees reach their professional potential by realizing their personal potential). To date, numerous amalgamations of psychological constructs have been conceptualized as reflective of emotional intelligence (see Bar-On, 1997; Schutte et al., 1998). For example, Bar-On (1997, 2000, 2013) defines emotional intelligence as an array of noncognitive capabilities, competencies, and skills that help us deal with the demands of the environment, but the related inventory, the EQ-I (Bar-On, 1997), primarily measures personality and mood variables such as self-regard, empathy, tolerance, and happiness. This atheoretical version of emotional intelligence may be distinct from other forms of intelligence, yet it appears to overlap existing operationalizations of meaningful psychological variables. Therefore, measuring this type of emotional intelligence may not provide a researcher or practitioner with the new information that might help predict positive life outcomes.

We believe that the proliferation of emotional intelligence models and the general appeal and popularity of this positive construct have led to a muddying of the waters. As a result, emotional intelligence now may be one of the most misunderstood and misrepresented constructs in psychology. For that reason, we return to the roots of emotional intelligence research and demonstrate how we learn to manage emotion-laden material for our benefit and the benefit of others.

In 1960, Mowrer addressed the prevailing thoughts about emotions undermining intelligence by suggesting that emotion was, in fact, "a high order of intelligence" (p. 308). Peter Salovey of Yale University and John Mayer of the University of New Hampshire (Mayer, DiPaolo, & Salovey, 1990; Salovey & Mayer, 1990) shared Mowrer's sentiment and theorized that adapting to life circumstances required cognitive abilities and emotional skills that guide our behavior. In their original 1990 papers, Salovey and Mayer constructed a theoretical framework for an

Peter Salovey

Source: Photo credit: Michael Marsland, Office of Public Affairs, Yale University. Reprinted with permission.

emotional intelligence. The framework comprised three core components: appraisal and expression, regulation, and utilization. These fledging ideas about a set of emotional abilities that might provide people with a reservoir of intellectual resources was well received by the general public and psychology scholars.

The Salovey and Mayer four-branch ability model of emotional intelligence (see Table 7.2; Mayer et al., 1990; Mayer & Salovey, 1997; Salovey & Mayer, 1990; Salovey et al., 2002) has been predicated on the belief that skills needed to reason about emotions and to use emotional material to assist reasoning can be learned. Branch 1 of the model involves skills needed to perceive and express feelings. More specifically, perception of emotions requires picking up on subtle emotional cues that might be expressed in a person's face or voice. For example, when chatting with a friend about an emotionally charged political topic, a person skilled in perceiving emotions can determine what aspects of the discussion are safe or unsafe territory based on the friend's nonverbal behavior. These skills in perceiving can be considered a threshold competency that needs to be acquired so that the other three emotional intelligence competencies can be developed.

Branch 2 of this ability model concerns using emotions and emotional understanding to facilitate thinking. Simply stated, people who are emotionally intelligent harness emotions and work with them to improve problem solving and to boost creativity. Physiological feedback from emotional experience is used to prioritize the demands on our cognitive systems and to direct attention to what is most important (Easterbrook, 1959; Mandler, 1975). In this regard, imagine that a woman has to make an important decision about a relationship. Should she invest more energy in a friendship that has been on the rocks, or should she cut her losses and end the friendship in a civil manner? How she feels physically and emotionally when she thinks about continuing or ending the friendship can provide some clues about how to proceed. This emotional information thus turns attention to alternatives about how to handle the friendship. Also, the more the emotions are used in efforts to make good decisions, the greater the increase in emotional intelligence.

Branch 3 of emotional intelligence highlights the skills needed to foster an understanding of complex emotions, relationships among emotions, and relationships between emotions and behavioral consequences. Someone displaying a heightened level of emotional understanding would know that hope is an antidote to fear (see Chapter 8) and that sadness or apathy are more appropriate responses to lost love than hating is. People with these skills understand that emotions such as jealousy and envy are destructive in their own right (due to their physiological and psychological repercussions) and that they fuel maladaptive interpersonal behavior that probably results in a proliferation of negative emotions. Appreciating the dynamic relationships among emotions and behaviors gives an emotionally intelligent person the sense that they can better "read" a person or a situation and act appropriately, given environmental demands. For example, imagine the emotional struggle of a man who is placed in the awkward situation of being asked by a close friend to betray the confidence of a classmate or work colleague. He might feel disappointment or disgust that the friend asked him to behave in an inappropriate manner. If he were tempted to break the trust, he might experience a wave of shame. Understanding these complex emotions then might help him choose the right course of action at that time.

The more we practice skills that are associated with Branches 1 through 3, the more emotional content there is to manage. Managing emotions, Branch 4, involves numerous mood regulation skills. These skills are difficult to master because regulation is a balancing act. With too much regulation, a person may become emotionally repressed. With too little, one's emotional life

Table 7.2   Salovey and Mayer's Four-Branch Ability Model of Emotional Intelligence

Branch 1: Perceiving Emotions

    Ability to identify emotion in a person's physical and psychological states

    Ability to identify emotions in other people

    Ability to express emotions accurately and to express needs related to them

    Ability to discriminate between authentic and inauthentic emotions

Branch 2: Using Emotions to Facilitate Thought

    Ability to redirect and prioritize thinking on the basis of associated feelings

    Ability to generate emotions to facilitate judgment and memory

    Ability to capitalize on mood changes to appreciate multiple points of view

    Ability to use emotional states to facilitate problem solving and creativity

Branch 3: Understanding Emotions

    Ability to understand relationships among various emotions

    Ability to perceive the causes and consequences of emotions

    Ability to understand complex feelings, emotional blends, and contradictory states

    Ability to understand transitions among emotions

Branch 4: Managing Emotions

    Ability to be open to feelings, both pleasant and unpleasant

    Ability to monitor and reflect on emotions

    Ability to engage, prolong, or detach from an emotional state

    Ability to manage emotions in oneself and others

Source: From Salovey, P., & Mayer, J. D., Emotional intelligence, *Imagination, Cognition, & Personality, 9*(3), pp. 185–211. Copyright © 1990. Reprinted with permission of Baywood Publishing Company.

becomes overwhelming. People who become very good at regulating their moods also are able to share these skills with others. Often the best parents, teachers, coaches, leaders, bosses, or role models can manage their emotions and at the same time instill confidence in others to be open to feelings and manage them appropriately.

Each of the four dimensions of the ability model is assessed with two sets of tasks in a measure called the Mayer-Salovey-Caruso Emotional Intelligence Test (the most recent version is the MSCEIT 2.0; Mayer, Salovey, & Caruso, 2002). The tasks concerned with perceiving emotions ask respondents to identify the emotions expressed in photographs of faces and the feelings suggested by artistic designs and landscapes. For the measurement of using emotions to facilitate thought, respondents are asked to describe feelings using nonfeeling words and to indicate the feelings that might facilitate or interfere with the successful performance of various tasks. The understanding-emotions dimension is assessed with questions concerning the manner in which emotions evolve and how some feelings are produced by blends of emotions. To tap the ability of managing emotions, the MSCEIT 2.0 presents a series of scenarios eliciting the most adaptive ways to regulate one's own feelings, as well as feelings that arise in social situations and in other people.

Practicing some or all of the 16 skills associated with the 4 branches of emotional intelligence is robustly associated with positive interpersonal functioning. For example, Lopes et al. (2004) examined the relationship between self-reported emotional intelligence (using the MSCEIT; Mayer, Salovey, & Caruso, 2001) and social behavior in a sample of college students. These researchers found these students' ($n = 118$) abilities to manage emotions were positively associated with the quality of their social interactions. Additional work with a small group ($n = 76$) of college students (Lopes, Salovey, Cote, Beers, & Petty, 2005) revealed that the strengths of emotional regulation skills were associated positively with interpersonal sensitivity (self-reports and peer nominations), with prosocial tendencies, and with the proportion of positive vs. negative peer nominations. These relationships remained meaningful after controlling for the Big Five personality traits, as well as verbal and fluid intelligence. Likewise, in a sample of 103 college students, Lopes, Salovey, and Straus (2004) found that individuals with high-level skills in managing emotions were more likely to report positive relationships with other people and perceived parental support and were less likely to report negative interactions with close friends. These associations remained statistically significant even when controlling for significant Big Five personality traits and verbal intelligence. Findings from these latter two studies (Lopes et al., 2005; Lopes, Salavoy, and Strauss, 2004) highlight the added value of emotional intelligence to understanding the nature of person-to-person interactions—that is, emotional intelligence tells us something about social functioning that personality traits and analytical intelligence do not explain. It is important to note that these links have not been found in some cross-cultural studies. Differences have thus far been found between German and Indian samples (Koydemir, Şimşek, Schütz, & Tipandjan 2013) and Eastern (Thai) versus Western (United States) samples (Young & Schwartz, 2014). (See Sharma, Biswal, Deller, & Mandal, 2009, for another example.)

As revealed in the previous section's review of research on emotion-focused coping, engaging more deeply in your emotional experiences (or perceiving, using, understanding, and managing emotions, to use the parlance of emotional intelligence researchers) has benefits in some cultural contexts, including the United States; culturally normative emotional expression may be helpful to a number of different races and ethnicities. Additionally, for people who demonstrate emotional intelligence, positive social functioning may be realized. Given that these two lines of research (Stanton's work on emotional approach and Salovey and Mayer's examination of emotional intelligence) establish the potential of working with your emotions, our attention now turns to whether emotional skills can be learned. More than 300 program developers (Salovey et al., 2002) have been intrigued by the teachability of emotional intelligence. On this issue, anecdotal evidence suggests that children, youth, and adults can be taught to use emotional experiences to enrich their daily lives and can be equipped to deal with the good and bad events they encounter. Time and more empirical scrutiny, however, will tell whether intentional skill development actually produces gains in emotional intelligence.

Further research also is needed to determine the neurological substrates of emotional intelligence. There is some evidence that efficient operation of the amygdala and the ventromedial prefrontal cortex may be implicated in emotional intelligence (see Damasio, 1994), but the interplay between brain structures in people with high emotional intelligence has not been elaborated on.

Who Is Emotionally Intelligent—And Does It Matter?
Jack Mayer

A Description of the High EI Individual

Generally speaking, emotional intelligence improves an individual's social effectiveness. The higher the emotional intelligence, the better the social relations. In a recent review, my colleagues and I described the emotionally intelligent person in these terms:

> The high EI individual, most centrally, can better perceive emotions, use them in thought, understand their meanings, and manage emotions, than others. Solving emotional problems likely requires less cognitive effort for this individual. The person also tends to be somewhat higher in verbal, social, and other intelligences, particularly if the individual scored higher in the understanding emotions portion of EI. The individual tends to be more open and agreeable than others. The high EI person is drawn to occupations involving social interactions such as teaching and counseling more so than to occupations involving clerical or administrative tasks.

> The high EI individual, relative to others, is less apt to engage in problem behaviors and avoids self-destructive, negative behaviors such as smoking, excessive drinking, drug abuse, or violent episodes with others. The high EI person is more likely to have possessions of sentimental attachment around the home and to have more positive social interactions, particularly if the individual scored highly on emotional management. Such individuals may also be more adept at describing motivational goals, aims, and missions (Mayer, Salovey, & Caruso, 2004).

Note that the specific kind of boost that emotional intelligence gives the individual will be subtle, and as a consequence, require some effort to identify. It will not be exhibited in all social circumstances.

Nonetheless, EI Is Important

Some of us accomplish certain tasks with great ease and sophistication; others of us simply can't do those tasks. This is the case with most challenges we face in life. Some of us are great chess players, while others of us have trouble just figuring out how the pieces move. Some of us are fabulous conversationalists, while others of us have trouble just saying hello.

Now, the world could do without the game of chess, and the world could do without fabulous conversationalists, but it would be a poorer place for it.

Emotional intelligence is an intelligence having to do with discerning and understanding emotional information. Emotional information is all around us. Emotions communicate basic feeling states from one individual to another—to signal urgent messages such as "let's get together" or "I am hurting" or "I'm going to hurt you."

What ability tests of emotional intelligence tell us is that only some people can pick up and understand and appreciate the more subtle versions of those messages. That is, only the high EI individual understands the full richness and complexities of these communications.

Emotional information is crucial. It is one of the primary forms of information that human beings process. That doesn't mean that everybody has to process it well. But it does mean that it is circulating around us, and certain people who can pick up on it can perform certain tasks very well that others cannot perform.

We all need emotional intelligence to help us through our emotionally demanding days. Even if we are not emotionally intelligent ourselves, we may rely on those higher in emotional intelligence to guide us.

But guide us to what? What is it that people high in emotional intelligence can see that so many others are blind to? The key to this lies in what those high in emotional intelligence are particularly good at doing themselves.

They're particularly good at establishing positive social relationships with others and avoiding conflicts, fights, and other social altercations. They're particularly good at understanding psychologically healthy living and avoiding such problems as drugs and drug abuse. It seems likely that such individuals, by providing coaching advice to others and by directly involving themselves in certain situations, assist other individuals and groups of people to live together with greater harmony and satisfaction.

So, perhaps even more important than scoring high on an emotional intelligence test is knowing one's level at this group of skills. Discovering one's level means that you can know whether and how much to be self-reliant in emotional areas, and when to seek others' help in reading the emotional information that is going on around oneself. Whether one is high or low in emotional intelligence is perhaps not as important as knowing that emotional information exists and that some people can understand it. Knowing just that, one can use emotional information by finding those who are able to understand it and reason with it.

This is the information age. All of us are dependent on information and using it wisely. The advent of the ability model of emotional intelligence enriches our knowledge of the information surrounding us—it tells us emotional information is there and that some people can see it and use it. The model encourages all of us to use emotional information wisely—whether through our own direct understanding, or through the assistance of those who do understand.

Source: Mayer, J. (2005). *Who is emotionally intelligent—and does it matter?* Retrieved from http://www.unh.edu/emotional_intelligence/. Reprinted with permission of Jack Mayer.

The Case of Maria

Maria is a gifted elementary school teacher who loves her job. Several years ago, I (SJL) had the privilege of observing her classroom teaching while I was working on a positive psychology project in her school. The first day I saw her work with students, I developed a hypothesis about effective teaching that has stuck with me: Good educators (at all levels) are emotionally intelligent teachers of knowledge and skills. That is, I believe that, irrespective of the focus of the course (e.g., math, chemistry, Spanish, literature, psychology), good teachers make sense of the emotional content in the room, and they make minor adjustments in their teaching approaches so that they can effectively share their knowledge with the group.

During my first visit to Maria's classroom, I was struck by how she could "read" a room. She seemed to know what each student needed at any given moment, and she seemed to have a sense of the general emotional tenor of the room. For example, before the "daily check-in" (her name for a quiz), Maria responded to the anxiety in the room with soothing comments and a quick relaxation exercise. Her ability to *perceive the emotions* of her students and respond to them in a strategic manner was demonstrated time and time again during my 5 hours of observation.

Based on my interactions with Maria, it seemed as though she also had a keen sense of her own emotional experience. She described herself as intuitive, and that seemed to fit . . . but there was more to it than that. Although she did seem instinctively to know what she and her students were feeling, she also was adept at using emotions to spark her creativity in the classroom. She could scrap her lesson plan and create an engaging activity on the spot if the students were getting bored or restless. And she had great timing—when she made these major shifts in her plan, the students were not aware that she went off the page to grab more attention.

Perhaps my view of Maria's high emotional intelligence was cemented the day I saw her settle a dispute among five students on the playground. The children were frustrated and tearful, and Maria seemed to understand their emotions and their fast-paced exchanges of accusations and explanations. Slowly, she calmed down the situation and helped each student save face . . . but then, all of a sudden, one of the students yelled, "You're not fair! I hate you!" At that moment, she encouraged the other children to return to the game, and she knelt down to talk to the infuriated student eye to eye. With time, his posture and grimace seemed to soften, and then he nodded his head and ran back to his friends. It was clear that her ability to *manage her own emotions* helped this boy manage his.

Maria shared her emotional intelligence with her students every day by modeling adaptive behavior. I believe that some of her students learned how to make the most of their emotions by watching her.

SOCIOEMOTIONAL SELECTIVITY: FOCUSING IN LATER LIFE ON POSITIVE EMOTIONS AND EMOTION-RELATED GOALS

The extent to which we are able to make the most of our emotional experiences is determined in part by personal and environmental demands such as our health status, social surroundings, and cultural norms. It now is becoming clear that humans' unique ability to monitor time across their entire span of life also may determine how much energy is dedicated to emotional goals. (See Chapter 8 for a related discussion on the influence of time perspective.) Indeed, in Stanford psychologist Laura Carstensen's (1998; Carstensen & Charles, 1998) socioemotional selectivity theory, she posits that our later years (the "golden years") may be valuable as we focus less on negative emotions, engage more deeply with the emotional content of our days, and savor the "good stuff" in life (e.g., establishing and enhancing relationships). Carstensen reasons that we are able to appreciate these benefits in our advanced years because we come to realize that we have a short amount of time left.

In her laboratory, Carstensen has demonstrated that young people and their older counterparts manage emotion-laden material quite differently. In tests of attention to novel stimuli, for example, the younger participants attended to negative images more quickly, whereas the older participants oriented faster to images laden with positive emotions (smiling face, happy baby, puppy) (Charles, Mather, & Carstensen, 2003). Regarding recall of emotional events, it appears that young people (college age and a bit older) remembered the positive and negative material to the same degree, but the older people had a positivity bias in which they recalled the positive material more quickly than the negative material (Charles et al., 2003; Reed & Carstensen, 2012). The "positivity effect" shown in these studies suggests that the process of interacting with emotions is different for young adults and older adults. This said, conflicting research results have been found with regard to this effect since its original introduction to the field. In a recent article,

Laura Carstensen

Source: Reprinted with permission of Laura Carstensen.

Reed and Carstensen (2012) address these conflicting research findings by looking closely at the conditions in the different studies conducted. To this point, they state, "Positivity appears when cognitive resources are available, when experimental task or stimuli do not activate automatic processing, and when information processing is unconstrained by external factors such as task instructions" (p. 7). In addition, when pressure is on or risk of failure is high, the positivity effect seems to disappear. Thus, some of the conflicting results may be artifacts of research studies and their characteristics, more than as a result of actual findings (Reed & Carstensen, 2012).

Irrespective of our tendencies to attend to and remember certain types of events, life provides all of us with blessings and burdens. Related to this point, Carstensen and her colleagues have found that there are age cohort effects for how we handle positive and negative daily life experiences. After monitoring the moods of 184 people (age 18 and up) for a week, Carstensen, Pasupathi, Mayr, and Nesselroade (2000) discovered that their older research participants not only did not "sweat the small stuff" (which is how they viewed negative events), but they also savored the positive events (experienced the good residuals of positive events for longer periods than their younger counterparts did). Given these findings, it appears that positive experiences and positive emotions become our priority as we age and consider our mortality. In addition, contrary to young people's fascination with future-oriented goals pertaining to acquiring information and expanding horizons, older people seem to orient to here-and-now goals that foster emotional meaning (Kennedy, Fung, & Carstensen, 2001; Reed & Carstensen, 2012).

The tendency to remember more positive than negative information may generalize across other cultures. Studies demonstrate that Chinese older adults have the same pattern of memory of positive and negative pictures (Chung & Lin, 2012), though they may not have the same pattern with regard to visual attention to positive images (Fung et al., 2008). In the study by Chung and Lin, Chinese older adults remembered fewer negative pictures in comparison to positive pictures, and they remembered fewer negative pictures in comparison to their U.S. counterparts. Researchers hypothesize that this may be partially due to the more negative view of aging held by older adults in the United States as compared to views of aging in China. With regard to attention, Fung and colleagues (2008) found that it was more common for older Chinese (but not younger) to look away from positive images, showing no attentional preference toward positivity. These interesting findings must be explored in greater detail to truly understand the process at hand. As with most situations, context appears to play some role in the equation.

As mentioned earlier, some of the results found may be a result of a perception by older adults that time is waning for them in general. Ersner-Hershfield, Mikels, Sullivan, and Carstensen (2008) compared experiences of poignancy (mixed emotions related to an ending or to losing something meaningful) in younger and older adults. Both younger and older adults in the experimental condition in this study were taken through a series of guided imagery scenarios of being in a personally meaningful location, ending with a final scenario that asked them to imagine that they were at this meaningful location for the very last time. Results showed that age was not a significant factor in the experience of poignancy, suggesting that "a meaningful limited-time situation such as an ending can produce poignancy regardless of age" (Ersner-Hershfield et al., p. 163). The researchers posited that the higher incidence of these feelings in older adults that have been reported previously may be more related to the feeling that time is limited (in life) as opposed to something organic to the aging process. This provides us with important information about processing complex emotions and directs us toward continuing to search for deep emotional experiences in younger groups, while at the same time looking toward the strengths of older adults as models for successful processing of deep emotional experiences.

Recall of positive experience, savoring the good times, and setting and investing in emotion-focused goals systematically influence social preferences, emotion regulation, and cognitive processing. Overall, therefore, looking at the aging process within various cultural groups may be able to provide us with valuable information about how best to strive for a deeper emotional life.

EMOTIONAL STORYTELLING: THE PENNEBAKER PARADIGM AS A MEANS OF PROCESSING INTENSE NEGATIVE EMOTIONS

Every now and again, we experience life events that shake us to our core. Traumatic events that cause emotional upheaval may outstrip the resources of good emotion-focused copers, the emotionally intelligent, and the young and old alike. It is quite likely (with a 95% probability) that, when we experience an overwhelming emotional event, we will share the experience with a friend or family member within the same day of its occurrence, typically in the first few hours (Rime, 1995). It is almost as if we were compelled to tell the story of our emotional suffering. Is it possible that we have learned that not talking about our intense emotions has dire consequences? This question and many related research hypotheses have served as the impetus for the work of

University of Texas psychologist James Pennebaker. In 1989, Dr. Pennebaker broke ground on this research area by making the following request of undergraduate research participants in an experimental group of a study:

> For the next four days, I would like . . . you to write about your deepest thoughts and feelings about your most traumatic experience in your life. In your writing, I'd like you to really let go and explore your very deepest emotions and thoughts. You might tie your topic to your relationships, including parents, lovers, friends, or relatives. You may also want to link your experience to your past, your present, or your future, or to who you have been, who you would like to be, or who you are now. You may write about the same general issues or experiences on all days of writing, or on different traumas each day. All of your writing will be completely confidential. (p. 215)

The control group participants were asked to write for 15 minutes a day for 4 days, but about a nonemotional topic (e.g., a description of the room they were seated in). All participants were asked to write continuously, without regard to spelling, grammar, and sentence structure. The immediate effects of the two interventions were such that the experimental group was more distressed. Then, over time (beginning 2 weeks after the study), the members of the emotional storytelling group experienced numerous health benefits, including fewer physician visits over the next year, than did the members of the control group.

Other researchers have found that there may be certain features within the narratives constructed for these purposes that can predict health outcomes (Ramírez-Esparza & Pennebaker, 2006). These researchers have found that when people use more positive-emotion words (such as *happy* or *laugh*) as part of expressive writing, their health improves more. In addition, participants who used cognitive words specifically associated with insight or causality made greater inroads toward better health as well. Thus, how and what we write may affect the benefits of these techniques.

Emotionally expressive writing may have benefits in many populations. In research looking at early survivors of breast cancer, findings showed that participants who were assigned to experimental groups with expressive writing regarding their cancer experience had improved quality of life (Craft, Davis, & Paulson, 2013). In addition, this type of emotional processing may have benefit in dealing with prejudice. Kwon (2013) asserts that use of emotional processing in this way may assist gay and lesbian individuals dealing with discrimination to develop more resilience as a sort of buffer to the effects of prejudice.

Finally, writing about emotions and emotional experiences may be particularly beneficial to individuals who prefer to use an emotion approach style of coping in dealing with problems in their lives (Austenfeld & Stanton, 2008). In a study of undergraduate students, Austenfeld and Stanton found that individuals who preferred an emotionally expressive style of coping made fewer visits to a health care provider when assigned to a group that used emotion-based writing as compared to more goal-oriented writing. This was not true for those who did not prefer this style, however; these individuals had fewer medical visits when participating in a group that instructed members to write about their "best possible selves" (Austenfeld & Stanton, 2008, p. 35). These results direct us to remember to attend to the vast array of individual differences that can affect the effectiveness of various strategies (Stickney, 2010). Again, it may be that psychological outcomes are partially determined by individuals' emotional preferences related to coping.

Emotional Storytelling After a Traumatic Event

In January 2000, the author of this account experienced overwhelming fear and guilt while scuba diving. Upon her return from the outing, she was visibly shaken. After hours of one-to-one conversation, she was encouraged to write for 15 minutes about her intense thoughts and feelings associated with the experience in a free-flowing manner with no regard for punctuation, grammar, or sentence structure.

My 4th dive ever. My 2nd dive in a year. Steve talked me into going on a night dive. I was nervous about it, esp. since my dive 2 days ago had a scary hyperventilating incident. I like Steve and I didn't want to seem a wimp so I said "sure," even though compounding my uneasiness was my discomfort over diving without my husband. I don't like to do anything w/o him if it is at all risky. If something happens to me, I want him there to see it, even if he can't stop it. His very presence gives me a lot of my nerve.

Over the back of the boat holding my regulator and mask. My fat strap slips over my head and the mask fills with water. It's more in my hand than on my head. I swallow sea water. I get the mask back on but was hyperventilating. The dive master seems far away but some guy name Walker came over to help me. He told me to fill my BCD and he held me as I lay on my back. He tried to distract me with small talk to calm me down. The dive master asked if I wanted back in the boat. I said no. So we tried to descend. More hyperventilating. This time I know it wouldn't stop. My body was in alarm mode and I would not be able to descend. The whole group resurfaced and I was back at the surface. Luckily I was only under about 10 feet.

The dive master said "What's wrong with her? " and I said I want back in the boat. They said the boat is over there. The dive master seemed to want me to swim to the boat that seemed far away while the group descended. The group refused to leave me at the surface so far from the boat. After the boat finally got close enough, I swam to it and Walker came to help me again. Once I was in the boat, everyone else started to get in, too. At first I thought someone else had panicked but soon realized the dive master had aborted the dive. I felt guilty and embarrassed that the other 6 people couldn't dive because of me. Guy and Steve tried to reassure me that it was okay and Walker said I had made the right decision and the last person he would blame is me. I was pretty quiet on the way back to La Sirena. Steve drove and chatted with Guy. I tried to participate but all I could think about was getting back to my husband and our room. My limbic system was still going off for a while after that. No more dives this trip.

Understandably, the diver experienced distress for several days, but the inferred long-term effects of the emotional storytelling were quite positive. The diver talks about this event on occasion and experiences little stress when doing so. She enjoys snorkeling to this day but has not had the opportunity to dive again.

Source: Reprinted with permission of story author.

This research procedure involving the mere act of written disclosure of emotional upheaval—what we generally call emotional storytelling—is now referred to as the Pennebaker paradigm (systematic written disclosure across brief sessions). This technique has been used to address the emotions associated with job loss (discussed in Chapter 15), diagnosis of illness, and relationship breakup (reviewed in Pennebaker, 1997). The positive long-term effects of emotional storytelling are fairly robust, yet it does appear that people with hostility (which typically suggests personal difficulty managing emotions) have greater positive immune response than people with low hostility (Christensen & Smith, 1998), and participants high in the trait of alexithymia (difficulty identifying and making sense of emotions) experienced more salutary effects than those low in the trait (Paez, Velasco, & Gonzales, 1999). We reference these findings in particular because they may suggest that people who typically do not have the tendency (or skills) to work with the emotionally laden content of life may benefit the most from this means of processing intense negative emotions.

The theoretical explanations for the benefits of emotional storytelling in response to traumatic events continue to be refined. It does appear that disinhibition (letting go of emotion-related stress), cognitive processing, and social dynamics (when disclosure occurs outside the laboratory) are at work (Niederhoffer & Pennebaker, 2002) when someone experiencing emotional upheaval shares his or her story. Others have stated, "emotional writing . . . reveals the natural abilities people have to construct stories" (Ramírez-Esparza & Pennebaker, 2006, p. 212). Plainly stated, "Putting upsetting experiences into words allows people to stop inhibiting their thoughts and feelings, to begin to organize their thoughts and perhaps find meaning in their traumas, and to reintegrate their social networks" (Niederhoffer & Pennebaker, 2002, p. 581). Some also have found benefit from using storytelling to teach children how to develop their own emotional frameworks and perhaps influence better attachment to parents (Frude & Killick, 2011). When parents allow their own emotional response to characters in a story to be seen, in addition to discussing potential emotions of the characters themselves, children may be better able to cope with varying emotions in their own lives through this modeling. We believe these explanations for the potency of emotional storytelling can be summed up as *strategically working with emotions within a social context.*

EMOTIONS AND CONTEXT

Like many psychological constructs and traits, it is difficult to discuss their level of import, use, and manifestation without a discussion of their existence within context. Individuals in different cultures within the United States and around the globe have different ways of viewing themselves and others and of interactions between the two. Emotional experience does not appear to be universal; as Markus and Kitayama (1991) state, "the experience of an emotion depend[s] on the current construal of the social situation" (p. 235). This refers to the precursors of certain emotions, as well as to specific manifestations of emotions (i.e., how a particular emotion is expressed). For example, in many Western cultures, avoiding expression of anger is thought of as undesirable so that one is not overcome by it at a later date (e.g., "blowing up"). Expression of anger may be something that is viewed as unacceptable or unnecessary in many Eastern cultures, however (Markus & Kitayama, 1991). In addition, intensity of emotional expressions (including positive emotions such as happiness) appears to be affected by cultural context. Lu and Gilmour (2004) assert that less intense emotional expression is more culturally normative and thus more functional for Asian individuals. Further, it is more common for Asian individuals to be dialectical in their emotional experience, such that they more commonly experience a positive correlation between positive and negative affect in comparison to Westerners (Spencer-Rodgers et al., 2010). Thus, emotional experience, emotional expression, and the benefits and deficits of their various manifestations must always be viewed from within a context in order to properly understand the experience of the individual.

WORKING WITH EMOTIONS TO BRING ABOUT POSITIVE CHANGE

Practicing psychologists have long discussed the role of emotions in the psychological change process. During our training as psychologists, we were encouraged to identify clients' emotions and reflect the emotional content of clients' stories through empathic statements we shared aloud. Emotions, as understood within the cultural context of our clients, are considered the indicators of quality of functioning; they helped us track how well a client was doing. Now, given the research discussed in this chapter, we train our graduate students to view emotions as determinants of positive change, not just markers of growth, and caution them to look for varying ways of expressing emotions in different cultural groups. Indeed, how well we and our clients handle emotional events sets, in part, the outer limits of personal well-being.

Now, with what we have learned in our roles as teachers and clinicians in mind, we share ideas that will reveal the potential benefits of strategically working with your emotions. First, we want you to approach the Personal Mini-Experiments as a psychologist gathering data about the phenomena discussed in this chapter. Be as objective as possible when you conduct each experiment, and determine whether your personal results line up with the research findings in this text. Then, make some attempts to hone your personal skills for dealing with the emotion-laden information you encounter every day by implementing the Life Enhancement Strategies.

PERSONAL MINI-EXPERIMENTS

Making the Most of Emotions in Everyday Life

In this chapter, we discuss the "how-tos" and benefits of engaging our emotions. Our review suggests that engaging our emotional selves leads to better and deeper living. Here are a few ideas (and don't forget about the Pennebaker writing exercise described on p. 171) for experimenting with making the most of emotions in your everyday life.

The Emotions Daily Journal. Based on your physiological reactions or the duration of the emotional experience, carefully identify the intense emotions (see Chapter 6 for listings of positive and negative feelings) that you feel every 4 waking hours for

2 days. Note these feelings in your paper or electronic calendar. At the end of each 4-hour segment, spend 5 minutes reflecting on these experiences to determine if you tend to *approach* or *avoid* provocative emotions. (Use the listing of emotional processing and expression items in Table 7.1 to track reactions. If necessary, create a 5-point Likert-type rating system to gauge your responses.) After 2 days' time, identify the benefits and pitfalls of moving toward and moving away from emotion-laden information.

"Acting as If" You Were Emotionally Intelligent for a Day. Think about the people in your life who manage their emotions very well. Make a list of these people and informally rank them from good to best in terms of their emotional intelligence. Then, pick a day of the week when you are sure to have a great deal of social interaction. Spend the day emulating one of your emotionally intelligent role models and act as if you were highly skilled in working with your emotions. When faced with problems or opportunities to excel, ask yourself, "What would my EI role model do in this situation?" and then do it! At the end of the day, identify the top three emotional skills you acted as if you had (see Table 7.2 on p. 164) for the list of the 16 skills of emotional intelligence). In the days that follow, use the three skills again and again until you feel like you have mastered them.

The Buoyant Grandparent Visit. Have you ever asked your grandmother or grandfather (or another family elder) how she or he stays optimistic, happy, compassionate, or working to create harmony despite all the life challenges that she or he has endured? Identify your most resilient or most buoyant family elder and ask this person, "What's important to you these days? What helps you to be in the moment? How do your friends figure into your daily life?" Emotional strategies and plans for spending time with family and friends are sure to be mentioned.

Emotions in Cultural Context. Make a list of the emotions you most often experience. Rank order them in terms of how much you value each. Is the experience of happiness a major priority in your life? Useful expression of anger? Attending to feelings of joy or fear? How did you learn about the importance of these emotions? How might individuals from cultures other than your own feel differently about this ranking? Think about people in your life from different races, genders, religions, or generations—might they have both similarities and differences to you with regard to expression of various emotions?

Life Enhancement Strategies

We encourage you to develop new emotional skills that you can apply in the important domains of your life.

Love

- Practice using more "feeling words" when interacting with friends and family. Adding this to your daily communication will encourage a more emotional approach.

- Set new goals for important relationships that might promote your emotional growth and that of the other person. Think about how your plans and those of others might differ depending on their cultural facets. Are there gender differences in terms of what may be most beneficial, for example? This might enhance the quality of the relationship over time.

Work

- Acknowledge the emotional undercurrents of communication at work. Share these observations in a nonconfrontational way with your coworkers and bosses and facilitate a dialogue about the roles of emotions in the workplace.

- Seek "emotional intelligence at work" seminars. Many human resources offices or local consulting services offer this type of seminar, and anecdotal evidence suggests that participants feel more efficacious in their use of emotional intelligence skills once they complete such training.

Play

- Become an emotional storyteller. Write down the stories of your good times and bad in a journal or share them with trusted friends. Storytelling may distance you from negative experiences in your life and bring you closer to people who are important to you.

- Learn and practice meditation skills. These skills are believed to "suspend time" and help us engage our emotional experiences more deeply.

AN EMOTIONAL BALANCING ACT

Dealing with the emotional aspects of life certainly is a balancing act (Salovey et al., 2002). Sometimes, intense emotional experiences that tax our psychological resources might result in avoidant responses . . . and this is probably adaptive. Dealing with negative emotions in a manner that results in rumination (obsessive thinking), however, may be quite maladaptive. Balancing approach and avoidance tendencies may result in the best functioning, though this is highly dependent on cultural context.

Some people are well versed in managing negative emotions but can't identify any intense positive emotions. Other people may ignore the important protective messages conveyed by negative emotions while remaining very open to "good" feelings. These unbalanced attempts at processing feelings may result in lots of missing data, which may lead to poor decision-making. In many cases, it may not even be possible to be open to only some emotions. In a study investigating individuals dealing with and without depression, distinct differences were found in reactions to both sad and happy movies. While the non-depressed individuals cried during the sad movie, and laughed during the humorous movie, the depressed individuals were much less likely to respond to either. It may be that in closing off access to some emotions (as may be a function of coping with depression to some extent), the depressed individuals were not able to access positive emotions either, like "turning off an emotional faucet" (R. Biswas-Diener, personal communication). Making the most of emotional experiences via emotion-focused coping, emotional intelligence, emotional goal setting, and emotional storytelling can help to create a balanced means of dealing with the information gained from all emotional experiences, while allowing us to retain access to all types of emotions as well.

Certainly, there are many productive and unproductive ways to deal with the emotion-laden information we process each day within our own contexts. It is important to learn how to work with emotions by diversifying your repertoire of coping skills and then determining what is effective and leads to desired life outcomes.

KEY TERMS

Emotional approach: Active movement toward, rather than away from, a stressful or emotional encounter.

Emotional avoidance: Active movement away from, rather than toward, a stressful or emotional encounter.

Emotional expression: Free and intentional display of feeling.

Emotional intelligence: According to Salovey and Mayer's four-branch ability model, the skills (1) to perceive and express feelings; (2) to use emotions and emotional understanding to facilitate thinking; (3) to understand complex emotions, relationships among emotions, and relationships between emotions and behavioral consequences; and (4) to manage emotions.

Emotional processing: The attempt to understand one's emotions.

Emotional storytelling: Written disclosure of emotional upheaval.

Pennebaker paradigm: Systematic written disclosure of emotional upheaval, often involving several timed sessions.

Poignancy: Mixed emotions related to an ending or to losing something meaningful.

Socioemotional selectivity theory: Carstensen's theory that, as compared to younger adults, older adults are more able to focus less on negative emotions, to engage more deeply with emotional content, and to savor the positive in life.

Positive Cognitive States and Processes

CHAPTER 8

Seeing Our Futures Through Self-Efficacy, Optimism, and Hope

FASCINATION WITH THE FUTURE

In the privacy of their personal thoughts, people can imagine wonderful visions of their tomorrows. Indeed, the future is often fascinating precisely because it holds seductive and positive possibilities. Unlike the past and present, therefore, the future offers the chance to change things—to make them different and better, or to strive to preserve what has been gained.

People want to feel as if they can "make things happen" to their satisfaction. This starts from the earliest baby and toddler days. As the weeks and years roll by, however, individuals are left with more and more past events that cannot be changed, and their present lives unfold so quickly that it seems as if they have little chance to make any real changes. On the other hand, the future remains a place where peoples' fantasies and desires can produce the proverbial happy endings.

Within the United States, parents and caregivers teach that the "real action" in life lies ahead. For those who grow up in difficult circumstances, the "American Dream" is that their children will have better lives. Therefore, the children in such environments are often taught to look ahead and to focus on what they can accomplish in the "land of opportunity." In the process of looking ahead, people run the risk of making their lives extremely busy. As a caveat to the general benefits of the future orientations we describe in this chapter, we encourage the reader to consider the thoughts of columnist Ellen Goodman in her essay, "Being Busy Not an End in Itself." Goodman makes a good case for occasionally taking time out from our busy, future-oriented thinking. Many cultures emphasize this mindfulness and taking time to smell the flowers on a more regular basis; perhaps those of us in the United States might take a lesson from these other cultural groups.

Being Busy Not an End in Itself
Ellen Goodman

BOSTON—A friend of mine once worked for a Hollywood executive as chief assistant in charge of the calendar. That wasn't the actual title, of course, but it was the job description.

This executive had a penchant for filling up her Palm Pilot weeks and months in advance. When the day would come, a day invariably brimming over with "unexpected emergencies," she would order another round of cancellations. And begin to fill in the future.

My friend came to think of this as a binge and purge cycle. Out of earshot, she described her boss as a time-bulimic.

I always remember this, because I wonder how many people suffer from timing disorders. How many make commitments *now* with the absolute and inaccurate certainty that we will have more time *then.* Do we look into the mirror and see an image as distorted as the anorexic who looks into the mirror?

This year, a pair of marketing professors from North Carolina published research about time and timing. The students surveyed said repeatedly they would have more free time on the same day of the next week or the next month than they had today. If you asked these students to add a commitment today, they would answer no. But ask them to do it in the future, and they were more likely to say yes.

These students were not just a bunch of cockeyed optimists. The same people had a much more realistic view of their budgets. They were less likely to commit to spending more money in the future than in the present.

But in this sense, time was not money. It was more malleable. When thinking about their spare time, they experienced what the researchers called "irrational exuberance." Even those on overload today would take on a fresh load in the future.

Americans talk a great deal about time-crunch. We ask each other, "How are you?" And we answer: "Busy." We export our "productivity," which has become the international gold standard of workaholism. We think of time as something that's been eaten away, not given away.

In just my own adulthood, Americans have lost Sundays to shopping and lost focus to multitasking. We spend lifetimes on hold.

In this world, the hero of the month must surely be Joseph Williams, the Baltimore lawyer who sued Sears, Roebuck when a no-show repairman left him waiting for four hours. He won a single dollar and a shiny principle: You can't waste my time.

But how many of us are also victims of our own timing disorder, keepers of irrational exuberance? Do we also fill in the future out of an irrational anxiety about "free" time?

"It's difficult to learn that time will not be more abundant in the future," wrote the researchers. Well, it is one thing for students to be fooled repeatedly. But it is quite another for those of us who are older. Time is, to put it quietly, *less* abundant. The refusal to learn a lesson comes with a higher price tag.

I wonder if other cultures suffer from our timing disorder, our "irrational exuberance." Busyness, we believe, is part of our creed. It was that founding father, Thomas Jefferson, who admonished us, "Determine never to be idle. No person will have occasion to complain of the want of time who never loses any. It is wonderful how much can be done if we are always doing."

But these days, I smile more at the words of that cranky radical, Henry David Thoreau, who replied, "It is not enough to be busy, so are the ants. The question is what are we busy about."

Source: Lawrence Journal-World, April 7, 2005. Copyright © 2005, The Washington Post Writers Group. Reprinted with permission.

Note: Ellen Goodman (ellengoodman@globe.com) is a columnist for the Washington Post Writers Group.

In the present chapter, we first examine three major, future-oriented temporal perspectives in positive psychology—**self-efficacy**, **optimism**, and hope. We explore the theories that guide these concepts, along with the scales that measure each and the associated research findings. Next, we discuss the potential balance among temporal orientations aimed at past, present, and future. Finally, we provide cautionary comments about how these future-oriented concepts may not apply to samples other than the Caucasian Americans who were the participants in much of the reported research.

SELF-EFFICACY

I Think I Can, I Think I Can . . .

After Stanford University psychologist Albert Bandura published his 1977 *Psychological Review* article titled "Self-Efficacy: Toward a Unifying Theory of Behavior Change," the self-efficacy concept spread in popularity to the point that it now may have produced more empirical research than any other topic in positive psychology (Bandura, 1977, 1982, 1997). What exactly is this concept that has proven so influential? To understand self-efficacy, some people have used the sentiments of the little train engine (from Watty Piper's [1930/1989] children's story, *The Little Engine That Could*) to epitomize self-efficacy. Recall that the tiny engine, thinking about how the little boys and girls on the other side of the mountain would not

Albert Bandura

Source: Reprinted with permission of Albert Bandura.

have their toys unless she helped, uttered the now-famous motivational words, "I think I can. I think I can. I think I can"—and then proceeded to chug successfully up the mountainside to deliver her payload. This belief that you can accomplish what you want is at the core of the self-efficacy idea.

The self-efficacy construct rests upon a long line of historical thinking related to the sense of personal control. Famous thinkers such as John Locke, David Hume, William James, and Gilbert Ryle have focused on willfulness, or volition, in human thinking (Vessey, 1967). Similar ideas have appeared in theories on achievement motivation (McClelland, Atkinson, Clark, & Lowell, 1953), effectance motivation (White, 1959), and social learning (Rotter, 1966). (For a review of personal competence, coping, and satisfaction, see Skinner, 1995.) It was this classic line of control-related scholarship upon which Bandura drew in defining the self-efficacy concept.

A Definition

Bandura (1997, p. vii) defined self-efficacy as "peoples' beliefs in their capabilities to produce desired effects by their own actions." Similarly, Maddux (2009a, p. 336) has described self-efficacy as "what I believe I can do with my skills under certain conditions." Based on an examination of what needs to be done in order to reach a desired goal (these are called *outcome expectancies*), the person supposedly then analyzes his or her capability to complete the necessary actions (these are called *efficacy expectancies*). For Bandura, outcome expectancies are viewed as far less important than efficacy expectancies; consistent with his perspective, studies have shown that outcome expectancies do not add much to efficacy expectancies when predicting various human actions (Maddux, 1991). Thus, situation-specific self-efficacy thoughts are proposed to be the last and most crucial cognitive step before people launch goal-directed actions.

Childhood Antecedents: Where Does Self-Efficacy Come From?

Self-efficacy is a learned human pattern of thinking rather than a genetically endowed one. It begins in infancy and continues throughout the life span. Self-efficacy is based on the premises of social cognitive theory, which holds that humans actively shape their lives rather than passively reacting to environmental forces (Bandura, 1986; Barone, Maddux, & Snyder, 1997a).

Social cognitive theory, in turn, is built on three ideas. First, humans have powerful symbolizing capacities for cognitively creating models of their experiences. Second, by observing themselves in relation to these cognitive models, people then become skilled at self-regulating their actions as they navigate ongoing environmental events. Thus, cognitive reactions influence the surrounding environmental forces that, in turn, shape subsequent thoughts and actions (i.e., there is a back-and-forth interchange of environmental and thinking forces). Third, people (i.e., their selves) and their personalities are a result of these situation-specific, reciprocal interactions of thoughts →environment → thoughts. Given these social cognitive ideas, therefore, a developing child uses symbolic thinking, with specific reference to the understanding of cause-and-effect relationships, and learns self-efficacious, self-referential thinking by observing how she or he can influence the surrounding circumstances (Maddux, 2009a).

Bandura (1977, 1989a, 1989b, 1997) proposed that the developmental antecedents of self-efficacy include the following:

1. Previous successes in similar situations (calling on the wellspring of positive thoughts about how well one has done in earlier circumstances)

2. Modeling on others in the same situations (watching other people who have succeeded in a given arena and copying their actions)

3. Imagining oneself behaving effectively (visualizing acting effectively to secure a wanted goal)

4. Undergoing verbal persuasion by powerful, trustworthy, expert, and attractive other people (being influenced by a helper's words to behave in a given manner)

5. Arousal and emotion (when physiologically aroused and experiencing negative emotions, our self-efficacy may be undermined, whereas such arousal paired with positive emotions heightens the sense of self-efficacy)

Cultural Context and Self-Efficacy

Some differences may exist in the experience of self-efficacy and its development. In specific domains, gender differences have been found in United States populations, for example. In a recent meta-analysis, women were found to exhibit higher self-efficacy in language arts than their male counterparts, whereas men had higher self-efficacy than women in areas of study such as math, social sciences, and computer sciences (Huang, 2013). Cultural norms, expectations, and stereotype threat (defined by Claude Steele as the threat one feels at being judged on performance in relation to negative stereotypes that exist about one's group) may be at work in the development (or lack thereof) of self-efficacy in these instances. Interestingly, other research has found that biological sex may not be the determining factor in the development of self-efficacy in the domains of math, science, and/or language arts. Instead, it appears that gender roles may be the main influence. Huffman, Whetten, and Huffman (2013) found in their study that masculinity (i.e., a more masculine gender expression and role assumption) predicted self-efficacy for technological pursuits regardless of biological sex. This means that both men and women who had more masculine gender role traits had higher self-efficacy in technology, whereas those of both genders with less masculinity had lower self-efficacy in this same area. This type of research is important in helping us to understand the role cultural context (and perhaps its tolerance or lack thereof for more fluid gender roles) may have in determining personal beliefs about one's abilities. Finally, the source of self-efficacy may differ between men and women in various pursuits. Self-efficacy for science appeared to stem from vicarious learning for female students but from mastery experiences for male students. More research in this area might help us to provide more culturally specific experiences for girls versus boys in order to fully develop self-efficacy in both (Sawtelle, Brewe, & Kramer, 2012).

Others have noted that differences may exist in levels of self-efficacy between individuals from individualist countries such as the United States and members of more collectivist groups. Kim and Park (2006) found that, within the United States, participants in their study rated their abilities as high even when they performed poorly in subjects such as math and science. The opposite was found in Japanese and Korean students, where low self-efficacy was found even in the face of high levels of performance on a difficult math test (Lee, 2009). Thus, culture may play a role in the type of persuasion one receives and the modeling available (e.g., women succeeding in fields where few role models are to be found), and this may have an effect on some of the developmental anteced-ents to self-efficacy mentioned by Bandura above.

One other point in this area seems worth making as our world grows more diverse: Certain groups have been limited in some ways with regard to their being "allowed" to engage in certain types of roles and activities throughout history because of disenfranchisement or actual laws that have prevented their participation. In "Thinking She Could Be the Next President," Rios, Stewart, and Winter (2010) discuss how presenting a diverse curriculum showing girls and women as lead-ers in addition to those of the male gender might influence girls' perspectives on what they can be in life. Self-efficacy, as described above, can be engendered by role models and by the very virtue of being able to imagine oneself in a particular situation. Presenting diverse examples across all curricula may allow a broader group of children to develop self-efficacy with regard to a broad range of activities and roles in the future.

The Neurobiology of Self-Efficacy

It is likely that the frontal and prefrontal lobes of the human brain evolved to facilitate the priori-tization of goals and the planful thinking that are crucial for self-efficacy (as well as hope, dis-cussed later in this chapter; see Newberg, d'Aquili, Newberg, & deMarici, 2000; Stuss & Benson, 1984). When faced with goal-directed tasks, especially the problem solving that is inherent in much of self-efficacy thinking, the right hemisphere of the brain reacts to the dilemmas as relayed by the linguistic and abstract left hemisphere processes (Newberg et al., 2000).

Experiments, most of which have been conducted on animals, also reveal that self-efficacy or perceived control can be traced to underlying biological variables that facilitate coping (Bandura, 1997). Self-efficacy yields a sense of control that leads to the production of neuroendocrines and catecholamines (neurotransmitters that govern automatic activities related to stress) (Bandura, 1991; Maier, Laudenslager, & Ryan, 1985). These later catecholamines have been found to mirror the level of felt self-efficacy (Bandura, Taylor, Williams, Mefford, & Barchas, 1985). So, too, does a sense of realistic self-efficacy lessen cardiac reactivity and lower blood pressure, thereby facilitat-ing coping.

Scales: Can Self-Efficacy Be Measured?

Bandura (1977, 1982, 1997) has held staunchly to the situational perspective that self-efficacy should reflect beliefs about using abilities and skills to reach given goals *in specific circumstances or domains.* In his words, "Efficacy beliefs should be measured in terms of particularized judg-ments of capacity that may vary across realms of activity, under different levels of task demands within a given domain, and under different situational circumstances" (Bandura, 1997, p. 42). Consistent with Bandura's emphasis upon situations, Betz and colleagues have developed and validated a 25-item measure that taps confidence in making career decisions (Betz, Klein, & Tay-lor, 1996; Betz & Taylor, 2000). Scores on this scale predict confidence in examining various careers (Blustein, 1989) and actual career indecision (Betz & Klein Voyten, 1997). Other career self-efficacy indices are available, including the Occupational Questionnaire (Teresa, 1991), which taps students' mastery of various vocations, and the Career Counseling Self-Efficacy Scale (O'Brien, Heppner, Flores, & Bikos, 1997), which measures counselors' confidence in deriving interventions for persons who are having difficulties with their career decisions. (See also Schwarzer and Renner [2000] for situation-specific "coping self-efficacy.") Likewise, numerous scales exist for measuring feelings of efficacy for various types of skills. These include the Alcohol Abstinence Self-Efficacy scale (McKiernan, Cloud, Patterson, Golder, & Besel, 2011) and the Internet Self-Efficacy Scale (Kim & Glassman, 2013). Efficacy is measured in other types of situations in studies such as Hyre and colleagues' (2008) Hurricane Coping Self-Efficacy questionnaire, developed following Hurricane Katrina, and the Cultural Self-Efficacy Scale, which was designed specifically for adolescents (Briones, Tabernero, Tramontano, Caprara, & Arenas, 2009). Scales assessing self-efficacy during specific life transitions also exist, including Lowe's (1993) Childbirth Self-Efficacy Scale and the Memory Self-Efficacy Scale for older adults (Berry, West, & Dennehey, 1989). And, finally, scales exist to measure certain types of social and emotional development, including the Emotional Self-Efficacy Scale (Pool & Qualter, 2012) and the Social Self-Efficacy Scale (Zullig, Teoli, & Valois, 2011).

Although Bandura consistently has argued against the trait perspective (in which psychological phenomena are viewed as enduring over time and circumstances), other researchers have developed such dispositional measures of self-efficacy (e.g., Sherer et al., 1982; see also Tipton & Worthington, 1984). Citing evidence that self-efficacy experiences involving personal mastery can generalize to actions that transcend any given target behavior (e.g., Bandura, Adams, & Beyer, 1977) and that some people are especially likely to have high self-efficacy expectations across several situations, Sherer et al. (1982) developed and validated a trait-like index called the Self-Efficacy Scale.

The Self-Efficacy Scale consists of 23 items to which respondents rate their agreement on a 14-point Likert scale (1 = Strongly disagree to 14 = Strongly agree). Examples of some items include the following: "When I make plans, I am certain I can make them work," "If I can't do a job the first time, I keep trying till I can," and "When I have something unpleasant to do, I stick to it until I finish it."

Factor analyses have revealed one factor reflecting *general self-efficacy* and a second one tapping *social self-efficacy*. The internal consistency of the scale (i.e., the degree to which individual items aggregate together) has ranged from alphas of .71 to .86. Lastly, the concurrent validity of the Self-Efficacy Scale has been supported by its positive correlations with scores on measures of personal control, ego strength, interpersonal competency, and self-esteem (Chen, Gully, & Eden, 2001; Sherer et al., 1982).

More recently, Chen et al. (2001) have developed an 8-item New General Self-Efficacy Scale, and its scores appear to relate positively to those on the Self-Efficacy Scale of Sherer et al. (although there are exceptions). This New General Self-Efficacy Scale may provide yet another valid self-report index for tapping cross-situational self-efficacy.

Contrary to the cross-situational perspective of the Self-Efficacy Scale, Bandura suggests that any measurement of the individual's sense of personal efficacy should be carefully tied to a given performance situation (see Bandura, 1995, 1997 for expositions of how to do this). Although the cross-situational efficacy scales produce significant correlations with other measures, it is when using such situation-specific measures that higher self-efficacy robustly and consistently has predicted (1) lower anxiety, (2) higher pain tolerance, (3) better academic performance, (4) more political participation, (5) effective dental practices, (6) continuation in smoking cessation treatment, and (7) adoption of exercise and diet regimes (Bandura, 1997).

Measuring self-efficacy has become a more common cross-cultural endeavor in recent years as well. A quick search of PsycINFO reveals a number of validation studies post-2006 that involve measuring this construct in a variety of populations. For example, Israelashvili and Socher (2007) focused on self-efficacy in counselors in an Israeli sample, and self-efficacy scales for children in Brazil (De Cássia Marinelli, Bartholomeu, Caliatto, & de Greggi Sassi, 2009) and Poland (Gambin & Święcicka, 2012) also exist. Other researchers have endeavored to examine self-efficacy across a variety of countries (e.g., Klassen et al., 2009; Wu, 2009). These and other similar studies point to the global relevance of strength-based research and applications of this construct and may lead us to a better understanding of how self-efficacy is developed and maintained in various cultural contexts.

Self-Efficacy's Influence in Life Arenas

Self-efficacy has produced huge bodies of research both inside and outside of psychology. In this section, we explore some of this research. For the reader interested in deeper explorations of self-efficacy research findings, we recommend Albert Bandura's *Self-Efficacy: The Exercise of Control* (1997) and the James Maddux–edited volume, *Self-Efficacy, Adaptation, and Adjustment* (1995).

Psychological Adjustment

Self-efficacy has been implicated in successful coping with a variety of psychological problems (Maddux, 1995). Lower self-efficacies have been linked with depression (Bandura, 1977; Pickett, Yardley, & Kendrick, 2012) and avoidance and anxiety (Williams, 1995). Higher self-efficacy is helpful in overcoming eating disorders and abuse (DiClemente, Fairhurst, & Piotrowski, 1995), and it also has been linked with life satisfaction in a variety of populations (see Charrow, 2006; Dahlbeck & Lightsey, 2008; Danielson, Samdal, Hetland, & Wold, 2009). Recent research suggests that self-efficacy may play a role in success of treatment aimed at interpersonal behavior of out-patients dealing with schizophrenia (Morimoto, Matsuyama, Ichihara-Takeda, Murakami, & Ikeda, 2012). Bandura was one of the first to take a positive, strengths-based approach when he posed that self-efficacy can play a protective role in dealing with psychological problems and, further, emphasized *enablement factors* that help people "to select and structure their environments in ways that set a successful course" (Bandura, 1997, p. 177). This latter view regarding enablement factors taps the positive psychology emphasis on enhancing strengths instead of lessening weaknesses.

Physical Health

Maddux (2009a) has suggested that self-efficacy can influence positive physical health in two ways. First, elevated self-efficacy increases health-related behaviors and decreases unhealthy ones; moreover, self-efficacy helps to maintain these changes (Lee, Kuo, Fanaw, Perng, & Juang, 2012; Maddux, Brawley, & Boykin, 1995). In this regard, theories pertaining to health behaviors all showcase self-efficacy. Examples of these theories include the protection motivation theory (Rogers & Prentice-Dunn, 1997), the reasoned action behavior theory (Ajzen, 1988), and the health belief model (Strecher, Champion, & Rosenstock, 1997).

Second, self-efficacy has an impact on various biological processes that relate to better physical health. Included in such adaptive biological processes are immune functioning (O'Leary & Brown, 1995), susceptibility to infections, the neurotransmitters that are implicated in stress management (i.e., catecholamines), and the endorphins for muting pain (Bandura, 1997).

Finally, self-efficacy may be particularly useful in dealing with individuals coping with disease or disorders. In a study with patients dealing with multiple sclerosis, researchers found that those who developed a certain level of self-efficacy for dealing with their disease and having control over it (as opposed to becoming overwhelmed by it) were more likely to engage in physical endeavors and had higher quality of life with regard to physical pursuits (Motl, McAuley, Wynn, Sandroff, & Suh, 2013). This is only one example of how self-efficacy interventions might influence daily life with a particular disorder.

Psychotherapy

Just as Jerome Frank (see Frank & Frank, 1991) made the case that hope is a common factor in successful psychotherapy, so, too, has it been reasoned that self-efficacy is a common factor across various psychological interventions (Bandura, 1986; Maddux & Lewis, 1995). As such, self-efficacy enhancement in the context of psychotherapy not only bolsters efficacious thinking for specific circumstances but also shows how to apply such thinking across situations that the client may encounter (Maddux, 2009a).

Psychotherapy may use one or more of the following five strategies discussed previously for enhancing self-efficacy:

1. Building successes, often through the use of goal setting and the incremental meeting of those goals (Hollon & Beck, 1994)

2. Using models to teach the person to overcome difficulties (e.g., Bandura, 1986)

3. Allowing the person to imagine himself or herself behaving effectively (Kazdin, 1979)

4. Using verbal persuasion by a trustworthy psychotherapist (Ingram, Kendall, & Chen, 1991)

5. Teaching techniques for lowering arousal (e.g., meditation, mindfulness, biofeedback, hypnosis, relaxation, etc.) to increase the likelihood of more adaptive, self-efficacious thinking

Development of Cultural Competence and Acculturation

Self-efficacy has also been studied with regard to belief in one's ability to succeed in a culture that differs somewhat from one's own home culture. **Bicultural self-efficacy**, for example, is described as a sense of assurance in one's own ability to participate and interact in a culture of origin and a second culture (Miller, Yang, Farrell, & Lin, 2011). Miller and colleagues discuss three ways that this might occur: (1) via language (e.g., translation); (2) through social relations (e.g., understanding norms and subtle nuances); and (3) via an ability to value things from both cultural frameworks (e.g., seeing benefits in individualist and collectivist worldviews). This type of self-efficacy has important implications for individuals who are not part of majority culture (namely White American culture) within the United States, as levels of this may impact an individual's willingness to engage within both cultures when obstacles occur. For example, Jordan, a second-generation Vietnamese American, may choose to retain aspects of his traditional Vietnamese culture (perhaps thereby preserving relationships with his more traditional parents) while at the same time learning and adopting some aspects of U.S. culture (perhaps allowing him to have better social relationships with majority group peers). This type of bicultural skill provides many benefits for the individual, including a decrease in acculturative stress (Miller et al., 2011).

Bicultural self-efficacy could also have potential benefits for members of a majority group attempting to learn more about a minority cultural group. Here an example might be Sadie, who is heterosexual, feeling confident about interacting with same-sex oriented peers as well as those who are heterosexual like herself. Bicultural self-efficacy in this direction may have benefits such as promoting ally behavior in groups with higher social power.

Related to the concept of bicultural self-efficacy is the more general *cultural self-efficacy* defined by Briones and colleagues (2009) as "the perception of one's own capability to mobilize motivation, cognitive resources and courses of action necessary in situations characterized by diversity" (p. 303). This concept is somewhat different than bicultural self-efficacy as it talks about one's comfort in navigating a situation in which various groups, some of which may differ from one's own, are present. Within a country such as the United States, this type of confidence might encourage more interaction between different cultural groups and subsequently increase empathy and understanding between these groups. As diversity has been shown to be profitable both socially and with regard to productivity, development of this type of self-efficacy seems beneficial on many levels.

(The reader can refer to the discussion of self-efficacy-based interventions in Chapter 14, which details various positive psychology change techniques.)

The Latest Frontier: Collective Self-Efficacy

Although the great majority of work on the self-efficacy concept has centered on individuals reacting to given circumstances, self-efficacy also can operate at the collective level and involve large numbers of people who are pursuing shared objectives (Bandura, 1997). Collective self-efficacy has been defined as "the extent to which we believe that we can work together effectively to accomplish our shared goals" (Maddux, 2009a, p. 340). Although there is no agreement about how to measure this collective efficacy, the relevant evidence does show that it plays a helpful role in classroom performances (Bandura, 1993) and work teams (Little & Madigan, 1997), to name but two examples. Our prediction is that collective efficacy will become even more influential with the growing focus of positive psychology on cooperative group efforts. For a real-life application of social learning theory and self-efficacy principles as embodied by television heroes, read the article "Changing Behavior Through TV Heroes."

Changing Behavior Through TV Heroes
Melissa Dittmann
Monitor Staff

Albert Bandura highlighted how serial dramas grounded in his social learning theory can lead people to make lifestyle changes and alter detrimental social practices.

Long-running TV and radio programs founded on social psychology are helping people around the world make positive changes in their lives, from encouraging literacy to raising the status of women in societies where they are marginalized, said renowned social cognitive psychologist Albert Bandura, PhD, at a presidential invited address at APA's 2004 Annual Convention in Honolulu. Bandura also received APA's Lifetime Achievement Award at the convention. . . .

Bandura's social learning theory—which emphasizes how modeling and enhancing people's sense of efficacy can help them improve their lives—is at the heart of numerous serial dramas now airing in Africa, Asia, and Latin America. And research is finding the dramas' gripping storylines and realistic characters are proving influential by encouraging people to adopt family planning methods, seek literacy programs, improve women's status, and protect against AIDS infection.

"These dramatic productions are not fanciful stories," said Bandura, APA president in 1973 and the David Starr Jordan Professor of Psychology at Stanford University. "They portray people's everyday lives, help them see a better future, and provide them with strategies and incentives that enable them to take the steps to realize it."

These dramas, incorporating Bandura's theory, involve a global effort, partnering television producers, writers, demographers and communication researchers in creating programs that change personal lifestyles and society.

The messages appear to inspire action: In Mexico, for example, nearly one million people enrolled in a study program to learn to read after watching a drama that promoted national literacy by showing people of different ages struggling to read and then becoming literate and managing their lives more effectively.

According to Bandura, the television programs spark such behavioral and social changes using four guiding principles:

- Contrasting role models with positive and negative models exhibiting beneficial or detrimental lifestyles and transitional models changing from detrimental to beneficial styles of behavior.

- Vicarious motivators that serve as incentives to change by showing the benefits of the positive lifestyles and the costs of the detrimental ones.

- Attentional and emotional involvement within the programs to sustain viewers' attention.

- Environmental supports with each program that contain an epilogue providing contact information for relevant community services and support groups.

For example, using these principles, a series of dramas targeted the high fertility rate in Tanzania, which is expected to nearly double its 36 million population in 25 years and has a fertility rate of 5.6 children per woman. After the dramas aired, researchers found that the greater exposure marital partners had to the dramas, the more they discussed the need to control family size and adopted family planning methods.

To help guide such productions, the drama producers study a region's culture and values to identify major social problems and obstacles to overcoming them. Writers and producers use this information to develop realistic characters and plots grounded in respect for human dignity and equity, which are codified in United Nations covenants.

(Continued)

(Continued)

"Global problems produce a sense of paralysis in people that they cannot do anything about them," Bandura said. "Our global applications illustrate how a collective effort combining the expertise of different players can have a worldwide impact on seemingly insurmountable problems."

Source: From Dittmann, M., Changing behavior through TV heroes, *APA Monitor*, September 2004, p. 70. Copyright © 2004 by the American Psychological Association. Reproduced with permission. No further reproduction or distribution is permitted without written permission from the American Psychological Association.

OPTIMISM

In this section, we discuss two theories that have received the overwhelming majority of the attention in regard to the construct of optimism. The first is learned optimism as studied by Martin Seligman and colleagues, and the second is the view of optimism as advanced by Michael Scheier and Charles Carver.

Learned Optimism—Seligman and Colleagues

The Historical Basis of Learned Optimism

Abramson, Seligman, and Teasdale (1978) reformulated their model of helplessness (see also Peterson, Maier, & Seligman, 1993) to incorporate the attributions (explanations) that people make for the bad and good things that happen to them. University of Pennsylvania psychologist Martin Seligman (Seligman, 1991, 1998b; see also Seligman, Reivich, Jaycox, & Gillham, 1995) later used this attributional or explanatory process as the basis for his theory of learned optimism.

A Definition of Learned Optimism

In the Seligman theory of learned optimism, the optimist uses adaptive causal attributions to explain negative experiences or events. Thus, the person answers the question, "Why did that bad thing happen to me?" In technical terms, the optimist makes external, variable, and specific attributions for failure-like events rather than the internal, stable, and global attributions of the pessimist. Stated more simply, the optimist explains bad things in such a manner as (1) to account for the role of other people and environments in producing bad outcomes (i.e., an external attribution); (2) to interpret the bad event as not likely to happen again (i.e., a variable attribution); and (3) to constrain the bad outcome to just one performance area and not others (i.e., a specific attribution).

Thus, the optimistic student who has received a poor grade in a high school class would say, (1) "It was a poorly worded exam" (external attribution), (2) "I have done better on previous exams" (variable attribution), and (3) "I am doing better in other areas of my life such as my relationships and sports achievements" (specific attribution). Conversely, the pessimistic student who has received a poor grade would say, (1) "I screwed up" (internal attribution), (2) "I have done lousy on previous exams" (stable attribution), and (3) "I also am not doing well in other areas of my life" (global attribution).

Figure 8.1   Learned Optimism Theory Viewed in Terms of Its Past Temporally Oriented Excusing Qualities as Compared to Future Temporally Oriented Optimism Qualities

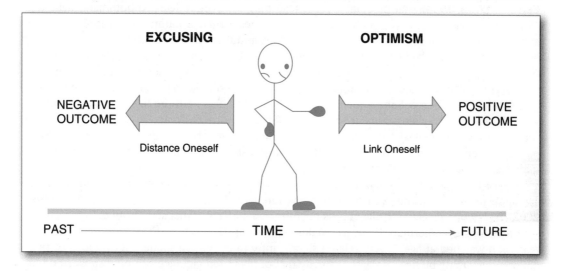

Seligman's theory implicitly places great emphasis upon negative outcomes in determining one's attributional explanations. Therefore, as shown in Figure 8.1, Seligman's theory uses an excuse-like process of "distancing" from bad things that have happened in the past, rather than the more usual notion of optimism involving the connection to positive outcomes desired in the future (as reflected in the typical dictionary definition, as well as in Scheier and Carver's definition, which we explore shortly in this chapter). Within the learned optimism perspective, therefore, the optimistic goal-directed cognitions are aimed at distancing the person from negative outcomes of high importance.

Childhood Antecedents of Learned Optimism

Seligman and colleagues (Abramson et al., 2000; Gillham, 2000; Seligman, 1991, 1995, 1998b) carefully described the developmental roots of the optimistic explanatory style. To begin, there appears to be some genetic component of explanatory style, with learned optimism scores more highly correlated for monozygotic than dizygotic twins (correlations = .48 vs. .0; Schulman, Keith, & Seligman, 1993).

Additionally, learned optimism appears to have roots in the environment (or learning). For example, parents who provide safe, coherent environments are likely to promote the learned optimism style in their offspring (Franz, McClelland, Weinberger, & Peterson, 1994). Likewise, the parents of optimists are portrayed as modeling optimism for their children (Bamford & Lagattuta, 2012), often by making explanations for negative events that enable the offspring to continue to feel good about themselves (i.e., external, variable, and specific attributions) and by providing explanations for positive events that help the offspring feel extra-good about themselves (i.e., internal, stable, and global attributions; Forgeard & Seligman, 2012). Moreover, children who grow up with learned optimism are characterized as having had parents who understood their failures and generally attributed those failures to external rather than internal factors (i.e., they taught their children adaptive excusing; see Snyder, Higgins, & Stucky, 1983/2005). On the other hand, pessimistic people had parents who also were pessimistic. Furthermore, experiencing childhood traumas (e.g., parental death, abuse, incest, etc.) can yield pessimism (Bunce, Larsen, & Peterson, 1995; Cerezo & Frias, 1994), and parental divorce also may undermine learned optimism (Seligman, 1991). (Not all studies have found the aforementioned negative parental contributions to the explanatory styles of the offspring of those parents, and thus these conclusions must be viewed with caution. For a balanced overview of parental contributions, see Peterson & Steen, 2002.) As a final thought, researchers note that there can sometimes be "too much of a good thing" with regard to use of optimistic explanatory style. Optimists tend to keep gambling even when losing over and over (Gibson & Sanbonmatsu, 2004). They may also be more likely to make mistakes when looking at risky situations in some cases (Sharot, Korn, & Dolan, 2011). Therefore, sometimes "temporary (realistic) pessimism may be more beneficial" (Forgeard & Seligman, 2012, p. 115). When we become optimistic to the point of disregarding potential problems and consequences, we may need to adjust our tendency.

Television watching is yet another potential source of pessimism. American children ages 2 to 17 watch an average of almost 25 hours of television per week (3.5 hours per day; Gentile & Walsh, 2002). As but one recent example of pessimism-related behaviors that stem from children's television watching, Zimmerman, Glew, Christakis, and Katon (2005) found that greater amounts of television watched at age 4 were related significantly to higher subsequent likelihoods of those children becoming bullies. Likewise, a steady diet of television violence can predispose and reinforce a helpless explanatory style that is associated with low learned optimism in children (Nolen-Hoeksema, 1987). Certain types of television programs may have a greater affect on children in this way. For example, shows aimed at "tweens" (i.e., 8 to 12 year olds), particularly shows that depict social conflict in middle and high school settings, seem to create anxiety in their viewers (Mares, Braun, & Hernandez, 2012). This leads to more pessimism experienced by these tweens when thinking about the high school context. These results were found even when this type of episode was watched only once! Discussions of how parents might deactivate some of these effects with simple conversations are important (Mares et al., 2012). This underlines the importance of parental involvement in the development of a more optimistic explanatory style.

Scales: Can Learned Optimism Be Measured?

The instrument used to measure attributional style in adults is called the Attributional Style Questionnaire (ASQ; Peterson et al., 1982; Seligman, Abramson, Semmel, & von Baeyer, 1979); the instrument for children is the Children's Attributional Style Questionnaire (CASQ; Kaslow, Tanenbaum, & Seligman, 1978; Seligman, 1995; Seligman et al., 1984). The ASQ poses negative or positive life events, and respondents are asked to indicate what they believe to be the causal explanation of those events on the dimensions of internal/external, stable/transient, and global/specific. Since the development of the ASQ, however, researchers have begun using expanded versions with more items (E-ASQ; see Metalsky, Halberstadt, & Abramson, 1987; Peterson & Villanova, 1988).

Beyond the explanatory style scales for adults and children, University of Michigan psychologist Chris Peterson and his colleagues (Peterson, Bettes, & Seligman, 1985) developed the Content Analysis of Verbal Explanation (CAVE) approach for deriving ratings of optimism and pessimism from written or spoken words (Peterson, Schulman, Castellon, & Seligman, 1992). The advantage of the CAVE technique is that it allows an unobtrusive means of rating a person's explanatory style based on language usage. In this latter regard, one can go back and explore the optimism/pessimism of famous historical figures in their speeches, diaries, or newspaper interviews from earlier decades (e.g., Satterfield, 2000). To demonstrate the predictive power of the CAVE, we describe an intriguing application of the technique to predict the performances of major league baseball teams (see "The CAVE and Predicting Baseball Outcomes").

What Learned Optimism Predicts

The various indices of learned optimism have spawned a large amount of research (see Carr, 2004), with the learned optimistic rather than pessimistic explanatory style associated with the following:

1. Better academic performances (Beard, Hoy, & Hoy, 2010; Peterson & Barrett, 1987; Seligman, 1998b)

2. Superior athletic performances (Seligman, Nolen-Hoeksema, Thornton, & Thornton, 1990)

3. More productive work records (Seligman & Schulman, 1986)

4. Greater satisfaction in interpersonal relationships (Fincham, 2000)

5. More effective coping with life stressors (Nolen-Hoeksema, 2000)

6. Less vulnerability to depression (Abramson et al., 2000)

7. Superior physical health (Peterson, 2000)

8. Greater life satisfaction (Szcześniak & Soares, 2011)

In terms of learned optimism-based interventions, the reader is referred to Chapter 14, where details are given about the change techniques for both children and adults (see also Seligman, Steen, Park, & Peterson, 2005). Additionally, a good overview of learned optimism interventions can be found in Jane Gillham's edited volume titled *The Science of Optimism and Hope* (2000). Easily understood analyses of learned optimism adult interventions can be found in Seligman's *Learned Optimism: How to Change Your Mind and Your Life* (1998b/2006) and his *Authentic Happiness* (2002). Child interventions are described in Seligman et al.'s *The Optimistic Child* (1995).

The CAVE and Predicting Baseball Outcomes

Martin Seligman, an avid Philadelphia Phillies baseball fan, decided to see whether his CAVE approach could be used to predict the outcomes of baseball teams. To accomplish this, his research group used the CAVE technique to analyze the optimistic explanatory styles inherent in the comments of National League baseball players reported in the *Sporting News* and the hometown newspaper sports sections from April though October of 1985. This was a huge task in that 12 National League team newspapers had to be read across the season—this involved 15,000 pages of reading! The

(Continued)

(Continued)

group then used the tabulated learned optimism scores for 1985 to predict various performance outcomes in the next 1986 season.

Of particular focus were the comments of the players on the New York Mets and the St. Louis Cardinals. When they lost, the Mets players' remarks conveyed an optimistic explanatory style. For example, star Mets pitcher Dwight Gooden explained a batter's home run with a simple, "He hit well tonight," and of his wild pitch, Gooden opined, "Some moisture must have gotten on the ball." Mets right fielder Darryl Strawberry said of a loss, "Sometimes you go through these kind of days." Compare these optimistic comments to the more pessimistic comments of St. Louis Cardinals' manager Whitey Herzog and team slugger Jack Clark. When asked why his team lost, Herzog replied, "We can't hit. What the hell, let's face it." And Clark commented on a fly ball he dropped by saying, "It was a real catchable ball."

When the explanatory styles of the Mets and Cardinals were used to predict performance in the next 1986 season, the optimistic comments of the Mets suggested success, and the pessimistic comments of the Cardinals predicted failure. This is precisely what happened. The Mets won the division, the playoffs, and the World Series in 1986, whereas the Cardinals lost more games than they won. The Mets' batting average for 1986 was .263 overall and .277 in pressure situations; the Cardinals, in comparison, had a batting average of .236 overall and .231 in pressure situations. Although we have described the results for only 2 of the 12 National League teams, the CAVE ratings of 1985 optimism were equally robust in predicting the outcomes of the other 10 teams. Because Seligman was skeptical about these findings, he replicated them, this time using 1986 comments to predict 1987 performance. He found the same results.

Seligman and his coworkers have performed similar studies on other sports to show the power of players' comments as measured by the CAVE approach to deriving explanatory style scores. More specifically, he has predicted the outcomes of NBA professional basketball teams and 1988 Olympic swimmer Matt Biondi. In yet another form of "sports," American politics (humor intended), Seligman also has found that optimistic explanatory style scores are strong predictors of success.

Note: All these applied studies are described in delightful detail in Seligman's 1991 book, *Learned Optimism.* From Seligman, M. E. P., *Learned Optimism,* copyright © 1990 by Martin E. P. Seligman.

Optimism—Scheier and Carver

Defining Optimism as Expectancies of Reaching a Desired Goal

In their seminal article published in *Health Psychology,* psychologists Michael Scheier and Charles Carver (1985, p. 219) presented their new definition of optimism, which they described as the stable tendency "[to] believe that good rather than bad things will happen." Scheier and Carver assumed that, when a goal was of sufficient value, then the individual would produce an expectancy about attaining that goal.

In their definition of optimism, Scheier and Carver (1985) purposefully do not emphasize the role of personal efficacy. They wrote,

Michael F. Scheier

Source: Reprinted with permission of Michael F. Scheier.

Our own theoretical approach emphasizes a person's expectancies of good or bad outcomes. It is our position that outcome expectancies per se are the best predictors of behavior rather than the bases from which those expectancies were derived. A person may hold favorable expectancies for a number of reasons— personal ability, because the person is lucky, or because others favor him. The result should be an optimistic outlook—expectations that good things will happen. (p. 223)

Thus, these generalized outcome expectancies may involve perceptions about being able to move toward desirable goals or to move away from undesirable goals (Carver & Scheier, 1999).

Childhood Antecedents of Optimism

The consensus is that there is a genetic basis to optimism as defined by Scheier and Carver (see also Plomin et al., 1992). Likewise, borrowing from Erikson's (1963, 1982) theory of development, Carver and Scheier (1999) suggest that their form of optimism stems from early childhood experiences that foster trust and secure attachments to parental figures (Bowlby, 1988). Parents have a role in the development of optimism on the "nurture side" of things. Various types of childhood experiences may lead a child to develop less optimism for the future. Some researchers have noted that children born to parents who live in a lower socioeconomic status may be exposed to more stress and a greater amount of negative emotional states due to this; exposure to socioeconomic difficulties in childhood predicts lower adult optimism as well (Heinonen et al., 2006). Sadly, children in these cases may expect the worst throughout life because they've often been right; this lower level of optimism appears to be somewhat stable throughout life, even if socioecomic status becomes higher in adulthood (Heinonen et al., 2006; Pedrotti, 2013a).

In a study asking college students why they scored high on a scale of dispositional optimism, participants credited factors such as belief in a higher power, feelings that the world was just, personal privileges and benefits in life, and feelings of hope as major reasons with regard to *why* they were optimistic overall (Sohl, Moyer, Lukin, & Knapp-Oliver, 2011). Many of these types of factors might find their origin in positive childhood experiences and beneficial parenting practices, thus giving a bit more evidence for a positive childhood leading to the development of optimism.

Scales: Can Optimism Be Measured?

Scheier and Carver (1985) introduced their index of optimism, the Life Orientation Test (LOT), as including positive ("I'm always optimistic about my future") and negative ("I rarely count on good things happening to me") expectancies. The LOT has displayed acceptable internal consistency (alpha of .76 in original sample) and a test–retest correlation of .79 over 1 month. In support of its concurrent validity, the LOT correlated positively with expectancy for success and negatively with hopelessness and depression.

After years of extensive research using the LOT, a criticism arose about its overlap with neuroticism (see Smith, Pope, Rhodewalt, & Poulton, 1989). In response to this concern, Scheier, Carver, and Bridges (1994) validated a shorter, revised version of the LOT known as the LOT-Revised (LOT-R). The LOT-R eliminated items that caused the neuroticism overlap concerns. Furthermore, relative to neuroticism, trait anxiety, self-mastery, and self-esteem, optimism as measured by the LOT-R has shown superior capabilities in predicting various outcome markers related to superior coping. For example, higher scores on the LOT-R have related to better recovery in coronary bypass surgery, dealing more effectively with AIDS, enduring cancer biopsies more easily, better adjustment to pregnancy, and continuing in treatment for alcohol abuse (Carver & Scheier, 2002; for a good review of the many beneficial correlates of optimism, see Scheier, Carver, & Bridges, 2001). Additionally, internal consistency of the LOT-R equals or exceeds the original LOT (alpha of .78); its test–retest correlations are .68 to .79 for intervals of 4 to 28 months.

In addition, some discussion has been generated regarding whether optimism should be considered a *unidimensional* characteristic (i.e., with optimism at one end of the continuum and pessimism at the other) versus a *bidimensional* construct (i.e., two different factors on two different continua). Studies have found varying results on the factor structure of the LOT-R, with Scheier et al. (1994) finding one factor (optimism) and Affleck and Tennen (1996) finding the two independent factors of optimism and pessimism. This may be a function of cultural context, as differing results have been found when looking cross-culturally. Findings show that the LOT-R seems to measure two factors (optimism and pessimism) in its Spanish translation, and with Brazilian Portuguese individuals as well (Ribeiro, Pedro, & Marques, 2012). In Hong Kong, German, and French-Canadian populations, the one-factor model (i.e., high or low optimism) has been found. Differing reliability coefficients have been found in different samples; specifically, English language versions of the LOT have been found to have reliability estimates that are higher than non-English language versions (Vassar & Bradley, 2010). Given this finding, it is important to acknowledge that measurement does not appear to be consistent across varying groups at this time (Li, 2012; Ribeiro et al., 2012). The categorizing of optimism as unidimensional in some groups and bidimensional in others might provide us with more information; more research is needed in this area.

New scales have been developed fairly recently, including a measure of personal and social optimism called the Questionnaire for the Assessment of Personal Optimism and Social Optimism–Extended (POSO-E; Schweizer & Koch, 2001). In addition, versions of the LOT for children have been developed, including the Youth Life Orientation Test (YLOT; Ey et al., 2004) and the Parent-Rated Life Orientation Test (PLOT; Lemola et al., 2010). In this second scale, parents rate the optimism of their young children.

What Optimism Predicts

The LOT-R, like the LOT, has generated a large amount of research. When coping with stressors, optimists (in Caucasian samples) appear to take a problem-solving approach[1] (Scheier, Weintraub, & Carver, 1986) and are more planful than pessimists (Fontaine, Manstead, & Wagner, 1993).

Furthermore, optimists tend to use the approach-oriented coping strategies of positive reframing and seeing the best in situations, whereas pessimists are more avoidant and use denial tactics (Carver & Scheier, 2002). Optimists appraise daily stresses in terms of potential growth and tension reduction more than their pessimistic counterparts do. Also, when faced with truly uncontrollable circumstances, optimists tend to accept their plights, whereas pessimists actively deny their problems and thereby tend to make them worse (Carver & Scheier, 1998; Carver, Scheier, & Segerstrom, 2010; Scheier & Carver, 2001). In other words, an optimist knows when to give up and when to keep plugging on, whereas the pessimist still pursues a goal when it is not a smart thing to do.

On the whole, the LOT-R has produced robust predictive relationships with a variety of outcome markers (for reviews, see Carver & Scheier, 1999, 2002; Carver, Scheier, Miller, & Fulford, 2009). For example, optimists as compared to pessimists fare better in the following situations:

1. Starting college (Aspinwall & Taylor, 1992)

2. Performing in work situations (Long, 1993) and vocational identity (Shin & Kelly, 2013)

3. Enduring a missile attack (Zeidner & Hammer, 1992) or other traumatic event in war (Thomas, Britt, Odle-Dusseau, & Bliese, 2011)

4. Caring for Alzheimer's patients (Hooker, Monahan, Shifren, & Hutchinson, 1992) and cancer patients (Given et al., 1993)

5. Undergoing coronary bypass surgeries (Fitzgerald, Tennen, Affleck, & Pransky, 1993) and bone marrow transplants (Curbow, Somerfield, Baker, Wingard, & Legro, 1993)

6. Coping with cancer (Carver et al., 1993; Colby & Shifren, 2013); AIDS (Taylor et al., 1992); and chronic pain (Ramírez-Maestre, Esteve, & López, 2012)

7. Coping in general (Carver, Scheier, & Segerstrom, 2010; Solberg Nes & Segerstrom, 2006)

8. Dealing with health issues in later life (Ruthig, Hanson, Pedersen, Weber, & Chipperfield, 2011)

Interestingly, some studies have found that optimism may be related to the suppression of the immune system in some cases (Segerstrom, 2006; Segerstrom & Sephton, 2010). Segerstrom found in a study with law students that while those with higher optimism had higher cellular immunity in times of low conflict, these same individuals had *lower* cellular immunity than those with lower optimism scores during times of high stress or extreme conflict. At present it is not clear if this is due to high expectations being disappointed, the fact that optimists set their sights on more difficult goals (with more difficult stressors), or some other explanation. Segerstrom suggests that regardless of the reason for this, "If optimists are more successful in fulfilling difficult but important goals, the short-term physiological costs may even be to their long-term benefit" (p. 657). In a follow-up to this study, Segerstrom and Sephton (2010) looked more carefully at cellular immune function to determine differences between "little optimism" (that is optimism about a specific situation) versus "big optimism" (general dispositional optimism) and found that differences exist in terms of what other constructs appear to mediate these experiences. Positive affect may be one such construct in circumstances involving little optimism, though it does not appear to have this mediating effect when looking at big optimism. In this follow-up study, it was found that when law students became more optimistic about law school (little optimism), their cellular immune function also increased; the results here are thought to be partly a result of the increase in positive affect that accompanied thinking more positively about their law school future (Segerstrom & Sephton, 2010). More research must be done in this area to further elucidate the complex interactions between optimism and immunity. Implications also exist for interventions to be created for specific circumstances. Perhaps thinking more positively about other experiences (e.g., childbirth, academic testing, going through a medical procedure, etc.) might help us to be healthier in these situations as well.

Culture, Optimism, and Pessimism

Varied findings in studies using the LOT and the LOT-R point to potential cultural nuances in looking at these constructs (e.g., Vassar & Bradley, 2010). Along these lines, both differences and similarities have been found with regard to research on optimism, pessimism, and their correlations to one another across different countries, different racial groups, and different genders. Additional uses for optimism and pessimism are also found in different cultural groups.

In African American samples, optimism seems to mirror Caucasian samples' usual associations with other constructs, including positive correlations to resilience (Baldwin, Jackson, Okoh, & Cannon, 2011) and effective parenting practices (Taylor, Larsen-Rife, Conger, Widaman, & Cutrona, 2010), and negative relationships to depressive symptoms (Odom & Vernon-Feagnas, 2010; Taylor, Budescu, & McGill, 2011) and stress/distress (Baldwin et al., 2011; Taylor et al., 2011). Optimism may be a buffer (along with other factors such as church-related support) against racism and discrimination experienced because of being African American (Odom & Vernon-Feagans, 2010). Furthermore, the way the women in this study perceived racism, as well as the effects racism had upon them, were moderated by their levels of optimism. This may be another example of a cultivated strength in a population that must deal with adversity and might be maximized by emulation in other groups who suffer similar indignities.

Some research has been conducted with the optimism construct in comparing Western and Eastern cultures. Using the learned optimism construct as measured by the ASQ, for example, Lee and Seligman (1997) found that Asian Americans and Caucasian Americans had similar levels of optimism, but the mainland Chinese students were less optimistic. Using the Scheier and Carver approach to operationalizing optimism (along with a version of the LOT), Edward Chang of the University of Michigan (1996a) found that Asian American and Caucasian American students did not differ on optimism, but the Asian Americans were higher in pessimism than their Caucasian American counterparts. In this same study, Chang found that, for the Caucasian Americans, their higher pessimism was associated with less problem solving—as one would expect. For the Asian Americans, on the other hand, *their higher pessimism was associated with greater problem solving.* In the words of Chang (2001a, p. 226), "Thus, what 'works' for Asian

Edward C. Chang

Source: Reprinted with permission of Edward C. Chang.

relative to Caucasian Americans simply might be different, *not necessarily more effective*" (emphasis added). (See Chapter 4 for a related discussion of Chang's work.) Thus, in Asian American samples, optimism and pessimism seem to interact differently than they do in Caucasian and African American samples.

Chang's recent research suggests that Asian Americans may also have more of a pessimistic bias toward some future events (Chang, Sanna, Kim, & Srivastava, 2010). Asian Americans were more likely to have a pessimistic outlook about positive physical health outcomes such as having "wrinkle-free skin." They did not show differences from Caucasian Americans on predictions of positive psychological (e.g., "I will be resilient"); negative physical (e.g., "I will suffer from gum disease"); or psychological (e.g., "I will suffer from depression") outcomes. Both groups had a more optimistic bias (Chang et al., 2010). Other researchers have found that social support may have a different function with regard to optimism in the lives of Asian Americans (Ayres & Mahat, 2012). These researchers found that having social support may increase the impact of optimism on the lives of individuals in this group. Thus, we cannot assume that this coping approach is manifested in the same degree among Asian Americans and Caucasian Americans, nor can we assume that having more optimism (and less pessimism) even produces the same coping repercussions for these two distinct groups.

Research on gender differences suggests that the cultural facet of gender impacts optimism and pessimism. One interesting study examined differences in *comparative optimism* (i.e., one's belief that the chance that good things will happen for him or her is greater than for others) and *personal optimism* (i.e., one's belief that good things will happen for him or her in general) and found that men scored higher than women on both of these constructs, even after controlling for personal experience with parental divorce (Helweg-Larsen, Harding, & Klein, 2011). This same difference, with men scoring higher on optimism and lower on pessimism, has also been found in other studies using samples in the United States and in Taiwan (Black & Reynolds, 2013; Chang, Tsai, & Lee, 2010). Even at the high school level, the same conclusion was reached: boys were more optimistic than girls overall (Pusker et al., 2010). Helweg-Larsen and colleagues (2011) considered why this might be the case and found, for example, that the men in their study also scored significantly higher on measures of personal control. It may be that as men feel they have more control over their futures, they also feel more positive about them. Historically, women across the globe have had less control over their lives and less social power and privilege. It may be that even today this affects the beliefs of many women on what the future holds. Though there may be cultural variations in terms of desire or expectation for personal control, we may want to investigate ways for women of some cultures (e.g., majority culture women in the United States) to have a more internal locus of control with regard to their future.

Turning to the interventions to enhance optimism, we again suggest that the reader examine our Chapter 14 discussion of implementing positive psychological change. Presently there appears to be one major therapy approach that expressly seeks to enhance the positive expectancies as conceptualized in the Scheier and Carver model of optimism. John Riskind and his colleagues (Riskind, Sarampote, & Mercier, 1996) have modified standard cognitive therapy to influence optimism and pessimism. Riskind has acknowledged that most cognitive therapy techniques aim to lessen negative thinking (pessimism) but do little to enhance positive thinking (optimism). On this point, it should be noted that a simple decrease in negative thinking does not change positive thinking, owing perhaps to the fact that negative and positive cognitions are not correlated (Ingram & Wisnicki, 1988). In the Riskind approach, cognitive techniques are used to challenge optimism-suppressing schemas as well as to enhance positive and optimistic thinking. Another technique suggested by Riskind et al. is positive visualization, wherein the client rehearses seeing positive outcomes for problematic circumstances (for overview, see Pretzer and Walsh, 2001). Because of the robust findings relating optimism to various health outcomes, we believe that the Scheier and Carver model will continue to expand in influence, especially in the area of interventions to help medical patients who are facing physical health challenges.

The Neurobiology of Optimism and Pessimism

Individuals higher and lower in optimism may differ in terms of the type of allele pair found on a receptor gene in the oxytocin system (Saphire-Bernstein, Way, Kim, Sherman, & Taylor, 2011). This points to the idea that brain structure may indeed influence one's ability to be optimistic. Individuals high in dispositional optimism also appear to have a weaker cortisol response upon waking up in the morning, compared to those lower in dispositional optimism; this result was found after holding other influencing factors constant (e.g., waking time, depressive symptoms, gender, etc.; Endrighi, Hamer, & Steptoe, 2011). Researchers are currently investigating the reasons for *unrealistic optimism* (i.e., optimism for a rosy outcome in the face of a non-rosy reality). Scientists have investigated the neurological mechanisms that appear to keep some of us optimistic even when we really shouldn't be. For example, Sharot et al. (2011) asked participants to rate their risk of developing various medical problems in the future (e.g., kidney stones, Alzheimer's, etc.) and then presented these same participants with the actual calculated risk of someone similar to them in terms of physicality and lifestyle developing these problems. The participants were then asked at a second interview to again estimate their likelihood of risk for these various diseases and medical conditions. When participants were allowed to become more optimistic as a result of the actual prediction offered to them (i.e., they had *over*estimated their likelihood of developing these problems), they were much more likely to move to a more accurate position in terms of assessing their risk in the second interview. When participants should logically have revised their view in a more pessimistic direction (i.e., they had *under*estimated their likelihood of developing these problems in the face of the actual probability), they did not change as much in their predictions from the first interview to the second (Sharot et al., 2011). Neurologically, less activity was noted in many brain regions in the unrealistically optimistic individuals. This provides interesting evidence for the *optimism bias* discussed by many researchers in this area of the field (see Sharot's [2011] book *The Optimism Bias: A Tour of the Irrationally Positive Brain*). Many researchers have pondered the evolutionary benefits of optimism (e.g., its positive correlations to coping, resiliency, etc.); findings such as this ask us to delve further into this very interesting area of study (Izuma & Adophs, 2011; Shah, 2012; Whelan & Garavan, 2013).

HOPE

In all of human history, there has been a need to believe that bad could be transformed into good, that ugly could become beautiful, and that problems could be solved. But civilizations have differed in the degree to which they have viewed such changes as possible. For example, consider the classic Greek myth of Pandora's box, a story about the origin of hope. There are two versions of this tale.

In one version, Zeus created Pandora, the first woman, in order to exact revenge against Prometheus (and against humans in general) because he had stolen fire from the gods. Pandora was endowed with amazing beauty and grace but also with the tendency to lie and deceive. Zeus sent Pandora with her dowry chest to Epimetheus (brother of Prometheus), who married her. In using what may be one of the earliest examples of reverse psychology, Zeus instructed Pandora not to open her dowry chest upon arriving on Earth. Of course, she ignored Zeus's order and opened the chest. Out spewed all manner of troubles into the world. Hope, however, remained in the chest—not to help humankind but to taunt it with the message that hope does not really exist. In this version, therefore, hope was but a cruel hoax.

A second version of this tale holds that all earthly misfortunes were caused by Pandora's curiosity rather than by any inherent evil nature. The gods tested her with instructions not to open the dowry chest. She was sent to Epimetheus, who accepted her despite the warning of Prometheus about gifts from Zeus. When Pandora opened the dowry chest, hope was not a hoax but a blessing and a source of comfort for misfortunes (Hamilton, 1969). And in this positive version of the story, hope served as an antidote to the evils (e.g., gout, rheumatism, and colic for the body, and envy, spite, and revenge for the mind) that escaped when the chest was opened. Whether hope was a hoax or an antidote, these two versions of this story reveal the tremendous ambivalence of the Greeks toward hope.

Pandora's Box
Source: Photos.com/Thinkstock.

A Definition

Given the considerable attention that C. R. Snyder's theory of hope (Snyder, 1994; Snyder, Harris, et al., 1991) has received in the last two decades, we explore this approach to explaining hopeful thinking in some detail. (Snyder, before his death in 2006, was professor of psychology at the University of Kansas and the senior author of this book.) An overview of the various theories of hope are set forth in Appendix A. Additionally, the book *Hope and Hopelessness: Critical Clinical Constructs* by Farran, Herth, and Popovich (1995) provides a good overview of various approaches for defining and measuring hope.

C. R. Snyder

Both the Snyder hope theory and the definition of hope emphasize cognitions that are built on goal-directed thought. We define hope as goal-directed thinking in which the person utilizes **pathways thinking** (the perceived capacity to find routes to desired goals) and **agency thinking** (the requisite motivations to use those routes).

Only those goals with considerable value to the individual are considered applicable to hope. Also, the goals can vary temporally—from those that will be reached in the next few minutes (short-term goals) to those that will take months or even years to reach (long-term goals). Likewise, the goals entailed in hoping may be approach oriented (that is, aimed at reaching a desired goal) or preventative (aimed at stopping an undesired event) (Snyder, Feldman, Taylor, Schroeder, & Adams, 2000). Lastly, goals can vary in relation to the difficulty of attainment, with some quite easy and others extremely difficult. Even with purportedly impossible goals, however, people may join together and succeed through supreme planning and persistent efforts. On this latter issue, coordinated and successful group efforts illustrate why we should refrain from characterizing extremely difficult goals as being based on "false hopes" (Snyder, Rand, King, Feldman, & Taylor, 2002).

Pathways thinking has been shown to relate to the production of alternate routes when original ones are blocked (Snyder, Harris, et al., 1991), as has positive self-talk about finding routes to desired goals (e.g., "I'll find a way to solve this"; Snyder, LaPointe, Crowson, & Early, 1998). Those who see themselves as having greater capacity for agency thinking also endorse energetic personal agency-focused self-talk statements (e.g., "I will keep going"; Snyder et al., 1998), and they are especially likely to produce and use such motivational talk when encountering impediments.

High hopers have positive emotional sets and a sense of zest that stems from their histories of success in goal pursuits, whereas low hopers have negative emotional sets and a sense of emotional flatness that stems from their histories of having failed in goal pursuits. High- or low-hope people bring these overriding emotional sets with them as they undertake specific goal-related activities.

The various components of hope theory can be viewed in Figure 8.2, with the iterative relationship of pathways and agency thoughts on the far left. Moving left to right from the developmental agency–pathways thoughts, we can see the emotional sets that are taken to follow specific goal pursuit activities. Next in Figure 8.2 are the values associated with specific goal pursuits. As noted previously, sufficient value must be attached to a goal pursuit before the individual will continue the hoping process. At this point, the pathways and agency thoughts are applied to the desired goal. Here, the feedback loop entails positive emotions that positively reinforce the goal pursuit process or negative emotions that curtail this process.

Figure 8.2 shows how the person may encounter a stressor along the route to the goal that potentially blocks the actual goal pursuit. Hope theory proposes that the successful pursuit of desired goals, especially when circumventing stressful impediments, results in positive emotions and continued goal pursuit efforts (i.e., positive reinforcement). On the other hand, if a person's goal pursuit is not successful (often because that person cannot navigate around blockages), then negative emotions should result (Ruehlman & Wolchik, 1988), and the goal pursuit process should be undermined (i.e., punishment). (For more information on hope, consult Shane Lopez's *Making Hope Happen* [2013]).

Such a stressor is interpreted differently depending on the person's overall level of hope. That is to say, high hopers construe such barriers as challenges and will explore alternate routes and apply their motivations to those routes. Typically, having experienced successes in working around

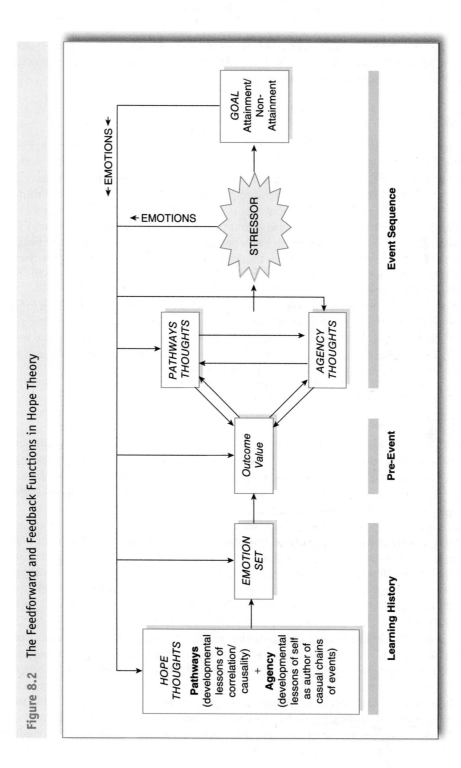

Figure 8.2 The Feedforward and Feedback Functions in Hope Theory

such blockages, the high hopers are propelled onward by their positive emotions. The low hopers, however, become stuck because they cannot find alternate routes; in turn, their negative emotions and ruminations stymie their goal pursuits.

Childhood Antecedents of Hope

More details on the developmental antecedents of the hope process can be found in Snyder (1994, pp. 75–114) and Snyder, McDermott, Cook, and Rapoff (2002, pp. 1–32). In brief, Snyder (1994) proposes that hope has no hereditary contributions but rather is entirely a learned cognitive set about goal-directed thinking. The teaching of pathways and agency goal-directed thinking is an inherent part of parenting, and the components of hopeful thought are in place in a child by age two. Pathways thinking reflects basic cause-and-effect learning that the child acquires from care-givers and others. Such pathways thought is acquired before agency thinking, with the latter being posited to begin around age one. Agency thought reflects the baby's increasing insights as to the fact that he or she is the causal force in many of the cause-and-effect sequences in his or her sur-rounding environment.

Snyder (1994, 2000a) has proposed that strong attachment to caregivers is crucial for imparting hope, and available research is consistent with this speculation (Shorey, Snyder, Yang, & Lewin, 2003). Traumatic events across the course of childhood also have been linked to the lessening of hope (Rodriguez-Hanley & Snyder, 2000), and there is research support for the negative impacts of some of these traumas (e.g., the loss of parents; Westburg, 2001).

The Neurobiology of Hope

Although Snyder and colleagues have held that hope is a learned mental set, this does not preclude the idea that the operations of hopeful thinking have neurobiological underpinnings, especially as related to goal-directed behaviors. Norman Cousins, in his 1991 best-selling book, *Head First: The Biology of Hope and the Healing Power of the Human Spirit,* wrote the following apt description of the brain and hope-related thinking:

> Brain researchers now believe that what happens in the body can affect the brain, and what happens in the brain can affect the body. Hope, purpose, and determination are not merely mental states. They have electrochemical connections that play a large part in the workings of the immune system and, indeed, in the entire economy of the total human organism. In short, I learned that it is not unscientific to talk about a biology of hope. (p. 73)

One exciting new idea here is that goal-directed actions are guided by opposing control pro-cesses in the central nervous system. According to Pickering and Gray (1999), these processes are regulated by the *behavioral inhibition system (BIS)* and the *behavioral activation system (BAS)*. The BIS is thought to be responsive to punishment, and it signals the organism to stop, whereas the BAS is governed by rewards, and it sends the message to go forward. A related body of research suggests a *behavioral facilitation system (BFS)* that drives incentive-seeking actions of organisms (see Depue, 1996). The BFS is thought to include the dopamine pathways of the midbrain that connect to the limbic system and the amygdala.

Another idea recently discussed by Lopez (2013) is the idea of the "prospection pipeline" (p. 41). Lopez discusses the process of hope as it may occur neurologically in the brain. Neuroscientists can track in the brain the process of a good idea or a future plan by watching the parts of the brain that light up as the idea forms and becomes realized. Lopez talks about creating hopes from memories, and thus the prospection pipeline begins in the hippocampus, where memories are examined and often used as the basis for new imaginings. Hope, a form of imagining in some ways, may start here as we begin to take stock of what has happened before and what that might mean we could do in the future. Once the ideas have been examined, the next stop along the pipeline might be the rostral anterior cingulate cortex (rACC), which works with the amygdala to determine how important our various mental images and plans are and to attach emotional meaning to them. As Lopez says, "It pushes you to make smart choices" (p. 43). The last stop on the pipeline is the prefrontal cortex. Thoughts and ideas that are deemed meaningful and emotionally provocative change into action in the prefrontal cortex. It is here that the hopeful pathway begins to emerge in a way that looks like Snyder and colleagues' (1991) operationalization of hope. Ideas about pathways, obstacles, and ways around obstacles begin to emerge in our minds, and we can then begin our journey along these pathways, motivated by that prospection pipeline that got us started on the process. Using neuroscience to understand processes such as this is invaluable in helping us to understand how to shape our future as we would like.

Scales: Can Hope Be Measured?

Using hope theory, Snyder and his colleagues developed several self-report scales. First, Snyder, Harris, et al. (1991) developed a 12-item trait measure for adults ages 16 and older in which 4 items reflect pathways, 4 items reflect agency, and 4 items are distracters. An example pathways item is "I can think of many ways to get out of a jam," and an example agency item is "I energetically pursue my goals." Respondents respond to each item on an 8-point Likert continuum (1 = Definitely false to 8 = Definitely true).

The internal consistency (alpha level) typically has been in the .80 range, and test–retest reliabilities have been .80 or above over time periods of 8 to 10 weeks (Snyder, Harris, et al., 1991). Furthermore, there are extensive data on the concurrent validity of the Hope Scale in regard to its predicted positive correlations with scales tapping such similar concepts as optimism, expectancy for attaining goals, expected control, and self-esteem, and there have been negative correlations with scales reflecting such opposite constructs as hopelessness, depression, and pathologies. Finally, several factor-analytic studies provide support for the pathways and agency components of the Hope Scale (Babyak, Snyder, & Yoshinobu, 1993).

The Children's Hope Scale (CHS; Snyder, Hoza, et al., 1997) is a six-item self-report trait measure appropriate for children age 8 to 15. Three of the six items reflect agency thinking (e.g., "I think I am doing pretty well"), and three reflect pathways thinking (e.g., "When I have a problem, I can come up with lots of ways to solve it"). Children respond to the items on a 6-point Likert continuum (1 = None of the time to 6 = All of the time). The alphas have been close to .80 across several samples, and the test–retest reliabilities for 1-month intervals have been .70 to .80. The CHS has shown convergent validity in terms of its positive relationships with other indices of strengths (e.g., self-worth) and negative relationships with indices of problems (e.g., depression). Lastly, factor analyses have corroborated the two-factor structure of the CHS (Snyder, Hoza, et al., 1997). Both Portuguese (Marques, Pais-Ribeiro, & Lopez, 2009), and Spanish (L. M. Edwards, November 14,

2013, personal communication) language versions of the CHS have recently been developed and determined psychometrically valid as well.

Snyder and colleagues (Snyder, Sympson, et al., 1996) also developed the State Hope Scale (SHS), a six-item self-report scale that taps here-and-now goal-directed thinking. Three items reflect pathways thinking (e.g., "There are lots of ways around any problem that I am facing now") and three items reflect agency thinking ("At the present time, I am energetically pursuing my goals"). The response range is 1 = Definitely false to 8 = Definitely true. Internal reliabilities are quite high (alphas often in the .90 range). Strong concurrent validity results also show that SHS scores correlate positively with state indices of self-esteem and positive affect and negatively with state indices of negative affect. Likewise, manipulation-based studies reveal that SHS scores increase or decrease according to situational successes or failures in goal-directed activities. Finally, factor analysis has supported the two-factor structure of the SHS (Snyder, Sympson, et al., 1996). Finally, hope scales have also been created involving specific domains of life (e.g., the Academic Hope Scale and the Math Hope Scale), and many of these measures have also been found to be psychometrically valid (Robinson & Rose, 2010).

What Hope Predicts

For a detailed review of the predictions flowing from Hope Scale scores, see Snyder (2002a). What is noteworthy about the results related to these predictions is that the statistically significant findings typically remain, even after mathematical correction for the influences of a variety of other self-report psychological measures, such as optimism, self-efficacy, and self-esteem. In general, Hope Scale scores have predicted outcomes in academics, sports, physical health, adjustment, and psychotherapy. For example, in the area of academics, higher Hope Scale scores obtained at the beginning of college have predicted better cumulative grade point averages and whether students remain in school (Snyder, Shorey, et al., 2002). In the area of sports, higher Hope Scale scores obtained at the beginning of college track season have predicted the superior performances of male athletes and have done so beyond the coach's rating of natural athletic abilities (Curry, Snyder, Cook, Ruby, & Rehm, 1997). In the area of adjustment, higher Hope Scale scores have related to various indices of elevated happiness, satisfaction, positive emotions, and getting along with others, to name a few (Marques, Lopez, & Mitchell, 2013; Snyder, Harris, et al., 1991). Additionally, hope has been advanced as the common factor underlying the positive changes that happen in psychological treatments (Snyder, Ilardi, Cheavens, et al., 2000). Recently, the basic premise that Snyder's scale predicts goal attainment was tested by Feldman, Rand, and Kahle-Wrobleski (2009). In this research, the agency portion of the Hope Scale was found to most successfully predict goal attainment in college students. The seemingly greater strength of agency (as compared to pathways and, at times, overall hope) in predicting other positive outcomes is something that has been found in other samples as well (e.g., Tong, Fredrickson, Chang, & Lim, 2010).

Hope, too, has been investigated in different cultures, and the results begin to elucidate our understanding of the contextual influences on this construct. Chang and Banks (2007) investigated the applicability of Snyder's (1994, 2002) hope model in a diverse population and found that predictors of hope and its factors of pathways and agency might vary between racial or ethnic groups. For example, in European Americans in this study, life satisfaction was the strongest predictor of agentic thinking, but it had no significant predictive power toward agentic thinking in the Asian American portion of the sample (Chang & Banks, 2007). In Latinos in Chang and Banks's sample, rational problem solving (i.e., a deliberate and rational approach to solving problems) was the strongest significant predictor of agentic thinking; this construct was not significantly predictive of this trait in European Americans. Positive affect was the strongest predictor of agentic thinking in Asian Americans, but it was not a significant predictor for Latinos or European Americans.

Differences between racial and ethnic groups in terms of the mean overall hope, agency, and pathways scores were also found in this comprehensive study (Chang & Banks, 2007). Some racial and ethnic minority groups appear to have higher mean scores in agentic and pathways thinking when compared to majority groups. Chang and Banks hypothesized that the types of obstacles faced by these different cultural groups (e.g., racism, discrimination) may differ substantially, and these experiences may lead some individuals to have more practice at dealing with obstacles in life, which may in turn lead to higher scores.

Recently, other researchers have looked at hope in a racially diverse sample within the context of the relationship between depression and suicidal behavior (Hirsch, Visser, Chang, & Jeglic, 2012). These researchers measured trait hope (via Snyder and colleagues' [1991] model), hopelessness, depression, and suicidal thoughts/behavior (including ideation, attempts, etc., over the lifetime). Findings showed different patterns of data when comparing different racial groups. In Latino and White samples, higher-hope individuals were less likely to have many suicidal behaviors as a result of their depression, but this was not found in the African American or Asian American participants. In these cases, hope (either high or low) was a better predictor of suicidal behavior than hopelessness (Hirsch et al., 2012). In addition, lack of hope (measured by the Beck Hopelessness Scale) was a better predictor of suicidal behavior (as opposed to depression) for both African American and White participants, though this was not found in the Latino or Asian samples. (Note: Some of Hirsch and colleagues' [2012] conclusions about Asian Americans must be tempered, as the sample size was small compared to the other racial groups). Thus, this study provides more evidence for the fact that hope may interact with other constructs differently in different racial groups (See Hirsch et al., [2012] for a more thorough description of hypotheses for why results occurred in this way).

Though more research needs to be conducted on various groups, this information, coupled with the findings regarding optimism in Chang's earlier (2001a) study, provides evidence that the links between hope, life satisfaction, optimism, and other psychological constructs related to adjustment seem to differ across racial and/or ethnic groups. Thus, these differences must be taken into account when attempting to develop interventions and explanations for these constructs.

In regard to interventions to enhance hope, see our discussion of the various approaches in Chapter 14. For the reader with considerable background in psychotherapy, a thorough overview of hope theory interventions can be found in Snyder's edited volume, *Handbook of Hope* (2000b). For the reader with less experience in psychotherapy, "how-to" descriptions for enhancing adults' hopes can be found in Lopez's *Making Hope Happen* (2013) and in Snyder's *The Psychology of Hope: You Can Get There From Here* (1994/2004). "How-to" descriptions for raising children's hopes are described in McDermott and Snyder's *The Great Big Book of Hope* (2000) and in Snyder, McDermott, et al.'s *Hope for the Journey: Helping Children Through the Good Times and the Bad* (2002).

The Latest Frontier—Collective Hope

As with the concept of self-efficacy, hope researchers also have expanded their construct to explore what is called collective hope (see Snyder & Feldman, 2000). Simply put, collective hope reflects the level of goal-directed thinking of a large group of people. Often, such collective hope is operative when several people join together to tackle a goal that would be impossible for any one person. Snyder and Feldman (2000) have applied the notion of collective hope more generally to the topics of disarmament, preservation of environmental resources, health insurance, and government.

Hope in Our Current Times

Hope has been a term frequently used by our current administration in the United States. After President Barack Obama was elected the first time, many in the United States commented that an era of new hope was being ushered in for all individuals living in the United States. With the election of our first non-White president, people in this country of all ages and races reported feelings of hope that opportunities long prevented by racism and discrimination were now opening to a larger group. President Obama himself titled his book *The Audacity of Hope*. In addressing the National Democratic Convention in Boston in 2004, well before his own election campaign, he stated,

> In the end, that's what this election is about. Do we participate in a politics of cynicism or a politics of hope? . . . I'm not talking about blind optimism here—the almost willful ignorance that thinks unemployment will go away if we just don't talk about it, or the health care crisis will solve itself if we just ignore it. No, I'm talking about something more substantial. It's the hope of slaves sitting around a fire singing freedom songs; the hope of immigrants setting out for distant shores; the hope of a young naval lieutenant bravely patrolling the Mekong Delta; the hope of a millworker's son who dares to defy the odds; the hope of a skinny kid with a funny name who believes that America has a place for him, too. Hope in the face of difficulty. Hope in the face of uncertainty. The audacity of hope!"

As hope has often been touted as false or foolish, it is an interesting change to be called upon by a leader to use hope as a tool to move forward and to work to solve problems within the United States. This points to an expansion of the understanding of positive characteristics such as hope, optimism, and self-efficacy and their use in our current era as traits that should be cultivated and used regularly, and it may represent a paradigm shift in our current world.

Life Enhancement Strategies

Self-efficacy, optimism, and hope provide the momentum needed to pursue a good life. Therefore, we encourage you to use the self-efficacy, optimism, and hope you already possess to improve functioning in important domains of your life.

Love

- Build new confidence in your relationships by observing someone who is quite skilled in managing friendships and romantic relationships. Emulate his or her behavior as appropriate.

- Approach your next visit with extended family with a flexible explanatory style. When positive events occur, be sure to identify your role in the family success.

- Set goals for important relationships that will help you grow closer to others. Be sure to identify multiple pathways and sources of agency for pursuing these aims.

Work

- Develop new skills for work or school by attending training or study sessions that will help you approach your assignments with increased confidence.

- When a new project is assigned to you, expect that the best will happen. Nurture those optimistic thoughts daily as you work toward successful completion of the project.

- Break down a big task into small goals and direct your energy toward pursuing small goal after small goal.

Play

- Watch an hour of educational television for children. Attempt to identify the many messages designed to enhance self-efficacy.

- Play a board game or a sport with a friend and attempt to respond to a poor outcome with a flexible explanatory approach.

- Identify a personal goal associated with your favorite leisure activity that you hope to attain in the next month. Identify and procure all the resources you need to make progress toward that goal.

PUTTING TEMPORAL FUTURES IN PERSPECTIVE

We now juxtapose the orientations that focus on the future (i.e., the ones we have explored in this chapter) with those that focus on either the past or the present. We do this because comparing these three orientations toward time may foster a better understanding of the possible role of a balanced temporal orientation in producing a productive and satisfying life (see Boniwell & Zimbardo, 2004).

There are advantages and disadvantages to each of the three temporal orientations—the past, the present, and the future. Let us begin, for example, with the past orientation, which often is characterized by an emphasis on pleasurable views of previous interpersonal relationships with friends and family. This somewhat sentimental perspective focuses on the happiness to be derived in warm personal interactions. However, there is no guarantee that the view of the past is positive; those who hold negative views about their pasts are filled with ruminations, anxieties, and depressive thoughts and feelings. Additionally, assessment of the use of this orientation must be viewed using a cultural lens. For example, from a Western perspective, the past orientation can produce a very conservative, overly cautious approach to one's life and a desire to preserve the status quo, making the person unwilling to experience new things. From an Eastern perspective, however, paying attention to the past might ensure safe passage of traditions and ritual from generation to generation.

Let us next explore the person who lives in the here and now. The person who lives for the present can be described in hedonistic terms that have both good and bad consequences. The individual who lives in the moment derives great pleasure in highly intense activities, relishes the thrills and excitements found in the here and now, and remains open to the ongoing adventures of the moment. The person focused on the present also may place a premium on excitement.

One aspect of enjoying the ongoing experience can be savoring (Bryant, 2004; Bryant & Veroff, 2006). Although savoring can be applied to the past or the future, one of the most robust types of savoring pertains to the enjoyment of the moment, perhaps even acting to stretch out an ongoing positive event. As balloonist Bertrand Piccard observed in his 1999 trip around the world, "During the last night, I savor once more the intimate relationship we have established with our planet. I feel so privileged that I want to enjoy every second of this air world" (Piccard, 1999, p. 44).

When considered from a Western perspective, the concerns that arise from this **present orientation** all reflect the fact that such a person may not think ahead about the potential liabilities of such excitement seeking. Although most of us probably do not remember our toddler years, it is likely that we then lived a here-and-now existence as we pursued our momentary whims and desires to the fullest. When adults are committed solely to this present orientation, however, some may suffer the negative consequences of hedonistic adventures. For example, addictions, injuries from accidents, and various temptations can destroy the career aspirations of the person who lives

Philip Zimbardo

Source: Reprinted with permission of Philip Zimbardo.

only with such a hedonistic present orientation. Such people take risks in a variety of arenas, including the driving of automobiles, sexual encounters, and drug use (Keough, Zimbardo, & Boyd, 1999). Much of our current description of the present orientation has a distinctly Western flavor; an Eastern perspective or an American Indian perspective would include a meditative appreciation of the calmness that flows from a here-and-now orientation (see Chapter 10 for discussions of optimal experiences of the present). If one considers these other cultural perspectives, many of these more negative possibilities are less likely to appear (if they appear at all).

Lastly, there is the future temporal perspective, which has formed the core theme of this chapter. The person with a future orientation thinks ahead to the possible consequences of his or her actions. As we have learned, future-oriented people form clear goals and conjure the requisite paths to reach those goals. They are likely to engage in preventive behaviors to lessen the likelihood of bad things happening in the future. Furthermore, as we have learned in the literature on self-efficacy, optimism, and hope reviewed in this chapter, such people are typically successful in life's endeavors—in academics, jobs, sports, health, and so on. Some future-oriented people may not do very well, however, at experiencing the enormous pleasure that can be derived from just being with others or recalling previous interpersonal activities. Additionally, future orientation may not be viewed in a positive light by all cultures.

In reading about the past, present, and future orientations, you may be intrigued about which orientation characterizes your own life. Stanford psychologist Philip Zimbardo (Zimbardo & Boyd, 1999) has developed and validated a trait-like measure of temporal orientation, the Zimbardo Time Perspective Inventory (see Appendix B). Although people have accentuated the past, present, or future at given moments, they also are disposed across situations to one of these temporal orientations. Thus, temporal orientations can have a trait-like quality.

In the Personal Mini-Experiments are two approaches to help you answer the question of how you use your time. First, we encourage you to try the "What's Ahead" exercise. In this exercise, you will monitor your thoughts for one day in order to see to what degree you are focused on the past, present, and future. Students who have tried this exercise report that they find the results surprising and worthwhile.

PERSONAL MINI-EXPERIMENTS

Balancing Your Perspective on Time

In this chapter, we discuss the benefits of future orientation and balancing time perspectives. Our review suggests that our orientation to time affects positive and negative outcomes alike. Here are a few ideas for experimenting with increasing your awareness of how you view time.

What's Ahead. Although you may have a rough idea about how much time you spend thinking about the future, we have found it useful for people actually to reflect on their days to produce an estimate of the time spent "in the past," "in the present," and "in the future." Mark a piece of lined paper with columns and rows (see the example following). From the top down in each column, write the hours of your day (1:00 a.m., 2:00 a.m., 3:00 a.m., etc.), and across the top in a row, write the words *Past, Present,* and *Future.* Now you have a chart on which you can note how many minutes in each hour were spent in thoughts of the past, present, or future. It helps to print this chart on a small piece of card stock that you can

(Continued)

(Continued)

Time	Past	Present	Future
7:00 a.m.			
8:00 a.m.			
9:00 a.m.			
10:00 a.m.			
11:00 a.m.			
12:00 p.m.			
1:00 p.m.			
And so on			
Totals			

place in your pocket or purse along with a small pencil for the hourly recording of your time spent in each perspective.

If you can, in the last minute of each hour from 7:00 a.m. to midnight (or whatever your waking hours may be), estimate the number of minutes you spent in that previous hour thinking about the past, present, or future. If you found yourself in a flow-like experience, totally engrossed in whatever you were doing, and the time just seemed to fly, count that under *Present*. Lastly, sum the number of past, present, or future minutes across the hours that you were awake. The next day, figure out how you spent most of your time. For most people, even during busy hours, considerable time was spent thinking ahead about goals and plans to reach those goals. We do this virtually from the moment we awaken and think about what we will be doing that day. Remember, there are no right or wrong ways to spend your time. Instead, the purpose is to sensitize you to the temporal foci of your thinking. Realize also that the results of this experiment may depend on the day of the week, your health, your age, whether you are on vacation, the time of year, where you live, your job, and so on. Most people who complete this exercise, however, are somewhat surprised by how much time they spend thinking about the future.

Toward a Balanced Time Perspective. After completing and scoring the Zimbardo Time Perspective Inventory (see Appendix B), identify the most meaningful event you will experience in the upcoming week (i.e., the event you are most looking forward to or the one you are most dreading). Once you have identified that event, daydream about how you will approach it with the temporal orientation you typically hold across situations (past-negative, past-positive, present-fatalistic, present-hedonistic, future). Jot down notes about how your orientation to time might affect the outcome of the event. Then, consider how you might approach the event if you held one of the other orientations. Are there benefits to this alternative orientation to time? Most people realize that perceptions of time can affect present and future experiences.

As part of the Personal Mini-Experiments, you can take the Zimbardo Time Perspective Inventory (Zimbardo & Boyd, 1999) presented in Appendix B. With this scale, you can ascertain the degree to which each of the following five temporal orientations best characterizes you across situations: (1) past-negative, (2) past-positive, (3) present-fatalistic, (4) present-hedonistic, or (5) future. By completing the "What's Ahead" Personal Mini-Experiment and the "Balance Exercise" associated with the Zimbardo Time Perspective Inventory, you should be able to see the past, present, and future temporal orientations in your life.

The key to having a balance in these three temporal perspectives is your ability to operate in the temporal orientation that best fits the situation in which you find yourself. This balance, according to Boniwell and Zimbardo (2004, p. 176), entails the following: "Working hard when it's time to work. Playing intensively when it's time to play. Enjoying listening to grandma's old stories while she is still alive. Viewing children though the eyes of wonder with which they see the world. Laughing at jokes and life's absurdities. Indulging in desire and passion."

Being flexible and capable of switching to an appropriate temporal orientation yields the most productive approach to how we spend our time. Having said this, however, it is clear that cultural context plays a large role in what type of temporal orientation feels right and is validated by the societies and communities of which we are a part. We touch on this important point in the next and final section of this chapter.

CULTURAL CAVEATS ABOUT TEMPORAL PERSPECTIVE

Much of the research presented in this chapter deals with a perspective on temporal orientations that reflects that of Caucasian Americans, who overwhelmingly have been the research participants in the various reported studies. Be clear, therefore, that some in the United States and members of other, non-Western cultures may *not* share the perspectives on self-efficacy, optimism, and hope that we have presented. (See Chapter 4 for a detailed discussion of culture and positive psychology; See Chapter 2 for more details on both Western and Eastern philosophies.) Not only may these non-Western perspectives differ in their implementation of self-efficacy, optimism, and hope, they also may not value these to the same degree that we have in writing about them in this chapter.

Additionally, in many cases the instruments we have described may not be sensitive to the nuances of non-Western people. Clearly, Caucasian cultural groups in the United States and other Western cultures place a priority on the mastery of their futures and emphasize action- or goal-oriented activities and the individual rather than the collective perspective (Carter, 1991). Moreover, the Caucasian Americans about whom we have reported in this chapter are judged by what they do more so than by what they are. So, too, are these research participants, in a manner similar to Western cultural bias (Stewart, 1972), probably focused on controlling their surrounding environments and, in so doing, view time in a linear manner (and consider planning for the future crucial).

Contrast the former perspective, for example, with the American Indian accentuation of the here and now (Trimble, 1976). For American Indians, time is seen as a kind of flowing and relative resource that is to be focused upon; instead of "going by the clock," things are done as needed (Soldier, 1992). Similarly, Cuban Americans, Mexican Americans, and Puerto Rican Americans all appear to prefer a present orientation to a future one (Chandler, 1979; Inclan, 1985; Szapozcnik, Scopetta, & King, 1978). Generally, American Indians, Latinos/Latinas, African Americans, and Asian Americans perceive time in a *polychronic* manner—many things are conceptualized as happening at once with people. Moreover, time is viewed as a plentiful resource, and human relationships take priority over it (Schauber, 2001). Contrast this with the European American culture, in which time is linear, sequential, and *monochronic* (also consider the value placed on time in the phrase "time is money"; Schauber, 2001).

There is considerable variation, however, even within the multicultural context of the United States as a whole, as has been noted at other points in this chapter. Furthermore, as we begin to flesh out the types of differences that exist within the U.S. culture regarding perspectives that relate to self-efficacy, optimism, and hope, it is probably accurate to infer that the differences are even larger when comparisons are made to cultures outside the United States.

In Eastern cultures (as exemplified by Asian countries), the traditional view is to see the self and other people as interrelated (Kim, Triandis, Kagitcibasi, Choi, & Yoon, 1994; Markus & Kitayama, 1991). Thus, contrary to the Western values, the Eastern view is to accentuate harmonious interdependence among interacting persons (see Chapter 2; Weisz, Rothbaum, & Blackburn, 1984). Furthermore, in the Eastern perspective, the experience of suffering is seen as a necessary part of human existence (Chang, 2001b). This emphasis on people serves to make temporal concerns far less important in Eastern cultures.

In closing this chapter by comparing persons from different cultural backgrounds, we seek to point out how important it is to consider the cultural context of the theories, research hypotheses, and conclusions, and of the participants involved in the study of any construct or process. It is important that future positive psychology thinkers *not* assume that Western-based theories and scales can and will translate in obvious ways to Eastern cultures (See Chapter 3 for a more thorough discussion of *conceptual equivalence*). We strongly believe that positive psychology should be a worldwide initiative, and thus we must take care to test any theories and measures across cultures before drawing inferences about "universally" applicable findings. As such, we are reminded of the wisdom inherent in the old proverb, "To be uncertain is to be uncomfortable, but to be certain sometimes can be ridiculous."

APPENDIX A: A SUMMARY OF HOPE THEORIES

Averill

Averill, Catlin, and Chon (1990) define hope in cognitive terms as appropriate when goals are (1) reasonably attainable (i.e., have an intermediate level of difficulty), (2) under control, (3) viewed as important, and (4) acceptable at social and moral levels.

Breznitz

Breznitz (1986) proposed five metaphors to capture the operations of hope in response to stressors, with hope as (1) a protected area, (2) a bridge, (3) an intention, (4) performance, and (5) an end in itself. He also cautioned that hope may be an illusion akin to denial.

Erikson

Erik Erikson (1964, p. 118) defined hope as "the enduring belief in the attainability of fervent wishes" and posed dialectics between hope and other motives, one of the strongest and most important being trust/hope versus mistrust, which is the infant's first task. Another broad dialectic, according to Erikson (1982), pertains to the generativity of hope versus stagnation.

Gottschalk

For Gottschalk (1974), hope involves positive expectancies about specific favorable outcomes, and it impels a person to move through psychological problems. He developed a hope scale to analyze the content of 5-minute segments of spoken words. This hope measurement has concurrent validity in terms of its positive correlations with positive human relations and achievement and its negative relationships to higher anxiety, hostility, and social alienation.

Marcel

Basing his definition on the coping of prisoners of war, Marcel (see Godfrey, 1987) concluded that hope gives people the power to cope with helpless circumstances.

Mowrer

Mowrer (1960) proposed that hope was an emotion that occurred when rats observed a stimulus that was linked with something pleasurable. Mowrer also described the antithesis of hope, or fear, which he said entailed a type of dread in which the animal lessened its activity level and that, as such, fear impedes their goal pursuits.

Staats

Staats (1989, p. 367) defined hope as "the interaction between wishes and expectations." Staats and colleagues developed instruments for tapping the affective and cognitive aspects of hope. To measure affective hope, the Expected Balance Scale (EBS; Staats, 1989) entails 18 items for which respondents use a 5-point Likert continuum. To measure cognitive hope, the Hope Index (Staats & Stassen, as cited in Staats, 1989) focuses on particular events and their outcomes and contains the subscales of Hope-Self, Hope-Other, Wish, and Expect. The Hope Index contains 16 items, and respondents use a 6-point Likert continuum (0 = Not at all to 5 = Very much) to rate both the degree to which they "wish this to occur" and "expect this to occur."

Stotland

Stotland (1969) explored the role of expectancies and cognitive schemas and described hope as involving important goals for which there is a reasonably high perceived probability of attainment. Using Stotland's (1969) model, Erickson, Post, and Paige (1975) designed a hope scale that consists of 20 general and common (i.e., not situation-specific) goals. This hope scale yields scores of average importance and average probability across these goals. There is little reported research, however, using this scale.

APPENDIX B: ZIMBARDO TIME PERSPECTIVE INVENTORY ITEMS

Directions: Read each item carefully. Using the 5-point scale shown below, please select the number to indicate how characteristic each statement is of you in the blank provided.

1	2	3	4	5
Very Uncharacteristic	Uncharacteristic	Neutral	Characteristic	Very Characteristic

_____ 1. I believe that getting together with one's friends to party is one of life's important pleasures.

_____ 2. Familiar childhood sights, sounds, smells often bring back a flood of wonderful memories.

_____ 3. Fate determines much in my life.

_____ 4. I often think of what I should have done differently in my life.

_____ 5. My decisions are mostly influenced by people and things around me.

_____ 6. I believe that a person's day should be planned ahead each morning.

_____ 7. It gives me pleasure to think about my past.

_____ 8. I do things impulsively.

_____ 9. If things don't get done on time, I don't worry about it.

_____10. When I want to achieve something, I set goals and consider specific means for reaching those goals.

1	2	3	4	5
Very Uncharacteristic	**Uncharacteristic**	**Neutral**	**Characteristic**	**Very Characteristic**

_____11. On balance, there is much more good to recall than bad in the past.

_____12. When listening to my favorite music, I often lose track of time.

_____13. Meeting tomorrow's deadlines and doing other necessary work comes before tonight's play.

_____14. Since whatever will be will be, it doesn't really matter what I do.

_____15. I enjoy stories about how things used to be in the "good old times."

_____16. Painful past experiences keep being replayed in my mind.

_____17. I try to live my life as fully as possible, one day at a time.

_____18. It upsets me to be late for appointments.

_____19. Ideally, I would live each day as if it were my last.

_____20. Happy memories of good times spring readily to mind.

_____21. I meet my obligations to friends and authorities on time.

_____22. I've taken my share of abuse and rejection in the past.

_____23. I make decisions on the spur of the moment.

_____24. I take each day as it is rather than try to plan it out.

_____25. The past has too many unpleasant memories that I prefer not to think about.

_____26. It is important to put excitement in my life.

_____27. I've made mistakes in the past that I wish I could undo.

_____28. I feel that it's more important to enjoy what you're doing than to get work done on time.

_____29. I get nostalgic about my childhood.

_____30. Before making a decision, I weigh the costs against the benefits.

_____31. Taking risks keeps my life from becoming boring.

_____32. It's more important for me to enjoy life's journey than to focus only on the destination.

_____33. Things rarely work out as I expected.

_____34. It's hard for me to forget unpleasant images of my youth.

(Continued)

(Continued)

1	2	3	4	5
Very Uncharacteristic	Uncharacteristic	Neutral	Characteristic	Very Characteristic

_____35. It takes joy out of the process and flow of my activities if I have to think about goals, outcomes, and products.

_____36. Even when I am enjoying the present, I am drawn back to comparisons with similar past experiences.

_____37. You can't really plan for the future because things change so much.

_____38. My life path is controlled by forces I cannot influence.

_____39. It doesn't make sense to worry about the future, since there is nothing I can do about it anyway.

_____40. I complete projects on time by making steady progress.

_____41. I find myself tuning out when family members talk about the way things used to be.

_____42. I take risks to put excitement in my life.

_____43. I make lists of things to do.

_____44. I often follow my heart more than my head.

_____45. I am able to resist temptations when I know that there is work to be done.

_____46. I find myself getting swept up in the excitement of the moment.

_____47. Life today is too complicated; I would prefer the simpler life of the past.

_____48. I prefer friends who are spontaneous rather than predictable.

_____49. I like family rituals and traditions that are regularly repeated.

_____50. I think about the bad things that have happened to me in the past.

_____51. I keep working at difficult, uninteresting tasks if they will help me get ahead.

_____52. Spending what I earn on pleasures today is better than saving for tomorrow's security.

_____53. Often luck pays off better than hard work.

_____54. I think about the good things that I have missed out on in my life.

_____55. I like my close relationships to be passionate.

_____56. There will always be time to catch up on my work.

1	2	3	4	5
Very Uncharacteristic	**Uncharacteristic**	**Neutral**	**Characteristic**	**Very Characteristic**

To obtain the scores for each of the five subfactors, (1) reverse code all the relevant items, (2) add the scores for each item that contributes to the specific subfactor, and (3) divide the subfactor total by the number of questions that constitute the subfactor.
Past-Negative = Items 4, 5, 16, 22, 27, 33, 34, 36, 50, and 54
Past-Positive = Items 2, 7, 11, 15, 20, 25, 29, 41, and 49
Present-Fatalistic = Items 3, 14, 35, 37, 38, 39, 47, 52, and 53
Present-Hedonistic = Items 1, 8, 12, 17, 19, 23, 26, 28, 31, 32, 42, 44, 46, 48, and 55
Future = Items 6, 9, 10, 13, 18, 21, 24, 30, 40, 43, 45, 51, and 56

Appendix B Source: Zimbardo, P. G. & Boyd, J. N. "Putting time in perspective: A valid, reliable individual-differences metric," in *Journal of Personality and Social Psychology,* 77(6), 1271–1288. Copyright 1999 by the American Psychological Association. Reproduced with permission.

NOTE

1. As noted later in this chapter and in Chapter 4, Asian Americans who are higher in pessimism are also higher in problem-solving (Chang, 2001).

KEY TERMS

Agency thinking: The requisite motivations to use routes to desired goals. (Compare with *pathways thinking.*)

Bicultural self-efficacy: Confidence in one's ability to navigate both one's culture of origin and a second culture. May include a comfort with language in both cultures (e.g., translation); appropriate social interaction (understanding cultural norms); and an ability to understand both worldviews.

Collective hope: Goal-directed thinking in which a group of people have the perceived capacity to find routes to desired goals and the requisite motivations to use those routes.

Collective self-efficacy: The degree to which a group of people believe they can work together to accomplish shared goals.

Cultural self-efficacy: the perception of one's own capability to mobilize motivation, cognitive resources, and courses of action necessary in situations characterized by diversity.

Future orientations: Perspectives in which one emphasizes future events and the consequences of one's actions. Future-oriented people focus on planning for things to come.

Learned optimism: Characteristic use of a flexible explanatory style in which one has learned to make external (outside oneself), variable (not consistent), and specific (limited to a specific situation) attributions for one's failures. In contrast, pessimists have learned to view failures as due to internal (characteristics of the self), stable (consistent), and global (not limited to a specific situation) attributions.

Optimism: One's expectancy that good things rather than bad will happen. It is a stable trait in some people and is independent of self-efficacy (Scheier & Carver, 1985).

Pathways thinking: The perceived capacity to find routes to desired goals. (Compare with *agency thinking*.)

Past orientation: A perspective in which one emphasizes past occurrences, pleasurable experiences, or previous relationships when thinking about time.

Present orientation: A perspective in which one emphasizes the here and now, looking to the present to experience pleasure and satisfy needs.

Self-efficacy: Belief that one's skills and capabilities are enough to accomplish one's desired goals in a specific situation.

Situational perspective: A view of psychological concepts (such as self-efficacy) as situationally, or context, specific—that is, that the specific setting influences how a psychological phenomenon is manifested. As the situation varies, the concept varies in turn. (Compare with *trait perspective*.)

Social cognitive theory: A theory suggesting that people's self-efficacy (confidence in their abilities) influences their actions and thoughts in such a way that it shapes their environment. For example, a young girl who thinks she might be good at basketball tries out for the team. Trying out for the basketball team, in turn, gives the child opportunities to develop her skills and gain confidence in her abilities. Then the child thinks more positively about her ability to do a variety of sports. Therefore, the child's beliefs influenced the type of environment in which she pursued goals.

Trait perspective: An approach to understanding a psychological concept (such as self-efficacy) as part of the enduring characteristics of a person—a part of their disposition that is evident across situations. (Compare with *situational perspective*.)

CHAPTER 9

Wisdom and Courage

Characteristics of the Wise and the Brave

God grant me the serenity to accept the things I cannot change, courage to change the things I can, and the wisdom to know the difference.

—Attributed to Reinhold Niebuhr

The serenity prayer has become the credo for many ordinary people who are struggling with life challenges. We open with this reference because it makes two points that we examine throughout this chapter. First, as the prayer reveals, the notions of wisdom and courage have been intermingled, historically, in literature. We will examine this link and the reasons for it. Second, the prayer suggests that the extraordinary qualities of wisdom and courage are available to everyone. This point is discussed in the context of the reviews pertaining to wisdom and courage.

WISDOM AND COURAGE: TWO OF A KIND

Some philosophers and theologians consider wisdom (prudence) and courage (fortitude) to be two of the four cardinal virtues (along with justice and temperance). These primary virtues, traditionally ranked in the order prudence, justice, fortitude, and temperance, "are cognitive and motivational dispositions that in themselves designate not only adaptive fitness for individuals' achievements, but also the idea of convergence of individual goal achievements with becoming and being a good person from a communal and social-ethical point of view" (Baltes, Glück, & Kunzmann, 2002, p. 328). The cardinal virtues facilitate personal development; good living through practicing them may foster the development of social resources that spark the growth of other people. Both wisdom and courage can inform human choices and fuel pursuits that lead to enhanced personal functioning and communal good. Courage also can help overcome obstacles that make the practice of other virtues more difficult.

Wisdom and courage often have been studied together, although their intermingling may cause difficulties in distinguishing them. This construct confusion is captured in a statement from the movie *The Wizard of Oz* (Haley & Fleming, 1939), in which the Wizard says to the Cowardly Lion, "As for you, my fine friend, you are a victim of disorganized thinking. You are under the unfortunate delusion that, simply because you run away from danger, you have no courage. You're confusing courage with wisdom."

Wisdom and strength both exemplify human excellence; they involve a challenge, they require sound decision making, they are culturally bound, and they typically contribute to the common good. Furthermore, as mentioned in the introduction to this chapter, ordinary people can demonstrate both of these extraordinary qualities. Without question, however, the scholarly discussion aimed at clarifying the relationship between wisdom and courage will be complex. In some cases, wisdom is characterized as the predecessor of courage. Moreover, in

The Cowardly Lion (played by Bert Lahr)

Source: © Bettmann/CORBIS.

the strongest form of the argument, St. Ambrose believed that "[f]ortitude without justice is a level of evil" (cited in Pieper, 1966, p. 125). Some people even reason that wisdom can make courage unnecessary. This view is described in the words of Staudinger and Baltes (1994):

> [W]e need courage only in those instances when in fact they [wisdom and faith] do not suffice—either because we simply lack them or because they are irrelevant to or ineffective against our distress. Knowledge, wisdom, and opinion can provide fear with its objects or deprive it of them. They do not impart courage but rather offer an opportunity to exercise it or do without it. (p. 57)

In contrast to this perspective, courage has been portrayed as a precursor of wisdom. The logic here is that the capacity for courageous action is necessary before one can pursue a noble outcome or common good that is defined by wisdom. Courage sometimes is viewed as the virtue that makes all virtuous behaviors possible. Irrespective of their relative power or import, we believe that a discussion of implicit and explicit theories of wisdom and courage will help in understanding their importance in our daily lives.

THEORIES OF WISDOM

Wisdom often is referenced in ancient maxims (e.g., Yang, 2001) and in philosophical reviews. For example, Robinson's (1990) review of early Western classical dialogues revealed three distinct conceptualizations of wisdom: (1) that found in persons seeking a contemplative life (the Greek term *sophia*); (2) that of a practical nature, as displayed by great statesmen (*phronesis*); and

(3) scientific understanding (*episteme*). Aristotle added to the list of types of wisdom by describing *theoretikes,* the theoretical thought and knowledge devoted to truth, and distinguishing it from *phronesis* (practical wisdom). (See the comments of classics professors as shared by Roger Martin.)

During the fifteenth, sixteenth, and seventeenth centuries in the Western world, two issues dominated the scholarly discussion of wisdom. Philosophers, theologians, and cultural anthropologists debated the philosophical versus pragmatic applications of virtue, along with the divine or human nature of the quality (Rice, 1958). Both issues relate to the question of whether wisdom is a form of excellence in living as displayed by ordinary people or is more aptly seen as a fuzzy philosophical quality possessed only by sages. These issues have yet to be resolved, although psychology scholars have suggested recently that ordinary people are capable of living a good life by applying wisdom.

Wisdom Difficult to Define, Attain
Roger Martin

One day, somebody said, "I enjoy reading your column, but I'm not always sure what it does for the university."

It was one of those hot-potato moments.

I thought fast and tossed this back:

"Universities create knowledge through research and distribute it through teaching.

"The column suggests that, in doing that, universities are one of the sources of wisdom. And that's a great thing. Right?"

I wasn't actually that articulate or concise.

But that's what I meant.

Later, I started to wonder if I was jiving.

I think of this piece I do as a knowledge column. I realized I'd defend it because I love to write about the ideas that come to bright people who passionately study one thing.

The possible jive I detected was in my attempt to connect knowledge with wisdom. I wondered whether that was legitimate.

I called two University of Kansas professors of classics, Tony Corbeill and Stan Lombardo, thinking that, because they study the ancient Greeks, they would have thought about the relationship of knowledge and wisdom.

In Greek mythology, knowledge is the domain of the god Hermes, Lombardo said. Hermes is both inventive and tricky, but he's a lightweight compared with Zeus, the Greek god of wisdom.

According to Corbeill, the wisdom of Zeus was given to humans by the god Apollo.

Apollo spoke through prophets who lived in his temple at Delphi. The prophets were always women. They weren't known for their clarity. Their wisdom often came out garbled, or they spoke in riddles.

(Continued)

(Continued)

In *Scientific American* last year, some researchers reported one possible reason. The prophets may have been sitting in a place where a lot of ethane, methane, and ethylene were leaking in.

Imagine sniffing a lot of glue and then channeling Zeus, and you've got the idea.

Whatever the source of the prophets' inspiration, it's significant to me that they weren't easy to understand.

Wisdom sometimes arrives at the door in odd packages, ones that mere mortals have trouble opening.

Another source of the idea that wisdom is difficult is the Greek poet Empedocles.

Empedocles says that, to get wisdom, you have to "sift knowledge through the guts of your being," according to Lombardo.

Now, the university used to love this word *wisdom.*

KU's fifth chancellor, Francis Huntington Snow, thought a KU education was in part about attaining it. He had these words carved on a building that once served as a KU library:

"Whoso Findeth Wisdom Findeth Life."

But the university seldom uses the word *wisdom* anymore, and it's not the exclusive property of scholars, not by a long shot.

Corbeill says, "It's rare for a polymath to be wise. What comes to mind are people who just learn language after language, for example, as if they're collecting them."

Nevertheless, I've been learning things for 25 years in order to write this column, and as the years have passed, I've become increasingly interested in wisdom—if not wise.

Given the difficulty of discovering wisdom, of breaking the puzzling code that contains it, my mule-headed persistence hasn't hurt a bit.

Source: Martin, R., Wisdom difficult to define, maintain, *Lawrence Journal-World*, May 21, 2004, www.news.ku.edu/archive. Reprinted with permission.

Although our understanding of wisdom has progressed slowly over modern times, this started to change during the late twentieth century. Although the first president of the American Psychological Association, G. Stanley Hall, wrote a book in 1922 in which he addressed the wisdom gained during the aging process, this work was considered the bailiwick of religion and moral philosophers until about 1975, when psychologists began to scrutinize the concept of wisdom. These scholarly efforts produced a better commonsense psychological understanding of wisdom. Implicit theories (folk theories of a construct that describe its basic elements) of wisdom first were described by Clayton (1975, 1976; Clayton & Birren, 1980) and then further explicated by German psychologist Paul Baltes's (1993) analysis of cultural-historical occurrences. Knowledge gained from these recent studies has informed the development of explicit theories (theories detailing the observable manifestations of a construct) of wisdom, the soundest of which presently include the balance theory of wisdom (Sternberg, 1998) and the Berlin wisdom paradigm (Baltes & Smith, 1990; Baltes & Staudinger, 1993, 2000). In the next section, we explore these implicit and explicit theories of wisdom.

Implicit Theories of Wisdom

Clayton's (1975) dissertation study was one of the first systematic examinations of the wisdom construct. She had people rate similarities between pairs of words believed to be associated with wisdom (e.g., *empathic, experienced, intelligent, introspective, intuitive, knowledgeable, observant*). Through a statistical procedure known as multidimensional scaling, she identified three dimensions of the construct: (1) affective (empathy and compassion), (2) reflective (intuition and introspection), and (3) cognitive (experience and intelligence).

In a later study, Sternberg (1985) asked 40 college students to sort cards (each describing one of 40 wise behaviors) into as many piles as they thought necessary to explain their contents. Again, a multidimensional scaling procedure was used, and the following six qualities of wisdom were identified: (1) reasoning ability, (2) sagacity (profound knowledge and understanding), (3) learning from ideas and environment, (4) judgment, (5) expeditious use of information, and (6) perspicacity (acuteness of discernment and perception). In yet another study, Holliday and Chandler (1986) determined that five factors underlie wisdom: (1) exceptional understanding, (2) judgment and communication skills, (3) general competence, (4) interpersonal skills, and (5) social unobtrusiveness.

The meaning of wisdom also is communicated in our everyday language. In this regard, Baltes (1993) analyzed cultural-historical and philosophical writings and found that wisdom (1) addresses important/difficult matters of life; (2) involves special or superior knowledge, judgment, and advice; (3) reflects knowledge with extraordinary scope, depth, and balance applicable to specific life situations; (4) is well intended and combines mind and virtue; and (5) is very difficult to achieve but easily recognized. More recently, researchers have asked children what *wisdom* means to them. A group of Austrian school children ages 6 to 10 (Glück, Bischof, & Siebenhüner, 2012) answered open-ended questions such as, "What are wise persons like?" Children in this study listed attributes that fell into the categories of (1) cognitive aspects (e.g., "clever," "astute"); (2) characteristics that addressed thinking of others (e.g., "friendly," "helpful"); (3) facets involved in appearance (e.g., "green eyes," "grey beard"); and (4) possession of real-world abilities (e.g., "gives good advice," "can teach you things"). They also listed some characteristics such as "old" in specific relation to age (Glück et al., 2012). Perhaps this points to the possibility that wisdom may be present at young ages, as so much overlap exists between these children's implicit definitions and those of their adult counterparts! One area of difference that Glück and colleagues note between these younger children is the absence of a "reflective" component of wisdom (e.g., life experience, or perspective-taking; p. 596). It may be that increased age comes with a better understanding of the value of these other, more abstract components.

Recently, 30 international "wisdom experts" (primarily from North America and Europe) completed surveys regarding components that they believed should be included in an operationalization of wisdom as a construct (Jeste et al., 2010). Several characteristics of wisdom emerged from these data as those that most experts agreed upon: "[Wisdom] is uniquely human; a form of advanced cognitive and emotional development that is experience driven; a personal quality, albeit a rare one, that can be learned, increases with age, can be measured and is not likely to be enhanced by medication" (Jeste et al., 2010, p. 668). These experts also noted distinctions between other constructs often believed to overlap with wisdom, namely intelligence and spirituality. Thus, these data provide us with a more comprehensive view of how wisdom is defined, at least within Western expert opinion.

Lastly, implicit definitions of wisdom also differ by cultural context. Sternberg (2012) specifically argues that cultural context must be consulted with regard to both conceptualization of this construct and in terms of its measurement as a result of this. Though some similarities exist across cultures, followers of Western and Eastern ideology differ on their views of what makes someone wise (Yang, 2008). Those from Eastern traditions may take the affective side into account in equal balance with the cognitive side of wisdom, whereas Westerners might stress cognition over affective dimensions (Takahashi, 2000; Takahashi & Overton, 2005). Personal qualities such as compassion, open-mindedness, humbleness, and others may be part of a description of a wise person in these Eastern cultures, while intelligence, problem solving, and planning may be more emphasized in Western cultures (Yang, 2008). In another study, three factors were found to be contained within implicit definitions of Asian participants: (1) altruism, (2) determination, and (3) serenity (Brezina, 2010). While there is some overlap between these factors and those found in Western societies (e.g., altruism might overlap with affective components in Western models), some differences also exist (e.g., the inclusion of serenity; Brezina, 2010). More research in this area might broaden our understanding of how this construct is similar and different in various cultural groups.

Explicit Theories of Wisdom

Although informed by implicit theories, explicit theories of wisdom focus more on behavioral manifestations of the construct. Explicit theories applied to wisdom are intertwined with decades-old theories of personality (Erikson, 1959) and cognitive development (Piaget, 1932), or they emphasize the application of pragmatic knowledge in pursuit of exceptional human functioning (Baltes & Smith, 1990; Baltes & Staudinger, 1993, 2000; Sternberg, 1998).

Robert Sternberg

Source: Reprinted with permission of Robert Sternberg.

In his (1932) stage theory of cognitive development, Jean Piaget describes the qualitatively different kinds of thinking that occur during childhood and adulthood. Children typically move from the sensorimotor stage (in which the child's world is experienced through sensing and doing) to the preoperational stage (in which the child's world is framed in symbolic thought) to the concrete operations stage (in which the child's experience begins to be understood through logical thought) during the first 12 years of life. During the formal operations stage, people develop the ability to reason by systematically testing hypotheses. Riegel (1973) built on Piaget's work and considered a form of postformal operational thinking referred to as the dialectical operations stage or, more simply, wisdom. These dialectical operations (logical argumentation in pursuit of truth or reality) associated with wisdom involve reflective thinking that attends to a balance of information and to truth that evolves in a cultural and historical context. Such reflective, or dialectical, thinking facilitates an integration of opposing points of view (Kitchener & Brenner, 1990), dual use of logical and subjective processing of information (Labouvie-Vief, 1990), and an integration of motivation and life experiences (Pascual-Leone, 1990).

Life-span theorists (e.g., Erikson, 1959) view wisdom as part of optimal development. For Erikson, wisdom reflects a maturity in which concerns for the collective good transcend personal interests. In Orwoll's (1989) study of people nominated as wise, this Eriksonian integrity was accompanied by elevated concerns for the collective good.

Both Sternberg's (1998) balance theory and Baltes's (Baltes & Smith, 1990; Baltes & Staudinger, 1993, 2000) Berlin wisdom paradigm are similar in that they emphasize the organization and application of pragmatic knowledge. Furthermore, both views of wisdom propose that wise people can discern views of others, develop a rich understanding of the world, craft meaningful solutions to difficult problems, and direct their actions toward achieving a common good.

Yale psychologist Robert Sternberg built on his previous work on intelligence and creativity (Sternberg, 1985, 1990) and proposed the balance theory of wisdom as specifying "the processes (balancing of interests and of responses to environmental contexts) in relation to the goal of wisdom (achievement of a common good)" (Sternberg, 1998, p. 350). More specifically, Sternberg theorized that the tacit knowledge underlying practical intelligence (i.e., "knowing how" rather than "knowing what") is used in balancing self and other interests within the environmental context to achieve a common good (R. Sternberg, personal communication, October 8, 2003). See Figure 9.1 for a diagram of Sternberg's wisdom model. In this model, the wise person goes through a process that may resemble high levels of moral decision making (Gilligan, 1982; Kohlberg, 1983). First, the person is challenged by a real-life dilemma that activates the reasoning abilities that were first developed in adolescence and then refined in adulthood. Then, the person's life history and personal values bear on his or her use of available tacit knowledge in balancing interests and generating wise responses. The person striving to be wise then examines possible responses to determine the extent to which solutions require adaptation to the environmental and cultural context, the shaping of the environment to fit the solutions, or the selection of a new environment where the solutions might work. Finally, if balance is achieved, then the common good is addressed with the proposed solution. (For a related discussion of wisdom as a "balance strength," see Bacon, 2005.)

According to Sternberg, wisdom involves forming a judgment when there are competing interests that lack a clear resolution. For example, a wise approach to resolving a conflict over a proposed ban of cigarette smoking on a college campus would consider the interests of all people (smokers, nonsmokers, students, faculty, visitors, etc.); review the options for serving the interests of those people; and act to best serve the common good. As such, balancing personal interests and actions and sharing a wise judgment may entail exceptional problem-solving ability.

In the Berlin wisdom paradigm, Baltes and his colleagues (Baltes & Smith, 1990; Baltes & Staudinger, 1993, 2000) define wisdom as the "ways and means of planning, managing, and understanding a good life" (Baltes & Staudinger, 2000, p. 124). Simply stated, "Wisdom is an expertise in conduct and meaning of life" (p. 124). The Baltes group (Baltes & Smith, 1990; Staudinger & Baltes, 1994) has identified five criteria that characterize wisdom (excellence) and wisdom-related (near-excellence) performance.

The two basic criteria, factual and procedural knowledge, indicate that wise performance necessitates expertise. According to Baltes, such expertise requires people to "know what" (i.e., have knowledge about topics such as human nature and development, individual differences, social relations and norms, etc.) and to "know how" (i.e., be able to develop strategies for dealing with problems and giving advice, resolving life conflicts, and planning for and overcoming obstacles that could thwart problem resolution). Factual knowledge, or the behavior that is the "product" of that knowledge, could be evaluated with the following question: "To what extent does this product show general (*conditio humana*) and specific (e.g., life events, institutions) knowledge about life matters and the human condition as well as demonstrate scope and depth in the coverage of issues?" (Staudinger & Baltes, 1994, p. 149). "Know how," or procedural knowledge, would be examined in light of the following question: "To what extent does this product consider decision strategies, how to define goals and to identify the appropriate means, whom to consult with and about strategies of advice giving?" (Staudinger & Baltes, 1994, p. 149). The three metacriteria that are specific to wisdom (life-span contextualism, relativism of values, and recognition and management of uncertainty) involve flexible thinking and dialectical processing. In particular, life-span contextualism requires that wise people consider the contexts of life (e.g., love, work, and play); cultural values; and the passage of time when reviewing problems and their associated solutions. Relativism of values and life priorities place the value differences across people and societies in perspective. Lastly, managing uncertainty provides the decision-making flexibility that is necessary for processing difficult information and coming up with appropriate solutions. These characteristics of wisdom also may be evaluated with additional probing questions (see Staudinger & Baltes, 1994).

To determine the quality of wisdom, Baltes challenges people with questions about resolving real-life problems. Then, the responses to such questions are transcribed and rated according to the five criteria of wisdom. Reliable wisdom scores can be calculated using this method. Specifically, Baltes asks people to consider how they would advise other people facing dilemmas (referred to as wisdom-related tasks requiring "life planning" or "life management") or to conduct a "life review" by describing their responses to problems experienced in their lives. For example, people are asked to consider the following: "In reflecting over their lives, people sometimes realize that they have not achieved what they had once planned to achieve. What should they do and consider?" (Baltes & Staudinger, 2000, p. 126). One "high-level" (i.e., wise) response to this question demonstrates the value perspective plays in drawing meaning from life:

> First, I would want to say that only very few and most likely uncritical people would say
> that they are completely satisfied with what they have achieved. . . . It depends very much
> on the type of goals we are considering, whether they are more of the materialistic or
> more of the idealistic kind. It also depends on the age of the person and the life
> circumstances in which he/she is embedded. . . . Next, one would start to analyze possible
> reasons for why certain goals are not attained. Often, it is the case that multiple goals
> were pursued at the same time without setting priorities and, therefore, in the end, things
> get lost. . . . It is important to gradually become realistic about goals. Often, it is helpful to
> talk to others about it. . . . Conditions external and internal to the person could be at work
> or sometimes it is also the match between the two that can lead to difficulties in life.
> (Staudinger & Leipold, 2003, p. 182)

Baltes and colleagues have continued to refine their definitions of wisdom in recent years and have added the concept of what they term *Sehnsucht* ("life longings") to their life-span view of

Figure 9.1 Sternberg's Balance Theory of Wisdom

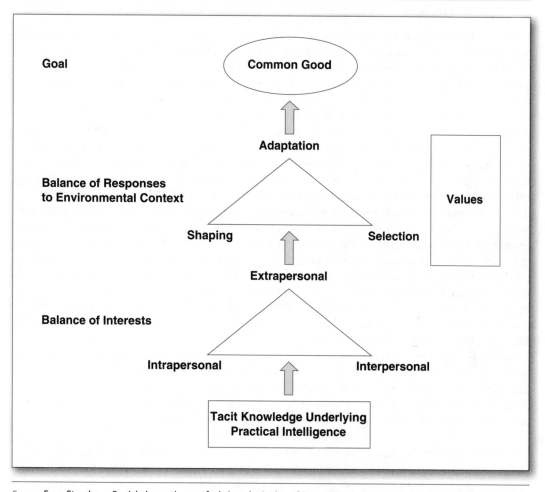

Source: From Sternberg, R., A balance theory of wisdom, in *Review of General Psychology,* 1998. Reprinted with permission.

positive traits that are experienced alongside such constructs as wisdom (Scheibe, Freund, & Baltes, 2007). These researchers define *life longings* as "the recurring strong feelings that life is incomplete or imperfect, coupled with a desire for ideal (utopian), alternative states and experiences of life" (Scheibe, Kunzmann, & Baltes, 2009, p. 176). Life longings are different than the concept of wisdom in that they are qualified as more idiographic experiential knowledge, as opposed to the more general focus of wisdom. This concept may be important as a supplement to discussing wisdom overall, particularly in older adults. (For a more detailed discussion of *Sehnsucht* see Scheibe et al., 2009.)

BECOMING AND BEING WISE

Developing Wisdom

Influential developmental theorists such as Piaget (1932), Jung (1953), and Erikson (1959) provided building blocks for twentieth-century wisdom theorists. As mentioned previously, Piaget's work has been extended beyond formal operations to include "dialectical operations" (Riegel, 1973). The work of Erikson and Jung gave modern theorists clues about how resolving conflict leads to enhanced discernment and judgment. In this regard, Erikson emphasized that wisdom is gained through resolving daily crises, specifically those involving integrity and despair. Jung, with his interests in family-of-origin issues, proposed that wisdom develops through the resolution of psychic conflicts pertaining to individuating from the family unit.

Theorists such as Baltes (1993), Labouvie-Vief (1990), and Sternberg (1998) suggest that wisdom builds on knowledge, cognitive skills, and personality characteristics (discussed by Piaget, Jung, Erikson, and others), and that it requires an understanding of culture and the surrounding environment. Moreover, wisdom develops slowly through exposure to wise role models. Sternberg proposed that knowledge, judicial thinking style, personality, motivation, and environmental context precede wisdom, and Baltes and Staudinger (2000) suggested that fluid intelligence, creativity, openness to experience, psychological-mindedness, and general life experiences "orchestrate" to produce wisdom. In Taiwan, general agreement exists on similar factors believed to underlie wisdom, and a list of several facilitative factors of wisdom in this culture has been developed. Ideas similar to those found in Western contexts include life and work experiences, observation and social interaction, and professional development and reading (Chen, Wu, Cheng, & Hsueh, 2011). Also included in this list, however, are unique ideas more normative of Eastern culture, including "family teaching" and religion (Chen et al., 2011, p. 178). In addition, this study found that experts believed in certain types of conditions or scenarios as being more conducive to the development of wisdom (similar to Sternberg's ideas that environmental context plays a role).

Others examined laypeople's ideas of how wisdom develops, and though variability exists in responses to questions in this vein, in general two main themes emerged from this data (Glück & Bluck, 2011). Similar to the experts' views, many individuals in this study asserted the belief that life experience mixed with tutelage from wise individuals breeds wisdom, while others added dealing with emotionally challenging incidents to these first two components. Life experience appeared to be positively correlated with the idea that emotional challenge was included in the development of wisdom, though growing older in and of itself did not factor into the explanations offered (Glück & Bluck, 2011).

Wisdom grows as people learn to think flexibly to solve problems, and such problem solving entails recognizing ideas according to place and culture. In turn, by recognizing that the answers to questions depend both on contextual factors and on the balancing of many interests, people become even more flexible in their thinking. On these points, Baltes and Staudinger (2000) also emphasize the importance of "guidance by mentors or other wisdom-enhancing 'others'" (p. 127), though such mentoring benefits are sometimes indirect and sometimes direct. Indeed, Staudinger and Baltes (1996) agree with the old adage, "Two heads are better than one," when it comes to responding wisely to life challenges. These same researchers also found that people who discussed dilemmas with loved ones (and others) and then were allowed time for reflection showed increases in their wisdom-related performances; moreover, the older participants benefited more from these interactive experiences than did the younger participants. Some of the benefits here may be linked to the fact that having distance from a problem appears to enhance wise behavior and reasoning (Kross & Grossman, 2012). In addition, neurobiological research on wisdom and decision making in groups has shown that when neural activity is combined across multiple individuals, accurate decisions are made more often (Eckstein et al., 2012). This supports the idea that _collective wisdom_ can be beneficial for many reasons.

The transmission of wisdom from generation to generation has been considered in other literature. Edmondson (2012) conducted a study of family interactions in the West of Ireland and found via ethnographic study that access to wisdom in the form of interactions with older members of the family provided younger members with more resilience and competence, even in the face of very difficult situations. The transmission of wisdom described here is not necessarily a mere sharing of advice, however, but also a modeling of the way in which people in older generations might _listen_ to the information provided and the ways in which they may use this to direct their behavior. Wisdom seemed to be bred from close observation, close relationships, and an emulating of wise characteristics found in others. It is also, according to accounts of the participants in this study, partially in the way that the information is transmitted between generations. One older participant remarked, "You must give them knowledge in a way that interests them, that they enjoy, that they feel they are able to take in" (Edmondson, 2012, p. 89). Those who are teachers, parents, and mentors may do well to remember that the methods of imparting information may be just as important as the information itself.

Wise People and Their Characteristics

Over centuries and cultures, the _sage_ was considered the carrier of wisdom (Assmann, 1994; Baltes, 1993). These mysterious and rare sages were purveyors of life guidance, but they often did little to teach life understanding and the skills needed for wisdom. Modern characterizations of the wise person suggest that the ordinary person can acquire expertise in life matters. In this latter regard, clinical psychologists have been found to possess high levels of wisdom (discussed subsequently; see Smith, Staudinger, & Baltes, 1994; Staudinger, Smith, & Baltes, 1992).

Monika Ardelt, a researcher who has studied aging, measured what she referred to as the "timeless and universal knowledge of wisdom" (2000, p. 71). California residents were the participants in her longitudinal study, the Berkeley Guidance Project. Her analysis of the characteristics that facilitate the development of wisdom revealed that a person's childhood does not have an impact on this development, whereas the quality of one's social environment in early adulthood does. She (1997) also found that wise people achieved greater life satisfaction than unwise people. More recently, Ardelt (2010) examined differences with regard to age and wisdom and found that few differences in wisdom score were found

Monika Ardelt

Source: Reprinted with permission of Monika Ardelt.

between older adults in general and current college students. Larger differences were found, however, when comparisons were made between older college-educated adults and current college students. Ardelt (2010) thus posits that "wisdom might increase with age for individuals with the opportunity and motivation to pursue its development" (p. 193).

While some take a more cognitive view of wisdom, others believe that wisdom may have an affective component that is neglected by this conceptualization (Labouvie-Vief, 1990; Levenson, 2009). These researchers believe that those who are truly wise integrate these two components. Some slight gender differences have been found, pointing toward a more cognitive bent in wise men and a more affective bent in wise women (Ardelt, 2010); this difference was larger when dealing with true-life contexts as opposed to being asked to abstractly think about a situation (Glück, Strasser, & Bluck, 2009).

In 1993, Orwoll and Achenbaum reviewed the role that gender played in the development of wisdom and concluded that wisdom combines traditional masculine and feminine sensibilities. In their review, they also reported that many of men's wise acts took place in public, whereas women's wise acts took place in private. In more recent research conducted by Ardelt (2009), however, the link between wisdom and gender has not been found. In a comprehensive study comparing men and women from two different age cohorts (college age versus adults older than 52 years of age), Ardelt found that some of the earlier findings discussed by Orwoll and Achenbaum were present only in the older cohort, leading to an explanation that this may reflect the different gender roles perceived by younger adults today. In addition, this study and others (e.g., Glück et al., 2009) found that when separating wisdom into affective and cognitive aspects, women in both age groups scored higher on affective aspects of wisdom. Those individuals deemed the most wise did not appear to differ along the variable of gender, giving support for the point made by several researchers, including Orwoll and Achenbaum (1993), that people who are wise have integrated cognitive and affective characteristics of wisdom (Aldwin, 2009; Ardelt, 2009).

Life-span researchers also have explored whether wisdom-related performances vary with chronological age (Smith & Baltes, 1990; Staudinger, 1999). In exploring the performances of 533 people, Baltes and Staudinger (2000) found that "for the age range from about 25 to 75 years of age, the age gradient is zero" (p. 128). In this study, therefore, there were no age differences in levels of wisdom. Wisdom does appear to decline, however, in the late 70s and beyond. Furthermore, researchers studying adolescents (e.g., Pasupathi, Staudinger, & Baltes, 1999) have reported that the decade between years 15 to 25 is a major time for acquiring wisdom. Taken alone, these findings suggest that adolescence and young adulthood are fertile times for wisdom development, and the late 70s and beyond bring about declines in wisdom. More research is needed to explain wisdom development during the 50-year period between 25 and 75.

The role of professional background also has been considered in regard to the expression of wisdom (see Smith et al., 1994; Staudinger et al., 1992). This research revealed that clinical psychologists had higher levels of wisdom-related performance than people in other professional jobs who were matched on educational level and age. Although the wisdom displayed by psychologists was elevated, it was not at the expert level. Based on these findings, the researchers concluded that professional specialization does play a role in the manifestation of wisdom. (Of course, it also may suggest that people predisposed to the development of wisdom self-select for certain professions—that is, those who are disposed toward being wise decide to pursue educations and careers in clinical psychology.)

It may also be that certain characteristics related to wisdom are cultivated more purposefully in some cultures. In investigating differences in wise strategies used to handle conflicts, samples from Japan and the Midwestern United States were compared. Researchers found that individuals in Japan showed evidence of wise traits throughout their life span (whereas those in the United States exhibited increased wisdom with increased age), and that younger and middle-aged Japanese adults showed greater utilization of wise strategies when compared to their U.S. counterparts (Grossman et al., 2012). These authors hypothesized that, due to the strong motivation within Japanese culture to avoid conflict, Japanese individuals become skilled at resolving conflicts in wise ways at an earlier age due to normative pressure to maintain group harmony. Individuals in the United States, however, may not have as much motivation to resolve conflicts, and as such they may not practice these strategies as frequently; wisdom related to resolving conflict accrues more quickly in Japanese individuals but takes a lifetime to develop in U.S. adults (Grossman et al., 2012). This provides more evidence for the old adage, "Culture matters."

Mary Pipher

Source: Reprinted by permission of Mary Pipher.

We have met thousands of psychologists during our careers, and we have had the privilege of working with a handful of applied psychologists who could be considered master therapists. In our estimation, these therapists are paragons of wisdom because not only are they prudent in their daily lives, they also are able to impart wisdom to some of the people they counsel and educate. One master therapist whom we have gotten to know through her writings is the popular author Dr. Mary Pipher; we encourage you to get to know her as well. Dr. Pipher's keen ability to provide perspective on complex issues has been demonstrated in books such as the 1995 bestseller *Reviving Ophelia,* a work that deals with the cultural pressures exerted on adolescent girls in America. Her wisdom as a therapist was shared broadly with psychologists-in-training in her 2003 book *Letters to a Young Therapist.* In this book, she shares pages and pages of "know-how," a basic criterion of wisdom, and she encourages readers to adopt a "back to the basics" approach when helping others. Similar to the advice given by the individuals in the study mentioned previously in the West of Ireland (Edmondson, 2012), she emphasizes the need to contextualize clients' problems and to recommend treatment strategies that fit with the person at *this* time in their lives. She also addresses the uncertainty that is part and parcel of life, and she describes numerous strategies for managing, or better yet, accepting, this uncertainty. Through her *Letters* book, which is an excellent primer on human change, Piper suggests that young therapists practice wisely and share their perspective-taking skills with their clients.

The Measurement of Wisdom

Several measurement approaches have been used in the models of wisdom described in this chapter. For example, developmental and personality theories of wisdom have yielded self-report questions and sentence completion tasks. The forms of wisdom involving expertise in the conduct and meaning of life have been tapped via problem-solving tasks. Sternberg (1998) has proposed that wisdom problems require a person to resolve conflicts. Consistent with his emphasis on pragmatism, Baltes (Baltes & Smith, 1990; Baltes & Staudinger, 1993) has constructed a series of difficult life problems such as the following: "Someone receives a telephone call from a good friend, who says that he or she cannot go on like this and has decided to commit suicide. What might one/the person take into consideration and do in such a situation?" (Baltes & Staudinger, 1993, p. 126). Respondents are encouraged to "think aloud" while considering the resolution of this problem. Their comments and solutions to the problem are evaluated by trained raters, based on the five criteria identified by the Baltes group (factual and procedural knowledge, life-span contextualism, relativism of values, and recognition and management of uncertainty).

A brief self-report measure of wisdom that includes Likert-type items recently was constructed and validated for inclusion in the Values in Action Classification of Strengths (Peterson & Seligman, 2004; see Chapter 3 for a discussion of the classification system). The items are not linked to any of the aforementioned theories, however, and they tap five aspects of wisdom: curiosity, love of learning, open mindedness, creativity, and perspective. Although all respondents complete the wisdom items, only people who have wisdom as one of their top five strengths (out of 24) receive feedback on their capacity for wise living.

A longer self-report measure called the Wisdom Development Scale (Brown & Greene, 2006) also shows promise as a measure of wisdom. This measure is connected to a different theory of wisdom (Brown, 2004) than those that have been mentioned in this chapter thus far, and it includes dimensions for self-knowledge (6 items), altruism (14 items), inspirational engagement (11 items), judgment (11 items), life knowledge (9 items), life skills (11 items), and emotional management (9 items). Psychometrics for this scale are adequate, though this measure has thus far been tested mainly in a college student population, and, as such, more research is necessary. The Wise Thinking and Acting Questionnaire (WITHAQ; Moraitou & Efklides, 2012) is an assessment that specifically taps the cognitive facet of wisdom. This scale contains three subscales: Practical Wisdom, Integrated Dialectical Thinking, and Awareness of Life Uncertainty, and has been found to be psychometrically sound with both older and young adults.

The aforementioned measures of wisdom do not include any items commonly associated with conventional intelligence tests or measures of creativity. The exclusion of these markers is deliberate because IQ and creativity are not necessarily associated with wisdom. Hence, the very intelligent or very creative person should not be automatically considered a wise person. Although implicit theories of wisdom and intelligence are similar (Sternberg, 1985), the two constructs can be distinguished by their roles in daily living. Intelligence provides the basic knowledge for accomplishing daily life-supporting tasks for oneself and others, whereas wisdom includes the know-how, judgment, and flexibility to resolve major life problems for the common good (Clayton, 1982; Sternberg, 1985). Clayton (1982) noted that crystallized intelligence is time bound (knowledge acquired today may be obsolete in 20 years), and wisdom is timeless (knowledge that endures in utility across decades and even centuries). Likewise, Sternberg (1985) characterized wisdom, more than intelligence, as involving interpersonal savvy (listening to and dealing with many different people) and day-to-day life management skills. In addition, wisdom need not be correlated with education or access to resources (Choi & Landeros, 2011). Separating wisdom from these other constructs may assist practitioners in avoiding bias about "who is wise" and in helping individuals from diverse life experiences to uncover strength and resilience in their day-to-day lives.

Benefits of Wisdom

As may be expected, wisdom is associated with many other positive psychological constructs. Studies with young adults have found that wisdom is related to having a coherent sense of self and a solid and consistent ego, which may be linked to other beneficial qualities both inter- and intrapersonally (Webster, 2010). In addition, wise individuals appear to have less investment in hedonistic pursuits (e.g., seeking pleasure) and more interest in reflection and personal growth (Bergsma & Ardelt, 2012; Webster, 2010). The wise also tend to reserve social judgment in favor of making attempts to understand the whole situation and its context before making conclusions; this may have implications for decreasing prejudice and the making of ultimate attributional errors (i.e., assuming that actions of all members of a group can be attributed to internal and stable conditions).

Recent studies have also found moderate and positive links to happiness and life satisfaction (Le, 2011; Walsh, 2012). One reason for this may be the fact that wise individuals appear to be more open to experience in general, as well as open to various attributions for different life experiences (both bad and good; Le, 2011). In addition, as others including Sternberg (2012) have suggested, having a wise outlook on life may allow an individual to be more flexible, adapting and changing as life requires.

The Neurobiology of Wisdom

Though it would seem to fit naturally in the discussion, wisdom has not often been included in neuroscience for various reasons, one of which is the perception that it falls outside the realm of biological science (Jeste & Harris, 2010). Recently, however, some researchers have begun to discuss brain regions that appear to be fundamental to the development of wisdom. In cases where traumatic brain injuries have been centralized in the frontotemporal lobe, deficits are found in ability to be socially appropriate, process emotions effectively, and control impulsivity; all of these are, as Jeste and Harris state, "the antithesis of wisdom" (2010, p. 1603). One potential sticking point related to the neurological bases of wisdom lies with the oft-found circumstance where wisdom appears to increase with age. This is contrary to many past biological findings with regard to brain activity; however, emerging research on neuroplasticity in aging adults appears to support the idea that brain function can increase in some ways as an individual gains more experience (Jeste & Harris, 2010). More research is needed in this developing area, but we are hopeful that wisdom will be included in future neurobiological discussions.

THEORIES OF COURAGE

Like wisdom, courage is appreciated in many cultures. Go to any corner of the earth, and you will find that courage is valued, though potentially manifested in very different ways. Read the works of Eastern philosophers and Western thinkers, and you will find that even the wisest people in the history of the world marveled at courage. Socrates is one of many who sought to understand this noble quality, as illustrated in his question to Laches: "Suppose we set about determining the nature of courage and in the second place, proceed to inquire how the young men may attain this quality by the help of study and pursuits. Tell me, if you can, what is courage," implored Socrates (Plato, trans., 1953, p. 85). Although this age-old question has long intrigued scholars and laypeople, it is only in the last few decades that researchers from diverse fields (e.g., Finfgeld, 1995; Haase, 1987; Putman, 1997; Rachman, 1984; Shelp, 1984) have established the requisite theoretical and scientific springboards needed for launching more comprehensive examinations of courage. In fact, as can be seen in Table 9.1, there are at least 18 different conceptualizations of courage.

Table 9.1 Selected Scholarly Definitions of Courage

Aquinas	Defined *fortitudo* as "firmness in mind in enduring or repulsing whatever makes steadfastness outstandingly difficult, that is, particularly serious dangers, primarily sustaining action to overcome fears of bodily harm and death and secondarily in persevering in attacking" (1273/1948, p. 123).
Aristotle	Defined *andreia* (military courage) as the disposition to act appropriately in situations that involve fear and confidence—a rationally determined mean between cowardice and foolhardiness (cited in Rorty, 1988).
Finfgeld	"Being courageous involves being fully aware of and accepting the threat of a long-term health concern, solving problems using discernment, and developing enhanced sensitivities to personal needs and the world in general. Courageous behavior consists of taking responsibility and being productive" (1998, p. 153).
Gergen & Gergen	"To be courageous, then, is to remain steadfast within the bosom of those relationships from which one's sense of personal esteem and identity are derived" (1998, p. 144).
Haitch	"Courage is two-sided: there is an aspect of standing firm or fighting, and an aspect of accepting intractable realities; courage is the psychic strength that enables the self to face danger and death" (1995, p. 86).
Hemingway	Grace under pressure (Parker, 1929).
Hobbes	"The contempt of wounds and violent death. It inclines men to private revenges, and sometimes to endeavor the unsettling of public peace" (cited in Rorty, 1988, p. x).
Kant	Defined *fortudido* as the "capacity and the resolved purpose to resist a strong but unjust opponent; and with regard to the opponent of the moral disposition within us" (cited in Rorty, 1988, p. 65).
Kennedy	(Describing senators with political courage) "Men whose abiding loyalty to their nation triumphed over personal and political considerations" (1956, p. 21).
Kohut	"Oppose the pressures exerted on them and remain faithful to their ideals and themselves" (1979, p. 5).
O'Byrne et al.	"Dispositional psychological courage is the cognitive process of defining risk, identifying and considering alternative actions, and choosing to act in spite of potential negative consequences in an effort to obtain 'good' for self or others, recognizing that this perceived good may not be realized" (2000, p. 6).

Plato	The ability to remember what is worth prizing and what is worth fearing (cited in Rorty, 1988).
Putman	Facing the fears associated with the loss of psychological stability (summarized from Putman, 1997).
Rachman	Persevering in the face of fear (summarized from Rachman, 1984).
Seligman	The capacity to rise to the occasion (Seligman, personal communication, January 7, 2001).
Shelp	"The disposition to voluntarily act, perhaps fearfully, in a dangerous circumstance, where the relevant risks are reasonably appraised, in an effort to obtain or preserve some perceived good for oneself or others, recognizing that the desired perceived good may not be realized" (1984, p. 354).
Snyder	"Responding to extraordinary times with behaviors that seem natural and called for in those circumstances. It is only later, when removed from courage-eliciting events, that the protagonist and others view the behaviors as particularly worthy of the label courageous. This view of courage obviously gives greater weight to situational than to personal factors and suggests that most people are capable of courage if faced with the appropriate circumstances" (Snyder, personal communication, October 17, 2005).
Woodard	"The ability to act for a meaningful (noble, good, or practical) cause, despite experiencing the fear associated with perceived threat exceeding the available resources" (2004, pp. 4–5).

Hemingway's definition (see Table 9.1) appears to be the most parsimonious, whereas Hobbes's view is the most critical of courage. Each of these definitions provides a different historical glimpse of what scholars and society valued in terms of persevering in the face of fear. One other scholarly description, that of the Roman statesman Cicero (as summarized by Houser, 2002), may be the view of courage that best transcends time (as suggested by a comparison to implicit and explicit views on courage detailed later in this chapter). Houser noted that Cicero saw courage as

(1) magnificence, the planning and execution of great and expansive projects by putting forth ample and splendid effort of mind; (2) confidence, that through which, on great and honorable projects, the mind self-confidently collects itself with sure hope; (3) patience, the voluntary and lengthy endurance of arduous and difficult things, whether the case be honorable or useful, and (4) perseverance, ongoing persistence in a well-considered plan. (p. 305)

Implicit Theories of Courage

To examine laypeople's views of courage, O'Byrne, Lopez, and Petersen (2000) surveyed 97 people and found considerable variation. For example, as seen in Table 9.2, some perceive courage as an

Kristin Koetting O'Byrne

Source: Reprinted with permission of Kristin Koetting O'Byrne.

attitude (e.g., optimism), and others see it as a behavior (e.g., saving someone's life). Some refer to mental strength; others write of physical strength. Some claim that courage involves taking a risk, whereas others accentuate the role of fear. Neither the risk component nor the fear component, however, is found in all descriptions of courage.

Across history and cultures, courage has been regarded as a great virtue because it helps people to face their challenges. Philosophers offered the earliest views on understanding courage. Over the past centuries, efforts to construct socially relevant views of courage have transported it from the hearts of the warriors on the battlefields to the daily experiences and thoughts of every person. Whereas Aristotle analyzed the physical courage of his "brave soldier," Plato marveled at the moral courage of his mentors. The philosophical focus seemed to shift to the deeds and traits of veterans of moral wars with Aquinas's (1273/1948) attention paid to steadfastness in the face of difficulty and Tillich's (1980) interpretation of courage as the reaffirmation of self and being. These latter two types of courage (physical and moral) have captured most philosophers' attentions, and the classification of courageous behavior has broadened over the years.

After reviewing work on courage, two groups of researchers developed similar classifications of courage. In their Values in Action classification system, Peterson and Seligman (2004) conceptualized courage as a core human virtue comprising such strengths as valor (taking physical, intellectual, and emotional stances in the face of danger); authenticity (representing oneself to others and the self in a sincere fashion); enthusiasm/zest (thriving/having a sense of vitality in a challenging situation); and industry/perseverance (undertaking tasks and challenges and finishing them).

In a similar model, O'Byrne et al. (2000) identified the three types of courage as physical, moral, and health/change (now referred to as *vital courage*). Physical courage involves the attempted maintenance of societal good by the expression of physical behavior grounded in the pursuit of socially valued goals (e.g., a firefighter saving a child from a burning building). Moral courage is the behavioral expression of authenticity in the face of the discomfort of dissension, disapproval, or rejection (e.g., a politician invested in a "greater good" places an unpopular vote in a meeting). Vital courage refers to the perseverance through a disease or disability even when the outcome is ambiguous (e.g., a child with a heart transplant maintaining his or her intensive treatment regimen even though the prognosis is uncertain).

Physical courage has evolved slowly from the Greek *andreia,* the military courage of the brave soldier in ancient Greece. Finding the rugged path between cowardice and foolhardiness distinguished a Greek soldier as courageous. This disposition to act appropriately in situations involving fear and confidence in the face of physical danger has been valued in many cultures for centuries (Rorty, 1988). For example, Ernest Hemingway was a major writer on the topic of courage in twentieth-century America. His fascination with physical courage in a variety of arenas, such as the

Table 9.2 Laypeople's Responses to the Question, "What Is Courage?"

Taking action (either mental, physical, or spiritual) that is difficult because it makes you uncomfortable (because it is dangerous, threatening, or difficult)

Doing something outside of one's comfort zone—fine line between courage and stupidity

Taking risks in the face of possible failure and uncertainty

Ability to take what life gives and make the best out of one's life (positive attitude involved)

Initiate risk-taking behavior in the face of a threatening situation toward one's emotional/psychological/spiritual/physical health

Standing up for what one believes in even if others don't feel the same

Standing up for oneself in the face of adversity or harm even when the consequences are known

Willingness to take risks, not knowing if one may fail or succeed (being brave)

Sacrificing, working, or helping a cause; faith

Proceeding in a situation even when one is unsure about the outcome; challenging the norm in the best interest of society

Ability to face threats/fears/challenges and overcome obstacles

Ability to contain one's fear enough to progress with a task

Self-confidence; belief in self and situations; making a choice and acting on it; strength

Bravery; act of strength/wisdom in moments of crisis

Using one's power to stand up for those who have none in the name of social justice

Defending a viewpoint that is different from the norm

Having the power and strength to face difficulties or challenges

Taking responsible risks; sacrificing part of oneself

Facing challenges rather than running away or pretending they don't exist

Displaying actions that go along with one's beliefs

Risking failure; determination in the face of failure

Form of assistance during a dangerous or life-threatening event

Speaking up when something that is not right is happening

Selfless behavior; displaying concern for others rather than oneself

Committing acts of perceived bravery that an ordinary person might not do

Being mentally/physically strong

Note: Major themes: taking risks (possible failure, negative consequences, uncertainty); particular attitude; facing challenges; and defending beliefs battlefield, the open sea, and the bullfighting arena, seemed to mirror the American fascination with staring danger in the face and persevering. In fact, the "Hemingway code" of living a life characterized by strength, knowledge, and courage provided a code of conduct for many Americans.

Jack Rachman's research on courage stemmed from his realization that courage was the mirror image of fear. He noticed that, when faced with physical jeopardy, some people dealt with the perceived danger better than others. Therefore, Rachman (1984) worked with paratroopers, decorated soldiers, and bomb squad members to gather information on the nature of fear and its counterpart, courage. He found that courageous people persevere when facing fear and thereafter make quick physiological recoveries. He also suggested that courageous acts are not necessarily confined to a special few, nor do they always take place in public. In regard to this latter point, he became intrigued by the inner battles and private courage displayed by his psychotherapy clients. He concluded that clearly there was more to courage than *andreia* and related physical conquest of danger.

One recent current example of this physical courage may be Captain Chesley B. "Sully" Sullenberger and the "Miracle on the Hudson" in 2009. Though his plane hit a flock of geese, this potential tragedy resulted in no loss of life due to Sullenberger's calm and steady bravery in the face of extreme danger. Similarly, the 19 Granite Mountain Hotshot firefighters who lost their lives fighting the Arizona wildfire in June of 2013 can be held up as examples of bravery and courage. These men knew the danger they were in and still pressed forward to try to stop the raging fire. Other examples would of course include the tens of thousands of service men and women who leave their families and friends to go to fight for our country every day, sometimes volunteering for extended tours of duty despite the daily threat of death. These individuals must feel the bite of fear on a regular basis and yet press onward due to their great courage.

Moral courage involves the preservation of justice and service for the common good. Fascinated by moral courage, John F. Kennedy spent years gathering stories of statesmen who followed their hearts and principles when determining what was "best" for the American people—even when constituents did not agree with their decisions or value their representations. Although Kennedy himself was a military hero, in his *Profiles in Courage* (1956), he seemed to give more attention and reverence to moral courage than to physical courage.

Authenticity and integrity are closely associated with the expression of personal views and values in the face of dissension and rejection. Exactly when should one take a stand? In one example, Rosa Parks said that she took a seat at the front of a bus because it was time to do so. Doctors and nurses, when facing difficult situations with patients and families, must be truthful and straightforward even when it would be easier, emotionally, to sugarcoat diagnoses and prognoses (see Finfgeld, 1998; Shelp, 1984). Not only does it take courage to speak the truth (Finfgeld, 1998), it also takes courage to hear the truth. Moral courage can take yet another form when an individual stands up for the rights of the underprivileged and the disadvantaged and confronts someone with power over him or her.

Moral courage might be considered the "equal opportunity" form of this virtue; we all experience situations in which a morally courageous response is provoked, and this behavior requires no special training. We may encounter discomfort or dissension and be challenged by the task of maintaining authenticity and integrity in those situations. Physical courage, on the other hand, is sparked only in special circumstances, and often those who engage in physically courageous behavior have received training that helps them overcome fear. (Thankfully, most of us, except for soldiers and first responders, are not called upon to put our lives at risk to protect the common good every day.) Similarly, vital courage is not needed unless we encounter disease or disability, and often professionals teach us how to battle the infirmity. So, how does a common person like you or me respond to situations that challenge our core assumptions about the world and about people? When discomfort or dissension is experienced, and prudence suggests that a stand needs to be taken, we have the opportunity to engage in behavior consistent with moral courage. Unfortunately, we (SJL and JTP) encounter many situations every month in which a person (who is present or not present) is not getting a "fair shake" because of someone's prejudice, be it ageism, racism, or sexism. (We guess that you witness bias of some sort once or more a month as well.) On occasion, we are able to muster up the moral courage to address the perceived injustice; we hope you can conjure up this kind of courage in similar situations in the future. Most of us will never have to summon the type of courage shown by Malala Yousafzai. All of us should be relieved that such a brave girl has recovered. Perhaps we can use her unfailing courage as an inspiration to be courageous in our own ways.

Malala Yousafzai's Courage
The New York Times

October 10, 2012 – If Pakistan has a future, it is embodied in Malala Yousafzai. Yet the Taliban so feared this 14-year old girl that they tried to assassinate her. Her supposed offense? Her want of an education and her public advocation for it.

Malala was on her way home from school in Mingora, Pakistan, in the Swat Valley, on Tuesday when a Taliban gunman walked up to the school bus, asked for her by name and shot her in the head and neck. On Wednesday, doctors at a military hospital removed the bullet that lodged in her shoulder. She remains in critical condition.

Malala was no ordinary target. She came to public attention three years ago when she wrote a diary for the BBC about life under the Taliban, which controlled Swat from 2007 to 2009 before being dislodged by an Army offensive. Last year, she won a national peace prize.

The Pakistani Taliban was quick and eager to take credit for Tuesday's attack. Malala "has become a symbol of Western culture in the area; she was openly propagating it," a spokesman, Ehsanullah Ehsan, told The Times. If she survives, the militants would try again to kill her, he vowed.

Malala has shown more courage in facing down the Taliban than Pakistan's government and its military leaders. Her father, who once led a school for girls and has shown uncommon bravery in supporting his daughter's aspirations, said she had long defied Taliban threats.

Pakistan's founder, Muhammad Ali Jinnah, envisioned a democratic and moderate Muslim nation. But extremism is engulfing the country, and too many people are enabling it or acquiescing to it. This attack was so abominable, however, that Pakistanis across the ideological spectrum reacted with outrage, starting with the president and prime minister. Even Jamaat ud Dawa, the charity wing of the militant Islamist group Lashkar-e-Taiba, which waged its own violent campaigns against India, couldn't stay silent. "Shameful, despicable, barbaric attempt," read a message on the group's official Twitter feed. "Curse be upon assassins and perpetrators."

(Continued)

(Continued)

The attack was an embarrassment for the Pakistani Army, which has boasted of pushing the Taliban from Swat. The army chief, Gen. Ashfaq Parvez Kayani, visited the hospital where Malala was being treated, and, in a rare public statement, he condemned the "twisted ideology" of the "cowards" who had attacked her.

Words only have meaning if they are backed up by actions. What will he and other leaders do to bring Malala's attackers to justice and stop their threat to ordinary citizens and the state?

In recent years, the Taliban destroyed at least 200 schools. The murderous violence against one girl was committed against the whole of Pakistani society. The Taliban cannot be allowed to win this vicious campaign against girls, learning and tolerance. Otherwise, there is no future for that nation.

Source: "Malala Yousafzai's Courage," Editorial. *The New York Times,* October 11, 2012. Copyright © 2012 The New York Times. All rights reserved. Used by permission.

Vital courage is at work as a patient battles illness through surgery and treatment regimens. Physicians, nurses, and other allied health professionals use their expertise to save human lives or to improve the quality of the lives of those whom they serve. Many researchers have examined vital courage (though not calling it such), and their work has captured the phenomenon that captivates us when we hear about someone facing chronic illness. Haase (1987) interviewed nine chronically ill adolescents in order to answer the question, "What is the essential structure of the lived-experience of courage in chronically ill adolescents?" She found that courage involves developing a deep personal awareness of the potential short-term and long-term effects of the illness.

Amputee a Driving Force in Getting People With Disabilities Moving

Julie Deardorff

The Chicago Tribune

12/21/2012— Army veteran Melissa Stockwell has one strong, healthy leg. The other is a scarred, 6-inch stump that she has proudly nicknamed "Little Leg."

The Bucktown woman throws birthday parties for this shortened limb, always dresses it in her favorite colors — red, white and blue — and has trouble imagining going through life any other way. "I've done more with one leg than I ever could have with two," she often says.

The first female soldier to lose a limb in Iraq, Stockwell, 32, has managed to turn a traumatic above-the-knee amputation into an uplifting experience, one that motivates people of all abilities. Since the injury she has shaken hands with presidents, won three consecutive paratriathlon world championships, run marathons, skied down mountains and raced 267 miles across Alaska in the longest wheelchair and handcycle race in the world.

Earlier this month she declared on her blog, "I'm going to be an Ironman," and signed up for Ironman Arizona, a punishing 2.4-mile swim and 112-mile bike ride, followed by a 26.2-mile run.

But Stockwell's physical feats only partly explain why a company like Trek, which ended its relationship with disgraced cyclist Lance Armstrong, now touts her as one of its "great athletes," calling her an inspirational role model.

Stockwell also empowers others to become more physically active, healthier and socially connected through her work as a prosthetist, fitting amputees in the U.S. and Guatemala with new limbs. In 2011 she co-founded Dare2Tri, a triathlon training group for people with disabilities, where she works as a coach and mentor, often swimming, biking or running alongside her athletes. Stockwell also is an instrumental part of Blade Runners, a running group for amputees, and is active in organizations ranging from the Wounded Warrior Project to the Challenged Athletes Foundation.

"Melissa understands what her role is on the planet," said her coach, Stacee Seay, national manager for TrainingBible coaching and the head coach for Dare2Tri. "Her injury does not define her, but it certainly, certainly makes her who she is today. She has taken what has happened to her and turned everything about it into a positive."

"Be known not for what happened to you but what you choose to become," Stockwell recently typed out on Twitter.

In interviews about courage with middle-aged adults with various physical illnesses, Finfgeld (1998) determined that courage involves becoming aware of and accepting the threat of a long-term health condition, solving any related problems through the use of insight, and developing enhanced sensitivities to oneself and others. Finfgeld (1995) also interviewed older adults who were demonstrating courage in the face of chronic illnesses and concluded that being courageous is a lifelong process that entails factors such as significant others, values, and hope.

Regarding the courage of physicians, Shelp (1984) found that this virtue, along with competence and compassion, is a very desirable characteristic of health care providers. Moreover, instilling courage through "encouragement" (p. 358) is required of anyone in a profession that exemplifies care and concern. Furthermore, Shelp states that the necessary components of courage are freedom of choice, fear of a situation, and the willingness to take risks in a situation with an uncertain but morally worthy end. We believe that vital courage frequently is exhibited by people who are suffering, by the health care providers who treat them, *and* by the many significant others who care for loved ones during hard times. This vital courage of family and friends who cared for an ailing significant other was one of the many backstories in Jerome Groopman's work, *The Anatomy of Hope: How People Prevail in the Face of Illness.* In this 2004 book, Dr. Groopman told the stories of people who were enduring illness. Often, the sick person was accompanied by a caring doctor and a loving support person. Those caregivers shared, albeit vicariously, in the suffering of the ill person; they faced their own fears, including the fear of the loss of the person who meant so much to them. Hence, vital courage in the face of suffering often is manifested by people other than the identified patient. Groopman's account of a mother with colon cancer and her teenage daughter's coping was particularly poignant. Indeed, the story of Frances and Sharon Walker (pseudonyms for an actual patient and her daughter), discussed in Chapter 2 of the Groopman text, revealed how courage can be seen in the virtuous behavior of those who are ill and the loved ones who suffer alongside them. Furthermore, this case demonstrated that, when one caregiver (the physician in this example) behaves in a cowardly manner, other caregivers might be challenged to rise to the occasion. Frances Walker, during her battle with cancer, was the model patient; she was determined to endure, and she was compliant with treatment. Sharon, her teenage daughter, believed that her mother would be cured, and the young woman was a constant source of comfort and support to her mother at every appointment. Unfortunately, Frances's oncologist was not honest with them; her cancer treatment was only palliative, not curative as he had boldly asserted. The colon cancer was indeed terminal, a fact the doctor probably knew when first rendering his diagnosis. When Frances was overwhelmed by her true prognosis, and the physician would not keep his appointments with her, young Sharon stood by her mother and stood up to the medical staff. She grappled with her fears about her mother's suffering and her dread of losing her loved one in the near future, and she overcame her hesitancy to challenge authority (the medical staff) when she realized she wasn't getting straight answers. Frances, the patient, and Sharon, the caregiver, embodied the vital courage necessary to fight an illness and maintain dignity.

Psychological courage, as Putman (1997) described it, is strength in facing one's destructive habits. This form of vital courage may be quite common in that we all struggle with psychological challenges in the forms of stress, sadness, and dysfunctional or unhealthy relationships. In light of these threats to our psychological stabilities, we stand up to our dysfunctions by restructuring our beliefs or systematically desensitizing ourselves to the fears. One striking argument that Putman advanced about psychological courage is that there is a paucity of training for psychological courage as compared to physical and moral courage. Putman goes on to say that pop culture presents many physically and morally courageous icons in literary works and movies, but exemplars of psychological courage are rare. Perhaps this is due to the negative stigma surrounding mental health problems and destructive behaviors. It is also possible, however, that the language surrounding vital courage is new relative to that for moral and physical courage (the latter having been acknowledged since the ancient Greeks). The people in Figure 9.2 exemplify moral, physical, and vital courage.

Other researchers have discussed the construct of civil courage, which is defined by Greitemeyer, Osswald, Fischer, and Frey (2007) as "brave behavior accompanied by anger and indignation that intends to enforce societal and ethical norms without considering one's own social costs" (p. 115). This form of courage is thought to combine facets of physical courage and moral courage, as defined by O'Byrne et al. (2000) and Pury, Kowalski, and Spearman (2007) (Greitemeyer et al.). As an example, someone exhibiting civil courage may decide to intervene in a situation where someone is under physical attack as a result of prejudice. Greitemeyer and colleagues state that this type of courage is separate from helping behaviors more commonly labeled as altruism (e.g., helping an individual who has dropped something) because of the common cost experienced by the individual who decides to help in these circumstances. In the example given here, the "helper"

Figure 9.2   Exemplars of Three Types of Courage

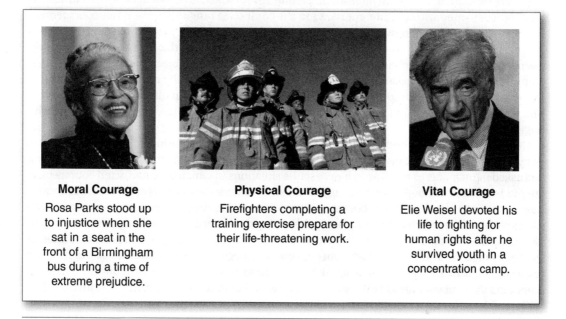

Moral Courage

Rosa Parks stood up
to injustice when she
sat in a seat in the
front of a Birmingham
bus during a time of
extreme prejudice.

Physical Courage

Firefighters completing a
training exercise prepare for
their life-threatening work.

Vital Courage

Elie Weisel devoted his
life to fighting for
human rights after he
survived youth in a
concentration camp.

Sources: Rosa Parks: Copyright © Reuters/CORBIS; Firefighters: Copyright © Comstock/Thinkstock; Elie Wiesel: Copyright © Ramin Talaie/Corbis.

who is exhibiting civil courage risks bodily harm in helping to fend off attackers but feels angered and morally and civilly obligated to stand up for what is right.

Consideration of the implicit views of courage and of modern scholars' theoretical examination of courage suggests that our understanding of this virtue has changed little in the 2,000 years since Cicero's work. Cicero's definition, summarized previously on page 234, is a timeless one. For example, his comments on courage take into account its multidimensional nature, going beyond the culturally lauded physical courage to honor the patience and perseverance necessary for vital courage and the magnificence inherent in moral courage. Today's implicit views and scholarly operationalizations of courage include references to the qualities of hope, confidence, and honor that appeared in Cicero's definition.

BECOMING AND BEING COURAGEOUS

Courageous behaviors follow the identification of a threat, after which there is a shift away from defining the problem as an insurmountable obstacle (Finfgeld 1995, 1998). Behavioral expectations, role models, and value systems also appear to determine if, when, and how courage unfolds.

Courageous behavior may result in a sense of equanimity, or calmness; an absence of regret about one's life; and personal integrity.

Using structured individual interviews, Szagun (1992) asked children ages 5 to 12 to rate the courage associated with 12 different risks (on a 5-point scale ranging from 1 = Not courageous to 5 = Very courageous); moreover, the researcher asked the children to judge courage vignettes. The younger children (ages 5 to 6) likened courage to the difficulty of the task at hand, along with being fearless. The older children (ages 8 to 9) likened courage to subjective risk taking and overcoming fear. Still older children (ages 11 to 12) reported that being fully aware of a risk at the time of acting is a necessary component of courage. Not surprisingly, given their developmental stages, the younger group rated physical risks as entailing more courage than other risks (e.g., psychological risks).

More recently, Szagun and Schauble (1997) investigated courage using an interview technique for younger children and an open-ended questionnaire for adolescents and adults. These researchers asked participants to recall and then describe situations in which they had acted courageously and to focus on the thoughts and feelings of those situations. Children were asked about courage through the use of a short story about a specific character. Results showed that the young children did not consider fear or overcoming fear in describing the experience of courage, but this propensity to equate courage with the experience of fear increased with age. As in past research (Szagun, 1992), younger research participants conceptualized courage as more physical risk taking, whereas older children focused on psychological risk taking as being necessary for courage. The older children also conceptualized courage as a multifaceted emotional experience that involves fear, self-confidence, and an urge to act.

Several researchers have attempted to determine how people become courageous and/or decide upon courageous action in the face of certain circumstances (Fagin-Jones & Midlarsky, 2007; Finfgeld, 1995, 1998; Haase, 1987). Corrupt times often test our courageous mettle, and perhaps in no other historical era was this more evident than during the Jewish Holocaust. Fagin-Jones and Midlarsky interviewed two groups of individuals: (1) non-Jewish "rescuers" who assisted and/or saved the lives of Jews during this time, despite the obvious threat to their own personal safety; and (2) non-Jewish "bystanders" who did not make efforts to assist Jews, though they also did not participate in direct persecution of them (p. 139). These researchers aimed to better understand the effect of various positive characteristics of personality (e.g., social responsibility) on the "courageous altruism" that took place during this time (Fagin-Jones & Midlarsky, 2007, p. 136). Results showed that rescuers could be distinguished from bystanders on measures of social responsibility, empathic concern, and risk taking, as well as altruistic moral reasoning. These findings further exemplify the idea that personal traits may lead some individuals toward more courageous actions. In January of 2010, one of the most famous of these rescuers passed away. Miep Gies, one of the incredible individuals who helped to hide Anne Frank and who was the keeper of Anne's diary, remained humble about the civil courage she showed by her involvement in helping the Franks until her death at 100 years old. Gies considered helping Anne Frank and her family to be not a choice but a duty (a key component of the concept of civil courage) and has been quoted as saying, "I am not a hero" (Goldstein, 2010). Nonetheless, history will always remember her as one.

Haase (1987) used a phenomenological, descriptive method of assessment to further his understanding of how people such as Gies and others become courageous. In an unstructured interview format with chronically ill adolescents, participants identified and described their courageous experiences. They were asked the following: "Describe a situation in which you were courageous. Describe your experience as you remember it, include your thoughts, feelings, and perceptions as you remember experiencing them. Continue to describe the experience until you feel it is fully described" (p. 66). This instruction reveals an assumption that all individuals have the capacity for and past experience with courage. Haase's findings regarding courage point to the development of attitudes and coping methods rather than descriptions of so-called born heroes. In particular, she found that, through daily encounters with "mini-situations" of courage (e.g., treatment, procedures, physical changes, and others that result from the illness), the adolescent comes to an awareness and resolution of the experience as one of courage. Increasingly, over time and experiences, the situation is viewed as difficult but not impossible. Through resolution of the situation of courage, the adolescent develops a sense of mastery, competence, and accomplishment and a feeling of growth. The mechanisms at the heart of Haase's work may also be found in use with psychotherapy. Some psychologists have spoken of the use of courage in therapeutic treatment, specifically with regard to having the "courage to risk positive change" (Campos, 2012, p. 209). As a part of transactional analysis, therapists who are proponents of this style of treatment state that one must take some risks in order to seek out change in one's life which requires courage. Campos (2012) and others write about building a "culture of courage" in which clients are encouraged to try to change themselves or their community in some way (p. 215).

Sean Hannah, Patrick Sweeney and Paul Lester (2007) have proposed a theory explaining how the individual may experience courage on a subjective level and how these experiences may lead to the development of what they call "a courageous mindset" (p. 129). In Hannah et al.'s model (see Figure 9.3), factors such as the perception of risk are impacted by external constructs such as social forces (e.g., normative influences) and positive states (such as hope, efficacy, or the experience of positive emotions), as well as more internal characteristics such as positive traits (e.g., openness to experience and conscientiousness) and values and beliefs (e.g., valor, loyalty, honor). Hannah and colleagues posit that these influences have a collective effect on how risk is perceived, how fear is experienced, and whether courageous behaviors are exhibited. In addition, they theorize that the subjective experience of these courageous behaviors may lead the individual to develop the "courageous mindset" (Hannah et al., 2007, p. 129) that in turn affects the occurrence of courageous action in future endeavors. Interestingly, other research has found that mood (e.g., positive or negative affect) may not be related to deciding to engage in helping behavior when moral courage is on the line (Kayser, Greitemeyer, Fischer, & Frey, 2009). These researchers found that though positive mood predicts helping behavior in many settings, mood did not appear to impact helping behavior in situations requiring moral courage. Other studies in this vein have shown that general helping behavior and moral courage helping behavior may have differential predictors (Kayser et al., 2009).

In *The Courage Quotient,* Robert Biswas-Diener (2012) talks more about courage for the layperson. Biswas-Diener states that most people think first of *physical* courage when the word is mentioned. Images of people rescuing babies from burning buildings or daredevils willing to risk death to perform physical feats are often the first things that come to our minds. When we compare everyday actions of ourselves or others we know to these types of images, it seems that courage is a scarce thing, something not often seen. Biswas-Diener makes the point, however, that courage can mean more than this, stating "When we understand courage as 'a quality of spirit or mind,' we can see that this mental attitude can apply as easily to a child facing her first day of school as to an executive who is willing to gamble on a new product. In the end courage is not found only in physical acts; it is fundamentally an attitude toward facing intimidating situations" (p. 5). If we are able to identify more courageous acts, we might also be able to emulate them in everyday situations. Bravery in trying something new, for example, is something that might be attempted in the workplace, in our relationships, and in setting difficult goals for ourselves. As we are able to pay more attention to more courageous acts in these domains, we may be better situated to become more courageous ourselves.

This is something we can try with our children as well. In my (JTP) house, we occasionally put up "The Bravery Tree" when inspiration for trying challenging new things seems to be needed. The Bravery Tree is just a makeshift shape of a tree, drawn with ribbons on our sliding glass door. Everyone in the family has a different branch, and each can earn Bravery Leaves for attempting acts of courage. A child might try a new food at the dinner table even though she thinks she won't like it. Another might challenge himself by playing in the "big kids" basketball game at recess. A third might try her best not to cry, though she misses her mother while she is at school that day. We talk about "brave faces" and what we can do to make ourselves feel brave. One of my children likes to roar, "I am not afraid!" Another just lifts her chin ever so subtly. Praising acts of bravery in our children that involve these more everyday feats may instill in them the idea that they are Courageous Individuals, that this is something *inside* of them. There is no telling what they might do with this mindset in the future.

United States Senator John McCain's View on Strengthening Courage—April 2004

"Moral courage we can strengthen. The first time you stand up to a bully, it's hard. The second time, it's not so hard. Physical courage sometimes you run out of. And when I ran out of courage and came back to my cell and tapped on my wall, it was my comrades that picked me up, that lifted me up, that sustained me, that gave me strength to go back and fight again." (Transcript of MSNBC's *Hardball With Chris Matthews*)

COURAGE RESEARCH

The Measurement of Courage

Over the last 30 years, numerous brief self-report measures of courage have been created for research purposes. Although several of these measures have some strong points, all warrant additional development.

In 1976, Larsen and Giles developed a scale to measure existential (akin to moral) and social (related to physical) courage. The existential courage domain is tapped by 28 items, and 22 items examine social courage. Psychometric support for this measure is limited, and little if any work has been done to refine the scale.

Figure 9.3 Subjective Experience of Courage

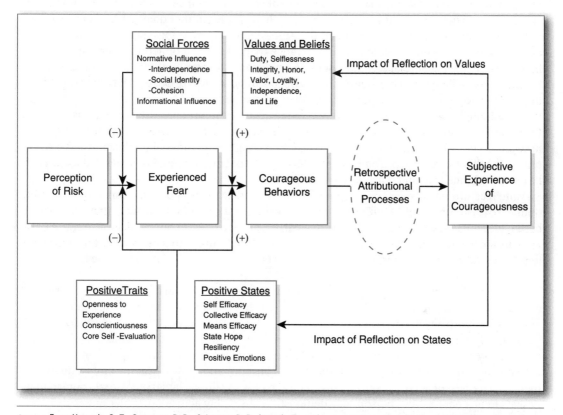

Source: From Hannah, S. T., Sweeney, P. J., & Lester, P. B. (2007). Toward a courageous mindset: The subject act and experience of courage, *The Journal of Positive Psychology, 2,* 129–135. Reprinted with permission by the Taylor & Francis Group.

Schmidt and Koselka (2000) constructed a seven-item measure of courage. Three items relate to general courage, and four assess what is considered panic-specific courage (possibly a subtype of vital courage). This scale meets basic standards for reliability, but evidence for its validity is limited.

Woodard (2004) used a carefully researched definition of courage as the willingness to act for a meaningful (noble, good, or practical) cause, despite experiencing fear (associated with perceived threat exceeding available resources), to develop a different measurement of courage. This psychometrically sound scale has since been revised (now called the Woodard-Pury Courage Scale [WPCS-23]), and new scoring calls for analysis of the items that address the willingness piece of this construct in four factors. These factors include the willingness to act in a courageous way for (1) one's job or self-interest; (2) one's beliefs (e.g., religious, patriotic); (3) individual social and/or moral situations; and (4) situations relevant to family (Woodard & Pury, 2007). Recent scale development has been completed by positive psychology research teams who were working on what originally were called "wellsprings" measures, and now referred to as the Values in Action Inventory of Strengths (Peterson & Seligman, 2004). The first version of a wellsprings measure included five items (e.g., "I have taken a stand in the face of strong resistance") that tapped courage. The current version measures four types of courage, including valor, authenticity, enthusiasm/zest, and industry/perseverance. Norton and Weiss (2009) have developed a final measure more recently that consists of items that ask individuals to judge their likelihood of acting when experiencing fear, regardless of situational characteristics. More research on psychometric characteristics must be conducted to determine its utility (Pury & Lopez, 2009), but this appears to be another promising research tool for assessing the construct of courage.

In addition, measures of distinct types of courage exist. Kastenmüller, Greitemeyer, Fischer, and Frey (2007) have developed a scale that specifically measures the construct of civil courage (see previous sections for a discussion of this concept). Though at the time of publication this scale is only offered in German, it provides more information about this type of courage and appears to be psychometrically sound (Kastenmüller et al.).

More recently, a new measure designed to assess courage in children has been developed. The Courage Measure for Children (CM-C; Norton & Weiss, 2009) is a 12-item scale that asks Likert-based questions regarding the likelihood of a participant acting in a courageous way (e.g., "If I am anxious about something, I will do it anyway" and "If something scares me, I try to get away from it."). In addition to a self-report version, a parent version of the CM-C is also available for corroboration (Muris, Mayer, & Schubert, 2010).

The development of measures of courage is in its early stages because a comprehensive theory of courage has not been proposed and carefully examined. It will be difficult to develop a model of courage, but this task should be no more difficult than that accomplished already by several wisdom researchers. An important issue here is whether measurement should assess courage as displayed in a courageous act or as embodied by the courageous actor. To compound matters, it is not clear whether we should focus on the tonic (constant) and phasic (waxing and waning) elements of courage, or both. This may depend on the type of courage assessed. Moral courage may possess tonic qualities, as a person may demonstrate it steadily across situations, and it also may possess phasic qualities, as it only *appears* when necessary. (Physical and vital courage may be tonic and phasic as well, but the phasic characteristics are more evident.) For example, tapping the tonic elements of moral courage could be achieved with straightforward questions; traditional scales could yield a meaningful representation of this strength. On the other hand, the phasic elements of moral courage, which only emerge in their pure form when needed in a given situation, may require the assessment techniques of observation, narrative reports, experience sampling methods, and critical incident reviews.

Relationships Between Fear and Courage

Although the link between fear and courage has been assumed for centuries, the relationship is not well understood. One of the first researchers to examine this link, Rachman (1984), observed that frightened people can perform courageous acts. Though courage and fearlessness often are regarded as synonymous, many (see Table 9.1) have argued that perseverance despite fear is the purest form of courage. Indeed, Rachman proposed that true courage is being willing and able to approach a fearful situation despite the presence of subjective fear. In this case, physiological responses may be measured to assess the presence of fear or stress in a given situation in order to determine how the courageous people respond.

Prior to his research on courage, Rachman's (1978) work focused on describing subjective fear and its associated bodily responses. As he developed a firm understanding of fear and its bodily manifestations and made the shift toward courage research, Rachman and his colleagues (Cox, Hallam, O'Connor, & Rachman, 1983; O'Connor, Hallam, & Rachman, 1985) studied the relationship between fear and courage. These researchers compared bomb disposal operators who had received decorations for gallantry to undecorated operators with comparable training and years of service. (The decoration served as a method of identifying individuals with the experience of courageous acts.) Based on Rachman's (1978) previous research, performances under stressors were determined by various subjective, behavioral, and psychophysiological measures. Comparisons revealed distinctive physiological responses under stress for the decorated as compared to the nondecorated bomb disposal operators, although there were no statistically significant differences found (Cox et al., 1983). In a subsequent experimental replication, O'Connor et al. (1985) demonstrated that, relative to comparison persons, the decorated operators maintained a lower cardiac rate under stress. The findings from these studies suggested that people who had performed courageous acts might respond (behaviorally and physiologically) to fear in a way that is different from people who had not demonstrated courage.

Rachman (1984), trying to understand why some people respond to fear in a manner that might be conducive to courageous behavior, studied beginning paratroopers. His assessment of subjective fear and corresponding physiological markers revealed that paratroopers reported a moderate amount of fear at the beginning of their program, but this fear subsided within their initial five jumps. Furthermore, it was found that the execution of a jump despite the presence of fear (i.e., courage) resulted in a reduction of fear.

This line of research begins to unravel the complex relationship between fear and courage. Given the common assumption that a prerequisite fear must be apparent for there to be courage, the link between fear and physical courage, moral courage, and vital courage needs further examination.

Benefits of Courage

There are many beneficial characteristics that seem to be correlated with the construct of courage. For example, in personality research, individuals who have the positive traits of agreeableness and openness also score higher on measures of courage (Muris et al., 2010). Courage was also found to correlate with the Big Five personality trait of extraversion in this study and to have a negative relationship with the trait of anxiety. In addition, courage exhibited in certain scenarios (e.g., educational settings) even in the face of fear of failure has other positive correlates, including a more adaptive coping style and higher levels of confidence, though there is a question of whether or not courage and confidence are distinct enough to be called different constructs (Martin, 2011). As more research is done on this interesting construct, it is likely that other positive correlates could emerge.

Courage and Culture

In closing, we would like to highlight the fact that there is a dearth of literature on the subject of courage and its manifestations in different cultures. Acts deemed "courageous" might differ from culture to culture. For example, the acts of suicide bombers in some areas of the world, or of those who choose to bomb abortion clinics within the United States, are at times considered courageous by the proponents of these cultural groups (e.g., extremist members of some religions). It is safe to say, however, that these might not be considered acts of courage by members of other cultural groups. In some cultural groups (e.g., Asian cultures), deciding to keep a personal opinion quiet in service of the pursuit of harmony of the group might be viewed as courageous, though speaking up at all costs might be viewed as courageous in other groups (e.g., Western cultures; Pedrotti, Edwards, & Lopez, 2009).

In addition, some cultural groups might find courage to be *necessary* more often than others. For instance, the young Pakistani hero Malala Yousafzai, discussed previously, was faced with extreme discrimination and danger, the likes of which might not be present for members of many other cultural groups. Within the United States, problematic race relations may require a basic level of courage from racial, ethnic, and other minorities in order to live day-to-day in our country despite violence directed disproportionately at these groups. As an example, the most recent FBI (2012) statistics regarding hate crimes in the United States show that in the 3,467 incidents of racial bias crimes in 2012, 66.2% were victims of anti-Black bias, versus 22% being victims of anti-White bias. Of the 1,376 hate crimes perpetrated because of sexual orientation bias, 98.1% were due to bias against lesbian, gay, and bisexual individuals, in comparison to 1.9% of heterosexual individuals being targeted due to this type of bias. Finally, courage may be a necessary component of life for women across the world as their safety is not commensurate to that enjoyed by men in most areas of the world (National Organization for Women, 2012; A Safe World for Women, 2013). In researching this necessary, though perhaps more quiet, courage that many of these individuals may need in order to live their daily lives, we may discover a new source of strength to emulate.

FINDING WISDOM AND COURAGE IN DAILY LIFE

Wisdom and courage, probably the most valued of the virtues, are in high demand in our world, and fortunately there is not a limited supply. Indeed, we believe that most people, through a mindful approach to life, can develop wisdom and courage. Feel free to test this hypothesis by completing the Personal Mini-Experiments. Then, create some mini-situations of wisdom and courage by implementing the Life Enhancement Strategies.

Can Courage Be Learned?
Vic Conant
President of Nightingale-Conant Corporation

If you look at the most revered people in history, the people who have done the most for the world, the people who have pushed society forward, you'll invariably find that a major characteristic of those individuals is courage. But what is courage?

S. J. Rachman, a Canadian psychologist specializing in fear and courage, says that many people think of courage as fearlessness. However, Rachman defines courage as perseverance in the face of fear and stress.

Courage is a personal strength, which equates to the ability to act when others of lesser courage will not. It's the ability to act in spite of fear and overwhelming opposition. It's the ability to act in spite of hardship, despair, and sometimes imminent personal physical danger.

Ask yourself, who's the most courageous individual you've personally known? Next, who's the most courageous person you can identify throughout history? Now, what were the courageous characteristics that caused you to choose these individuals? My personal favorite is Winston Churchill. At the end of World War I, Churchill was in charge of the British navy. After a major naval defeat, he was removed from office and then had to endure more than 20 years of rejection of his political views. He admittedly suffered some very low times. But he never wavered on his beliefs. His views were eventually proven correct when the Germans swept through Europe, and Churchill was the obvious choice to become Britain's wartime prime minister.

Everyone automatically looked to him in this time of need because they knew where he stood, and they witnessed him display courage in battle, putting himself in harm's way over and over again. His personal courage and determination helped inspire an entire nation to continue to resist a force that at the time must have seemed to most insurmountable. And yet Churchill wasn't a likely person to become courageous. According to Stephen Mansfield, in his book *Never Give In: The Extraordinary Character of Winston Churchill,* Churchill didn't have physical strength or towering stature. He was neglected, ridiculed, and misused by friends and family alike. He was brought up in the leisure class, which seldom produces principled men of vision. However, in spite of all that, he developed a staggering moral and physical bravery.

Mansfield goes on to say about courage, "It cannot be taught, though it can be inspired. And it normally springs from something like faith or resolve—a commitment to something larger than oneself. It can burst forth instantly as though awakened by a sudden jolt. But, more often, it waits in silence until aroused by some pressing challenge. What is certain of courage, though," he says, "is that true leadership is impossible without it."

Churchill himself said, "Courage is rightly esteemed the first of human qualities, because it is the quality that guarantees all others."

Mansfield is right to say that it would be difficult to teach someone to operate at, as he says, "the staggering level of courage of a Churchill or a Gandhi or a Martin Luther King." However, it's been proven that courage can be learned, and that is incredibly important for any of us who would like to increase our courage in some area of our lives.

Among S. J. Rachman's research, he observed the military bomb-disposal officers serving in the British army in Northern Ireland. He discovered that these men were able to cultivate a great capacity for courage, even if they initially lacked a high degree of self-confidence or a natural ability to persist under pressure. He found that the ability to persist and function well in the face of great danger was largely the result of intense and specialized training for their job. Not only being prepared, but *knowing you are prepared.*

Denis Waitley describes fear as one of the strongest motivating emotions we can experience. Yet we do have the power to choose an even stronger motivation that can override fear and cause us to act courageously.

(Continued)

(Continued)

Denis used to be a Navy pilot, and he observed the training of our astronauts. After some of the most arduous and intense training ever devised, astronauts have been able to act efficiently and effectively, even in incredibly dangerous situations. As Neil Armstrong said after he walked on the moon, "It was just like a drill. It was just like we planned it."

It's apparent that we can become more courageous with enough preparation. If we venture, we do so by faith, because we cannot know the end of anything at its beginning. Isn't this the ultimate reason that doubt and fear are able to eat away at our courage? We're fearful because we cannot know the end of anything at its beginning, and we start imagining the worst possible scenarios. So, it seems our best chance to overcome fear and become courageous is to prepare and then have faith. Now, in what area of your life would you like to become more courageous?

Source: Reprinted with permission of Vic Conant, Chairman of Nightingale Conant Corporation. For information about Nightingale-Conant visit nightingale.com

PERSONAL MINI-EXPERIMENTS

In Search of the Wisdom and Courage of Everyday

In this chapter, we discuss two of the most celebrated human strengths, wisdom and courage. Our review suggests that both these qualities, although extraordinary, are manifested in one's daily life. Here are a few ideas for finding wisdom and courage in everyday people.

The Wisdom Challenge. Consider your views on the following life event. Think aloud and write them down. "A 15-year-old girl wants to get married right away. What should one/she consider and do?" (Baltes, 1993, p. 587). What questions would you want to ask before offering a comment? Write them down. Then, informally evaluate how well your questions address the five criteria of wisdom (factual and procedural knowledge, life-span contextualism, relativism of values, and recognition and management of uncertainty).

Today's Superheroes. Identify real-life superheroes, people you know, who exemplify each type of courage—physical, moral, vital, and civil. Write a brief biography of each person, and, if you are inclined, write a note to these people telling why you think they possess courage. You may be surprised by how easy it is to find people who demonstrate courage, as well as how uncomfortable courageous people are with the label.

Everyday Courage. Look for opportunities to be courageous in your everyday life, and watch for examples from others as well. Don't just focus on big and loud acts, look for quiet courage and bravery as well. Challenge yourself to be brave and start now! Focus on personal and cultural definitions of courage and on ideas about whose common good needs to be considered when identifying courage. Sometimes a great deal of wisdom is needed in determining this.

Life Enhancement Strategies

Pursuits of wisdom and courage have been chronicled in many historical and fictional accounts. For example, Buddha abandoned everything that he knew and loved in order to seek enlightenment, a state of wisdom and love that has defined the Buddhist traditions. And, as we referenced at the beginning of this chapter, the Cowardly Lion trekked through the magical forest in hopes that the Wizard of Oz would grant him the courage that he thought he lacked.

We believe that, over the journey that is your life, you can develop the wisdom and courage to make your life more fulfilling and to contribute to a greater good. By no means do we think it is easy to develop these qualities, but other ordinary people have been able to do so by facing life's challenges . . . and with mindful practice, so can you.

As in most chapters, we categorize the life enhancement strategies across three of life's important domains—love, work, and play. We share two suggestions for each domain, one related to wisdom and one to courage.

Love

- Balancing your love life with your work life will take a tremendous amount of wisdom. Identify one person in your family who is the best role model for using wisdom to balance his or her love life with his or her work life. Interview this person and determine the four wise acts in which he or she engages to maintain that balance.

(Continued)

(Continued)

- Face the fear often associated with dating and making new friends by introducing yourself to twice as many people today as you did yesterday. You can increase and broaden the impact of this challenge to yourself by making sure that some of these new faces look different than your own.

Work

- Share your wisdom about succeeding academically and socially with freshmen at your college or university. Your perspective on how to adapt may prove valuable to other students, particularly those who may not have others in their lives to share this type of wisdom (e.g., first generation college students).

- Stand up for what is just when your rights or the rights of others are violated. Take opportunities to display your moral and civil courage, especially in situations where someone who has less power than you is being mistreated (e.g., situations involving racism, sexism, heterosexism, ageism, etc.).

Play

- Balance your work or school demands with your leisure activities. Reflect on the past week and determine how well you balanced your daily living.

- Pursue recreational interests with a passion, but do not confuse rashness or fearlessness with courage.

THE VALUE OF WISDOM AND COURAGE

"To understand wisdom fully and correctly probably requires more wisdom than any of us have" (Sternberg, 1990, p. 3). Likewise, to understand courage may require a good bit of wisdom. This chapter provides a brief review of what we know about these strengths. Undoubtedly, despite our effort to demonstrate that everyday people embody both of these extraordinary characteristics, the number of times that you are exposed either directly or by the media to images of unwise and rash behavior may outnumber the times that you see virtuous behavior. Given that many people are enamored of the stupid behavior of the unwise and the apparent fearlessness of contestants on past television shows such as *Fear Factor,* we feel compelled to make an even stronger case for celebrating virtue: Wisdom and courage have evolutionary value, whereas stupidity and rash fearlessness thin the herd.

A clear argument for the adaptive value of wisdom is made by Csikszentmihalyi and Rathunde (1990). Wisdom guides our action, and through that wisdom we make good choices when challenged by the social and physical world. This practiced wisdom is intrinsically rewarding and beneficial to the common good; it promotes the survival of good ideas, of oneself, and of others. Indeed, wise ideas and wise people may stand the test of time. A similar case can be made for courage. Physical courage and vital courage often extend lives. So, too, do moral and civil courage preserve the ideals of justice and fairness.

KEY TERMS

Authenticity: A dimension of courage in the Values in Action classification system. Authenticity involves acknowledging and representing one's true self, values, beliefs, and behaviors to oneself and others.

Balance theory of wisdom: A theory developed by Sternberg (1998) that specifies the processes used to balance personal interests with environmental context to achieve a common good. The processes involve using tacit knowledge and personal values to form a judgment of or resolution for competing interests.

Berlin wisdom paradigm: A theory developed by Baltes et al. suggesting that wisdom requires knowledge and insight into the self and others within a cultural context and is "the ways and means of planning, managing, and understanding a good life" (Baltes & Staudinger, 2000, p. 124). The paradigm addresses life-span contextualism, relativism of values, and managing uncertainty.

Civil courage: Described by Greitemeyer, Osswald, Fischer, and Frey (2007) as "brave behavior accompanied by anger and indignation that intends to enforce societal and ethical norms without considering one's own social costs" (p. 115).

Dialectical operations: The use of logical argumentation, discussion, and reasoning as a method of intellectual investigation. Dialectical thinking involves examining and resolving opposing or contradictory ideas and integrating subjective information, motivation, and life experiences.

Enthusiasm/zest: A dimension of courage in the Values in Action classification system. It involves thriving, or having motivation, in challenging situations or tasks.

Explicit theories: Explicit theories examine the externally visible aspects of a construct. For example, in the study of wisdom, explicit theories examine behaviors thought to demonstrate wisdom, such as problem-solving ability. These theories focus on the observable characteristics of a construct.

Implicit theories: Theories that examine the nature or essence of a construct, such as courage, that cannot be directly seen or revealed. Implicit theories or "folk theories" seek to explain through describing characteristics, qualities, and/or dimensions of the desired construct.

Industry/perseverance: A dimension of courage in the Values in Action classification system. It involves undertaking tasks or having initiative and determination to start and complete challenges.

Life-span contextualism: A component of the Berlin wisdom paradigm that requires understanding a problem in terms of its context. These contexts can be aspects of life, such as love, work, and play, as well as cultural and temporal contexts (time and place in society).

Managing uncertainty: A component of the Berlin wisdom paradigm. Using this skill means understanding that any problem-solving strategy or solution involves limitations and requires decision-making flexibility.

Moral courage: Part of O'Byrne, Lopez, and Petersen's (2000) classification of courage; the authentic expression of one's beliefs or values in pursuit of justice or the common good despite power differentials, dissent, disapproval, or rejection.

Phasic: Pertaining to a nonenduring characteristic, a quality that is subject to change depending on the situation, context, or when it is needed.

Physical courage: Part of O'Byrne, Lopez, and Petersen's (2000) classification of courage; an attempted physical behavior or action that seeks to uphold the values of a society or the common good.

Psychological courage: Described by Putman (1997) as a form of vital courage that involves the strength to acknowledge and face personal weaknesses, destructive habits, or threats to one's own psychological stability.

Relativism of values: A component of the Berlin wisdom paradigm; involves understanding that values and priorities are different across people, societies, and time. The value of any idea may vary depending on the context in which it is presented.

Tonic: Pertaining to an enduring characteristic or trait-like quality.

Valor: A dimension of courage in the Values in Action classification system. It involves taking a physical, emotional, or intellectual stance in the face of danger or fear.

Vital courage: Part of O'Byrne, Lopez, and Petersen's (2000) classification of courage, formerly *health/change courage*; a person's persistence and perseverance through a disease, illness, or disability despite an uncertain outcome.

Mindfulness, Flow, and Spirituality

In Search of Optimal Experiences

Perhaps our favorite definition of *insanity* is "doing the same thing over and over again and expecting different results" (attributed to both Albert Einstein and Benjamin Franklin). Why would we engage in the same behavior again and again if we know that the eventual outcome will be negative? Well, passive habits are easy to establish and hard to break (see Bargh & Chartrand, 1999). For example, many of us have done this more than once: turned on the television to "see what's on," watched "nothing" for 3 hours, and then wished we had those 180 minutes back. That kind of habitual, mind-numbing experience may have some short-lived, stress-relieving benefits, but more often it distracts us from what is happening in our worlds. Mindless pursuit of less-than-meaningful goals or unchallenging ones leaves people feeling bored and empty. Conversely, intentional, moment-to-moment searches for optimal experiences give us joy and fulfillment. These positive pursuits may bring about sanity in daily life that is grounded in competence and happiness (Hsu & Langer, 2013; Langer, 1989, 1997; Myers, 2000).

This chapter directs your attention to the moment-to-moment experiences that make up each and every day of our lives. A discussion of mindfulness, flow, and spirituality is framed as searches for optimal experiences. We believe that too many of us walk through everyday life unaware—out of sync with the significance of our experiences and with our emotional selves. Hence, we need to learn more about the psychology of deeper living, a psychology with many applications that teaches about the depths of enjoyment, contentment, and meaningfulness that can be achieved through engagement with everyday life. In fast-paced and future-focused cultural groups (such as the majority culture in the United States), mindfulness is often undervalued. Many American Indian groups, however, have often been shown to have a more present focus in terms of their orientation to time (Ho, 1987), which allows them to cultivate and create mindful experiences on a moment-to-moment basis. Asian cultural practices, specifically Buddhism, also encourage mindfulness and reward its achievement. All cultural groups might take a lesson from the strength found in American Indian and Asian cultural values with regard to living in the moment and paying attention to the present.

In our pursuit of an understanding of optimal experiences, we discuss the searches for novelty, absorption, and the sacred, and we highlight the possible benefits of a more intentional existence (produced with the aid of sound interventions promoting mindfulness, flow, and spirituality). We begin by considering how the moments of our existence hold the potential for giving our lives pleasure and meaning.

MOMENT-TO-MOMENT SEARCHES

In a fast-paced, twenty-first-century world, it is easy to lose sight of the thousands of moments passing in front of our very eyes. Yet each of these moments is accessible (or can be captured), and each has untapped potential; they all are part of our search for optimal experiences. Daniel Kahneman, a psychologist who won the 2002 Nobel Prize in economics, values the currency that is time and understands the relationship between individual moments and the broader experience of life, as suggested by this excerpt from one of his recent addresses:

> Now, there are about 20,000 moments of 3 seconds in a 16-hour day, so this is what life consists of; it consists of a sequence of moments. Each of these moments is actually very rich in experience, so if you could stop somebody and ask, "What is happening to you right now?" a great deal is happening to us at any one of these moments. There is a goal, there is a mental content, there is a physical state, there is a mood, there might be some emotional arousal. Many things are happening. And then you can ask, "What happens to these moments?" (Mitchell, 2003, para. 11)

We certainly can agree that moments are plentiful in daily life. And the potential that each moment holds is reflected in the thoughts, feelings, and physiological forces connected to each moment. From a positive psychology perspective, a day presents 20,000 opportunities for engagement, for overcoming the negative, and for pursuing the positive.

To test our contention that each moment of life is novel and potential packed, try slowing down your day a bit by taking a stroll through a neighborhood . . . with a 3-year-old child. A 3-year-old (who is well rested and generally content) can turn a two-block walk into a grand adventure that lasts about five times longer than you expected. The typical child will attend to everything in his or her line of vision and will happily share thoughts about what is being experienced. When the next "moment" arrives (e.g., another child runs across the path), this child can move on to experience it without any "analysis paralysis" (i.e., "Should I attend to that or to this?"). Undoubtedly, sauntering through a neighborhood with a toddler will draw your attention to the slices of life that are there to be experienced. By adding a bit of intentionality to your belief that each moment has potential, we believe you can actively pursue, on a daily basis, a richer life experience that includes more novelty (*mindfulness*), absorption (*flow*), and attention to the sacred (*spirituality*).

MINDFULNESS: IN SEARCH OF NOVELTY

Some of the best examples of mindfulness are manifested in the everyday behaviors of people. This was indirectly illustrated in the research of Amy Wrzesniewski, a positive psychologist interested in how people function optimally at work (cited in Lopez & Snyder, 2009; Wrzesniewski,

McCauley, Rozin, & Schwartz, 1997; also see Chapter 15.). She found that a third of the hospital cleaners in a metropolitan medical center considered their work a "calling" and therefore did everything they could to make the health care experience positive for patients and staff. These members of the cleaning team essentially reconstrued their jobs by mindfully making moment-to-moment choices about what was worthy of attention, thereby also exercising some control over their duties. Their mindfulness resulted in benefits for others. For example, cleaners who felt they had a calling were quite vigilant in their attempts to keep the hospital sanitary. These cleaners would make generous efforts to make the stays of the long-term patients more bearable by changing the placement of pictures in the rooms and repositioning other objects to give patients new views of their surroundings. Each day, the cleaners found novel ways to improve the hospital environment. (See the story about a hospital orderly told by the senior author [CRS] in Chapter 15.)

Ellen Langer, a social psychologist at Harvard University, made sense out of mindfulness behavior by observing the everyday behavior of people from all walks of life (students, business people, retirees, children). In the context of a research study that examined the effects of perceived control on older adults in a residential care facility, Langer and her colleague Judith Rodin (Langer & Rodin, 1976; Rodin & Langer, 1977) gave a group of residents a "pep talk" about making their own decisions and then allowed these participants each to choose a houseplant to tend over the coming months. Another group of residents received a talk focused on how staff would help them with daily activities and decisions. These participants also received plants, but they were told that the staff would care for them. Over the 3 weeks postintervention, the individuals who were encouraged to make choices and to care for their plants were more alert and happier. They found novelty in every day as their plants and their lives changed little by little.

Langer's follow-up with the facility 18 months later revealed a striking finding: only half as many people in the group encouraged to make choices had died, relative to the group encouraged to take advantage of staff support (7 out of 44 versus 15 out of 43). Langer explained this finding by highlighting the value of "minding" daily choices and the houseplant; this observation launched her into a career dedicated to mindfulness research.

Ellen Langer

Source: Reprinted with permission of Ellen Langer.

In more recent research, Langer (2009b) has conducted studies showing that being mindful about various aspects of our lives can have great health and well-being benefits. In her most recent book, *Clockwise: Mindful Health and the Power of Possibility,* Langer states that many age-related declines and maladies may be at least in part related to the type of mindset that elderly develop as a result of negative stereotypes about older groups that exist in some cultures. Langer states that in being more mindful about not accepting these stereotypes, we may age "better," and she has shown results to this effect in the various studies she depicts. In tuning out what they are *supposed to do* and tuning in to what they *are doing,* older adults may have more realistic and potentially less pathological views of themselves; this may have the effect of improving well-being and possibly health overall (Langer, 2009b).

Mindfulness as a State of Mind

Mindfulness, which sometimes is considered a new-age concept, is comparable to the age-old process of cultivating awareness (of everyday happenings and physiological and psychological sensations) in Buddhist traditions and to the modern therapeutic technique of increasing attention in order to identify distorted thinking (an aspect of cognitive and cognitive–behavioral therapies; Miller, 1995). This said, there are some important differences in Westernized mindfulness and its use in the Buddhist tradition (Keng, Smoski, & Robins, 2011). Whereas in Westernized ideas of mindfulness, this construct may be studied rather independently, it is often viewed as only one component on the road to true enlightenment within Buddhism. In addition, mindfulness must be introspective in Buddhist teachings as opposed to more of an external awareness of surroundings in Western teachings (Keng et al., 2011). Understanding this distinction is important to note, as this is an excellent example of how the definition and utility of a construct is informed by culture.

Although a very commonly discussed psychological phenomenon, mindfulness has not always been very well understood (Bishop et al., 2004). Therefore, we have done our best in what follows to elaborate on Langer's (2009a, 2009b) definition of mindfulness and to describe the benefits of the practice of mindfulness meditation. First, here is Langer's definition of mindfulness, written 25 years after she conducted the study with the elderly residents of the residential care facility:

> [I]t is important to take at least a brief look at what mindfulness is and is not: It is a flexible state of mind—an openness to novelty, a process of actively drawing novel distinctions. When we are mindful, we become sensitive to context and perspective; we are situated in the present. When we are mindless, we are trapped in rigid mind-sets, oblivious to context or perspective. When we are mindless, our behavior is rule and routine governed. In contrast, when mindful, our behavior may be guided rather than governed by rules and routines. Mindfulness is not vigilance or attention when what is meant by those concepts is a stable focus on an object or idea. When mindful, we are actively varying the stimulus field. It is not controlled processing (e.g., 31×267), in that mindfulness requires or generates novelty. (p. 214)

In short, mindfulness is an active search for novelty, whereas mindlessness involves passively zoning out to everyday life. "Automatic pilot" is a form of mindlessness that is attributable to the repetition of behaviors.

Drawing novel distinctions (being mindful) requires us (1) to overcome the desire to reduce uncertainty in daily life, (2) to override a tendency to engage in automatic behavior, and (3) to engage less frequently in evaluations of self, others, and situations. Regarding uncertainty, Langer (2009b) argues that "aspects of our culture currently lead us to try to reduce uncertainty" (p. 280). Our desire to control our surroundings by reducing uncertainty often leads to more uncertainty. For example, a child's effort to hold a spirited kitten or puppy demonstrates this point well. The more the child attempts to hold the little pet still, the more it tries to wriggle away. This also happens in daily life when we attempt to hold things (and people's behavior) still in our attempt to reduce uncertainty. Given that life is not static, Langer contends that we should exploit the uncertainty and proposes that mindfulness "makes clear that things change and loosens the grip of our evaluative mind-sets so that these changes need not be feared" (p. 215). Uncertainty keeps us grounded in the present, and awareness of all that is happening in the present creates more uncertainty.

The automaticity of behavior provides quick, well-honed responses to familiar situations. For example, what do most people do when a phone rings? No matter what else is going on around them, many people automatically reach for their phones and answer them. This response is considered the "one best way" to deal with the given situation—but is it? Do we necessarily need to answer the phone when it rings, irrespective of what else we are doing, or has it become an automatic, mindless behavior? Automaticity of behavior relies on the assumption that the quick, well-rehearsed behavior is the easiest behavior in which to engage. In fact, in the case of the ringing phone, the less automatic behavior (e.g., continuing to chat with friends, working on homework, leaving your house so you are not late for class) may be the most efficient way to behave. Perhaps we are distracted from the novelty of the stimuli right before us when a phone rings. What happens if the phone's ringing becomes a signal or a reminder to search for the novelty right in front us? What happens if we don't answer the phone?

Langer, Blank, and Chanowitz (1978) explored the automaticity of behavior by sending an interdepartmental memorandum to university offices that requested that the recipient handle the memo in a particular manner ("Please return this immediately to Room 247") and another memo that demanded particular handling ("This memo is to be returned to Room 247"). To examine the effects of novelty on behavior, half the memos were formatted in the usual form for interoffice memos, whereas the other half of the memos were formatted in a distinctly different manner. In the end, 90% of the memos that looked like the typical interoffice missive were returned to Room 247; 60% of those that looked a bit different from the typical memo were returned. The automaticity of behavior is quite evident given that the majority of the memos were returned. The potency of attention to novelty, however, also was suggested given that a smaller percentage of uniquely formatted memos was returned. Hence, mindfulness will occur when we become less automatic in our daily behavior and search for novelty.

Making evaluations requires us to cast judgment on ourselves, others, and life situations, as "events do not come with evaluations; we impose them on our experiences and, in so doing, create our experience of the event" (Langer, 2009b, p. 283). Mindfulness may battle our evaluative nature and lead us to make fewer unnecessary judgments, even positive ones. Here-and-now living does require a refined ability to discriminate between subtleties, but this need not lead to an evaluation. For example, on a walk through a park, a statue may catch your eye and grab a few minutes of your attention. During that short span of time, you may mindfully make numerous observations that discriminate between weathered portions of the statue and less weathered portions, or you may notice that it looks taller from one perspective than another. There is no need or benefit for you to mindlessly activate your criteria for quality artwork and pass judgment on the statue, labeling it as either good art or bad art.

Miller's focus on avoiding evaluation of internal events as well as external ones is shared by Bishop and his colleagues (2004). Bishop et al.'s (2004) operationalization of mindfulness, although similar to Langer's (2009b), does discourage continued evaluation of the self, and it draws more attention to the cognitive and emotional components of mindful engagement. In the Bishop et al. two-component system, *self-regulated attention* is honed on current personal experience, and *emotional openness* facilitates the acceptance and appreciation of all internal experiences. Hence, mindfulness from this perspective borrows somewhat from more traditional Buddhist teachings and involves metacognition and emotional awareness.

Turning from Langer's (2009b) and Bishop et al.'s (2004) definitions and discussions of mindfulness, we consider a nuts-and-bolts operationalization of mindfulness that often is used by mindfulness meditation practitioners (Kabat-Zinn, 1990; Shapiro, 2009; Shapiro, Schwartz, & Santerre, 2002). Mindfulness, in the practice community, is parsimoniously described as attending nonjudgmentally to all stimuli in the internal and external environments. In moments of mindfulness, some "mindfulness qualities" (Shapiro et al., 2002) come into consciousness; see Table 10.1. Many of these qualities are positive psychological processes discussed elsewhere in this book.

Table 10.1   Mindfulness Qualities

Nonjudging: Impartial witnessing, observing the present moment by moment without evaluation and categorization

Nonstriving: Non-goal-oriented, remaining unattached to outcome or achievement, not forcing things

Acceptance: Open to seeing and acknowledging things as they are in the present moment; acceptance does not mean passivity or resignation, rather a clearer understanding of the present so one can more effectively respond

Patience: Allowing things to unfold in their time, bringing patience to ourselves, to others, and to the present moment

Trust: Trusting oneself, one's body, intuition, emotions, as well as trusting that life is unfolding as it is supposed to

Openness:[1] Seeing things as if for the first time, creating possibility by paying attention to all feedback in the present moment

Letting go: Nonattachment, not holding on to thoughts, feelings, experiences; however, letting go does not mean suppressing

Gentleness: Characterized by a soft, considerate and tender quality; however, not passive, undisciplined, or indulgent

Generosity: Giving in the present moment within a context of love and compassion, without attachment to gain or thought of return

Empathy: The quality of feeling and understanding another person's situation in the present moment—their perspectives, emotions, actions (reactions)—and communicating this to the person

Gratitude: The quality of reverence, appreciating and being thankful for the present moment

Lovingkindness: A quality embodying benevolence, compassion, and cherishing, a quality filled with forgiveness and unconditional love

Source: Shapiro, S. J., Schwartz, G. E. R., & Santerre, C. (2002). Meditation and positive psychology, in C. R. Snyder & S. J. Lopez (Eds.), *The handbook of positive psychology*, pp. 632–645, New York: Oxford University Press. Copyright © Oxford University Press, Inc. Used by permission of Oxford University Press, Inc.

Note: These categories are offered heuristically, reflecting the general idea that there are mindfulness qualities that should be part of the intention phase as well as the attention phase of a pathway model. A commitment (intention phase) is made to bring the qualities to the practice, and then the qualities are themselves cultivated throughout the self-regulation practice itself (attention phase). See Kabat-Zinn (1990, pp. 33–40) for detailed definitions of the first seven qualities (cognitive in nature) and Shapiro and Schwartz (2000) for the other five (more affective in nature).

1. Openness: Derived from beginner's mind, defined as "a mind that is willing to see everything as if for the first time" (Kabat-Zinn, 1990, p. 35).

Living With Mindfulness
The Women's Heart Foundation

Reactions to stress can have a negative effect on health. [They] can lead to high blood pressure, a rapid resting pulse rate, and . . . heart rhythm disturbances. Reactions to stress can weaken the immune system, which then leads to a variety of illnesses. It is important to learn how to handle stress.

Mindfulness meditation has been shown to help a person manage stressful situations by increasing one's awareness and by making the mind more receptive to one's current situation and internal states. It is a method of fully embracing with minimal resistance to one's current life situation and internal states.

One can bring about increased awareness to any activity. Here are some examples:

Being Mindful of Emotions

With mindfulness meditation, one can learn to be less judgmental. Being less judgmental helps to bring about a more relaxed state. One can learn to watch anger and other emotional states with compassion. This enables one to eventually let go of these states or at least keep from intensifying them.

Being Mindful of Eating

Increasing one's awareness of eating may benefit those who are trying to make changes in their eating habits. Here is how to increase your awareness of eating:

- Look at the food you are about to eat. Focus on what it consists of. Ask yourself, "Do I still want to take this food into my body?"

- Pay close attention to every bite. Food eaten mindfully will be easier to digest, and you will be less likely to overeat.

(Continued)

(Continued)

- Just after eating, notice how the food you ate affects your digestive system. Does it agree with you? Notice how you feel when eating a low-fat meal versus a high-fat meal . . . a candy bar snack versus a raw vegetable snack.

Mindful Stretching Exercises

Gentle stretching and strengthening exercises done very slowly with moment-to-moment awareness of breathing and of the sensations that arise is yoga. Yoga seeks to unite the body, mind, and spirit. This can result in improved health and vitality.

Mindful Breathing and Sitting as a Meditation

Mindful breathing and sitting (meditation) help to relax and focus the mind. Just 5 minutes a day can make you feel more refreshed and energetic. Here are some guidelines for practicing mindful breathing and sitting:

1. Make a special time and place for "non-doing."

2. Adopt an alert and relaxed body posture.

3. Look dispassionately at the reactions and habits of your mind.

4. Bring your attention to your breathing by counting silently "1" on inhalation and "2" on exhalation, "3" on inhalation, etc. When you reach number 10, return to number 1. (If you go beyond the number 10, then you know your mind has wandered.)

5. When your mind wanders, name what it wanders to, and come back to the breathing.

6. Once you have practiced focusing on your breathing, you can use sensation, sound, or watching thoughts as your point of concentration.

You cannot prevent stressful situations in life, but you can control your reactions to them. Practicing mindfulness can help.

Source: "Beliefs Surrounding Mindfulness," poem from the Buddhist faith. Mindfulness is used by many Eastern cultures. The positive use of mindfulness outlined herein was extrapolated from the teachings of Jon Kabat-Zinn. Reprinted with permission. Grateful acknowledgement to the Women's Heart Foundation, which is dedicated to improved survival and quality of life (www.womensheart.org).

The Benefits of Mindfulness

The deliberative practice of mindfulness often takes the form of mindfulness meditation. The aim of mindfulness meditation, generally speaking, is the "development of deep insight into the nature of mental processes, consciousness, identity, and reality, and the development of optimal states of psychological well-being and consciousness" (Walsh, 1983, p. 19) through "opening up." The results of several studies examining the effects of mindfulness meditation are discussed here in order to consider the potential benefits of intentionally searching for novelty. In the past, this body of research was criticized because few rigorous, randomized, controlled studies had been published (Bishop, 2002), but today more randomized clinical trials using the techniques below (and others) have been conducted, and with promising results (for an overview of these, see Keng et al., 2011; See Table 10.1 for some examples from this overview).

Jon Kabat-Zinn (1982, 2005) of the University of Massachusetts adapted some of the ancient Eastern meditation practices and created a form of mindfulness meditation that has been used in the successful treatment of chronic pain and anxiety. In one study, Kabat-Zinn and Skillings (1989) examined the effects of an 8-week, mindfulness-based stress reduction program (MBSR) on stress hardiness (commitment, control, challenge; Kobasa, 1990) and sense of coherence (the ability to find the world meaningful and manageable; Antonovsky, 1987) in hospital patients. The researchers found improvement in both hardiness and coherence over the course of the intervention. In turn, patients with the largest improvements in sense of coherence made the biggest gains in psychological and physical symptom reduction. At the 3-year follow-ups (Kabat-Zinn & Skillings, 1992), the initial gains were maintained, and even further improvement was made in the extent to which patients considered their worlds manageable. Mindfulness meditation practices also appear to decrease our tendency to respond automatically to various stimuli (Wang et al., 2012). In a study conducted in China, participants were involved in an 8-week course involving mindfulness as a component. Participants who were involved in the mindfulness training were better able to resist automatic responses on the Stroop color test and other memory tasks. In addition, in a randomized controlled study, Shapiro, Schwartz, and Bonner (1998) tested the effects of mindfulness meditation on 78 premedical and medical students. Their results revealed increased levels of empathy and decreased levels of anxiety and depression in the meditation group as compared to the wait-list control group. Furthermore, these results held during the students' stressful examination period. The findings were replicated when participants in the wait-list control group received the mindfulness intervention.

Studies involving Mindfulness-Based Cognitive Therapy (MBCT) also have led to positive discoveries. MBCT is also an 8-week, standardized treatment developed to attempt to hold depression at bay in cases of remission (Segal, Williams, & Teasdale, 2002). This group intervention follows the premises of general cognitive therapy in which the goal is to weaken associations between negative thoughts and depressive emotions, but it differs in the sense that it focuses more on awareness of the thoughts and emotions as opposed to the evaluation of legitimacy of these thoughts (Keng et al., 2011). Many beneficial outcomes have been observed through use of MBCT, including reductions in depressive relapse (Teasdale et al., 2000), decreasing depressive symptoms in bipolar individuals (Williams, Russell, & Russell, 2008) and in lessening symptoms of social phobia (Piet, Hougaard, Hecksher, & Rosenberg, 2010; again, see Keng et al., 2001).

Brown and Ryan (2003) conducted a clinical intervention study with cancer patients, targeting an increase in positive emotional states and decreased anxiety. The researchers demonstrated that increases in mindfulness over time related to declines in mood disturbances and stresses.

Biegel, Brown, Shapiro, and Schubert (2009) used a mindfulness-based stress-reduction technique on adolescents dealing with various psychiatric diagnoses and compared this in a randomized clinical trial to a control group. The group who received the mindfulness-based stress-reduction program in this study reported decreases in depressive and anxious symptom-atology and decreased somatic complaints, as well as increases in quality of sleep and positive feelings about themselves.

The benefits of mindfulness meditation go beyond stress relief. For example, Duncan, Coatsworth, and Greenberg (2009) propose a model of mindful parenting that includes "moment-to-moment awareness" (p. 255) of the parent–child relationship with the goal of interacting with more compassion toward our children. More recently, researchers have found that mindful adults are also preferred by children, perhaps because of their more compassionate approach, and may have less self-devaluation following these interactions (Langer, Cohen, & Djikic, 2012). Astin (1997) demonstrated significant increases in spiritual experience after mindfulness meditation interven-tions in a group of undergraduate students. Similarly, Shapiro and colleagues (1998), in a random-ized controlled study, found that higher scores were obtained on a measure of spiritual experience in a meditation group as compared to a control group. Furthermore, these results were replicated when the control group received the same intervention.

As mindfulness-based therapies and treatments have become more common in the past decade, some researchers have also been investigating their relevance and use across multiple populations. Sobczak and West (2013) discuss some important considerations for therapists who have a diverse clientele. Mindfulness may be particularly useful when dealing with adversity and becoming aware of one's emotions so that they might be processed at a deeper level (Fuchs, Lee, Roemer, & Orsillo, 2013; Sobczak & West, 2013). As some individuals in underserved populations (e.g., racial and ethnic minorities and/or those in lower socioeconomic status groups) might face a greater amount of adversity due to discrimination, acculturative stress, and poverty, mindfulness-based treatments provide an excellent opportunity to attend to emotions surrounding these inci-dences. This said, some racial and ethnic groups may have less usefulness for emotions and/or negative values for expressing them in the way majority cultural groups would. Others may have difficulty allowing emotions about issues such as discrimination or prejudice to surface in their conscious mind, as they are likely to bring up stress. These issues must be attended to in the therapy setting so as to provide multiculturally competent mindfulness strategies. In addition, Sobczak and West (2013) note that some components of being mindful may have to be tempered somewhat depending on environment. In the case of an individual living in a lower socioeconomic neighborhood with the threat of violence, it may not be functional to stop assessing or judging threat in the environment. In these cases, validating that keeping vigilant and assessing danger is sensible and allowing the client to become aware of emotions related to this and process them will be key.

Finally, some research points to the fact that being mindful in one's daily life might increase the ability to multitask (Ie, Haller, Langer, & Courvoisier, 2012). Though this might seem somewhat counterintuitive, this research showed that increases in cognitive flexibility as a result of trait mindfulness appear to be linked to a greater ability to multitask in every day life. (To explore the benefits of mindfulness in your relationships, try the Personal Mini-Experiments.)

Neurological Findings With Mindfulness

In the past few years, much attention has been paid to the neuroscience behind mindfulness, with particular interest paid to its neurological benefits (Tang & Posner, 2013). Improving mind-fulness is related to better spatial abilities regardless of gender (Chiesa, Calati, & Serretti, 2011;

Geng, Zhang, & Zhang, 2011); increased ability for awareness (Jerath, Barnes, Dillard-Wright, Jerath, & Hamilton, 2012); and potential increased neuroplasticity in the brain (Berkovich-Ohana, Glicksohn, & Goldstein, 2012). In order to delineate clinical implications of the use of mindfulness, some studies have mapped the neurological process of mindfulness, though there is not consistent agreement in this area. In neuroscience, emotional regulation is thought to occur in two distinct ways. A "top-down" approach to this is where cognitive reappraisal of a situation occurs in order to modulate the emotional impact of the stimulus; this contrasts with a "bottom-up" approach in which the base reaction to the stimulus is modulated without the need to cognitively reappraise and utilize higher order functioning (Chiesa, Serretti, & Jakobsen, 2013). Researchers do not agree on whether the process of mindfulness follows a bottom-up or a top-down procedure, as evidence of both seems to exist. It may be that mindfulness helps to regulate emotions in a top-down fashion in those who have just learned mindfulness techniques, but this becomes more of a bottom-up strategy in longer-term users (Chiesa et al., 2013). In support of this hypothesis is a finding that individuals who possess high trait mindfulness appear to control emotional reactions to sources of threat by producing less cortisol (a bottom-up process), even in the face of a social stressor (Brown, Weinstein, & Creswell, 2012). Those who are taught mindfulness strategies may use a more top-down process until these strategies become more automatic for them. More research continues to be produced on this exciting topic, and the next step will be to determine application of these findings.

Cultivating Mindfulness

The fostering and encouragement of mindfulness is something that many groups have been doing throughout history. In some Native American traditions (specifically Cherokee), the practice of *ayeli* is described as a "centering technique" that can be used to help individuals to become more mindful (Garrett, Brubaker, Rivera, Gregory, & Williams, 2011; Garrett & Garrett, 2002). This practice involves both breathing and meditation techniques that allow participants to sit in the moment and to allow balance and integration to assist them in increasing personal wellness. A large part of this technique involves orienting oneself to value relations to other things.

The cultivation of mindfulness may be of especial use to those studying in the field of psychology, specifically counseling psychology trainees and interns. Schure, Christopher, and Christopher (2008) conducted a long-term qualitative study in which counseling students were taught the arts of hatha yoga, qigong (meditation and movement from a Chinese tradition), and sitting meditation and then assessed for changes in their lives through the use of open-ended interview questions. Students who engaged in these mindfulness-inducing techniques reported positive changes in interpersonal, physical, cognitive, and affective arenas and felt that these changes enhanced their abilities as counselors (Schure et al.). In a second study, Greason and Cashwell (2009) found that a higher degree of mindfulness in counseling psychology trainees predicted higher levels of counseling self-efficacy and empathy in these students. These researchers posit that the effects of mindfulness on counseling self-efficacy might be mediated by attention, specifically, and discuss it as a skill to pursue cultivating during the training of counselors.

Mindfulness may also be of interest in looking at the development of what Thomas (2006) calls "cultural intelligence (CQ)" (p. 78). Speaking mostly of CQ's use in business settings, Thomas discusses the use of mindfulness as a primary ingredient in developing this useful construct. Similar in some ways to social intelligence (Kihlstrom & Cantor, 2000) and emotional intelligence

(Goleman, 1995), Thomas defines CQ as "the ability to interact effectively with people who are culturally different" (p. 80). This concept views mindfulness as a link between behavior and knowledge that accounts for the ability to have awareness in the moment, which can assist one in achieving an effective cross-cultural interaction. This mindful behavior may be manifested in different ways, such as being aware of one's biases, noting context in various situations, and tuning in to different worldviews and perspectives as they may affect these interactions (Thomas, 2006). Thus, mindfulness may be a construct of particular use in our increasingly diverse society today.

Lastly, mindfulness is something that can be taught to children as well as adults. In one study, children were encouraged to take time to reflect moment to moment on various experiences. Results showed that children who were taught these strategies had better self-regulation skills and were also able to solve problems and think more creatively (Zelazo & Lyons, 2012). More research here might have benefits for children in many different situations.

FLOW: IN SEARCH OF ABSORPTION

Flow experiences have been observed throughout time, across cultures, and in countless creative and competitive endeavors. Such experiences are vividly described in accounts of the responses of the world's great artists, scientists, and religious figures to the challenge of seemingly overwhelming tasks. For example, historical accounts suggest that Michelangelo worked on the ceiling of the Vatican's Sistine Chapel for days at a time. Totally absorbed in his work, he would go without food and sleep and push through discomfort until he ultimately passed out from exhaustion. He was consumed by work, neglecting self-care and the needs of others. (Legend has it that Michelangelo went weeks without changing his clothes, including his boots. One of his assistants supposedly observed the skin of his foot peel down as a boot was removed.)

PERSONAL MINI-EXPERIMENTS

In Search of Optimal Experiences

In this chapter, we discuss mindfulness, flow, and spirituality. Our review suggests that intentional pursuits of novelty, absorption, and the sacred can lead you to the good life. Here are a few ideas for experiments aimed at helping you initiate these searches and explore the benefits.

Searching for Novelty: Increasing Mindfulness in Your Relationships. According to Table 10.1, numerous behaviors are associated with mindfulness. For example, *nonjudging* is impartial witnessing, observing the present moment by moment without evaluation and categorization. *Nonstriving* involves non-goal-oriented behavior, remaining unattached to outcome or achievement, not forcing things. What would happen if you practiced these behaviors for one day in a significant relationship? Try no judgments and no "forcing things." Be an impartial witness, remain unattached to outcomes for one day, and attempt careful introspection. Then, at the end of the day, ask your partner what differences he or she has noticed in your behavior.

Searching for Absorption: Finding Flow in Your School Day. Have you ever wondered how much your screen time (time in front of television, surfing the Internet, instant messaging) affects your ability to immerse yourself in your schoolwork? Take a break from all screen time (except academic use of computers) for 2 days and determine whether your ability to concentrate increases or decreases. If focused attention increases during this trial period, be sure to decrease screen time during busy times in your academic semester.

Searching for the Sacred: Being More Spiritual in Daily Life. Often, the search for the sacred is cast as a grand journey toward a life-changing goal, but it actually requires small daily steps. Jon Haidt at New York University (http://people.stern.nyu.edu/jhaidt/) created the following exercises to help folks start the search. Try these brief exercises and see how they work for you:

- For 5 minutes a day, relax and think about the purpose of life and where you fit in.

- For 5 minutes a day, think about the things you can do to improve the world or your community.

- Read a religious or spiritual book, or go to a religious service every day.

- Explore different religions. You can do this by going to a library, looking on the Internet, or asking your friends about their religions.

- Spend a few minutes a day in meditation or prayer.

- Invest in a book of affirmations or optimistic quotes. Read a few every day.

Mihaly Csikszentmihalyi

Source: Christopher Csikszentmihalyi.

Mihaly Csikszentmihalyi was intrigued by the stories about artists who lost themselves in their work. Studying the creative process in the 1960s (Getzels & Csikszentmihalyi, 1976), Csikszentmihalyi was struck by the fact that, when work on a painting was going well, the artist persisted single-mindedly, disregarding hunger, fatigue, and discomfort—yet rapidly lost interest in the artistic creation once it had been completed (Nakamura & Csikszentmihalyi, 2009, p. 195). Csikszentmihalyi (1975/2000) also noted that forms of play (e.g., chess, rock climbing) and work (e.g., performing surgery, landing a plane) often produced similar states of engagement. Over the last 30 years, Csikszentmihalyi has interviewed and observed thousands of people, and his views on the concept of flow guide us in our discussion of this state of "full-capacity" living that is believed to be directly linked to optimal development and functioning.

The Flow State

Decades of qualitative and quantitative research (summarized in Nakamura and Csikszentmihalyi, 2009) have explored the underpinnings of intrinsic motivation. Indeed, psychology has grappled with the issue of why people pursue particular goals with great fervor in the absence of external rewards (e.g., money and praise). Csikszentmihalyi (e.g., 1978, 1997, 1975/2000) examined this issue in order to understand "the dynamics of momentary experience and the conditions under which it is optimal" (Nakamura & Csikszentmihalyi, 2009, p. 197). Csikszentmihalyi conducted extensive interviews of people from many walks of life; he also developed and used the experience sampling method, in which research participants are equipped with programmable watches, phones, or hand-held computers that signal them, at preprogrammed times throughout the day, to complete a measure describing the moment at which they were paged. To date, the conditions of flow appear to be remarkably similar across work settings, play settings, and cultures. These conditions of flow include (1) perceived challenges or opportunities for action that stretch (neither underutilizing or overwhelming) existing personal skills and (2) clear proximal goals and immediate feedback about progress.

Many of Csikszentmihalyi's early research participants described their optimal momentary experiences as being "in flow," hence his use of the term to describe the phenomenon. Based on the early interviews, Csikszentmihalyi (1975/2000) mapped out the landscape of deep flow experiences by graphically representing the relationship between perceived challenges and skills. Three regions of momentary experiences were identified: (1) *flow,* where challenges and skills matched; (2) *boredom,* where challenges and opportunities were too easy relative to skills, and (3) *anxiety,* where demands increasingly exceeded capacities for action (see Figure 10.1).

Under the flow conditions of perceived challenge to skills, clear goals, and feedback on progress, experience unfolds from moment to moment, and the subjective state that emerges has the following characteristics (as listed in Nakamura and Csikszentmihalyi, 2009):

- Intense and focused concentration on what one is doing in the present moment

- Merging of action and awareness

- Loss of reflective self-consciousness (i.e., loss of awareness of oneself as a social actor)

- A sense that one can control one's actions; that is, a sense that one can in principle deal with the situation because one knows how to respond to whatever happens next

- Distortion of temporal experience (typically, a sense that time has passed faster than normal)

- Experience of the activity as intrinsically rewarding, such that often the end goal is just an excuse for the process

Figure 10.1   The Original Model of the Flow State

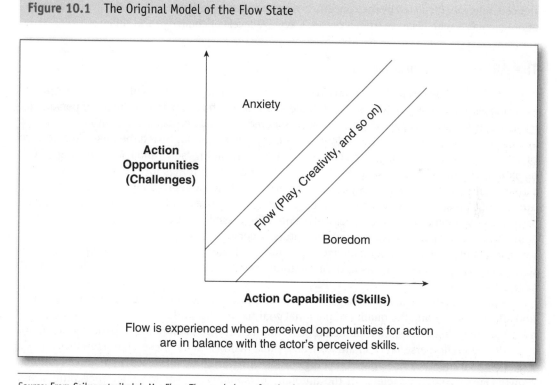

Flow is experienced when perceived opportunities for action are in balance with the actor's perceived skills.

Source: From Csikszentmihalyi, M., *Flow: The psychology of optimal experience.* Copyright © 1990 by Mihaly Csikszentmihalyi.

The search for absorption in momentary experiences is primarily an intentional attentional process. Intense concentration is dedicated to the present activity, followed by the merging of action and awareness. The loss of self-consciousness occurs as flow emerges. Maintaining the flow state is quite challenging given the many distractions from the outside world and the self-talk that may involve criticism of performance. (Hence, a mindful, nonjudgmental approach to personal performance may be necessary for achieving deep flow.) When considering the quality of flow state, the variable of interest is time spent absorbed, with more engagement in flow being better for the individual.

The conceptualization of flow has not changed much over the last quarter century of research. The model of balancing perceived challenge and skill has been refined, however, by Delle Fave, Massimini, and colleagues (Delle Fave & Massimini, 1988, 1992; Massimini & Carli, 1988; Massimini, Csikszentmihalyi, & Carli, 1987), who, by using the experience sampling method, discovered that the quality of a momentary experience intensifies as challenges and skills move beyond a person's *average* levels. For example, if you play chess with a typical 6-year-old, the experience will not present you with an average or above-average challenge that requires higher-level skills. If you play chess with someone with considerably more experience and skill, however, you experience a great challenge, your skills will be stretched, and flow is more likely. See Figure 10.2 for a depiction of a flow model that takes into account these characteristics of flow. Apathy is experienced when perceived challenges and skills are below a person's average levels; when they are above, flow is experienced. Intensity (depicted by the concentric rings) of each experience (e.g., anxiety, arousal, relaxation) increases with distance from a person's average levels of challenge and skill.

The Autotelic Personality

The majority of flow research has focused on flow states and the dynamics of momentary optimal experiences. Csikszentmihalyi (1975/2000) did hypothesize, however, that a cluster of personality variables (e.g., curiosity, persistence, low self-centeredness) may be associated with the ability to achieve flow and with the quality of flow that is experienced. He suggested the possible existence of an autotelic personality (from the Greek words *autos,* meaning "self," and *telos,* meaning "end"), as exhibited by a person who enjoys life and "generally does things for [his or her] own sake, rather than in order to achieve some later external goal" (Csikszentmihalyi, 1997, p. 117). The amount of time spent in flow has been used as a rough measure of this personality type (Hektner, 1996), but this operationalization does not account for possible environmental influences on flow. A more nuanced operationalization of the autotelic personality focused on the disposition to be intrinsically motivated in high-challenge, high-skill situations. This conceptualization of the autotelic personality has been measured via quantitative methods (Csikszentmihalyi, Rathunde, & Whalen, 1993).

The autotelic personality in teenagers within the United States appears to be related to positive and affective states and the quality of personal goal statements (Adlai-Gail, 1994). In a sample of adults in the United States, Abuhamdeh (2000) found that, when compared to people who do not have the autotelic personality characteristics, those who do have these characteristics have a preference for high-action-opportunity, high-skills situations that stimulate them and encourage growth. Furthermore, people with the autotelic personality appear to experience little stress when in the flow quadrant (see Figure 10.1), whereas the reverse is true for adults without these characteristics.

Cultural Comparisons and Considerations in the Flow Experience

As our globe seemingly grows smaller, we become more and more aware of the fact that different conditions and contexts may be necessary to maximize strengths in individuals from different cultural backgrounds (Markus & Kitayama, 1991). Though flow has been studied more often in Western contexts (Moneta, 2004a), some cross-cultural differences have been found in looking at various groups. Moneta (2004b) found that Chinese students in Hong Kong did not experience

Figure 10.2   The Current Model of the Flow State

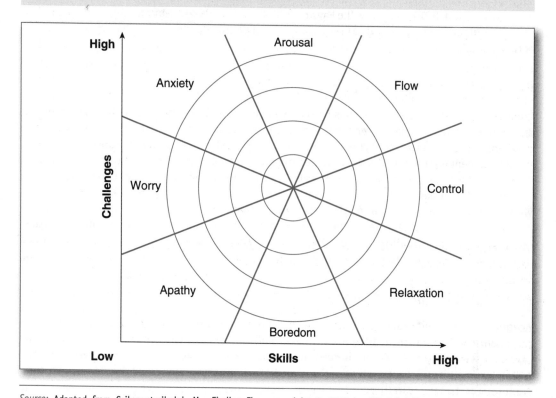

Source: Adapted from Csikszentmihalyi, M., *Finding Flow,* copyright © 1997 by Mihalyi Csikszentmihalyi. Reprinted by permission of Basic Books, a member of Perseus Books, L.L.C.

flow in accordance with the optimal challenge/skill conditions that Csikszentmihalyi's (2000) model found in Western populations; instead, these participants preferred skill level to be higher than challenge level. They evaluated high-challenge situations negatively, which Moneta (2004b) postulates could be because of the higher values of prudence (among other traits) in this culture. Similarities have also been found across cultures. Asakawa (2004) investigated autotelic personality and flow experience in general in Japanese college students and found that Csikszentmihalyi's (2000) flow model was a good fit for these individuals (i.e., high challenge plus high skill produced flow experiences as in Western samples). In 2010, Asakawa found that the Japanese college students who were more autotelic and had more flow experiences also scored higher on measures of self-esteem, scored lower on scales measuring anxiety, and had better coping strategies (Asakawa, 2010). Factors that seemed to contribute to flow included college engagement (including academic work and college life in general) and were positively linked to more frequency of the flow experience. In addition, these Japanese participants scored higher in *Jujitsu-kan,* a Japanese concept meaning possession of a sense of fulfillment. Finally in this study, it appears that Japanese individuals experienced flow far less often in comparison with data that have been collected in other studies with U.S. and German participants. More research in this area is necessary for us to fully understand how flow may work in non-Western, and/or non-majority cultural groups (Asakawa, 2010; Ishimura & Kodama, 2006). Again, this contributes to our understanding of how context and cultural values may dictate what circumstances are necessary to achieve an actual flow state.

Longitudinal Flow Research

Longitudinal research on flow reveals how flow experiences are associated with achievement (in academics, work, or sports) over time. For example, Csikszentmihalyi et al. (1993) tracked the development of talented teenagers through high school. These researchers found that commitment to a talent area at age 17 was predicted by the student's identification of this talent area as a source of flow 4 years previously, as well as by the amount of flow and anxiety experienced at the time of the initial data gathering (when the students were 13 years old). Similarly, Heine (1996), who studied students skilled in mathematics, found that those who experienced flow in the first part of a math course performed better in the second half (controlling for initial abilities and grade point average). These findings suggest that commitment, persistence, and achievement exhibited by teenagers are associated with previous experiences of flow.

Fostering Flow and Its Benefits

According to the flow model, experiencing absorption provides intrinsic rewards that encourage persistence in and return to an activity. Hence, skills related to that activity might be enhanced over time. Therefore, the goal of intervention researchers interested in the applications of flow is to help people identify those activities that give them flow and to encourage people to invest their attentions and energies in these activities.

Flow researchers (e.g., Csikszentmihalyi, 1990, 1997; Csikszentmihalyi & Robinson, 1990; Jackson & Csikszentmihalyi, 1999; Nakamura & Csikszentmihalyi, 2009; Perry, 1999) have assisted people in their search for absorption by describing two paths to becoming more engaged with daily life: (1) finding and shaping activities and environments that are more conducive to flow experiences and (2) identifying personal characteristics and attentional skills that can be tweaked to make flow more likely.

In his consultation practices, Csikszentmihalyi has modified numerous work environments to increase the chances of producing flow. For example, he worked with the Swedish police to identify obstacles to flow in their daily work routines and then to make their work more conducive to flow on the beat. (Specifically, officers were encouraged to walk the beat alone on occasion, rather than with their partners, so that they could become more absorbed in their work.) Flow principles also have been incorporated into the design of workplaces and into the organization of displays at art venues, including those at the J. Paul Getty Museum in Southern California, to increase the enjoyment of visits to these sites.

Several clinical researchers (e.g., Inghilleri, 1999; Massimini et al., 1987) have used the experience sampling method and flow principles to help individuals discover and sustain flow. This use of the experience sampling method data provides feedback on momentary experiences and identifies activities and environments in which optimal experience can be increased.

Perhaps the best application of flow principles has occurred at the Key School in Indianapolis, Indiana, where the goal is to foster flow by influencing both the environment and the individual (Whalen, 1999). In the school's Flow Activities Center, students have regular opportunities to actively choose and engage in activities related to their own interests and then pursue these activities without demands or distractions, creating what has been described as "serious play" (Csikszentmihalyi et al., 1993). In support of students' searches for absorption, teachers encourage students to challenge and stretch themselves; teachers also provide new challenges to the children to foster growth. (See the Personal Mini-Experiments for a flow experiment and the Life Enhancement Strategies for tips for enhancing flow within the domains of your life.)

As always, taking note of cultural background is an essential part of developing an effective intervention for various groups. More research needs to be done in this area to determine if different conditions foster opportunities for different cultural groups to experience flow in their daily lives (Moneta, 2004b).

New Areas of Investigation Involving Flow: Gaming and Internet Use

In this "technological age," the use of the Internet for social media, gaming, and other functions is of interest in numerous contexts. Many people, from professionals to adolescents and children, spend hours online engaging in technological pursuits. While some of these activities may have purposes (e.g., doing research for a school paper, investigating ratings of elementary schools), many people seem to spend time on the Internet just for the sake of being online. Those who study digital gaming have proposed that the flow state is experienced by some during this type of activity (Boyle, Connolly, Hainey, & Boyle, 2012; Procci, Singer, Levy, & Bowers, 2012; Sherry, 2004). This same conclusion has been drawn by some who study Internet shopping and browsing behavior (Hsu, Chang, & Chen, 2012). The loss of awareness of time, desire to keep playing despite physical discomfort, and the experience of action and awareness merging are reported by those who engage in these types of activities (Procci et al., 2012). One distinction that has been made in this literature, however, is the fact that flow is described as a *constructive* or *beneficial* construct. As some of these Internet-related behaviors may take on an almost addiction-like quality, perhaps those engaging in them cannot accurately be described as experiencing flow in the way Csikszentmihalyi describes it (Thatcher, Wretschko, & Fridjhon, 2008; Voiskounsky, 2010). More research and better measurement is needed here (Procci et al., 2012), and future developments may help to clarify this distinction.

Life Enhancement Strategies

Every day you make thousands of choices about how to focus your attention and spend your time. We hope that you choose to become more intentional in your searches for novelty, for absorption, and for the sacred (as you define it in your life.)

(Continued)

(Continued)

As in most chapters, we categorize the life enhancement strategies across three of life's important domains—love, work, and play. Three suggestions for each domain are shared here, one related to each of the topics of this chapter.

Love

- Orient yourself to the mindfulness relationship skills presented in Chapter 12.

- Identify an activity that helps you and a friend achieve flow at the same time. Then, spend more time jointly engaged in that activity.

- Find out how a significant other defines the sacred and ask that person how he or she pursues it.

Work

- Practice making nonjudgmental observations when working with classmates or colleagues.

- Volunteer for assignments and projects that challenge or stretch your existing skills. These tasks are more likely to bring about flow than are easy assignments.

- Find a spiritual haven at work or school that allows you to pursue the sacred during your breaks in the day.

Play

- Read a book on mindfulness meditation (e.g., Kabat-Zinn, 1990) and practice some of the basic skills.

- Pursue recreational activities that are known to induce flow: playing chess, riding a mountain bike, climbing a rock wall, learning a second language, etc.

- Make your search for the sacred a communal experience; invite friends to join you in your favorite spiritual pursuit.

SPIRITUALITY: IN SEARCH OF THE SACRED

Glancing at someone engaged in everyday behavior can evoke thoughts about spirituality. For example, imagine a picture of an older woman kneeling with a look of utter concentration on her face. Her search for the sacred (that which is set apart from the ordinary and worthy of veneration) may be inferred from her behavior; this is the case if a church interior appears in the background of the woman's image . . . or if a garden serves as the backdrop. This search for the sacred can happen anywhere, any time because, like flow and mindfulness, spirituality is a state of mind, and it is universally accessible.

The term *search for the sacred* is a widely accepted description of spirituality. (Religion and religious behaviors represent the many ways in which the search for the sacred becomes organized and sanctioned in society; for example, through the attendance of religious services and the frequency and duration of prayer.) In 2000, Hill et al. defined spirituality as "the feelings, thoughts, and behaviors that arise from a search for the sacred" (p. 66). Pargament and Mahoney (2009) also defined spirituality "as a search for the sacred" and elaborated that "people can take a virtually limitless number of pathways in their attempts to discover, conserve and transform the sacred" (p. 612). These pathways to the sacred also may be described as spiritual strivings, which include personal goals associated with the ultimate concerns of purpose, ethics, and recognition of the transcendent (Emmons, Cheung, & Tehrani, 1998).

Kenneth Pargament

Source: Reprinted with permission of Kenneth Pargament.

Psychology researchers agree with the foregoing definitions of spirituality, and there is general support for the belief that spirituality is a positive state of mind experienced by most people. Peterson and Seligman (2004) contend that spirituality is a strength of transcendence, stating, "Although the specific content of spiritual beliefs varies, all cultures have a concept of an ultimate, transcendent, sacred, and divine force" (p. 601). Similarly, Pargament and Mahoney (2009) argue that spirituality is a vital part of society and psychology within the United States:

> First, spirituality is a "cultural fact" (cf. Shafranske & Malony, 1990): The vast majority of Americans believe in God (95%), believe that God can be reached through prayer (86%), and feel that religion is important or very important to them (86%) (Gallup Organization, 1995; Hoge, 1996). Second, in a growing empirical body of literature, the important implications of spirituality for a number of aspects of human functioning are being noted. Included in this list are mental health (Koenig, 1998), drug and alcohol use (Benson, 1992), marital functioning (Mahoney et al., 1999), parenting (Ellison & Sherkat, 1993), the outcomes of stressful life experiences (Pargament, 1997), and morbidity and mortality (Ellison & Levin, 1998; Hummer, Rogers, Nam, & Ellison, 1999). . . . There are, in short, some very good reasons why psychologists should attend more carefully to the spiritual dimension of peoples' lives. (p. 647)

Despite its ubiquitous nature and scholarly agreement on its definition, psychological researchers and the general public continue to muddy the waters when discussing spirituality. For example, Peterson and Seligman's (2004) Values in Action Classifications of Strengths lumped spirituality together with similar, yet different, concepts such as religion and faith. And, in a large group of research participants, nearly 75% identified themselves as being both spiritual and religious (Zinnbauer et al., 1997). The fuzziness of the construct under-mines efforts to understand the actual effects of searching for the sacred on a person's functioning.

THE TRUE BENEFITS OF SPIRITUALITY?

Many positive psychologists (e.g., Lopez & Snyder, 2009; Peterson & Seligman, 2004) have hypoth-esized that a deep understanding of ourselves and our lives is enhanced by our search for the sacred. Indeed, as noted previously, spirituality is associated with mental health, managing sub-stance abuse, marital functioning, parenting, coping, and mortality (summarized in Pargament & Mahoney, 2009; Thoresen, Harris, & Oman, 2001). One examination of spiritual strivings reveals that these pathways to the sacred may lead to (or at least are associated with) well-being (Emmons et al., 1998). Though much research in this area has been conducted with individuals who identify with a variety of Christian religions, the same links have been found between religiosity and hap-piness in Muslim undergraduates (Sahraian, Gholami, Javadpour, & Omidvar, 2013). Better overall mental health may be another benefit, though the function of spirituality in cultural context is important to distinguish here (Dein, Cook, & Koenig, 2012). Another examination of spiritual striv-ings suggests the search for the sacred may lead to what we consider to be the true benefits of spirituality in our lives: purpose and meaning (Mahoney et al., 2005). Finally, a higher level of spiritual commitment may increase levels of hope and optimism (over and above variance pre-dicted by a personality measure; Ciarrocchi, Dy-Liacco, & Deneke, 2008). Despite the findings that demonstrate the benefits of searching for the sacred, the mechanisms by which spirituality leads to positive life outcomes are not clear.

The connection between spirituality and other positive states may be bidirectional as well. While much of the literature has investigated the effects of spirituality on positive traits and emo-tions, Saroglou, Buxant, and Tilquin (2008) looked at this relationship from another angle and found that positive emotions are also predictive of spirituality and religiousness. These researchers found that when positive emotions were induced in individuals in their study, scores on measures of both religiousness and spirituality were found to be higher than in those individuals who had neutral emotions. As spirituality is associated with many other positive characteristics (Pargament & Mahoney, 2009), increasing this construct in the individual may have implications for the devel-opment of other beneficial experiences.

Other research shows that spirituality and religiosity may be particularly beneficial in times of strife, or when coping is necessary. Links have been found between these constructs and better coping in patients dealing with schizophrenia (Mohr et al., 2011); struggling with cancer (Holt et al., 2011); dealing with chronic illness (Dalmida, Holstad, Diorio, & Laderman, 2012; Harvey & Cook, 2010); living with chronically ill children (Allen & Marshall, 2010); and taking care of elders (Koerner, Shirai, & Pedroza, 2013). In addition, spirituality may be a useful part of therapeutic treatment in some cultural groups, namely African American (Alawiyah, Bell, Pyles, & Runnels, 2011; Boyd-Franklin, 2010) and Latino (Koerner et al., 2013) individuals. Individuals dealing with low socioeconomic status who are also religious show better physical health and higher well-being than one would expect given their environments (Steffen, 2012). Finally, Rowles and Duan (2012) have found that although perceived racism appears to lead toward lack of feelings of encouragement in African Americans, the effects of this may be buffered somewhat by the presence of spirituality in the lives of these individuals. This is a hopeful finding as perceived racism has so many negative effects (both psychological and physical) on the recipient and represents another situation in which spirituality may aid in coping.

THE SEARCH CONTINUES

"Zoning out," experiencing apathy and boredom, and feeling as though we lack direction in our lives are signs that we are not actively engaged with daily experience. What if we use these signs of disengagement as prompts to initiate searches for novelty, absorption, and the sacred? For example, next time you are driving and lose track of a stretch of road, take that as a nudge to search for novelty in the next few miles of highway. Seek out new experiences with people who are different from you. When you find yourself thinking, "I'm bored," lose yourself in the activity that brings you the most flow, and make a commitment to engage in activities such as this on a more regular basis. Finally, when you feel aimless, turn your attention to your search for the sacred, or use the benefits of spirituality when dealing with strife or frustration.

Practicing mindfulness, flow, and spirituality may have benefits for your psychological and physical health, your academic or work performance, and your sociocultural well-being. These practices may have a more profound effect on us. Indeed, these searches may lead us to a greater appreciation for diversity and a deeper existence, one that is filled with meaning.

KEY TERMS

Autotelic personality: A cluster of traits exhibited by a person who enjoys life and who "generally does things for [his or her] own sake, rather than in order to achieve some later external goal" (Csikszentmihalyi, 1997, p. 117). From the Greek words *autos,* meaning "self," and *telos,* meaning "end."

Experience sampling method: A research method used to study flow experiences. Participants are signaled via watches, phones, or hand-held computers and asked to answer questions about their experiences at each moment they are paged.

Mindfulness: Openness to novelty and sensitivity to context and perspective. Mindfulness involves cultivating an awareness of everyday happenings and physiological and psychological sensations; overcoming the desire to reduce uncertainty in everyday life; overriding the tendency to engage in automatic behavior; and engaging less frequently in evaluating oneself, others, and situations.

Spirituality: As commonly defined, the thoughts, feelings, and behaviors that fuel and arise from the search for the sacred.

Prosocial Behavior

CHAPTER 11

Empathy and Egotism

Portals to Altruism, Gratitude, and Forgiveness

In this chapter, we explore how empathy and egotism can lead to altruism, gratitude, and forgiveness (see Figure 11.1). As a prelude to describing how this can occur, we share a story.

Figure 11.1 Empathy and Egotism as Portals to Altruism, Gratitude, and Forgiveness

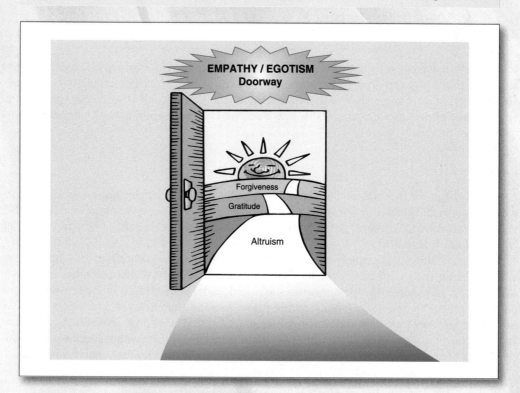

Rick went to 12 different schools before graduating from high school. Every year, around the month of October, his family moved because his dad was transferred or promoted, lost his job, or found a new job. Forced to interact with a new group of kids each year, Rick was the outsider— looking yet again for friendship from different peers. Painfully aware of his plight as the "new kid," he became fascinated with the lives of the children around him. He watched, listened, and learned to see the world from the perspectives of these other kids. Not particularly talented in any area, Rick was not much of a threat to the other children of these "little societies" into which he was thrust.

Although he longed to become a real participant in the lives of the other kids, a single year in each location was not enough time for the other children to let him into their lives. Unable to make solid friendship bonds in this short time period, Rick instead became sensitive to the emotional plights and needs of the other kids. This sense of empathy made him want to help the other children, but they did not see him as a legitimate source of help because he was an outsider. In short, his understanding and empathy produced a compassion and desire to help others, but he could not successfully fulfill this need.

It was only when he grew up and for the first time had the luxury of staying in the same place that Rick could use his empathy to actually help others. Indeed, his empathy fostered his altruism, gratitude, and forgiveness in the context of these later, enduring, adult relationships. In truth, however, he also felt good (enhanced ego and self-esteem) when he expressed these constructs. This story's protagonist is the senior author of this book. Perhaps you have had similar childhood experiences.

ALTRUISM

In this section, we begin by defining *altruism*. Next, we explore the egotism (or esteem) motive and show that it also can drive various types of altruistic actions. We then discuss the **empathy– altruism hypothesis** and follow with discussions of the genetic and neural underpinnings of empathy and of cultural variations of this construct. We close with approaches for enhancing and measuring altruism.

Defining Altruism

Altruism is behavior that is aimed at benefiting another person. Altruistic behavior can be motivated by personal egotism, or it can be prompted by "pure" empathic desire to benefit another person, irrespective of personal gain (for overviews, see Batson, 1991; Batson, Ahmad, & Lishner, 2009; Cialdini et al., 1978).

The topic of altruism is a timely one due to the recent economic downturn in the United States. Volunteerism is thought to be a naturally related concept to altruism (Haski-Leventhal, 2009), and some reports have showed that volunteerism and helping those in need has waned in the wake of the poor economy. The *New York Times* reported that across the United States as a whole, "72% of Americans said they were devoting less time to volunteering and other civic activities, like providing food and shelter to those in need" (Strom, 2009, para. 7). In some reports within specific states, however, it has been suggested that practices related to economic difficulties (e.g., mandatory furlough days, shortened workweeks, etc.) have provided volunteering opportunities for some individuals. *USA Today* (July 10, 2009) reported that in Utah, mandatory flex schedules that called for state workers to work four 10-hour days per week to save on electricity and maintenance costs have left many of these workers free to volunteer on their nonworking Fridays. In California, the Office of the Governor (July 28, 2009) reported that "800,000 more Californians volunteered their time in 2008 than in the previous year" (para. 1). Holland (January 25, 2009) suggests in the *New York Times* that volunteering might be an important use of time for those who have lost their jobs due to the economic crisis, stating that volunteering is an ideal way to continue to accrue valuable work experience. In this way, perhaps strife can be the creator of opportunities to practice a strength.

The Egotism Motive

Egotism is the motive to pursue some sort of personal gain or benefit through targeted behavior. Egotism has been heralded as one of the most influential of all human motives. Not surprisingly, therefore, egotism is seen as driving a variety of human actions, including altruism. In this regard, noted Western thinkers such as Aristotle (384–322 BC), St. Thomas Aquinas (1125–1274), Thomas Hobbes (1588–1679), David Hume (1711–1776), Adam Smith (1723–1790), Jeremy Bentham (1748–1832), Friedrich Nietzsche (1844–1900), and Sigmund Freud (1856–1939) have weighed in on the debate as to whether egotism, the sense of empathy, or both, fuel altruistic human actions (see Batson et al., 2009).

Since the Renaissance, a prevailing view has been that altruism is best explained by the motive of egotism. So, too, have several modern scholars reasoned that egotism fuels altruistic behavior (for review, see Wallach & Wallach, 1983). The essence of this position is that we care for other people because it benefits us to do so (Mansbridge, 1990). Furthermore, no matter how noble the altruism may appear, those in the egotism–altruism camp believe that all altruistic actions produce an underlying benefit to the person who is doing the good deeds. Thus, the prevailing motive here is, "I help because it benefits me."

Forms of Egotism-Motivated Altruism

The forms of such self-beneficial egotism may be straightforward, as when helping another person results in public praise for the individual rendering the aid. In another variant of praise, the helper may receive material rewards or honors for altruistic deeds. In this latter regard, in 2005 the rocker Bob Geldof of the Irish musical group Boomtown Rats took the initiative to hold Live 8 concerts all over the globe. His efforts raised roughly $100 million for the starving people of Africa. Because of this and his continued altruistic work, Geldof was nominated for the 2006 and the 2008 Nobel Peace Prize.

There are other examples of self-benefits where the helpers receive no external rewards for their altruistic actions. For example, it is distressing to see another person in some sort of anguishing situation; accordingly, we may help that person to lessen our own sense of personal torment. Or we simply may feel good about ourselves when we act kindly toward another individual. Yet another possibility is that we may escape a sense of guilt for not helping when we step in and lend a hand to a needy person. Moreover, consider the soldier who throws himself upon a live grenade and saves his nearby comrades' lives. Surely this is an act of "pure" altruism, isn't it? Perhaps not, if this soldier imagined the praise and the medals that would be bestowed upon him for his act of courage, or perhaps our hero conjured the image of potential benefits coming to him in the after-life because of his heroism (Batson et al., 2009).

In posing these various ego-based explanations, we do not mean to be cynical about the helping actions of people. Rather, we are uncovering the many subtle forms that such egotism-based help-ing can take. Although we have posed several variants, such egotistical or self-benefiting actions involving altruism basically take one of the following three forms:

- The helping person gets public praise or even a monetary reward, along with self-praise for having done that which is good.

- The helping person avoids social or personal punishments for failing to help.

- The helping person may lessen his or her personal distress at seeing another's trauma.

Remember also that, even though the helping person is motivated by personal egotism, the bottom line is that the person renders aid to a fellow human being in need.

The Empathy Motive and the Empathy–Altruism Hypothesis

Empathy is an emotional response to the perceived plight of another person. One view of empathy is that it involves the ability to match another person's emotions. Instead of this mimic-like reproduction of another person's emotions, however, empathy may entail a sense of tenderheartedness toward that other person. University of Kansas social psychologist C. Daniel Batson has described this latter empathy in his 1991 book, *The Altruism Question.* For Batson, altruism involves human behaviors that are aimed at promoting another person's well-being.

Batson and colleagues do not deny that some forms of altruism may occur because of egotism, but their shared view is that, under some circumstances, these egotistical motives cannot account for the helping (see Batson et al., 2009). Indeed, in careful tests of what has come to be called the empathy–altruism hypothesis (see Batson, 1991), findings show that there are instances in which egotism does *not* appear to explain such helping behaviors. One example addresses the argument that people help at least partially in order to avoid aversive arousal and negative emotions that may occur as a result of not helping another (Batson, 1991). Recent research has found, however, that even when physical (Batson, 1991) or psychological (Stocks, Lishner, & Decker, 2009) escape from such a situation is made easy, individuals higher in empathy still help those in need. Thus, the evidence appears to strongly support the view that having empathy for another leads to a greater

C. Daniel Batson

Source: Reprinted with permission of C. Daniel Batson.

likelihood of helping that other person (for reviews, see Batson, 1991; Batson et al., 2009; Dovidio, Allen, & Schroeder, 1990; Eisenberg & Miller, 1987).

Because of the efforts of Batson and other recent scholars, "pure" altruism arising from human empathy has been viewed as a viable underlying motive for helping, in contrast to the previous emphasis on egotism as the sole motive. In the words of Piliavin and Charng (1990),

> There appears to be a paradigm shift away from the earlier position that behavior that appears to be altruistic must, under closer scrutiny, be revealed as reflecting egoistic motives. Rather, theory and data now being advanced are more compatible with the view that true altruism—acting with the goal of benefiting another—does exist and is a part of human nature. (p. 27)

Void of egotistical gains, therefore, humans at times are sufficiently moved by their empathies to help other people. If we ever need an example of positive psychology in action, this surely is it.

The Genetic and Neural Foundations of Empathy

The method for measuring genetic heritability is to compare the concordances of empathy scores in monozygotic (identical) twins with the scores of dizygotic (fraternal) twins. For adult males, the empathy correlations for monozygotic and dizygotic twins were found to be .41 and .05, respectively (Matthews, Batson, Horn, & Rosenman, 1981; for similar results, see Rushton, Fulker, Neale, Nias, & Eysenck, 1986). Although both of these studies have been criticized because of concerns that their analytic procedures produced overly elevated heritability scores (e.g., Davis, Luce, & Kraus, 1994), other studies have found monozygotic correlations in the range of .22 to .30, as compared to dizygotic correlations of .05 to .09 (Davis et al., 1994; Zahn-Wexler, Robinson, & Emde, 1992). The latter correlations still suggest a modest level of heritability for empathy.

Recent research has revealed that areas of the prefrontal and parietal cortices are essential for empathy (Damasio, 2002). Empathy requires the capacity to form internal simulations of another's bodily or mental states. Given that people who have damage to their right somatosensory cortices no longer can judge others' emotions, it follows that they have lost a skill that is crucial for empathy (Adolphs, Damasio, Tranel, Cooper, & Damasio, 2000). Likewise, damage to the prefrontal cortex leads to impairments in appraising the emotions of other people (Bechara, Tranel, Damasio, & Damasio, 1996). Furthermore, beginning in the 1990s, researchers discovered "mirror neurons" that react identically when an animal performs an action or witnesses another animal performing the same action (Winerman, 2005). In the words of neuroscientist Giacomo Rizzolatti, who was the first to discover these mirror neurons, "The neurons could help to explain how and why we . . . feel empathy" (in Winerman, 2005, p. 49). We must be careful in generalizing these findings to humans, however, because the methodologies to date have involved attaching electrodes directly to brains, and for ethical reasons this only has been done with monkeys.

Other research seems to suggest that altruistic actions could be the result of trait-like behavior, as opposed to being state-like, leading people to act in this way more frequently. Fetchenhauer, Groothuis, and Pradel (2010) theorize that altruists may be actually able to recognize the trait of altruism in one another and benefit evolutionarily from selecting a similarly altruistic mate. These authors state that in this way, "some individuals pursue ultimate genetic self-interest through psychological adaptations that embody a genuine concern for others" (p. 84). These ideas present another view of altruism as something more than just learned behavior within the current time of a single individual's life; rather, it may be an evolutionary benefit developed over time.

Cultural Variations in Altruism

Even among human subjects, we as researchers and scholars must be careful about generalizing findings across cultural groups. Many have discussed the idea that personal identities and values may determine the definition of constructs and the manifestation of them, as well as the value of various constructs as being beneficial (Chang, 2001b; Leu, Wang, & Koo, 2011; Pedrotti, Edwards, & Lopez, 2009; Uchida, Norasakkunkit, & Kitayama, 2004). In the following section, we report differences found between genders, cultural ideologies, and religious backgrounds.

The concepts of altruism and empathy have been investigated with regard to gender in several recent studies. Visser and Roelofs (2011) conducted a study in which participants of male and female genders were asked to distribute a fixed number of tokens between themselves and a fictional other person based on different scenarios (often called a Dictator Game). Part of the information given to the participants was the ingroup or outgroup status of the other in relation to them. Here, women as a group were found to be less sensitive to the "price of giving" in making decisions about dividing the tokens, meaning that they gave altruistically more often than men (Visser & Roelofs, 2011, p. 490). This effect, however, appeared to be heightened by possession of particular Big Five personality factors (e.g., Agreeableness, Conscientiousness, etc.), leading to a conclusion that gender may explain only part of the equation about this seeming tendency toward being more altruistic in this setting. Similar results were found in other studies involving Dictator Games in which female players were more likely than male players to give up half of the endowment given to them in the game, particularly when playing the game in a room with other women (Cadsby, Servátka, & Song, 2010). Women have also been found to be more appreciative of altruistic traits when choosing a male partner for a short-term relationship (i.e., a date), though this trait did not affect male preference in choosing a partner (Barclay, 2010). Both genders, however, appeared to value altruism in long-term relationships. Thus, women and men may differ in some ways in terms of altruistic acts and their value for them in some settings. More research is needed here, however.

Cultural variations may also be found in looking at different norms and ideologies between groups. Batson and colleagues (Batson et al., 2009) posit that *collectivism* as an ideology may in fact be a form of altruism or prosocial behavior that affects an entire community. In prioritizing the welfare of others above one's own welfare, helping behavior becomes a part of the normed social structure; not behaving in a way that serves the greater good is punished, while engaging in helping behavior is rewarded. Looking toward cultures who model this WE perspective rather than a ME perspective may reveal other routes toward cultivating altruistic behaviors (see Chapter 2). Research conducted by Oda, Hiraishi, Fukukawa, and Matsumoto-Oda (2011) supports this premise, as can be seen in their study of Japanese undergraduates. Oda and colleagues looked at both external and internal factors determining a prosocial mindset and found that individuals who exhibited prosociality toward others received significantly more social support from mothers, siblings, and friends/acquaintances. These results were found with regard to prosocial behavior directed at friends and acquaintances but in some cases also extended to prosocial behavior toward strangers. In addition, internal traits such as self-sacrifice and private self-consciousness were found to be related to prosocial behavior. Oda and colleagues (2011) term this collectivist society an "altruism niche" (p. 283) and state that it is the function of prosociality being rewarded and valued within the Japanese society.

Lastly, the concepts of religiosity and spirituality have long been under investigation as potential correlates to empathy and prosocial behavior (Galen, 2012; Saroglou, 2012). Many have found proposed links between religion and spirituality and altruistic behaviors, but the relationship between the two may be more complex than was originally thought. Huber and MacDonald (2012) found that empathy was linked to religiousness and that altruism was most strongly linked to spiritual experiences and spiritual cognitions. These same authors, however, found that non-religious spiritual cognitions were also strongly linked to empathy in particular. Galen (2012) conducted a thorough review of the literature in this area and concluded that the links found between religion and prosociality are more likely due to methodological problems and faulty interpretations of results. Still others dispute Galen's (2012) account of the literature surrounding the "religious prosociality hypothesis." Saroglou (2012), for example, agrees that religion is more often associated with prosociality when it relates to what Galen terms "ingroup favouritism" (p. 878). In other words, when individuals think of being prosocial to others from their same religious group, they may respond more favorably to taking these tasks on. Conversely, when the group they are helping is seen as an outgroup, taking these actions may not seem as favorable. Additionally, these data were gathered by self-report, and as such may be influenced in some ways by the wish of the respondents to appear socially desirable in their actions. Saroglou and others (e.g., Myers, 2012) take issue with the idea that prosociality directed toward an ingroup is not actually altruism since it also benefits the individual member (i.e., primarily egoistic). In addition, these authors state that, regardless of the reasons why the prosocial behavior occurs, there is still a link between prosocial behavior and level of religiosity (Saroglou, 2012). Thus, the relationships between religiousness, spirituality, and these prosocial tendencies may be more nuanced than previously assumed.

The main point that must be taken from each of these areas of study is that cultural facets and varying levels of identification within them may make a difference when attempting to understand the nature and function of helping behavior.

Cultivating Altruism

For clues to how to help someone become more altruistic, we call upon the very processes of egotism and empathy that we have used to explain altruism.

Egotism-Based Approaches to Enhancing Altruistic Actions

In our experiences working with clients in psychotherapy, we have found that people often may incorrectly assume that feeling good about themselves is not part of rendering help. At least for some individuals living in the United States, this attitude may reflect the Puritan heritage with its emphasis on suffering and total human sacrifice for the good of others. Whatever the historical roots, however, it is inaccurate to conclude that helping another and feeling good about oneself are incompatible. Thus, this is one of the first lessons we use in enabling people to realize that they can help and, because of such actions, have higher self-esteem. Furthermore, we have found that people seem to take delight in learning that it is legitimate to feel good about helping others.

One way to unleash such positive feelings is to have the person engage in community volunteer work. Local agencies assisting children, people with disabilities, older people who are alone, the homeless and other low-income groups, and hospitals all need volunteers to render aid. Although this form of helping may begin as a voluntary experience, we have witnessed instances in which our clients have changed their professions to involve activities where they support others *and get paid for it*. Our more general point, however, is that it feels good to help other people, and this simple premise has guided some of our efforts at channeling people into volunteer positions.

One note of caution with these egoistically based approaches must be stated, however. Though it is true that egoistic approaches result in benefits to others as much as those that are based more purely on helping, the benefits *to the helper* may differ. Research shows that there may be some distinction between those who set out to help another in order to attain this sort of egoistic gain and those who act due to less egoistic motivation. Konrath, Fuhrel-Forbis, Lou, and Brown (2012) studied motivations in older adults toward volunteer work and found that those whose primary motivations were for self-gain had higher mortality risk four years after the study was conducted in comparison to those whose primary motivations were more directed at helping others. This was especially true in individuals who volunteered on a more regular basis. Thus, though egoistic motivations may provide some of the same benefits that "true" altruists obtain, there may still be greater benefits from acting outside of self-interest.

Empathy-Based Approaches to Enhancing Altruistic Actions

A way to increase people's likelihood of helping is to teach them to have greater empathy for the circumstances of other people. How can such empathy be promoted? One simple approach is to have a person interact more frequently with people who need help. Then, once the individual truly begins to understand the perspectives and motives of the people who are being helped, this insight breaks down the propensity to view interpersonal matters in terms of "us versus them."

Another means of enhancing empathy is to point out similarities with another person that may not be obvious. These similarities can be as simple as having grown up in the same part of the country, having done work of the same type, having endured comparable hardships, and so on. The shared characteristics of people often are much greater than any of us may realize, and these parallels in life circumstances make people understand that we all are part of the same "grand journey" (see Chapter 2).

It is also important to understand, however, that similarity is not the only characteristic that can breed empathy. In our day-to-day life, the word *different* is often used synonymously with *strange* or some other negative trait. From a young age, we train children to spot similarities and highlight differences, but at the same time we often pretend that differences, specifically those pertaining to facets such as race or disability, are invisible. Many researchers have shown that difference is not invisible, even to very small children (e.g., Bigler & Liben, 2006), but in acting as though it is, we as parents and educators accidentally malign the idea of "difference" in general. As Bigler and Liben have discussed in their research, this may make it less likely for dissimilar individuals to spend time with one another, even during childhood. We would take this one step further and posit that this lack of closeness may in turn decrease empathy. If we can help our children to develop wide and diverse social circles, perhaps we can allow empathy to develop toward a broader group of people. This may mean that altruistic acts have a farther reach as well.

One final approach for promoting empathy involves working with those people who especially want to see themselves as different from others (see Snyder & Fromkin, 1980). Uniqueness is something that most people desire to some degree (see Chapter 2) but that, taken to an extreme, makes it very difficult for the person to make contact and interact with others. Such people must be taught that they do share characteristics with others and how their illusory specialness needs may be preventing them from deriving pleasure from interacting with other people (Lynn & Snyder, 2002; Vignoles, 2009). One personal mini-experiment that you can perform on yourself is to imagine another person and then list all the things (physical, psychological, etc.) that you have in common with this person. This exercise, in our experience, increases the propensity of a person to "walk in the shoes" of another—with greater empathy the result.

Values-Based Approaches to Enhancing Altruistic Actions

Other researchers have looked toward historical accounts of "helpers" such as those who protested against Nazi ideology and practices or who engaged in the Civil Rights movement (Fagin-Jones & Midlarsky, 2007; Hitlin, 2007; see discussion of altruistic courage in chapter 9). Researchers have found some individuals may incorporate helping into their personal identity such that anything other than altruistic behavior in these types of situations does not feel authentic and thus isn't considered as a viable behavioral option (Colby & Damon, 1995). As such, personal values may affect altruistic behavior. Hitlin (2007) found that in individuals who value prosocial acts so strongly that this becomes a piece of their identity, volunteering becomes an important source of self-esteem. Working to engender personal responsibility for acting prosocially may impact the development of altruism in this way.

Similarly, we find examples of heroism in prosocial acts. Those people described often as "in the line of duty," such as firefighters, ambulance workers, and the police, put themselves in harm's way for others on a regular basis (Zimbardo, 2007). Members of the military and war heroes are other examples of this type of prosocial behavior, of which there are many living in our current times. In extreme situations (e.g., war, disaster, etc.), it may be that this type of prosocial behavior is in some ways "required," due to the values of the context in which these situations occur. These types of helping jobs, though they may tend to draw individuals who already value prosocial behavior to them, at the same time promote further development of prosocial qualities. Emulating these real-life heroes may have an effect on the development of altruism as well. Franco, Blau, and Zimbardo (2011) believe we can stimulate our "heroic imagination," which is "a collection of attitudes about helping others in need, beginning with caring for others in compassionate ways, but also moving toward a willingness to sacrifice or take risks on behalf of others or in defense of a moral cause" (p. 11). Maybe anyone has the capacity to act in a heroic way.

Helping behavior may be habit forming. Even after taking parental volunteer action into account, Rosen and Sims (2011) found that those children who volunteered or were involved in some kind of fundraising were 3.1% more likely to make cash gifts to various organizations as adults. Interestingly, the effect of having volunteered (donating an average of $329 more per year) is significantly greater than the effect posed by fund-raising alone ($122 greater than those who did not have these experiences in childhood). This same pattern was found with regard to volunteer work as an adult, with individuals who volunteered or fund-raised during childhood as 8.3% and 6%, respectively, more likely to volunteer their time as adults; this again was found after excluding parental volunteer activity. Rosen and Sims acknowledge that more research needs to be done in this area, yet it is important to note that it seems that involving children in altruistic actions when they are young may have important implications for continuation of this prosocial behavior. We explore yet more ways to increase altruism in the following Personal Mini-Experiments.

PERSONAL MINI-EXPERIMENTS

Exercises in Altruism, Gratitude, and Forgiveness

As suggested in previous exercises, experiment and see what works for you.

Altruism for Thy Neighbor. If you look around your local neighborhood, you will find people who could use a helping hand. The key is to surprise other people and do them favors that they are not expecting. Here are some suggestions:

- Mow the lawn of an elderly person.
- Volunteer to babysit for a single parent who is working hard to make ends meet.
- Speak up for someone whose voice is not as likely to be heard as yours. Put any privilege you have (e.g., socioeconomically, racially, gender-wise, etc.) to good use to help others.
- Offer to read for persons who cannot see.
- Give blood or go to a local hospital and see what volunteer work can be done there.

You get the idea. Do for others, and make a note of the feelings that altruism engenders in you.

Count Your Blessings (see Emmons & McCullough, 2003). At the beginning and end of each day, list five things for which you are grateful and then take a few minutes to meditate on the gift inherent in each. One means of elucidating this sense of appreciation is to use the stem phrases, "I appreciate _____ because _____."
In the first blank, list the person, event, or thing for which you are grateful, and in the second blank state the reasons for each of the things for which you have expressed gratitude. Discuss the effects of one week of this practice with a classmate, and tweak the exercise as you wish.

Gone but Not Forgiven. If you are contemplating forgiving a person who is no longer alive, or if you cannot locate him or her, use a technique from Gestalt therapy. In this technique, called the "empty chair exercise," one sits facing an empty chair. Then, one imagines the target person sitting in that chair and speaks to the person as though he or she were really there. Occasionally, we may want to forgive ourselves for some transgression that ended up causing us personal harm. The empty chair exercise is a good one for addressing oneself. You can also write yourself a letter and actually mail it to yourself.

Measuring Altruism

There is a variety of self-report instruments for assessing the altruism of people from childhood through adulthood. Perhaps the best-known self-report instrument is the Self-Report Altruism Scale, a validated 20-item index for adults (Rushton, Chrisjohn, & Fekken, 1981). If one desires an observational index, the Prosocial Behavior Questionnaire (Weir & Duveen, 1981) is a 20-item rating index that can be used by teachers to report prosocial behaviors (using a three-point continuum of applicability ranging from "does not apply" to "applies somewhat" to "definitely applies"). (For a similar index to the Prosocial Behavior Questionnaire, see the Ethical Behavior Rating Scale, a 15-item teacher rating instrument by Hill and Swanson [1985].)

Another promising self-report instrument for adults is the Helping Attitude Scale, a 20-item measure that taps beliefs, feelings, and behaviors related to helping (Nickell, 1998). The Helping Attitude Scale appears to meet the psychometric criteria for scale reliability and validity, and initial findings show that women have more positive attitudes about helping than do men. The Helping Attitude Scale can be examined in its entirety in Appendix A.

In addition, researchers often use various decision-making games of give and take borrowed from the field of economics to determine if participants in their studies are likely to act in a more prosocial way or a more egoistic way in various scenarios. These scenarios attempt to measure altruism from a more behavioral standpoint. The standard Dictator Game, in which a participant is given a number of tokens and told to divide those tokens between themselves and another person given various circumstances (e.g., the other person is a member of the same group or another group, the other person holds all the tokens or the participant holds all the tokens, etc.), is one way in which prosocial behavior is often measured. Other games, such as the Voluntary Contributions Mechanism, are very similar to this procedure. Some note that there are issues with measuring altruism in this way, including interviewer bias and assumptions made for various behaviors (Lightman, 1982).

GRATITUDE

In this section, we discuss the concept of gratitude, which received scant attention prior to the last two decades. We first define gratitude and discuss cultural variations of this construct, then we discuss how it can be cultivated and measured, review its physiological bases, and close with a real-life example.

Defining Gratitude

The term *gratitude* is derived from the Latin concept *gratia,* which entails some variant of grace, gratefulness, and graciousness (Emmons, McCullough, & Tsang, 2003). The ideas flowing from this Latin root pertain to "kindness, generousness, gifts, the beauty of giving and receiving" (Pruyser, 1976, p. 69). In the words of noted University of California–Davis researcher Robert Emmons (2005, personal communication), gratitude emerges upon recognizing that one has obtained a positive outcome from another individual who behaved in a way that was (1) costly to him or her, (2) valuable to the recipient, and (3) intentionally rendered. As such, gratitude taps into the propensity to appreciate and savor everyday events and experiences (Bryant, 1989; Langston, 1994).

In Emmons's definition, the positive outcome appears to have come from another person; however, the benefit may be derived from a nonhuman action or event. For example, the individual who has undergone a traumatic natural event, such as a family member's survival of a hurricane (see Coffman, 1996), feels a profound sense of gratitude. In a related vein, it has been suggested that events of larger magnitude also should produce higher levels of gratitude (Trivers, 1971). Other researchers have found that *quality* not quantity is more important in gratitude experiences. For example, Wood, Brown, and Maltby (2011) found that participants in their study ranked their level of gratitude in any one particular instance relevant to other situations in which they had been thankful for something. When participants were not used to getting help from friends, they felt more grateful when someone did help them, and vice versa. Along these same lines, Ortony, Clore, and Collins (1988) have reasoned that gratitude should be greater when the giving person's actions are judged praiseworthy and when they deviate positively from that which was expected.

In yet another example of gratitude, a person may have come through a major medical crisis or problem and discover benefits in that experience (Affleck & Tennen, 1996). This process is called *benefit finding*. This may be especially helpful in the short term in dealing with the stress that occurs as a result of some trauma (Wood, Britt, Wright, Thomas, & Bliese, 2012).

As is the case with altruism, it is likely that the ability to empathize is a necessary condition for feeling gratitude toward another person (M. McCullough, 2005, personal communication). Gratitude is viewed as a prized human propensity in the Hindu, Buddhist, Muslim, Christian, and Jewish traditions (Emmons et al., 2003). On this point, philosopher David Hume (1888, p. 466) went so far as to say that *in*gratitude is "the most horrible and unnatural of all crimes that humans are capable of committing." According to medieval scholar Thomas Aquinas (1273/1981), not only was gratitude seen as beneficial to the individual, but it also serves as a motivational force for human altruism.

Of the many famous thinkers who commented on gratitude, only Aristotle (trans. 1962) viewed it unfavorably. In his opinion, magnanimous people are adamant about their self-sufficiencies and, accordingly, view gratitude as demeaning and reflective of needless indebtedness to others.

Cultural Variations in Gratitude

Research focused on cross-cultural comparisons between East Asian participants from Korea and Japan and participants from the United States (primarily White American samples) shows that expressions of gratitude and reactions to these expressions may differ between East and West. The words "thank you," for example, are shown to produce more positive reactions in the United States samples as compared with those participants from Korea, especially when the attention of the recipient of the gratitude is drawn specifically toward it (Park & Lee, 2012). Other research found that Koreans preferred the use of apology phrases as opposed to a "thank you," whereas those in the United States (again, primarily White Americans) had the opposite reaction (Lee & Park, 2011). Lee and Park state that this preference has to do with perception of which words would help soothe a threat to personal "face" (i.e., saving face); while Koreans felt that "I'm sorry" best accomplished this task, those in the United States felt that "thank you" was more effective. Similar results were found in the samples in Japan (Ide, 1998; Long, 2010).

Differences have been found between racial groups within the multicultural context of the United States as well. The use of gratitude-enhancing strategies to influence happiness or well-being also appears to differ between Asian Americans and their White American counterparts. In a study by Boehm, Lyubomirsky, and Sheldon (2011), researchers assigned participants to groups that employed different happiness-enhancing techniques. In the condition using gratitude expression as a vehicle for increasing happiness, marked differences were found between these cultural groups, with White Americans benefiting much more greatly from these techniques as compared with the Asian American participants. This may be because Asian Americans hold similar beliefs regarding gratitude to those in Asian countries, as suggested previously by Lee, Park, and others (Ide, 1998; Lee & Park, 2011; Long, 2010; Park & Lee, 2012). This has special significance for practitioners in terms of reminding them to consider the value placed on particular constructs when working with clients from non-majority racial and ethnic backgrounds.

Having a cultural identity as someone who is religious may also effect one's levels of gratitude in life. Research has found that religiousness is positively correlated with gratitude in general (Sandage, Hill, & Vaubel, 2011; Tsang, Schulwitz, & Carlisle, 2012) and that specific gratitude toward God (within Western Christian religion) "enhances the psychological benefit of gratitude" (Rosmarin, Pirutinsky, Cohen, Galler, & Krumrei, 2011, p. 389). Rosmarin and colleagues also found that the interaction of religious commitment and religious gratitude is particularly sensitive in being able to predict emotional well-being, above and beyond general gratitude. Thus, this cultural facet may be a protective one in this area.

Finally, it must be noted that multiple cultural facets (e.g., race + religious affiliation) may also play a dynamic role in effecting understanding, manifestation, and utility of various constructs. In light of the benefits purported to be received as a result of spiritual gratitude, Krause (2012) studied the role of gratitude toward God in Western Christian tradition within elderly populations from three different racial and ethnic groups: African Americans, White Americans, and Mexican Americans. Older African Americans and older Mexican Americans reported feeling more grateful to God than older White Americans, but though the reason for this gratitude among African Americans and White Americans appeared to be a function of perception of the receipt of spiritual support, this model did not hold true for the Mexican American sample. Krause calls for more research into this area of Mexican American religiosity and gratitude, as it appears that ethnicity may play a role in the use of gratitude in a religious setting.

Cultivating Gratitude

We begin this section with the words of the writer Charles Dickens (1897, p. 45): "Reflect on your present blessings, of which every man has many, not on your past misfortunes, of which all men have some." In more recent times, psychologists Robert Emmons and Michael McCullough have explored a variety of ways to help people enhance their sense of gratitude (for reviews, see Bono, Emmons, & McCullough, 2004; Emmons & Hill, 2001; Emmons & McCullough, 2004; Emmons &

Michael McCullough

Source: Copyright © Elisabeth McCullough. Reprinted with permission.

Robert A. Emmons

Source: Reprinted with permission of Robert A. Emmons.

Shelton, 2002; McCullough, Kilpatrick, Emmons, & Larson, 2001). These interventions aimed at enhancing gratitude consistently have resulted in benefits. For example, in comparison to people who recorded either neutral or negative life stresses in their diaries, those who kept weekly gratitude journals (i.e., recorded events for which they were thankful) were superior in terms of (1) the amount of exercise undertaken, (2) optimism about the upcoming week, and (3) feeling better about their lives (Emmons & McCullough, 2003). Furthermore, those who kept gratitude journals reported greater enthusiasm, alertness, and determination, and they were significantly more likely to make progress toward important goals pertaining to their health, interpersonal relationships, and academic performances. Those who were in the "count your blessings" diary condition also were more likely to have helped another person. Finally, in a third study in Emmons and McCullough's (2003) trilogy, people with neuromuscular conditions were randomly assigned to either a gratitude condition or a control condition. Results showed that those in the former condition were (1) more optimistic, (2) more energetic, (3) more connected to other people, and (4) more likely to have restful sleep.

In Japan, a form of meditation known as Naikan has been found to enhance a person's sense of gratitude (Krech, 2001). Using Naikan, one learns to meditate daily on three gratitude-related questions: First, what did I receive? Second, what did I give? And third, what troubles and difficulties did I cause to others? In Western societies, we may be rather automatic in our expectations of material comforts; gratitude meditation helps to bring this process more into awareness so we can learn how to appreciate such blessings.

The effectiveness of gratitude interventions may be moderated by the level of positive affect in the lives of participants (Froh, Kashdan, Ozimkowski, & Miller, 2009). Jeffrey Froh and colleagues asked a sample of children and adolescents to write a letter of thanks to someone for whom they were grateful and to then deliver that letter in person. They then compared youth in their study who were high in positive affect with those that were low in positive affect in terms of the effectiveness of this gratitude exercise. Results showed that those youth who were low in positive affect were able to make greater increases in their level of gratefulness and had higher positive affect post-intervention. Thus, gratitude may be even more important to cultivate in individuals who are lower in regular positive emotional experiences. Similar results were found in a study with adults in which participants were asked to write gratitude letters once a week for three weeks (Toepfer, Cichy, & Peters, 2012). This more sustained letter-writing procedure resulted in increases in happiness and life satisfaction and decreases in depression in a majority population sample. Keeping a diary focused on gratitude in addition to attending workshops on this subject has also been found to be helpful and to result in higher environmental mastery and greater life satisfaction (Carson, Muir, Clark, Wakely, & Chander, 2010). Finally, Chan (2010; 2011) designed a culturally competent gratitude intervention to be used with schoolteachers in Hong Kong. Chan used a very similar procedure to the studies discussed previously, though he changed the format somewhat, using elements of Naikan mediation questions (Chan, 2010). In addition, he emphasized a less self-focused attention with regard to thinking about gratitude to accommodate cultural norms in these participants (Chan, 2011). In both of these studies, Chan showed that as gratitude increased, life satisfaction did as well. In addition, emotional exhaustion was found to decrease, thus revealing an additional benefit of gratitude. Chan's studies are to be emulated in their careful attention to cultural differences; here these changes in the intervention were able to help show the beneficial impact of gratitude in this non-Western population. In summary, there are multiple ways in which formal interventions can increase feelings of gratitude and their beneficial correlates.

In addition, other factors may influence the increase of gratitude in some groups. Cohort effects, for example, may influence the level of gratitude that people feel toward various sources. In a study looking at differences in gratitude in children pre- and post-9/11, Gordon, Musher-Eizenman, Holub, and Dalrymple (2004) found that mention of gratitude toward rescue workers (such as police and firefighters); the United States and its values (e.g., freedom); and people other than family members were each significantly higher in children after the 9/11 terrorist attacks. In addition, post-9/11 discussions of gratitude included less reference to material items (such as toys), leading Gordon and colleagues to hypothesize that "at least in the months following the terrorist attacks, children may have reprioritized their lives in a manner similar to adults" (p. 549) with regard to gratitude. Thus, times of strife may lead to emphasis of different priorities and might offer opportunities to build on positive traits such as gratitude.

Gratitude can also be cultivated from a young age. In their 2013 book *Making Grateful Kids: A Scientific Approach to Helping Youth Thrive*, Jeffrey Froh and Giacomo Bono discuss ideas designed to help parents, mentors, and teachers to assist children in developing gratitude. These authors also give suggestions that children can try themselves on their road to more satisfying life via the development of gratitude.

One additional comment is noteworthy in regard to gratitude and motivation. In an interview, Dr. Emmons (2004) was asked about the most common *incorrect* assumption that people make about his work on gratitude. In response, he observed that many people assume that gratefulness is synonymous with lack of motivation and greater complacency in life. He then noted that he had never seen a case where gratitude was linked to passivity. On the contrary, gratitude is an active and affirming process,

Jeffrey Froh

Source: Reprinted with permission of Jeffrey Froh.

and we share some of the clinical approaches we have used to facilitate it in the Personal Mini-Experiments on pp. 296–297 (see also Bono et al., 2004). We also present an editorial on the importance of thanking others.

Thanking Your Heroes
Rick Snyder

It was 1972, and I had just taken a job as an assistant professor at KU. There was one person who had sacrificed her whole life to make it possible for me to reach this point. She worked her regular job, along with part-time jobs, to see that I could go to college. She was a hero in every sense, giving so that I could have a better life than what she had experienced.

This hero was my mother. She told me that my life as an academician was to be her reward. She planned to visit Lawrence later that year, but that visit never happened. Diagnosed with a form of quickly spreading cancer, she spent her last months bedridden in Dallas, Texas.

I visited as much as I could, and we talked about things that were important to both of us. Unfortunately, I never told her that she was my hero. Almost every day over the past 30 years, I have regretted this omission. If you still have a chance to deliver this message to an important hero in your life, do it right now.

Source: From Snyder, C. R., Thanking your heroes, *Lawrence Journal-World*, October 4, 2004.

Measuring Gratitude

Several approaches have been taken to measure gratitude. One tactic was to ask people to list the things about which they felt grateful (*Gallup Poll Monthly*, 1996). This simple method allowed researchers to find those events that produced gratefulness. Another strategy was to take the stories that people wrote about their lives and code these vignettes for gratefulness themes. Some attempts also have been made to measure gratitude behaviorally. For example, whether children said "thank you" during their door-to-door Halloween trick-or-treat rounds was used as an unprompted index of gratitude (Becker & Smenner, 1986). Similarly, the grateful responses of people receiving food in a soup kitchen have been quantified (Stein, 1989).

Working in the context of an overall index called the Multidimensional Prayer Inventory, Laird and his colleagues (Laird, Snyder, Rapoff, & Green, 2004) have developed and validated a three-item Thanksgiving self-report subscale on which people respond along a 7-point response scale (1 = Never to 7 = All of the time) to each item. The three Thanksgiving items are "I offered thanks for specific things," "I expressed my appreciation for my circumstances," and "I thanked God for things occurring in my life." This Thanksgiving subscale of the Multidimensional Prayer Inventory obviously is worded in terms of religious prayer, and higher scores have correlated with stronger religious practices, such as prayer.

Finally, there are three trait-like self-report measures of gratitude that do not inherently link the wording of the items to religious prayer. The first such measure is the Gratitude, Resentment, and Appreciation Test (GRAT), a 44-item index developed and validated by Watkins, Grimm, and Hailu (1998). The GRAT taps the three factors of resentment, simple appreciation, and social appreciation. The second is the Gratitude Adjective Checklist (GAC; McCullough, Emmons, & Tsang, 2002), and it asks participants to state how well three adjectives (grateful, appreciative, and thankful) describe them. This scale is often used as a secondary measure of gratitude in conjunction with some other inventory.

The trait self-report index that appears to be most promising is the Gratitude Questionnaire (GQ-6) (McCullough et al., 2002; see also Emmons et al., 2003). The GQ-6 is a six-item questionnaire (see Appendix B for the entire scale) on which respondents endorse each item on a 7-point Likert scale (1 = Strongly disagree to 7 = Strongly agree). Results show that the six items correlate strongly with each other, and one overall factor seems to tap the scale content. Scores of the GQ-6 correlate reliably with peers' rating of target persons' gratitude levels; people scoring high on this scale report feeling more thankful and more grateful (Gray, Emmons, & Morrison, 2001). Additionally, this sense of appreciation as tapped by the GQ-6 endured over a 21-day interval (McCullough, Tsang, & Emmons, 2004).

Froh and colleagues (2011) assessed the validity of all three of the above adult-normed scales (the GQ-6, GAC, and the GRAT-short form) for use with children and adolescents. Results showed that similar relationships were found as with adult research participants on positive affect and life satisfaction, but that age appeared to mediate the relationships with depression and negative affect. More research is needed here as cultivating and investigating gratitude in younger populations has many benefits (Froh et al., 2011; Froh & Bono, 2013).

The Psychophysiological Underpinnings of Gratitude

Although we could not locate research relating directly to psychophysiology and gratitude, research does exist on appreciation. Whereas gratitude typically refers to another person's actions, appreciation may or may not entail another individual. These two concepts certainly are quite similar, however, and it is for this reason that we briefly explore here the psychophysiology of appreciation. Although frustration typically elicits disordered and erratic heart rhythms, reflecting a lack of synchrony between the parasympathetic and sympathetic branches of the autonomic nervous system, appreciation produces a more coherent pattern of heart rhythms (McCraty & Childre, 2004). This coherent, "calming" pattern of heartbeats per minute can be observed in Figure 11.2 (see Tiller, McCraty, & Atkinson, 1996).

Appreciation also has produced another form of physiological coherence—the synchrony between alpha brain wave activity (taken from electroencephalograms [EEGs]) and heartbeats. In research by McCraty and colleagues (McCraty, 2002; McCraty & Atkinson, 2003), for example, under experimental manipulations of appreciation relative to baseline, the synchrony of heartbeat and EEG was higher in the left hemisphere. As shown in Figure 11.3, where the lighter shading signifies the greater degree of synchrony between heartbeat and EEG alpha brain waves, a shift can be seen from the right frontal area at baseline to the left hemisphere in the appreciation manipulation condition. In this regard, McCraty and Childre (2004) have noted that the left hemisphere has been implicated in other research with positive emotions (e.g., Lane et al., 1997). Although there obviously is much more research to be done in this area, it is promising that the

Figure 11.2 Heart Rhythms Under Frustration and Appreciation

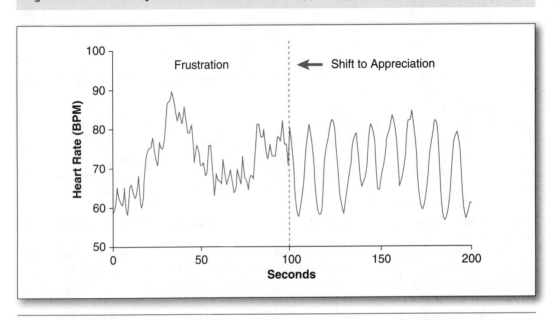

Source: From McCraty and Childre, The grateful heart, in R. A. Emmons & M. E. McCullough (Eds.), *The psychology of gratitude.* Copyright © 2004 by HeartMath®. Used by permission of Oxford University Press, Inc.

gratitude-related human response of appreciation appears to have a coherent (McCraty's term) psychophysiological pattern.

FORGIVENESS

Once a quiet, relatively unexplored concept, there has been an explosion of interest in forgiveness since the 1990s. Part of the reason for this tremendous expansion of theory and research relates to the fact that philanthropist John Templeton initiated calls for grants involving research on forgiveness from the Templeton Foundation. Mr. Templeton believed forgiveness was sufficiently important as a concept to spend his own money to facilitate more research on it!

In this section, we first introduce the various definitions of forgiveness and discuss its individual and cultural variations, then we describe how it can be cultivated, review its measurement, and end with an overview of its evolutionary and neurobiological bases.

Defining Forgiveness

Scholars have differed in their definitions of forgiveness (McCullough, Pargament, & Thoresen, 2000a, 2000b; Worthington, 2005). Although views of the exact nature of forgiveness vary, the

Figure 11.3 Alpha Brain Wave Activity and Heartbeat Synchrony Under Baseline and Appreciation Conditions

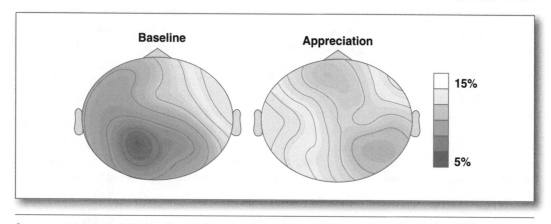

Source: From McCraty and Childre, The grateful heart, in R. A. Emmons & M. E. McCullough (Eds.), *The psychology of gratitude.* Copyright © 2004 by HeartMath®. Used by permission of Oxford University Press, Inc.

Note: Lighter shading signifies greater synchrony between brain waves and heartbeat.

consensus is that it is beneficial to people (see Worthington, 2005). We discuss the major ways of defining forgiveness in the remainder of this section, starting with the most liberal and inclusive definition and moving to relatively more circumscribed ones.

Thompson and Colleagues

In the theory espoused by Thompson and her colleagues (Thompson et al., 2005), forgiveness is a freeing from a negative attachment to the source that has transgressed against a person. Of all forgiveness theories, Thompson's is the most inclusive in that the source of the transgression, and thus the target of any eventual forgiveness, may be one-self, another person, or a situation that is viewed as out of one's control.

McCullough and Colleagues

According to McCullough (2000; McCullough et al., 1998), forgiveness reflects increases in prosocial motivation toward another such that there is (1) less desire to avoid the trans-gressing person and to harm or seek revenge toward that individual, and (2) increased desire to act positively toward the transgressing person. Changes in motivation are viewed as being at the core of this theory (McCullough et al., 2000a,

Laura Yamhure Thompson

Source: Reprinted with permission of Laura Yamhure Thompson.

2000b), with the person becoming more benevolent over time; moreover, forgiveness is seen as applicable only when there is another person who has engaged in a transgression.

Enright and Colleagues

The scholar with the longest track record in studying forgiveness is Robert Enright, who defined forgiveness as "a willingness to abandon one's right to resentment, negative judgment, and indifferent behavior toward one who unjustly hurt us, while fostering the undeserved qualities of compassion, generosity, and even love toward him or her" (Enright, Freedman, & Rique, 1998, pp. 46–47). For Enright (2000; Enright et al., 1998), it is crucial that the forgiving person develop a benevolent stance toward the transgressing person. As he put it, "The fruition of forgiveness is entering into loving community with others" (Enright & Zell, 1989, p. 99). Furthermore, Enright was adamant in stating that forgiveness cannot be extended to situations and thus must be directed only at people. On this point, he wrote, "Forgiveness is between people. One does not forgive tornadoes or floods. How could one, for instance, again join in a loving community with a tornado?" (Enright & Zell, 1989, p. 53).

Tangney and Colleagues

In 1999, Tangney and her colleagues (Tangney, Fee, Reinsmith, Boone, & Lee, 1999) suggested that forgiveness reflected

> (1) cognitive-affective transformation following a transgression in which (2) the victim makes a realistic assessment of the harm done and acknowledges the perpetrator's responsibility, but (3) freely chooses to "cancel the debt," giving up the need for revenge or deserved punishments and any quest for restitution. This "canceling of the debt" also involves (4) a "cancellation of negative emotions" directly related to the transgression. In particular, in forgiving, the victim overcomes his or her feelings of resentment and anger for the act. In short, by forgiving, the harmed individual (5) essentially removes himself or herself from the victim role. (p. 2)

The Tangney model suggests that the giving up of the negative emotions is the crux of the forgiving process.

Individual and Cultural Variations in Forgiveness

Researchers suggest that the way in which individuals conceptualize forgiveness plays an important role in their assignment of value to this construct and ultimately their use of it in their daily lives. Ballester, Muñoz Sastre, and Mullet (2009) state that differences may occur in how one defines forgiveness (e.g., as "pardoning" or agreeing with the offender versus moving on with a relationship after a transgressor has seen the error of their ways) and that having different conceptualizations may interfere with healthy relationships between transgressors and victims. If, for example, a transgressor

June Tangney

Source: Reprinted with permission of June Tangney.

knows that a victim feels that forgiveness is a pardoning of behavior, they may be able to work harder to emphasize their fault in the situation or assure the victim that this type of behavior will not recur, and thus forgiveness may be more comfortably granted as well as received (Ballester et al., 2009).

Actions that the transgressor takes (or decides not to take) may make a difference in whether forgiveness occurs as well. Past research shows that when a transgressor apologizes (either verbally or by offering some kind of compensation) forgiveness is more likely to follow (Exline & Baumeister, 2000; Howell, Dopko, Turowski, & Buro, 2001). This said, the effectiveness of an apology is often influenced by the personality factors of the person who committed the bad act—namely, how much Agreeableness they possess (Tabak, McCullough, Luna, Bono, & Berry, 2011). In addition, others have shown that apologies are more effective when they are in line with the victim's self-construal. For example, Fehr and Gelfand (2010) found that those individuals who are more independent in their self-construal tend to be more forgiving when a transgressor clearly states what he or she will do to "make things right" and recreate equality in the relationship. Individuals in this study who were more relational in their construal responded more positively to empathy as opposed to compensation. Studies have also found that even children were more likely to reconcile with a brother or sister who has committed some "crime" against them when the sibling apologized and when that apology was not mandated by parents or authority figures (Schleien, Ross, & Ross, 2010). Thus, knowing the mindset from which the victim comes might make a difference in whether forgiveness occurs.

Finally, there are differences across developmental stages that account for the qualitative experience and likelihood of forgiveness. Most studies find that the older you are, the more willing you are to forgive and that this tendency to forgive becomes more dispositional (as opposed to situational) with age (Steiner, Allemand, & McCullough, 2011; Steiner, Allemand, & McCullough, 2012). Other studies, however, show that as a rule the number and seriousness of transgressions seem to decrease in older adulthood, and thus this may partially explain these findings (Steiner et al., 2011).

Identification with various cultural facets and contexts (e.g., race, ethnicity, gender, religion, etc.) may also drive different definitions or values placed on forgiveness as a concept. In some cultures, forgiveness may be more of an *inter*personal process, and in others it may be more of an *intra*personal process; these different conceptualizations may have implications for cross-cultural interactions with regard to forgiveness (Kadiangandu, Gauché, Vinsonneau, & Mullet, 2007; Hook, Worthington, Utsey, Davis, & Burnette, 2012). Others have stated that forgiveness may be more common in Eastern cultures as compared to Western cultures and that situational factors and cultural norms (such as a value of harmony) may play more of a role in likelihood of forgiving in certain cultures as well (Paz, Neto, & Mullet, 2008). Karremans and colleagues (2011) found that in collectivist nations such as Japan and China, norms of social harmony dictated forgiveness, even in situations where Western-oriented individuals would be less likely to forgive. In addition, in these collectivist societies, people believe that some sort of reconciliation attempt or conciliatory behavior is a necessary precursor to forgiveness (Hook et al., 2012; Watkins et al., 2011).

Other cultural facets may affect propensity and experience of forgiveness as well. With regard to gender, results have been mixed. One study found that men have stronger initial responses to forgiveness prompts than women (Root & Exline, 2011). This may suggest that women exert more time and effort toward forgiving; they also appear to respond to multiple types of forgiveness prompting. In addition, other studies have found that forgiveness is "a more manifest subject in everyday life" for adult women (Ghaemmaghami, Allemand, & Martin, 2011, p. 192). In still another study, women in heterosexual marriages reported perceptions that their partners were more forgiving, in comparison with male partners' perception of their female partners' forgiveness (Miller & Worthington, 2010). Thus, this is an area that may benefit from more study.

Race and ethnicity also may have some effect on willingness and propensity to forgive, depending on such factors as racial identity development. Leach, Baker, and Zeigler-Hill (2011) found that African American participants' propensity to forgive White transgressors was predicted at least in part by their current stage of Cross's (1971) Black Racial Identity development model. This may be true for other cultural identity facets as well. Other studies have found that the link between forgiveness and health may be stronger in African Americans as compared to White Americans (McFarland, Smith, Toussaint, & Thomas, 2012).

Finally, having a personal identity that includes religiosity may affect propensity to forgive and the definition associated with this concept. As many religions, including Christian, Hindu, and Buddhist, promote forgiveness, this is unsurprising; however, religious beliefs may dictate what forgiveness means, and this meaning may differ from the way in which the field of psychology defines it. For example, in many religious traditions the idea of "forgive and forget" (i.e., forgive and then reconcile) go hand in hand. In the field of psychology, particularly in the majority culture, however, forgiveness does not always include the reconciliation piece of this concept (Frise & McMinn, 2010). Moreover, the centrality of the role religion plays in the life of an individual is likely to mediate the relationship between whether or not the idea of forgiveness necessarily translates to everyday life outside of the individual's religious experience (Huber, Allemand, & Huber, 2011).

Cultivating Forgiveness

In this section, we explore how forgiveness can be taught. Accordingly, we show how three sources—another person, oneself, or even a situation or circumstance—can be used as targets in forgiveness instruction.

Forgiving Another Person

In this most typical category of forgiveness, forgiving another individual, one can imagine the lyrics of a blues song in which one partner in a relationship has been "done wrong" (e.g., the other partner had an affair). In our therapy experiences with couples dealing with forgiveness in the wake of infidelities, we have found that the model of Gordon, Baucom, and Snyder is a useful one (2004, 2005; Gordon & Baucom, 1998). In this model, in which forgiveness is the goal, the first step is to promote a non-distorted, realistic appraisal of the relationship of the two people. The second step is the attempt to facilitate a release from the bond of ruminative, negative affect held toward the violating (transgressing) partner. Finally, the third step is to help the victimized partner lessen his or her desire to punish the transgressing partner. Over time, forgiveness makes it possible for the hurt and the outpouring of negative feelings to diminish—especially for the victimized partner. Likewise, the treatment enhances the empathy for the transgressing partner, and the therapist tries to make both people feel better about themselves.

Forgiveness parallels the stages of recovery from psychological trauma. Over time, the couple progresses from the initial impact stage to a search for meaning or understanding of what happened to them. Finally, the couple moves to a recovery stage, in which they "get on with their lives" (Gordon et al., 2005). In the impact stage, there is typically a rampage of negative emotions—hurt, fear, and anger. At this time, the partners may swing from numbness to very bad feelings. Then, in the meaning stage, the partners search desperately to comprehend why the affair happened. Surely, the couple reasons, there must be some meaning in this relationship-shaking event. Last, the couple slowly begins to recapture a sense of control over their lives; a major goal in this stage is to keep the affair from ruling every waking thought of these two people. To forgive does not necessarily mean that the couple decides to stay together—but at least the forgiving process enables them to make more informed decisions about what to do next.

Another productive approach for helping couples to deal with infidelity is the forgiveness model of Everett Worthington of Virginia Commonwealth University (see Ripley & Worthington, 2002; Worthington, 1998; Worthington & Drinkard, 2000). This model is based on helping the partners through the five steps of the acronym REACH: Recall the hurt and the nature of the injury caused, promote Empathy in both partners, Altruistically give the gift of forgiveness between partners, Commit verbally to forgive the partner, and Hold onto the forgiveness for each other.

Forgiving Oneself

A clinician will be alerted to the potential need for forgiveness of the self when a client is feeling either shame or guilt. In this regard, shame reflects an overall sense that "I am a bad person." As such, shame cuts across particular circumstances, and it reflects an all-encompassing view of the self as powerless and worthless. In contrast, guilt taps a situation-specific negative self-view, for example, "I did a bad thing" (Tangney, Boone, & Dearing, 2005). A person who feels guilt has a sense of remorse and typically regrets something that he or she has done. To correct for such guilt, some sort of reparative action is warranted, such as confessing or apologizing. The process of helping a person to deal with shame is a more difficult one for the helper than is the treatment for guilt. This follows because shame cuts through more situations than the single-situational focus of guilt.

Self-forgiveness has been defined as "a process of releasing resentment toward oneself for a perceived transgression or wrongdoing" (DeShea & Wahkinney, 2003, p. 4). Given that we all must live with ourselves, it can be seen that the consequences of not forgiving oneself can be much more severe than the consequences of not forgiving another person (Hall & Fincham, 2005). Interventions to lessen counterproductive criticism of the self are aimed at helping the individual take responsibility for the bad act or actions and then

Everett L. Worthington, Jr.

Source: Reprinted with permission of Everett L. Worthington, Jr.

let go so that she or he can move forward with the tasks in life. In fact, any client who is absorbed in very negative or very positive self-thoughts feels "caught." Accordingly, helpers attempt to help their clients understand how their self-absorbed thoughts and feelings interfere with positive living. Holmgren (2002) has captured this sentiment:

> To dwell on one's own past record of moral performance, either with a sense of self-hatred and self-contempt or with a sense of superiority, is an activity that is overly self-involved and devoid of any real moral value. The client will exercise his moral agency much more responsibly if he removes his focus from the fact that he did wrong and concentrates instead on the contribution he can make to others and on the growth he can experience in the moral and nonmoral realms. (p. 133)

Jacinto and Edwards (2011) outline four therapeutic stages that they believe one must process through on the road to self-forgiveness. The first of these is *recognition*, and it refers to the awareness of the individual that self-forgiveness is justified. Second, the stage of *responsibility* is a basic "owning" of the transgressions the individual feels he or she has committed. Third, the stage of *expression* is an active emotion-approach stage in which the individual works on expressing the emotions related to the incident and dialogs about these feelings. Finally, the stage of *recreating* helps individuals create a new self-image that acknowledges the past but looks toward and informs the future (Jacinto & Edwards, 2011).

Forgiveness of a Situation

Recall the Enright position (described previously) that forgiveness should be applied only to people, not to inanimate objects such as tornadoes. We disagree with this premise; our views are consistent with the Thompson model of forgiveness, in which the target can be another person, oneself, or a situation.

Dr. Snyder's recounting of a psychotherapy case he had some 20 years after the publication of the first edition of this book shows how forgiveness can be applied to a situation. Dr. Snyder resided in Lawrence, Kansas, at the time, where tornadoes occasionally descend on the local community. In this particular instance, a tornado had damaged houses and injured the inhabitants. After this tornado, Dr. Snyder saw a man in therapy who held severe angry and bitter thoughts toward the tornado for destroying his house and making him feel psychologically victimized. In the course of treatment, the goal was to help this man to stop ruminating about the tornado and to stop blaming it for having ruined his life (Snyder, 2003). Therefore, the man was taught to let go of his resentment toward the tornado. This was part of a larger treatment goal aimed at teaching this person to release the bitterness he felt about a series of "bad breaks" that he had received in life. Moreover, he came to understand that the tornado had struck other houses and families, but those people had picked up the pieces and moved on with their lives. For this client, ruminations about the tornado kept him stuck in the past, and he realized that letting go was part of moving forward so as to have hope in his life (see Lopez, Snyder, et al., 2004; Snyder, 1989).

For professionals who have done considerable psychotherapy, this case will not seem unusual. Clients often point to their life circumstances as the causes of their problems (i.e., they blame the happenings in their lives). For such clients, therefore, a crucial part of their treatment entails instruction in stopping thoughts about earlier negative life events so that they instead can look ahead toward their futures (Michael & Snyder, 2005; Wade, 2010).

Before turning to our next topic, we offer one more interesting area of research related to the potential negative antecedents of forgiveness in some circumstances. According to Gordon, Burton, and Porter (2004) victims of domestic violence who were able to forgive their abusive partners were more likely to return to the violent situation. This finding held even when other factors (e.g., lack of belief in divorce, concerns about alternatives to the relationship) were controlled. Based on this pattern of data, these researchers caution clinicians to take care in linking the ideas of forgiveness and reconciliation. As discussed above, many may find these two concepts to be joined, and in these situations this belief that reconciliation is necessary may drive an abused woman toward returning as a component of her forgiveness process (Gordon et al, 2004). In addition, other studies have found that the tendency to forgive a violent partner is predictive of continued aggression (both physical and psychological) within marriages (McNulty, 2011).

Some researchers have shown that there may be some less positive antecedents to self-forgiveness as well. Wohl and Thompson (2011) found that some maladaptive behaviors may be maintained through the process of self-forgiveness. In their study, these researchers looked at smokers and found that those higher in self-forgiveness were more likely to continue smoking and resist change toward a healthier lifestyle. This may be in part because the negative emotion associated with not forgiving oneself for this type of behavior spurs the individual to change; when the negative emotion is dissipated by self-forgiveness, the need to change is no longer warranted (Wohl & Thompson, 2011). With regard to cultural differences in self-forgiveness, though shame is often touted as a negative and non-functional emotion in Western society, many Eastern cultures promote shame as a functional reaction in some social situations (Okano, 1994). In light of these cultural contexts, lack of an "appropriate" level of shame or "too much" self-forgiveness may isolate an individual from their culture as it goes against norms in these societies.

Thus, these examples highlight the importance of understanding the function (or dysfunction) of forgiveness in more detail before promoting it in all situations. For more insights into raising one's forgiveness, we recommend that you return to the Personal Mini-Experiments.

Measuring Forgiveness

Each of the previously discussed theories of forgiveness is associated with an individual differences self-report measure that has been validated. We cover these measures in the same order as we discussed the theories.

Thompson et al. (2005) developed the Heartland Forgiveness Scale (HFS) as an 18-item trait measure of forgiveness. There are six items to tap each of the three types of forgiveness—self, other, or situation—and respondents use a 7-point scale (1 = Almost always false of me to 7 = Almost always true of me). This scale is reprinted in its entirety in Appendix C. Scores on the HFS have correlated positively with scores on other forgiveness measures; people scoring higher on the HFS also show more flexibility and trust, as well as less hostility, rumination, and depression.

McCullough et al. (1998) developed the Transgression-Related Interpersonal Motivations Inventory (TRIM) as a 12-item self-report measure (respondents use a 5-point continuum from

1 = Strongly disagree to 5 = Strongly agree), with the items tapping either (1) the motive to avoid contact with the transgressing person or (2) the motive to seek revenge against the transgressor. The TRIM can be regarded as a transgression-specific index of forgiveness. This scale is shown in Appendix D.

Enright has developed two forgiveness measures, the first of which is a 60-item version called the Enright Forgiveness Inventory (EVI; Subkoviak et al., 1995). The EVI assesses the respondent's thoughts about a recent interpersonal transgression. A second Enright-inspired measure is the 16-item Willingness to Forgive Scale (WTF; Hebl & Enright, 1993). The WTF gives a valid estimate of the degree to which a person is willing to use forgiveness as a problem-solving coping strategy.

Tangney and colleagues (1999) have developed a trait self-report index called the Multidimensional Forgiveness Inventory (MFI). The MFI entails 16 different scenarios involving transgressions; 72 items tap these 9 subscales: (1) propensity to forgive self, (2) propensity to forgive others, (3) propensity to ask for forgiveness, (4) propensity to blame self, (5) propensity to blame others, (6) time to forgive self, (7) time to forgive others, (8) sensitivity to hurt feelings, and (9) anger-proneness.

The Evolutionary and Neurobiological Bases of Forgiveness

In many places throughout this book, we emphasize the communal nature of human beings. We live in groups, and part of such contact unfortunately involves instances in which one person strikes out against another in an injurious manner. In subhuman creatures, animals may at times engage in submissive gestures that stop the aggression cycle (deWaal & Pokorny, 2005; Newberg, d'Aquili, Newberg, & deMarici, 2000). In an analogous fashion, forgiveness may break the violence cycle in humans. Lacking such mechanisms to lessen the potential for aggression and retaliative counteraggression, humans may risk an escalating cycle that threatens the demise of the entire group. In this sense, there is an evolutionary advantage to forgiving actions in that they lower the overall level of hostility (Enright, 1996; Komorita, Hilty, & Parks, 1991), thereby enhancing the survival chances of the larger group. Indeed, people who display forgiveness toward their transgressors produce positive feelings in surrounding people who were in no way involved in the confrontation (Kanekar & Merchant, 1982), thereby stabilizing the social order. In short, forgiveness represents a process that has an adaptive evolutionary advantage in that it helps to preserve the social structure.

Newberg et al. (2000) have described the underlying neurophysiology of the forgiveness process. First, by necessity, forgiveness involves a person's sense of self because it is this source that is damaged during transgression by another. (Incidentally, perception of the self is crucial from an evolutionary standpoint because it is the self that the person strives to preserve over time.) The sense of self is located in the frontal, parietal, and temporal lobes, which receive input from the sensory system and the hippocampus. Second, injury to the self is registered via sensorimotor input, and this input is mediated by the limbic system, the sympathetic nervous system, and the hypothalamus. Third, initiation of the reconciliation process by the person transgressed against involves activation of the temporal, parietal, and frontal lobes, along with limbic system input. Some research suggests that the ventromedial prefrontal cortex plays a key role when deciding to forgive a deception (Hayashi et al., 2010). Finally, the actual outward direction of the forgiveness occurs through the limbic system and is associated with positive emotions.

PERSONAL BENEFITS OF ALTRUISM, GRATITUDE, AND FORGIVENESS

Altruism

As already discussed, there are many positive correlates of prosocial behavior. Specifically, helping others seems to be linked to feelings of well-being for a variety of reasons. Research shows that positive mood or affect often stimulates altruism and other types of helping behavior (Isen, 2000). In addition, even when people are experiencing negative moods, helping others seems to help them self-regulate these negative emotions, thus leading to more positive moods at home; in the workplace (Glomb, Bhave, Miner, & Wall, 2011); and in the face of disaster (Yang & Chen, 2011). Altruism has been found to be correlated positively with the personality characteristics of Agreeableness and Openness to Experience, and also with honesty and humility (LaBouff et al., 2012; Zettler, Hilbig, & Haubrich, 2011) as well.

Gratitude

Many researchers have shown that positive traits have been associated with self-reported gratitude. Higher scores on gratitude assessments have correlated positively with elevated positive emotions, vitality, optimism, hope, and satisfaction with life (McCullough et al., 2002; Szczesniak & Soares, 2011. Moreover, higher gratitude has correlated positively with empathy, sharing, forgiving, and giving one's time for the benefit of others. Those who scored higher in gratitude are less concerned with material goods; are more likely to engage in prayer and spiritual matters (McCullough et al., 2002); and may have better physical health (Hill, Allemand, & Roberts, 2012) and lower depressive symptoms (Lambert, Fincham, & Stillman, 2012). Other researchers have found that grateful reframing of negative events assisted individuals in developing emotional closure toward unpleasant memories of these events (Watkins, Cruz, Holben, & Kolts, 2008). These benefits are experienced by both adults and adolescents (see Froh et al., 2010; Froh, Sefick, & Emmons, 2008), though some cultural differences may exist regarding these benefits (Boehm et al., 2011). Some research reports differences in the way children express gratitude (de Lucca Freitas, Pieta, & Tudge, 2011); this area is ripe for more investigation.

Forgiveness

Many researchers have found correlations between forgiveness and well-being (Moorhead, Gill, Minton, & Myers, 2012), as well as between forgiveness and physical health (Green, DeCourville, & Sadava, 2012; Hannon, Finkel, Kumashiro, & Rusbult, 2012). In addition, those who forgive are said to be less ruminative, less depressed, and possess less narcissistic entitlement (Strelan, 2007; Takaku, 2001). Other research has found that longevity is also associated with practicing forgiveness (Toussaint, Owen, & Cheadle, 2012), as is satisfaction within relationships (Braithwaite, Selby, & Fincham, 2011). As noted previously, consequences of forgiveness may not always be positive

(Wohl & Thompson, 2011). Therefore, though forgiveness can lead to great things for many, caution must be taken in looking carefully at the situation before employing strategies in this area.

THE SOCIETAL IMPLICATIONS OF ALTRUISM, GRATITUDE, AND FORGIVENESS

In this portion of the chapter, we turn to the societal repercussions of altruism, gratitude, and forgiveness. As you will learn in this section, these three processes play crucial roles in helping groups of people live together with greater stability and interpersonal accord.

Empathy/Egotism and Altruism

Given that the feeling of empathy appears to propel human beings toward "pure" (i.e., nonegotistical) helping or altruistic actions, this motivation generally has positive implications for people living in groups. That is to say, as long as we can feel empathy, we should be more willing to help our fellow citizens.

Unfortunately, however, we often act either consciously or unconsciously so as to mute our sense of empathy toward other people. Consider, for example, the residents of major urban settings who walk down the street and do not even appear to see people who are homeless stretched out on the pavement or sidewalk. Faced daily with such sights, it may be that the inhabitants of cities learn to mute their empathies. City dwellers thus may avoid eye contact or walk to the other side of the street in order to minimize their interactions with such down-and-out people and/or their reactions to seeing individuals in these situations.

To compound matters, social psychologists have shown that residents of large cities can diffuse any sense of personal responsibility for helping others, a phenomenon known as the "innocent bystander effect" (Darley & Latane, 1968; Latane & Darley, 1970). At times, therefore, urban dwellers may rationalize and deceive themselves that they have behaved morally when, in fact, they have not rendered help to their neighbors (Rue, 1994; Snyder, Higgins, & Stucky, 1983/2005; Wright, 1994).

Realize, however, that even professionals whose training and job descriptions entail helping others may undergo similar muting of their sensibilities. For example, both nurses and schoolteachers may experience burnout when they feel blocked and repeatedly sense that they cannot produce the positive changes that they desire in their patients or students (Maslach, 1982; Maslach & Jackson, 1981; Snyder, 1994/2000). Medical students and other health care professionals often show a decrease in altruistic mindsets and empathy as they move though their educational processes (Burks & Kobus, 2012). In our estimation, positive psychology must find ways to help people to remain empathic so they can continue to help others, perhaps through mindfulness training and self-reflection (Burks & Kobus, 2012). Furthermore, we should explore avenues for enhancing empathy so we can address large-scale problems such as AIDS and homelessness (Batson, Polycarpou, et al., 1997; Dovidio, Gaertner, & Johnson, 1999; Snyder, Tennen, Affleck, & Cheavens, 2000).

This research can also help us as individuals and as a society by further investigating the use of empathy within multicultural and cross-cultural interactions. As noted earlier in this chapter, one way to promote empathy is to interact more closely with others. As one gets to know another's plight or situation, it may be that feelings of empathy come more easily. Thus, in interacting with individuals from cultural backgrounds other than your own, *ethnocultural empathy* may be cultivated and measured (see Wang et al., 2003). Wang and colleagues define this concept as "empathy directed toward people from racial and ethnic cultural groups who are different from one's own ethnocultural group" (p. 221). Development of this type of empathy seems to be aided by close interactions with members of groups who are different from oneself (Batson et al., 1997; Pedrotti & Sweatt, 2007). In surrounding ourselves with others who are similar to us, we enjoy comfort and familiarity, but this same action can also lead to a lack of understanding about the situations of others who are unlike us. This can, at times, lead to scapegoating and stereotyping (Hamilton, 1981; Mio, Barker, & Tumambing, 2009). By engaging with others from different backgrounds, we learn about history and ways in which certain groups and individuals (perhaps particularly those who have been marginalized in the past) have been treated and mistreated. In helping to cultivate ethnocultural empathy in our children and in ourselves, we lay a foundation for a more understanding world.

Turning to the role of egotism-based benefits as they are implicated in the altruism process, our view is that it would be wise to teach people that there is nothing wrong with deriving benefits from or feeling good about helping others. In fact, it is unrealistic to expect that people always will engage in pure, non-ego-based motives as they go about their helping activities. In other words, if people indeed do feel good about themselves in rendering aid to others, then we should convey the societal message that this is perfectly legitimate. Although it certainly is worthwhile to engender the desire to help because it is the right thing to do, we also can impart the legitimacy of rendering help on the grounds that it is a means of deriving some sense of gratification. We should remember both the former and the latter lessons as we educate our children about the process of helping other people.

Empathy/Egotism and Gratitude

If we can understand and take the perspective of another person to a greater degree, it is more likely that we will express our sense of gratitude for that other person's actions. Research shows that taking time to voice appreciation for one's friends, spouse, and family can have large benefits for these relationships. Those who feel that their romantic partners appreciate them report that they in turn feel more grateful back, creating a context of gratitude within the relationship (Gordon, Impett, Kogan, Oveis, & Keltner, 2012). In addition, being more appreciative of a partner is also associated with more commitment and more responsivity to a partner's needs (Bartlett, Condon, Cruz, Baumann, & Desteno, 2012; Gordon et al., 2012). This may be the case even in situations where this gratitude is not expressed out loud (Gordon, Arnette, & Smith, 2011). In addition, expressing gratitude toward a partner has been found to improve not only the recipient's perception of the relationship, but the *expresser's* perception of the relationship as well (Lambert, Clark, Durtschi, Fincham, & Graham, 2010). Thus, gratitude can be good for many aspects of relationships.

Beyond individual and personal relationships, a sense of gratitude might be felt toward something larger. In our work with various students over the years, many have reported their profound feelings of gratefulness at living in the United States after traveling to other, less well-off countries as part of study-abroad programs or missionary projects. A common theme in the responses of these students upon their return is their awareness of how much they had taken for granted before their travels. Having clean air and water, medical supplies, access to education, and protection of basic personal rights are some of the positive things they seem to notice upon their return. Taking the time to appreciate what we have and working to develop this type of everyday gratitude for these rights and commodities is something we can all do toward building a more grateful attitude. This, of course, has benefits for others and for ourselves.

Empathy/Egotism and Forgiveness

Empathy also is a precursor to forgiving another (McCullough et al., 1998; McCullough, Worthington, & Rachal, 1997; Worthington, 2005). The authors of this book have worked with psychotherapy clients for whom either empathy or egotism served as the routes for unleashing forgiveness. For example, consider the person who is filled with anger at something hurtful that another person has done and who must first learn to see the issue from the perspective of that other person (i.e., empathize) before coming to the point of forgiving him or her.

In a situation related to this point, a man, Michael, who received a very dire medical diagnosis chose not to impart the seriousness of this diagnosis or its life-threatening nature to his close friends, among which were this author (JTP) and her family. Upon his death, many of us felt anger mixed with our sadness at losing this great friend. We felt cheated, at some level, at not being able to say goodbye and to instead be jolted by the suddenness (to us) of his death. In light of Michael's very caring and nurturing nature, however, it was likely his true belief was that he was sparing his friends from worry during the time that he was ill, especially as his death was inevitable. Reframing this "transgression" as a caring gesture towards loved companions allowed us to "forgive" him for not telling us the truth.

So too can we forgive—let go of negative ruminations about another person or event—in order to feel better about ourselves. As an example of this egotistical type of forgiveness, consider young people who have gotten into difficulties by breaking the law during their earlier teenage years. To feel better about themselves when they reach young adulthood, these young people may decide to do volunteer work to aid teens with legal problems. Such teenagers often desperately want and need to feel forgiven for their transgressions, and adults in their 20s who have been through similar circumstances make ideal sources of such forgiveness. In this latter regard, these young adults not only can empathize with the teens, they also can feel good about themselves for providing such forgiveness.

Engaging in regular acts of forgiveness may also enhance our social relationships within our communities (Hook, Worthington, & Utsey, 2009). In cultures whose ideologies are more collectivistic, forgiveness is a necessary part of achieving social harmony, which is highly valued within these groups. Hook and colleagues present the concept of "collective forgiveness" (p. 821) and discuss its usefulness in maintaining and repairing relationships that have been ruptured due to some transgression. With this type of forgiveness, the decision to forgive may be "largely to promote and maintain group harmony rather than [attain] inner peace" (Hook et al., p. 821).

Moral Imperatives: Altruism, Gratitude, and Forgiveness

As we have noted throughout this chapter, empathy and egotism often are precursors of altruism, gratitude, and forgiveness toward another. This notion of the empathy/esteem portal is depicted visually in Figure 11.1. Once a person has expressed altruism, gratitude, or forgiveness toward a recipient, however, the cycle does not stop. Consider, for example, the reactions of the recipient to gratitude. When the recipient of the gratitude expresses thanks or some other type of appreciation, the giver of the benevolent behavior is rewarded and thereafter may behave prosocially in the future (Gallup, 1998). Likewise, it is possible that some people render prosocial behavior at least in part because they enjoy the reinforcement they receive for it (Eisenberg, Miller, Shell, McNalley, & Shea, 1991).

In this process, depicted in Figure 11.4, the recipient is likely to reciprocate the altruism, gratitude, or forgiveness and, in so doing, may well experience empathy and esteem toward the giver. Moreover, the recipient of the altruism, gratitude, or forgiveness is likely to behave in moral ways toward other people in general (see the right-hand side of Figure 11.4). In other words, when altruism, gratitude, or forgiveness is exchanged, then the recipient should practice the virtues of positive psychology in subsequent interpersonal interactions. In this way, there are ripple effects of altruism, gratitude, and forgiveness. The underlying sentiment here may be, "When I am treated with respect, I will do the same to others."

In Adam Smith's (1790/1976) classic book, *The Theory of Moral Sentiments,* he suggested that gratitude and related constructs such as altruism and forgiveness are absolutely crucial in establishing a moral society. As such, gratitude is a moral imperative in that it promotes stable social interactions that are based on mutual reciprocity and respect (see again Figure 11.4). Using the line of thought developed by Smith, sociologist Georg Simmel (1950) reasoned that gratitude, in particular, reminds people of their need to reciprocate and of their inherent interrelationships to each

Figure 11.4 Altruism, Gratitude, and Forgiveness From Giver to Recipient to Others

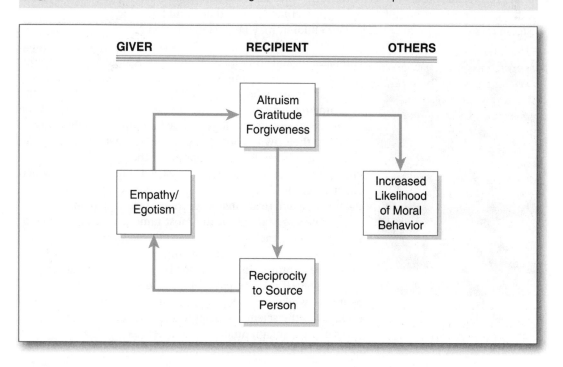

other. On this point, Simmel penned the beautiful sentiment that gratitude is "the moral memory of mankind. . . . [I]f every grateful action . . . were suddenly eliminated, society (at least as we know it) would break apart" (1950, p. 388). Thus, gratitude and its neighboring concepts of altruism and forgiveness facilitate a society in which there is a sense of cohesion and the ability to continue to function when both good and bad things happen to its citizens (for related discussion, see Rue [1994] and Snyder & Higgins [1997]).

"I HAVE A DREAM": TOWARD A KINDER, GENTLER HUMANKIND

Dr. Martin Luther King, Jr. once said, "Life's most persistent and urgent question is, 'What are you doing for others?'" This chapter covers a trilogy of some of the finest behaviors of people—their altruism, gratitude, and forgiveness. It appears that empathy for the target person often is an important precursor to these behaviors. When we have empathy for another, we are more likely to help that person, to feel grateful for his or her actions, and to be forgiving when he or she transgresses. But in feeling such empathy, people also can fulfill their egotism needs. Thus, it need not be an either–or proposition when it comes to the motives of empathy and egotism that unleash altruism, gratitude, and forgiveness.

An implication here is that a kinder and gentler humankind will be one where each of us can understand the actions of others, feel their pains and sorrows, and yet also feel good about our own motives as we help our neighbors. In addition, working hard to channel that empathy toward actions that give equal rights to all helps us to stand up for those who need assistance and calls us to lend power to those who have less. These are all ideas that stem from the legacy left to our country by Dr. King. Certainly, empathy is a crucial lesson that should be added to the lessons in esteem that are taught to children. Our children may be able to feel good about themselves and get along better with others because of their understanding, compassion, and ethnocultural empathy. A large part of development of this empathy might be broadening our circles of interaction with those who we perceive to be dissimilar to us and encouraging our children to do the same. Indeed, much of the future of positive psychology will be built upon people who can attend to their own egotism needs and also get along with and respect each other. Relationships are at the core of positive psychology, and our goal is a more "civilized" humankind in which altruism, gratitude, and forgiveness are the expected, rather than the unexpected, reactions between interacting people.

In what may be one of the most famous oral discourses of modern times, the "I Have a Dream" speech of Dr. King, his empathy and altruism/gratitude/forgiveness thoughts and feelings were captured in his call for brotherhood and sisterhood (King, 1968). If positive psychology is to share in such a dream, as it surely aspires to do, then we must continue our quest to understand the science and applications that flow from the concepts of altruism, gratitude, and forgiveness.

Martin Luther King, Jr.
Source: Copyright © Corbis.

Life Enhancement Strategies

Altruism, gratitude, and forgiveness can help you to live a more satisfying life. Here, we offer some tips for being more giving, grateful, and forgiving in all three life arenas.

Love

- Doing things for others can help others to feel love, even if they are outside your normal social context. Spreading this goodwill to those who are different than you can begin to foster true connections between you and others.

- A loving relationship is built on praise for one's mate when they do positive things; therefore, it is crucial to say "thank you" and to not take the positive for granted. Your expressed gratitude for your partner keeps the sense of caring alive through an atmosphere of appreciation.

- There may be instances in a loving and intimate relationship where one partner transgresses and forgiveness is needed for the relationship to endure. Try to become the partner and/or friend who practices forgiveness during difficult times.

Work

- Share your strengths and talents with others in an effort to help them on their work or school projects.

- Gratitude can be even more important than money as management's way of rewarding workers. If you are given the responsibility of leading a team, give daily thanks for the contributions of others.

- Colleagues are going to be more willing to take chances, to try new things, and to work hard if they know that they will be forgiven should they make an occasional unintended mistake. Spread forgiveness in the workplace or classroom.

Play

- By their very nature, play and leisure activities entail a sense of freedom. Give that sense of freedom to others by making sure that time for play and recharging is afforded to people of all socioeconomic groups.

- Sometimes we are given peeks into others' pleasure. When friends and family are having fun around the house, don't be shy about expressing your gratitude for the "good times."

- Forgive the small rule infractions that are bound to result in competition. Don't let the small stuff get in the way of your fun.

APPENDIX A: THE HELPING ATTITUDE SCALE

Instructions: This instrument is designed to measure your feelings, beliefs, and behaviors concerning your interactions with others. It is not a test, so there are no right or wrong answers. Please answer the questions as honestly as possible. Using the scale below, indicate your level of agreement or disagreement in the space which is next to each statement.

1	2	3	4	5
Strongly Disagree	Disagree	Undecided	Agree	Strongly Agree

_____ 1. Helping others is usually a waste of time.

_____ 2. When given the opportunity, I enjoy aiding others who are in need.

_____ 3. If possible, I would return lost money to the rightful owner.

_____ 4. Helping friends and family is one of the great joys in life.

_____ 5. I would avoid aiding someone in a medical emergency if I could.

_____ 6. It feels wonderful to assist others in need.

_____ 7. Volunteering to help someone is very rewarding.

_____ 8. I dislike giving directions to strangers who are lost.

_____ 9. Doing volunteer work makes me feel happy.

_____ 10. I donate time or money to charities every month.

_____ 11. Unless they are part of my family, helping the elderly isn't my responsibility.

_____ 12. Children should be taught about the importance of helping others.

_____ 13. I plan to donate my organs when I die, with the hope that they will help someone else live.

_____ 14. I try to offer my help with any activities my community or school groups are carrying out.

_____ 15. I feel at peace with myself when I have helped others.

_____ 16. If the person in front of me in the checkout line at a store was a few cents short, I would pay the difference.

_____ 17. I feel proud when I know that my generosity has benefited a needy person.

_____ 18. Helping people does more harm than good because they come to rely on others and not themselves.

_____ 19. I rarely contribute money to a worthy cause.

_____ 20. Giving aid to the poor is the right thing to do.

To score the Helping Attitude Scale, reverse the scores for items 1, 5, 8, 11, 18, and 19, then add up all twenty scores to obtain the total score. This score could range from 20 to 100, with a neutral score of 60.

Appendix A Source: From Nickell, G. S., The helping attitude scale, presented at the 106th Annual Convention of the American Psychological Association. Reprinted by permission of Dr. Gary Nickell.

APPENDIX B: THE GRATITUDE QUESTIONNAIRE—SIX ITEMS FROM GQ-6

Instructions: Using the scale below as a guide, write a number beside each statement to indicate how much you agree with it.

1	2	3	4	5	6	7
Strongly Disagree	Disagree	Slightly Disagree	Neutral	Slightly Agree	Agree	Strongly Agree

_____1. I have so much in life to be thankful for.

_____2. If I had to list everything that I felt grateful for, it would be a very long list.

_____3. When I look at the world, I don't see much to be grateful for.*

_____4. I am grateful to a wide variety of people.

_____5. As I get older, I find myself more able to appreciate the people, events, and situations that have been part of my life history.

_____6. Long amounts of time can go by before I feel grateful to something or someone.*

Appendix B Source: From McCullough, M. E., Emmons, R. A., & Tsang, J., "The grateful disposition: A conceptual and empirical topography," *Journal of Personality and Social Psychology, 82*(1), 112–127. Copyright © 2002 by the American Psychological Association. Reproduced with permission. No further reproduction or distribution is permitted without written permission from the American Psychological Association.

*Items 3 and 6 are reverse scored.

APPENDIX C: THE HEARTLAND FORGIVENESS SCALE (HFS)

Directions: In the course of our lives, negative things may occur because of our own actions, the actions of others, or circumstances beyond our control. For some time after these events, we may have negative thoughts or feelings about ourselves, others, or the situation. Think about how you *typically* respond to such negative events. In the blank lines before each of the following items, please write the number (using the 7-point scale below) that best describes how you *typically* respond to the type of negative situation described. There are no right or wrong answers. Please be as honest as possible.

1	2	3	4	5	6	7
Almost Always False		More Often False of Me		More Often True of Me		Almost Always True

_____ 1. Although I feel badly at first when I mess up, over time I can give myself some slack.

_____ 2. I hold grudges against myself for negative things I've done.

1	2	3	4	5	6	7
Almost Always False		More Often False of Me		More Often True of Me		Almost Always True

_____ 3.	Learning from bad things that I've done helps me get over them.
_____ 4.	It is really hard for me to accept myself once I've messed up.
_____ 5.	With time, I am understanding of myself for mistakes I've made.
_____ 6.	I don't stop criticizing myself for negative things I've felt, thought, said, or done.
_____ 7.	I continue to punish a person who has done something that I think is wrong.
_____ 8.	With time, I am understanding of others for the mistakes they've made.
_____ 9.	I continue to be hard on others who have hurt me.
_____10.	Although others have hurt me in the past, I have eventually been able to see them as good people.
_____11.	If others mistreat me, I continue to think badly of them.
_____12.	When someone disappoints me, I can eventually move past it.
_____13.	When things go wrong for reasons that can't be controlled, I get stuck in negative thoughts about it.
_____14.	With time, I can be understanding of bad circumstances in my life.
_____15.	If I'm disappointed by uncontrollable circumstances in my life, I continue to think negatively about them.
_____16.	I eventually make peace with bad situations in my life.
_____17.	It's really hard for me to accept negative situations that aren't anybody's fault.
_____18.	Eventually, I let go of negative thoughts about bad circumstances that are beyond anyone's control.

Appendix C Source: From Thompson, L. Y., Snyder, C. R., Hoffman, L., Michael, S. T., Rasmussen, H. N., Billings, L. S., Heinze, L.,...Roberts, D. E., Dispositional forgiveness of self, others, and situations, *Journal of Personality, 73.* Copyright © 2005. John Wiley & Sons. Reprinted with permission.

Reverse-Scored Items
Items 2, 4, 6, 7, 9, 11, 13, 15, and 17 are reverse scored.

Overall HFS Score
A total forgiveness score is derived by summing the numbers given in response to items 1 through 18 (using the reverse scores for items 2, 4, 6, 7, 9, 11, 13, 15, and 17).

Subscales
Self: Items 1 through 6 compose the forgiveness-of-self subscale.
Other: Items 7 through 12 compose the forgiveness-of-other subscale.
Situations: Items 13 through 18 compose the forgiveness-of-situations subscale.

APPENDIX D: THE TRANSGRESSION-RELATED INTERPERSONAL MOTIVATIONS SCALE (TRIM)

Directions: For the following questions, please indicate your current thoughts and feelings about the person who hurt you. Use the following scale to indicate your agreement with each of the questions.

1	2	3	4	5
Strongly Disagree	**Disagree**	**Neutral**	**Agree**	**Strongly Agree**
_____ 1. I'll make him/her pay.				
_____ 2. I keep as much distance between us as possible.				
_____ 3. I wish that something bad would happen to him/her.				
_____ 4. I live as if he/she doesn't exist, isn't around.				
_____ 5. I don't trust him/her.				
_____ 6. I want him/her to get what he/she deserves.				
_____ 7. I find it difficult to act warmly toward him/her.				
_____ 8. I avoid him/her.				
_____ 9. I'm going to get even.				
_____10. I cut off the relationship with him/her.				
_____11. I want to see him/her hurt and miserable.				
_____12. I withdraw from him/her.				

Avoidance Motivations
Add up the scores for items 2, 4, 5, 7, 8, 10, and 12.

Revenge Motivations
Add up the scores for items 1, 3, 6, 9, and 11.

KEY TERMS

Altruism: Actions or behaviors that are intended to benefit another person.

Egotism: The motive to pursue some sort of personal gain or benefit through targeted behavior.

Empathy: An emotional response to the perceived plight of another person. Empathy may entail the ability to experience emotions similar to the other person's or a sense of tenderheartedness toward that person.

Empathy–altruism hypothesis: The view, borne out by Batson's (1991) findings, that empathy for another person leads to a greater likelihood of helping that person.

Forgiveness (as defined by Thompson and colleagues): A freeing from a negative attachment to the source of the transgression. This definition of forgiveness allows the target of forgiveness to be oneself, another person, or a situation.

Forgiveness (as defined by McCullough and colleagues): An increase in prosocial motivation such that there is less desire to avoid or seek revenge against the transgressor and an increased desire to act positively toward the transgressing person. This theory of forgiveness is applicable only when another person is the target of the transgression.

Forgiveness (as defined by Enright and colleagues): The willingness to give up resentment, negative judgment, and indifference toward the transgressor and to give undeserved compassion, generosity, and benevolence to him or her. Enright and colleagues also limit their definition of forgiveness to people and do not include situations.

Forgiveness (as defined by Tangney and colleagues): A process involving "(1) cognitive-affective transformation following a transgression in which (2) the victim makes a realistic assessment of the harm done and acknowledges the perpetrator's responsibility, but (3) freely chooses to 'cancel the debt,' giving up the need for revenge or deserved punishments and any quest for restitution. This 'canceling of the debt' also involves (4) a 'cancellation of negative emotions' directly related to the transgression. In particular, in forgiving, the victim overcomes his or her feelings of resentment and anger for the act. In short, by forgiving, the harmed individual (5) essentially removes himself or herself from the victim role" (Tangney, Fee, Reinsmith, Boone, & Lee, 1999, p. 2).

Gratitude: Being thankful for and appreciating the actions of another. Gratitude emerges upon recognizing that one has received a positive outcome from another person who behaved in a manner that was costly to him or her, valuable to the recipient, and intentionally rendered.

CHAPTER 12

Attachment, Love, and Flourishing Relationships

In our clinical work, we see people from all walks of life who talk about feelings of loneliness. For some clients, the conversation focuses on longing for loved ones "back home," along with concerns about finding good friends in a new place. For too many, the loneliness and a sense of alienation stem from relationships that have soured. There are sons who do not feel connected to their fathers, boyfriends who feel invisible to their partners, wives who "don't know" their partners anymore, and aging parents who haven't seen their children in years. All these people tell painful stories of loss. When our basic needs for love, affection, and belongingness are not met (Maslow, 1970; see Figure 12.1), we feel lonely and worthless. This pain has long-term effects because our growth is stymied when we feel detached and unloved.

We start our discussion of attachment, love, and flourishing relationships with comments on loneliness because much of the positive psychology of social connection was built on scholarship pertaining to traumatic separation (Bowlby, 1969) and failed relationships (Carrere & Gottman, 1999).

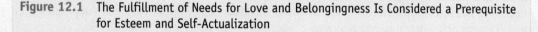

Figure 12.1 The Fulfillment of Needs for Love and Belongingness Is Considered a Prerequisite for Esteem and Self-Actualization

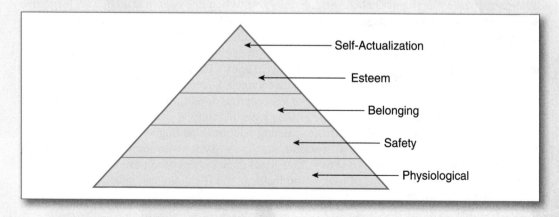

Only recently have scholars pursued research questions such as, "What are the characteristics of successful relationships?" (e.g., Gable, Reis, & Elliot, 2003; Harvey, Pauwels, & Zicklund, 2001).

Attachment and love are necessary components of flourishing relationships, but they are not sufficient for the maintenance of such relationships. In this regard, attachment and love must be accompanied by what we refer to as *purposeful positive relationship behaviors*.

In this chapter, we discuss the *infant-to-caregiver attachment* that forms the foundation for future relationships, the *adult attachment* security that is closely linked to healthy relationship development, the *love* that is often considered a marker of quality of relationships, and the *purposeful positive relationship behaviors* that sustain interpersonal connections over time and contribute to *flourishing relationships*. Along the way, we describe a hierarchy of social needs that demonstrates how meaningful relationships develop into flourishing relationships. Important to note as well is the impact of cultural context on our experience of love, its manifestations, and the emotions that accompany it (de Munck, Korotayev, de Munck, & Khaltourina, 2011; Gareis & Wilkins, 2011; Shiota, Campos, Gonzaga, Keltner, & Peng, 2010). We also describe real-life exemplars of "person-growing" relationships (relationships that promote the optimal functioning of both participants). Moreover, we discuss people who have experienced the best aspects of the interpersonal world. Finally, we summarize the findings on the biology of social support.

INFANT ATTACHMENT

Attachment is a process that probably starts during the first moment of an infant's life. It is the emotional link that forms between a child and a caregiver, and it physically binds people together over time (Ainsworth, Bell, & Stayton, 1992). John Bowlby (1969), a clinician who worked with delinquent and orphaned children, identified numerous **maladaptive parental behaviors** (chaotic, unplanned attempts to meet a child's needs; lack of physical availability) and **adaptive parental behaviors** (responsiveness to a child's behavioral cues, e.g., smiling) that were believed to be causally linked to functional behavior and emotional experiences of children. For example, inconsistency in responses to children is associated with children's frustration and later anxiety. On the other hand, consistency in caregivers' responses to children's cues is linked to children's contentment and later development of trust. Adaptive and maladaptive parental behaviors lead to the development of an **attachment system** that regulates the proximity-seeking behaviors connecting infants and caregivers in physical and emotional space. When this system is disrupted, formative social and emotional milestones may not be met (Howard, Martin, Berlin, & Brooks-Gunn, 2011). This two-way connection has been described as "a unique, evolutionarily-based motivational system (i.e., independent of the gratification of libidinal needs and drives) whose primary function is the provision of protection and emotional security" (Lopez, 2003, p. 286).

Through the study of children who became disconnected from their caregivers, Bowlby (1969) realized that insecure attachment is a precursor to numerous developmental struggles. A child with insecure attachment to at least one caregiver may have difficulty in cooperating with others and in regulating moods. These problems make existing relationships fragile and new relationships hard to build. Conversely, children with sound attachment systems become more appealing to their caregivers and other people. Over time, that attachment system becomes more sophisticated, and mutually beneficial patterns of interaction facilitate the psychological development of such children and their caregivers.

A classic behavioral assessment strategy designed by Mary Ainsworth (1979) has allowed psychologists to look into the attachment phenomenon. In the **Strange Situation** assessment, a child is exposed to a novel situation in the company of his or her caregiver, and then the caregiver is removed and reintroduced to the situation twice. During this process, the child participant's reactions are assessed. Here are the basic steps in the assessment paradigm (Steps 2 through 7 last 3 minutes each):

1. Caregiver and child are invited into a novel room.

2. Caregiver and child are left alone. Child is free to explore.

3. Stranger enters, sits down, talks to caregiver, and then tries to engage child in play.

4. Caregiver leaves. Stranger and child are alone.

5. Caregiver returns for the first reunion, and stranger leaves unobtrusively. Caregiver settles child, if necessary, and then withdraws to a chair in the room.

6. Caregiver leaves. Child is alone.

7. Stranger returns and tries to settle child, if necessary, and then withdraws to the chair.

8. Caregiver returns for the second reunion, and stranger leaves unobtrusively. Caregiver settles child and then withdraws to the chair.

Trained observers code behavioral responses in this strange situation and render one of the following assessments of the quality of the attachment: **secure attachment, insecure-avoidant attachment**, or **insecure-resistant/ambivalent attachment**. (See Table 12.1 for a description of adult attachment classification systems that have been refined over the years.) The secure attachment pattern is characterized by a balance between exploration of the environment and contact with the caregiver. As the strange situation unfolds, the child will engage in more proximity-seeking and contact-maintaining behavior with the caregiver, exploring the environment only to return for comfort when necessary. Insecure patterns involve increasing tension between the child and caregiver over the course of the strange situation. Children with insecure-avoidant patterns avoid the caregiver when he or she is reintroduced into the situation, and those with the insecure-resistant/ambivalent pattern passively or actively demonstrate hostility toward the caregiver while simultaneously wanting to be held and comforted. (In the following Personal Mini-Experiments, conduct the jungle gym observation to test your ability to evaluate attachment in relationships.)

Quality of attachment patterns, as measured by the Strange Situation assessment approach, has predicted aspects of children's functioning many years later. For example, a study of preschool children indicated that those who were securely attached were more able to cope with parental absence and to relate to actual strangers more readily. Insecurely attached children seem tongue-tied when communicating with adults, and they had general difficulty relating to their caregivers (Bretherton & Waters, 1985). Other researchers (e.g., Belsky & Nezworski, 1988; Howard et al., 2011; Sprecher & Fehr, 2010) have identified long-term consequences of insecure attachment, such as relationship problems, emotional disorders, mental disorders, and conduct problems.

More research is needed with participants of different cultural groups to see if these theories hold true in groups with more collectivistic orientations. For example, though a one-on-one or two-on-one ratio of caregiver to child is often thought of as "normal" in Western cultural groups, there may be more caregivers involved in the lives of children raised in a collectivist society. Grandparents, aunts, uncles, older cousins, and other extended family may more commonly provide regular caregiving for children in addition to parents in non-Western cultural groups, and children and mothers may remain more physically close in these cultural groups. Supporting this cultural influence, some have found that parental absence and other factors may have different meanings for these children (Rothbaum, Weisz, Pott, Miyake, & Morelli, 2000). Other studies have found that there may be some similar characteristics of reaction to the Strange Situation assessment that exist across cultures. Jin,

Table 12.1 Three Prominent Classification Systems of Adult Attachment Styles

Main & Goldwyn (1984, 1998)	Description
Secure/Autonomous	Interviewee demonstrates coherent, collaborative discourse. Interviewee values attachment but seems objective regarding any particular event/relationship. Description and evaluation of attachment-related experiences are consistent whether experiences are favorable or unfavorable.
Dismissing	Interview is not coherent, and interviewee is dismissing of attachment-related experiences and relationships. Interviewee "normalizes" these experiences with generalized representations of history unsupported or actively contradicted by episodes recounted. Transcripts also tend to be excessively brief, violating the maxim of quantity.
Preoccupied	Interview is not coherent, and interviewee is preoccupied with or by past attachment relationships/experiences. Interviewee appears angry, passive, or fearful and uses sentences that are often long, grammatically entangled, or filled with vague uses. Transcripts are often excessively long, violating the maxim of quantity.
Unresolved/ Disorganized	During discussions of loss or abuse, interviewee shows striking lapse in the monitoring of reasoning or discourse. For example, the person may briefly indicate a belief that a dead person is still alive in the physical sense or that this person was killed by a childhood thought. Interviewee may lapse into prolonged silence or eulogistic speech.
Hazan & Shaver (1987)	**Description**
Secure	I find it relatively easy to get close to others and am comfortable depending on them and having them depend on me. I don't often worry about being abandoned or about someone getting too close to me.
Avoidant	I am somewhat uncomfortable being close to others; I find it difficult to trust them completely, difficult to allow myself to depend on them. I am nervous when anyone gets too close, and often love partners want me to be more intimate than I feel comfortable being.
Anxious/Ambivalent	I find that others are reluctant to get as close as I would like. I often worry that my partner doesn't really love me or won't want to stay with me. I want to merge completely with another person, and this desire sometimes scares people away.

Bartholomew & Horowitz (1991)	Description
Secure	It is easy for me to become emotionally close to others. I am comfortable depending on others and having others depend on me. I don't worry about being alone or having others not accept me.
Dismissing	I am comfortable without close emotional relationships. It is very important for me to feel independent and self-sufficient, and I prefer not to depend on others or have others depend on me.
Preoccupied	I want to be completely emotionally intimate with others, but I often find that others are reluctant to get as close as I would like. I am uncomfortable being without close relationships, but I sometimes worry that others don't value me as much as I value them.
Fearful	I am uncomfortable getting close to others. I want emotionally close relationships, but I find it difficult to trust others completely, or to depend on them. I worry that I will be hurt if I allow myself to become too close to others.

Source: From Hazan & Shaver (1987). Adapted from E. Hesse in *Handbook of attachment: Theory, research, and clinical applications.* Copyright 1999 by Guilford Press. Also appeared in Lopez & Snyder (2003) *Positive Psychology Assessment.*

Jacobvitz, Hazen, and Jung (2012) conducted a study in which Korean infants were exposed to the same parameters as in Ainsworth's original assessment. Korean infants reacted similarly to the children in the Ainsworth sample, though some differences existed in both babies' and mothers' behavior following the situation. In addition, the incidence of some *insecure* attachment styles (particularly avoidant classifications) has been found to be significantly lower in both Korean (Jin et al., 2012) and Japanese samples (Miyake, Chen, & Campos, 1985). Though more research is needed, it appears that at least some factors of the development of attachment may be culture-specific.

PERSONAL MINI-EXPERIMENTS

In Search of Love and Flourishing Relationships

In this chapter, we discuss attachment, love, and flourishing relationships. Our review suggests that sound relationships are built on a foundation of secure attachments and that they are maintained with love and purposeful positive relationship behaviors. Here are a few ideas for personal experiments aimed at helping you develop a better understanding of secure, loving relationships—including your own.

(Continued)

(Continued)

The Jungle Gym Observations of Attachment. Conduct your own Strange Situation (Ainsworth, 1979) observations at a jungle gym at the local playground. As a child begins to play and is separated from the caregiver by physical distance, note the frequency of proximity-seeking and contact-maintaining behavior exhibited by that child. Hypothesize how the child will react when he or she takes a break from playing . . . or when the caregiver roams a little farther away from the jungle gym (to supervise another child or find a bench). Note whether the child's behavior is consistent with your attachment-related hypotheses. Remember to integrate cultural context into your observation. Are you using an ethnocentric bias with your assumptions?

The Relationship of Two Circles. According to self-expansion theorists (Aron, Aron, & Smollan, 1992), a relationship between two people can be evaluated based on the degree of overlap of two circles representing the two persons in the relationship. To consider the degree of expansion and inclusion in your relationship (the less the two circles overlap, the less inclusion; the more they overlap, the more inclusion), draw a circle that represents your partner, and then draw a circle that represents you and your relationship to your partner. Consider the meaningfulness of the degree of overlap (inclusion and self-expansion) by discussing it with your partner. Note that the optimal degree of overlap may vary as a function of cultural context.

Making the Most of Good News. Over the course of your relationship, you may become a master of capitalizing on joyful occurrences by providing active/constructive responses (see Figure 12.2) to your partner's attempts to share positive events. To foster this purposeful positive relationship skill, do the following to make the most of the positive daily events in your romantic partner's life:

- Listen actively and empathically to the account of the positive event.

- Make efforts to understand the significance of the event for your partner's cultural context (e.g., Does this have special significance for this person as a woman or man? Does this have special significance for the person as a racial or ethnic minority? Other cultural significance?).

- Mirror your partner's enthusiasm about the positive event (while he/she shares it with you) by engaging in authentic expressions of excitement and delight (e.g., smiling, saying "Great!" or "Wow!," reaching for your partner's hand).

- Ask two constructive questions about the positive event ("How did you feel when it happened?" "How did it happen? Tell me everything!" and other, more specific questions).

- Reintroduce the positive event into conversation later in the day or on the next day to stretch out the benefits of something good having happened in your partner's life.

Figure 12.2 Capitalizing on Daily Positive Events

How would your friend/relative/partner characterize your habitual responses to their good news?

Active/Constructive

My friend/relative/partner reacts to the positive event enthusiastically.

My friend/relative/partner seems even more happy and excited than I am.

My friend/relative/partner often asks a lot of questions and shows genuine concern about the good event.

Passive/Constructive

My friend/relative/partner tries not to make a big deal out of it but is happy for me.

My friend/relative/partner is usually silently supportive of the good things that occur to me.

My friend/relative/partner says little, but I know he/she is happy for me.

Active/Destructive

My friend/relative/partner often finds a problem with it.

My friend/relative/partner reminds me that most good things have their bad aspects as well.

My friend/relative/partner points out the potential down sides of the good event.

Passive/Destructive

Sometimes I get the impression that my friend/relative/partner doesn't care much.

My friend/relative/partner doesn't pay much attention to me.

My friend/relative/partner often seems uninterested.

Source: Modified portion of the Perceived Responses to Capitalization Attempts Scale. From Gable, S. L., Reis, H. T., Impett, E. A., & Asher, E. R., Capitalizing on daily positive events, *Journal of Personality and Social Psychology, 87.* Copyright © 2004. Reprinted with permission.

Note: Shelly Gable of UCLA divides the possible responses into the four categories described above. She has found that the first response style is central to capitalizing, or amplifying, the pleasure of the good situation and contributing to an upward spiral of positive emotion.

Attachment is a dynamic force that connects children to their caregivers. Moreover, secure attachment provides the safe environment in which children can take chances, engage in learning activities, initiate new relationships, and grow into healthy, socially adept adults. In the following example, this secure attachment provided the springboard that helped "Crystal" to grow into a happy adult with a thriving family.

Crystal and her brother were always close. He saw her as a little baby who needed more attention, and as she grew up, she saw him as someone she could count on. Crystal warmly greeted her brother when he met her after school to walk her home. Since their early childhood, she found comfort in her relationship with her older brother. Today, she is fond of telling her children stories about the many good times and occasional bad times she shared with her sibling. In this story, Crystal was able to pinpoint that her older brother helped her to feel secure and loved.

In a recent study using data from the Cross-National Adolescent Project, researchers found that adolescents as a group viewed encouragement, affection, and instrumental support from their parents as signs that their parents loved them (McNeely & Barber, 2012). These types of behaviors were interpreted as loving by adolescents in all of the 12 cultural groups studied in this investigation. It is important to note, however, that cross-cultural and multicultural differences were found across participants in other areas. For example, in cultural groups classified in this study as Eastern or Southern (e.g., Bogotá, Dhaka, Gaza, and Bangalore), adolescents most frequently cited actions that showed trust, respect, and guidance as those that made it clear to them that they were loved by their parents; the opposite was found within the majority of Western cultural groups (e.g., United States, Ogden, Adelaide), where the same three parental actions were least often designated as signs of love (McNeely & Barber, 2012). In addition, this study looked at differences between male and female adolescents and found that, though there were few gender differences, adolescent girls are more likely to state that listening and talking and showing physical affection were actions parents performed that told these girls they were loved. Conversely, male adolescents more often cited being given monetary support as a sign of love from their parents (McNeely & Barber, 2012). These cross-cultural and gender differences are important to note as it is clear that no one set of parental behaviors can be cited as "healthy" or as evidence of love in all groups. Instead, as with most other psychological constructs, culture factors in to these perceptions. As few studies have been conducted using both an emic and etic approach (i.e., one that looks at culture as a potential variable), some research on attachment in this area may be flawed, and, as such, methodology must be reviewed carefully alongside of findings (Chao, 1994).

ADULT ATTACHMENT SECURITY

Personal perspectives on attachment are carried through childhood and adolescence and into stages of adulthood in the form of an internal working model of self and others (Bowlby, 1988; Shaver, Hazan, & Bradshaw, 1988). Early in their social development, children integrate perceptions of their social competence, appeal, and lovability (the self model) with their expectations regarding the accessibility, responsiveness, and consistency of caregivers (the other model). These models are relatively stable over developmental periods because they are self-reinforcing. That is, the internal models consist of a set of cognitive schema through which people see the world, gather information about self and others, and make interpersonal decisions. The model is a "conscious 'mindful state' of generalized expectations and preferences regarding relationship intimacy that guide participants' information processing of relationship experiences as well as their behavioral response patterns" (Lopez, 2003, p. 289). If people carry forward a secure mindful state, they see the world as safe and others as reliable. Unfortunately, negative or insecure schema also may be perpetuated. For example, people who see the social world as unpredictable and other people as unreliable have difficulty overcoming their desires to keep others at a distance, and they may falter in participating in high-quality love relationships later in adulthood (McCarthy, & Maughan, 2010).

Numerous theorists (e.g., Bartholomew & Horowitz, 1991; Hazan & Shaver, 1987; Main & Goldwyn, 1984, 1998; Shaver & Mikulincer, 2006; Sprecher, & Fehr, 2010) have extended attachment theory across the life span in an effort to understand how adults relate to other adults as well as to the children for whom they will serve as caregivers. Developmental psychologists Mary Main and colleagues have conducted interviews of mothers who participated in the Strange Situation assessment and found that adult attachment can best be described by a system comprising four categories: secure/autonomous, dismissing, preoccupied, and unresolved/ disorganized. The interview used by Main (George, Kaplan, & Main, 1985; Main & Goldwyn, 1984, 1998), the Adult Attachment Interview, has become the gold standard for clinical assessment of adult attachment. (Social psychologists researching attachment tend to use self-report measures such as those reviewed by Brennan, Clark, and Shaver in 1998.)

Phillip Shaver

Source: Reprinted with permission of Phillip Shaver.

Social psychologists Cindy Hazan and Phillip Shaver have studied attachment in the context of adult romantic relationships. They found (Hazan & Shaver, 1987) that the three categories of secure, avoidant, and anxious, akin to Ainsworth's (1979) groups, effectively described the nature of adult attachments to a significant other. In 1991, Bartholomew and Horowitz expanded the three categories of adult attachment to four by differentiating two types of avoidant attachment: dismissive and fearful. Most recently, Brennan et al. (1998) considered Bartholomew and Horowitz's system from a different perspective. They conceptualized attachment on the two dimensions of attachment-related avoidance and attachment-related anxiety. The secure style is low on both dimensions, the dismissing style is high on avoidance and low on anxiety, the preoccupied style is low on avoidance and high on anxiety, and the fearful style is high on both avoidance and attachment anxiety. Table 12.1 on pp. 328–329 describes the adult attachment classification systems.

Secure adult attachment, as characterized by low attachment-related avoidance and anxiety, involves a comfort with emotional closeness and a general lack of concern about being abandoned by others. Feeling secure in one's attachment to other significant adults has numerous benefits. Most importantly, this approach provides the pathways to survival and healthy development. By successfully recruiting care from significant others, children and adults become stronger and more able to cope with threats (Bowlby, 1988). Adults who are lower in attachment anxiety may also have less intense and prolonged grieving experiences (Jerga, Shaver, & Wilkinson, 2011) and even a higher amount of physical energy (Luke, Sedikides, & Carnelley, 2012). Moreover, by pursuing growth experiences within the context of safe, secure relationships, we can pursue optimal human functioning, or flourishing (Lopez & Brennan, 2000; Luke et al., 2012).

Attachment style may also provide links to emotional regulation and experiences of happiness and positive affect. Adults who were classified as secure in their attachment style were found to have higher levels of well-being in comparison to those who exhibit a preoccupied style of attachment (Karreman & Vingerhoets, 2012). This appears to be due in part to the higher levels of resilience exhibited by securely attached adults and their ability to cognitively reframe various situations (e.g., reevaluate an emotional circumstance as less emotional).

Certain styles of attachment may also predict the development of compassionate love, which is described as "an attitude toward another containing feelings, cognitions, and behaviors that are focused on caring, concern, tenderness, and an orientation toward supporting, helping, and understanding the other" (Sprecher & Fehr, 2010, p. 559). This type of love is thought to be particularly intense in relationships with romantic partners but can be felt for strangers as well; it is linked to altruism, sympathy, empathy, and other positive characteristics. This type of caring appears to be positively predicted by a secure dispositional style as opposed to one that is more avoidant or dismissing, furthering the idea that a healthy attachment style has other benefits in relationship initiation and maintenance.

Adult attachment security provided "Mari" in our next example with a lively confidence that helped her initiate new relationships and sustain existing ones. Mari introduced herself to her new group of colleagues by sharing a few interesting facts about her life. She had a close-knit family hundreds of miles away and a boyfriend a thousand miles away. Despite her recent goodbyes, she seemed to have a great deal of emotional energy to give to her new friendships. Her first week on the job included three lunch dates with coworkers and numerous quick cell phone calls from her mother and her boyfriend.

Each of you has developed and maintained an attachment system, and based on our cultural context and our history and system, we process new social and emotional stimuli everyday. It determines who is or is not "let in," emotionally. Furthermore, it determines the depths of love.

LOVE

The capacity for love is a central component of all human societies. Love in all its manifestations, whether for children, parents, friends, or romantic partners, gives depth to human relationships. Specifically, love brings people closer to each other physically and emotionally. When experienced intensely, it makes people think expansively about themselves and the world.

Susan Hendrick

Source: Reprinted with permission of Susan Hendrick.

The definitive history of love (Singer, 1984a, 1984b, 1987) highlights the following four traditions, denoted by Greek terms, that define this primary emotional experience: (1) **eros**, the search for the beautiful; (2) **philia**, the affection in friendship; (3) **nomos**, submission and obedience to the divine; and (4) **agape**, or the bestowal of love by the divine. Contrary to the arguments of some researchers (Cho & Cross, 1995; Hatfield & Rapson, 1996), and, contrary to the depictions of history in Hollywood movies, it is notable that Singer did not believe that romantic love played a major role in world culture.

Other notable scholars, such as Texas Tech University psychologists Susan Hendrick and Clyde Hendrick (1992, 2009), hypothesized that only during the last 300 years or so have cultural forces led people to develop a sense of self that has made them capable of loving and caring for a romantic partner over a lifetime. Despite the uncertainty about the place of romantic love in history, its role in the future of the world is clear. Indeed, love for a companion is considered central to a life well lived, as described in this quotation:

"Romantic love may not be essential in life, but it may be essential to joy. Life without love would be for many people like a black-and-white movie full of events and activities but without the color that gives vibrancy and provides a sense of celebration" (Hendrick & Hendrick, 1992, p. 117).

Given the intense interest in romantic love, we highlight some of the psychological research that explores this type of loving. We describe three conceptualizations of romantic love that may foster an understanding of how it develops between two people.

Passionate and Companionate Aspects of Romantic Love

Romantic love is a complex emotion that may be best parsed into *passionate* and *companionate* forms (Berscheid & Walster, 1978; Hatfield, 1988), both of which are valued by most people. Passionate love (the intense arousal that fuels a romantic union) involves a state of absorption between two people that often is accompanied by moods ranging from ecstasy to anguish. Companionate love (the soothing, steady warmth that sustains a relationship) is manifested in a strong bond and an intertwining of lives that brings about feelings of comfort and peace. These two forms can occur simultaneously or intermittently rather than sequentially (from passionate to companionate).

Romantic love is characterized by intense arousal and warm affection. In a study of college students who were probably in the early stages of romantic relationships, nearly half named their romantic partners when asked to identify their closest friend (Hendrick & Hendrick, 1993). This finding suggests that passionate and companionate love can coexist in the new relationships of young people. Likewise, in a study of couples married for as long as 40 years, Contreras, Hendrick, and Hendrick (1996) found that companionate love *and* passionate love were alive, and that passionate love was the strongest predictor of marital satisfaction (of all variables measured in the study). Sexual satisfaction may be a part of this passionate love and has been found to be a very strong predictor of relationship well-being in both same-sex couples and opposite-sex couples (Holmberg, Blair, & Phillips, 2010).

The Triangular Theory of Love

In developing the triangular theory of love, psychologist Robert Sternberg (1986) theorized that love is a mix of three components: (1) passion, or physical attractiveness and romantic drives; (2) intimacy, or feelings of closeness and connectedness; and (3) commitment, involving the decision to initiate and sustain a relationship. Various combinations of these three components yield eight forms of love. For example, intimacy and passion combined produce romantic love, whereas intimacy and commitment together constitute companionate love. Consummate love, the most durable type, is manifested when all three components (passion, intimacy, commitment) are present at high levels and in balance across both partners.

Some of the research exploring Sternberg's theory of love has focused on the predictive value of these three ingredients of love in United States samples. In a study of 104 heterosexual couples (average length of marriage was 13 years, ranging from 2 months to 45 years), both husbands' and wives' intimacy, followed by passion, predicted marital satisfaction (Silberman, 1995). Additionally, research on U.S. adults' views about their relationships found that commitment was the best predictor of relationship satisfaction in these opposite-sex relationships, especially for the long-term partnerships (Acker & Davis, 1992). Certain personality characteristics may also be related to the three factors in Sternberg's model and as such may be partial determinants of relationship length as well (Ahmetoglu, Swami, & Chamorro-Premuzic, 2010). This research found that the Big Five factor of Agreeableness was associated with all three components in the Sternberg model and that Conscientiousness had positive links to both commitment and intimacy. Relationship length was linked differently to passion (negative correlation) and commitment (positive correlation); this finding supports Sternberg's ideas that passion may diminish after time in a relationship, though commitment may still be strong (Ahmetoglu et al., 2010).

Interestingly, cross-cultural analysis of the importance of these different types of love have elucidated differences across cultural groups. In a study comparing U.S., Russian, and Lithuanian participants, researchers found that while the U.S. participants identified "friendship and comfort love" as a key component of romantic love, these features were non-existent in the other two samples (de Munck et al., 2011). Multiculturally, recent studies of an African American sample indicate that Sternberg's theoretical components may also be important to members of this cultural group (Curran, Utley, & Muraco, 2010). In the past, the presence and function of love has been downplayed in depictions of the romantic relationships of racial and ethnic minority individuals (Curran et al., 2010), thus more research is needed in this area with non-White samples to determine if other similarities and differences exist. More recently, the triangular theory of love has been explored in young adult, male, same-sex couples as well and has found support for the same three-factor solution (Bauermeister et al., 2011). As more research is conducted in samples outside the majority, we may be able to better elucidate the experience of love overall.

The Self-Expansion Theory of Romantic Love

Informed by Eastern conceptualizations of love, Arthur Aron and Elaine Aron (1986) developed a theory that humans have a basic motivation to expand the self; moreover, they posited that the emotions, cognitions, and behaviors of love fuel such self-expansion. People seek to expand themselves through love: "The idea is that the self expands toward knowing or becoming that which includes everything and everyone, the Self. The steps along the way are ones of including one person or thing, then another, then still another" (Aron & Aron, 1996, pp. 45–46).

According to the self-expansion theory (Aron & Aron, 1996), relationship satisfaction is a natural by-product of self-expansive love. Being in a loving relationship makes people feel good. They then associate those positive feelings with the relationship, thereby reinforcing their commitment to the relationship. The positive consequences of being in love are clear. Aron, Paris, and Aron (1995) studied a group of college students over a 10-week period, and the researchers monitored the reactions of the students to falling in love (if they happened to do so during that particular semester). Those students who fell in love experienced increased self-esteem and self-efficacy. People who were "newly in love" (i.e., in a romantic relationship for 18 months or less, with high scores on the Passionate Love Scale) appeared to seek out positive feedback on a selection task more often than those not newly in love and tended to also have less avoidance of a negative consequence (Brown & Beninger, 2012). This may support the idea that being in love encourages the type of risk-taking involved with sharing oneself with others because of the potential benefit of obtaining positive reinforcement (e.g., the positive consequences of love) from these self-expansive behaviors. On a more cognitive level, self-expansion means that each partner has made a decision to include another in his or her self. This investment in each other adds to relationship satisfaction. (In the

Personal Mini-Experiments, conduct the Relationship of Two Circles experiment to determine the extent to which love has been a self-expanding force in your life.)

Comments on Love Research

Psychological theories of love—and, more specifically, scholarly ideas about romantic love—provide insights into a mysterious phenomenon. The work of positive psychologists interested in love tells the story of how people first unite and then how positive feelings help to maintain relationships over time. We now turn to another example, the marriage of "Kai" and "Libby," which has taught many people about the potency of love. Each afternoon, Kai and Libby can be seen walking their yellow Labrador retriever in their neighborhood. They chat nonstop about their days at work and about their dreams for the future. They are both near 60, but they have the look of high school friends excitedly planning their lives. Over dinner with friends, they flirt with each other, make occasional overtures, and tell funny stories about themselves and their relationship. When they are at their best, and the relationship is really going well, they make you think that their love will last forever.

It is also important to acknowledge that all relationships do not have the qualities described above with Kai and Libby. Some relationships are instead marked by distrust, negative emotions, and lack of commitment. In these cases, it may be that dissolution of the relationship is a predictor of more positive emotions. Lewandowski and Bizzoco (2007) investigated undergraduate students who had recently experienced the ending of a relationship and found that positive growth and more positive emotions were related to the dissolution of a relationship described as low in Aron and Aron's (1996) quality of *self-expansion*. Though much research has focused on the more negative aspects of dissolution of a relationship, there can be benefits in ending a relationship that is not working.

The scholarship on love also describes stories of love (Sternberg, 1998) and the meaning of "I love you" (Hecht, Marston, & Larkey, 1994; Marston, Hecht, & Robers, 1987). Our stories of love develop throughout our lives and are carried by us into relationships; theoretically, these stories define the quality of our interactions with our significant others. Sternberg, upon interviewing a large sample of couples, found that there are at least 26 "love stories" (e.g., a fantasy story, a horror story) that are largely unconscious views of romance and relationships that guide our interpersonal choices. By becoming more aware of the stories of love we have told ourselves over the years, we are more able to make mindful choices in approaching and enhancing relationships.

Analysis of the meaning of the statement "I love you" (Hecht et al., 1994; Marston et al., 1987) reminds us how subjective and personal our views of love can be. Have you ever thought about what you mean when you say "I love you"? Most people have not examined the many meanings of "I love you," and that spurred Dan Cox, a student in my (SJL's) positive psychology seminar, to ask his colleagues to describe exactly what they meant when they last said those three words to someone. The many meanings of this sentiment included "I understand," "I support you," "Thanks," "I am sorry," and more global statements, such as "This is a good life" and "It is good to be with you." The variability in the meaning of those three little words suggests there is much we don't know about the emotion that connects us to others.

Cultural context can also sharply define how love is expressed and the value it has in romantic relationships, as well as how it is defined as a construct. Landis and O'Shea (2000) examined the concept of passionate love across several countries (as well as comparing locations within those countries) and found that this construct appeared to have unique factor structures across different cultural groupings. It is important to recognize that different cultural practices, such as arranged marriages, may dictate to some extent the value love has within a society. Some researchers have found differences in constructs such as emotional investment (Schmitt et al., 2009) or in the experiences of passionate or companionate love among different cultural groups (Doherty, Hatfield, Thompson, & Choo, 1994; Gao, 2001). In addition, using the words "I love you" may be more common in some cultures than in others. Gareis and Wilkins (2011) found that verbal expression of love, particularly a public declaration of this love, was much less common in Germany when compared with U.S. participants. In this study, the researchers found that Germans often reserved the words "I love you" for more private and formal circumstances, whereas participants in the U.S. used this phrase more commonly and outside of romantic relationships as well as within them. More research must be done in this area to better understand the experiences and correlates of the different types of love in various groups.

Research on love throughout different cultural groups does not account for all the subjectivity that defines the richness of the experience, nor does it identify the many reasons why some relationships fail and why some flourish. The next section highlights the behaviors, rather than positive emotions, that determine the success of most close relationships.

FLOURISHING RELATIONSHIPS: A SERIES OF PURPOSEFUL POSITIVE RELATIONSHIP BEHAVIORS

Positive psychologists specializing in close relationships (Harvey et al., 2001; Reis & Gable, 2003) are exploring what makes existing relationships flourish and what skills can be taught directly to partners to enhance their interpersonal connections. (Try to develop some of these behaviors by completing the brief exercises in the Life Enhancement Strategies.) In this section, we discuss theories and research evidence on flourishing relationships, which are good relationships that continue to get better due to concerted effort of both partners.

Building a Mindful Relationship Connection

Well-minded relationships are healthy and long lasting. This belief led University of Iowa social psychologist John Harvey and his colleagues (Harvey & Ormarzu, 1997; Harvey et al., 2001) to develop a five-component model of minding relationships. This model shows how closeness, or the satisfaction and relationship behaviors that contribute to one another's goals in life, may be enhanced. (See Table 12.2 for a summary of these components and their maladaptive counterparts.)

Table 12.2   Minding Relationship Behavior: Adaptive and Nonadaptive Steps

Adaptive	Nonadaptive
Via an in-depth knowing process, both partners in step in seeking to know and be known by the other.	One or both partners out of step in seeking to know and be known by the other.

Adaptive	Nonadaptive
Both partners use the knowledge gained in enhancing relationship.	Knowledge gained in knowing process is not used or not used well (may be used to hurt other).
Both partners accept what they learn and respect the other for the person they learn about.	Acceptance of what is learned is low, as is respect for the other person.
Both partners motivated to continue this process and do so indefinitely, such that synchrony and synergy of thought, feeling, and action emerge.	One or both partners are not motivated to engage in the overall minding process or do so sporadically; little synchrony and synergy emerge.
Both partners in time develop a sense of being special and appreciated in the relationship.	One or both partners fail to develop a sense of being special and appreciated in the relationship.

Source: From Harvey, J. H., Pauwels, B. G., & Zicklund, S., Relationship connection: The role of minding in the enhancement of closeness, in C. R. Snyder & S. J. Lopez (Eds.), *The handbook of positive psychology.* Copyright © 2002 by Oxford University Press, Inc. Used by permission of Oxford University Press, Inc.

Life Enhancement Strategies

Additional tips for bringing more security and love into your life are listed here. Although we focus on aspects of romantic love in this chapter, we address many forms of love in this list of strategies.

Love

- Identify a couple in your life that you believe has an excellent relationship. Arrange to spend some time with them so you can observe relationship behaviors that work for them. If you know the couple well, ask them specific questions about how they maintain their relationship. Emulate some of these behaviors in your own significant relationships.

- When you are in an ongoing relationship, develop a list of what makes your partner feel appreciated and attempt to enhance the culture of appreciation in your relationship with five purposeful acts each day.

Work

- Take a mindfulness meditation course (see Chapter 10 for a description) with a partner and apply your newfound skills when attending to your own behavior and to the relationship. Generalize these skills to behavior with colleagues at work.

(Continued)

(Continued)

- Ignore old advice about not making friends at work. Vital friendships (which may involve philial love) in the workplace can enhance your engagement with your work.

Play

- Children benefit socially and emotionally from having at least one caring adult in their lives. Volunteer some time with a child or youth service and attempt to form a connection with at least one young person. Over time, the benefits of the relationship may become increasingly mutual.

- We often become friends with people who are similar to us. While this "birds of a feather, flock together" tendency is natural, we may be able to capitalize more via self-expansion when we stretch ourselves to include dissimilar others in our close social circles or romantic relationships. Challenge yourself to step outside of your usual social circles and to extend yourself to others who are different than you in some ways.

Minding is the "reciprocal knowing process involving the nonstop, interrelated thoughts, feelings, and behaviors of persons in a relationship" (Harvey et al., 2001, p. 424). As described in Chapter 10, mindfulness is a conscious process that requires moment-to-moment effort. This need for consciousness in minding relationships is reflected in the first component of the model, *knowing and being known*. According to the model, each partner in the relationship must want to know the other person's hopes, dreams, fears, vulnerabilities, and uncertainties. Furthermore, each partner must monitor the balance between his or her own self-expression and that of the partner and give preference to learning about the other person rather than focusing on his or her own personal information. People who are successful at knowing and being known in their relationships demonstrate an understanding of how time brings about change and of how change necessitates renewed opportunities and attempts to learn about the other person.

John H. Harvey

Source: Reprinted with permission of John H. Harvey.

The second component of relationship minding involves partners *making relationship-enhancing attributions for behaviors.* Attributing positive behaviors to dispositional causes and negative behaviors to external, situational causes may be the most adaptive approach to making sense of another person's behavior. Over time, people in well-minded relationships develop the proper mixture of internal and external attributions and become more willing to reexamine attributions when explanations for a partner's behavior don't jibe with what is known about the loved one. Making charitable attributions (i.e., going beyond the benefit of the doubt; T. Krieshok, personal communication, June 21, 2005) occasionally can resolve conflicts before they become divisive.

Accepting and respecting, the third component of the minding model, requires an empathic connection (see Chapter 11), along with refined social skills (such as those described in the next section). As partners become more intimate in their knowledge of one another and share some good and bad experiences, mindful acceptance of personal strengths and weaknesses is necessary for the continued development of the relationship. When this acceptance is linked with respect, it serves as an antidote for contemptuous behavior that can dissolve a relationship (Gottman, 1994).

The final components of the model are *maintaining reciprocity and continuity in minding.* Regarding reciprocity in minding, "Each partner's active participation and involvement in relationship-enhancing thoughts and behaviors" (Harvey et al., 2001, p. 428) is necessary for maintaining a mutually beneficial relationship. A lack of conscious engagement displayed by one partner can lead to frustration or contempt on the part of the other partner. Continuity in minding also may require planning and strategizing to become closer as the relationship matures. Partners who frequently check in on the other's goals and needs are likely to identify what is working and what is not working in the minding process (see Snyder, 1994/2000).

Mindfulness is a skill that can be taught and, as such, relationship minding can be enhanced (Harvey & Ormarzu, 1997). The mutual practice of mindfulness techniques (discussed in Chapter 10) could benefit partners who are attempting to apply Harvey's relationship-enhancing guidance.

Creating a Culture of Appreciation

John Gottman (1994, 1999) has spent a lifetime "thin-slicing" relationship behavior (Gladwell, 2005). He measures bodily sensations of partners, "reads" the faces of husbands and wives as they interact, and watches people talk about difficult issues while he dissects every aspect of the exchange. He has become so good at his craft that he can use his analyses of brief interactions to predict relationship success (divorce versus continued marriage) with a 94% accuracy.

Gottman achieved this feat of prediction by studying thousands of married couples across many years of their relationships. (Although his original work focused on heterosexual married couples, Gottman's lab's Web site, www.johngottman.com, indicates that current studies focus on same-sex couples. The applicability of Gottman's findings to people from diverse backgrounds currently is unclear.) The standard research protocol involves a husband and wife entering the "love lab" and engaging in a 15-minute conversation while being closely observed by the researchers and monitored by blood pressure cuffs, EKGs, and other devices. Gottman's seminal finding from observations of couples was derived with the assistance of mathematicians (Gottman, Murray, Swanson, Tyson, & Swanson, 2003) who helped him discover what is referred to as the "magic ratio" for marriages. Five positive interactions to one negative interaction (5:1) are needed to maintain a healthy relationship. As the ratio approaches 1:1, however, divorce is likely.

Achieving the 5:1 ratio in a relationship does not require avoiding all arguments. Partners in master marriages can talk about difficult subjects and do so by infusing warmth, affection, and humor into the conversation. On the other hand, a lack of positive interactions during challenging discussions can lead couples to emotional disconnections and to mild forms of contempt.

A Lot of Love in the Lovemaking: Avoiding Chaos, Relationshipwise

Mark D. Fefer

Professor John Gottman is the doctor of love, at least love of the conventional sort—he's an internationally known researcher on what makes marriage last and what makes it fall apart. In his work at the University of Washington, he has managed to apply strict scientific rigor to what seems like the most subjective of areas, and he's popularized his findings in a string of best-selling books (*The Seven Principles for Making Marriage Work* is the most recent).

At his "love lab" near the UW, Dr. Gottman videotapes married couples as they go about a lazy day "at home" and monitors physiological signs like heart rate and blood pressure as they discuss areas of conflict. By toting up the "positive" and "negative" interactions, checking "repair attempts" during fights, watching for incidents of contemptuous behavior, etc., Gottman is able to predict the ultimate fate of the pair with over 90 percent accuracy, he says.

However, as a single guy, I wanted to know how I can keep from getting into a bad marriage in the first place. Wouldn't that save us all a lot of trouble? Warm and affable, the professor met me at the Grateful Bread bakery near his home to discuss the issue.

Seattle Weekly: You study a lot of couples that are on the rocks. And you talk about the four behaviors that foretell divorce—criticism, contempt, defensiveness, stonewalling. But I'm sure that, at one time, most of these couples were in love and gushing about each other. How can I know if my current relationship is going to end up like that?

Dr. Gottman: People used to think, "Well, you're in love, you're blissed out, you're not going to be doing a lot of real nasty . . . not going to be contemptuous toward your partner, not going to be disrespectful." Not true. If you keep going back and looking at relationships earlier and earlier, to the newlywed phase, the same variability [in behavior] exists for couples there as for later on. Even in the dating relationship—researchers have looked—the same signs are predictive. If you've been going together for 6 months, you can take a look at what's going on and decide if you want to be in that relationship or not.

So how do I make that decision? How can I know if a relationship is right or not? First, what is the quality of the friendship? Are you guys really friends? In other words, is it easy to talk? Like, before you know it, four hours have gone by. It's really a lot like same-sex friendship. It's about being interested in one another, remembering stuff that's important to one another, being affectionate and respectful, and it's about noticing when your friend needs something from you.

Then there's the quality of sex, romance, and passion. Do you feel special to this person? Do you feel attractive? Are you really attracted and turned on by them? Is there a lot of love in the lovemaking? Does it feel passionate?

But everybody feels this stuff at first, don't they? That's the surprising thing: People get married and they don't really like each other, and they're not having good sex together, and they don't feel like their partner's really that interested in them . . . they get married anyway! They're not taking a hard look at their relationship.

OK, but so what if it's really passionate at first—isn't that going to fade? The common belief that passion and good sex start early and then fade is totally wrong—totally wrong. Passion can grow over time in a relationship if people pay attention to it. [In our studies of long-term couples] the thing that came out among those who had a great sex life was friendship—"We've remained really close friends, we're really buddies, we try to understand and help each other."

What about fighting? From what you've written, it seems like fighting in itself isn't bad, right? Right. Conflict does exist in the very beginnings of romantic relationships; it comes out. [But] what's the balance in terms of destructive vs. constructive? Constructive conflict is about accepting influence from your partner, compromising. Destructive conflict is about insulting, being domineering, being defensive, denying any responsibility, withdrawing. Those predict a bad end to the relationship.

How do you get through a time when you're feeling distant, or you're not so sure about the relationship, or you're arguing a lot? Can you repair effectively? It's kind of a sense of confidence. You develop a feeling that you can weather any storm—not that you like the storms. Conflict is inevitable, but coping with it is a way of building the friendship.

Should I feel wildly in love, swept off my feet? You'd be surprised what a small percentage of relationships have had that. Psychologists have called it "limerance," that stage. You're mostly just projecting on your partner what you wish would be there. And when we started interviewing newlyweds about it, couples who had experienced it didn't necessarily have better relationships. It didn't seem necessary or sufficient, except that it is so pleasant to go through. It's very good if you can build from there.

What else should I be on the watch for? There's something called "negative sentiment override." You tend to be walking around with a chip on your shoulder, hypervigilant for put-downs, for ways your partner is saying, "I don't really love you, you're not that special to me." And if you're in that state, it's bad, particularly if you're a male, because that's something that is going to be very difficult to change. And it's really just a question of perception. Two women may be identical in how angry they get, but the one guy is saying, "Boy, she's really stressed right now, but it's OK; I get that way myself sometimes." The other guy's saying, "Nobody talks to me like that; this, who needs this." What determines the perception, we've discovered, is friendship. If you feel like your partner respects you, is interested in you, turns toward you, then you're in positive sentiment override.

Why are we so bad at this? More than half of all marriages end in divorce. Are we just choosing badly? Are we just bad at being married like we're bad drivers? There are lots of ways to destroy things, and usually only a few ways to really maintain things and keep them working. Things fall apart—this is the entropy idea. Chaos is the more likely event. It really takes a lot of energy to maintain a system that's working well.

Source: From Fefer, M. D., A lot of love in the lovemaking: Avoiding chaos, relationshipwise, *Seattle Weekly*, February 13–19, 2002. Reprinted with permission.

Drawing from his decades of research and his "sound marital house" theory, Gottman, Driver, and Tabares (2002) developed a multidimensional therapeutic approach to couples counseling that moves partners from conflict to comfortable exchanges. The goals of the therapy include the enhancement of basic social skills and the development of an awareness of the interpersonal pitfalls associated with the relationship behaviors of criticism, contempt, defensiveness, and stonewalling. Over time, these four behaviors that undermine relationships are replaced with complaint (i.e., a more civil form of expressing disapproval), a culture of appreciation, acceptance of responsibility for a part of the problem, and self-soothing. These skills also are mentioned in Gottman's (1999) book, *The Seven Principles for Making Marriage Work*.

Based on our reading of Gottman's work, his advice regarding the creation of a culture of appreciation in a relationship may be his most basic, yet most potent, advice to couples of all ages, backgrounds, and marital statuses. The purposeful positive relationship behavior of creating a culture of appreciation is potentially powerful because of (1) the positive reception of the partner and the partner's behavior that it promotes and (2) the contemptuous feelings that it prevents. Creating a culture of appreciation helps to establish an environment where positive interactions and a sense of security are the norms. Expressing gratitude (see Chapter 11) to a partner is the primary means for creating a positive culture. Saying thanks for the small behaviors that often go unnoticed (e.g., picking up around the house, taking the trash out, making the morning coffee, cleaning out the refrigerator) makes a partner feel valued for his or her daily efforts around the home. Sharing appreciation for small favors (e.g., taking an extra turn in the car pool, making a coworker feel welcome in the home) and for big sacrifices (e.g., remembering a least favorite in-law's birthday, giving up "rainy day" money for a home expense) honors a partner's contributions to the relationship and the family.

Capitalizing on Positive Events

During most of the twentieth century, research into relationships focused on negative, or *aversive,* processes such as resolving conflict and dysfunctional communication. Relationship research was grounded in the assumption that these processes are the primary determinants of relationship success. Harvey and Gottman have worked diligently to highlight the role of positive relationship behaviors that often have been overlooked. This focus on the positive, or *appetitive,* processes in relationships may be the primary reason that their theories and research findings are so robust. Aversive processes are the eliminating of negative relationship behaviors; appetitive processes are the promoting of positive relationship behaviors. Shelly Gable and Howard Reis (Gable & Reis, 2001; Gable et al., 2003; Reis & Gable, 2003) have demonstrated that these two processes are independent and that they must be conceptualized and researched as independent processes if we are to fully understand human relationships.

It may also be that some events that seem inherently negative have unintended positive consequences for relationships. Stigma and discrimination are more commonly found within the relationship experiences of non-heterosexual couples (Frost, 2011; Kamen, Burns, & Beach, 2011). Though some define these stigmatizing experiences as having a negative impact on their relationships, many participants "framed stigma as bringing them closer to their partners and strengthening the bond within their relationships" (Frost, 2011, p. 1). Going through these difficult times and supporting each other throughout them may provide some same-sex couples with strength in the face of strife, and being in a relationship while experiencing this strife may assist in individual coping responses (Fingerhut & Maisel, 2010).

Gable et al. (2003) noted that differentiating between appetitive and aversive processes provides a new lens for viewing research on the success of close relationships. Then, in a program of research summarized in Gable, Reis, Impett, and Asher (2004), the researchers addressed the appetitive relationship processes directly by answering the question, "What do you do when things go right?" In a series of studies, Gable and colleagues found that the process of capitalization, or telling others about positive events in one's life, is associated with personal benefits (enhanced positive affect and well-being) as well as interpersonal benefits (relationship satisfaction and intimacy). The personal gains are attributable to the process of reliving the positive experience, and they are enhanced when a partner responds enthusiastically (i.e., active/constructively; see Figure 12.2) to the good news. Improvement in interpersonal relations is contingent upon the quality of the partner's response to the loved one's good news. In Gable et al.'s research, active and constructive responses by partners were found to be the most beneficial.

Shelly Gable

Source: Reprinted with permission of Shelly Gable.

Praise: Encouraging Signs
Willow Lawson

Summary: Your partner's level of encouragement is a good indicator of how your relationship is going.

Hurdles like jealousy and miscommunication can determine whether a relationship succeeds. But what about how couples "cope" when something positive happens? According to a new set of studies, the way we respond to our mate's good fortune is a strong predictor of marital satisfaction and, at least in the short term, whether a couple will break up.

Shelly Gable, an assistant professor of psychology at the University of California at Los Angeles, examined how couples share everyday positive events because she felt that the lion's share of relationship research focused on how couples handle conflict and trauma. "Thankfully, positive events happen more often than negative ones," she says. "And satisfying and stable relationships are about more than a lack of conflict, insecurity, and jealousy."

In one study, Gable analyzed how men and women respond to a positive event in their partner's life, such as a promotion at work. A partner might respond enthusiastically ("That's wonderful, and it's because you've had so many good ideas in the past few months"). But he or she could instead respond in a less-than-enthusiastic manner ("Hmmm, that's nice"), seem uninterested ("Did you see the score of the Yankees game?") or point out the downsides ("I suppose it's good news, but it wasn't much of a raise").

The only "correct" reaction according to Gable's research—the response that's correlated with intimacy, satisfaction, trust and continued commitment—is the first response, the enthusiastic, active

(Continued)

(Continued)

one. Basking in good news or capitalizing on the event seems to increase the effect of happy tidings by reinforcing memory of the occurrence. This is true for both men and women, and holds regardless of whether they are dating or married and whether the positive event is large or small.

Gable says an occasional passive response from a partner probably isn't the end of the world, and she speculates that most of us are able to make excuses for our partners in such situations. "The problem is when that's the chronic response," she says. "If a partner doesn't respond actively and constructively, the person who's trying to disclose something immediately feels less positive and feels less intimacy. Basically they feel less understood, validated, and cared for."

Source: An Excerpt from "Praise: Encouraging Signs," by Willow Larson, *Psychology Today,* January/February 2004. Reprinted with permission from *Psychology Today,* copyright © 2004 Sussex Publishers, LLC.

The purposeful positive relationship behavior of capitalizing on positive events for intrapersonal benefits is straightforward. It merely involves telling trusted friends and family about your daily "good stuff." If there are people who attempt to undermine such excitement by pointing out the downside of a positive event ("That promotion will cause you to work harder and longer. Are you sure you are up for that? Really?"), then it is best to avoid telling them the good news. The habit of offering active, constructive responses (mirroring enthusiasm, asking meaningful questions about the event) to the good news of others also is easily developed (see Making the Most of Good News in the Personal Mini-Experiments). And, the more you model this capitalizing behavior, the more likely it is that your partner and other people in your circle of friends and family will reciprocate and practice it themselves.

Few couples master each and every purposeful positive relationship behavior described in this chapter, but some couples seem to dance effortlessly through each day. When you ask them, "How do you make your relationship work?" you get an answer that makes you realize how hard they work at it. In this regard, we turn to the example of "Mitch" and "Linda," who tell the story of the work that goes into their flourishing relationship. "For as long as we have been married, I have sent Linda flowers every Friday," Mitch reported. Linda chimed in that Mitch keeps up with her "new" favorite flowers and honors the tradition even when they are on vacation. "We have been in remote villages living among the locals, and that man will spend an entire Friday seeking out a bouquet of flowers." Mitch expresses his appreciation for Linda through flowers, and Linda shares her gratitude by showering him with thanks and praise, as if it is the first time she had ever received such a gift.

THE NEUROBIOLOGY OF INTERPERSONAL CONNECTION

Neuropsychoanalyst Allan Schore (1994, 2003) and health psychologist Shelley Taylor (Taylor, Dickerson, & Klein, 2002) have gathered and integrated indirect and direct evidence on the neurobiology of interpersonal connection from their own laboratories, as well as from other researchers. Schore, building on the assumptions of attachment theory, argues that the social environment, mediated by actions of and attachment to the primary caregiver, influences the evolution of structures in a child's brain. More specifically, Schore proposed that the maturation of a region of the right cortex, the orbitofrontal cortex (which may store the internal working models of attachment), is influenced by interactions between the child and the caregiver. As the orbitofrontal cortex matures, self-regulation of emotions is enhanced. The brain–behavior interactions suggest that an upward spiral of growth may explain how infant attachment sometimes produces emotionally healthy adults. That is, when a child and his or her caregiver have a secure attachment, the part of the brain that helps with the regulation of emotions and behavior is stimulated. As the child's security is maintained, the brain development is promoted, and the abilities to empathize with others and to regulate intrapersonal and interpersonal stress are enhanced. Equipped with well-honed self-regulation skills, the child can develop and sustain healthy friendships and, eventually, healthy adult relationships. (For additional discussion of work related to the link between attachment and neurobiology, we suggest Siegel's [1999] *The Developing Mind*.)

Taylor and colleagues (Taylor et al., 2002), intrigued by the health benefits of social contact and social support (for a review, see Seeman, 1996), reviewed research on social animals and humans to determine the biological mechanisms associated with interpersonal experiences. Like Schore (1994, 2003), Taylor et al. hypothesized that a nurturing relationship between a child and a caregiver promotes the development of regulatory activity, in this case in the hypothalamic-pituitary-adrenocortical (HPA) system (which is activated via hormone secretion). The same biological system may regulate adult social functioning, but little is known about how this system matures over the decades. It is becoming clearer, however, that gender differences in the way the neuroendocrine system works to transform social support into health benefits are associated with the presence of oxytocin in women.

Other researchers are beginning to study neural links to long-term romantic love. When participants involved in intense romantic relationships lasting more than 10 years were shown pictures of their loved partner, effects occurred in many areas of the brain that are associated with bonding and attachment, including regions rich in dopamine (Acevedo, Aron, Fisher, & Brown, 2012). These effects were not found when participants were shown pictures of other close individuals (e.g., long-term friends) or strangers. Activation in this study was also found in the dorsal-striatum, which is an area of the brain linked to behavior aimed at achieving goals that lead to rewards. This "suggests regions that are active when partners enact behaviors that maintain and enhance their relationships" (Acevedo et al., 2012, p. 157). These results point to the close association between attachment and the development of long-term romantic relationships and give more insight into what neural correlates may sustain this type of relationship. In addition, the experience of being in love may protect individuals from stress at the biological level and lead to better response to negative emotions (Schneiderman, Zilberstein-Kra, Leckman, & Feldman, 2011). The vagus nerve, which is the tenth cranial nerve, plays a key role in regulating the amount of physiological stress felt by an individual. Strong reactivity of this nerve leads to better protection of other bodily processes from the effect of stress. Researchers have found that individuals in love seem to have better regulation of their vagal-cardiac response and that this may "be one mechanism through which love and attachment reduce stress and promote well-being and health" (Schneiderman et al., 2011, p. 1314). Finally, though some have thought that the type of neurobiological reactions such as these described here are better explained by *desire* as opposed to *love*, new research points to distinctive neuroimaging patterns when observing effects of love versus desire (Diamond & Dickenson, 2012).

Neuroscientists and psychologists will continue to explore how neurobiology and positive social behavior are intertwined. As the positive psychology of close relationships incorporates neurobiological findings, we will draw closer to knowing how good relationships become great.

MORE ON FLOURISHING RELATIONSHIPS

As noted in the beginning of this chapter, _infant-to-caregiver attachment_ and _adult attachment security_ are linked to healthy relationship development. Given the literature revealing the neuro-biological underpinnings of attachment (Schore, 1994; Taylor et al., 2002), it appears that interpersonal connection stimulates the brain activity that helps to create the regulatory systems that lead to the development of empathy, enjoyment of positive interactions, and management of the stress associated with negative interactions. The result of this complex brain–behavior interplay is the creation of a foundation of interpersonal experiences and skills on which future relationships are built (see Figure 12.3).

Love, the positive emotion that links us, often is considered a marker of the quality of relationships. We believe that the love we have for another motivates us to engage in _purposeful positive relationship behaviors_ that sustain interpersonal connections over time. As relationships grow stronger, they flourish and facilitate the personal development of both participants. (See Chapter 5 for a discussion of the life tasks of adults.) Love may have different origins and yet still produce the same beneficial effects for those who experience it. Though in Western contexts many believe that control and choice must dictate a marriage connection (as opposed to an arranged marriage) and

Figure 12.3 The Makings of Flourishing Relationships

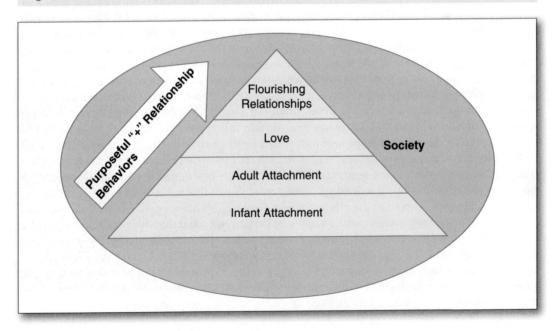

lead to the development of love, other research has found that love, satisfaction, and commitment in arranged marriages have just as high ratings as those found in love-based marriages (Regan, Lakhanpal, & Anguiano, 2012). Findings such as these remind us to be objective as scientists, even when studying something as subjective-seeming as *love*, and to remember the biases our world-views often create.

Another look at Figure 12.3 reveals the makings of flourishing relationships and summarizes our comments in this section. The hierarchy of social needs presented in this figure suggests that attachment, love, and flourishing relationships are desired by all people but achieved only by some. Indeed, we believe that, of all the individuals who are attached to a caregiver at infancy, only some develop secure adult attachments. Though the stability of attachment style across the life span has been questioned (Feeney & Noller, 1996), those who experience attachment in early childhood are often the ones who achieve secure attachment in adulthood (McCarthy & Maughan, 2010).

Progressing up the hierarchy, the need for sustained romantic love is met by those who have realized at least a modicum of secure adult attachment. With the benefits generated by applying *purposeful positive relationship behaviors* (see arrow in Figure 12.3), a couple can parlay love into a flourishing relationship.

FUTURE OF LOVE

In recent times, love has made its way into the papers and the courts as the definition of what makes a "marriage" has become a central issue within the federal court system. Same-sex couples within the United States have been fighting for the right to be legally married for years, and this fight has recently gained some traction. At the time of this writing, 19 states, including the District of Columbia, have legalized gay marriage. Conversely, however, several states in the past few years have had ballot measures to disallow marriage between same-sex couples. Rothblum, Balsam, and Solomon (2011) asked same-sex couples who were granted civil unions to reflect on the significance of this type of legal recognition of their relationship. Participants in this qualitative research cited many tangible benefits of civil unions, such as financial security and assistance with health care costs, but it is the psychological benefits that are more revealing to the topic at hand in this chapter. One respondent in this study stated, "After the civil union, we definitely felt a strengthening of our relationship bond" (Rothblum et al., 2011, p. 397), and others commented on "an increased sense of stability, commitment, and security" (p. 312). Others relished in using the terms "husband" and "wife" for one another and felt that the increased legitimacy to their relationship allowed them to feel more supported and loved within their families and within society. Finally, some couples commented on their increased well-being as a function of validation: "I think the rest of the country has no clue how restrictive the cultural disapproval or ignorance can feel. The Union said, 'We are valid! We

Source: Kobby Dagan / Shutterstock.com

belong!' in a way that we had not experienced" (Rothblum et al., 2011, p. 397). These positive antecedents of the legal and public legitimizing of relationships via civil unions are important to the field of positive psychology as they represent potential pathways toward a greater level of well-being and decreased feelings of stigma for same-sex couples. This said, some couples in the study by Rothblum and colleagues noted that a civil union was not equivalent to an actual legalized marriage. The "separate-but-not-equal" status was a constant reminder of the discrimination that they coped with on a day-to-day basis (Rothblum et al., 2011, p. 312). As the topic of legalizing gay marriage at the federal level is likely to make its way to the U.S. Supreme Court in the near future, those making these decisions may do well to take the positive antecedents of legitimacy for *all* relationships into account.

BUILDING A POSITIVE PSYCHOLOGY OF CLOSE RELATIONSHIPS

The study of insecure attachment, lost love, and failed relationships has produced significant findings that are relevant to our lives. Indeed, relationship researchers have been successful in uncovering what does not work and have attempted to teach people how to correct their relationship problems. Nevertheless, most would agree that we all struggle with identifying the right things to do in relationships. The positive psychology of close relationships builds on the work of the past (including the knowledge that secure attachment and love are prerequisites for healthy relationships), but it is important to note that some of this research has not included a broad spectrum of individuals in terms of cultural background (Chao, 1994; Curran et al., 2010). More research needs to be done in this area. In addition, positive psychology research on the construct of love incorporates a focus on appetitive processes and sets an agenda for the future—an agenda that will hopefully produce research that will tell the story of flourishing relationships for *all* individuals.

KEY TERMS

Adaptive parental behaviors: Parents' appropriate responsiveness to a child's behavioral cues (e.g., smiling).

Agape: The bestowal of love by the divine.

Appetitive processes: The promotion of positive relationship behaviors.

Attachment system: The sum of emotional and physical proximity-seeking behaviors toward the caregiver, developed by the child as a result of adaptive and maladaptive parent behaviors. Regulates the pattern of attachment characteristic of the child.

Aversive processes: The eliminating of negative relationship behaviors.

Companionate love: A form of romantic love characterized by the soothing and steady warmth that sustains a relationship.

Compassionate love: An attitude toward another containing feelings, cognitions, and behaviors that are focused on caring, concern, tenderness, and an orientation toward supporting, helping, and understanding the other.

Consummate love: The most durable type of love, manifested when all three components (passion, intimacy, commitment) are present at high levels and in balance across both partners.

Eros: Romantic love, including the search for and possession of the beautiful.

Flourishing relationships: Good relationships that continue to get better due to the concerted effort of both partners.

Insecure-avoidant attachment: In the Strange Situation assessment, an attachment pattern characterized by a tension between the caregiver and child, resulting in the child's avoidance of the caregiver when reintroduced.

Insecure-resistant/ambivalent attachment: In the Strange Situation assessment, an attachment pattern characterized by a tension between the caregiver and child, resulting in the child's passive or active demonstration of hostility toward the caregiver while simultaneously wanting to be held and comforted.

Maladaptive parental behaviors: Parents' chaotic or unplanned attempts to meet a child's needs.

Minding: A form of relationship maintenance that includes knowing and being known, making relationship-enhancing attributions for behaviors, accepting and respecting, and maintaining reciprocity and continuity.

Nomos: A type of love characterized by submission and obedience to the divine.

Passionate love: A form of romantic love characterized by the intense arousal that fuels a romantic union.

Philia: A type of love characterized by affection and friendship.

Secure attachment: In the Strange Situation assessment, a form of attachment that involves a balance between exploration of the environment and contact with the caregiver.

Self-expansion theory of romantic love: A theory developed by Arthur and Elaine Aron suggesting that humans have a basic motivation to expand the self. The Arons hypothesize that the emotions, cognitions, and behaviors of love fuel such self-expansion.

Strange Situation: An assessment strategy first used by Mary Ainsworth to study children's attachment styles. The strange situation exposes a child to a novel situation in the company of his or her caregiver; the caregiver is then removed and reintroduced to the situation twice while the researcher assesses the child participant's reactions.

Triangular theory of love: Robert Sternberg's theory that all types of love are made up of different combinations of passion, intimacy, and commitment.

Understanding and Changing Human Behavior

CHAPTER 13

Balanced Conceptualizations of Mental Health and Behavior

During the 1950s, psychology addressed the full spectrum of human behavior through its scholarship and practice. In 1955, Erich Fromm explored the "sane society," defining mental health as "the ability to love and to create" (Fromm, p. 69). During the same period, social psychologist Marie Jahoda (1958) characterized mental health as the positive condition that is driven by a person's psychological resources and desires for personal growth. She described these six characteristics of the mentally healthy person:

1. A personal attitude toward self that includes self-acceptance, self-esteem, and accuracy of self-perception

2. The pursuit of one's potentials

3. Focused drives that are integrated into one's personality

4. An identity and values that contribute to a sense of autonomy

5. World perceptions that are accurate and not distorted because of subjective needs

6. Mastery of the environment and enjoyment of love, work, and play

Fromm and Jahoda wrote volumes on their views of positive mental health and good living. These various efforts to advance ideas regarding positive mental health took place during the same general time period in which psychiatrists drafted a small, pocket-sized book titled *Diagnostic and Statistical Manual* (*DSM*; American Psychiatric Association, 1952).

At the beginning of the twenty-first century, it is clear that the focus on the positive has lagged behind the attention paid to the negative. Only recently has the work of Fromm and Jahoda been rediscovered, contextualized, and incorporated into refined conceptualizations of positive mental health. At the same time, the *DSM* has grown tremendously over the last five decades, to the point that the most recent version is an impressive and influential 947-page document covering the symptoms of mental illness (American Psychiatric Association, 2013).

Why have the efforts to conceptualize positive mental health and optimal human functioning lagged behind the work on mental illness? One explanation is that the attainment of positive mental health is a passive process, whereas the remediation of mental illness is an active process that demands more resources. Another explanation is that the maintenance of mental health does not warrant the same careful attention (from theorists and practitioners) as does the alleviation of suffering. In this regard, it is easy to see why our feelings of compassion are activated in the presence of someone with heightened vulnerabilities (Frankl, 1959; Leitner, 2003). Such attention to profound human suffering has captivated Eastern philosophers for thousands of years, and it defined the meaning of life for some Western thinkers for most of the twentieth century (see Chapter 2). Therefore, the positive mental health of our fellow human beings does not evoke such strong feelings in us. Although these are plausible reasons for our intense focus on mental illness and the associated limited attentions to positive mental health, a more parsimonious explanation is that we are fascinated by **abnormal behaviors**.

In this chapter, we explore our seeming preoccupation with abnormal behavior and how this has contributed to a limited understanding of positive functioning. We offer recommendations for developing more balanced conceptualizations of behaviors that focus on positive and negative psychological characteristics as influenced by environmental, developmental, and cultural contexts. In short, we believe that conceptualizations of behaviors need to be more balanced. Accordingly, we address the obstacles to such balance and present resources that may help in the development of more comprehensive clinical thinking.

MOVING TOWARD BALANCED CONCEPTUALIZATIONS

All clinicians struggle to make sense of the complexity of clients' behaviors. Beginning clinicians report that the sheer volume of information that they collect in a 50-minute session overwhelms them. This challenge is intensified by the fact that such clinical information typically is shared in an emotionally charged interpersonal exchange. Novices and master clinicians alike develop strategies to collect, organize, and interpret the clinical data they collect. We may focus too much or too little on particular aspects and determinants of our clients' behaviors. When conceptualizing a case, rendering a diagnosis, and developing and implementing a treatment plan, we must strike a balance in the type and amount of information we gather and process. Specifically, we emphasize the need to address the following issues that contribute to less-than-optimal mental health care:

- Abnormal behavior seems to more easily gain the attention of the clinician, and aspects of normal behavior and healthy functioning (i.e., what is working in person's life) may not be considered meaningful in the diagnostic and treatment process.

- Attributions for behavior may overemphasize the internal characteristics of a person, whereas the environmental influences on behavior are not adequately addressed (this neglect of the environment may also undermine the impact of cultural context on the individual).

- Weaknesses and negative emotions often are deemed more salient to the diagnostic and treatment process than are strengths and positive emotions.

- Current behavior may not be considered in light of developmental history and milestones. Specifically, we may not address thoroughly the question, "Is this person's behavior consistent with expectations for his or her developmental history and age?"

- Behaviors often are interpreted without attention to information about the cultural contexts that could influence whether the behaviors are considered adaptive or maladaptive.

By resolving these challenges, we can produce more balanced views of people within an appropriate cultural context, and observe how our views about them change. We share here our ideas for improving the conceptualizations of human behavior, but first we attempt to explain the human fascination with abnormal behaviors.

OUR FASCINATION WITH ABNORMAL BEHAVIOR

Students from all majors vie for seats in the abnormal psychology course that will explain why their roommates are scared to leave the dorm room or why Aunt Nita never takes a bath! Like you, these students also quietly wonder, "Is that normal . . . and how do I know for sure?" Why is this normality question asked so often? And how can it be answered with any degree of confidence?

As practicing psychologists, we would have some serious money if we had a dollar for every time we've been asked the question, "Is that normal?" This question has been posed so many times that we have tried to understand the motivation behind the query. Here are our thoughts. A small percentage of people have prurient interests in all behaviors that deviate from the norm. They want to experience, understand, and discuss them. Most people who ask this question, however, seem to have a mixture of curiosities and concern. This natural desire to know appears whenever we seek to understand a phenomenon, psychological or otherwise. Furthermore, sometimes abnormal behavior makes us uncertain about another's welfare, or perhaps even our own. For example, if you walk past a man who is screaming obscenities at the top of his lungs, you may be both curious about why he is doing this and nervous about coming into close contact with him. There is a dance of ambivalence about such interactions, but we believe the underlying fascination with the abnormal is a part of our healthy attempts to make sense out of the world and to ensure the well-being of other people and ourselves.

To answer the question, "Is that normal?" and to further examine abnormal behavior, we must define the criteria for abnormality. Immediately, however, we bump into a problem, because there is no widely accepted definition of *abnormal*, nor can it be appropriately applied without some knowledge of cultural context. Nevertheless, three criteria commonly serve as markers of abnormal behavior in a social context. First, the behavior is *atypical* or *aberrant*, which means that it deviates from what is considered standard or expected within the cultural context. Second, the behavior is considered *maladaptive*—that is, the behavior does not typically lead to socially or culturally sanctioned goals. Third, the behavior often is accompanied by *psychological distress*— worry, rumination, and uncomfortable thoughts and feelings.

So, in response to the question, "Is that normal?" the *frequency, function,* and *effects* of the particular behavior must be considered. Furthermore, the context of the behavior must be carefully scrutinized. Consider, for example, a grown woman who is kissing the tarmac at an airport. Surely this is atypical behavior. But, if this is a soldier returning to her home country after a battle in a foreign land, then this behavior may seem perfectly reasonable and normal. Indeed, such a gesture may be adaptive in that it shows love for one's country as well as relief at coming home. Simply put, the normality conclusion depends on the context of a person's action. Consider another example. You see a man with his face upraised and hands clasped, appearing to be talking to someone who is not there. Is this abnormal behavior? Perhaps not if you know that this person is religious and is engaging in prayer. Looking at cultural context (as defined by religion in this case) is obviously another very important factor to take into account with regard to what is "abnormal." When we judge behaviors or practices without taking culture into account, we open ourselves up toward a biased assessment of others.

Yet another determinant of the abnormality label is whether there is a powerful and influential person in the societal context who is willing to speak out and ostracize a given action by another person. In this regard, Becker (1963) made the important point that a behavior is not necessarily deviant because it merely violates a rule, but rather it often is the reaction of one or more people to that behavior that ultimately determines the label. Furthermore, on occasion there may be no rule or norm violation at all, but the fact that an influential person in the society initiates a "splitting off" process can produce the abnormal label for just about any person. So, we must consider the situational context, the time of the action, and the potential powerful enforcer of the label when considering the application of the label "abnormal" (Snyder & Fromkin, 1980). These examples suggest that consistent identification of abnormal behavior might prove quite difficult. Nevertheless, we do attempt to categorize such behaviors.

Our preoccupation with abnormal behaviors may serve positive functions, such as promoting understanding of the world and helping to keep people safe. But this preoccupation seldom leads to a clear answer to the question, "Is that normal?" More times than not, our response to the question is, "It depends." Indeed, as just discussed, it depends on the context of the behavior. Moreover, it depends on additional factors discussed in the next sections of this chapter: the severity of the behavior, the developmental factors that defined the person's behavioral repertoire, and the environmental and cultural contexts that frame the behavior. Failure to consider the multiple qualities of a behavior may make the behavior seem more threatening than it needs to be. Equally important for the theme of the present book, our propensity to categorize behavior as abnormal may contribute to the insufficient attention paid to those qualifying factors that may lead to the application of a label on the positive side of the spectrum. We believe the positive side of human experiences also deserve considerable attention because strengths and well-being are the basic ingredients of mental health.

NEGLECT OF THE ENVIRONMENT AND OF THE POSITIVE

The desire to understand behavior often leads to a question such as, "Why did he do that?" In search of the answer, however, we unfortunately often forgo asking the actor directly and instead attempt to answer the question from our seat as the observer. When we do this, we expose ourselves to potential errors in thinking that may lead to limited consideration of important environmental influences. Accordingly, the flaws in thinking associated with the **fundamental attribution** error and the **fundamental negative bias** contribute to our tendency to over-pathologize behavior and to view behavior in a manner that is not comprehensive, culturally competent, or valuing of potential strengths.

When trying to explain the behavior of others in social situations, we are prone to ignore external situational or environmental factors, and instead we attribute the behavior to the other person's internal characteristics (e.g., personality or abilities). This occurs even when the diagnosing clinician knows little about the person and how that person views the environment. This flawed tendency is referred to as the **fundamental attribution error** (Nisbett, Caputo, Legant, & Maracek, 1973). On the other hand, when we explain our own behavior, we are more comprehensive in our conceptualization in that we probably take the environmental variables into account. For example, have you ever received a bad grade on an examination in school? Whereas an outside observer might conclude that you did poorly because you are stupid, you would hasten to give more situation-based explanations, such as the teacher's poor explanation of the material or the instructor's tricky, misleading wording of the test questions.

The **fundamental negative bias** involves the *saliency* (stands out vs. does not stand out), the *value* (negative vs. positive), and the *context* (vague vs. well-defined) of any given behavior (Wright, 1988). Specifically, when a behavior stands out, is considered negative, and occurs in a vague context, the primary factor guiding the perception of the behavior is its negative quality. Imagine that a friend tells you that her boyfriend was rude to her family during a holiday visit home. With this small amount of information, you know that the behavior is atypical—that it stands out—and negative. With little contextual information, your attention is drawn to the value of the behavior, and you may be left thinking that your friend's boyfriend is a hostile guy. (The same is true for behavior that stands out in a sparse context and is considered positive; the positive quality will define and determine the reactions to the behavior.)

We, as humans and as clinicians, also tend to view scenarios, disorder, and "abnormality" from our own worldview, and this vantage point is different for members with different cultural facets (e.g., different races, ethnicities, genders, sexual orientations, socioeconomic statuses, and so on; Hays, 2008; Mio, Barker, & Tumambing, 2009). While seeing visions, for example, may be an abnormal behavior in White majority culture within the United States, it may not have the same status from an American Indian cultural viewpoint; in taking care to assess symptoms from within a cultural context, we can more fully offer effective intervention (American Psychological Association, 1993). The field as a whole has tended to neglect culture in conceptualizations of behavior until recently (Sue & Sue, 2008); however, culture is an essential environmental factor to include when viewing behavior in general.

By addressing these biases in our views of behavior, we can create an understanding of the influence of environmental stressors on our functioning. With our increased attention to the environment, we also become more aware of environmental resources that may interact with strengths and result in positive functioning.

Asking Questions: The Four-Front Approach

Recent developments in classifying the full spectrum of human functioning hold much promise. In Beatrice Wright's **four-front approach** (1991; Wright & Lopez, 2002), she aims at developing a comprehensive conceptualization about a person's weaknesses and strengths, as well as stressors and resources in the environment. To this end, she encourages observers to gather information about the following four fronts of behavior:

1. Deficiencies and undermining characteristics of the person

2. Strengths and assets of the person

3. Lacks and destructive factors in the environment

4. Resources and opportunities in the environment

Multiple and complex methods can be used to gather this information, but collaborating with the *actor* (the person being observed) can reveal the answers to these four questions: (1) What deficiencies does the person contribute to his or her problems? (2) What strengths does the person bring to deal effectively with his or her life? (3) What environmental factors serve as impediments to healthy functioning? and (4) What environmental resources accentuate positive human functioning? The idea of checking in with the actor personally is an important component to this approach as it allows them to say for themselves what they consider a strength or a deficit *from their own perspective*, thus allowing for a more culturally competent understanding. This balanced approach to conceptualization, refined by the authors of this text (Lopez, Snyder, & Rasmussen, 2003; Snyder & Elliott, 2005; Snyder, Ritschel, Rand, & Berg, 2006), encourages the search for personal strengths as well as environmental resources.

The Case of Michael

Throughout the remainder of this chapter, one of the authors (SJL) tells you about Michael, a 41-year-old, gay, Caucasian male client who was seen in counseling for 4 years. Michael, who was referred by a physician treating him for cancer, reported that he had moderate depression. This depression not only produced sadness, it also caused problems in maintaining relationships and cooperating with his care providers. He started our lengthy relationship with the statement, "I desperately need help with my life." I responded, "What kind of help do you need?" About 100 sessions later, Michael's life story remained intriguing, and I learned something new about him at every meeting. I give a glimpse into Michael's life here and in three other places in this chapter.

Michael told me that he needed help with "everything." I encouraged him to be more specific, and he reached into his jeans pocket and pulled out two pages of handwritten notes about his struggles. He was very descriptive about each and every concern and its effects. It was clear why Michael felt that the world was against him. His car had been totaled, he was having major side effects from medications and treatment, the heat was not working in his apartment, and so forth. Although his depression was quite complicated (due to his family history, illness, and side effects of treatment), it was clear that aspects of his situation, and to some extent the quality of his environment, were exacerbating his symptoms.

Near the middle of our first session, I said, "These problems would be overwhelming for anyone. How do you cope?" He looked at me as if he were uncertain about how to respond. Then, I asked him how he handled a particular problem on his list. He was just as descriptive in his storytelling about coping as he was in his accounting of his struggles. At the very end of the session,

I said, "Next time, we will talk about your strengths." Part of me knew that he would bring a list of strengths to the next session, and he did. With pages of notes about Michael's strengths and struggles and his environmental stressors and resources, I was able to develop a basic understanding of his depression, his battle with cancer, and the vitality that kept him moving toward a more positive future.

THE LACK OF A DEVELOPMENTAL EMPHASIS

Developmental psychologists focus on the origins and functions of behavior (see Chapter 5 for further discussion of human development). Their scientific efforts shed light on normal developmental processes such as cognitive operations (Piaget, 1932); moral judgment (Gilligan, 1982; Kohlberg, 1983); and personality (Allport, 1960; Mischel, 1979). Most of what we know about the origins of everyday behavior we owe to the insights of developmental (and evolutionary) psychologists. Moreover, during the last 25 years, developmental psychopathology scholars (e.g., De Los Reye, 2013; Olson et al., 2013; Sameroff, Lewis, & Miller, 2000; Wenar & Kerig, 1999) have begun to unravel the mystery of why some people develop particular disorders and others do not.

Although developmental research has answered many questions about learning and growth over time, some aspects of development remain unexplained and warrant further study. For example, we know very little about how people mature in very specific environments (e.g., a dorm on campus) or how they grow during discrete periods of their lives (e.g., a semester or 4 years of college life). In this regard, a theory about adolescent/adult development during college (developed by Chickering, 1969) contextualizes normal and abnormal behaviors in the unique setting of a college campus.

Although laypeople may be fascinated with such basic questions as, "What happens when bad things happen to good people?" developmental theories often fail to address such basic issues. Such bad things, or "insults," as professionals in the field sometimes describe them, might include traumatic stressors such as abuse or seemingly less painful events such as significant academic failures or relationship breakups. Of particular note here is Allen Ivey and Mary Bradford Ivey's (1998, 1999) developmental counseling and therapy approach, which makes sense out of the life events that potentially could positively or negatively change basic developmental processes.

Normalizing Negative and Positive Behavior

In Chickering's (1969; Chickering & Reisser, 1993) theory of the development of college students, the focus is on a circumscribed time period (years in college for traditional and nontraditional learners) and a specific environment (the college academic and social setting). Beyond survival, Chickering proposed that the primary human goal involves the establishment of an identity—the refinement of a unique way of being (called *individuation*). Within the Chickering model, students move toward these goals via seven pathways, or vectors; moreover, Chickering makes the point that movement along multiple pathways at one time is quite likely. Developing competence (moving from low-level competence in intellectual, physical, and interpersonal domains to high competence in each area) is identified as a primary developmental driver for young people. (Acquiring competency and developing human strengths are interchangeable and serve as foundations for future growth.) With increased confidence in their resourcefulness, students can pursue Chickering's six other developmental goals. These goals include:

1. **Managing emotions,** or growing from little awareness of feelings and limited control over disruptive emotions to increased understanding of feelings and flexible control and constructive expression

2. **Moving through autonomy toward interdependence,** or moving from poor self-direction and emotional dependence to instrumental independence and limited need for reassurance

3. **Developing mature interpersonal relationships,** or growing from intolerance of differences and few relationships to an appreciation of differences and healthy relationships

4. **Establishing identity,** or changing from personal confusion and low self-confidence to a self-concept clarified through lifestyle and self-acceptance

5. **Developing purpose,** or transitioning from unclear vocational goals and distracting self-interests to clear goals and more communal activities

6. **Developing integrity,** or changing from unclear beliefs and values to clear and humanizing values

Chickering's (1969) developmental vectors describe the pathways and goals associated with growth that takes place during a discrete period in a fairly special environment. Understanding optimal functioning during this period can reveal generalizable skills that can be used in other periods and settings. It is important to note, of course, that these six vectors were designed from a Western point of view, and a phrase such as "as is appropriate within the student's cultural context" might be added today to each of the six items above to make them more culturally competent. Appropriateness of levels of autonomy, the way in which emotions are managed in a culturally normative fashion, and what a "mature relationship" looks like are just some of the factors above that might differ as a function of cultural background. We recommend one basic question to pose to fellow college students to discover what resources they have for the future: "What got you ready for college?" Consider Chickering and Reisser's (1993) probing questions to determine where you are on your developmental path:

Briefly describe a change in yourself that had a major impact on how you lived your life. What was the "old" way of thinking or being, vs. the "new" way? What did you move *from,* and what did you move *to?* How did you know that a significant change had occurred? What were the important things (or persons) that *helped* the process? What did the person(s) *do?* What was the experience that catalyzed the shift? Were there any *feelings* that helped or accompanied the process? (Chickering & Reissner, 1993, p. 45) Today, in the interest of also taking culture into account, we would add a few additional questions, such as, how did this affect relationships with your family or other members of your culture? Or, what role did culture play in your change process?

When considering the positive and negative circumstances of each person's experiences and environments that may have contributed to his or her current adaptivity and dysfunctionality, the work by Ivey and Ivey (1998, 1999) may be quite useful. In this regard, the Iveys' developmental counseling and therapy provides a here-and-now conceptualization in which pathological behaviors are seen as logical responses to life events. (Aspects of the developmental focus and a traditional diagnostic system are juxtaposed in Table 13.1.) Furthermore, Ivey and Ivey posit that there are many categories for understanding behavior and experiences, and they urge clinicians to reach the most accurate understandings by viewing each person as a whole.

In framing their approach, the Iveys (1999) state that the "contextual self includes relational dimensions of personal and family developmental history, community and multicultural issues, and physiology" (p. 486). Therefore, understanding the individual requires gaining information about him or her along numerous contextual dimensions. Conceptualization of a person's behavior within the Ivey system involves building a framework of background information. For example, when working with someone who has experienced childhood trauma, the Iveys would gather information about environmental or biological insults (Masterson, 1981). The Iveys then recommend examining the connections between such insults and other stress and pain, along with how subjective experiences of stress and pain relate to sadness and depression. Such an examination obviously emphasizes the origins and severity of a person's suffering. Next in this approach, strategies that can be used to combat a negative mood are examined. From the Iveys' point of view, the way in which a personality style helps a person navigate current interpersonal relationships ultimately is linked to a person's psychological well-being. More recently, Ivey and colleagues have discussed using this model with a diversity-sensitive approach. While the developmental and counseling therapy model has always held multiculturalism, social justice, and advocacy at the core of its work, new suggestions on how to use these techniques in a multiculturally competent way are available. Zalaquett and colleagues (2013) give a very thorough overview of the theory, the microskills, and the interviewing strategies needed—a must-read for counselors considering employing this approach.

The Case of Michael

Michael's strengths of "being loving" in relationships and "persevering" in the face of illness and an avalanche of daily obstacles were touchstones throughout his treatment. These strengths seemed to be products of the adversity he experienced during his childhood and adolescence, or, at the very least, they were galvanized during that time.

Table 13.1 The Contrast Between Traditional and Developmental Meaning-Making Systems

Issue	Traditional Pathological Meaning	Developmental Meaning
Locus of problem	Individual	Individual/family/cultural context
Pathology	Yes	No, logical response to developmental history
Developmental and etiological constructs	Peripheral	Central

(Continued)

Table 13.1 (Continued)

Issue	Traditional Pathological Meaning	Developmental Meaning
Culture	Beginning awareness	Culture-centered
Helper role	Hierarchy, patriarchy	Egalitarian, construction
Cause	Linear, biology vs. environment	Multidimensional, considers both biology and environment
Family	Not emphasized	Vital for understanding individual development and treatment
Treatment	Not emphasized	Central issue

Source: Reprinted from Ivey, A., & Ivey, M. B (1998), Reframing DSM-IV: Positive strategies from developmental counseling and therapy, *Journal of Counseling & Development, 76,* 336. The American Counseling Association. Reprinted with permission. No further reproduction authorized without written permission from the American Counseling Association.

About the quality of "being loving," Michael remarked, "I think I was born with it." He held on to this loving approach as if it were a prized possession even though, from his perspective, this love was not returned by some of the most important people in his life (his stepmother, his brother, and the first person on whom he had a crush). Over the course of counseling, Michael found that he could be loving to the people who did not return his affection and still find some satisfaction in life. It took 41 years for him to realize that his strength was not encumbered by the behaviors of others.

His perseverance took many forms, but I tend to describe it as vital courage. In the face of threats to his psychological well-being and severe illnesses, Michael plugged on. I remember asking him when he had discovered his vital courage. The question clearly brought up a moving memory. Through tears, he told me the story of his stepmother's repeated efforts to "dehumanize me and make me feel like I would never become anything." The many insults that Michael experienced made him more determined to make a good life for himself. When he was diagnosed with cancer, he was reminded of his commitment to himself. With that in mind and a history of using his strengths, he promised himself and all of his care providers, "I am going to beat this thing."

DIFFICULTIES UNDERSTANDING BEHAVIOR IN A CULTURAL CONTEXT

The surgeon general's report, *Mental Health: Culture, Race, Ethnicity* (U.S. Department of Health and Human Services, 2001), emphasizes the importance of acknowledging that there are culture-bound syndromes, that culture influences coping strategies and social supports, and that individuals may have multiple cultural identities (see Figure 13.1 for an example of how grief expressions may differ across cultures). Indeed, "culture counts," as it plays a crucial role in determining an individual's thoughts and actions. (See Chapter 4 for an extended discussion of developing strengths and living well in a cultural context.) Clinicians engaging in diagnosis must pay keen attention to the cultural context in forming impressions of any person. Being careful to take culture into account, which we strongly endorse, runs counter to the **universality assumption**, which holds that what is deemed true for one group may be considered true for other people, irrespective of cultural differences.

Despite the surgeon general's directive to contextualize all behavior, and the clarion call made by multicultural psychologists to consider the cultural factors associated with human functioning, psychologists and laypeople alike may hold the universality assumption. In this regard, psychologists Madonna Constantine and Derald Wing Sue reason that notions of hopefulness and suffering may not be universal. On this issue, Constantine and Sue (2006) wrote that

[some] Buddhists (many of whom may have an Asian cultural background), for instance, tend to believe that hopelessness is the nature of the world and that life is characterized by suffering. Moreover, present-day suffering is thought to be retribution for transgressions in past lives. Thus, the way to overcome the hopelessness and suffering of the world is through meditation, which will lead to the final state of nirvana, or a higher plane of existence (Obeysekere, 1995). It can be surmised that it is neither optimism nor "realistic optimism" (Schneider, 2001) that results in satisfaction with life for Buddhists. Instead, Western perceptions of depressive affect in Buddhists, in fact, may be the

Figure 13.1   *The Jazz Funeral* by Susan Clark depicts how grief and joy intermingle following the death of a New Orleans local. Contrary to the universality assumption, grief looks different across cultures, as do many positive emotions.

Source: Reprinted with permission of Susan Clark.

"psychology of the norm" for individuals who adhere to Buddhist philosophy, and an ideal state of well-being would be equivalent to a heightened state of existence. (p. 229)

The empirical data stemming from the research of University of Michigan psychologist Edward Chang (1996a; 1996b; Chang & Banks, 2007; Chang, Maydeu-Olivares, & D'Zurilla, 1997) directly challenge the universality assumption and demonstrate that acting on this false belief could have quite negative consequences. (See Chapters 4 and 8 for more discussion of Dr. Chang's research.) Chang's research demonstrates that optimism, pessimism, problem solving, and possibly psychological and physical symptoms are conceptualized differently and behave differently across cultures. Given these findings, interventions that benefit one group may be benign or harmful to another.

Determining How "Culture Counts"

Awareness of cultural nuances lends insight into how people of varied backgrounds generate psychological well-being. In addition, examining how adverse experiences could promote adaptive psychological functioning in all people might provide vital clues about how optimal human functioning develops.

Cultural values (from various identity facets such as race, ethnicity, sexual orientation, gender, socioeconomic status, nation of origin and others; Hays, 2008) provide the context in which behaviors, thoughts, and feelings are deemed normal or abnormal (Banerjee & Banerjee, 1995; Constantine, Myers, Kindaichi, & Moore, 2004); these values and their influence on meaning making of experiences contribute to optimal human functioning (Pedrotti et al., 2009; Sue & Constantine, 2003). For example, explicit demonstrations of religious faith are considered quite normal in many cultures. In the predominately Catholic parishes of southern Louisiana, home of an ethnic enclave of Cajuns, people put crucifixes above all doorways to ward off evil. In the Cajun culture, this practice is viewed as a common and normal approach to putting one's faith to work to protect personal welfare and ensure well-being. In addition, some assessments of what is normal may differ as a function of cultural facets that do not involve race and ethnicity or nation of origin. A man from a lower socioeconomic status, for example, may view his ability to overcome obstacles to achieve his goals as a "normal" and necessary part of his life; someone outside this socioeconomic status may call this ability "extraordinary" and in this way "abnormal" to some extent, though still a positive trait. Considering worldview as it is developed from these different cultural facets is essential in understanding behavior (Pedrotti, 2013a).

Focusing specifically on the functioning of people of color in the United States, Constantine and Sue (2006) identified two large classes of variables (see Table 13.2), discussed in previous literature (e.g., Helms & Cook, 1999; Sue & Sue, 2012), that interact in complex environments and contribute to the psychological and social well-being of people of color. Constantine and Sue asserted that these dimensions should be included in psychological conceptualizations pertaining to persons of color.

Zalaquett, Fuerth, Stein, Ivey, and Ivey (2008) comment on the *DSM-IV-TR*'s (American Psychiatric Association, 2000) "limited consideration of social and cultural factors in defining psychiatric disorders" (p. 366). In the most current iteration of this manual, *DSM-5* (American Psychiatric Association, 2013), some cultural facets are alluded to in some areas, but more overall attention to the fact that culture influences experience and development is still needed. People of color, women, same-sex-oriented individuals, and other groups may experience environmental factors such as social injustices (e.g., racism, sexism, heterosexism, classism, etc.) on a regular basis, and these situational variables naturally affect behavior (Zalaquett et al.). Some research has found that dealing with this sort of discrimination may actually hone one's skills at coping (Fingerhut & Maisel, 2010). This heightened coping ability is, unfortunately, not the case in all situations, however, and particular characteristics (e.g., racial identity) may mediate this relationship (Forsyth & Carter, 2012; Pieterse & Carter, 2010). Viewing behavior in isolation without attending to environment then can lead to inappropriate over-pathologizing in these clients.

The Case of Michael

"I am looking for support outside my family and my docs." That is how Michael started one of our sessions during the 3rd year of our work. We had developed a sort of shorthand in our sessions by then. Michael slid his handwritten notes to me as the session started; he always had them, and I always read them as we kicked off our meetings.

"What have you tried?" I asked, and Michael listed his many attempts to build his social network. "I think I have tried everything except going to church!" he said with an edge. Michael and I had discussed his religious beliefs and his spirituality at great length over the years. His spirituality was a source of strength, but his religion and, more precisely, his childhood church, were a source of great pain, as he had felt ostracized after coming out as a gay teen. "Why did you bring up church?" I inquired. I learned that Michael's new case manager had made a big sales pitch about the value of the social support of fellow parishioners. In response, Michael was justifiably angry about the "one size fits all" recommendation. After talking about his frustration with his case manager, we returned to his plans for finding more social connectedness. The discussion soon focused on the gay culture in his small town. Similar to any culture, his town's gay community had norms for behavior, and people held expectations about how single males reached out for support. Our next two sessions were devoted to reviewing Michael's efforts to better create a healthy social network in his community.

Table 13.2   Optimal Human Functioning of People of Color in the United States: Variables That Interact in Environmental Contexts

Cultural Values, Beliefs, and Practices

   Collectivism

   Racial and/or ethnic pride

   Spirituality and religion

   Interconnectedness of mind/body/spirit

   Family and community

Strengths Gained Through Adversity

   Heightened perceptual wisdom

   Ability to rely on nonverbal and contextual meanings

   Bicultural flexibility

THE LIMITS OF THE CATEGORICAL DIAGNOSTIC SYSTEM

Once data have been collected in a balanced fashion, clinicians must turn to the task of rendering a diagnosis that describes a client's behavior and symptom patterns. In today's mental health practice, clinicians summarize this valuable data in the form of a categorical diagnosis. In this section, we examine the limitations of a categorical diagnostic system and recommend that dimensions be used to more comprehensively describe our fellow men and women. In the most current version of the *DSM*, the *DSM-5* (American Psychiatric Association, 2013), dimensions are considered in some areas. In the diagnosis of any depressive disorder, for example, the last few iterations of the *DSM* have offered guidelines for assessing mild, moderate, and severe depression (see Table 13.3).

We have been grouping behaviors into the categories "abnormal" and "normal" for as long as people have possessed language capabilities, but this does not necessarily mean that we are reliably and accurately distinguishing between the two. For example, recent factor analyses of data from a sample of individuals who were diagnosed with personality disorders and a sample of individuals with a "normal" personality revealed that personalities reflected in the two groups were more alike than different (see Maddux & Mundell, 1999, for a review). Similarly, Oatley and Jenkins (1992) found that "normal" and "abnormal" emotional experiences were not discretely classified. Specifically, the distress associated with everyday stresses often is hard to distinguish from the criteria of emotional disorders.

Regarding the real-world challenge of making diagnoses by categorizing clients' behaviors, there is evidence of a lack of consistency and accuracy among practicing psychologists. On this point, McDermott (1980) found that when 72 psychology graduate students and psychologists

Table 13.3 Severity Specifications for Depressive Disorders in *DSM-5* (APA, 2013)

Specify current severity:

Severity is based on the number of criterion symptoms, the severity of those symptoms and the degree of functional disability.

Mild: Few if any symptoms in excess of those required to make the diagnosis are present, the intensity of the symptoms is distressing but manageable, and the symptoms result in minor impairment in social or occupational functioning.

Moderate: the number of symptoms, intensity of symptoms, and/or functional impairment are between those specified for "mild" and "severe."

Severe: the number of symptoms is substantially in excess of that required to make the diagnosis, the intensity of the symptoms is seriously distressing and unmanageable, and the symptoms markedly interfere with social and occupational functioning.

Source: Reprinted with permission from the *Diagnostic and Statistical Manual of Mental Disorders*, Fifth Edition. Copyright © 2013. American Psychiatric Association. All rights reserved.

(24 novices, 24 interns, 24 experts) were presented with the same three case studies, diagnostic agreement was no better than that predicted by chance. A total of 370 diagnostic statements were rendered, and there was no specific pattern of agreement within or between the participant groups.

Barone, Maddux, and Snyder (1997b) acknowledged the difficulties in categorizing human functioning. These scholars went on to observe that, despite the fact that all people experience problems, these personal difficulties are best represented as occurring on a continuum from none to slight to moderate to extreme degrees. The inevitable variability of clients' problems cannot be easily explained, however, by using discrete categories. On this latter point, it is impossible to create a true dichotomy between normal and abnormal functioning because almost every theoretical orientation to psychology acknowledges that it is the *degree* of the dysfunctional behavior that largely drives the distinction between normality and abnormality. Even Freud, who often is criticized for pathologizing behaviors, was clear in stating that conceptualizations depend on the degree to which an unconscious conflict or desire interferes with normal functioning, not on the mere presence or absence of that conflict or desire.

It has often been noted in the past that there may be socially significant problems associated with the categorical system in the American Psychiatric Association's *Diagnostic and Statistical Manual* (*DSM*) (2000, 2013). That is, as mental health professionals, we can become preoccupied with forcing people into negative categories and thereby make little or no attempt to understand the person in a more comprehensive manner. To confound the problem, the labels given to these negative categories then serve as a social wedge between persons who are so labeled and all others who are not. Negative labeling can create stereotypical expectations that can influence how professionals conceptualize and interact with individuals; it can also influence how these labeled individuals may think about themselves.

Once the label of the diagnostic group is applied, the perception of within-group differences tends to be diminished, whereas the perception of between-group differences is enhanced (Wright, 1991). Remember the story about the Sneetches from Dr. Seuss (1961)? In the beginning of that tale, young readers probably view the Sneetches (Star-bellied or Plain-bellied) as a group, as being almost identical to each other, as suggested in Dr. Seuss's singsong verse:

Now the Star-bellied Sneetches had bellies with stars.

The Plain-bellied Sneetches had none upon thars.

The stars weren't so big; they were really quite small.

You would think such a thing wouldn't matter at all. (p. 3)

The story soon reveals that the small characteristic, the star, did matter quite a bit in the society of Sneetches. The Star-bellied Sneetches viewed themselves as quite similar to one another and quite different from and superior to the Plain-bellied Sneetches. Young readers also quickly become intrigued with the subtle difference between groups, typically making the star a more salient characteristic of the Sneetches and pointing out that one group (whichever has the star at a given time) seems to be happier than the other group. Often, clinicians and laypeople behave like Dr. Seuss's target audience. We overemphasize the meaningfulness of a label, we accentuate the similarities among the group members possessing the label, and we overestimate the differences between the labeled group members and another group of people.

Because diagnostic labels traditionally have been negative, clinicians may ignore the ideographic and potentially positive characteristics of people. This has been particularly true in diagnosing people of color, women, same-sex-oriented individuals, and other groups who have historically lacked power (Pedrotti & Edwards, 2010). Wright (1991; Wright & Lopez, 2002) asserts that information consistent with the diagnostic label will be remembered more easily than inconsistent information. Thus, simply by applying the negative label, professionals attend to and seek information about individual deficits rather than strengths, thereby decreasing accuracy and comprehensiveness in conceptualizing a person's complete psychological make-up. In less privileged cultural groups (e.g., non-White, female, etc.) these negative labels also set up a deficit model from which it may be hard to recover (Sue & Sue, 2012).

Some changes to the current *DSM* address some of these issues. For example, sections for each diagnosis titled "Development and Course" exist to assist the clinician in being able to view the diagnosis within a developmental context to some extent, providing a "normal" developmental course of the disorder (APA, 2013). In addition, sections titled "Gender-Related Diagnostic Issues" and "Culture-Related Diagnostic Issues" have been added to multiple diagnoses, and these sections detail information relevant to culture and gender with regard to the specific diagnosis. In addition, a method of assessing culture and its impact on diagnosis and development of disorder has been added as part of the new assessment section in the *DSM-5* (APA, 2013). This Cultural Formulation Interview assesses many different facets of the cultural experience of a client. Though not a required assessment (though we might argue it should be), this type of resource does provide multiculturally conscious and competent clinicians with a way to collect good data on cultural background. Interestingly, this interview system has a section titled "Stresses *and Supports*" (italics added) that appears to be the first incidence of a more balanced assessment. Specifically this section instructs the interviewer to ask their client, "Are there any kinds of support that make your [PROBLEM] better, such as support from family, friends or others?" (APA, 2013, p 753). This type of question reflects a more balanced investigation of experience, which is what we are advocating for here.

Second, the multiaxial system has been dispensed with in the current version of the *DSM* (APA, 2013). The previous distinctions of Axes I, II, and III have been eliminated with the intent of incorporating medical and health issues into the clinician's understanding of the patient or client's diagnosis. These changes to the *DSM* help in some ways to situate diagnostic labels into context as opposed to looking at them as occurring within a vacuum.

Considering New Personality Dimensions

Given the general limitations of a categorical system and the neglect of positive behaviors in the current categorical systems, alternative conceptualizations might advance our understanding of psychological phenomena. In this regard, the dimensional approach puts human behavior on a continuum, thereby allowing the examination of individual differences in negative and positive behavior. It is important to clarify here that viewing psychological behavior does not involve juxtaposing "good" and "evil" on the same continuum. Such a use of dimensional systems may only lead back to the categorizing of behaviors. One view is that it is more informative to consider the degree to which behaviors are adaptive or maladaptive.

Another use of the dimension system involves examining negative and positive behaviors on separate dimensions. Indeed, such an approach is supported by related research. Scores on measures of positive behaviors (e.g., life satisfaction) and scores on measures of negative behaviors (e.g., depression) correlate negatively and modestly, around −.40 or −.50 (see Frisch, Cornell, Villanueva, & Retzlaff, 1992). Accordingly, a report from the United States Surgeon General (U.S. Department of Health and Human Services, 1998) indicated that mental illness and mental health are not opposite ends of the same continuum.

In their 1995 book, *New Personality Self-Portrait,* Oldham and Morris (1995) describe a dimensional approach to conceptualizing personality disorders that have historically been considered the most intractable forms of mental disorders. They contend that each of the 14 personality disorders listed in the *DSM* can be viewed as residing on its own continuum of adaptation. At one end of these continua lie less acute, more adaptive presentations of these personality types or styles; on the other end of the continua, we find the actual, less adaptive manifestations of the personality disorders (e.g., borderline, paranoid, histrionic). Oldham and Morris posit that, at any point in time, an individual may move along this continuum, depending on the environmental and endogenous stressors in his or her life. In this conceptualization, an individual may exhibit dysfunctional behaviors that are more indicative of the actual disorder at times of high stress, whereas a clinical presentation may be characterized by a more adaptive symptomatology in times of less stress. Thus, an individual may meet the *DSM-5* (APA, 2013) criteria for histrionic personality disorder during extremely stressful periods but might be described merely as "dramatic" at times of low life stress.

As another example, someone with obsessive-compulsive personality disorder in stressful situations may be described as "conscientious" on the lower end of the continuum (see Figure 13.2). In fact, these characteristics may be quite helpful to the individual living at the adaptive end of the continuum. A person who is conscientious as described by Oldham and Morris may find that possessing this quality allows him or her to be responsible and reliable. A person with features of narcissistic personality disorder may find that certain aspects of this behavior allow him or her to be self-confident and thereby able to function at a superior level. An important point to remember is that it is only when these characteristics become extreme or non-functional within the environment or cultural context do they cease to be beneficial to a person.

This personality continuum can be used to differentiate between individuals who possess less or more florid symptomatology in their daily lives. With the current *DSM-5* conceptualization, however, to be diagnosed as "having" a disorder, one must possess a majority of the criteria delineated. An individual possessing one less than the specified number of criteria may be experiencing quite a high level of stress but nevertheless may not receive services because the requisite number of criteria have not been met. The Oldham and Morris (1995) conceptualization leaves room for individuals to be diagnosed according to the degree of dysfunction as well as the degree of positive use of resources. In addition, it may provide more client-friendly terminology for discussion of personality disorder diagnoses during sessions and allow clinicians to help clients identify strengths and weaknesses in their set of behaviors.

The Alternative *DSM-5* Model for Personality Disorders appears in the new *DSM*. In this alternative model, personality disorders are defined in terms of a general set of criteria, including separate criteria for personality function and pathological personality traits. In addition, criteria for pervasiveness and stability and alternative explanations for personality pathology are listed (APA, 2013, p. 761–763). Specific personality disorder diagnosis criteria are also listed for the various

Figure 13.2   Oldham and Morris's (1995) Dimensional Conceptualization of Personality Disorders

Personality Style		Personality Disorder
Conscientious	⟶	Obsessive-Compulsive
Self-Confident	⟶	Narcissistic
Dramatic	⟶	Histrionic
Vigilant	⟶	Paranoid
Mercurial	⟶	Borderline
Devoted	⟶	Dependent
Solitary	⟶	Schizoid
Leisurely	⟶	Passive-Aggressive
Sensitive	⟶	Avoidant
Idiosyncratic	⟶	Schizotypal
Adventurous	⟶	Antisocial
Self-Sacrificing	⟶	Self-Defeating
Aggressive	⟶	Sadistic
Serious	⟶	Depressive

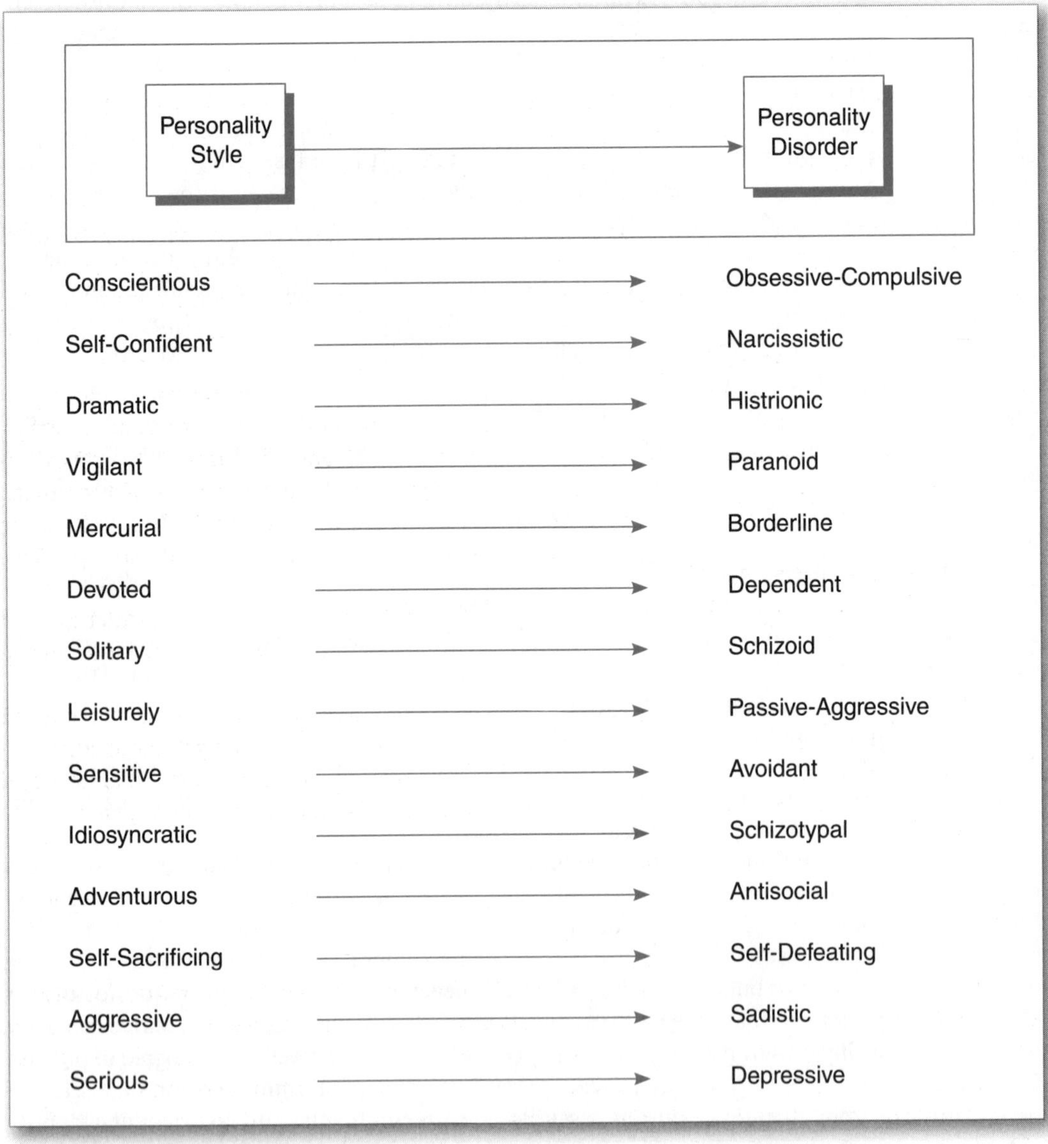

Source: The Personality Style-Personality Disorder Continuum from *The New Personality Self Portrait: Why You Think Work, Love, and Act the Way You Do* by John M. Oldham & Lois B. Morris. Copyright © 1995 by John M. Oldham & Lois B. Morris. Used by permission of Bantam Books, an imprint of Random House, a division of Random House LLC. All rights reserved.

personality disorders. Though there is still a heavy focus on the negative and on specific criteria for most disorders (as well as almost no mention of the positive in this dimensional system), it may signify a directional change with regard to how we view personality disorders in general. Perhaps in future iterations of the *DSM* a more balanced view (i.e., one that includes positive traits as well) will emerge.

The Case of Michael

Over our 4 years of work, Michael taught me a great deal about the meaningfulness and meaninglessness of labels. It would have been technically accurate to describe him as an "impoverished gay male suffering from cancer and depression." But this did not tell half the story of Michael's existence. Indeed, his strengths defined him much more than his weaknesses did. Furthermore, as Michael pointed out, these diagnostic terms did not help him make positive changes in his daily life. "I am not poor. Other people can't classify me as poor," Michael told me when his case manager recommended that he claim impoverishment and seek assistance with his utility bills. Michael certainly did not have much of an income—around $9,000 a year—but he did believe that he had the right to define his own circumstances.

Regarding the terms *suffering, cancer,* and *depression,* at one time or another Michael proclaimed, "The diagnosis doesn't fit." "Suffering is subjective," he reminded me, "and I have felt like I was suffering for a long time." Many of our discussions about diagnoses addressed the classification of depression (records from previous counseling, prior to the development of his cancer, indicated that Michael had a history of recurrent episodes of major depression). "But I am coping much better with my depression; doesn't that mean anything in your diagnostic workup?" This was one of Michael's many questions that I could not answer well.

Occasionally, I call Michael to have "booster sessions." Each time, I am impressed with how well he is coping with challenges that might overwhelm other people. We typically talk about how he is using his strengths and building a stronger network of friends.

My work with Michael, which was conducted early in my career, taught me about the need to go beyond the client's report of symptoms and to test the limits of the existing diagnostic framework. In time, good mental health care routinely will require us to consider clients' resources and to contextualize their behaviors when we render diagnoses and carry out treatment plans.

GOING BEYOND THE *DSM-5* FRAMEWORK

Traditionally, conceptualizations of disorders have focused on symptomatology and dysfunction—those things that are not "working" in a person's life. This focus on negative aspects has occurred at the expense of identifying strengths, and it has not helped people in their pursuit of optimal human functioning (Lopez et al., 2006). This limited view of psychology undermines the ultimate goal of any psychodiagnostic system: *to understand the person's needs and resources and to facilitate the implementation of helpful therapeutic interventions.* Accordingly, Maddux (2009b) points out that the utility of a classification system is closely linked to its ability to lead subscribers to the development and selection of effective treatment. This aspect of the *DSM*'s utility has been repeatedly questioned (see Raskin & Lewandowski, 2000; Rigazio-DiGilio, 2000). Furthermore, the *DSM* system does not explain connections among environment, culture, behavior, thoughts, emotion, external supports, and functioning. Therefore, the *DSM* system can only "suggest somewhat vaguely *what* needs to be changed, but it cannot provide guidelines for *how* to facilitate change" (Maddux, 2009b, p. 67).

Going beyond the *DSM* framework requires clinicians to implement the numerous strategies described in this chapter: using the four-front approach, infusing developmental data into conceptualizations, counting culture's effects on mental health in a more central way, and considering adopting new, more dimensional models for all behavior as opposed to categorizing it. Over time, diagnostic practice may evolve into a process that incorporates more meaningful data into a robust system of describing behavior and mental health. Until then, clinicians can make small steps to account for positive and negative aspects of a person's functioning. For example, Ivey and Ivey (1998) suggest that one of the first steps toward transcending pathology is to change the language we use to describe client functioning. This includes discovering what is working in a person's life and finding ways to capitalize on personal strengths. Indeed, simply asking about strengths can have a profound effect on the client, the therapeutic relationship, and, ultimately, the clinical conceptualization, as suggested by Snyder et al. (2003):

> By asking about strengths, the diagnostician is fostering several positive reactions in the client. First, the client can see that the helper is trying to understand the whole person. Second, the client is shown that she or he is not being equated with the problem. Third, the client is not reinforced for "having a problem" but rather is encouraged to look at her or his assets. Fourth, the client can recall and reclaim some of the personal worth that may have been depleted prior to coming to the mental health profession. Fifth, a consideration of the client's strengths can facilitate an alliance of trust and mutuality with the mental health professional; in turn, the client is open and giving of information that may yield a maximally productive diagnosis. By asking about strengths, therefore, a positive assessment is at once healing and buoyant in its focus. (p. 38)

Determining "what is not working" and "what is working" for a person honors the client's life experiences and guides clinicians to treatment approaches that make sense (see Chapter 14 for a further discussion of interventions). In addition, committing oneself to using the Cultural Formulation Interview as offered in the new *DSM* with all clients would be a laudable statement for clinicians to make. And, with the ongoing development of positive psychology research and practice, clinicians will be able to link balanced conceptualizations to applications that will help clients achieve optimal mental health within their own cultural contexts.

Attending to All Behavior

Practicing psychologists get to know people on deep, meaningful levels. We are entrusted with stories that begin, "I wish I had. . . ." and those that start with "I am glad I did. . . ." We learn about hidden regrets and secret dreams. We are able to borrow the worldview of another to try to see life through his or her eyes. We hear about missed opportunities and planned "next shots." We see and feel deep suffering, and we are carried away by unbridled exuberance. We find out not only that abnormal behavior is fascinating but that *all behavior is intriguing*.

Contextualizing what you see by considering the influences of developmental processes, environmental conditions, and cultural nuances helps create a more balanced, accurate picture of a person and his or her struggles and triumphs. So, next time someone asks you, "Is that normal?" answer, "It depends." Ask a few more questions, and remember to consider context and to put yourself in the shoes of the person being judged. This is what we try to do in working with people.

KEY TERMS

Abnormal behaviors: A hard-to-define term, most definitions of which include behaviors that are atypical or aberrant, maladaptive, or accompanied by psychological distress. It is also important to consider a person's context and culture when deciding whether their behavior is abnormal.

Developing competence: One of Chickering's developmental goals of college students; involves going from low-level competence in intellectual, physical, and interpersonal domains to high competence in each area.

Developing integrity: One of Chickering's developmental goals of college students; developed when a person changes from unclear beliefs and values to clear and humanizing values.

Developing mature interpersonal relationships: One of Chickering's developmental goals of college students; involves growing from intolerance of differences and few relationships to an appreciation of differences and healthy relationships.

Developing purpose: One of Chickering's developmental goals of college students; involves transitioning from unclear vocational goals and distracting self-interests to clear goals and more communal activities.

Developmental counseling and therapy: Ivey and Ivey's theory of counseling, in which the here and now is examined and information gathered about a variety of contextual

dimensions in the process of conceptualizing clients' situations. In this theory, pathological behaviors are understood as logical responses to life events.

Establishing identity: One of Chickering's developmental goals of college students; involves changing from personal confusion and low self-confidence to a self-concept clarified through lifestyle and self-acceptance.

Four-front approach: A diagnostic approach that encourages assessment of a person's strengths as well as weaknesses. Observers using this approach gather information on (1) deficiencies and undermining characteristics of the person, (2) strengths and assets of the person, (3) lacks and destructive factors in the environment, and (4) resources and opportunities in the environment.

Fundamental attribution error: The tendency to ignore external situational or environmental factors and instead attribute the behavior of another to that person's internal characteristics (i.e., personality or abilities). In contrast, people are likely to explain their own behavior in terms of situational or environmental influences rather than personal characteristics.

Fundamental negative bias: The tendency to perceive as negative behavior that stands out, is considered negative, and occurs in a vague context. Behavior is remembered according to its saliency (stands out vs. doesn't stand out), its value (negative vs. positive), and its context (vague vs. well-defined).

Managing emotions: One of Chickering's developmental goals of college students; involves going from little awareness of feelings and limited control over disruptive emotions to increased understanding of feelings, flexible control, and constructive expression.

Moving through autonomy toward interdependence: One of Chickering's developmental goals of college students; involves moving from poor self-direction and emotional dependence to instrumental independence and limited need for reassurance.

Universality assumption: The assumption that what is deemed true for one group can be considered true for other people, irrespective of cultural differences.

CHAPTER 14

Preventing the Bad and Promoting the Good

IN THE WORDS OF A PSYCHOTHERAPY CLIENT . . .

Eager to get started, a new psychotherapy client passionately announced, "I want to stop the bad things that keep happening, but that's not all. . . . I want more good!" Her words tap the two broad topics that we explore in this chapter.

The first category, stopping the bad, involves efforts to prevent negative things from occurring later, and it can be divided into primary and secondary preventions. **Primary preventions** lessen or eliminate physical or psychological problems *before* they appear. **Secondary preventions** lessen or eliminate problems *after* they have appeared. The latter process often is called psychotherapy.

The second category, making more good, involves enhancing what people want in their lives; it, too, can be divided into primary and secondary types. **Primary enhancements** establish optimal functioning and satisfaction. **Secondary enhancements** go even farther, however, to build upon already-optimal functioning and satisfaction to achieve peak experiences. Primary enhancements make things good (create optimal experiences), whereas secondary enhancements make things the very best that they can be (create peak experiences).

PRIMARY PREVENTION: "STOP THE BAD BEFORE IT HAPPENS"

Primary preventions (see Figure 14.1) reflect actions that people take to lessen or remove the likelihood of subsequent psychological difficulties (Heller, Wyman, & Allen, 2000) or physical problems (Kaplan, 2000). With primary preventions, people are not yet manifesting any problems, and it is only later that such problems will appear if appropriate protective, or prophylactic, steps are not taken (Snyder, Feldman, Taylor, Schroeder, & Adams, 2000). When primary prevention is aimed at an entire population, it is called **universal prevention** (e.g., childhood immunizations); when focused on a particular at-risk group, it is called **selective prevention** (e.g., home visitations for children with low birth weight; Munoz & Mendelson, 2004).

Figure 14.1 · Primary and Secondary Preventions

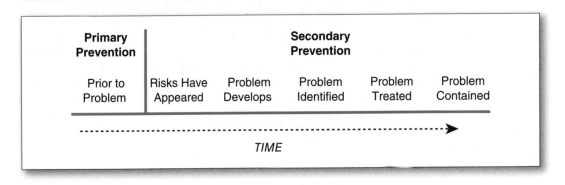

If each of these primary and secondary approaches to prevention and enhancement were to have a slogan, we would suggest the following:

- Primary prevention: "Stop the bad before it happens."

- Secondary prevention (psychotherapy): "Fix the problem."

- Primary enhancement: "Make life good."

- Secondary enhancement: "Make life the best possible."

Primary prevention activities are based on hope for the future. As Snyder, Tennen, Affleck, & Cheavers (2000, p. 256) put it, "*We would suggest that prevention is, at its core, an act of hope*—a positive, empowered view of one's ability to act so as to attain better tomorrows." Primary prevention sometimes may occur at the governmental level. By setting and enforcing laws that allow people to succeed because of their merits and efforts, for example, a government can lessen subsequent negative consequences for its citizens (Snyder & Feldman, 2000). With legislation against prejudicial hiring practices based on such things as racism, sexism, and heterosexism, individual citizens are likely to remain satisfied because they perceive that they have equal opportunities to obtain desirable jobs. Likewise, when citizens perceive that laws allow equitable opportunities to pursue goal-directed activities, they then should (1) become less frustrated and aggressive (an aspect of the frustration-aggression hypothesis [Zillman, 1979]); (2) continue to exert effort in their work settings and personal lives (the negative outcome here has been called *learned helplessness* [Peterson, Maier, & Seligman, 1993]); and (3) be less likely to attempt suicides (Rodriguez-Hanley & Snyder, 2000). On the last point, in a multicountry study, Krauss and Krauss (1968) examined the degree to which citizens sensed that their governments blocked them in various goal-pursuit activities. The researchers found that greater perceived blockages correlated significantly with higher suicide rates across countries.

The United States government's recent passing of the Affordable Health Care Act is also an attempt at primary prevention. If all individuals are able to seek more routine medical care regardless of their socioeconomic status, more serious health crises may be prevented at higher rates.

The U.S. Department of Health and Human Services (2013) estimates that 7 out of every 10 deaths of Americans are due to chronic diseases, many of which might be prevented by more consistent medical care. Some of these preventative measures (e.g., mammograms for women, regular physicals, STI counseling, etc.) may assist in decreasing the occurrence of certain diseases in the population at large.

Finally, whatever can be done locally and nationally to raise educational levels also will serve primary prevention purposes by lessening the chances that citizens will be physically unhealthy and psychologically unhappy (Diener, 1984; Veroff, Douvan, & Kulka, 1981). Furthermore, any actions taken to promote employment should prevent people from incurring psychological and physical maladjustments (Mathers & Schofield, 1998; Smith, 1987; see also Chapter 15 on the beneficial aspects of work).

Is Primary Prevention Effective?

On the whole, primary preventions are quite effective (Albee & Gullotta, 1997; Durlak & DuPre, 2008; Garber et al., 2009; Mrazek & Haggerty, 1994; Reddy, Newman, De Thomas, & Chun, 2009; Yoshikawa, 1994). To understand the magnitude of the effects of primary prevention efforts, consider the results of a meta-analysis (a statistical technique that allows researchers to combine the results of many studies to discover common trends) conducted by Durlak and Wells (1997). Durlak and Wells examined the effectiveness of prevention programs on children's and adolescents' behavioral and social problems; they found that the preventions yielded effective outcomes similar in magnitude (and in some cases superior) to medical procedures such as cancer chemotherapy and coronary bypass surgery. Moreover, Durlak and Wells (1997) observed that, relative to control group participants, those in the prevention programs were anywhere from 59% to 82% better off in terms of reduced problem behaviors and increased competencies. More recently, Durlak and DuPre (2008) reviewed over 500 studies conducted on prevention and promotion programs. In this analysis, they were able to delineate 23 contextual factors that affected successful implementation of these programs, including variables related to who was providing the service, the community in which the program was provided, and the amount of support in place for the program. These data are extremely useful for future endeavors in developing effective primary prevention.

Components of Effective Primary Preventions

Heller and his colleagues (2000, pp. 663–664) offered five suggestions for implementing successful primary preventions. First, the targeted populations should be given knowledge about the risky behavior to be prevented. Second, the program should be attractive; it should motivate potential participants to increase the desirable behaviors and decrease the undesirable ones. Third, the program should teach problem-solving skills, as well as how to resist regressing into previous counterproductive patterns. Fourth, the program should change any norms or social structures that reinforce counterproductive behaviors. On this latter point, social support and approval often are needed in order to overcome the rewarding qualities of problematic behaviors. Fifth, data should be gathered to enable evaluation of the program's accomplishments. These evaluation data then can be used to make a case for implementing primary prevention programs in other settings.

Other researchers have investigated various components in prevention programs as specific "active ingredients" in the change process. Collins and Dozois (2008) list (1) inclusion of parents in treatment, (2) approaches that focus on interpersonal interactions, and (3) incorporation of cognitive–behavioral interventions as offering specific benefits toward effective prevention programs. Studies such as this that investigate particular mechanisms of change are particularly helpful at determining future evidence-based treatments and programming (Kazdin, 2008).

Head Start: An Example of Primary Prevention

Perhaps the most noteworthy example of primary prevention is the Head Start program, which began in the 1960s as a part of President Lyndon Johnson's War on Poverty. Head Start was implemented in response to widespread concerns that poor American children were not receiving sufficient cognitive and intellectual stimulation to benefit adequately from their schooling. Unfortunately, some children often were failing from the moment they began school.

The goal of Head Start is to provide poor children with a level of preparation that mirrors that of their economically more advantaged counterparts. In addition to its education components, Head Start offers nutritious meals, medical screenings, and parental education. The parental training has proved to be especially efficacious. Results have showed that, when children attend Head Start for at least 3 days per week for 2 years or more, and when parents are involved, social and academic benefits are reliable and last over time (Ramey & Ramey, 1998). Head Start also shows children and parents that they need not slip into previous counterproductive behaviors; moreover, this program shows that a better life is possible for the children. Finally, compared to the various other prevention programs, Head Start has received repeated and extensive testing to show that it works. Perhaps the most crucial result has been that children in the program have performed better academically than their counterparts who did not participate in Head Start (Ramey & Ramey, 1998). Though some of this research is several years old, current data show that Head Start is no less effective today (Hillemeier, Morgan, Farkas, & Maczuga, 2013). In comparison to children not involved in Head Start, those involved in the program continue to be better off. Investing in this type of program is an investment in the future generation.

Primary Preventions for Racial and Ethnic Minorities

Racial and ethnic minorities have been disenfranchised for many decades, thus placing them at risk for various difficulties that might not exist for members of majority racial background. In addition, research on programs that have been deemed effective at large (such as Head Start) has sometimes found disparities in the quality of care between racial groups, with African Americans in particular receiving the lowest quality of care (Hillemeier et al., 2013). Due to this, programs aimed specifically at racial and ethnic minority individuals are both valuable and necessary. In a modification of Bierman's (1997) risk reduction programs for rural children, Alvy (1988) developed an effective parent training program for African American parents, taking into account their unique cultural background and norms. This program emphasized pride, study skills, discipline, and obedience to authorities. Likewise, the parents were taught the importance of family support for their children. Alvy was careful to use a multiracial staff and to consult both locally and nationally with African American experts. A similarly effective program has been implemented for the parent training of Mexican American mothers (D. L. Johnson, 1988).

Another primary prevention that is currently under evaluation is a promising program called Chicago Urban Resiliency Building (CURB; Saulsberry et al., 2013). This Internet-based program is aimed at providing preventative intervention for African American and Latino adolescents who are at risk for depression. CURB uses a model based on the idea that health behaviors and beliefs are embedded in culture and, as such, it uses culturally competent means to reach these youth. The fact that the community and family members are approached in culturally sensitive ways appears to be a major factor in the success of CURB and similar programs. Also, the programs all emphasize that the support of the surrounding community is crucial to the adoption of new attitudes (pride, studying, discipline, etc.). Examination of the effectiveness of such programs must be continued to broaden their utility to minority racial and ethnic groups.

Primary Preventions for Children

Several primary prevention programs target at-risk children and youth. The work of Shure and Spivak (Shure, 1974; Shure & Spivak, 1988; Spivak & Shure, 1974) has been exemplary in teaching problem-solving skills to children likely to use inappropriate, impulsive responses when encountering interpersonal problems. Such children were projected to have unhappy lives in which they would resort to crime and aggressive behaviors. As an antidote to these predicted problems, the children were taught to come up with ways other than aggressive outbursts to reach their goals. These successful problem-solving primary prevention programs have been expanded to middle schools (Elias et al., 1986) and to teenage children identified as likely to abuse drugs (Botvin & Toru, 1988); become pregnant (Weissberg, Barton, & Shriver, 1997); or contract HIV (Jemmot, Jemmot, & Fong, 1992). Many programs also teach skills that promote mental health and emotional and social abilities in children and adolescents (Dobrin & Kállay, 2013; Hayes, Bach, & Boyd, 2010; Leadbetter, Gladstone, Yeung Thompson, Sukhawathanakul, & Desjardins, 2012). For example, Gillham, Reivich, Jaycox, and Seligman (1995) implemented a 12-week primary prevention program for fifth- and sixth-grade children. The prevention program helped children to identify negative, self-referential beliefs and to change their attributions to more optimistic and realistic ones. Relative to a control group of children who did not receive this prevention package, those in the experimental group were significantly lower in depression; these findings were directly linked to their learning to make more optimistic attributions. (For analogous findings with high school students, see Clarke et al., 1995.) The Seligman program is especially laudatory because it continually has assessed its effectiveness in terms of the positive outcomes of the participant children, who otherwise would be at risk for serious depression.

Primary Preventions for the Elderly

Prevention programs for the elderly can focus on many different objectives, including screening to lessen the probability of later physical or mental health problems (Ory & Cox, 1994); checking living arrangements to remove physical hazards that can lead to falls and other accidents (Stevens et al., 1992); and attempts to maximize the elders' work, social, and interpersonal engagements (Payne, 1977). One such intriguing prevention program, called Grandma Please, involves grandchildren who telephone their grandparents after school (Szendre & Jose, 1996). Although its results have been mixed, the program is based on the compelling premise that keeping the elderly involved and actively participating in their families prevents them from spiraling into lives of isolation and depression. Unfortunately, these programs for the elderly have not necessarily produced uniformly beneficial results. For example, Baumgarten, Thomas, Poulin de Courval, and Infante-Rivard (1988) assumed that having older adults volunteer to help their debilitated neighbors would be beneficial to these helpers, but in fact the researchers found no such positive results. Related to this failure, it may be that spending time with family is more important in such prevention activities for elders than spending time meeting new friends (Thompson & Heller, 1990).

The recognition and prevention of depression in the elderly has become a greater focus in recent years (Madhusoodanan, Ibrahim, & Malik, 2010; Oyama et al., 2010). Just the fact that depression has been recognized as a preventable disorder for the elderly is progress to some extent; historically, depression has been treated as a sort of inevitability of old age (Madhusoodanan et al., 2010). Thankfully, today, physicians are becoming more aware of the need to assess for depression in ways that can likely help older adults to live more fulfilling lives. In addition, current studies are investigating various lifestyle changes that may help to prevent disease on multiple fronts. Researchers cite healthy diet, social interaction, education, and exercise as some factors that may help to prevent various difficulties in elderly populations (Madhusoodanan et al., 2010).

Obviously, more research is needed to understand what types of preventions actually work with the elderly, and this will become especially important as the large cohort of baby boomers (people born after the end of World War II in 1945) moves into the senior years.

Caveats About Primary Preventions

Several factors make it difficult to implement primary prevention programs. First, people tend to believe that the future will result in good things happening to them, whereas bad things will happen to other people. This phenomenon has been called the illusion of uniqueness (Snyder & Fromkin, 1980), or unique invulnerability (Snyder, 1997). One approach to lessening this inaccurate view is to give people actuarial information about how typical it is to encounter some problems. This makes it seem more "normal" to have the problem, and the recipient of such information then may be more willing to seek help before the problem grows to such a large size that is difficult to treat.

In an empirical test of this approach, Snyder and Ingram (1983) told college students, half of whom were high in test anxiety, about the high prevalence of anxiety among college students. Results showed that only the highly test-anxious students then perceived their anxiety as normal and that they then were more likely to seek treatment. A similar approach is to show short television spots in which famous athletes or movie stars disclose that they sought treatment for a problem and now are better (Snyder & Ingram, 2000b). In short, by normalizing the problem, people suffering from it may become more willing to seek help.

Another force undermining prevention activities is the difficulty in convincing people that these programs are effective and worth the effort. People tend to remain passive and to believe that "things will work out." Furthermore, funding agencies may not see the payoff—that doing something now will result in benefits years later. One way to correct this misperception is to conduct research to show the direct payoffs in terms of increased productivity and money saved by the agencies where the preventions may be applied (businesses, government organizations, etc.) (Snyder & Ingram, 2000b). If research shows a company that primary prevention efforts actually would save money in the long run, the company is likely to invest money in these activities. Durlak and DuPre (2008) offer five factors that affect the implementation process: (1) community aspects (e.g., politics, funding); (2) provider characteristics (e.g., self-efficacy, proficiency); (3) characteristics of the innovation itself (e.g., compatibility, adaptability); (4) features relevant to the prevention delivery system (e.g., positive work climate, shared decision making, communication, leadership); and (5) factors related to the prevention support system (e.g., training, technical assistance). Paying attention to these aspects when developing prevention programs can assist in making sure that components are optimized in terms of their potential to impact a population in "real life."

Lastly, even though advances have been made in the area of prevention, there is a sizable lag time until such findings are published and become part of the knowledge base in psychology (Clark, 2004). Although we have considerable knowledge about how to intervene against psychopathologies (because of the previous widespread application of the pathology model), we have far less understanding of prevention to promote health and lessen the probability of future problems among identified populations (Holden & Black, 1999; Sajatovic, Sanders, Alexeenko, & Madhusoodanan, 2010). Groups such as postpartum women, military personnel who have experienced trauma, immigrants, and oncology patients have had exposure to trauma and/or vulnerability in some way and must be studied more often (Sajatovic et al., 2010). Nevertheless, primary prevention can be applied effectively to target behaviors involving both psychological and physical health. Primary prevention can help keep physical illnesses at bay and enhance the psychological quality of life in subsequent years (Casey, 2013; Durlak & DuPre, 2008; Kaplan, 2000; Kaplan, Alcaraz, Anderson, & Weisman, 1996; Kaplan & Anderson, 1996).

SECONDARY PREVENTION (PSYCHOTHERAPY): "FIX THE PROBLEM"

Secondary prevention addresses a problem as it begins to unfold (see Figure 14.1). Snyder et al. (2000, p. 256) have described secondary prevention as occurring when "the individual produces thoughts or actions to eliminate, reduce, or contain the problem once it has appeared." Therefore, time in relation to the problem is a key differentiating factor in these two types of prevention, with primary prevention involving actions *initiated before a problem has developed* and secondary prevention involving actions *taken after the problem has appeared*. In secondary prevention, it is not even necessary to know exactly why the problem is occurring as long as the process is able to halt the danger or problem. Consider the historical account of the outbreak of cholera in nineteenth-century London. Although John Snow did not know the actual causal factor for the outbreak at the biochemical level, he did know enough to effectively curtail the epidemic by removing the handle of the water pump at Broad Street! Snow's hunch was that cholera was carried by something in the water supply that was coming from the water at this pump site. Indeed, Snow was able to prevent the spread of cholera by cutting off its source (described in Munoz & Mendelson, 2004).

Secondary prevention is synonymous with psychotherapy interventions. Although most people probably realize that there are numerous forms of psychotherapies, it may surprise many to learn that helpers presently are practicing more than 400 different types of interventions (Roth, Fonagy, & Parry, 1996).

We view psychotherapy as a prime example of secondary prevention because people who come for such treatments know that they have specific problems that are beyond their capabilities to handle, and this is what leads them to obtain help (Snyder & Ingram, 2000a). Indeed, the related literature reveals that specific problems and life stressors trigger the seeking of psychological assistance (Norcross & Prochaska, 1986; Wills & DePaulo, 1991). Of course, when psychotherapy is successful, it also may produce the primary prevention characteristic of lessening or preventing recurrence of similar problems in the future.

Is Secondary Prevention Effective?

From the earliest summaries of the effectiveness of psychotherapies (e.g., Smith, Glass, & Miller, 1980) to more contemporary ones (see Ingram, Hayes, & Scott, 2000; Wampold, 2011, 2013), there is consistent evidence that psychotherapy improves the lives of adults and children. When we say that psychotherapy "works," we mean that there is a lessening of the severity and/or frequency of the client's problem and symptoms. On average, for example, a person who has undergone psychotherapy has improved by a magnitude of 1 standard deviation (that is, she or he is about 34% better off) on various outcome markers, relative to the person who has not undergone psychotherapy (Landman & Dawes, 1982; Shapiro & Shapiro, 1982). Thus, there is strong scientific support for the effectiveness of what are called *evidence-based treatments* for adults (Chambless et al., 1996; Chambless et al., 1998; Chambless & Hollon, 1998); children (Casey & Berman, 1985; Kazdin, Siegel, & Bass, 1990; Roberts, Vernberg, & Jackson, 2000; Weisz, Weiss, Alicke, & Klotz, 1987); the elderly (Gallagher-Thompson et al., 2000; Woods & Roth, 1996); and racial and ethnic minorities (Malgady, Rogler, & Costantino, 1990). Furthermore, most clients who have undergone psychotherapy treatments report being very satisfied with their experiences (Seligman, 1995), though this may vary by racial group to some extent (Sue & Sue, 2012). Wampold makes the assertion that the biggest piece of the puzzle of whether therapy is actually effective in any given situation is the level of effectiveness of the *therapist*. In a symposium given in 2011 to the American Psychological Association at their annual convention, Wampold cited characteristics such as strong interpersonal skills, powers of persuasion, and the abilities to be reflective and offer optimism as key traits that an effective therapist must possess. In addition, Wampold states that having research backing to one's strategies is essential.

For the reader interested in overviews of effective treatments for depressions, bipolar disorders, phobias, generalized anxiety disorders, panics, agoraphobias, obsessive-compulsive disorders, eating disorders, schizophrenia, personality disorders, alcohol dependency and abuse, and sexual dysfunctions, we recommend the book *What Works for Whom? A Critical Review of Psychotherapy Research,* edited by Anthony Roth and Peter Fonagy (1996/2005). Effective interventions for specific problems are summarized in Appendix A on pp. 402–403. Finally, it must be noted that in 2012 the American Psychological Association approved a resolution that recognized psychotherapy as effective (the policy document created as a result of this approval can be found in the *Journal of Psychotherapy Integration* in the September 2013 issue; see this document for more current information on research in this area).

All this said, throughout the history of psychotherapy there have been varying opinions on which treatments are "best" (e.g., Eysenck, 1952; Strupp, 1964), and, as many have noted, the "evidence" used in these studies that appears to back one type of treatment or another is often fraught with error (Wampold, 2013). Bruce Wampold, in a recent article titled "The Good, the Bad, and the Ugly: A 50-Year Perspective on the Outcome Problem" (2013), notes that defining what is a "good outcome" is inherently culturally based and thus can often be flawed. Wampold uses Strupp's (1964) list of what constitutes a good outcome of therapy as an example here, noting that one criteria of positive functioning listed at this time was "full *heterosexual* functioning with potency and pleasure" (p. 10, italics added). Today we would not consider this to be a universally positive outcome and recognize that heterosexual functioning is not the only healthy expression of sexuality. This said, there are very likely other criteria we might use today that are still culturally biased and contained and that we might someday come to believe are also wrong. Thus, all discussions of "effective" treatment must be couched in a discussion of cultural context (Kirmayer, 2012). Readers may find Whaley and Davis's article in the September 2007 issue of the *American Psychologist,* "Cultural Competence and Evidence-Based Practice in Mental Health Services," to be a useful resource to this end.

Looking ahead to the future, one final point that must be made here is the fact that secondary prevention is not always accessible to all populations that may benefit from it. Lower socioeconomic groups of both adults and children have been shown to benefit from secondary prevention as much as other groups, but they participate in therapeutic interventions less often (Santiago, Kaltman, & Miranda, 2013). As part of our ethics code as psychologists calls for us to make sure that the profession is accessible to all, we have work to do in this area. Determining strategies to alter programs to make them more culturally competent across socioeconomic groups and attractive and available to all is necessary for future work in this area.

Common Components of Secondary Preventions

On the effectiveness of psychotherapy, noted psychiatrist and psychotherapy researcher Jerome Frank (1968, 1973, 1975) suggested that hope was the underlying process common to all successful psychotherapy approaches. Building on Frank's pioneering ideas, Snyder and his colleagues (Snyder, Ilardi, Cheavens, et al., 2000; Snyder, Ilardi, Michael, & Cheavens, 2000; Snyder, Parenteau, Shorey, Kahle, & Berg, 2002) have used hope theory (see Chapter 8) to show how pathways and agency goal-directed thinking facilitate successful outcomes in psychotherapy. We elaborate on the application of these agency and pathways processes to psychotherapy next.

Placebo effects in psychotherapy research represent how much clients will improve if they are motivated to believe that change will happen. Therefore, if the size of the placebo therapeutic outcome effect is compared to the size of therapeutic effect for clients who get no such motivational expectancies, we can produce what amounts to an agency (or motivation) effect. Likewise, if we take the full treatment outcome effect (comprising agency plus the pathways of treatment) and subtract the placebo effect (agency), a pathways-like effect remains. The typical agency effect size has been shown to be .47 standard deviation in magnitude (i.e., clients are 16% better off than had they received no treatment), and the pathways effect has been .55 standard deviation in magnitude (i.e., clients are 19% better off than had they received no treatment; data taken from Barker, Funk, & Houston, 1988). Summing these agency and pathways effects produces an overall hope effect size of 1.02 standard deviation (i.e., clients are about 35% better off than had they received no treatment). As shown in Figure 14.2, we can see that about half of the robust psychotherapy outcome effect relates to agency motivation and the other half of the psychotherapy effect relates to the pathways learned in the specific interventions.

Secondary Prevention Programs for Adults

Most psychotherapy approaches have used what Insoo Kim Berg and Phillip de Shazer (1992) call "problem talk" rather than "solution talk." That is to say, the traditional focus has been on decreasing negative thoughts and behaviors rather than focusing on the building of positive thoughts and behaviors (Lopez, Floyd, Ulven, & Snyder, 2000). Even though the pathology approach to thinking about human behavior still is the prevailing model, in recent years many therapists have begun to attend to clients' strengths. Likewise, a client sometimes must unlearn negative thoughts and behaviors before learning positive ones.

Before turning to examples of the newer therapeutic approaches of positive psychology, it would be useful to describe previous approaches that have proven effective in lessening client problems. In this regard, some psychotherapy interventions involve self-management (Rokke & Rehm, 2001). One such is Bandura's self-efficacy model, discussed previously in Chapter 8. According to this model, a client can learn efficacy beliefs through (1) actual performance accomplishments in the problematic area, (2) modeling another person who is coping effectively, (3) verbal persuasion by the helper, and (4) controlling negative cognitive processes by learning to implement positive moods (Forgas, Bower, & Moylan, 1990). It is important to note that there are specific target problems in such self-efficacy approaches.

A second type of self-management involves Meichenbaum's (1977) self-instructional training, which typically is aimed at the problem of anxiety. The initial stage of this approach is gathering information about the problem, including maladaptive cognitions. This is accomplished when the helper asks the client to imagine the problem and then describe the ongoing internal dialogue. In the second stage of Meichenbaum's treatment approach, the client is taught more

Figure 14.2   Primary and Secondary Enhancements

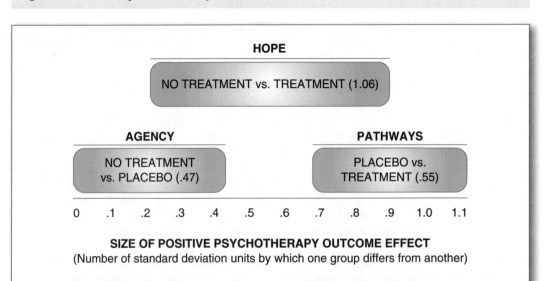

adaptive internal dialogues. Lastly, the client practices these new coping dialogues in order to strengthen the likelihood of actually using them.

A third self-management approach is Kanfer's (1970) three-stage self-control model, which often is used with anxiety problems. In the first stage, self-monitoring, the client observes the problematic behavior in the context of its antecedents and consequences. In the second stage, self-evaluation, the client learns to compare the ongoing problematic behavior with the desired, improved standard of performance and to realize that she or he is falling below this standard. In the third stage, self-reinforcement, the client learns to reinforce himself or herself (with rewards and punishments) for controlling the undesired behavior. Additionally, the client must be committed to change and must perceive that the given behaviors are under his or her control.

We cannot describe all the major psychotherapeutic approaches in detail here. For reviews of these various approaches, see the *Handbook of Psychological Change: Psychotherapy Processes & Practices for the 21st Century* (2000a), edited by C. R. Snyder and R. E. Ingram, and the recently updated 6th edition of *Bergin and Garfield's Handbook of Psychotherapy and Behavior Change,* edited by M. J. Lambert (2013). The major psychotherapy models have included psychodynamic approaches, behavioral techniques, cognitive–behavioral strategies, humanistic models, and family system approaches, along with the possible use of psychotropic medications (Plante, 2005).

We now turn to approaches to secondary prevention that are described within the new field of positive psychology. For a review of these approaches to psychotherapy, we recommend *Positive Psychology in Practice,* edited by P. A. Linley and S. Joseph (2004; 2nd edition in press).

Seligman has used his learned optimism theory as an attributional retraining framework for developing a therapeutic approach for depression. For overviews of his adult therapy, we suggest Seligman's 1991 book, *Learned Optimism,* and his 2002 book, *Authentic Happiness.*

Seligman's attributional retraining for adults starts with teaching people the "ABCs" related to negative events in their lives. Specifically, A is for the adversity, B is for the belief about the underlying reason for the bad event, and C is the consequence in terms of feelings (usually negative or depressed). Seligman then teaches the adult to add a D to the ABC sequence; this D represents the client's learning to dispute the previous counterproductive, depression-producing belief with compelling, accurate evidence. For example, in the following sequence, consider a hypothetical client named Jack:

Adversity = Jack's perception that his friend Miguel has been ignoring him.

Belief (of Jack) = Miguel does not like him because Jack is "no fun."

Consequence = Jack feels lousy.

With disputation training to learn other explanations for Miguel's behavior, Jack will be able to feel better about himself. For example, consider this next sequence, in which disputation is added:

Adversity = Miguel does not talk with Jack all afternoon at work.

Belief (of Jack) = Miguel doesn't like Jack.

Consequence = Jack feels bad.

Disputation = Jack invokes the more optimistic attribution that Miguel has also been quiet with other people at work. Additionally, Jack notes that, in fact, Miguel did speak with him during the coffee break that morning. Thus, having made these more optimistic attributions, Jack is able to feel much better about the situation.

In addition to learned optimism therapy, some attention has been given to implementing what has been called "hope therapy" in one-on-one settings (Lopez et al., 2000; Lopez et al., 2004; McDermott & Snyder, 1999); with couples (Worthington et al., 1997); and in groups (Klausner et al., 1998). For example, Klausner and her colleagues (Klausner et al., 1998; Klausner, Snyder, & Cheavens, 2000) have developed a valid group intervention for depressed older adults. Specifically, in a series of 10 group sessions, learning the goal-directed activities that are inherent in hope theory has diminished depression and raised physical activity levels for depressed older persons. Moreover, these improvements based on hope treatment were superior to those attained by a comparison group who underwent Butler's (1974) reminiscence group therapy (this approach entails elders recalling earlier, pleasurable times in their lives). Also, using hope theory as a base, Cheavens and her colleagues (Cheavens, Feldman, Gum, Michael, & Snyder, 2006; Cheavens et al., 2001) have developed an effective eight-session intervention for depressed adults.

In another therapeutic hope application, outpatients visiting a community mental health center were given a pretreatment therapy preparation based on hope theory (i.e., they were taught the basic principles of this theory), and these clients then received the normal psychotherapy interventions implemented at this facility. Results showed that the people who were given the pretreatment instructions in hope theory improved in subsequent treatments more than those who did not receive such pretreatment preparations (Irving et al., 2004). It should be emphasized that all clients in this study received comparable actual treatments, but the one group that was given pretreatment education in hope theory profited more from their interventions. In yet another hope intervention, Trump (1997) devised a treatment process using a videotape of hopeful narratives of women who had survived childhood incest. Results showed that viewing this tape increased the hope levels of women seeking treatment relative to those who viewed a control tape. Finally, hope has been shown to be a moderating variable between symptoms of depression and negative life events in young adults, such that individuals high in hope have fewer depressive symptoms despite dealing with possibly psychologically injurious situations (Visser, Loess, Jeglic, & Hirsch, 2013). Thus, hope may be a valuable component to use in the therapeutic process in many situations.

As shown in Appendix B (p. 404), which is a worksheet for use in implementing hope therapy for adults, the client undergoing the therapy initially is probed for his or her goals in differing life arenas. Next, the client is asked to select a particular life domain on which to work. Over the ensuing sessions, the therapist then helps the client to clarify the goals by making lucid marker points for assessing progress in attaining these goals. Various pathways for reaching the goals are then taught, along with ways to motivate the person to actually use those routes. Impediments to the desired goals are anticipated, and the clients are given instructions in how to institute backup routes to the goals. As reaching different goals is practiced over time, the clients learn how to apply hope therapy naturally in their everyday goal pursuits. The overall purpose is to teach clients how to use hope therapy principles to attain ongoing life goals, especially when they encounter blockages (Cheavens, Feldman, Woodward, & Snyder, 2006).

Secondary Preventions for Racial and Ethnic Minorities

The following comments about psychotherapy for racial and ethnic minority clients should be considered in light of the fact that people of color often seek treatment at a lower rate than White individuals. Members of non-White groups represent roughly 30% of the U.S. population (U.S. Census Board, 2010), but they make up a much smaller percentage of those who seek mental health care services (Jimenez, Cook, Bartels, & Alegría, 2013; Vessey & Howard, 1993). This problem is magnified by the fact that the members of some racial and ethnic minority groups who do enter psychotherapy are more likely than White clients to terminate treatment early (Gray-Little & Kaplan, 2000). Another factor that sometimes comes into play here has to do with the match between therapist and client with regard to race and ethnicity. In some groups, lack of racial match between client and therapist has not been a significant determinant of outcome or early termination of treatment (e.g., African American clients); however, it has adversely affected the number of sessions attended by clients in other racial groups (e.g., White American, Mexican American, and Asian American clients), and it has affected treatment outcomes in some (e.g., Asian American and Mexican American clients; Sue, 1998). Some of this may have to do with linguistic or other differences, but another hypothesis is that we still have some way to go with regard to multicultural competence in understanding folks from different racial groups than our own. Thus, good education in this area for all therapists is a must when trying to broadly enhance the benefits of secondary prevention.

We mention these facts in part to highlight that the system has not always been effective in reaching and helping people of color. Furthermore, so little research has been done with psychotherapy clients who are African American, American Indian, Latino/a, or Asian American that we presently cannot make statements about the best approaches for treatments for these groups. In commenting on the lack of sufficient samples of racial and ethnic minority clients, Gray-Little and Kaplan (2000, p. 608) have written, "Our review has left us feeling like the dinner guest who remarked that the food was disappointing and 'such small portions.'" Whaley and Davis (2007) provide suggestions for increasing cultural competence in evidence-based practice and discuss making cultural adaptations with non-White populations. These authors posit that the move toward *effectiveness* studies (as opposed to the former focus on *efficacy*) may assist cultural adaptations as well. Some researchers state that inclusion of more non-White individuals in the samples of empirical studies regarding effective treatments will address this dearth in the literature, while others argue that adaptations to treatments are necessary for true cultural competence with diverse individuals (Whaley & Davis, 2007). The interested reader may look toward a review conducted by Miranda and colleagues (2005) titled "State of the Science on Psychosocial Interventions for Ethnic Minorities." Obviously, one of the missions of positive psychology should be to understand the reasons for the underutilization of mental health professionals by members of racial and ethnic minority groups, as well as to increase the propensity of minority individuals to seek such services and remain in treatment.

Secondary Preventions for Children

For overviews of secondary preventions for children, check the two Internet sites http://www.state .hi.us/doh/camhd/index.html and http://www.clinicalchildpsychology.org. We now turn to specific positive psychology interventions for children. Previously in this chapter, we discussed the Seligman approach to optimism as it was used in a primary prevention program for depression in

5th and 6th graders (see Jaycox, Reivich, Gillham, & Seligman, 1994). In his 1995 book, *The Optimistic Child,* Martin Seligman shows teachers and parents how to instruct children in attaining the necessary life skills so as to diminish depression. This program also improves self-reliance, school performance, and physical health.

There also have been exploratory intervention programs to raise the hope of children using hope theory as developed by Snyder and colleagues. In these programs, children are taught to set clear goals and to find several workable routes to those goals. The children then are taught to motivate themselves to use the routes to their desired goals. In their book *Hope for the Journey,* Snyder, McDermott, Cook, and Rapoff (2002) use stories to implant hopeful thoughts and behaviors in children. Furthermore, initial programs in grade schools (McDermott et al., 1996) and junior high schools (Lopez, 2000) have used stories to promote modest increases in hope. McNeal (1998) reported that children's hope increased after 6 months of psychotherapy, and Brown and Roberts (2000) found that a 6-week summer camp resulted in significant improvements in children's hope scores (these changes remained after 4 months). (For another overview of hope interventions for children, read *The Great Big Book of Hope* by McDermott and Snyder [2000].)

Secondary Preventions for the Elderly

Depression is the most frequent problem among older persons who come for psychotherapy. As Blazer (1994) puts it, depression is analogous to the common cold in the psychological life of the elderly, though, as noted previously, depression should not be treated as "normal" to the aging process (Madhusoodanan et al., 2010). The most prevalent therapeutic approach with the elderly is the cognitive–behavioral one (Thompson, 1996), although the psychodynamic (Newton, Brauer, Gutmann, & Grunes, 1986); interpersonal (emphasizing communication skills; Klerman, Weissman, Rounsaville, & Chevron, 1984); and reminiscence (Butler, 1974) approaches also have been used effectively. Because the elderly typically confront negative events that are almost inevitable (the lessening of income and health, loss of friends and spouse, etc.), the development of more adaptive views about one's circumstances and self is especially applicable (Gallagher-Thompson et al., 2000). In this approach, it is important to make sure that the elderly client (1) has appropriate expectancies of what will transpire in treatment, (2) can hear and see clearly in the sessions, and (3) has sessions structured to move slowly enough for the needed lessons to be absorbed. Although the usual approach is to conduct such treatment in a one-on-one setting, group formats also can work. In this regard, the psychoeducational approach with older adults will be increasingly important in the future. (For a manual in conducting such a class, see Thompson, Gallagher, and Lovett, 1992). Oyama and colleagues (2010) developed a community-based screening program for elderly in Japan who are at risk for depression and suicide. Aimed at individuals ages 60 and older, and looking at a very large sample, this program showed that a screening program such as this can be helpful at risk reduction in the area of suicide due to untreated depression (Oyama et al., 2010). Gender effects did play a role here, with this program being much more effective for men than women.

A Caveat About Secondary Preventions

Unfortunately, there is a stigma linked to seeing a mental health professional for psychotherapy. Although most people probably do not refrain from seeing other health professionals, such as ophthalmologists or surgeons, they are reticent about seeing a psychiatrist or professional psychologist.

A noteworthy example of this stigma occurred during the 1972 presidential elections when Democratic candidate George McGovern selected Senator Thomas Eagleton as his vice-presidential running mate. When the American public discovered that Senator Eagleton had been treated for clinical depression with electroconvulsive shock therapy, there was a concern that a depressed person would be "a heartbeat away from the presidency" should something happen to McGovern (if he were to be elected president). The stigma associated with the depression eventually led McGovern to remove Eagleton from the ticket.

Another example comes from former first lady Rosalynn Carter (Carter, 1977), who wrote,

> When I was growing up in Plains, GA, I did not hear the words "mental health" or "mental illness." Over the years, I picked up that a neighbor of ours had had a "nervous breakdown," and that another friend was "not quite right" and that a distant cousin was locked up in a state institution where, I assumed, everyone was crazy. I remember vividly when my cousin came home once to visit his family. I suppose I remember the occasion with such clarity because he chased me down the road—and I have never been more terrified. I do not know why I had to get away. . . . As a nation, we are still running away from persons who have had or still have mental and emotional disorders. And the stigma attached to their plight is an undeserved disgrace. . . . In sum, mental illness is still not acceptable in our society. (p. D4)

The media occasionally touches on this issue through television shows such as *The Bob Newhart Show* and *Frasier* or movies such as *Analyze This,* and we laugh at the humor inherent in the behaviors of the quirky psychotherapists in these programs. Such media does nothing to reduce the stigma, however, and it may well feed into the negative stereotypes. Indeed, there is little doubt that this stigma remains in U.S. society because most people still refrain from speaking of their mental health care. The tragedy here is that this stigma prevents many people from seeking needed treatment. Moreover, if people were able to seek treatment in the early phases of their psychological problems, then the likelihood of their having effective treatment outcomes would be improved. As it is, however, people may wait until the psychological problem becomes so severe that it is extremely difficult to intervene effectively. Perhaps positive psychology can work to lessen such prejudicial beliefs by making people think of psychotherapy not only as solving problems, but also as building on one's strengths and talents in order to become more productive and happier. In other words, with the growth of positive psychology, the stigma associated with psychotherapy may lessen because people come to view treatment as involving processes to accentuate their assets.

PRIMARY ENHANCEMENT: "MAKE LIFE GOOD"

Primary enhancement involves the effort to establish optimal functioning and satisfaction. As shown on the left side of Figure 14.3, primary enhancement involves attempts either to increase hedonic well-being by maximizing the pleasurable or to increase eudaemonic well-being by setting and reaching goals (Ryan & Deci, 2001; Waterman, 1993). Whereas hedonic primary enhancements tap indulgence in pleasure and the satisfaction of appetites and needs, eudaemonic primary enhancements emphasize effective functioning and happiness as a desirable result of the goal-pursuit process (Seligman, 2002; Shmotkin, 2005). In this regard, it should be noted that factor-analytic research has supported the distinction between hedonic and eudaemonic human motives (Compton, Smith, Cornish, & Qualls, 1996; Keyes, Shmotkin, & Ryff, 2000).

Before describing the various routes to primary enhancement, some comments are necessary about the role of evolution. In an evolutionary sense, particular activities are biologically predisposed to produce satisfaction (Buss, 2000; Gailliot, 2012; Pinker, 1997). An evolutionary premise is that people experience pleasure under the circumstances favorable to the propagation of the human species (Carr, 2004; Cohn & Fredrickson, 2009). Accordingly, happiness results from close interpersonal ties, especially those that lead to mating and the protection of offspring. Indeed, research shows that happiness stems from (1) a safe and supportive living unit with people who work together, (2) an environment that is fertile and productive of food, (3) the "stretching" of our bodies through exercise, and (4) the pursuit of meaningful goals in one's work (Diener, 2000; Kahneman, Diener, & Schwartz, 1999; Lykken, 1999).

One more caveat is warranted. Many of the experiences placed in the category of primary enhancement also could fit into the category of secondary enhancement, which involves peak experiences. The line between an optimal experience and a peak experience may be very subtle. In addition, experiences and their magnitude and value vary from cultural group to cultural group. Keeping in mind cultural facets such as socioeconomic status, nation of origin, gender, and others is important in understanding these concepts.

Primary Enhancement: Psychological Health

Many people on their deathbeds may think, "I wish I had spent more time with my family." This suggests that *our relationships are crucial for life satisfaction* (as noted in Chapters 1 and 12). Indeed, for most people, interpersonal relationships with lovers, family, and good friends provide the most powerful sources of well-being and life satisfaction (Berscheid & Reis, 1998; Reis & Gable, 2003).

Figure 14.3 Common Components of Successful Psychotherapy: The Agency and Pathways of Hope

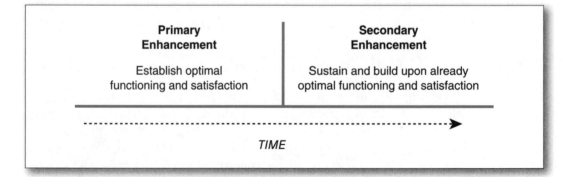

Engaging in shared activities that are enjoyable enhances psychological well-being (Watson, Clark, & Tellegen, 1988), especially if such joint participation entails arousing and novel activities (Aron, Norman, Aron, McKenna, & Heyman, 2000; Tomlinson & Aron, 2013). Likewise, it is beneficial for couples to tackle intrinsically motivated activities in which they can share aspects of their lives and become absorbed in the ongoing flow of their behaviors (Csikszentmihalyi, 1990; Graham, 2008).

Beyond the relationship with one's mate, primary enhancement satisfactions also can come from other relationships, such as those with family and friends. Arranging living circumstances to be within close physical proximity to kin can produce the social supports that are so crucial for happiness. So, too, can the close network of a few friends produce contentment. There are compelling evolutionary arguments (Argyle, 2001) and supportive empirical research (Demir & Davidson, 2012; Diener & Seligman, 2002) as to why such kin and friend relationships are crucial for happiness.

Another relationship that produces happiness is involvement in religion and spiritual matters (Delle Fave, Brdar, Vella-Brodrick, & Wissing, 2013; Myers, 2000; Piedmont, 2004). In part, this may reflect the facts that religiosity and prayer are related to higher hope (Laird, Snyder, Rapoff, & Green, 2004; Snyder, 2004b) and that religious faith and various other religious practices can be predictive of hope and optimism (Ciarrocchi, Dy-Liacco, & Deneke, 2008). Additionally, some of the satisfaction from religion probably stems from the social contacts it provides (Carr, 2004). And it may be particularly beneficial when the religion one practices is thought of as the normative one within a country's national context (Stavrova, Fetchenhauer, & Schlösser, 2013). Happiness also may result from the spirituality stemming from the individual's relationship with a higher power (Saroglou, Buxant, & Tilquin, 2008). On this point, there is accruing scientific evidence of a possible genetic link to human spirituality needs (see Hamer, 2004).

Gainful employment also is an important source of happiness (Argyle, 2001; see also Chapter 15). To the degree to which people are satisfied with their work, they also are happier (there is an overall correlation of .40 between being employed and level of happiness; Diener & Lucas, 1999). The reason for this finding is that, for many people, work provides a social network, and it also allows for the testing of talents and skills. To attain such satisfactions from work, however, it is crucial that a job has considerable variety in the activities undertaken. Moreover, the job duties should match the worker's skills and talents. Furthermore, it helps if there is a supportive boss who fosters autonomy (Warr, 1999) and at the same time enables the individual worker to understand and embrace larger company goals (Hogan & Kaiser, 2005). Some recent research posits that being self-employed may not bring these same benefits, for a number of reasons. In a multicountry study, El Harbi and Grolleau (2012) found that self-employment is significantly and negatively related to happiness within a nation overall. This may, according to these authors, be the result of other characteristics of nations high in self-employment, including an entrepreneurial culture that may lead to increased pressure and frustration.

Leisure activities also can bring pleasure (Argyle, 2001; Hood & Carruthers, 2007). Relaxing, resting, and eating a good meal all have the short-term effect of making people feel better. Recreational activities such as sports, dancing, and listening to music allow people to make enjoyable contacts with others. Although it may seem inconsistent with the term *leisure,* people often are quite active when they participate in recreational activities. Thus, sometimes happiness comes from stimulation and a sense of positive arousal, whereas at other times happiness reflects a quiet, recharging process. Iwasaki (2007) notes that leisure seems to be connected to quality of life overall in both multicultural and cross-cultural contexts; therefore, this is another area that many might pursue in enhancing one's life. In addition, certain types of leisure activities may be more beneficial than others. In a study looking across several nations, activities such as listening to music, attending a sporting or cultural event, getting together with family, and reading books all showed a positive effect on happiness (Wang & Wong, 2013).

Whatever the particular primary enhancement activities may be, those actions that are totally absorbing are the most enjoyable. Csikszentmihalyi and his colleagues (Csikszentmihalyi, 1990; Nakamura & Csikszentmihalyi, 2009) have studied the circumstances that lead to a sense of total engagement. Such activities typically are intrinsically fascinating, and they stretch talents to satisfying levels in which persons lose track of themselves and the passage of time. This type of primary enhancement has been called a flow experience, and artists, surgeons, and other professionals report such flow in their work (see Chapter 10 for further discussion of flow).

Yet another route to attaining a sense of contentment is through here-and-now contemplation of one's external or internal environment. Indeed, a common thread in Eastern thought is that immense pleasure is to be attained through "being" or experiencing. Even in Western societies, meditation upon internal experiences or thoughts has gained many followers (Shapiro, Schwartz, & Santerre, 2002). Meditation has been defined as "a family of techniques which have in common a conscious attempt to focus attention in a nonanalytic way, and an attempt not to dwell on discursive, ruminating thought" (Shapiro, 1980, p. 14). For example, mindfulness meditation (Langer, 2009a) involves a nonjudgmental attention that allows a sense of peacefulness, serenity, and pleasure. Kabat-Zinn (1990) has posed the following seven qualities of mindfulness meditation: nonjudging, acceptance, openness, nonstriving, patience, trust, and letting go (see Chapter 10). Likewise, in what is called *concentrative meditation,* awareness is restricted by focusing on a single thought or object, such as a personal mantra, breath, word (Benson & Proctor, 1984), or even a sound (Carrington, 1998). Interestingly, people who have just engaged in mindfulness mediation or who are experts in this type of meditation appear happier even to others who observe them (Choi, Karremans, & Barendregt, 2012)!

Another process that is meditation-like in its operation is savoring. Savoring involves thoughts or actions that are aimed at appreciating and perhaps amplifying a positive experience of some sort (see Bryant, 2004; Bryant & Veroff, 2006), and it appears to be "an important mechanism through which people derive happiness from positive events" (Jose, Lim, & Bryant, 2012, p. 176). According to Fred Bryant (2005), who is the psychologist who coined this term and produced the major theory and research on it, savoring can take three temporal forms:

1. Anticipation, or the enjoyment of a forthcoming positive event

2. Being in the moment, or thinking and doing things to intensify and perhaps prolong a positive event as it occurs

3. Reminiscing, or looking back at a positive event to rekindle the favorable feelings or thoughts

Furthermore, savoring can take the form of:

- Sharing with others

- Taking "mental photographs" to build one's memory

- Congratulating oneself

- Comparing with what one has felt in other circumstances

- Sharpening senses through concentration

- Becoming absorbed in the moment

- Expressing oneself through behavior (laughing, shouting, pumping one's fist in the air)

- Realizing how fleeting and precious the experience is

- Counting one's blessings

As an example of savoring, consider the comments (taken from his diary) of Bertrand Piccard (1999) as he contemplated the last night of his record-breaking 1999 balloon trip around the world:

> During the last night, I savor once more the intimate relationship we have established with our planet. Shivering in the pilot's seat, I have the feeling I have left the capsule to fly under the stars that have swallowed our balloon. I feel so privileged that I want to enjoy every second of this air world. . . . Very shortly after daybreak, [the balloon] will land in the Egyptian sand . . . [and I will] immediately need to find words to satisfy the public's curiosity. But right now, muffled in my down jacket, I let the cold bite of the night remind me that I have not yet landed, that I am still living one of the most beautiful moments of my life. . . . The only way that I can make this instant last will be to share it with others. (p. 44)

There is yet more that people can do beyond savoring. In this regard, University of North Carolina psychologist Barbara Fredrickson (2001) developed her pioneering broaden-and-build model (see Chapter 6 for a more detailed discussion of the model) after observing that negative emotions such as anger and anxiety tend to constrict a person's thought and action repertoires. That is to say, when feeling negative emotions, people become concerned with protection, and their thoughts and actions become limited to a few narrow options aimed at remaining "safe." On the other hand, Fredrickson proposed that, when experiencing positive emotions, people open up and become flexible in their thinking and behaviors. Thus, positive emotions help to produce a "broaden-and-build" mentality in which there is a positive carousel of subsequent emotions, thoughts, and actions. Therefore, anything a person can do to experience joy, perhaps through play or other activities, can yield psychological benefits.

In her research, Fredrickson (1999, 2001, 2002, 2013) has induced positive emotions by having research participants remember a joyful event, listen to a favorite piece of music, watch a good movie, or receive positive self-referential feedback, to name but few examples. These positive emotional inducements, in turn, make people happier, more perceptive, better at problem solving, more facile in social interactions, more creative, and so on. The broaden-and-build cycle is depicted in Chapter 6, in Figure 6.3 (p. 140). The positive emotions open the person to surrounding circumstances as well as to the important, task-relevant cues in those circumstances. Furthermore, the positive emotions remind the person of other related, successful episodes in his or her life, thereby enhancing the perceived probability of doing well in the present circumstances. Therefore, Fredrickson's broaden-and-build process sets a positive carousel in motion.

Stephen Ilardi

Source: Reprinted with permission of Stephen Ilardi.

Psychologist Steve Ilardi and his colleagues at the University of Kansas have initiated a new treatment for the prevention of depression and the enhancement of personal happiness called the Therapeutic Lifestyle Change (TLC) (Ilardi, 2009; Ilardi & Karwoski, 2005; for more about this program, visit www.psych.ku.edu/tlc). The basic tenet of TLC is that engaging in certain approaches to one's lifestyle, especially those activities that were natural parts of the lives of our ancestors who lived ages ago, brings about a lessening of depression and the enhancement of happiness.

The components of TLC are exercise, omega-3 fatty acid supplements, exposure to light, decreased rumination and worrying, social support, and good sleep. First, 35 minutes of aerobic exercise at least three times a week is recommended. The idea here is to get one's heart rate to 120 to 160 beats per minute. Second, over-the-counter omega-3 fatty acid supplements (fish oils) can be purchased at a drugstore. It appears that our ancestors consumed higher quantities of fish than we do today. Third, try to obtain at least 30 minutes of bright sunlight per day. This can be done naturally by being outside in the sunlight or by sitting next to a special light box that emits very bright light (10,000 lux). Fourth, stop ruminating. Things that work to lessen such worrying include calling a friend, exercising, putting one's negative thoughts in a journal, or engaging in other pleasant activities. Fifth, be sure to stay around other people. This also helps to distract you from rumination. Sixth, get at least 8 hours of sleep per night. Do this by creating a bedtime ritual, and be sure to avoid caffeine and alcohol for several hours before retiring. In summary, TLC appears to be a promising new approach (based upon age-old human actions) that may enhance our happiness and assist in the treatment of depression (Botanov et al., 2012). Also, it should be noted that TLC inherently seems to involve many of the processes already discussed in this section on the primary enhancement of psychological health.

Martin Seligman and his colleagues have undertaken a program of research aimed at finding interventions that are effective as primary enhancements (see Seligman, Steen, Park, & Peterson, 2005). In particular, Seligman recruited 577 adults who visited the Web site of his book *Authentic Happiness* (Seligman, 2002). Most of these people were Caucasian, had some college education, and were between 35 and 54 years old. Fifty-eight percent were women. Before and after undergoing the primary enhancement intervention, each participant took self-report measures of happiness. (Although participants were randomly assigned to several conditions, we focus on one control and three primary enhancement intervention conditions.)

The control comparison condition was a placebo exercise in which the participants wrote for a week about their early memories. Participants assigned to the gratitude intervention were given a week to "deliver a letter of gratitude in person to someone who had been especially kind to them but had never been properly thanked" (Seligman et al., 2005, p. 416). Participants assigned to the condition involving three good things in life were to write for a week about three things that went well each day, noting the underlying causes of each positive thing. Lastly, a group of participants was asked to examine their character strengths in a new way for a week.

Results showed that each of these three primary enhancement interventions had robust positive effects in terms of raising the participants' happiness levels relative to the levels of the participants in the placebo control condition. The gratitude activity produced the largest increases in happiness, but these lasted for only a month. The writing about three good things that had happened and the use of the signature strengths in a new way also made people happier, and these positive changes endured for as long as 6 months.

Taken together, these findings suggest that psychologists can help in the development and implementation of primary enhancement interventions that raise the happiness levels of people. In their closing comments about these pioneering findings, Seligman et al. (2005, p. 421) concluded, "Psychotherapy has long been where you go to talk about your troubles. . . . We suggest that psychotherapy of the future may also be where you go to talk about your strengths."

Before we close this section on primary enhancement in psychological health, the following observation may surprise you: One goal that does not appear to qualify for primary enhancement is the pursuit of personal financial wealth. Beyond providing for life's basic necessities, money does little to raise well-being (Diener & Biswas-Diener, 2002; Diener, Ng, Harter, & Arora, 2010; Myers, 2000; Sengupta et al., 2012). Think about the people you know. Chances are that the ones who are consumed with acquiring wealth probably are not all that happy. Indeed, as we noted in our earlier chapter on the antecedents of happiness (Chapter 6), acquiring great monetary riches is not the royal road to satisfaction in life.

Primary Enhancement: Physical Health

Exercise is a common route for attaining a sense of physical conditioning, fitness, and stamina. An important aspect of physical exercise and fitness is that it gives people greater confidence in their capacities to carry out the activities that form their daily routines. Beyond the physiological improvements that result from exercising, the resulting confidence also enhances happiness and well-being (Biddle, Fox, & Boutcher, 2000). Although short-term exercise raises positive moods, it is long-term exercise that produces greater happiness (Argyle, 2001; Sarafino, 2002). In this sense, exercise could be added to the previous section on primary enhancement and psychological health.

Part of the motivation to exercise may be to look good and to attain an improved physical image (Leary, Tchividjian, & Kraxberger, 1994). Another underlying motive to exercise may be the desire for good physical health. On this point, some people find pleasure in taking vitamins and eating nourishing foods. Our current First Lady, Michelle Obama, has touted the benefits of physical exercise in reducing the risk of obesity for children in particular. As part of her Let's Move program (www.letsmove.gov), Mrs. Obama discusses the social effects of obesity on children; obese children often suffer from social discrimination and stigma, which may lead to lower self-esteem. In this way, good physical health may help both physically and socially.

Regular physical activities produce both psychological and physical benefits. For example, physical activity relates to the following benefits (taken from Mutrie & Faulkner, 2004, p. 148): (1) lessened chance of dying prematurely, (2) diminished probability of dying prematurely from heart disease, (3) reduced risk of developing diabetes, (4) less likelihood of developing high blood pressure, (5) smaller chance of developing colon cancer, (6) weight loss and control, and (7) healthy bones, muscles, and joints.

A Caveat About Primary Enhancement

People should take care in primary enhancements not to overdo these activities. When seduced by the pleasures derived from building strengths, a person may lose a sense of balance in his or her life activities. As with any activity, moderation may be needed.

SECONDARY ENHANCEMENT: "MAKE LIFE THE BEST POSSIBLE"

Compared to primary enhancement, in which the person seeks optimal performance and satisfaction via the pursuit of desired goals, in secondary enhancement the goal is to augment already-positive levels to reach the ultimate in performance and satisfaction (see the right side of Figure 14.3). In a temporal sense, secondary enhancement activities take place after basic levels of performance and satisfaction have been reached in primary enhancement. Again, variation in different cultural contexts or between individuals with different status on various cultural facets (e.g., socioeconomic status) is inevitable.

Secondary Enhancement: Psychological Health

Secondary enhancement of psychological health enables people to maximize their pleasures by building on their preexisting positive mental health. Peak psychological moments often involve important human connections, such as the birth of a child, a wedding, the graduation of a loved one, or perhaps the passionate and companionate love of one's mate.

There are psychological group experiences that are used to help people achieve the extreme pleasures of in-depth relating with others. As early as the 1950s, for example, the training groups, or T-groups, as they were called (Benne, 1964), emphasized how people could gather together to fully experience their positive emotions (Forsyth & Corazzini, 2000). Such groups were sometimes called "sensitivity training" (F. Johnson, 1988).

The existentialist contemplation of the meaning in life is yet another approach to achieving a transcendently gratifying experience. Viktor Frankl (1966, 1992), in considering the question, "What is the nature of meaning?" concluded that the ultimate in experienced life meaning comes from thinking about our goals and purposes. Furthermore, he speculated that the ultimate satisfaction comes from contemplating our purpose during times in which we are suffering. Positive psychology researchers have reported that such meaning in life is linked to very high hope (Feldman & Snyder, 2005). In addition, studies have found that having stability in daily meaning in life appears to be related to higher life satisfaction (both personal and in relationships), more social connectedness, and higher overall positive affect (Steger & Kashdan, 2013). For the reader interested in self-report instruments related to meaning in life, we recommend the Purpose in Life Test (Crumbaugh & Maholick, 1964, 1981); the Life Regard Index (Battista & Almond, 1973); and the Sense of Coherence Scale (Antonovsky & Sagy, 1986).

Sometimes, secondary psychological enhancements occur in contexts where people can compete against each other. These "normal competitions" (see Snyder & Fromkin, 1980) involve engagements in competitive contests. There are rules for these contests, and, over time, one or more people emerge as winners. The high level of pleasure that such winners experience often is described as "pure joy."

Occasionally, the very highest levels of pleasure are derived from involvements that are larger than any one person alone can attain (Snyder & Feldman, 2000). Working together, people can strive for achievements that would be unthinkable for any one individual (see Lerner, 1996). Then, as part of this collective unit, people can experience a sense of meaning and emotions that are of the grandest scale. History is filled with such instances of collective triumph in the face of adversity. Likewise, literature often details the sheer ecstasy experienced by the people who have worked together to overcome difficult and challenging blockages to reach their collective goals. Some psychologists have begun utilizing wilderness coping experiences in which a small group of people learn the supreme joys of cooperating as a group to successfully complete various challenges (e.g., diving, kayaking, rafting, mountain climbing, etc.) in raw, natural settings.

Helping other people can make people feel very good about themselves. Tips for facilitating volunteering among people can be found in the Personal Mini-Experiments section. In our experience, volunteering is one of the most gratifying human activities, and we encourage you to explore the suggestions presented.

Yet another transcending experience involves seeing another person doing something that is so special that it is awe-inspiring or elevating. In such instances, it is as if we have been treated to witnessing the very best that is possible in people, and watching this produces a state of profound wonder and awe (see Haidt, 2000, 2002). Consider an actual example of such an event that was witness by Dr. Snyder, one of the authors of this book. As he stated,

> Here is what happened. I had been having a very bad day. Not only had things gone badly in my work (I had received word that my grant application had been rejected), but I also was feeling lousy physically. I went to lunch with my colleagues in the student union, only to find that they, too, were in foul moods. Suddenly, a young man in a University of Kansas athletic letter jacket ran over to a table across the aisle and administered the Heimlich maneuver to an older man who was choking. The cafeteria immediately grew quiet as people witnessed this heroic act that may have saved the man's life. Once the food was dislodged from the man's throat, the silence was broken as people applauded the young man's act. Looking a bit embarrassed, he smiled and scurried off. I felt a tremendous psychological lift that lasted throughout the rest of that day (and over the next several days). It was one of the most moving events in which I ever have been involved, and my only role was to witness this amazing, selfless action. Without a doubt, to observe such a truly exceptional act can produce a type of secondary enhancement.

Finally, through the arts—such as music, dancing, theatre, and painting— great pleasures are afforded to the masses. The viewing of stellar artistic performances can lift audiences to the highest levels of satisfaction and enjoyment (Snyder & Feldman, 2000). We also encourage older adults to recapture some of the joys and pleasures that came with the exploration and attainment of new skills when they were younger. (See the Personal Mini-Experiment, "Renewing the 'Wonder Years,'" for suggestions for recapturing the amazement of acquiring new skills.)

PERSONAL MINI-EXPERIMENTS

Enhancing Your Daily Life

Throughout this chapter, we make the case that people can make changes that will make their lives better. You can put this thesis to the test by engaging in these three mini-experiments.

Finding Pleasure in Helping Another. Popular responses to the question, "What brings you pleasure?" typically cite engaging in some sort of hedonic activity—watching a good movie, eating a favorite meal, playing a favorite sport or game, or having sex with one's partner. What about helping activities that bring pleasure? Examples of such altruistic actions have included volunteering as an aide at a local hospital, serving as a Big Brother or Big Sister to a grade school student or junior high student, helping an older person with yard work, tutoring a student who is having difficulty in a given subject matter, running an errand for a disabled person, reading to a person who is blind, being an ally for the cause of a disenfranchised group, and taking a child to a sporting event. Certainly both hedonic and helping activities bring personal pleasure. For you, which type of activity brings more pleasure? Engage in one of each kind of activity (hedonic and helping), and then write a paragraph explaining why you think one brought you more pleasure than the other. Think about what it may mean for the way you spend your time. Although most of us may think we know what brings us pleasure, this exercise shows that we may have some lessons to learn from positive psychology.

Stepping Outside of Your Comfort Zone. While at face value this title does not seem as though this exercise would produce positive emotion or pleasure, learning about groups that are different from our own can expand our opportunities for pleasurable social involvement. Knowing more about a wide variety of cultural groups can help us to feel more comfortable in cultivating relationships with a larger social circle. In addition, by having a better understanding of the histories of other groups, all of us can more confidently help groups that have traditionally been marginalized or disenfranchised. Strike up a conversation with someone you view as different from you. Visit a religious service or community different from your own. Read a novel about a group to which you do not belong. Stretch yourself.

Renewing the "Wonder Years." After the teenage years have passed, most adults cease to find new skills. What a shame this is! Do you recall the wonder and excitement that you had as a child when you learned to walk, tie your shoes, count to 10, ride a bike, fly a kite, drive a car, and so on? Perhaps our youth is called "the wonder years" in large part because of the excitement and sense of marvel that attended all the new skills we mastered. But why did this stop around age 20? We do not think it needs to. Indeed, the point of this positive psychology experiment is to help you regain the joys that come with acquiring new skills. Our instructions here are quite simple: *Learn a new skill that you always have wanted to learn.* Chances are you have talents of which you are not fully aware or which you have not used. Cultivating them is one of the most satisfying and rewarding changes you can make in your adult life. So go ahead and recapture the spirit of trying new things that used to be a normal part of your daily experience as a child or adolescent. Take some chances.

Secondary Enhancement: Physical Health

Secondary enhancement of physical health pertains to the peak levels of physical health—levels that are beyond those of well-conditioned people. People who seek secondary enhancement strive for levels of physical conditioning that far surpass those typically obtained by people who simply engage in exercise. Be clear, however, that such persons need not be Olympic-level athletes who compete against other elite athletes with the goal of achieving the very best performance in a sport. While many athletes who pursue the highest levels of competition may see physical fitness as a means of enhancing the probability of winning, people who typify the secondary enhancement of physical health in and of itself are motivated to reach very high levels of physical prowess per se. This superior level of physical fitness mirrors what Dienstbier (1989) has defined as *toughness* and may have implications for decreased stress (Gerber et al., 2013).

Caveats About Secondary Enhancement

As strange as it may sound, people may become almost addicted to the peak experiences that reflect secondary enhancement. There is a natural balancing force, however, in that the mundane activities of life necessitate that people attend to them. This leaves people with only limited amounts of time to pursue primary and secondary enhancements.

We also have a serious concern about the use of personal coaches to help people attain the peak experiences of secondary enhancement. Our concern is that only the wealthy will be able to afford such coaches, which would be antithetical to the spirit of equity that we believe should guide the field of positive psychology. The proliferation of personal positive psychology coaches should occur in such a way that people from all socioeconomic groups can have access to them. As we have said elsewhere, positive psychology should be for the many rather than the few (Snyder & Feldman, 2000).

THE BALANCE OF PREVENTION AND ENHANCEMENT SYSTEMS

In this chapter, we describe the prevention and enhancement intercessions separately. Primary and secondary preventions entail efforts to see that negative outcomes do not happen, whereas primary and secondary enhancements reflect efforts to ensure that positive outcomes will happen. Unchained from their problems via primary and secondary preventions, people then can turn their attentions to primary and secondary enhancements related to reaching optimal, even peak, experiences and life satisfactions (Snyder, Thompson, & Heinze, 2003). Together, preventions and enhancements form a powerful dyad for coping and excelling.

It is noteworthy that prevention and enhancement parallel the two major motives in all of psychology. Namely, prevention mirrors those processes aimed at avoiding harmful outcomes, and enhancement mirrors the processes that focus upon attaining beneficial outcomes. The juxtaposing of the avoidance and approach systems has a long heritage in psychology; it includes the early ideas about defenses in Freud's (1915/1957) psychoanalytic theory, behavioral research (Miller, 1944) and phenomenological research (Lewin, 1951) on the topic of human conflict, and, more recently, health psychology (Carver & Scheier, 1993, 1994).

Although the avoidance system has been portrayed as counterproductive (for review, see Snyder & Pulvers, 2001), these earlier views have ignored the possibility that, via avoidant thinking, people are proactively thinking and behaving to avoid a later bad outcome. Indeed, this latter definition is at the core of the primary and secondary prevention approaches in which obvious benefits do result. Instead of suggesting that avoidance is always "bad," we close this chapter by suggesting that the avoidant and approach processes (or, as they sometimes are called, the aversive and appetitive processes) both act to help people cope. Thus, prevention and enhancement intercessions provide challenges that people must balance in their daily lives.

APPENDIX A: EFFECTIVE SECONDARY PREVENTIONS (PSYCHOTHERAPIES) FOR ADULT PROBLEMS

Problem	Effective Psychotherapy Treatments
Depression	Social skills training to change depression-eliciting environments; cognitive therapy to alter counterproductive thinking; hope training to change goal-directed thinking; interpersonal/marital training to alter depression-maintaining styles of interacting
Bipolar depression	Medication (lithium carbonate), plus cognitive–behavioral therapy aimed at refuting elated or depressive thinking; family intervention to lower stress and to enhance problem solving and communication
Social phobias	Cognitive behavioral therapy that challenges threat orientations, plus practice in pairing social avoidance behaviors with coping skills and relaxation

Problem	Effective Psychotherapy Treatments
Simple phobias	Step-by-step, intensive exposure to fear-inducing stimuli, paired with coping skills and relaxation in the context of behavior therapy
Panic/ Agoraphobia	Cognitive behavioral therapy with slowly increasing exposure to anxiety-eliciting stimuli, plus family support, coping skills/relaxation training, and disputation of threat-inducing thought patterns
Generalized anxiety disorders	Cognitive behavioral therapy with therapeutic support to challenge threat-inducing thought patterns, plus pairing anxiety-eliciting stimuli with skills/relaxation training
Obsessive-compulsive disorders	Behavior therapy with graded exposure to obsession-eliciting cues and pairing of compulsion with coping skills/relaxation, all in the context of family support
Anorexia	Teaching less destructive approaches to assert autonomy; psychodynamic therapy to understand early relationships with caregivers and gain insight into present relationship problems (including with helper)
Bulimia	Cognitive behavioral therapy aimed at teaching self-monitoring and problem solving, understanding the precursors of the binge–purge cycle, and disputing the thinking that guides binging–purging
Post-traumatic stress disorders	Pairing of coping skills/relaxation with graded exposure to stimuli that evoke traumatic memories in the context of behavior therapy
Relationship difficulties	Marital behavioral therapy in which exchange contracts are used, plus skills training in problem solving and communication; couples therapy focused on emotional needs, with special focus on discussing unfulfilled attachment needs and the associated feelings of sadness
Alcohol addiction	Multimodal interventions, with family involvement being important; teaching of self-control in drinking contexts; attendance at Alcoholics Anonymous (AA); stress-management training, perhaps along with social skills training
Insomnia	Sleep restriction, plus graded withdrawal of any medications, relaxation training, and disputing of thought patterns that perpetuate insomnia
Smoking cessation	Cognitive behavioral therapy in which client is given psychoeducation, plus teaching of scheduled smoking, gradual withdrawal, and relapse prevention
Heart disease	Cognitive behavioral therapy, psychoeducation, and family support; dietary counseling, plus physical exercise program and coping/relaxation training
Chronic pain	Cognitive behavioral therapy, relaxation, and guided imagery training; family work to avoid reinforcing invalid thoughts and behaviors; positive reinforcement for more active lifestyle; gradual reduction of pain medication

APPENDIX B: HOPE THERAPY WORKSHEET

Domain	Importance Rating	Satisfaction Rating
Academic		
Family		
Leisure		
Personal growth		
Health/Fitness		
Romantic		
Social relationships		
Spiritual		
Work		

My selected domain is:

What would I have to do to increase my satisfaction in this domain?

What is my goal?

What is my pathway to the goal?

How much do I believe that I can make it? (circle one)

    A little   Medium   Very much

How much energy do I have to accomplish my goal? (circle one)

    A little   Medium   Very much

What makes me think I can attain my goal?

What will slow me down or stop me from reaching my goal?

What is my backup plan?

What are the first three steps to my goal?

    1.
    2.
    3.

KEY TERMS

Eudaemonic primary enhancements: Enhancements that increase well-being through the setting and reaching of goals. These enhancements are the desirable result of the goal-pursuit process, which results in effective functioning and happiness.

Hedonic primary enhancements: Enhancements that increase well-being by maximizing pleasure. This often involves the satisfaction of appetites.

Illusion of uniqueness: The common belief that, in the future, good things will happen to oneself but bad things will happen to other people. This belief is also called *unique invulnerability*.

Meditation: A collection of techniques aimed at focusing the attention in a nonanalytic way that avoids ruminative, rambling, or digressive thought.

Primary enhancements: Enhancements made to establish optimal functioning and satisfaction.

Primary preventions: Actions intended to stop or lessen the likelihood of physical or psychological problems before they appear.

Savoring: Thoughts and actions aimed at appreciating and perhaps amplifying a positive experience.

Secondary enhancements: Enhancements that build upon already-optimal functioning and satisfaction to achieve peak experiences.

Secondary preventions: Actions that lessen, eliminate, or contain problems after they appear.

Selective prevention: Primary prevention focused on a particular at-risk population.

Unique invulnerability: See *Illusion of uniqueness*.

Universal prevention: Primary prevention aimed at an entire community.

PART VII

Positive Environments

CHAPTER 15

Positive Schooling and Good Work

The Psychology of Gainful Employment and the Education That Gets Us There

We spend a large chunk of our time on this earth either in school or at work. Though our values are often set at home, both school and work contribute highly to our understanding of how the world works and what we should be doing in it. In addition, school and work are opportunities for identification of our strengths and our weaknesses. According to Erik Erikson (1959) and his psychosocial stage of Industry versus Inferiority, it is in school that we first start to notice that we are perhaps better than some at reading, or not as good as others at jumping rope. This indexing of strengths and skills continues on to adolescence and adulthood when we might begin to pick an area of study or an occupation defined in part by the strengths we have and the skills we hope to develop. At both school and work, there is potential for further enhancement of strength and skill; there is also, unfortunately, equal chance for stagnation and discouragement depending on the type of environment instilled. In the following, we discuss what components make up a *positive schooling* or *good work* experience.

Positive Schooling

If you can read this, thank a teacher.

—Car bumper sticker

Because schools play a major role in promoting the tenets of positive psychology, we begin with the topic of schooling. *Schooling,* an older word for "education," conveys the importance of the entire community in teaching children. This is why we use the word *schooling* in the title of this chapter. We begin by addressing the unfortunate negative views held by some people about teachers and their work and explore the characteristics of those few truly bad teachers. Next, we describe the support (or lack thereof) for education in America. Thereafter, we devote most of the chapter to an examination of the six components of effective schools. We then summarize the educational application developed by positive psychology pioneer Donald Clifton and take a look at some amazing teachers who exemplify positive teaching. Last, we share ideas about thanking teachers who have made positive differences in the lives of their students.

"TEACHERS CAN'T GET JOBS IN THE REAL WORLD!"

The very existence of this sentiment suggests that teachers are not recognized for their efforts (Buskist, Benson, & Sikorski, 2005). Not only do teachers receive relatively low salaries for professional work, they also are the targets of derisive comments. One day, Dr. Snyder was waiting in line to purchase some stamps at the post office when a gentleman ahead of him complained loudly to his friend about "those lazy professors on the hill." According to Dr. Snyder,

> Being one of "those lazy professors," I kept quiet, just wanting to get the stamps. Then, this same fellow announced for all in the lobby to hear, "Those professors wouldn't be teaching if they were good enough to get real jobs!" He followed that with a doozy: "As we all know, those who can't make it in the real world are the ones who end up teaching!" No longer could I bite my tongue, and a lively exchange ensued. (CRS)

Although there is no merit to "Those who can't, teach" statements (such as "Those who can, do; those who can't, teach" or "Those who can't teach, teach teachers"), it is likely that all of us unfortunately have endured some bad teachers. We also, however, have had some truly wonderful teachers. In this regard, many of the ideas in this chapter come from award-winning teachers who have used positive psychology principles in their classroom efforts (see Snyder, 2005b). These instructors are talented . . . they could succeed in many life arenas beyond the classroom. As such, we dedicate this chapter to "Those who can, teach!"

NEGATIVE PSYCHOLOGY: "THOSE WHO CAN'T, SHOULDN'T BE TEACHING"

We agree that some instructors are so bad that they should not go near classrooms. Such teachers are the ones

> who, when given the honor and the privilege to teach, bore rather than inspire, settle for the lowest common denominator rather than aspire to the highest possible numerator, take the job for granted rather than being continually amazed at the blessing—sins against all the minds they have closed, misinformed and alienated from education. (Zimbardo, 2005, p. 12)

That these bad teachers can do harm is more than sheer speculation; the related research consistently shows that poor teachers have adverse effects on their students (for an overview, see Jennifer King Rice's 2003 book, *Teacher Quality*). In fact, the low quality of teachers has been found to be the most influential of all school-related factors in terms of undermining students' learning and their attitudes about education in general (Rice, 2003). Furthermore, Darling-Hammond and Youngs (2002) reported that indices of teacher achievements and adequate preparation were robust predictors of students' achievements in the areas of mathematics and reading. To concretize the impact of teacher quality, consider the finding that the difference between having had a bad teacher and a good teacher reflects an entire grade level in student achievement (Hanushek, 1994). Overall, therefore, poor teachers leave behind trails of intellectual boredom and disrespect.

Although negative teachers are relatively rare, even one is too many. It would be bad enough if these poor teachers only impaired the learning of their students, but they also may inflict psychological pain and damage. Students tragically may become the unwilling participants in self-fulfilling prophecies in which they fail in both the academic and interpersonal spheres. Thus, as impassioned as we are about seeing to it that positive psychology fills the minds and classrooms of our teachers and their students, so, too, are we adamant about wanting poor teachers identified very early in their careers and either taught to change or shown the door out of the classroom.

Should your own education have included one or more poor teachers, we have prepared an exercise for you. We encourage you to follow the steps outlined in the Personal Mini-Experiments, which may help you to "bury" the bad influences of your previous poor teachers. These teachers did enough damage when you were in their classes; we developed this exercise to lessen the likelihood of any lingering negative effect on your life.

"NO CHILD LEFT BEHIND" AND BEYOND

In a letter to John Adams (anthologized in Barber & Battistoni, 1993, p. 41), Thomas Jefferson shared his vision of changing the ideal at the time of "privilege by inheritance" to a more natural type of aristocracy based on talent. Since those early times, the ideal within the United States has been that public education should make one's life outcomes less dependent upon family status and more dependent on the use of public education. Thus, schools were idealized as making huge differences in the lives of our children.

PERSONAL MINI-EXPERIMENTS

The Power of Positive (and Negative) Teachers

Throughout this chapter, we are reminded of the powerful effects of teachers on our lives. Here, we ask that you consider the effects of a bad teacher and a good teacher on your life.

Letting Go of a Bad Teacher. Think back over your days in grade school, junior high school, high school, college, and perhaps even graduate school. Think about one teacher

(Continued)

(Continued)

in particular who made you deplore going to school, not to mention learning. Take a blank piece of paper and see how much you can remember about this teacher. Write down what she or he looked like, along with the grade and place where you met. Describe how this teacher ran the class. What were the most negative things you can remember this teacher doing? Did this teacher make fun of you in front of the other students? Would this teacher not trust or believe you? Did this teacher make you feel dumb? Did this teacher give you the impression that he or she couldn't care less about you and your success in life?

Once you have written a fairly good summary of this negative teacher, turn the page over and write what you took away from that class and that instructor. Do messages that started in that class still play in your mind today? Do you think certain things about yourself even now because of something that happened with that teacher? When you have answered these questions, then say to yourself, "I am going to bury any influence this teacher had on the way I think." Then, repeat several times, "I am going to stop the bad lessons that [teacher's name] taught me!" Feel free to make any other statements that you want—just as if this old teacher were sitting in a chair across from you.

When you have finished making your statements to this bad teacher, grab a shovel and go outside and dig a hole. That's right, dig a hole! Now, put the shovel down and say good-bye to the bad things you learned from this teacher. Next, take the sheet of paper on which you wrote about this teacher and tear it into many pieces. Then, throw the pieces of paper into the hole and cover it over with dirt. Walk away—don't forget the shovel—and vow to yourself that this lousy teacher never again will influence your life. Finally, buy yourself a treat to celebrate this ritual.

Saying Thank You to a Good Teacher. We again ask that you look back over your school days. But this time, recall those teachers who were superb. They were so good that you actually looked forward to going to their classes. You enjoyed learning from these teachers. Now, take a blank piece of paper and write the name of a good teacher at the top of the page. Then, write everything you can remember about this teacher. Write down what this teacher looked like, the grade and place where you met, and how this teacher ran the class. What were some of the most positive things that you can remember this teacher doing?

Once you have a good summary of this positive teacher, turn the page over and write what you took away from this teacher. Are there any messages that you still play in your mind that were cultivated in that teacher's class? Because of things that happened with that teacher, do you now hold certain positive views of yourself? Perhaps this teacher made you feel smart or clever. Did this teacher make a point to give you credit when you did well? Did this teacher truly care that you succeeded in life? Do you still practice certain positive behaviors that you owe to your interactions with this teacher?

Once you have completed this assignment for one or more teachers, try to find out where they can be reached today. Some still may be teaching. Others probably will be retired. With the advent of e-mail, it has become easier to contact people whom we met earlier in our lives. Now, write a thank-you note to each of these positive teachers. You will feel great for having done this, and we can assure you that the teacher will get a tremendous lift from your message. There is nothing more gratifying to a teacher than to be told that she or he played a positive role in the life of a former student. We often do not take the time to thank the truly important people in our lives for the things they have done on our behalf. Your former teachers will treasure your note all the more if you describe specific instances where they helped you. So, too, will they cherish hearing about the successes and accomplishments in your life.

Unfortunately, this romanticized view of schools in the United States often has been more a dream than a reality. It is ironic that President Lyndon Johnson believed strongly in the power of schools as the "great equalizer" (a phrase popularized by nineteenth-century educational philosopher and leader Horace Mann) of people. Accordingly, he commissioned a huge study, the results of which he (and others) believed would show once and for all that the quality of school resources (e.g., facilities, curricula, books) was responsible for the superior educational outcomes of White Americans, compared to those of people of color. Contrary to these expectations, however, the publication of the Coleman Report (technically called the Equality of Educational Opportunity Report) in 1966 (Coleman et al., 1966) led to the conclusion that "schools do not make much of a difference" in the outcomes of students (see Fritzberg, 2001, 2002). This was an extremely disturbing bottom line for educators as well as President Johnson.

Do the findings of the Coleman Report mean that there is nothing that can be done in the way of schooling to improve the learning of students? Fortunately, the answer is no, and we already have touched upon the factor that does seem to yield better student learning: teacher quality. Before we address what can be done to improve the quality of our teachers, however, we describe the present environment of education in the United States.

With the passage of the No Child Left Behind Act in 2001, the emphasis increasingly has been upon accountability of teachers and school systems for producing targeted learning and performance objectives. For an excellent overview of this approach, we suggest the edited volume *No Child Left Behind? The Politics and Practice of Accountability* by Peterson and West (2003).

As we have noted, research shows that the quality of teachers is crucial to better learning-related outcomes (Rice, 2003). How, then, can we increase the number of qualified teachers in our schools? As with many issues, money appears to play an important role here, with relevant research showing that school districts with higher salaries and better physical facilities are likely to attract and keep the higher-quality teachers (Hanushek, Kain, O'Brien, & Rivkin, 2004; Murnane & Steele, 2007). Murnane and Steele state that "the most urgent problem facing American education . . . is the unequal distribution of high-quality teachers" (p.18) and discuss the trend for children in lower socioeconomic brackets and in non-White groups to more often be the recipients of low-quality teaching. While it must be acknowledged that teaching in schools with fewer resources is difficult at best, this leaves less privileged children at a lifelong disadvantage.

It appears that legislation to increase taxes to pay for schools and teachers is not receiving strong support among U.S. voters. We see two harmful implications of this trend. First, only the most affluent school districts will be able to pay the high salaries necessary to attract the best teachers (thus furthering the gap between socioeconomic statuses in receiving quality education). Obviously, this perpetuates the problem of the lack of outstanding teachers in poor school districts. Second, wealthier families are sending their children to private schools. Accordingly, the public schools are left to get by with lower-quality teachers. This said, President Obama's administration appears to be investing in the teachers in the United States to a greater extent than in years past. For example, the American Jobs Act included a $30 billion fund to avert the layoffs of teachers. As Arne Duncan, U.S. secretary of education, stated in 2011 with regard to teacher education reform and improvement,

> Over the next ten years, 1.6 million teachers will retire, and 1.6 million new teachers will be needed to take their place. This poses both an enormous challenge and an extraordinary opportunity for our education system: if we succeed in recruiting, preparing, and retaining great teaching talent, we can transform public education in this country and finally begin to deliver an excellent education for every child. (U.S. Department of Education, 2011)

THE COMPONENTS OF POSITIVE SCHOOLING

Positive schooling is an approach to education that consists of a foundation of care, trust, and respect for diversity, where teachers develop tailored goals for each student to engender learning and then work with him or her to develop the plans and motivation to reach his or her goals. Before we review the components of this approach, we acknowledge briefly some of the major educators who have paved the way for it. Noted philosophers such as Benjamin Franklin, John Stuart Mill, Herbert Spencer, and John Dewey focused on the assets of students (Lopez, Janowski, & Wells, 2005). Alfred Binet (Binet & Simon, 1916) often is considered the father of the concept of mental age, but he also emphasized the enhancement of student skills rather than paying attention only to the remediation of weaknesses. Likewise, Elizabeth Hurlock (1925) accentuated praise as more influential than criticism as a determinant of students' efforts. Lewis Terman (Terman & Oden, 1947) spent his whole career exploring the thinking of truly brilliant learners, and Arthur Chickering (1969) sought to understand the evolution of students' talents. (See Chapter 13 for a discussion of Chickering's views of college student development.) More recently, Donald Clifton identified and then expanded on the particular talents of students, rather than focusing on their weaknesses (see Buckingham & Clifton, 2001; Clifton & Anderson, 2002; Clifton & Nelson, 1992; Rath & Clifton, 2004).

We next explore the major components of positive schooling (see Buskist et al., 2005; Lopez et al., 2005; Ritschel, 2005). Figure 15.1 is a visual representation of the lessons that are common in positive schooling. This figure shows the positive psychology schoolhouse as being built of six parts, from the ground up. We begin with the foundation, where we describe the importance of care, trust, and diversity. Then, the first and second floors of our positive schoolhouse represent teaching goals, planning, and the motivation of students. The third floor holds hope, and the roof represents the societal contributions and paybacks produced by our positive psychology school graduates.

Care, Trust, and Respect for Diversity

We begin with a foundation that involves caring, trust, and respect for diversity. It is absolutely crucial to have a supportive atmosphere of care and trust because students flourish in such an environment. In attending award ceremonies for outstanding teachers, we have noticed that both the teachers and their students typically comment on the importance of a sense of caring. Students need as role models teachers who consistently are responsive and available. Such teacher care and positive emotions provide the secure base that allows young people to explore and find ways to achieve their own important academic and life goals (Shorey, Snyder, Yang, & Lewin, 2003). In addition, social acceptance by teachers has been found to contribute to overall school satisfaction (Baker, 1998; Gilman, Huebner, & Buckman, 2008), which has been found to be related to more satisfaction with life (Mahoney, Cairns, & Farmer, 2003) and fewer issues related to mental health (Locke & Newcomb, 2004). Better behavior in class is also linked with perceived acceptance from teachers for both boys and girls (Khan, Haynes, & Rohner, 2010).

Trust in the classroom has received considerable attention among educators, and the consensus is that it yields both psychological and performance benefits for students (Bryk & Schneider, 2002; Collins, 2001). Trust is crucial from the earliest grades on up. In their influential 2003 book, *Learning to Trust: Transforming Difficult Elementary Classrooms Through Developmental Discipline,* Marilyn Watson (an educational psychologist) and Laura Ecken (an elementary school teacher) tackle the thorny problem of classroom management and discipline in the elementary schools. Their approach is to establish trusting relationships with the most difficult students, with the logic that this then will have ripple effects that spread to the rest of the class.

Watson and Ecken (2003) advocate what they call developmental discipline. This notion is derived from the principles of attachment theory (see Chapter 12), which advocates helping those students who have insecure attachments to caregivers. Watson and Ecken write that

> the building of caring and trusting relationships becomes the most important goal in the socialization of these children. Of course, while we are building these relationships, we must find nonpunitive ways to prevent the children who are aggressive and controlling from harming others and to encourage self-reliance and confidence in those who are withdrawn and dependent. (p. 12)

For the reader interested in how to establish trust in secondary school classrooms with at-risk students, we also suggest Vicki Phillips' 1998/2011 volume, *Empowering Discipline.*

Instructors must make sure that there is a sense of trust in their classrooms. They must avoid becoming cynical about students because this undermines the trust that is so crucial for learning.

Figure 15.1   The Components of Positive Schooling

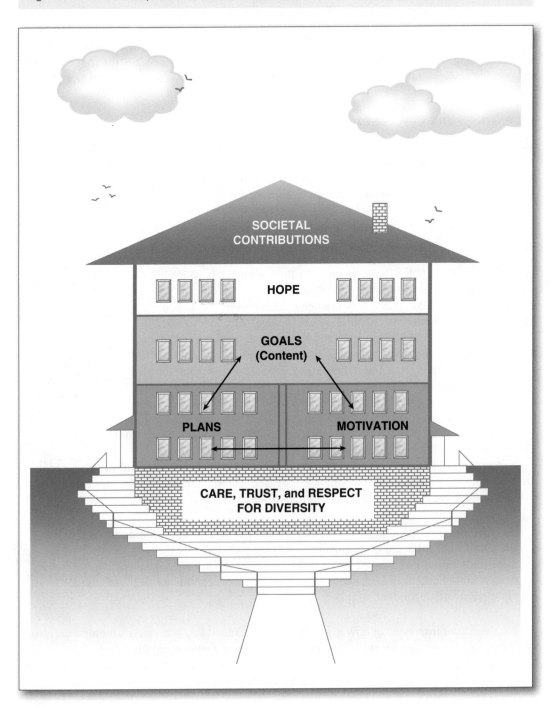

Often, students would rather misbehave (and suffer any punishment) than look dumb in front of their peers. In their interactions with students, therefore, positive teachers try to find ways to make students look good. Unless students sense the teacher's respect, they will not take the risks that are so important for learning. At times, the very best teaching occurs when the instructor is quiet and listens to the views of the students in a class. Award-winning teacher Jeanne Stahl of Morris Brown College has commented, "Silence is the best approach when you are not sure where a student is coming from or heading" (Stahl, 2005, p. 91). In addition, teachers must be willing to step outside their own worldviews and make room for ideas that come from backgrounds different than their own. Remembering cultural context in judging ideas, views, and behaviors, and avoiding invalidation of experiences (especially those related to experiences of discrimination and prejudice) are essential components of providing an environment of trust. In these cases, affirmation and caring can promote a sense of trust within the classroom (Baker, 1998).

Another aspect of the positive psychology foundation for schooling involves the importance of diversity of student backgrounds and worldviews in the classroom. This starts by encouraging students to become sensitive to the ideas of people from racial, ethnic, or age cohorts that are different from their own. This can be accomplished by revealing to students that they have much in common with those who are different from them. At the same time, it is important to emphasize that differences between individuals and groups are not necessarily problematic; there is room for more than one viewpoint, and trying to see things from different vantage points can broaden our minds. Along these lines, it is crucial to make certain that the views of all the different constituencies in a class are given voices in the classroom. Ethnocultural empathy, or the ability to feel for groups outside of our own cultural background, can be established through close contact with others who are different from oneself (see Chapter 11). Teachers who encourage students to be inclusive in their social circles can effectively broaden the cultural experiences of all their students. In addition, teachers can make sure to give voice to groups from all backgrounds. In past years, there has been an attempt to highlight various groups' achievements by devoting different months to each (e.g., February is Black History Month). While there are many benefits to reminding ourselves in these ways to be inclusive, stretching beyond the one-month-per-group approach is likely more effective. By teaching children about the history and accomplishments of all groups we give them the best chance to become culturally competent adolescents and adults. Finally, in sharing positive information about a variety of racial and ethnic groups, we allow children from all groups to take pride in their heritage.

A superb approach for developing a collaborative atmosphere is to implement the "jigsaw classroom," which was designed by University of California–Santa Cruz professor emeritus Elliot Aronson (Aronson & Patnoe, 1997). In this approach, students and teachers use group-based goals and students from different backgrounds are placed in work units where they must share information in order for the group—and therefore each member—to succeed. In the jigsaw classroom, each student has part of the information that is vital to the success of the group as a whole, and thus there is strong motivation to include each student's input. The jigsaw classroom teaches cooperation rather than competition; the related research shows that students learn the content along with respect for their fellow students. The jigsaw classroom also helps keep students from becoming "grade predators" who want to succeed through invidious competitions and social comparisons with each other (Aronson, 2000; Aronson, Blaney, Stephin, Sikes, & Snapp, 1978).

Before leaving this section on diversity, we emphasize how crucial it is to have compensatory programs aimed at students who may have difficulty in learning. We discuss such programs in detail in Chapter 14. One point that is not emphasized in that chapter, and that must be a part of positive psychology schooling, is that we must have programs to stimulate our truly gifted students. Very often, the unfortunate attitude prevails that gifted students already have such tremendous advantages that we should "just leave them alone." We applaud the words of Martin Seligman (1998d), who said that

> it is not just psychology that has neglected gifted and talented children. [Neglect is] found throughout society—even up to the top policy makers in the government. I had a striking encounter with a high official of the U.S. Department of Education at a meeting of the Council of Science Society Presidents recently. He had given a speech on the Clinton administration's uphill, but laudable, policy of attempting to raise the average science and math scores of all American children.
>
> "The future of American science and math depends not only on a scientifically literate citizenry but more crucially on the very talented young people who will become our future scientists and mathematicians," I commented. "What are you doing to help these children?"
>
> "Gifted children take care of themselves," he replied.
>
> This widespread belief is both mistaken and dangerous. It consigns a very large number of gifted children to fall by the wayside in despair and frustration. Intellectual giftedness comes in many guises, and parents, peers, and schools all too often fail to recognize or support high talents—and worse, reject them into mediocrity. This neglect is not benign; it squanders a precious, irreplaceable national resource under the banner of "anti-elitism."
>
> Psychology must take up their cause again. (p. 3)

Having made this point about stimulating our brightest students, we close this section by noting that the foundation of positive psychology schooling rests upon an atmosphere in which teachers and students have respect and care for various points of view and backgrounds. Such respect flows from teachers to students and from students to teachers.

Goals (Content)

The component of goals is represented by the second floor of the strengths schoolhouse (see Figure 15.1). Through exploring the responses of students from kindergarten to college, Stanford University professor Carol Dweck has put together an impressive program of research showing that goals provide a means of targeting students' learning efforts. Moreover, goals are especially helpful if agreed upon by the teacher and students (Dweck, 1999; Locke & Latham, 2002). Perhaps the most conducive targets are the stretch goals, in which the student seeks a slightly more difficult learning

Carol Dweck

Source: Photo by Steve Goldband. Reprinted with permission.

goal than attained previously. Reasonably challenging goals engender productive learning, especially if the goals can be tailored to particular students (or groups of students).

It is important for students to feel some sense of input in regard to their teachers' conduct of classes. Of course, the instructors set the classroom goals, but in doing so they are wise to consider the reactions of their previous students. The success of class goals involves making the materials relevant to students' real-life experiences whenever possible (Snyder & Shorey, 2002). Tailoring to students' experiences makes it more likely that students will become involved in and learn the material (see Dweck, 1999).

It also helps to make the goals understandable and concrete, as well as to take a larger learning goal and divide it into smaller subgoals that can be tackled in stages. Likewise, as we noted with respect to diversity issues in the previous section, goal setting is facilitated when teachers allow part of students' grades to be determined by group activities in which cooperation with other students is essential. Again, Aronson's jigsaw classroom (www.jigsaw.org) paradigm is very useful in setting such goals.

Plans

In Figure 15.1, the first floor of the strengths schoolhouse is divided into plans and motivation, both of which interact with the educational goals on the second floor (and with content). Like building science on accumulating ideas, teaching necessitates a careful planning process on the part of instructors.

One planning approach we will discuss is championed by noted social psychologist Robert Cialdini of Arizona State University (see Cialdini, 2005). Once Professor Cialdini has established a teaching goal regarding given psychological content, he then poses mystery stories for students. Through solving the mystery, the student learns the particular content. The inherent need for closure (see Kruglanski & Webster, 1996) regarding the mysteries also motivates the students; motivation is the companion to planning, which we discuss in the next section. Likewise, because the mystery stories have beginnings, middles, and ends, there is the inherent desire on the part of students to get to the conclusion (see Green, Strange, & Brock [2002] on the drive to traverse a narrative).

Another consideration in raising students' motivations is to make the material relevant to them (Buskist et al., 2005). At the most basic level, when the course information is relevant, students are more likely to attend class, pay attention, and make comments during the lectures (Lowman, 1995; Lutsky, 1999). To increase the relevance of material, instructors can develop classroom demonstrations and at-home exploration (such as the Personal Mini-Experiments and Life Enhancement Strategies in this book) of various phenomena applicable to situations that the students encounter outside the classroom. Some instructors conduct surveys at the beginning of a semester in which they ask students to

Robert Cialdini

Source: Reprinted with permission of Robert Cialdini.

describe positive and negative events that have happened in their lives. Then, the instructor can use the more frequently cited events to construct classroom demonstrations (Snyder, 2004). Or, once the instructor has described a phenomenon, students can be asked to give examples from their own diverse experiences.

Motivation (Plus Enlivening the Course Contents for Students)

Teachers must be enthused about their materials in order to carry out the plans that they have made for their classes (see the interactive arrow between plans and motivation on the first floor of Figure 15.1). Instructors are models of enthusiasm for their students. Therefore, when instructors make lesson goals and plans interesting to themselves, their students easily can pick up on this energy.

Motivated teachers are sensitive to the needs and reactions of their students. Strengths-based instructors also take students' questions very seriously and make every effort to give their best answers. If the teacher does not know the answer to a student question in the moment, he or she should make every effort to find it. When teachers follow through to locate the answer to a question and present it at the next class period, students typically are very appreciative of such responsiveness.

Teachers also raise the motivational level when they take risks and try new approaches in class (Halperin & Desrochers, 2005). When such risk-taking results in a classroom exercise that does not work, the instructor can have a good laugh at himself or herself. Humor raises the energy for the next classroom exercise, along with the effort level of the teacher. A strengths-based teaching motto is, "If you don't laugh at yourself, you have missed the biggest joke of all" (Snyder, 2005a).

Anything an instructor can do to increase students' accountability also can raise their motivation (Halperin & Desrochers, 2005). Relatedly, students who expect to be called upon by their instructors typically are prepared for each class—they read the material and follow the lecture (McDougall & Granby, 1996). We have often found in our own teaching that students will perform at whatever level you expect; this is true if a teacher's expectations are high . . . or low.

Lastly, praise is very motivating. It is best to deliver this privately, however, because an individual student may feel uncomfortable when singled out in front of peers. Public praise also may raise the propensities of students to compete with each other. An office visit or a meeting with the student outside the classroom is a good time to note the student's good work or progress. Furthermore, e-mail is a ready-made vehicle for privately delivering positive feedback that may be motivating. The opportunities for appropriately interacting with and motivating students are many, and positive teachers often try to convey energizing feedback.

Hope

If the previously mentioned lessons regarding goals, planning, and motivation have been applied in a classroom, then there will be a spirit of inquiry that students will pick up on (Ritschel, 2005). As Auburn University award-winning teacher William Buskist and his colleagues (2005) put it,

An essential aspect of our teaching is to pass the torch—to share our academic values, curiosities, and discipline-focused enthusiasm and to encourage students to embrace these values and qualities and to own them. Teaching is not about being dispassionate dispensers of facts and figures. Teaching is about influence. It is about caring deeply about ideas and how those ideas are derived, understood, and expressed. It is about caring deeply for the subject matter and for those students with whom we are sharing it. And it is through such passionate caring that we inspire students. (p. 116)

When students acquire this spirit, their learning expands to increase their sense of empowerment. Thus, students are empowered to become lifelong problem solvers. This "learning how to learn" pulls from goals-directed pathways thinking as well as from the "I can" motivation. Therefore, positive psychology schooling not only imparts the course contents, it also produces a sense of hope in the student learners. (See Chapter 8 for a detailed discussion of hope.) Hope is depicted in the attic of the positive schoolhouse in Figure 15.1. A hopeful student believes that she or he will continue to learn long after stepping out of the classroom. Or perhaps it is more apt to say that hopeful thinking knows no walls or boundaries in the life of a student who never stops learning.

Societal Contributions

A final positive psychology lesson is that students understand that they are part of a larger societal scheme in which they share what they have learned with other people. As shown in the potentially

William Buskist

Source: Reprinted with permission of William Buskist.

nourishing cloud above the metaphorical schoolhouse in Figure 15.1, these societal contributions represent the lasting "paybacks" that educated people give to those around them—whether this means teaching children to think positively or sharing insights and excitement with the multitude of others with whom they come into contact over the course of their lifetimes. Consider this comment from a student involved in one of our (JTP's) diversity-focused courses in college:

By learning more about how to be multiculturally competent myself, I can now share that information with my friends and family. When my friends judge based solely on their own worldviews, I can be the one who says, "Have you thought about it from this perspective?" This makes me feel like I am making a difference as an ally out there in the world!

The feeling of empowerment is obvious in her tone. Positive education thus turns students into teachers who continue to share what they have learned with others and who have an appreciation for diversity in thoughts and ideas. In this way, the benefits of the learning process are passed on to a wide range of other people. In positive schooling, therefore, students become teachers of others. For a stellar example of positive schooling, see Appendix A, which covers the StrengthsQuest Program.

TEACHING AS A CALLING

Just as negative teachers have damaged the process of learning, so, too, have positive teachers unleashed the enthusiasm and joys of education. These teachers in positive schooling see their

Rebecca Mieliwocki

Reprinted with permission of Rebecca Mieliwocki.

efforts as a calling rather than work (Wrzesniewski, McCauley, Rozin, & Schwartz, 1997). A calling is defined as a strong motivation in which a person repeatedly takes a course of action that is intrinsically satisfying (see Buskist, Benson, & Sikorski, 2005). When positive psychology tenets are applied to teaching, we believe that the instructors behave as if they had callings in that they demonstrate a profound and strong love for teaching.

Every year, Council of Chief State School Officers (CCSSO) gives out their National Teacher of the Year Award. Past winners include teachers at all grade levels and from states all over the United States. The 2012 winner of this prestigious award was Rebecca Mieliwocki, a middle school English teacher in Burbank, California. At the end of her speech, Mieliwocki said to all teachers, "You have been born with a gift for teaching and you've been given the gift of working with children. You have a front row seat to the future. You build that future one child at a time." Here we include an article written about this positive example of a teacher with a calling.

2012 National Teacher of the Year: "Great Teachers Lead With Both Their Heads and Their Hearts"

By Celeste Busser

National Education Foundation

Speaking to a crowd of nearly 8,000 fellow educators gathered at the National Education Association's (NEA) Representative Assembly (RA), 2012 National Teacher of the Year Rebecca Mieliwocki delivered captivating, moving and inspirational words about the power teachers have to shape and transform the lives of their students.

An English teacher at Luther Burbank Middle School in Burbank, Calif., Mieliwocki told delegates she is proud to represent teachers. "So here I stand, one teacher symbolizing millions," she said. "One imperfect, enthusiastic, hard-working and committed example of the millions more just like me. One voice to stand for all of us . . . We may have forgotten how important our teachers were in restoring America's public education system but it's not too late to shift our focus to what really matters."

"Rebecca's commitment to reach and motivate each of her students is an inspiration, and I am proud to count her among the millions of NEA members who rise to the occasion each day on behalf of their students," said NEA President Dennis Van Roekel. "As we honor Rebecca today, let's not lose sight of what drives her: a fundamental commitment to her students' success. The key to raising achievement for all students is to ensure that caring, committed and qualified teachers like Rebecca, and there are many of them, are empowered to lead and transform the teaching profession."

"If we want real change, lasting change, if we want back the power, the pride, the soaring achievement that is an exceptional public education, then the revolution begins with us," emphasized Mieliwocki.

Mieliwocki received the prestigious title of National Teacher of the Year for her unconventional teaching practices and her deep commitment to helping students succeed. President Barack Obama honored her and all of the State Teachers of the Year at a White House ceremony in April.

"You have been born with a gift for teaching and you've been given the gift of working with children. You have a front row seat to the future. You build that future one child at a time," concluded Mieliwocki.

Mieliwocki has been teaching for 14 years and has spent nine years in her current position. She holds a Bachelor of Arts in Speech Communication from California Polytechnic State University and her professional clear credential in Secondary English Education from California State University Northridge. She is the 2005 California League of Middle Schools Educator of the Year for Southern California, a 2009 PTA Honorary Service Award Winner and a Beginning Teacher Support and Assessment mentor.

Source: Busser, C., 2012 National teacher of the year: "Great teachers lead with both their hearts and their heads," National Association Education. Retrieved from http://www.nea.org/grants/52482.htm

For all master teachers, their calling represents a perceived privilege: the chance to make a positive difference in the lives of students (Buskist et al., 2005). The student and teacher together undertake an amazing journey. This journey is illustrated in Figure 15.2.

GIVING BACK TO TEACHERS

Our final observations about positive schooling pertain to the role that you can play in making teachers better. You can do several things to help teachers in particular and the school system in general. First, you can work with teachers to help in whatever ways possible to improve your own children's learning. Learning obviously happens outside of school hours as well, and we encourage you to try various activities with the children in your life to reinforce and practice the ongoing lessons taught at school.

Teach your children to be respectful of others' viewpoints and to appreciate differences as well as similarities between themselves and others. Help them to realize that their viewpoint is not the only one. Likewise, if you are able, volunteer to help with various school activities. Your children and their friends and classmates will be impressed by the fact that learning is not something about which only their teachers care.

You also can visit with the teachers in your local elementary, junior high, and high schools and ask them what they need to make their teaching more effective. If new computers or other school

Figure 15.2 The Parallels of Books and Teachers

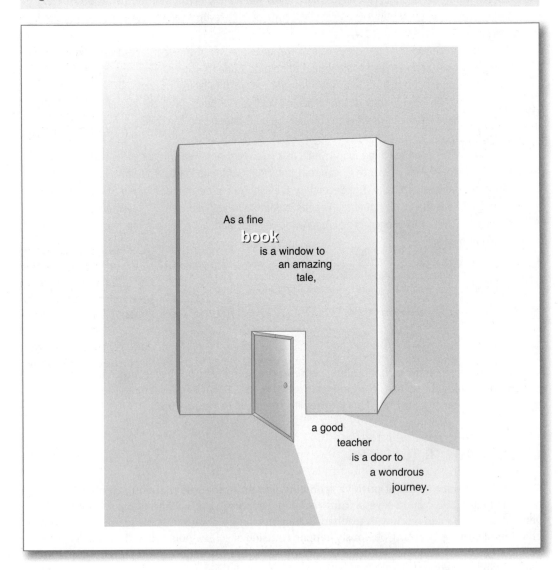

As a fine
book
is a window to
an amazing
tale,

a good
teacher
is a door to
a wondrous
journey.

supplies are needed, perhaps a bake sale or car wash held by parents and community members could raise the necessary money. See what other supplies the teachers may need for their classrooms. Maybe your old books could be donated to the school library. Do what you can to see that needed items or services are obtained. Ask that teachers be multiculturally competent in their teaching. If you have expertise in this area, share it with your local schools. If you have special skills in other areas, volunteer to come into class and give demonstrations to students. You may want to become politically active to increase local school taxes in order to raise teacher pay and benefits or build new classrooms. You can be part of the positive psychology solution to making the schools better in your community.

In a similar spirit, we ask that you close this chapter with an exercise aimed at saying thank you to those special teachers in your local community. Please try "Saying Thank You to a Good Teacher" (in the Personal Mini-Experiments). This "payback" takes very little time, but it would be tremendously meaningful to the teacher(s) whom you remember. Don't forget that these teachers were there for you at many crucial points in your life, so take some time now and reach out to them. It does not matter whether they are retired or not, because a thank you at any time is greatly appreciated by your former teachers.

GAINFUL EMPLOYMENT

It was Sigmund Freud who first made the bold statement that a healthy life is one in which a person has the ability to love and to work (O'Brien, 2003). In the many decades since Freud presented these ideas, the psychological literature has reinforced the importance of positive interpersonal relationships and employment. After reviewing the growing body of literature on the role of one's job in producing a healthy life, we searched for a phrase that captured the essence of the many benefits that can flow from work. In the end, we decided to use the phrase gainful employment.

Although many people awaken only to dread getting up and going to work, gainfully employed people actually look forward to it. Gainful employment is work that is characterized by the following nine benefits:

1. Variety in duties performed

2. A safe working environment

3. Income for the family and oneself

4. A purpose derived from providing a product or service

5. Happiness and satisfaction

6. Positive engagement and involvement

7. A sense of performing well and meeting goals

8. The companionship of and loyalty to coworkers, bosses, and companies

9. A working environment that respects and appreciates diversity

In this remainder of this chapter, we explore the growing body of positive psychology findings related to work and look at gainful employment from the perspectives of the employee, the boss, and the company.

GAINFUL EMPLOYMENT: HAPPINESS, SATISFACTION, AND BEYOND

As shown in Figure 15.3, nine benefits are derived from gainful employment. We place happiness and satisfaction at the center because of their key role (see Amick et al., 2002; Burnette & Pollack, 2013; Keller & Semmer, 2013; Kelloway & Barling, 1991). As Jane Henry (2004) describes it,

> The centrality of work to well-being is not surprising when you think of the number of benefits it offers, notably: an identity, opportunities for social interaction and support, purpose, time filling, engaging challenges, and possibilities for status apart from the provision of income. (p. 270)

Not surprisingly, the literature on job satisfaction is huge. Consider, for example, Locke's estimate, made in 1976, that more than 3,300 articles had been published on job satisfaction. Further, a PsycINFO search of the years 1976 though 2000 yielded 7,855 articles on job satisfaction (Harter, Schmidt, & Hayes, 2002).

If a person is happy at work, chances are that his or her overall satisfaction with life will be higher (Hart, 1999; Judge & Watanabe, 1993). The correlation of job satisfaction with overall happiness is about .40 (Diener & Lucas, 1999). Employed people consistently report being happier than their counterparts without jobs (Argyle, 2001; Warr, 1999).

Why should work, happiness, and satisfaction go hand in hand? In the next sections, we explore the various work factors that appear to be linked to greater happiness. Although we acknowledge the strong role that happiness and satisfaction play in overall gainful employment, we hasten to add that there often is a reciprocal relationship in that factors may influence each other to produce a sense of gainful employment. For example, as we explain in the next section, performing well at work heightens the sense of satisfaction. But so, too, does the sense of satisfaction contribute to an employee's better performance in the work arena.

Performing Well and Meeting Goals

How often has someone commented to you, "You are really grumpy. Did you have a bad day at work?" Or it can go the other way: "Wow, you are in a great mood. Did things go well at the office?" Without question, perhaps particularly in the career-focused culture of the United States, what happens at work spills over into various other aspects of our lives.

One school of thought about the happy worker is that such an employee has a sense of effectiveness and efficiency in performing his or her work activities (Herzberg, 1966). To test the notion that performance on the job relates to satisfaction, Judge, Thoresen, Bono, and Patton (2001) performed a meta-analysis (a statistical procedure for testing the robustness of results across many studies) of 300 samples (about 55,000 workers). They found a reliable relationship of approximately .30 between performance and general satisfaction.

By far the most research related to the sense of performing well has emerged from Bandura's influential self-efficacy construct (see Chapter 8 for a review of the role of self-efficacy in promoting work happiness). Career self-efficacy, which is defined as the personal confidence in one's capacity to handle career development and work-related goal activities, has been significantly

Figure 15.3 Nine Characteristics of Gainful Employment

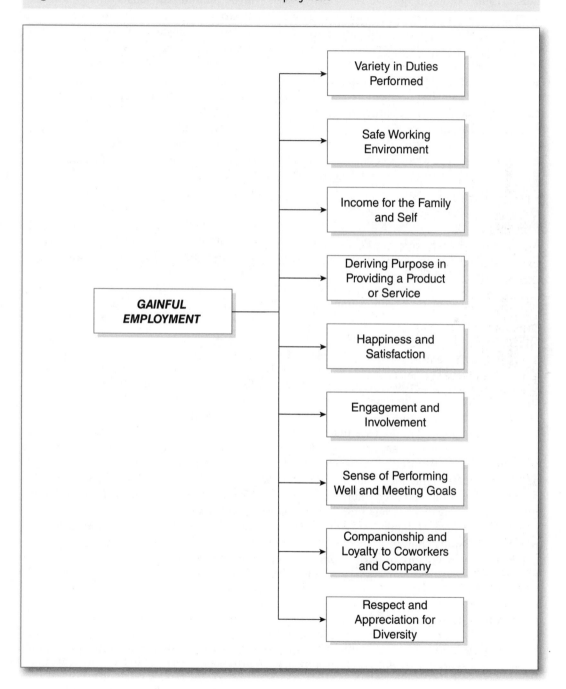

related to both success and satisfaction with one's occupational efforts and decisions (Betz & Luzzo, 1996; Donnay & Borgen, 1999). Self-efficacy can be built in individuals through a variety of means. Student athletes who had more support from various academic services felt more confident in making decisions about possible career choices (Burns, Jasinski, Dunn, & Fletcher, 2013). Other investigations have shown that students who have family members that contribute meaningfully (both financially and in terms of advice and help) to the career decision-making process develop higher levels of self-efficacy in the career arena (Metheny & McWhirter, 2013). Finally, career self-efficacy has been studied in several different racial and ethnic groups. We now know that level of acculturation may positively affect development of feelings of self-efficacy with regard to career in Latino youth (Ojeda et al., 2012). For Asian Americans and African Americans, programs designed to increase career self-efficacy were successful when they contained constructivist approaches—i.e., when participants were able to make personal meaning out of various factors that influenced career choice and decisions (Grier-Reed & Ganuza, 2011).

Performing well at work is more likely to occur when workers have clear goals. As shown in relevant literature (e.g., Emmons, 1992; Snyder, 2000), lucid goals offer satisfaction when they are met. Accordingly, when work goals are clearly delineated and employees can meet established standards, heightened personal pleasure and a sense of accomplishment result. In this regard, the high-hope leader's clear goal setting and facile communication provide lucid short- and long-term objectives for the work group. A high-hope boss also can provide greater satisfaction at work. This sequence unfolds this way: The high-hope boss clearly identifies achievable work subgoals, which in turn increases workers' motivation and the chances of reaching larger organizational goals (Snyder & Shorey, 2004). In this process, the hopeful leader also facilitates workers' willingness to embrace the company's overall objectives (Hogan & Kaiser, 2005).

Most research in this area has investigated the links between happiness and successful work performance by looking at success as the predictor and the happiness of the individual as the result (i.e., good work performance leads to a happier life). Boehm and Lyubomirsky (2008) investigated this relationship in the other direction, asking instead if happy people might have more career success overall. After reviewing a number of different studies in this area of research, they concluded that it is often the case that happiness is a precursor to career success. According to this review, happy people are often regarded as stronger performers by others in the workplace (Cropanzano & Wright, 1999). Further, Boehm and Lyubomirsky cite studies such as that by Burger and Caldwell (2000) that found happy individuals were more likely to receive a second interview for a job when compared to counterparts who were less happy. Happiness may also be a positive motivator for individuals striving for various career-related goals (Haase, Poulin, & Heckhausen, 2012). Boehm and Lyubomirsky also reported on a study by Roberts, Caspi, and Moffitt (2003). The results of this study showed a trend for those who scored higher on well-being measures in late adolescence as having more positive work outcomes in early adulthood. Thus, the relationship between happiness and performance may be bidirectional.

Deriving Purpose by Providing a Product or Service

One's work is an important potential source of purpose in life. A major underlying force that drives such purpose is the sense of providing needed products or services to customers. Workers want, sometimes in very small ways, to feel that they are making a contribution to other people and to their society.

Although we talk about her important research later in this chapter, we note here that Amy Wrzesniewski and her colleagues (e.g., Wrzesniewski, McCauley, Rozin, & Schwartz, 1997) have described how workers, from the very highest organizational status to the lowest, can perceive their work as a calling (a vocation to which the employee brings a passion—a commitment to the work for its own sake).

Engagement and Involvement

Engagement is the employee's involvement with his or her work, whereas satisfaction is what we might call employee enthusiasm at work (Harter et al., 2002). Engagement is said to occur when employees find that their needs are being met. Specifically, engagement reflects those circumstances in which employees "know what is expected of them, have what they need to do their work, have opportunities to feel something significant with coworkers whom they trust, and have chances to improve and develop" (Harter et al., 2002, p. 269). Similarly, Warr (1999) has reported that the most engaging jobs are those with special duties and in which there is a good match between the required activities and the skills and personalities of the employees. For example, in a meta-analysis of roughly 300,000 employees in more than 50 companies, responding positively to the engagement item, "I have the opportunity to do what I do best" was related reliably to work productivity and success (Harter & Schmidt, 2002). Furthermore, in their overall analyses, Harter and his colleagues (2002) found a reliable correlation of .37 between employee performance and several items measuring engagement at work.

Engaged involvement at work bears a resemblance to the concept of flow, which entails any circumstances in which a person's skills facilitate success at challenging tasks (Csikszentmihalyi, 1990; Csikszentmihalyi & Csikszentmihalyi, 1988; Nakamura & Csikszentmihalyi, 2009; see Chapter 10). In the flow state, the worker can become so engrossed and involved with the work tasks that she or he loses track of time. What is especially important for our present discussion is that these flow experiences are more likely to happen at work than during leisure activities or relaxation at home (Haworth, 1997). In addition, it appears that flow and job satisfaction are strongly related (Maeran & Cangiano, 2013). (This does not imply, however, that flow cannot happen in arenas outside of work, because research shows that it can [Delle Fave, 2001].) Recent research shows that engagement is a necessary ingredient of a successful work experience. Targeting individuals that are low in engagement may be a very effective way of increasing positive feelings about work and self-efficacy for various work-related tasks (Ouweneel, Le Blanc, & Schaufeli, 2013).

Related to the concepts of engagement and satisfaction is the concept of commitment to a particular work organization of which one is a member. Herrbach (2006) found that individuals who experienced more positive affect at work were more likely to experience a higher level of affective commitment (i.e., "A favorable evaluation of one's work environment" p. 633) in their respective organizations. This relationship was found to exist over and above the influence of a tendency to experience more positive affect overall; the positive affect at work appeared to be the active component in this relationship (Herrbach, 2006).

Variety in Job Duties

If the tasks performed at work are sufficiently varied, satisfactions come more easily. Indeed, boredom at work can cast a pall. People should maintain as much variety and stimulation as possible in their work activities (Hackman & Oldham, 1980). One fairly common practice for maintaining variety in workers' duties in industrial and technological job settings is *cell manufacturing*. In cell manufacturing, groups of multiskilled workers take responsibility for an entire sequence in the production process (Henry, 2004). These work teams then put their identifying insignia on the product or portion of the product. Cell manufacturing has been used with some success in the construction of automobiles by work teams. (There have been concerns about this approach costing more, however, which has lessened its popularity among some companies).

Lacking variability in work, the employee may lapse into what recently has been called *presenteeism* (in contrast to *absenteeism*). In presenteeism, the employee may physically be at work, but because of the mental health problems that often result from aversive and repetitive work experiences, he or she is unproductive and unhappy (as reported by Dittmann [2005] in citing the views of Daniel Conti, the employee assistance director of J. P. Morgan Chase). Faced with repetitious and tedious tasks and inflexible schedules, employees can become demoralized and lose their motivation. Others discuss presenteeism as resulting from having too many tasks and not enough time or resources to complete them (Merrill et al., 2012). Presenteeism may look different across cultures (Garczynski, Waldrop, Rupprecht, & Grawitch, 2013; Lu, Lin, & Cooper, 2013). In recent times, large organizations have made efforts to accommodate various working styles, encourage telecommuting, and make room for flexing of schedules for individuals with families. These efforts are in place to decrease the presenteeism that may occur when one is required to be present physically every day (Gosselin, Lemyre, & Corneil, 2013). Presenteeism is also something to think about with regard to what we ask our students to do in university settings. Some research shows that this phenomenon can occur in this venue as well (Matsushita et al., 2011).

When seeking a new job, it may be advisable to take a position that offers great variety but lower pay instead of a higher-paying position that involves unchangeable, repetitive activities. The old maxim that "variety is the spice of life" is nowhere more applicable than in work settings.

Income for Family and Self

Without question, a minimum income is necessary to provide for the needs of one's family and oneself. As discussed in Chapter 6, however, money is overrated as a source of happiness. Indeed, two survey studies show that people seem to understand that happiness and meaning in life are not related in any major degree to the amount of money they make (King & Napa, 1998).

Whether this "rational" approach to monetary rewards and work is actually practiced, however, remains questionable (King, Eells, & Burton, 2004). For example, making money has been rated as more important than having a cohesive philosophy of life (Myers, 1992, 2000). Additionally, though interpersonal relationships have been valued above work (Twenge & King, 2003), people in the United States still may think of quality of life in terms of how much money they make. The present generation of workers in the United States is spending more time on the job than their parents did (Schor, 1991). Furthermore, when making important life decisions, people are most likely to cite financial reasons (Miller, 1999). It seems as if we are of two minds about acquiring monetary wealth, and this ambivalence is played out in our work.

In past years, many families adhered to a traditional breadwinner–caregiver model aligned along traditional gender roles. Thus, often women were the ones charged with maintaining relationships, home, and children. Today, women make up approximately 47% of the labor force in the United States (U.S. Bureau of Labor Statistics, 2012). In addition, 55.8% of mothers with children under the age of 1 were in the labor force according to data from 2011 (U.S. Bureau of Labor Statistics, 2012). As more and more women enter the workplace at higher levels and salaries than ever before, the balance has changed. Today, both genders in opposite-sex partners are faced with making decisions about how to best preserve important partner and family relationships (Mundy, 2012: Perrone, Wright, & Jackson, 2009). Some of these ideas are being modeled to their children, who watch them carry out the day-to-day balancing act of work and home. Daughters in families who have mothers with less traditional and more prestigious careers gain more ideas about how to balance family and work early on in their developmental trajectory (Fulcher & Coyle, 2011). These young girls show more flexible attitudes about how this balance may occur in family life, thus benefitting from the modeling they observed at home (Fulcher & Coyle, 2011). It will be important for us to advantage our sons with these same flexible attitudes in the future if we are to maximize the preservation of relationships of any kind while still maintaining a sense of self-efficacy about these important life roles.

One promising trend in this area is the development of the Positive Parenting Program (Triple P). This program consists of small group sessions in which parents learn how to balance family life with the pursuit of money through work (Dittmann, 2005). Australian psychologist Matthew Sanders (Sanders, Markie-Dadds, & Turner, 2003; Sanders, Mazzucchelli, & Studman, 2004; Sanders & Turner, 2005) originated Triple P, and his intention was to lessen the negative effects of parents' long work hours on their children. Workers must make sure that the pursuit of money does not undermine important family pleasures and obligations. Indeed, if both parents work furiously to make money and do not attend to their offspring, the unfortunate result may be that their children end up behaving in the very same way when they grow up and have children. The irony here is that the same work that is meant to provide the financial resources to raise a family may grow like a cancer and cause problems in the family it is intended to support.

Companionship and Loyalty to Coworkers and Bosses: Friends at Work

Another reason that work may be associated with happiness is seen in the case of people whose friendship networks are located entirely within the employment setting. Work offers people a chance to get out of the house and interact with others. Because workers may share experiences such as encountering obstacles and celebrating triumphs in the work setting, there are reasons for them to form bonds with each other.

For the last 30 years or so, corporate America has discouraged the development of friendships at work. This practice was based on the assumption that socializing among coworkers, especially fraternizing between a worker and a manager, would lead to poor productivity. This assumption was not examined by systematic research until Tom Rath and colleagues at Gallup developed the Vital Friends Assessment and surveyed 1,009 people about the effects of friendships on their happiness, satisfaction, and productivity (Rath, 2006). The work of the Gallup researchers, presented in the book *Vital Friends,* confirmed that the sense of community at a given workplace is a contributing factor to happiness and satisfaction on the job (Mahan, Garrard, Lewis, & Newbrough, 2002; Royal & Rossi, 1996). Furthermore, Rath found that if you have a best friend at work you are likely to have fewer accidents, increased safety, more engaged customers, and increased achievement and productivity. These findings are attributable to the fact that people with a best friend at work are seven times more likely to be psychologically and physically engaged on the job (Rath, 2006).

Safe Work Environments

Part of happiness at work is a safe and healthy physical environment where it is obvious that management cares about the welfare of workers. In the previously discussed meta-analytic report by Harter et al. (2002), perceived safety of the workplace was one of the most robust predictors of employee satisfaction.

Are there reasons to be concerned about work and actual physical health? The answer to this question is a resounding yes. Many physical injuries occur at work; moreover, there are high-risk professions where serious accidents are quite prevalent. Keeping workers physically safe and injury free leads to better physical health in other areas of life (Hofmann & Tetrick, 2003; Tetrick & Pieró, 2012). We do not leave the pain and suffering of a workplace-induced physical impediment at the door of the factory at quitting time.

Respect and Appreciation for Diversity in the Workplace

As racial and ethnic diversity continues to increase in the workplace, a discussion of the relationship between the presence of this diversity and other factors (e.g., job performance, workplace climate, job satisfaction, etc.) becomes necessary. The concept of "diversity management" (Thomas, 1990, p. 107) is described as using various management techniques that increase the positive outcomes associated with having more diversity in the workplace. Pitts (2009) conducted a study in which results showed that proper use of diversity management was predictive of better group performance in the workplace and higher levels of job satisfaction for all employees (though particularly for people of color). In addition, Cunningham (2009) found in measuring responses from 75 NCAA athletic departments across the United States that racial diversity and overall performance were positively associated. This study found that the relationship was stronger in athletic departments that used "proactive diversity management" strategies (p. 1448). These strategies include viewing diversity as a broad and multifaceted concept, keeping communications lines open, and making sure that diversity is emphasized as a part of mission statements and organizational goals. In addition, organizations that use this type of management are proactive in attempting to address potential problems. Finally, making sure that leaders are heterogeneous in their cultural backgrounds ensures that responsibility for important decisions is spread across a number of different types of individuals (Cunningham, 2009). Other, more recent research has found diversity management to be beneficial across countries, as measured by studies on samples from the United States (see Madera, 2013; Wyatt-Nichol & Antwi-Boasiako, 2012); the United Kingdom (Tatli, 2011); Australia (Fenwick, Costa, Sohal, & D'Netto, 2011); and others (Lauring, 2013). Strategies such as these are vital to increasing a positive work experience for all groups, especially as diversity continues to increase in the workplace.

At the recent Asian Pacific Conference on Applied Positive Psychology held at the City University of Hong Kong, a presentation was offered by Rainbow Cheung, the general manager of Employee Development Service of Hong Kong Christian Service and Four Dimensions Consulting, Ltd. Ms. Cheung and her colleagues developed a survey entitled the Positive Organizational Index that is designed to measure the level of use of good practices in an organization that lead to a more positive experience for their employees (please see Appendix B for a detailed description of this index and its uses). As an example of an organization that scored high in this area, Ms. Cheung noted the Hong Kong–based company, Richform Holdings, Ltd. The CEO of this organization, Dr. Jimmy Lau Fu-Shing, stated in Richform's promotional materials, "We are not a charity—we are a small company and we have to make profits. But we have found that [using positive organizational strategies] can be competitive and advantageous." At Richform, employees (or associates, as they are called) enjoy longer lunch breaks; paternity leave; access to free, healthy snacks; and various self-care perks such as Chinese medicine consultations. In addition, Richform provides a "parents gratitude" allowance, which is offered in response to the cultural expectations in China that grown children will take care of their aging parents. This particular allowance provides extra salary when an employee's parent reaches the age of 65 (R. Cheung, January 9, 2014, personal communication). The results of the efforts made at Richform are obvious in employees' satisfaction with their positions. As Dr. Lau noted, "What is the single best thing done as a company? We have differentiated our company by caring for stakeholders." These stakeholders—their employees—appear more than grateful for these benefits, which is shown partially in very low turnover in staff and a very high level of employee satisfaction (Cheung, 2014).

In summary, the good news is that several factors in the work setting can contribute to a greater sense of happiness and satisfaction in particular and to gainful employment in general. Equally important is the fact that unhappiness with one's work is not inevitable; we expand on this theme in the remainder of this chapter. Caring about employees and their families can be mutually beneficial for workers and the companies with which they are affiliated. Please see Appendix B for an initiative that is currently ongoing in Hong Kong. Through use of their new Positive Organization Index, they are making changes in companies to ensure a more positive experience at work.

HAVING OR BEING A GOOD BOSS

The boss is a crucial resource in helping employees to have productive and satisfying job experiences. Notice that we include being a good boss in our section heading; we do so because many readers will find themselves in the role of boss at some point in their careers—if they are not already there. Supervisors who provide clear job definitions and duties and support to employees foster job satisfaction and production (Warr, 1999). Managers and leaders who are focused on employees' strengths (Buckingham & Clifton, 2001); good at communicating the company goals; and facile at giving feedback contribute to employees' positive experiences. High-hope bosses also enjoy their social interactions with employees; moreover, they often take an active interest in how employees are doing, both at work and outside it (Snyder & Shorey, 2004). In addition, bosses who implement the leadership strategies discussed previously regarding proactive diversity management can increase positive experiences for their employees across racial and ethnic groups (Cunningham, 2009; Madera, 2013).

Bruce J. Avolio

Source: Reprinted with permission of Bruce J. Avolio.

It also is helpful for a boss to be genuine and authentic in inter-actions with employees (Avolio, Luthans, & Walumbwa, 2004; Gardner & Schermerhorn, 2004; George 2003; Luthans & Avolio, 2003). But what, exactly, is authenticity? An **authentic boss** fosters trust and positive emotions, high engagement, and motivation to reach shared goals among employees. Authentic leaders hold deep personal values and convictions that guide their behaviors. In turn, their employees respect and trust them, and these positive views are reinforced as the authentic boss encourages differing views and interacts collaboratively with workers. Thus, authentic bosses value diversity in their employees and want to identify and build on employee talents and strengths (Luthans & Avolio, 2003). The authentic boss sets high standards for his or her own behavior and models integrity and honesty to employees. Through such mode-ling, the authentic work leader is able to establish a sense of employee teamwork. So, too, does the authentic boss set clear goals and foster employee hope (Snyder & Shorey, 2004). As noted previously, a good boss also encourages workers to be team players (Hogan & Kaiser, 2005). In summary, authenticity in bosses appears to be associated with gainful employment and a variety of positive outcomes in the workplace.

In our consultation work with various organizations over the years, we have observed these "top 10" characteristics common to the very best bosses:

- They provide clear goals and job duties to employees.

- They have personal awareness of biases and power differentials and strive toward cultural competency.

- They are genuine and authentic in their interactions with everyone.

- They are ethical and demonstrate moral values in their interactions with people.

- They are honest and model integrity.

- They find employee talents and strengths and build on them.

- They trust workers and facilitate their employees' trust in them.

- They encourage diverse views from diverse employees and can take feedback about themselves.

- They set high but reasonable standards for employees and for themselves.

- They are not just friends to employees but can deliver corrective feedback so that it is heard.

What is intriguing about these qualities is the degree to which the employees seem to agree that they are important to them, too. Employees attribute this consistency of views to the fact that they talk among themselves about what they like and do not like in their superiors. Furthermore, when a boss has these characteristics, this appears to play a huge role in employees' productivity and happiness at work.

Productivity, satisfaction, and sense of engagement all seem to go together in a positive workplace. Without a doubt, the boss plays a crucial role in making such positive outcomes happen. Think about these characteristics of a good boss and then apply them to your work setting. Do these qualities apply to your supervisors? Do you think that you yourself have many of these qualities? Although you may not be a boss right now, whether or not you possess these "top 10" characteristics may determine if you become one and if you succeed in this role.

THE STRENGTHS-BASED APPROACH TO WORK

In this section, we describe and explore a bold, trend-setting approach for matching employee duties to their strengths and talents that has been spearheaded at Gallup. Gallup has been a long-time champion of the strengths-based approach, and its leaders practice a "strengths-finder" strategy to hiring and cultivating employees. Instead of spending millions of dollars to repair or "fix" deficiencies in their employees' skills, the leaders of Gallup suggest that such money and energy is better spent on discovering employees' strengths and talents and then finding job duties that provide a good match for those talents (Hodges & Clifton, 2004). The focus is not on changing worker weaknesses and deficiencies but on building on their assets. As Buckingham and Coffman (1999, p. 57) put it, "Don't waste time trying to put in what was left out. Try to draw out what was left in. That is hard enough."

Match People, Don't Fix Them

The underlying premise of the strengths-based approach to work is a simple one: Instead of "fixing" all employees so that each has the same basic level of skills, find out what a worker's talents are and then assign the worker to jobs where those talents can be used, or shape the job activities around the workers' talents and skills. As obvious as this approach may seem, when Gallup performed a survey in different countries, the response was surprising when respondents were asked, "Which would help you be more successful in your life—knowing what your weaknesses are and attempting to improve your weaknesses, or knowing what your strengths are and attempting to build on your strengths?" (Hodges & Clifton, 2004, p. 256). Timothy Hodges and Donald Clifton of Gallup summarized the responses to these questions and found that the majority of respondents across different countries answered in favor of "improving your weaknesses." In terms of the percentages of respondents who favored the building on strengths approach, these researchers found the following: United States = 41%; Great Britain = 38%; Canada = 38%; France = 29%; Japan = 24%; and China = 24%. Obviously, most people still favor the traditional "fix it" model.

The Stages of This Approach

According to Clifton and Harter (2003), there are three stages in the strengths-based approach to gainful employment. The first stage is the identification of talents, which involves increasing the employee's awareness of his or her own natural or learned talents. If you are interested in finding these talents in yourself, we suggest Gallup's online assessment (http://www.strengthsfinder.com), which is described in Chapter 3. (The authors of this text have completed the measure on this Web site and found the results to be very useful. Note that there may be a charge for this if you have not purchased a book containing a Clifton StrengthsFinder code.)

The second stage is the integration of the talents into the employee's self-image; the person learns to define himself or herself according to these talents. Gallup has developed books aimed at helping particular groups of people to integrate their talents. There is an enjoyable volume for workers across potential employment areas (see Buckingham & Clifton, 2001), a workbook for students (see Clifton & Anderson, 2002), a book for people in sales (see Smith & Rutigliano, 2003), and one for members and leaders of faith-based organizations (see Winseman, Clifton, & Liesveld, 2003).

The third stage is the actual behavioral change, in which the individual learns to attribute any successes to his or her special talents. In this stage, people report being more satisfied and productive precisely because they have begun to own and accentuate their strengths.

Does It Work?

Does the strengths-based approach work for the betterment of employees? The answer appears to be a firm yes. In a survey of 459 people who took the Clifton StrengthsFinder assessment through the aforementioned Web site (Hodges, 2003), 59% agreed or strongly agreed with the item, "Learning about my strengths has helped me to make better choices in my life"; 60% agreed or strongly agreed with the item, "Focusing on my strengths has helped me to be more productive," and 63% agreed or strongly agreed with the item, "Learning about my strengths has increased my self-confidence."

Beyond these self-reported benefits, the strengths-based approach also has produced positive workplace results for "hard" markers—i.e., with regard to actual productivity. For example, in a study of the Toyota North American Parts Center California (Connelly, 2002), the warehouse workers completed the Clifton StrengthsFinder and then attended lunchtime sessions aimed at answering any related questions. Also, the managers of this company took a 4-day course in this approach. Relative to the previous 3 years, in which per-person productivity increased or decreased by less than 1%, the year following this strengths-based intervention saw a 6% increase in productivity. Other examples of actual work improvements stemming from the strengths-based approach can be reviewed in Hodges and Clifton (2004). In summary, the strengths-based approach has yielded considerable empirical support within the last decade.

CAPITAL AT WORK

University of Nebraska positive psychologist Fred Luthans has proposed a new way of thinking about resources or capital, one that can be applied to the workforce. This view of capital places the greatest emphasis on the individual worker. As Carly Fiorian of Hewlett-Packard has put it, "The most important ingredient in the transformed landscape is people" (in Luthans & Youssef, 2004, p. 143). In the spirit of positive psychology research and applications, Luthans begins with the traditional view of economic capital and then expands into new frontiers of positive psychological thinking. We share the evolution of his thinking in the next sections.

Traditional Economic Capital

As shown in Figure 15.4, traditional economic capital involves an organization's answer to the question, "What do you have?" The answer usually has been a list of the concrete facilities that make a given company unique. Included here would be buildings or plants, equipment, data, patents, technology, and so forth. Obviously, this type of capital is very expensive in terms of monetary outlay. Often, a marker of the success of an organization is that other companies attempt to copy these sources of capital (euphemistically called *benchmarking*). Because modern technology now enables the products of an industry leader to be copied by reverse engineering, however, the traditional advantages enjoyed by an organization that develops a new product have been greatly curtailed. Historically, these physical resources of economic capital have received most of the attention in analyses of work settings (Luthans, Luthans, & Luthans, 2004), but this is changing in the twenty-first century.

Fred Luthans

Source: Reprinted with permission of Fred Luthans.

Human Capital

Human capital refers to the employees at all levels of an organization. In this regard, business phenom Bill Gates has commented that the most important assets of his company "walk out of the door every night." In making such a comment, he is emphasizing how the skills, knowledge, and abilities of his employees reflect the ultimate assets that set Microsoft above its competitors. Thus, in the older economic capital model, the guiding question for an organization was, "What do you have?" whereas the core question in the human capital perspective is, "What do you know?" The answer to the latter query entails human capital—employee assets such as experience, education, skills, talents, knowledge, and new ideas (Luthans et al., 2004). The knowledge inherent in human capital is made up of the explicit skills of workers. Such skills and tacit knowledge are organization specific; for example, Nike has been characterized as superb at brand management, General Electric is skilled at global cooperation, and Microsoft has been lauded for having employees who excel at trying new ideas (Luthans & Youssef, 2004).

In the United States workforce, human capital increasingly involves workers of diverse racial and ethnic backgrounds. In the words of John Bruhn (1996),

> A healthy organization is one in which an obvious effort is made to get people with different backgrounds, skills, and abilities to work together toward the goals or purpose of the organization. While we have not accomplished this at the societal level, it is achievable at the organizational level. (p. 11)

The need for cultural diversity is being understood both at the managerial and worker levels (Cunningham, 2009; Thomas, 1990). University of Michigan professor Taylor Cox (1994) has suggested four good reasons for such diversity of social capital. First, diverse backgrounds within an organization enhance the overall level of energy and talent, thereby raising the problem-solving

Figure 15.4 Types of Capital

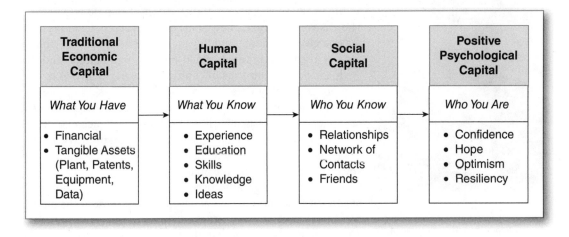

potential of the organization. Second, a core value of United States society is equal opportunity; it is therefore ethically and morally right to enhance diversity among workers. Third, cultural diversity raises the performance of all workers. Fourth, the legislation pertaining to equal pay, civil rights, pregnancy and age discrimination, and individuals with disabilities mandates diversity as a legal requirement. A multiculturally competent workplace augments these benefits (Youssef-Morgan & Hardy, 2014).

Social Capital

Closely related to human capital is social capital, with respect to which the key question is, "Who do you know?" Throughout all levels of an organization, an important set of assets taps into the relationships, network of contacts, and friends of workers (see Figure 15.4). Such social capital makes an organization facile in setting goals and solving any challenges that may arise. Because employees know with whom they should talk both within and outside the company, they can reach their goals even under difficult circumstances. Thus, advice is a precious commodity in social capital.

Positive Psychological Capital

The last and newest form of capital discussed by social scientists is positive psychological capital, which for Luthans and his colleagues (Luthans et al., 2004; Luthans & Youssef, 2004; Youssef-Morgan & Hardy, 2014) comprises four positive psychology variables (see Figure 15.5). These four variables involve Bandura's (1997) efficacy (confidence in one's ability to reach a desired goal; see Chapter 8), Snyder's (2002a) hope (the capacity to find pathways to desired goals, along with the motivation or agency to use those pathways; see Chapter 8), Seligman's (2002) optimism (the ability to attribute good outcomes to internal, stable, and pervasive causes; see Chapter 8), and Masten's (2001) resiliency (the capacity to endure and succeed in adversity; see Chapter 5).

Luthans argues that, as we move into the twenty-first century, it is time for businesses to lessen their dependency on the traditional sources of capital (e.g., economic) (Luthans et al., 2004; Luthans & Youssef, 2004). Instead, he suggests that there already are compelling theoretical reasons, along with beginning reports from research programs (see Luthans, Avolio, Walumbwa, & Li, 2005), to move

Figure 15.5   Positive Psychological Capital

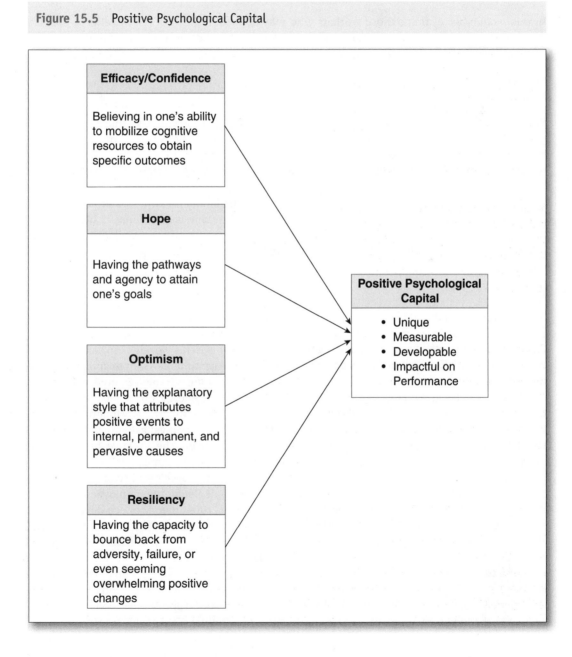

to these psychological forms of capital. We explore one form of psychological capital—hope—in greater detail in the next section.

THE DARK SIDE: WORKAHOLICS, BURNOUTS, AND JOBS LOST

In this section, we examine those workers who may be most in need of the benefits of positive psychology: people who work all the time, those who have burned out at their jobs, and those who have lost their jobs.

Workaholics

Some people, referred to as workaholics, become obsessed by their work—so much so that they cannot attend to the responsibilities of their friends and family. Workaholism also entails staying late on the job long after others have departed and working much harder than others, almost to the point of seeking perfectionism (McMillan, O'Driscoll, Marsh, & Brady, 2001). Researchers have found that those who score high on measures of characteristics of workaholics experience less pleasure in leisure activities and have greater conflict between work and family (Bakker, Demerouti, & Burke, 2009; Brady, Vodanovich, & Rotunda, 2008). For a workaholic, there is no balance in life activities, and this person even may begin to exhibit the Type A behavior pattern of hypervigilance with regard to time constraints and angry outbursts at coworkers (Houston & Snyder, 1988).

Burnout

Do you ever feel as though you work harder and harder at your job, yet the things that you need to get done just seem to grow despite your best efforts? Do you feel tired at work? Does your job lack any sense of reward? Perhaps you have watched your own parents working long and hard and have adopted their workaholic approach for yourself. If these sentiments seem to apply, you may be suffering from burnout (Pines, Aronson, & Kafry, 1981; Rodriguez-Hanley & Snyder, 2000).

Burnout is cyclical. Initially, the employee has a high level of energy, but this begins to wane over time. The employee encounters severe time constraints in getting the work done, there are barriers to the work goals, and the bosses tend not to give rewards and yet ask more and more of the employee because she or he is getting things done. Paradoxically, the effective, hard-working person is asked to do more. As this cycle continues, the employee becomes totally exhausted in both mind and body, and the burnout truly undermines the employee's ability to carry out the necessary duties of the job. When his or her energy is totally depleted, the employee needs time to recover and recharge (see Baumeister, Faber, and Wallace's [1999] theory of ego depletion).

Various approaches have been used to reduce burnout in work settings (Godfrey, Bonds, Kraus, Wiener, & Toch, 1990). Techniques found to be effective in lowering work stress have included training in goal setting, problem resolution, time management, aerobic exercise, relaxation techniques, and coping in general (Hudson, Flannery-Schroeder, & Kendall, 2004). In a meta-analysis of several such programs to reduce stress in work settings, the short-term interventions produced robust effects (technically, the effect sizes were .38 to .53) in reported employee moods and health; moreover, the long-term interventions produced even more robust effects (Kaluza, 1997).

Losing Your Job

Unfortunately, an all-too-common reality is that people lose their jobs. Being out of work is a very serious matter both psychologically and physically. Research shows that older workers may be particularly affected by these issues, especially when work is lost involuntarily (e.g., layoffs; Lippmann, 2008).

Research has actually linked unemployment to early death (Voss, Nylen, Floderus, Diderichsen, & Terry, 2004). In a program of long-running research on identical twins, Dr. Margaretha Voss of the Karolinska Institute in Stockholm, Sweden, has studied more than 20,600 men and women. One finding was that those who reported having been unemployed were more likely to die in the subsequent 10 to 24 years than were those who had not been unemployed. This finding among women who reported having been unemployed appeared to be linked to suicides, whereas for men the causes were undetermined. Dr. Voss had found in her previous research that early death (before age 70) was more likely for men and women who had been unem-

Christina Maslach

Source: Reprinted with permission of Christina Maslach.

ployed at some point in their lives, but the latest findings showed that women with unemployment histories were almost four times more likely to commit suicide than their employed counterparts.

WHAT CAN BE DONE TO IMPROVE YOUR WORK?

To help you think somewhat more deeply about your job, we encourage you to study Figure 15.6. We use the boxes in this figure as an aid in going through the steps to improve one's work.

Making the Job Better

In our clinical interactions with people who were exploring issues related to their work, we have found it useful to ask about the first thoughts that a person has, early in the morning, about going to work. If you feel good about your job and look forward to work, we congratulate you on this fortuitous state of affairs. Even if you do like your job, however, we suggest that it helps to look constantly for ways to make it better. In Figure 15.6, this is represented by the left-hand route, labeled "Make Job Better."

Some additional discussion of the various decision points on the "Make Job Better" side is warranted. We believe that employees often have much more power and latitude than they typically realize in making positive changes in their jobs. This is especially true if you have performed well in your job. Your value to your boss may be far greater than you think. One change, however, may

Figure 15.6   A Decision Tree for Improving One's Work

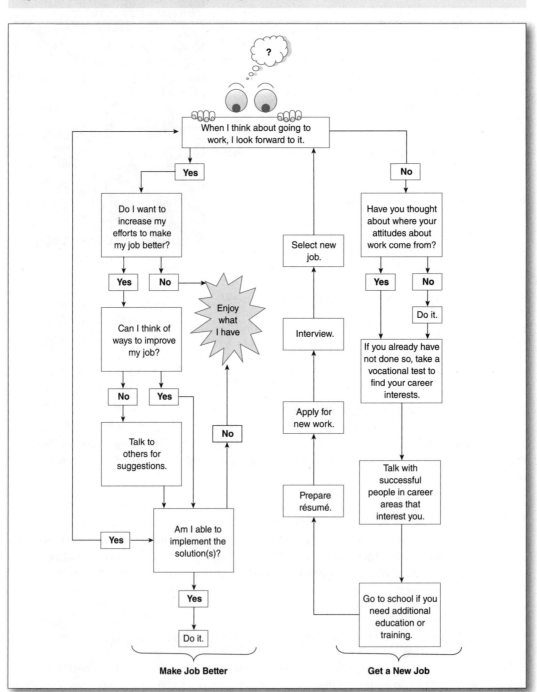

be tricky: You may think that getting a raise would greatly increase your job satisfaction; as we have discussed, however, money is not as important as is commonly believed.

If a raise is not a panacea, are there other changes in your job that would make your life more enjoyable? Perhaps you could ask for a better office, longer or more frequent vacations, time to spend with family, a larger expense account, an assistant, a company car, or increased and varied retirement benefits. Flexible work schedules are very important for workers' mental health and well-being (Dittmann, 2005). Another possibility here is working from home. See the Personal Mini-Experiments to explore the possibility of working from home.

PERSONAL MINI-EXPERIMENTS

Becoming Gainfully Employed

We hope you have realized how crucial work is to our personal well-being and satisfaction. The following activities encourage you to consider the roots of some of your vocational interests and to experiment with the ideas for making your work situation better.

Can You Work From Home? Whether you are working (or will work) part or full time, perhaps you should consider what more and more professionals are doing—working from home. If your reaction to this suggestion is that the activities of your job necessitate your physical presence, then this may not be a good idea. But if your concern is something along the lines of "My boss wouldn't even consider that," or "I wouldn't be able to work at home because I would just goof off," there are ways to address this. Keep in mind that bosses are most concerned about productivity; how or where you get the job done is often less important than that you do. Eliminating the commute from your daily routine and increasing the flexibility of your schedule may lead to greater productivity. It may also allow you to feel more balanced between work and family, which may in turn benefit your productivity by making you more focused and less guilt-ridden.

Are You a "Chip Off the Old Block" When It Comes to Work Attitudes? As you think about your own work and your attitudes toward it, have you ever thought about where and how you got your work beliefs? The answer, as with many things, may come from your developmental experiences. Here is an exercise that we have used with our clients to help them to uncover the roots of their work attitudes. Begin by writing down your answers to the following questions:

1. How important is work in your life? (Give details.)

2. What has been your attitude about work throughout your life? (Give details.)

(Continued)

(Continued)

3. Do you enjoy working? If so, why? If not, why not?

4. If you have children, what are you trying (or what did you try) to teach them about the role of work in their lives?

5. Based on what you have seen of them so far, do you think your children have followed your ideas about work?

Once you have answered these questions, think about the people who raised you. These may be your biological parents, stepparents, or a multitude of others who take on the role of caregiver for children. Think about the caregiver who was the biggest influence on you when you were growing up. Once you have a good image in your mind of this person, then do a mental role play in which you ask that person the same questions you just answered. Write down the answers that you expect your primary caregiver to give to these questions. Now, assuming that this primary caregiver is still alive and otherwise accessible, visit the person or give him or her a call. Ask these same five questions and write down his or her answers.

At this point, you can see whether or not you are a "chip off the old block." Write each of the five questions in a column on the left side of a piece of paper, then make three columns to the right. Head the first column "My Attitudes About Work"; the second column, "My Imagined Attitudes for My Caregiver"; and the third column, "My Caregiver's Actual Attitudes About Work." In our experience, most people are amazed at the similarity of the attitudes across the three columns. This means that we truly do adopt the attitudes and beliefs of our primary caregivers when it comes to work. A workaholic caregiver will impart his or her values about work to his or her offspring. Likewise, the caregiver who has found great meaning in a calling often transmits the quest for a purpose-driven life to his or her offspring. Remember, if you do not particularly like the attitudes that you have about work, this exercise also provides an excellent starting point for making some changes.

Where Did You Get Your Vocational Interests? Do you know how your interests relate to those of successful people in various lines of work? Are your career choices really ones that you have made, or have other people, such as your parents (or friends, teachers, etc.) made these decisions for you (Saccuzzo & Ingram, 1993)? As a beginning point, please think about each of the following people and rate the percentage of influence that each has had on your career choice to date:

Person	Influence Percentage
Mother	_____
Father	_____
Sister	_____
Brother	_____
Spouse/Mate	_____
Teachers	_____
Friends	_____
Other	_____
YOU	_____
Total	_____ (This should be 100%)

Are you surprised to see who is wielding the most influence in your career selection? Our point is not that you should ignore the input of other people, but rather that you should become more aware of these influences and then decide whether you need or want to take more control of this process.

A good guide for improving your work situation is to consider the various factors that we have discussed previously as contributing to gainful employment (see Figure 15.3, p. 427). Look for ways of attaining the following in your job: (1) variety in duties performed, (2) a safe working environment, (3) sufficient income, (4) a sense of purpose, (5) personal happiness and satisfaction, (6) positive engagement, (7) a sense that you are performing well and meeting the goals, (8) companionship and friendship, and (9) an environment that respects and appreciates diversity. Some of these nine characteristics of gainful employment may be more important to you than others. Accordingly, you should try to maximize the fulfillment of your needs in the most important areas.

A last strategy that comes from the "Make Job Better" side of Figure 15.6 is to learn to enjoy what you have. Appreciation and savoring (Bryant, 2005; Bryant & Veroff, 2006; Hurley & Kwon, 2013) are important positive psychology attributes, and you may want to take more time to simply realize and enjoy what you have.

Applying for a New Job

As you can see in Figure 15.6, if your answer is "no" to the question of awakening and looking forward to work, then you go to the right side of the guide, labeled "Get a New Job," and follow the steps outlined there.

It may take courage to launch a search for a new position. A key to this process is to remain flexible as you consider various options. You can think about a wide sample of potentially influential people in regard to your attitudes about work. Previous readers have found the "Where Did You Get Your Vocational Interests?" Personal Mini-Experiment to be useful in ascertaining the factors that influenced their work attitudes. This topic is important enough that we have prepared two exercises to assist people, which are presented in the Personal Mini-Experiments. In "Chip Off the Old Block," you can see to what degree you learned your work attitudes from your parents or caregivers.

The next step in Figure 15.6 is to take a vocational/interest test (if you have not already done so) to see how your interests align with various career trajectories. In our experience, the problem for some people is that they have been pursuing jobs that were not matched to their interest patterns. Our suggestion, especially if you are a college student who is reading this book as part of a course, is to walk over to the student services center and ask to talk to someone about getting career counseling. The key notion here is that you should be pursuing a career in which the activities truly tap your interests (and strengths, as noted previously). Vocational tests, such as those you might take at a center like this, have been carefully validated to give you a sense of what your career interests may be. They can also give you an idea of how your particular interests may relate to those of people who are happy and successful in various careers (for general overviews, see Swanson & Gore [2000]; for specific discussions of cross-cultural and ethnic issues, see Fouad [2002]). The counselor will talk with you about your pattern of interests, and, although you may think that you know what these are, you may be in for a surprise. You also will receive helpful feedback about how your interests fit with various professions. The decision about what direction to take will remain yours, but it will be an informed one, unlike that of the typical college student who selects a major and therefore delimits subsequent jobs by a hit-and-miss process of accumulating hours in that major.

Assuming that you do know what jobs are appropriate for you based on your interests and talents, then it may help to conduct informational interviews with people who are doing well in such careers. Find out what their jobs really entail, and then get their advice about finding jobs in the same area. At this stage, you may realize that you need to go back to school to get a new or different degree that will open doors to the jobs that you covet. If you do have the appropriate education, the next step is to prepare a résumé and have other people read it to make sure that it is in its best form. You may want to go to an employment agency for help in your job search, but whether or not you do, the next step is to get your application and résumé to as many employers as possible.

The next stage involves interviews. Prepare carefully for these. Before an interview, practice with people whom you can trust to give you candid feedback. Learn everything you can about a company and its personnel before the interview. Dress appropriately for the setting. During the interview, show enthusiasm for the job. Listen to what your interviewers are saying, and pay attention. If you do not have the answer to a question, don't try to fake it—admit that you do not know but will learn! And, know your strengths; most interviewers will ask about them.

Congratulations! You now are being offered a job. It is at this stage that you have the most power to influence the content of your job offer. Think about things other than money. Pay attention to the gainful employment factors shown in Figure 15.3 as you negotiate with your potential new employer (for an overview of the application, interview, and negotiation process, see Snyder, 2002b). Finally, select the job you want to take—the one that best fulfills your gainful employment needs.

Cultivating other psychological constructs as discussed in the section on positive psychological capital may prove to be especially helpful during this process as well. Obviously, and particularly because of the current economy, one could follow all the correct steps and yet still have difficulty in landing a position that suits one's needs both financially and in terms of personal satisfaction. When faced with these circumstances, using the explanatory style of learned optimism (Seligman, 1998b); relying on goal strategies as cultivated by use of the hope model (Snyder et al., 1991); drawing on resilience stores (Masten et al., 2009); and believing in oneself via the enhancement of self-efficacy (Maddux, 2009a) may be of great benefit to individuals who are having difficulty finding work.

The Power to Change

In helping people who were less than happy with their work circumstances, we have found that, almost without exception, they eventually realized that they had more options and alternatives than they initially imagined. Therefore, as you work your way through this guide, realize that you can do things to make your job better. An important principle of positive psychology is that we can effectively change our lives—of which work is a crucial aspect—for the better.

WHEN WORK BECOMES A CALLING: THE TALE OF A HOSPITAL ORDERLY

One point that comes across loud and clear is that a person need not be gainfully employed in a high-paying, high-status position to gain enormous satisfaction from the work itself. An example may help to bring this point to life. In 1999, a close friend of one of the authors of this textbook underwent a complex operation and recounted his experience here.

> I was in the medical center for 2 weeks, and during that time I had the pleasure of interacting with many people who were wonderful in how they conducted themselves in their jobs. There was a high-status surgeon with his team of "baby docs" who followed him everywhere, as well as my world-class gastroenterologist. Small armies of other physicians and nurses also made my life more bearable. But as marvelous and accomplished as these professionals were, they did not leave the same impression on me as did a person who arguably was the very lowest in the status hierarchy.
>
> This amazing woman was an orderly who worked the graveyard shift from midnight until 8 a.m. These were the times when my pain medication often was not working well, when the bed seemed especially hard and uncomfortable, and when I longed to escape the

suffering. It was during these dark hours that this orderly, a physically small woman, would fluff my pillow and talk with me about how things would be better. I asked her about her job, which seemed mostly to involve emptying bedpans, cleaning up messes, and replacing dirty gowns and blankets.

This orderly also was proud of what she did. Very proud. She saw herself as an important part of the health care team, and she was. She said that her job was to make sure that the postoperative patients were comfortable during the wee hours of the morning. When I wanted to scream because of the pain, she would tell me about my family, who would be showing up at sunrise.

This orderly expressed pleasure in the tasks that were part of her job, even those some might consider mundane. Many times I remember thanking her for the kindnesses she had delivered, and the next time I awakened, her prophecy had come true—there stood my wife, family members, and friends, and I was feeling better.

Each night, she brought a fresh selection of cut flowers in a small vase and placed it on the table beside my bed. I asked her about these flowers, and she said that she went to a nearby grocery store when she came to work in the evening. The store was going to throw away these cut flowers that they would not use, so instead she brought them to work to make small floral arrangements for "her" patients. I would look at these flowers in the early morning hours, and their beauty was magnified when I learned the story that went with them.

Amy Wrzesniewski

Source: Reprinted with permission of Amy Wrzesniewski.

My point in telling the story of this orderly is to show how any job, even one seemingly low status, can be a source of dignity and self-respect. Any task, when done well, can bring pleasure to the worker and those whom that person serves. I never will forget this orderly.

As positive psychology pioneer Martin Seligman (2002) notes in describing workers such as this one, they do not see themselves as just having jobs; instead, they have callings. Credit should be given to Amy Wrzesniewski of New York University for her groundbreaking research on the notion of calling (see Wrzesniewski, McCauley, Rozin, & Schwartz, 1997; Wrzesniewski, Rozin, & Bennett, 2001). Again, in the words of Seligman (2002),

Individuals with a calling see their work as contributing to the greater good, to something larger than they are, and hence the religious connotation is entirely appropriate. The work is fulfilling in its own right, without regard for money or for advancement. When the money stops and the promotions end, the work goes on.

Traditionally, callings were reserved to very prestigious and rarified work—priests, Supreme Court justices, physicians, and scientists. But there has been an important discovery in the field: Any job can become a calling, and any calling can become a job. (p. 168)

THE PSYCHOLOGY OF GAINFUL EMPLOYMENT AND THE EDUCATION THAT GETS US THERE

As mentioned in the beginning of this chapter, much of our life is spent in either a work or school setting. Many friends are made through these venues, and the experiences we have in them shape our lives. Therefore, if you are unhappy in your original choice of major, your current line of work, or just the specific scholastic or workplace environment in which you currently exist, take time to look into other options. As noted above, change can help us find our true callings or direct us along the path that can help us to find these callings. If you are a future teacher reading this book, be mindful of the impact, be it good or bad, that you may have on the lives of countless children. If you are a future boss of any kind, take care to infuse the tenets of positive workplaces into your practices and policies. And, regardless of your position, take chances to find your callings and to do your best at serving them.

APPENDIX A: EXAMPLE OF POSITIVE SCHOOLING: THE STRENGTHSQUEST PROGRAM

StrengthsQuest is a program to develop and engage high school and college students so that they can succeed in their academic pursuits in particular and in their lives in general. This program owes its existence to positive psychologist Donald Clifton, who began his work on this approach as a professor of education psychology at the University of Nebraska–Lincoln in the 1950s. Before elaborating on his theory and related educational program, we salute this remarkable man. Don Clifton has been commended by the American Psychological Association as a "father" of the strengths-based approach in psychology and the "grandfather" of positive psychology (McKay & Greengrass, 2003). Contrary to the intellectual and applied currents of the 1950s through 1990s, which swam in the murky water of weakness-oriented psychology, Professor Clifton always seemed to have a crucial and different question: "What would result if we studied what is right rather than wrong with people?"

This question is at the core of the StrengthsQuest Program (see Clifton & Anderson, 2002). Of course, this positive approach contrasts with the traditional approach to education, wherein students are explicitly and implicitly taught that they must "fix" their deficiencies, and, if they do not, they are flunked (Anderson, 2005). In terms of hope and related motivations discussed in the previous section, the StrengthsQuest Program energizes students. This follows from students' realizations that they are perceived as having the necessary natural cognitive talents to succeed in school.

The StrengthsQuest Program begins by having students complete the Clifton Strengths-Finder, an online, computerized assessment of the five areas of their greatest natural talents.

The assessment involves 180 items; for each item, the respondent selects the most applicable descriptor of a pair (e.g., "I read instructions carefully" vs. "I like to jump right into things"). The student also rates the degree to which the selected statement is better than the one with which it is paired. There are 34 possible themes (as shown in Table 3.1, pp. 56–58), and the student learns which five themes are the most applicable to him or her.

To date, more than 100 studies have used the StrengthsFinder assessment approach in accurately predicting a variety of outcome markers (Schmidt & Rader, 1999). Moreover, this technique has undergone considerable empirical construct validation (Lopez, Hodges, & Harter, 2005).

Next, the students complete (either online or in a printed format) the workbook *StrengthsQuest: Discover and Develop Your Strengths in Academics, Career, and Beyond* (Clifton & Anderson, 2002). This workbook helps students (as well as teachers, counselors, residence hall coordinators, and others who work with students) to understand and build their signature strengths in ongoing school efforts. Lastly, the students undertake more in-depth training by signing onto the Strengths-Quest Web site (www.strengthsquest.com).

In the second and third stages of this educational approach, students work on their signature strengths as revealed in their five most robust StrengthsFinder themes. Clifton and his colleagues, including the researchers at the Gallup Organization (which the Clifton family owns and operates), based this second phase on their research findings that the very best achievers and students (1) clearly recognize their talents and develop them, (2) apply strengths in those areas where there are good matches to natural talents and interests, and (3) come up with ways to apply their assets in the pursuit of desired goals. This part of the program is similar to the goals and pathways components discussed in the previous section on positive schooling (Anderson, 2005).

Parallel with these three findings in the Clifton approach, students appear to go though three distinct stages (as reflected in papers written by students undergoing this program; Clifton & Harter, 2003). In the first stage, it appears that students identify their talents. In the second stage, they have revelations about integrating these areas of strengths into their self-conceptualizations. And in the third stage, they make behavioral changes (Buckingham & Clifton, 2001). As the program advances, participating students notice examples of things they are doing that reflect their natural predilections and talents (e.g., taking a leadership role in difficult situations, giving instructions to others, learning particular new skills in given areas very easily). Not only do students recognize their talents, they also increasingly begin to "own" them.

APPENDIX B: POSITIVE WORKPLACES IN HONG KONG: BUILDING POSITIVE ORGANIZATIONS, ENGAGING THE HEART OF EMPLOYEES

Building Positive Organizations, Engaging the Heart of Employees— Insights Gained From the Survey on Positive Organizational Index

In recent years, every business has been facing a lot of social and economic challenges. This causes many managers and employees to suffer varying degrees of difficulty and work pressure. In fact, it is an indisputable fact that Hong Kong "wage earners" have to face long working hours, demanding work, office interpersonal tensions, and work pressure. Failure to respond positively will easily provoke labor conflicts and inevitably, employees will harbour thoughts of leaving the organizations. In the face of all these challenges, we need to strive to change whatever changeable and at the same time learn to face the unchangeable realities with a positive mindset.

Hong Kong's First Positive Organizational Index

As a pioneer and leading provider of "Employee Assistance Program" in Hong Kong, the Employee Development Service (EDS) of Hong Kong Christian Service recognizes that the operation of an organization not only affects the economic development of the organization itself or society, but also the physical and mental well-being of its employees. In order to promote sustainable development in-organizations so that they can utilize their positive energy and resilience to manage difficulties in the domains of corporate governance, employee relations, staff quality, leadership, and staff's personal well-being, the EDS and Four Dimensions Consulting Limited had conducted a comprehensive literature review on research and theories related to positive organization from the international community including *Positive Organizational Scholarship: Foundations of a New Discipline* (Cameron, Dutton, & Quinn, 2003) and *The Oxford Handbook of Positive Organizational Scholarship* (Cameron and Spreitzer, 2012) and developed a "Positive Organizational Index." This is the first set of indicators in Hong Kong and overseas designed to measure the level of positivity among organizations. The Index is deduced from a rigorous analysis and the insights gained from literature survey of theories and researches conducted by over 150 experts and scholars on positive organizations. This index consists of 69 effective positive strategies grouped under five core areas namely, P.R.I.D.E., where P stands for Positive Practice, R for Relationship Enhancement, I for Individual Attributes, D for Dynamic Leadership and E for Emotional Well-being.

What Is a Positive Organization?

A positive organization is a fresh lens that focuses on good practice of an organization without ignoring the negatives. It emphasizes on building strengths and capabilities of an organization leading to "generative positive cycles" that enhance it to move towards sustainable excellence. The five core dimensions of Positive Organization are:

Positive Practice: Effective measures are taken to maximize the organization's positive corporate governance, human resource management, and sustainable development even under constraints or undesirable situations.

Relationship Enhancement: Good relationship, high quality connection and positive team synergy are maintained among employees in the workplace.

Individual Attributes: The best of human conditions are nurtured in the workplace by building on employees' strengths and cultivating corporate and individual integrity.

Dynamic Leadership: Positive leadership strategies are implemented in the process of change to maximize the workforce's positive energy and resilience.

Emotional Well-being: Concerted efforts are made to keep up the employees' physical and psychological well-being and boost their positive emotions.

As a matter of fact, the survey has provided evidence indicating that the higher an organization's score on positive organizational index, the better performance it has at organizational level (significance level: $p < 0.01$). This includes effectiveness, efficiency, quality, business ethics, interpersonal relationships, adaptability and profitability, and so on. At the same time, the employees' physical and mental health statuses are comparatively better (significance level: $p < 0.01$). To sustain excellence and retain employees, it is imperative for organizations to invest in both "hardware" and "software" and foster balanced development of the positive strategies in the five areas of the Index. Additionally, organizations should be more proactive in enhancing their employees' psychological capital and positive energy on regular basis, instead of solving problems when they come up. By doing so, employees can probably possess higher resilience and enthusiasm in the face of challenges and adversity.

About the Writer

Ms. Rainbow K. H. Cheung is the general manager of Employee Development Service of Hong Kong Christian Service and Four Dimensions Consulting, Ltd. She is an experienced registered social worker who is one of the promoters for establishing the very first employee assistance program in Hong Kong. She specializes in positive organizational psychology, motivational interviewing, employee counseling, mental health first aid, and critical incident stress management.

Reprinted with permission of Ms. Rainbow K. H. Cheung General Manager, Four Dimensions Consulting Limited.

KEY TERMS

Authentic boss: A supervisor who is one of "those individuals who are deeply aware of how they think and behave and are perceived by others as being aware of their own and others' values/morals perspective, knowledge, and strengths; aware of the context in which they operate; and who are confident, hopeful, optimistic, resilient, and high on moral character" (Avolio et al. 2004, p. 4).

Burnout: An employee's feeling that, despite working hard, he or she is unable to do everything that needs to be done. The employee is tired and perceives a lack of reward from his or her job.

Calling: A strong motivation in which a person repeatedly takes a course of action that is intrinsically satisfying. For example, a person who experiences a calling to

teach teaches because the job is personally fulfilling, not just because of the paycheck.

Career self-efficacy: Personal confidence in one's capacity to handle career development and work-related activities

Commitment: the amount of psychological attachment a worker feels toward the organization for which they work.

Developmental discipline: An attempt, based on attachment theory, at socialization that involves building caring and trusting relationships with students who have insecure attachments with their primary caregivers.

Engagement: An employee's involvement with his or her work. Engagement often depends on employees knowing what is expected of them, having what they need to do their work, having a chance to improve and develop, and having opportunities to develop relationships with coworkers.

Gainful employment: Work that contributes to a healthy life by providing variety, a safe working environment, sufficient income, a sense of purpose in work done, happiness and satisfaction, engagement and involvement, a sense of performing well and meeting goals, and companionship and loyalty to coworkers, bosses, and companies.

Human capital: The skills, knowledge, education, experience, ideas, and abilities of employees that are assets to a company.

Positive psychological capital: Assets to a company that result from employees' efficacy (confidence in one's ability to reach desired goals); hope (the capacity to find pathways to desired goals, along with the motivation to use those pathways); optimism (the attribution of good outcomes to internal, stable, and pervasive causes); and resiliency (the capacity to endure and succeed in adversity).

Positive schooling: An approach to education that consists of a foundation of care, trust, and respect for diversity, where teachers develop tailored goals for each student to engender learning and then work with that student to develop the plans and motivation to reach his or her goals. Positive schooling includes

the agendas of instilling hope in students and contributing to the larger society.

Presenteeism: A state in which employees may be physically at work but, because of mental health problems resulting from aversive and repetitive work experiences, are unproductive and unhappy.

Social capital: Assets of a company or person that result from their social relationships, network of contacts, and friends—i.e., assets based on "who you know."

Strengths-based approach to gainful employment: The strengths-based approach to employment involves increasing an employee's awareness of his or her natural and learned talents, integration of these talents into the employee's self-image, and behavioral change in which the employee learns to attribute successes to his or her talents.

Stretch goals: Reasonably challenging goals in which the student seeks a slightly more difficult learning goal than attained previously.

Traditional economic capital: The physical facilities and assets of a company, such as plants and buildings, equipment, data, patents, and technology.

Workaholics: People so engaged in and obsessed by work that they are unable to disengage from it and attend to responsibilities of families and friends.

A Positive Look at
The Future of Psychology

CHAPTER 16

The Future of Positive Psychology

A Conversation Between the Authors

WHAT ARE THE THINGS POSITIVE PSYCHOLOGY NEEDS TO KEEP IN MIND IN ORDER TO CHANGE WITH THE TIMES AND REMAIN VIABLE?

SHANE: For too long psychologists did not value positive emotions and human strengths. We saw them as psychological surplus that people really didn't need to have a good life. Over the last two decades, we have realized that to understand humans we have to make sense of things like joy, hope, and love. There is so much for researchers and practitioners to do to demystify the positive side of life. That will keep us busy for centuries.

Now, how will positive psychology change with the times? A global positive psychology is taking shape. It is not enough to understand the lived experience of Caucasian college students in the middle of the United States. We have to see how theories and past results hold up around the globe. We really need to know more about the payoff of positive emotions and strengths for people of all cultural backgrounds. That work will take time.

As we become more culturally competent, we will be able to meet another challenge. We have to help leaders transform schools and businesses. These hubs of our communities need to function like human development centers. Each day, people should leave school and work feeling better than when they got there. Positive psychology can help with that.

JENNIFER: I agree, particularly with regard to the cultural context piece you just touched on. I think that as the field diversifies in terms of who is doing the research, there is more of an understanding about the different worldviews and experiences that are out there. When psychology as a field was occupied almost solely by men of European and European American backgrounds, that was the only view being studied. Since students at that time might have been from the same cultural context as the researchers, perhaps there wasn't as much questioning of the results from a cultural perspective; the ideas fit with these students' conceptualizations as well. Today, as our field is growing more diverse and including women, people of color, sexual minorities, and other groups, we are seeing that these cultural differences often mean different worldviews and understandings of what is healthy. I think you and I have had different experiences in the field based on our cultural contexts, though we're roughly the same age. Differences in gender and race have made our paths and our understandings different.

HOW DOES CULTURAL CONTEXT PLAY INTO THE WAY IN WHICH YOU USE AND DEVELOP YOUR OWN STRENGTHS?

SHANE: In my practice, I tell my clients, "Do what works as long as it doesn't hurt someone else." This honors my clients' approach to change and growth and reminds them that there are other people in the world that they need to consider as they move forward. What works depends on the cultural context. What makes a child's life better in one country might be different from what works for a child in another country. And, what makes neighborhood children happy might differ due to the cultural backgrounds of their families.

When we do what works for us and makes us happy, we should be sensitive to how our actions might affect the pursuit of happiness of people around us. That kind of cultural sensitivity would benefit us all. What have your experiences been?

JENNIFER: I gain a lot of strength from my culture. I come from a line of people who were tested to stay strong in the face of difficulty. The members of the Japanese American side of my family were imprisoned in the internment camps during World War II, and so I was taught my whole life that our culture gave us strength, that Teramotos are resilient. For me, that was a really good basis. I have always thought of myself as possessing strength in that way, and it was a good way to build other strengths as well. When I began work as a young, female, professor of color in the university system, I really had to use hope and optimism to focus on what I wanted for my future. I had goals to be a successful professional as well as a parent at some point in the future, and so I had to work around a few obstacles to try to move toward those goals. I think my status on these varying cultural facets made it imperative for me to use various strengths and gave me opportunities to further develop them.

HOW DO YOU USE POSITIVE PSYCHOLOGY IN YOUR DAY-TO-DAY LIFE, SEPARATE FROM YOUR SCHOLARLY PURSUITS?

SHANE: The two things most of us want from life are a good job and a happy family. I use what I know about positive psychology to make my work and home life better. Both at work and home, I try to help others do what they do best, and I praise and recognize them for their effort and good work. Those basic strategies go a long way to make my life better.

My work on hope has certainly influenced my relationships. I try to help my friends and family chase the goal that's most important to them and lend them some hope when they need it.

Because of what I know about positive psychology, I make more time for positive emotions in my life. I don't let good feelings evaporate the way I used to. That has made a big difference. How about for you?

JENNIFER: A lot of my use of positive psychology comes in the form of parenting techniques these days. As you know, I have three young children, and I find that thinking about them from a balanced perspective helps me maintain much-needed patience sometimes! Also, when I am thinking from a positive psychological perspective, it gives me greater insight as to what qualities I want to instill in them. How can I make sure they are empathic towards others? How can I help them to learn to be courageous? How can I model hope and optimism for them in ways they will find helpful to their future pursuits? And how can I make sure that I teach these things as culturally bound, so that they understand that others may have different opinions and strategies that are just as viable? The answers to these questions occur to me through the use of strengths. I use my own experience in hope and optimism to coach them to develop theirs. When an obstacle arises, I try to frame it as such and help them to look for ways around this to a better outcome. I also use my own strengths to seek out a diverse social group for them. I want them to see that people from all different groups can be doctors, mothers, janitors, teachers, and, of course friends. I tell them stories of courage from their family histories and praise them when they exhibit empathy and other positive traits.

I also use positive psychology at my job on a daily basis. I use hope strategies to plan out my time and make sure I can complete my tasks. I try to use empathy and kindness toward students from different situations so that I can understand where they are coming from. And I try to be brave when I am engaged in social activism on our campus to further goals of cultural competence. It's not always easy to remind myself to use my strengths; I can get bogged down sometimes when things get really busy. But that's when I turn to mentors and others to regain my perspective.

WHAT HELPS YOU TO STAY POSITIVE IN THE FACE OF NEGATIVITY?

SHANE: As a positive psychologist, you get to meet amazing people who have overcome tremendous odds in their quest for a good life. When I am overwhelmed by life, I think about those courageous people. They are all around us. In the last week alone I got to visit with my friend who has had two heart transplants. She is amazingly healthy, working as a baker, and moving to the Northwest. I chatted with two friends who are starting new businesses. They can't get loans from the bank to help, but they have figured out ways to launch a start-up anyway. These are the people that I let guide me when I feel lost. What do you use to guide you?

JENNIFER: I had the opportunity to listen to Dr. Clarence Jones speak at my university this last year. Dr. Jones is a lawyer and a social activist and was one of the former speechwriters for Dr. Martin Luther King, Jr. I got to have lunch with him with a small group of students and faculty, and I asked him how he kept going when negativity threatened to stop his progress toward a more just world. Dr. Jones gave a few different examples of things he relied on when he felt bogged down: religion, friends, family. But then he recounted a short fable about all the animals in the jungle trying to talk about the death of their king, the lion. The king had been killed by hunters, and the other animals were not sure if talking about the death was a good idea. Would the hunters come back? Would it be too hard? At last, they decided they had to speak about it. And Dr. Jones said that the moral of the story was that *"if the surviving lions don't tell their stories, the hunters get all the credit."* That really stuck with me in a lot of areas, particularly with regard to social justice and continuing to be positive so as to push forward in that area. But it can be applied to positive psychology in general, too. If we don't keep talking about what is GOOD in the world, all that is left is the bad.

WHAT DO YOU THINK HAS CHANGED THE MOST IN THIS PART OF THE FIELD SINCE ITS REBIRTH ALMOST 15 YEARS AGO?

SHANE: People seem to readily accept the findings of positive psychology researchers today. Fifteen years ago, it was difficult to convince people that strengths and positive emotions mattered. Today, people are eager to learn how to make their lives better not just by relieving anxiety and fending off depression, but by actively seeking happiness.

JENNIFER: Yes, and I think that the more accessible positive psychology is to the larger group, the more successful it will continue to be. I think we've started to make some moves toward being more inclusive and asking questions about how culture fits into the picture a bit more. That's a big change I've seen in the last few years, and it helps to make positive psychology and its constructs more relevant to groups that have often been marginalized by psychology. I think that if we continue in this vein, we can create a more multiculturally competent positive psychology.

WHAT WOULD YOU TELL A STUDENT WHO WANTS TO BE A POSITIVE PSYCHOLOGIST?

SHANE: There are some graduate programs that will help you become a well-trained positive psychologist. The Master of Applied Positive Psychology at the University of Pennsylvania is highly regarded. It seems to be a great fit for students with a desire to practice and a bit of an entrepreneurial spirit. The PhD program in Positive Developmental Psychology is the one I would choose if I were to do graduate school over again. The faculty members are committed to training the positive psychology scholars of the future.

Most of the questions I get from students have to do with job opportunities as a positive psychologist. I typically tell students to aim their education at becoming a really great psychologist who can add value with their knowledge of positive psychology. If you can bring deep positive psychology knowledge and skills to a job at a school, or a Veteran's Administration hospital, or in private practice, you will be highly valued as a professional.

JENNIFER: Yes, positive psychology and the identification of strengths can be used in so many contexts. When I was completing my doctoral internship at the VA in Topeka, Kansas, people used to ask, "You do positive psychology—how can you work at such a *hopeless* place?" and I was always very surprised by this understanding of the VA because it was one of the most hopeful places I'd ever been. The veterans there were trying so hard to get better; they believed they could and that they had strength enough to do it. And they were very appreciative that I, as a budding positive psychology scholar, could see those strengths in them. You can use positive psychology anywhere. I learned that from my mentors, including you, Shane, and that was an important piece of my education.

WHAT'S THE MOST IMPORTANT PIECE OF WISDOM YOU RECEIVED FROM YOUR MENTORS ABOUT POSITIVE PSYCHOLOGY?

SHANE: That's easy. *Do what you do best.* That's the best advice I got from my best mentors and bosses. When you do what you do best, you feel better, learn faster, and get more done. I have built my life around this piece of wisdom. I make decisions about what to do and who to hang out with based on what I do best.

JENNIFER: Something helpful that I've learned from my mentors is that I should turn to my strengths when I hit an obstacle—the fact that I can use hope, that I can find an optimistic explanation for a bad situation, that I can look for opportunities to be courageous, find environments that are conducive to flow for me. Another piece for me is the idea that I can find ways to build more strengths by looking to mentors and other models. When I recognize an area of growth for myself, I tend to look around and think to myself, "Who do I know who is great at this?" and then try to emulate some of their strengths. A nice side effect of that is that I notice strengths more often in my friends and family. My father, who is one of my greatest mentors, gave me what I think is the best piece of advice I've ever gotten: *Keep learning.* That can be applied to any area in life, I think, and if you are on the lookout for opportunities to use your strengths, you will be able to keep developing them.

OUR VISION OF THE FUTURE FOR POSITIVE PSYCHOLOGY

The future of positive psychology is what we make it. Together, we can make schools the happiest places on earth where we learn and grow while pursuing our goals. We can turn workplaces into meaning factories. We can raise healthy, happy families. And we can make sure that this vision can be translated into many different cultural contexts so that everyone can benefit from positive psychology.

References

A Safe World For Women. (2013). The Safeworld International Foundation. *A Safe World for Women*. Retrieved from http://www.asafeworldforwomen.org/about.html

Abramson, L. Y., Alloy, L., B., Hankin, B. L., Clements, C. M., Zhu, L., Hogan, M. E., & Whitehouse, W. G. (2000). Optimistic cognitive style and invulnerability to depression. In J. Gillham (Ed.), *The science of optimism and hope* (pp. 75–98). Philadelphia: Templeton Foundation Press.

Abramson, L. Y., Seligman, M. E. P., & Teasdale, J. D. (1978). Learned helplessness in humans: Critique and reformulation. *Journal of Abnormal Psychology, 87*, 49–74.

Abuhamdeh, S. (2000). *The autotelic personality: An exploratory investigation*. Unpublished manuscript, University of Chicago.

Acevedo, B. P., Aron, A., Fisher, H. E., & Brown, L. L. (2012). Neural correlates of long-term intense romantic love. *Social Cognitive and Affective Neuroscience, 7*, 145–159.

Acker, M., & Davis, M. H. (1992). Intimacy, passion and commitment in adult romantic relationships: A test of the triangular theory of love. *Journal of Social and Personal Relationships, 9*, 21–50.

Adlai-Gail, W. (1994). *Exploring the autotelic personality*. Unpublished doctoral dissertation, University of Chicago.

Adolphs, R., Damasio, H., Tranel, D., Cooper, G., & Damasio, A. R. (2000). A role for somatosensory cortices in the visual recognition of emotion as revealed by three-dimensional lesion mapping. *Journal of Neuroscience, 20*, 2683–2690.

Affleck, G., & Tennen, H. (1996). Construing benefit from adversity: Adaptational significance and dispositional underpinnings. *Journal of Personality, 64*, 899–922.

Ahmed, A. S. (1999). *Islam today: A short introduction to the Muslim world*. New York: I. B. Tauris & Co., Ltd.

Ahmetoglu, G., Swami, V., & Chamorro-Premuzic, T. (2010). The relationship between dimensions of love, personality, and relationship length. *Archives of Sexual Behavior, 39*, 1181–1190.

Ahuvia, A. (2001). Well-being in cultures of choice: A cross-cultural perspective. *American Psychologist, 56*, 77–78.

Ainsworth, M. D. S. (1979). Infant–mother attachment. *American Psychologist, 34*, 932–937.

Ainsworth, M. D. S., Bell, S. M., & Stayton, D. J. (1992). Infant–mother attachment and social development: "Socialization" as a product of reciprocal responsiveness to signals. In M. Woodhead, R. Carr, & P. Light (Eds.), *Becoming a person* (pp. 30–55). London: Routledge.

Ajzen, I. (1988). *Attitudes, personality, and behavior*. Chicago: Dorsey.

Aknin, L. B., Dunn, E. W., & Norton, M. I. (2012). Happiness runs in a circular motion: Evidence for a positive feedback loop between prosocial spending and happiness. *Journal of Happiness Studies, 13*, 347–355.

Alawiyah, T., Bell, H., Pyles, L., & Runnels, R. C. (2011). Spirituality and faith-based interventions: Pathways to diaster resilience for African American Hurricane Katrina survivors. *Journal of Religion and Spirituality in Social Work: Social Thought, 30*, 294–319.

Albee, G. W., & Gullotta, T. P. (Eds.). (1997). *Primary prevention works*. Thousand Oaks, CA: Sage.

Albom, M. (2002). *Tuesdays with Morrie: An old man, a young man, and life's greatest lesson*. New York: Broadway.

Aldwin, C. M. (2009). Gender and wisdom: A brief overview. *Research in Human Development, 6*, 1–8.

Allen, D., & Marshall, E. S. (2010). Spirituality as a coping resource for African American parents of chronically ill children. *MCN: The American Journal of Maternal/Child Nursing, 35*, 232–237.

Allport, G. W. (1960). *Personality and social encounter*. Boston: Beacon Press.

Alvy, K. T. (1988). Parenting programs for black parents. In L. A. Bond & B. M. Wagner (Eds.), *Families in transition: Primary prevention programs that work* (pp. 135–169). Newbury Park, CA: Sage.

American Psychiatric Association. (1952). *Diagnostic and statistical manual of mental disorders*. Washington, DC: Author.

American Psychiatric Association. (1994). *Diagnostic and statistical manual of mental disorders* (4th ed.). Washington, DC: Author.

American Psychiatric Association. (2013). *Diagnostic and statistical manual of mental disorders* (5th ed.). Washington, DC: Author.

American Psychological Association. (1993). Guidelines for providers of psychological services to ethnic, linguistic, and culturally diverse populations. Retrieved from http://www.apa.org/pi/oema/resources/policy/provider-guidelines.aspx

American Psychological Association. (2003). Guidelines on multicultural education, training, research, practice, and organizational change for psychologists. *American Psychologist, 58*, 377–402.

American Psychological Association. (2013). Recognition of psychotherapy effectiveness. *Journal of Psychotherapy Integration, 23*, 320–330.

Amick, B. C., III, McDonough, P., Chang, H., Rogers, W. H., Duncan, G., & Pieper, C. (2002). The relationship between all-cause mortality and cumulative working life course psychosocial and physical exposures in the United States labor market from 1968–1992. *Psychosomatic Medicine, 64*, 370–381.

Anderson, E. (2005). Strengths-based educating. *Educational Horizons, 83*, 80–89.

Antonovsky, A. (1987). *Unraveling the mystery of health: How people manage stress and stay well*. San Francisco: Jossey-Bass.

Antonovsky, A., & Sagy, S. (1986). The development of a sense of coherence and its impact on responses to stress situations. *Journal of Social Psychology, 126*, 213–225.

Aquinas, T. (1948). *Introduction to St. Thomas Aquinas: The Summa Theologica, The Summa Contra Gentiles*. (A. Pegis, Ed.). New York: Random House. (Original work published 1273)

Aquinas, T. (1981). *Summa theologica*. Westminster, MD: Christian Classics. (Original work published 1273)

Ardelt, M. (1997). Wisdom and life satisfaction in old age. *Journals of Gerontology: Psychological Sciences and Social Sciences, 52*, 15–27.

Ardelt, M. (2000). Antecedents and effects of wisdom in old age: A longitudinal perspective on aging well. *Research on Aging, 22*, 350–394.

Ardelt, M. (2009). How similar are wise men and women? A comparison across two age cohorts. *Research in Human Development, 6*, 9–26.

Ardelt, M. (2010). Are older adults wiser than college students? A comparison of two age cohorts. *Journal of Adult Development, 17*, 193–207.

Argyle, M. (1987). *The psychology of happiness*. London: Methuen.

Argyle, M. (2001). *The psychology of happiness* (2nd ed.). London: Routledge.

Aristotle. (1962). *Nichomachean ethics*. (M. Ostwald, Trans.). Indianapolis, IN: Bobbs-Merrill.

Aron, A., & Aron, E. N. (1986). *Love and the expansion of self: Understanding attraction and satisfaction*. New York: Hemisphere.

Aron, A., Aron, E. N., & Smollan, D. (1992). Inclusion of other in the self scale and the structure of interpersonal closeness. *Journal of Personality and Social Psychology, 63*, 596–612.

Aron, A., Norman, C. C., Aron, E. N., McKenna, C., & Heyman, R. E. (2000). Couples' shared participation in novel and arousing activities and experienced relationship quality. *Journal of Personality and Social Psychology, 78*, 273–284.

Aron, A., Paris, M., & Aron, E. N. (1995). Falling in love: Prospective studies of self-concept change. *Journal of Personality and Social Psychology, 69*, 1102–1112.

Aron, E. N., & Aron, A. (1996). Love and expansion of the self: The state of the model. *Personal Relationships, 3*, 45–58.

Aronson, E. (2000). *Nobody left to hate: Teaching compassion after Columbine*. New York: Freeman.

Aronson, E. (2003). *The social animal* (9th ed.). New York: Worth.

Aronson, E., Blaney, N., Stephin, C., Sikes, J., & Snapp, M. (1978). *The jigsaw classroom.* Beverly Hills, CA: Sage.

Aronson, E., & Patnoe, S. (1997). *The jigsaw classroom: Building cooperation in the classroom* (2nd ed.). New York: Addison Wesley Longman.

Aronson, J., & Rogers, L. (2008). Overcoming stereotype threat. In S. J. Lopez (Ed.), *Positive psychology: Exploring the best in people, Volume 3: Growing in the face of adversity* (pp. 109–121). Westport, CT: Greenwood Publishing Group.

Asakawa, K. (2004). Flow experience and autotelic personality in Japanese college students: How do they experience challenges in daily life? *Journal of Happiness Studies, 5,* 123–154.

Asakawa, K. (2010). Flow experience, culture, and well-being: How do autotelic Japanese college students feel, behave, and think in their daily lives?. *Journal of Happiness Studies, 11,* 205–223.

Ashby, F. G., Isen, A. M., & Turken, A. U. (1999). A neuropsychological theory of positive affect and its influence on cognition. *Psychological Review, 106,* 529–550.

Aspinwall, L. G., & Staudinger, U. M. (Eds.). (2002). *A psychology of human strengths: Fundamental questions and future directions for a positive psychology.* Washington, DC: American Psychological Association.

Aspinwall, L. G., & Taylor, S. E. (1992). Modeling cognitive adaptation: A longitudinal investigation of the impact of individual differences and coping on college adjustment and performance. *Journal of Personality and Social Psychology, 61,* 755–765.

Asplund, J., Agrawal, S., Hodges, T., Harter, J., & Lopez, S. J. (2014). *Clifton StrengthsFinder Technical Report.* Washington, DC: Gallup.

Asplund, J., Lopez, S. J., Hodges, T., & Harter, J. (2007). *Technical report: Development and validation of the Clifton StrengthsFinder 2.0.* Omaha, NE: Gallup.

Assmann, A. (Ed.). (1994). *Wisdom: Archeology of communication.* Munich, Germany: Fink Verlag.

Astin, J. A. (1997). Stress reduction through mindfulness meditation: Effects on psychological symptomatology, sense of control, and spiritual experiences. *Psychotherapy & Psychosomatics, 66,* 97–106.

Austenfeld, J. L., & Stanton, A. L. (2004). Coping through emotional approach: A new look at emotion, coping, and health-related outcomes. *Journal of Personality, 72,* 1335–1363.

Austenfeld, J. L., & Stanton, A. L. (2008). Writing about emotions versus goals: Effects on hostility and medical care utilization moderated by emotional approach coping processes. *British Journal of Health Psychology, 13,* 35–38.

Averill, J. R. (1990). Inner feelings, works of the flesh, the beast within, diseases of the mind, driving force, and putting on a show: Six metaphors of emotion and their theoretical extensions. In D. E. Leary (Ed.), *Metaphors in the history of psychology* (pp. 104–132). New York: Cambridge University Press.

Averill, J. R., Catlin, G., & Chon, K. K. (1990). *Rules of hope.* New York: Springer-Verlag.

Avolio, B., Luthans, F., & Walumbwa, F. O. (2004). Authentic leadership: Theory-building for veritable sustained performance (Working paper). Gallup Leadership Institute, University of Nebraska, Lincoln.

Ayres, C. G., & Mahat, G. (2012). Social support, acculturation, and optimism: Understanding positive health practices in Asian American college students. *Journal of Transcultural Nursing, 23,* 270–278.

Babyak, M., Snyder, C. R., & Yoshinobu, L. (1993). Psychometric properties of the Hope Scale: A confirmatory factor analysis. *Journal of Research in Personality, 27,* 154–169.

Bacon, S. F. (2005). Positive psychology's two cultures. *Review of General Psychology, 9,* 181–192.

Baker, J. A. (1998). The social context of school satisfaction among urban, low-income, African-American students. *School Psychology Quarterly, 13,* 25–44.

Bakker, A. B., Demerouti, E., & Burke, R. (2009). Workaholism and relationship quality: A spillover-crossover perspective. *Journal of Occupational Health Psychology, 14,* 23–33. doi: 10.1037/a0013290

Baldwin, D. R., Jackson, D., Okoh, I., & Cannon, R. L. (2011). Resiliency and optimism: An African

American senior citizen's perspective. *Journal of Black Psychology, 37*, 24–41.

Ballester, S., Sastre, M. T. M., & Mullet, E. (2009). Forgivingness and lay conceptualizations of forgiveness. *Personality and Individual Differences, 47*, 605–609. doi: 10.1016/j.paid .2009.05.016

Baltes, M. M., & Carstensen, L. L. (1996). The process of successful aging. *Aging in Society, 16*, 397–422.

Baltes, P. B. (1993). The aging mind: Potential and limits. *The Gerontologist, 33*, 580–594.

Baltes, P. B., Glück, J., & Kunzmann, U. (2002). Wisdom: Its structure and function in regulating successful life-span development. In C. R. Snyder & S. J. Lopez (Eds.), *The handbook of positive psychology* (pp. 327–347). New York: Oxford University Press.

Baltes, P. B., & Smith, J. (1990). The psychology of wisdom and its ontogenesis. In R. J. Sternberg (Ed.), *Wisdom: Its nature, origins, and development* (pp. 87–120). New York: Cambridge University Press.

Baltes, P. B., & Staudinger, U. (1993). The search for a psychology of wisdom. *Current Directions in Psychological Science, 2*, 75–80.

Baltes, P. B., & Staudinger, U. (2000). Wisdom: A metaheuristic (pragmatic) to orchestrate mind and virtue toward excellence. *American Psychologist, 55*, 122–136.

Bamford, C. M., & Lagattuta, K. H. (2012). Looking on the bright side: Children's knowledge about the benefits of positive versus negative thinking. *Child Development, 83*, 667–682.

Bandura, A. (1977). Self-efficacy: Toward a unifying theory of behavior change. *Psychological Review, 84*, 191–215.

Bandura, A. (1982). Self-efficacy mechanism in human agency. *American Psychologist, 37*, 122–147.

Bandura, A. (1986). *Social foundations of thought and action.* New York: Prentice Hall.

Bandura, A. (1989a). Human agency in social cognitive theory. *American Psychologist, 44*, 1175–1184.

Bandura, A. (1989b). Regulation of cognitive processes through perceived self-efficacy. *Developmental Psychology, 25*, 729–735.

Bandura, A. (1991). Self-efficacy mechanism in physiological activation and health-promoting behavior. In J. Madden IV (Ed.), *Neurobiology of learning, emotion and affect* (pp. 229–270). New York: Raven.

Bandura, A. (1993). Perceived self-efficacy in cognitive development and functioning. *Educational Psychologist, 28*, 117–148.

Bandura, A. (1995). *Manual for the construction of self-efficacy scales.* Available from Albert Bandura, Department of Psychology, Stanford University, Stanford, CA 94305–2130.

Bandura, A. (1997). *Self-efficacy: The exercise of control.* New York: Freeman.

Bandura, A. (2000). Social cognitive theory in context. *Journal of Applied Psychology: An International Review, 51*, 269–290.

Bandura, A., Adams, N. E., & Beyer, J. (1977). Cognitive processes mediating behavioral change. *Journal of Personality and Social Psychology, 35*, 125–139.

Bandura, A., Barbaranelli, C., Vittorio Caprara, G., & Pastorelli, C. (2001). Self-efficacy beliefs as shapers of children's aspirations and career trajectories. *Child Development, 72*, 187–206.

Bandura, A., Taylor, C. B., Williams, S. L., Mefford, I. N., & Barchas, J. D. (1985). Catecholamine secretion as a function of perceived coping self-efficacy. *Journal of Consulting and Clinical Psychology, 53*, 406–414.

Banerjee, T., & Banerjee, G. (1995). Determinants of help-seeking behavior in cases of epilepsy attending a teaching hospital in India: An indigenous explanatory model. *International Journal of Social Psychiatry, 41*, 217–230.

Bao, K. J., & Lyubomirsky, S. (2013). Making it last: Combating hedonic adaptation in romantic relationships. *The Journal of Positive Psychology, 8*, 196–206.

Barber, B. R., & Battistoni, R. M. (1993). *Education for democracy: A sourcebook for students and teachers.* Dubuque, IA: Kendall/Hunt.

Barclay, P. (2010). Altruism as a courtship display: Some effects of third-party generosity on audience perceptions. *British Journal of Psychology, 101*, 123–135.

Bargh, J., & Chartrand, T. (1999). The unbearable automaticity of being. *American Psychologist, 54*, 462–479.

Barker, S. L., Funk, S. C., & Houston, B. K. (1988). Psychological treatment versus nonspecific factors: A meta-analysis of conditions that engender comparable expectations of improvement. *Clinical Psychology Review, 8,* 579–594.

Bar-On, R. (1997). The *Bar-On Emotional Quotient Inventory (EQ-i): A test of emotional intelligence.* Toronto, Ontario: Multi-Health Systems.

Bar-On, R. (2000). Emotional and social intelligence: Insights from the Emotional Quotient Inventory. In R. Bar-On & J. D. A. Parker (Eds.), *The handbook of emotional intelligence* (pp. 363–388). San Francisco: Jossey-Bass.

Bar-On, R. (2013). The application of emotional intelligence in the reduction of risk factors: New perspectives in career counseling and development. *Counseling: Giornale Italiano di Ricerca e Applicazioni, 6,* 7–23.

Barone, D., Maddux, J. E., & Snyder, C. R. (1997a). The social cognitive construction of difference and disorder. In D. Barone, J. E. Maddux, & C. R. Snyder (Eds.), *Social cognitive psychology: History and current domains* (pp. 397–428). New York: Plenum.

Barone, D., Maddux, J. E., & Snyder, C. R. (1997b). *Social cognitive psychology: History and current domains.* New York: Plenum.

Bartholomew, K., & Horowitz, L. M. (1991). Attachment styles among young adults: A test of a four-category model. *Journal of Personality and Social Psychology, 61,* 226–244.

Bartlett, M. Y., Condon, P., Cruz, J., Baumann, J., & Desteno, D. (2012). Gratitude: Prompting behaviours that build relationships. *Cognition and Emotion, 26,* 2–13.

Batson, C. D. (1991). *The altruism question: Toward a social-psychological answer.* Hillsdale, NJ: Lawrence Erlbaum.

Batson, C. D., Ahmad, N., & Lishner, D. A. (2009). Empathy and altruism. In S. J. Lopez & C. R. Snyder (Eds.), *Oxford handbook of positive psychology* (pp. 417–426). New York: Oxford University Press.

Batson, C. D., Polycarpou, M. P., Harmon-Jones, E., Imhoff, H. J., Mitchener, E. C., Bednar, L. L., . . . Highberger, L. (1997). Empathy and attitudes: Can feeling for a member of a stigmatized group improve feelings toward the group? *Journal of Personality and Social Psychology, 72,* 105–118.

Battista, J., & Almond, R. (1973). The development of meaning in life. *Psychiatry, 36,* 409–427.

Bauermeister, J. A., Johns, M. M., Pingel, E., Eisenberg, A., Santana, M. L., & Zimmerman, M. (2011). Measuring love: Sexual minority male youths' ideal romantic characteristics. *Journal of LGBT Issues in Counseling, 5,* 102–121.

Baumeister, R. F., Bratslavsky, E., Finkenhaur, C., & Vohs, K. D. (2001). Bad is stronger than good. *Review of General Psychology, 5,* 323–370.

Baumeister, R. F., Faber, J. E., & Wallace, H. M. (1999). Coping and ego depletion. In C. R. Snyder (Ed.), *Coping: The psychology of what works* (pp. 50–69). New York: Oxford University Press.

Baumeister, R. F., & Leary, M. R. (1995). The need to belong: Desire for interpersonal attachment as a fundamental human motivation. *Psychological Bulletin, 117,* 497–529.

Baumeister, R. F., & Vohs, K. D. (2002). The pursuit of meaningfulness in life. In C. R. Snyder & S. J. Lopez (Eds.), *The handbook of positive psychology* (pp. 608–618). New York: Oxford University Press.

Baumgarten, M., Thomas, D., Poulin de Courval, L., & Infante-Rivard, C. (1988). Evaluation of a mutual help network for the elderly residents of planned housing. *Psychology and Aging, 3,* 393–398.

Beard, K. S., Hoy, W. K. W., & Hoy, A. (2010). Academic optimism of individual teachers: Confirming a new construct. *Teaching and Teacher Education, 26,* 1136–1144.

Bechara, A., Tranel, D., Damasio, H., & Damasio, A. R. (1996). Failure to respond autonomically to anticipated future outcomes following damage to prefrontal cortex. *Cerebral Cortex, 6,* 215–225.

Becker, H. S. (1963). *Outsiders.* New York: Free Press.

Becker, J. A., & Smenner, P. C. (1986). The spontaneous use of *thank you* by preschoolers as a function of sex, socioeconomic status, and listener status. *Language in Society, 15,* 537–546.

Behnke, A. O., Ames, N., & Hancock, T. U. (2012). What would they do? Latino church leaders and domestic violence. *Journal of Interpersonal Violence, 27,* 1259–1275.

Belgrave, F. Z., Chase-Vaughn, G., Gray, F., Addison, J. D., & Cherry, V. R. (2000). The effectiveness of a culture and gender-specific intervention for increasing resiliency among African American preadolescent females. *Journal of Black Psychology, 26.* 133–147.

Bell, C. C., & McBride, D. F. (2012). Prevention of mental and substance use and abuse disorders and comorbidity in African Americans. *Alcoholism Treatment Quarterly, 30,* 293–306.

Bellah, R. N., Madsen, R., Sullivan, W. M., Swidler, A., & Tipton, S. M. (1985). *Habits of the heart: Individualism and commitment in American life.* Berkeley: University of California Press.

Belsky, J., & Nezworski, T. (Eds.). (1988). *Clinical implications of attachment.* Hillsdale, NJ: Lawrence Erlbaum.

Benedikovičová, J., & Ardelt, M. (2008). The three dimensional wisdom scale in cross-cultural context: A comparison between American and Slovak college students. *Studia Psychologica, 50,* 179–190.

Benne, K. D. (1964). History of T-group in the laboratory setting. In L. P. Bradford, J. R. Gibb, & K. D. Benne (Eds.), *T-group and laboratory method: Innovation in re-education* (pp. 80–135). New York: Wiley.

Benson, H., & Proctor, W. (1984). *Beyond the relaxation response.* New York: Putnam/Berkley.

Benson, P. L. (1992). Religion and substance use. In J. F. Schumaker (Ed.), *Religion and mental health* (pp. 211–220). New York: Oxford University Press.

Benson, P. L., Leffert, N., Scales, P. C., & Blyth, D. A. (1998). Creating healthy communities for children and adolescents. *Applied Developmental Science, 2,* 138–159.

Benson, P. L., & Saito, R. N. (2000). The scientific foundations of youth development. In N. Jaffe (Ed.), *Youth development: Issues, challenges, and directions* (pp. 125–147). Philadelphia: Public/Private Ventures.

Benson, P. L., & Scales, P. C. (2009). The definition and preliminary measurement of thriving in adolescence. *Journal of Positive Psychology, 4.* 85–104.

Berg, I. K., & de Shazer, S. (1992). Making numbers talk: Language in therapy. In S. Friedman (Ed.), *The new language of change: Constructive collaboration in psychotherapy* (pp. 5–24). New York: Guilford Press.

Bergsma, A., & Ardelt, M. (2012). Self-reported wisdom and happiness: An empirical investigation. *Journal of Happiness Studies, 13,* 481–499.

Berkovich-Ohana, A., Glicksohn, J., & Goldstein, A. (2012). Mindfulness-induced changes in gamma band activity—Implications for the default mode network, self-reference, and attention. *Clinical Neurophysiology, 123,* 700–710.

Bernstein, D. M., & Simmons, R. G. (1974). The adolescent kidney donor: The right to give. *American Journal of Psychiatry, 131,* 1338–1343.

Berry, J. M., West, R. L., & Dennehey, D. M. (1989). Reliability and validity of the Memory Self-Efficacy Questionnaire. *Developmental Psychology, 25,* 701–713.

Berscheid, E., & Reis, H. T. (1998). Attraction and close relationships. In D. T. Gilbert, S. T. Fiske, & G. Lindsey (Eds.), *The handbook of social psychology* (4th ed., Vol. 2, pp. 193–281). New York: McGraw-Hill.

Berscheid, E., & Walster, E. (1978). *Interpersonal attraction* (2nd ed.). Reading, MA: Addison Wesley.

Bess, K. D., Fisher, A. T., Sonn, C. C., & Bishop, B. J. (2002). Psychological sense of community. In A. T. Fisher, C. C. Sonn, & B. J. Bishop (Eds.), *Psychological sense of community: Research, applications, and implications* (pp. 3–22). New York: Kluwer Academic/Plenum Publishers.

Betz, N. E., Klein, K., & Taylor, K. M. (1996). Evaluation of a short form of the Career Decision-Making Self-Efficacy Scale. *Journal of Career Assessment, 4,* 47–57.

Betz, N. E., & Klein Voyten, K. (1997). Efficacy and outcome expectations influence career exploration and decidedness. *Career Development Quarterly, 46,* 179–189.

Betz, N. E., & Luzzo, D. A. (1996). Career assessment and the Career Decision-Making Self-Efficacy scale. *Journal of Career Assessment, 4,* 413–428.

Betz, N. E., & Taylor, K. M. (2000). *Manual for the Career Decision-Making Self-Efficacy Scale and CDMSE-Short Form.* Unpublished document, Ohio State University, Columbus.

Biddle, S. J. H., Fox, K. R., & Boutcher, S. H. (Eds.). (2000). *Physical activity and psychological well-being*. London: Routledge.

Biegel, G. M., Brown, K. W., Shapiro, S. L., & Schubert, C. M. (2009). Mindfulness-based stress reduction for the treatment of adolescent psychiatric outpatients: A randomized clinical trial. *Journal of Consulting and Clinical Psychology, 77,* 855–866. doi: 10.037/a0016241

Bierman, K. L. (1997). Implementing a comprehensive program for the prevention of conduct problems in rural communities: The Fast Track experience. *American Journal of Community Psychology, 25,* 493–514.

Bigler, R. S., & Liben, L. S. (2006). A developmental intergroup theory of social stereotypes and prejudice. In R. V. Kail (Ed.) *Advances in child development and behaviour* (pp. 39–89). San Diego: Elsevier Academic Press.

Binet, A., & Simon, T. (1916). *The development of intelligence in children.* (E. S. Kit, Trans.). Baltimore: Williams & Williams.

Bishop, S. R. (2002). What do we really know about mindfulness-based stress reduction? *Psychosomatic Medicine, 64,* 71–84.

Bishop, S. R., Lau, M., Shapiro, S., Carlson, L., Anderson, N. D., Carmody, J., et al. (2004). Mindfulness: A proposed operational definition. *Clinical Psychology: Science and Practice, 11,* 230–241.

Biswas-Diener, R. (2012). *The courage quotient: How science can make you braver.* San Francisco: John Wiley & Sons.

Biswas-Diener, R., & Diener, E. (2006). From the equator to the north pole: A study of character strengths. *Journal of Happiness Studies, 7,* 293–310.

Bjornesen, C. A. (2000). Undergraduate student perceptions of the impact of faculty activities in education. *Teaching of Psychology, 27,* 205–208.

Black, B. (2001). The road to recovery. *Gallup Management Journal, 1,* 10–12.

Black, D. S., Sussman, S., Johnson, C., & Milam, J. (2012). Psychometric assessment of the Mindful Attention Awareness Scale (MAAS) among Chinese adolescents. *Assessment, 19,* 45–52.

Black, J., & Reynolds, W. M. (2013). Examining the relationship of perfectionism, depression, and

optimism: Testing for mediation and moderation. *Personality and Individual Differences, 54,* 426–431.

Blazer, D. (1994). Epidemiology of late-life depression. In L. Schneider, C. F. Reynolds, B. Lebowitz, & A. Friedhoff (Eds.), *Diagnosis and treatment of depression in late life* (pp. 9–19). Washington, DC: American Psychiatric Association.

Bliss, D., & Ekmark, S. S. (2013). Gender differences in spirituality in persons in alcohol and drug dependence treatment. *Alcoholism and Treatment Quarterly, 31,* 25–37.

Blum, D. (1998, May 1st). Finding strength: How to overcome anything. *Psychology Today.* Retrieved from http://www.psychologytoday.com/articles/199805/finding-strength-how-overcome-anything

Blustein, D. L. (1989). The role of goal instability and career self-efficacy in the career exploration process. *Journal of Vocational Behavior, 35,* 194–203.

Boehm, J. K., & Lyubormirsky, S. (2008). Does happiness promote career success? *Journal of Career Assessment, 16,* 101–116. doi: 10.1177/1069072707308140

Boehm, J. K., Lyubomirsky, S., & Sheldon, K. M. (2011). A longitudinal experimental study comparing the effectiveness of happiness-enhancing strategies in Anglo Americans and Asian Americans. *Cognition and Emotion, 25,* 1263–1272.

Bokser, B. Z. (1989). *The Talmud: Selected writings.* New York: Paulist Press.

Boniwell, I., & Zimbardo, P. G. (2004). Balancing one's time perspective in pursuit of optimal functioning. In P. A. Linley & S. Joseph (Eds.), *Positive psychology in practice* (pp. 165–180). Hoboken, NJ: Wiley.

Bono, G., Emmons, R. A., & McCullough, M. E. (2004). Gratitude in practice and the practice of gratitude. In P. A. Linley & S. Joseph (Eds.), *Positive psychology in practice* (pp. 464–481). Hoboken, NJ: Wiley.

Botanov, Y., Keil, K. M., Ilardi, S. S., Scheller, V. K., Sharp, K. L., & Williams, C. L. (2012). Successful treatment of depression via therapeutic lifestyle change: Preliminary controlled-trial results. Poster presentation at the annual conference of the Association for Psychological Science, Chicago.

Botvin, G. J., & Toru, S. (1988). Preventing adolescent substance abuse through life skills training. In R. H. Price, E. L. Cowen, R. P. Lorion, & J. Ramos-McKay (Eds.), *Fourteen ounces of prevention: A casebook for practitioners* (pp. 98–110). Washington, DC: American Psychological Association.

Bowers, E. P., Geldhof, G., Schmid, K. L., Napolitano, C. M., Minor, K., & Lerner, J. V. (2012). Relationships with important nonparental adults and positive youth development: An examination of youth self-regulatory strengths as mediators. *Research in Human Development, 9,* 298–316.

Bowlby, J. (1969). *Attachment and loss. Vol. I: Attachment.* London: Tavistock.

Bowlby, J. (1988). *A secure base: Parent–child attachment and healthy human development.* New York: Basic Books.

Boyd-Franklin, N. (2010). Incorporating spirituality and religion into the treatment of African American clients. *The Counseling Psychologist, 38,* 976–1000.

Boyle, E. A., Connolly, T. M., Hainey, T., & Boyle, J. M. (2012). Engagement in digital entertainment games: A systematic review. *Computers in Human Behavior, 28,* 771–780.

Bradburn, N. M. (1969). *The structure of psychological well-being.* Chicago: Aldine.

Brady, B. R., Vodanovich, S. J., & Rotunda, R. (2008). The impact of workaholism on work-family conflict, job satisfaction, and perception of leisure activities. *The Psychologist-Manager Journal, 11,* 241–263. doi:10.1080/10887150 802371781

Braithwaite, S., Selby, E. A., & Fincham, F. D. (2011). Forgiveness and relationship satisfaction: Mediating mechanisms. *Journal of Family Psychology, 25,* 551–559.

Brennan, K. A., Clark, C. L, & Shaver, P. R. (1998). Self-report measures of adult attachment: An integrative overview. In J. A. Simpson & W. S. Rholes (Eds.), *Attachment theory and close relationships* (pp. 46–76). New York: Guilford Press.

Bretherton, I., & Waters, E. (Eds.). (1985). *Growing points of attachment theory and research.* Chicago: University of Chicago Press.

Brezina, I. (2010). Folk conceptions of wise person's personality in Asian cultures. *Studia Psychologica, 52,* 347–353.

Breznitz, S. (1986). The effect of hope on coping with stress. In M. H. Appley & P. Trumbull (Eds.), *Dynamics of stress: Physiological, psychological, and social perspectives* (pp. 295–307). New York: Plenum.

Briones, E., Tabernero, C., Tramontano, C., Caprara, G. V., & Arenas, A. (2009). Development of a cultural self-efficacy scale for adolescents (CSES-A). *International Journal of Intercultural Relations, 33,* 301–312. doi: 10.1016/j.ijintre1 .2009.03.006

Brown, C. L., & Beninger, R. J. (2012). People newly in love are more responsive to positive feedback. *Psychological Reports, 110,* 753–763.

Brown, D. E. (1991). *Human universals.* Philadelphia: Temple University Press.

Brown, K., Weinstein, N., & Creswell, J. (2012). Trait mindfulness modulates neuroendocrine and affective responses to social evaluative threat. *Psychoneuroendocrinology, 37,* 2037–2041.

Brown, K. J., & Roberts, M. C. (2000). *An evaluation of the Alvin Ailey Dance Camp, Kansas City, Missouri.* Unpublished manuscript, University of Kansas, Lawrence.

Brown, K. W., & Ryan, R. M. (2003). The benefits of being present: Mindfulness and its role in psychological well-being. *Journal of Personality and Social Psychology, 84,* 822–848.

Brown, N. J. L., Sokal, A. D., & Friedman, H. L. (2013). The complex dynamics of wishful thinking: The critical positivity ratio. *American Psychologist, 68,* 801–813.

Brown, S. C. (2004). Learning across campus: How college facilitates the development of wisdom. *Journal of College Student Development, 45,* 134–148.

Brown, S. C., & Greene, J. A. (2006). The Wisdom Development Scale: Translating the conceptual to the concrete. *Journal of College Student Development, 47,* 1–19.

Bruhn, J. G. (1996). Creating an organizational climate for multiculturalism. *Health Care Supervisor, 14,* 11–18.

Brummett, B. R., Wade, J. C., Ponterotto, J. G., Thombs, B., & Lewis, C. (2007). Psychosocial well-being and a multicultural personality disposition. *Journal of Counseling & Development, 85,* 73–81.

Bryant, F. B. (1989). A four-factor model of perceived control: Avoiding, coping, obtaining, and savoring. *Journal of Personality, 57,* 773–797.

Bryant, F. B. (2004, May). *Capturing the joy of the moment: Savoring as a process in positive psychology.* Invited address at the meeting of the Midwestern Psychological Association, Chicago.

Bryant, F. B. (2005, February). *Pleasure—Happiness in the present.* Invited international Internet lecture, Authentic Happiness Coaching (www.authentichappinesscoaching.com), Bethesda, MD.

Bryant, F. B., & Veroff, J. (1982). The structure of psychological well-being: A sociohistorical analysis. *Journal of Personality and Social Psychology, 43,* 653–673.

Bryant, F. B., & Veroff, J. (2006). *The process of savoring: A new model of positive experience.* Mahwah, NJ: Lawrence Erlbaum.

Bryk, A. S., & Schneider, B. (2002). *Trust in schools: A core resource for improvement.* New York: Russell Sage.

Buckingham, M., & Clifton, D. O. (2001). *Now, discover your strengths.* New York: Free Press.

Buckingham, M., & Coffman, C. (1999). *First, break all the rules: What the world's greatest managers do differently.* New York: Simon & Schuster.

Bunce, S. C., Larsen, R. J., & Peterson, C. (1995). Life after trauma: Personality and daily life experiences of traumatized people. *Journal of Personality, 63,* 165–188.

Bundick, M. J. (2011). Extracurricular activities, positive youth development, and the role of meaningfulness of engagement. *The Journal of Positive Psychology, 6,* 57–74.

Burger, J. M., & Caldwell, D. F. (2000). Personality, social activities, job-search behavior, and interview success: Distinguishing between PANAS trait positive affect and NEO extraversion. *Motivation and Emotion, 24,* 51–62.

Burks, D. J., & Kobus, A. M. (2012). The legacy of altruism in health care: The promotion of empathy, prosociality and humanism. *Medication Education, 46,* 317–325.

Burnette, J. L., & Pollack, J. M. (2013). Implicit theories of work and job fit: Implications for job and life satisfaction. *Basic and Applied Social Psychology, 35,* 360–372.

Burns, G. N., Jasinski, D., Dunn, S., & Fletcher, D. (2013). Academic support services and career decision-making self-efficacy in student athletes. *The Career Development Quarterly, 61,* 161–167.

Buskist, W., Benson, T., & Sikorski, J. F. (2005). The call to teach. *Journal of Social and Clinical Psychology, 24,* 110–121.

Buss, D. (2000). The evolution of happiness. *American Psychologist, 55,* 15–23.

Butler, R. (1974). Successful aging and the role of life review. *Journal of the American Geriatric Society, 22,* 529–535.

Cabrera, N. L., & Padilla, A. M. (2004). Entering and succeeding in the "Culture of College": The story of two Mexican heritage students. *Hispanic Journal of Behavioral Sciences, 26,* 152–170.

Cadsby, C. B., Servátka, M., & Song, F. (2010). Gender and generosity: Does degree of anonymity or group gender composition matter? *Experimental Economics, 13,* 299–308.

Cameron, K. S., Dutton, J., & R. E. Quinn (Eds.). (2003). *Positive organizational scholarship: Foundations of a new discipline.* San Francisco: Berrett-Koeller Publisher.

Cameron, K. S., & Spreitzer, G. M. (2012). *The Oxford handbook of positive organizational scholarship.* New York: Oxford University Press.

Campbell, R. L., & Christopher, J. C. (1996a). Beyond formalism and altruism: The prospects for moral personality. *Developmental Review, 16,* 108–123.

Campbell, R. L., & Christopher, J. C. (1996b). Moral development theory: A critique of its Kantian presuppositions. *Developmental Review, 16,* 1–47.

Campbell, R. L., Christopher, J. C., & Bickhard, M. H. (2002). Self and values: An interactivist foundation for moral development. *Theory & Psychology, 12,* 795–822.

Campbell-Sills, L., Cohan, S. L., & Stein, M. B. (2006). Relationship of resilience to personality, coping, and psychiatric symptoms in young adults. *Behaviour Research and Therapy, 44,* 585–599.

Campos, L. P. (2012). Cultivated cultures of courage with transactional analysis. *Transactional Analysis Journal, 42,* 209–219.

Caprara, G., Di Giunta, L., Pastorelli, C., & Eisenberg, N. (2013). Mastery of negative affect: A hierarchical model of emotional self-efficacy beliefs. *Psychological Assessment, 25,* 105–116.

Carr, A. (2004). *Positive psychology: The science of happiness and human strengths.* New York: Brunner-Routledge.

Carrere, S., & Gottman, J. (1999). Predicting divorce among newlyweds from the first three minutes of a marital conflict discussion. *Family Process, 38,* 293–301.

Carrington, P. (1998). *The book of meditation.* Boston: Element Books.

Carson, J., Muir, M., Clark, S., Wakely, E., & Chander, A. (2010). Piloting a gratitude intervention in a community mental health team. *Groupwork: An Interdisciplinary Journal for Working with Groups, 20,* 73–87.

Carstensen, L. L. (1998). A life-span approach to social motivation. In J. Heckhausen & C. S. Dweck (Eds.), *Motivation and self-regulation across the lifespan* (pp. 341–364). Cambridge, England: Cambridge University Press.

Carstensen, L. L., & Charles, S. T. (1998). Emotion in the second half of life. *Current Directions in Psychological Science, 7,* 144–149.

Carstensen, L. L, Pasupathi, M., Mayr, U., & Nesselroade, J. R. (2000). Emotional experience in everyday life across the adult life span. *Journal of Personality and Social Psychology, 79,* 644–655.

Carter, R. (1977, November 29). Mentally ill still carry stigma. [*New York Times* feature]. *Lawrence Journal-World,* p. D4.

Carter, R. T. (1991). Cultural values: A review of empirical research and implications for counseling. *Journal of Counseling & Development, 70,* 164–173.

Carver, C. S., Pozo, C., Harris, S. D., Noriega, V., Scheier, M. F., Robinson, D. S., et al. (1993). How coping mediates the effect of optimism on distress: A study of women with early stage breast cancer. *Journal of Personality and Social Psychology, 65,* 375–390.

Carver, C. S., & Scheier, M. F. (1993). Vigilant and avoidant coping in two patient samples. In H. W. Krohne (Ed.), *Attention and avoidance: Strategies in coping with aversiveness* (pp. 295–320). Seattle, WA: Hogrefe & Huber.

Carver, C. S., & Scheier, M. F. (1994). Situational coping and coping dispositions in a stressful

transaction. *Journal of Personality and Social Psychology, 66,* 184–195.

Carver, C. S., & Scheier, M. F. (1998). *On the self-regulation of behavior.* New York: Cambridge University Press.

Carver, C. S., & Scheier, M. F. (1999). Optimism. In C. R. Snyder (Ed.), *Coping: The psychology of what works* (pp. 182–204). New York: Oxford University Press.

Carver, C. S., & Scheier, M. F. (2002). Optimism. In C. R. Snyder & S. J. Lopez (Eds.), *The handbook of positive psychology* (pp. 231–243). New York: Oxford University Press.

Carver, C. S., Scheier, M. F., Miller, C. J., & Fulford, D. (2009). Optimism. In S. J. Lopez & C. R. Snyder (Eds.), *Oxford handbook of positive psychology* (pp. 303–311). New York: Oxford University Press.

Carver, C. S., Scheier, M. F., & Segerstrom, S. C. (2010). Optimism. *Clinical Psychology Review, 30,* 879–889.

Carver, C. S., Scheier, M. F., & Weintraub, J. K. (1989). Assessing coping strategies: A theoretically based approach. *Journal of Personality and Social Psychology, 56,* 267–283.

Casey, B. R. (2013). Innovations in primary prevention: Emerging research from CDC's prevention research centers. *Journal of Primary Prevention, 34,* 3–4.

Casey, R. J., & Berman, J. S. (1985). The outcome of psychotherapy with children. *Psychological Bulletin, 98,* 388–400.

Cassell, E. J. (2009). Compassion. In S. J. Lopez & C. R. Snyder (Eds.), *Oxford handbook of positive psychology* (pp. 393–403). New York: Oxford University Press.

Catak, P. (2012). The Turkish version of Mindful Attention Awareness Scale: Preliminary findings. *Mindfulness, 3,* 1–9.

Catalano, R. F., Berglund, M. L., Ryan, J. A. M., Lonczak, H. S., & Hawkins, J. D. (1998). *Positive youth development in the United States: Research findings on evaluations of positive youth development programs.* Retrieved from http://aspe.hhs.gov/hsp/ PositiveYouthDev99/

Catalano, R. F., Berglund, M. L., Ryan, J. A. M., Lonczak, H. S., & Hawkins, J. D. (2002). Positive youth development in the United States: Research findings on evaluations of positive youth development programs. *Journal of the American Academy of Political and Social Science, 591,* 98–124.

Catalino, L. I., & Fredrickson, B. L. (2011). A Tuesday in the life of a flourisher: The role of positive emotional reactivity in optimal mental health. *Emotion, 11,* 938–950.

Ceci, S. J., & Papierno, P. B. (2005). The rhetoric and reality of gap closing: When the "have-nots" gain but the "haves" gain even more. *American Psychologist, 60,* 149–160.

Cederblad, M., Dahlin, L., Hagnell, O., & Hansson, K. (1995). Intelligence and temperament as protective factors for mental health: A cross-sectional and prospective epidemiological study. *European Archives of Psychiatry and Clinical Neuroscience, 245,* 11–19.

Cerezo, M. A., & Frias, D. (1994). Emotional and cognitive adjustment in abused children. *Child Abuse and Neglect, 18,* 923–932.

Chambless, D. L., Baker, M., Baucom, D. H., Beutler, L. E., Calhoun, K. S., Crits-Christoph, P., et al. (1998). Update: On empirically validated therapies, II. *Clinical Psychology, 51,* 3–16.

Chambless, D. L., & Hollon, S. D. (1998). Defining empirically supported therapies. *Journal of Consulting and Clinical Psychology, 66,* 7–18.

Chambless, D. L., Sanderson, W. C., Shoham, V., Bennett Johnson, S., Pope, K. S., Crits-Christoph, P., . . . McCurry, S. (1996). An update on empirically validated therapies. *Clinical Psychology,* 49, 5–18.

Chan, D. K. (1994). COLINDEX: A refinement of three collectivism measures. In U. Kim, H. C. Triandis, C. Kagitcibasi, S. Choi, & G. Yoon (Eds.), *Individualism and collectivism: Theory, method, and applications* (pp. 200–210). Thousand Oaks, CA: Sage.

Chan, D. W. (2010). Gratitude intervention and subjective well-being among Chinese school teachers in Hong Kong. *Educational Psychology, 30,* 139–153.

Chan, D. W. (2011). Burnout and life satisfaction: Does gratitude intervention make a difference among Chinese school teachers in Hong Kong? *Educational Psychology, 31,* 809–823.

Chancellor, J., & Lyubomirsky, S. (2011). Happiness and thrift: When (spending) less is (hedonically) more. *Journal of Consumer Psychology, 21,* 131–138.

Chandler, C. R. (1979). Traditionalism in a modern setting: A comparison of Anglo and Mexican-American value orientations. *Human Organization, 38,* 153–159.

Chang, E. C. (1996a). Cultural differences in optimism, pessimism, and coping. Predictors of subsequent adjustment in Asian American and Caucasian American college students. *Journal of Counseling Psychology, 43,* 113–123.

Chang, E. C. (1996b). Evidence for the cultural specificity of pessimism in Asians vs. Caucasians: A test of the negativity hypothesis. *Personality and Individual Differences, 21,* 819–822.

Chang, E. C. (2001a). A look at the coping strategies and styles of Asian Americans: Similar and different? In C. R. Snyder (Ed.), *Coping with stress: Effective people and processes* (pp. 222–239). New York: Oxford University Press.

Chang, E. C. (2001b). Cultural influences on optimism and pessimism: Differences in Western and Eastern construals of the self. In E. C. Chang (Ed.), *Optimism & pessimism: Implications for theory, research, and practice* (pp. 257–280). Washington, DC: American Psychological Association.

Chang, E. C., & Banks, K. H. (2007). The color and texture of hope: Some preliminary findings and implications for hope theory and counseling among diverse racial/ethnic groups. *Cultural Diversity and Ethnic Minority Psychology, 13,* 94–103. doi: 10.1037/1099-9809.13.2.94

Chang, E. C., Maydeu-Olivares, A., & D'Zurilla, T. J. (1997). Optimism and pessimism as partially independent constructs: Relationship to positive and negative affectivity and psychological well-being. *Personality and Individual Differences, 23*(3), 433–440.

Chang, E. C., Sanna, L. J., Kim, J. M., & Srivastava, K. (2010). Optimistic and pessimistic bias in European Americans and Asian Americans: A preliminary look at distinguishing between predictions for physical and psychological health outcomes. *Journal of Cross-Cultural Psychology, 41,* 465–470.

Chang, L., Tsai, Y., & Lee, G. (2010). Gender differences in optimism: Evidence from Yahoo Kimo Taiwan's Business News Polls Centre. *Social Behavior and Personality, 38,* 61–70.

Chao, R. I. (1994). Extending research on the consequences of parenting style for Chinese Americans and European Americans. *Child Development, 72,* 1832–1843.

Charles, S. T., Mather, M., & Carstensen, L. L. (2003). Aging and emotional memory: The forgettable nature of negative images for older adults. *Journal of Experimental Psychology: General, 132,* 310–324.

Charrow, C. B. (2006). Self-efficacy as a predictor of life satisfaction in older adults. (Doctoral dissertation). Retrieved from ProQuest (#AAI3200607)

Cheavens, J., Feldman, D., Woodward, J. T., & Snyder, C. R. (2006). Hope in cognitive therapies: Working with client strengths. *Journal of Cognitive Psychotherapy: An International Quarterly, 20,* 135–145.

Cheavens, J. S., Feldman, D. B., Gum, A., Michael, S. T., & Snyder, C. R. (2006). Hope therapy in a community sample: A pilot investigation. *Social Indicators Research, 77,* 61–78.

Cheavens, J., Michael, S. T., Gum, A., Feldman, D., Woodward, J. T., & Snyder, C. R. (2001). *A group-based intervention for depressed adults.* Unpublished manuscript, University of Kansas, Lawrence.

Chen, G., Gully, S. M., & Eden, D. (2001). Validation of a new general self-efficacy scale. *Organizational Research Methods, 4,* 62–83.

Chen, L.-M., Wu, P.-J., Cheng, Y.-Y., & Hsueh, H. (2011). A qualitative inquiry of wisdom development: Educators' perspectives. *The International Journal of Aging & Human Development, 72,* 171–187.

Chency, D., Seyforth, R., & Smuts, B. (1986). Social relationships and social cognition in non-human primates. *Science, 234,* 1361–1366.

Cheng, D. H. (2000). *On Lao Tzu.* Belmont, CA: Wadsworth.

Cheung, R. (2014, January). *Energizing and transforming organizations through positive organizational initiatives.* Plenary session given at the Asian Pacific Conference on Applied Positive Psychology. Hong Kong.

Chiang, W.-T. (2012). The suppression of emotional expression in interpersonal context. *Bulletin of Educational Psychology, 43,* 657–680.

Chiavarino, C., Rabellino, D., Ardito, R. B., Cavallero, E., Palumbo, L., Bergerone, S., Gaita, F., & Bara, B. G. (2012). Emotional coping is a better predictor of cardiac prognosis than depression and anxiety. *Journal of Psychosomatic Research, 73,* 473–475.

Chickering, A. W. (1969). *Education and identity.* San Francisco: Jossey-Bass.

Chickering, A. W., & Reisser, L. (1993). *Education and identity.* San Francisco: Jossey-Bass.

Chiesa, A. A., Calati, R., & Serretti, A. (2011). Does mindfulness training improve cognitive abilities? A systematic review of neuropsychological findings. *Clinical Psychology Review, 31,* 449–464.

Chiesa, A. A., & Serretti, A. A. (2010). A systematic review of neurobiological and clinical features of mindfulness meditations. *Psychological Medicine, 40,* 1239–1252.

Chiesa, A. A., Serretti, A., & Jakobsen, J. (2013). Mindfulness: Top-down or bottom-up emotion regulation strategy?. *Clinical Psychology Review, 33,* 82–96.

Cho, W., & Cross, S. E. (1995). Taiwanese love styles and their association with self-esteem and relationship quality. *Genetic, Social, & General Psychology Monographs, 121,* 283–309.

Choi, N. G., & Landeros, C. (2011). Wisdom from life's challenges: Qualitative interviews with low- and moderate-income older adults who were nominated as being wise. *Journal of Gerontological Social Work, 54,* 592–614.

Choi, Y., Karremans, J. C., & Barendregt, H. (2012). The happy face of mindfulness: Mindfulness medication is associations with perceptions of happiness as rated by outside observers. *Journal of Positive Psychology, 7,* 30–35.

Choubisa, R., & Singh, K. (2011). Psychometrics encompassing VIA-IS: A comparative cross cultural analytical and referential reading. *Journal of The Indian Academy of Applied Psychology, 37,* 325–332.

Christensen, A. J., & Smith, T. W. (1998). Cynical hostility and cardiovascular reactivity during self-disclosure. *Psychosomatic Medicine, 55,* 193–202.

Christensen, A. L., & Rosenberg, N. K. (1991). A critique of the role of psychotherapy in brain injury rehabilitation. *Journal of Head Trauma Rehabilitation, 6,* 56–61.

Christopher, J. C. (1999). Situating psychological well-being: Exploring the cultural roots of its theory and research. *Journal of Counseling & Development, 77,* 141–152.

Christopher, J. C. (2001). Culture and psychotherapy: Toward a hermeneutic approach. *Psychotherapy: Theory, Research, Practice, and Training, 38,* 115–128.

Christopher, J. C. (2003, October). *The good in positive psychology*. Paper presented at the International Positive Psychology Summit, Washington, DC.

Christopher, J. C. (2004). Moral visions of developmental psychology. In B. Slife, F. C. Richardson, & J. Reber (Eds.), *Critical thinking about psychology: Hidden assumptions and plausible alternatives*. Washington, DC: American Psychological Association.

Christopher, J. C. (2005). Situating positive psychology. *Naming and nurturing: The e-newsletter of the Positive Psychology Section of the American Psychological Association's Counseling Psychology Division, 17,* 3–4.

Christopher, J. C., & Hickinbottom, S. (2008). Positive psychology, ethnocentrism, and the disguised ideology of individualism. *Theory & Psychology, 18,* 563–589. doi: 10.1177/0959354308093396

Christopher, J. C., & Howe, K. (2014). Future directions for a more multiculturally competent (and humble) positive psychology. In J. T. Pedrotti & L. M. Edwards (Eds.), *Perspectives on the intersection of multiculturalism and positive psychology*. New York: Springer Science + Business Media.

Christopher, J. C., Nelson, T., & Nelson, M. D. (2004). Culture and character education: Problems of interpretation in a multicultural society. *Journal of Theoretical and Philosophical Psychology, 23,* 81–101.

Chung, C., & Lin, Z. (2012). A cross-cultural examination of the positivity effect in memory: United States vs. China. *The International Journal of Aging & Human Development, 75,* 31–44.

Cialdini, R. B. (2005). What's the best secret device for engaging student interest? The answer is in the title. *Journal of Social and Clinical Psychology, 24,* 22–29.

Cialdini, R. B., Schaller, M., Houlihan, D., Arps, K., Fultz, J., & Beaman, A. L. (1978). Empathy-based helping: Is it selflessly or selfishly motivated? *Journal of Personality and Social Psychology, 52,* 749–758.

Ciarrocchi, J. W., Dy-Liacco, G. S., & Deneke, E. (2008). Gods or rituals? Relational faith, spiritual discontent, and religious practices as predictors of hope and optimism. *Journal of Positive Psychology, 3,* 120–136. doi: 10.1080/17439760701760666

Clark, D. A. (2004). Design considerations in prevention research. In D. J. A. Dozois & K. S. Dobson (Eds.), *The prevention of anxiety and depression* (pp. 73–98). Washington, DC: American Psychological Association.

Clarke, G. N., Hawkins, W., Murphy, M., Sheeber, L. B., Lewinsohn, P. M., & Seeley, M. S. (1995). Targeted prevention of unipolar depressive disorder in an at-risk sample of high school adolescents: A randomized trial of a group cognitive intervention. *Journal of the American Academy of Child and Adolescent Psychiatry, 34,* 312–321.

Clauss-Ehlers, C. S. (2008). Sociocultural factors, resilience, and coping: Support for a culturally sensitive measure of resilience. *Journal of Applied Developmental Psychology, 29,* 197–212. doi: 10.1016/j.appdev.2008.02.004

Clayton, V. (1975). Erikson's theory of human development as it applies to the aged: Wisdom as contradictory cognition. *Human Development, 18,* 119–128.

Clayton, V. (1976). *A multidimensional scaling analysis of the concept of wisdom*. (Unpublished doctoral dissertation). University of Southern California, Los Angeles.

Clayton, V. (1982). Wisdom and intelligence: The nature and function of knowledge in later years. *International Journal of Aging and Human Development, 15,* 315–321.

Clayton, V., & Birren, J. E. (1980). The development of wisdom across the life span: A reexamination of an ancient topic. In P. B. Baltes & O. G. Brim (Eds.), *Life-span development and behavior* (Vol. 3, pp. 103–135). New York: Academic Press.

Cleary, T. (1992). Introduction. In T. Cleary (Trans.), *The essential Confucius* (pp. 1–11). New York: HarperCollins.

Clifton, D. O. (1997). *The self-reflection scale*. Princeton, NJ: Gallup Organization.

Clifton, D. O., & Anderson, E. (2002). *StrengthsQuest: Discover and develop your strengths in academics, career, and beyond*. Washington, DC: Gallup Organization.

Clifton, D. O., & Harter, J. K. (2003). Strengths investment. In K. S. Cameron, J. E. Dutton, & R. E. Quinn (Eds.), *Positive organizational scholarship* (pp. 111–121). San Francisco: Berrett-Koehler.

Clifton, D. O., & Nelson, P. (1992). *Soar with your strengths*. New York: Delacorte Press.

Coffman, S. (1996). Parents' struggles to rebuild family life after Hurricane Andrew. *Issues in Mental Health Nursing, 17*, 353–367.

Cohen, R. (1991). *Negotiating across cultures*. Washington, DC: United States Institute of Peace Press.

Cohn, M. A., & Fredrickson, B. L. (2009). Positive emotions. In S. J. Lopez & C. R. Snyder (Eds.), *Oxford handbook of positive psychology* (pp. 13–24). New York: Oxford University Press.

Colby, A., & Damon, W. (1995). The development of extraordinary moral commitment. In M. Killen & D. Hart (Eds.), *Morality in everyday life: Developmental perspectives* (pp. 342–370). New York: Cambridge University Press.

Colby, D. A., & Shifren, K. (2013). Optimism, mental health, and quality of life: A study among breast cancer patients. *Psychology, Health & Medicine, 18*, 10–20.

Coleman, J. S., Campbell, E. Q., Hobson, C. J., McPartland, J., Mood., A. M., Wienfeld, F. D., et al. (1966). *Equality of Educational Opportunity*. Washington, DC: U.S. Government Printing Office.

Collins, J. (2001). *Good to great*. New York: HarperCollins.

Collins, K. A., & Dozois, D. J. A. (2008). What are the active ingredients in preventative interventions for depression? *Clinical Psychology: Science and Practice, 15*, 313–330.

Compton, W., Smith, M., Cornish, K., & Qualls, D. (1996). Factor structure of mental health measures. *Journal of Personality and Social Psychology, 76*, 406–413.

Connelly, J. (2002). All together now. *Gallup Management Journal, 2*, 13–18.

Constantine, M., & Sue, D. W. (2006). Factors contributing to optimal human functioning of people of color in the United States. *The Counseling Psychologist, 34*, 228–244.

Constantine, M. G., Myers, L. J., Kindaichi, M., & Moore, J. L. (2004). Exploring indigenous methods of mental health treatment: The roles of healers and helpers in promoting psychological, physical, and spiritual well-being in people of color. *Counseling & Values, 28*, 110–125. doi: 10.1177/0011000005281318

Contreras, R., Hendrick, S. S., & Hendrick, C. (1996). Perspectives on marital love and satisfaction in Mexican American and Anglo couples. *Journal of Counseling and Development, 74*, 408–415.

Costa, P. T., & McCrae, R. R. (1988). Personality in adulthood: A six-year longitudinal study of self-reports and spouse ratings on the NEO Personality Inventory. *Journal of Personality and Social Psychology, 54*, 853–863.

Cousins, N. (1991). *Head first: The biology of hope and the healing power of the human spirit*. New York: Penguin.

Cox, D., Hallam, R., O'Connor, K., & Rachman, S. (1983). An experimental analysis of fearlessness and courage. *British Journal of Psychology, 74*, 107–117.

Cox, T. (1994). *Cultural diversity in organizations: Theory, research, and practice*. San Francisco: Berrett-Koehler.

Craft, M. A., David, G. C., & Paulson, R. M. (2013). Expressive writing in early breast cancer survivors. *Journal of Advanced Nursing, 69*, 305–315.

Cropanzano, R., & Wright, T. A. (1999). A 5-year study of change in the relationship between well-being and job performance. *Counseling Psychology Journal: Practice and Research, 51*, 252–265.

Cross, W. E. (1971). The Negro to Black conversion experience: Toward a psychology of Black liberation. *Black World, 20*, 13–27.

Crumbaugh, J. C., & Maholick, L. T. (1964). An experimental study in existentialism: The psychometric approach to Frankl's concept of noogenic neurosis. *Journal of Clinical Psychology, 20*, 200–207.

Crumbaugh, J. C., & Maholick, L. T. (1981). *Manual of instructions for the Purpose in Life Test*. Murfreesboro, TN: Psychometric Affiliates.

Csikszentmihalyi, M. (1978). Attention and the holistic approach to behavior. In K. S. Pope &

J. L. Singer (Eds.), *The stream of consciousness* (pp. 335–358). New York: Plenum.

Csikszentmihalyi, M. (1990). *Flow: The psychology of optimal experience*. New York: Harper & Row.

Csikszentmihalyi, M. (1997). *Finding flow*. New York: Basic Books.

Csikszentmihalyi, M. (1975/2000). *Beyond boredom and anxiety*. San Francisco: Jossey-Bass.

Csikszentmihalyi, M., & Csikszentmihalyi, I. S. (Eds.). (1988). *Optimal experience: Psychological studies of flow in consciousness*. New York: Cambridge University Press.

Csikszentmihalyi, M., & Rathunde, K. (1990). The psychology of wisdom: An evolutionary interpretation. In R. J. Sternberg (Ed.), *Wisdom: Its nature, origins, and development* (pp. 25–51). New York: Cambridge University Press.

Csikszentmihalyi, M., Rathunde, K., & Whalen, S. (1993). *Talented teenagers*. Cambridge, England: Cambridge University Press.

Csikszentmihalyi, M., & Robinson, R. (1990). *The art of seeing*. Malibu, CA: J. Paul Getty Museum and the Getty Center for Education in the Arts.

Cummins, R. A. (2011). Comparison theory in economic psychology regarding the Easternlin Paradox and Decreasing Marginal Utility: A critique. *Applied Research in Quality of Life, 6*, 241–252.

Cunningham, G. B. (2009). The moderating effect of diversity strategy on the relationship between racial diversity and organizational performance. *Journal of Applied Social Psychology, 39*, 1445–1460.

Curbow, B., Somerfield, M. R., Baker, F., Wingard, J. R., & Legro, M. W. (1993). Personal changes, dispositional optimism, and psychological adjustment to bone marrow transplantation. *Journal of Behavioral Medicine, 16*, 423–443.

Curran, M. A., Utley, E. A., & Muraco, J. A. (2010). An exploratory study of the meaning of marriage for African Americans. *Marriage & Family Review, 46*, 346–365.

Curry, L. A., Snyder, C. R., Cook, D. L., Ruby, B. C., & Rehm, M. (1997). The role of hope in student-athlete academic and sport achievement. *Journal of Personality and Social Psychology, 73*, 1257–1267.

Curry, R. O., & Valois, K. E. (1991). The emergence of an individualist ethos in American society. In R. O. Curry & L. B. Goodheart (Eds.), *American chameleon: Individualism in trans-national context* (pp. 20–43). Kent, OH: Kent State University Press.

Cushman, P. (1990). Why the self is empty: Toward a historically situated psychology. *American Psychologist, 45*, 599–611.

Daab, W. Z. (1991, July). *Changing perspectives on individualism*. Paper presented at the International Society for Political Psychology. Finland: University of Helsinki.

Dahlbeck, D. T., & Lightsey, O. R. Jr. (2008). Generalized self-efficacy, coping, and self-esteem as predictors of psychological adjustment among children with disabilities or chronic illnesses. *Children's Health Care, 37*, 293–315. doi: 10.1080/02739610802437509

Dahlsgaard, K., Peterson, C., & Seligman, M. E. P. (2005). Shared virtue: The convergences of valued human strengths. *Review of General Psychology, 9*, 203–213.

Dalmida, S., Holstad, M., DiIorio, C., & Laderman, G. (2012). The meaning and use of spirituality among African American women living with HIV/AIDS. *Western Journal of Nursing Research, 34*, 736–765.

Damasio, A. R. (1994). *Descartes' error*. New York: Grosset/Putnam.

Damasio, A. R. (2002). A note on the neurobiology of emotions. In S. G. Post, L. G. Underwood, J. P. Schloss, & W. B. Hurlbut (Eds.), *Altruism and altruistic love: Science, philosophy, and religion in dialogue* (pp. 264–271). New York: Oxford University Press.

Damon, W. (2004). What is positive youth development? *The Annals of the American Academy of Political and Social Science, 591*, 13–24.

Danielson, A. G., Samdal, O., Hetland, J., & Wold, B. (2009). School-related social support and students' perceived life satisfaction. *Journal of Educational Research, 102*, 303–320. doi: 10.3200/JOER.102.4.303-320

Danner, D. D., Snowdon, D. A., & Friesen, W. V. (2001). Positive emotions in early life and longevity: Findings from the nun study. *Journal of Personality and Social Psychology, 80*, 804–813.

Darley, J. M., & Latane, B. (1968). Bystander intervention in emergencies: Diffusion of responsibilities. *Journal of Personality and Social Psychology, 8,* 377–383.

Darling-Hammond, L., & Youngs, P. (2002). Highly qualified teachers: What does scientifically based research tell us? *Educational Researcher, 31,* 13–25.

Davidson, A. R., Jaccard, J. J., Triandis, H. C., Morales, M. L., & Diaz-Guerrero, R. (1976). Cross-cultural model testing: Toward a solution of the etic-emic dilemma. *International Journal of Psychology, 11,* 1–13.

Davis, M. H., Luce, C., & Kraus, S. J. (1994). The heritability of characteristics associated with dispositional empathy. *Journal of Personality, 62,* 369–391.

De Cássia Marinelli, S., Bartholomeu, D., Caliatto, S. G., & de Greggi Sassi, A. (2009). Children's self-efficacy scale: Initial psychometric studies. *Journal of Psychoeducational Assessment, 27,* 145–156. doi: 10.1177/0734282908325551

De Los Reye, A. (2013). Strategic objectives for improving understanding of informant discrepancies in developmental psychopathology research. *Development and Psychopathology, 25,* 669–682.

de Lucca Freitas, L. B., Pieta, M. A. M., & Tudge, J. R. H. (2011). Beyond politeness: The expression of gratitude in children and adolescents. *Psicologia Reflexão e Critica, 24,* 757–764.

de Munck, V. C., Korotayev, A., de Munck, J., & Khaltourina, D. (2011). Cross-cultural analysis of models of romantic love among U.S. residents, Russians, and Lithuanians. *The Journal of Comparative Social Science, 45,* 128–154.

DeBate, R. D., Severson, H. H., Cragun, D. L., Gau, J. M., Merrell, L. K., Bleck, J. R., . . . Hendricson, W. (2013). Evaluation of a theory-driven e-learning intervention for future oral healthcare providers on secondary prevention of disordered eating behaviors. *Health Education Research, 28,* 472–487.

Dein, S., Cook, C. H., & Koenig, H. (2012). Religion, spirituality, and mental health: Current controversies and future decisions. *Journal of Nervous and Mental Disease, 200,* 852–855.

Delle Fave, A. (2001, December). *Flow and optimal experience.* Paper presented to Economic and Social Research Council Individual and Situational Determinants of Well-Being, Seminar 2: Work, employment, and well-being. Manchester, England: Manchester Metropolitan University.

Delle Fave, A., Brdar, I., Vella-Brodrick, D., & Wissing, M. P. (2013). Religion, spirituality, and well-being across nations: The eudaemonic and hedonic happiness investigation. In H. H. Knoop & A. Delle Fave (Eds.). *Well-being and cultures: Perspectives from positive psychology* (pp. 117–134). New York: Springer Science + Business Media.

Delle Fave, A., & Massimini, F. (1988). Modernization and the changing contexts of flow in work and leisure. In M. Csikszentmihalyi & I. Csikszentmihalyi (Eds.), *Optimal experience* (pp. 193–213). Cambridge, England: Cambridge University Press.

Delle Fave, A., & Massimini, F. (1992). The experience sampling method and the measurement of clinical change: A case of anxiety disorder. In M. deVries (Ed.), *The experience of psychopathology* (pp. 280–289). Cambridge, England: Cambridge University Press.

Demir, M., & Davidson, I. (2012). Toward a better understanding of the relationship between friendship and happiness: Perceived responses to capitalization attempts, feelings of mattering, and satisfaction of basic psychological needs in same-sex best friendships as predictors of happiness. *Journal of Happiness Studies, 14,* 525–550.

Depue, R. (1996). A neurobiological framework for the structure of personality and emotions: Implications for personality disorder. In J. Clarkin & M. Lenzenweger (Eds.), *Major theories of personality* (pp. 347–390). New York: Guilford Press.

DeShea, L., & Wahkinney, R. L. (2003, November). *Looking within: Self-forgiveness as a new research direction.* Paper presented at the International Campaign for Forgiveness Conference, Atlanta, GA.

de Tocqueville, A. (2003). *Democracy in America.* London: Penguin. (Original work published 1835)

DeWaal, F. B. M., & Pokorny, J. J. (2005). Primate conflict and its relations to human forgiveness. In E. L. Worthington (Ed.), *Handbook of forgiveness* (pp. 17–32). New York: Taylor & Francis.

Diamond, L. M., & Dickenson, J. A. (2012). The neuroimaging of love and desire: Review and future directions. *Clinical Neuropsychiatry: Journal of Treatment Evaluation, 9,* 39–46.

Dickens, M. (1897). *My father as I recall him.* Westminster, England: Roxburghe Press.

DiClemente, C. C., Fairhurst, S. K., & Piotrowski, N. A. (1995). Self-efficacy and addictive behaviors. In J. E. Maddux (Ed.), *Self-efficacy, adaptation, and adjustment: Theory, research, and application* (pp. 109–142). New York: Plenum.

Diener, E. (1984). Subjective well-being. *Psychological Bulletin, 95,* 542–575.

Diener, E. (2000). Subjective well-being: The science of happiness and a proposal for a national index. *American Psychologist, 55,* 34–43.

Diener, E. (2013). The remarkable changes in the science of well-being. *Perspective on Psychological Science, 8,* 663–666.

Diener, E., & Biswas-Diener, R. (2002). Will money increase subjective well-being? *Social Indicators Research, 57,* 119–169.

Diener, E., & Diener, M. (1995). Cross-cultural correlates of life satisfaction and self-esteem. *Journal of Personality and Social Psychology, 68,* 653–663.

Diener, E., Diener, M., & Diener, C. (1995). Factors predicting the well-being of nations. *Journal of Personality and Social Psychology, 69,* 653–663.

Diener, E., & Emmons, R. A. (1984). The independence of positive and negative affect. *Journal of Personality and Social Psychology, 47,* 1105–1117.

Diener, E., Emmons, R. A., Larsen, R. J., & Griffin, S. (1985). The Satisfaction With Life Scale. *Journal of Personality Assessment, 49,* 71–75.

Diener, E., & Larsen, R. J. (1984). Temporal stability and cross-situational consistency of affective, behavioral, and cognitive responses. *Journal of Personality and Social Psychology, 47,* 871–883.

Diener, E., & Lucas, R. (1999). Personality and subjective well-being. In D. Kahneman, E. Diener, & N. Schwartz, N. (Eds.). *Well-being: The foundations of hedonic psychology* (pp. 213–229). New York: Russell Sage.

Diener, E., Lucas, R. E., & Oishi, S. (2002). Subjective well-being: The science of happiness and life satisfaction. In C. R. Snyder & S. J. Lopez (Eds.), *The handbook of positive psychology* (pp. 63–74). New York: Oxford University Press.

Diener, E., Lucas, R., & Scollon, C.N., (2006). Beyond the hedonic treadmill: Revising the adaptation theory of well-being. *American Psychologist, 61,* 305–314. doi: 10.1037/0003066X.61.4.305

Diener, E., Ng, W., Harter, J., & Arora, R. (2010). Wealth and happiness across the world: Material prosperity predicts life evaluation, whereas psychosocial prosperity predicts positive feeling. *Journal of Personality and Social Psychology, 99,* 52–61.

Diener, E., Oishi, S., & Lucas, R. E. (2009). Subjective well-being: The science of happiness and life satisfaction. In S. J. Lopez & C. R. Snyder (Eds.), *Oxford handbook of positive psychology* (pp. 187–194). New York: Oxford University Press.

Diener, E., & Seligman, M. E. P. (2002). Very happy people. *Psychological Science, 13,* 81–84.

Diener, E., Suh, E. M., Lucas, R. E., & Smith, H. (1999). Subjective well-being: Three decades of progress. *Psychological Bulletin, 125,* 276–302.

Dienstbier, R. A. (1989). Arousal and physiological toughness: Implication for mental and physical health. *Psychological Review, 96,* 84–100.

D'Imperio, R. L., Dubow, E. F., & Ippolito, M. F. (2000). Resilient and stress-affected adolescents in an urban setting. *Journal of Clinical Child Psychology, 29,* 129–142.

Dittmann, M. (2004, September). Changing behavior through TV heroes. *APA Monitor on Psychology, 35,* 70.

Dittmann, M. (2005). Building a mentally healthy work force. *Monitor, 36,* 36–37.

Dobrin, N., & Kállay, É. (2013). The investigation of the short-term effects of a primary prevention program targeting the development of emotional and social competencies in preschoolers. *Cognition, Brain, Behavior: An Interdisciplinary Journal, 17,* 15–34.

Doherty, R. W., Hatfield, E., Thompson, K., & Choo, P. (1994). Cultural and ethnic influences on love and attachment. *Personal Relationships, 1,* 391–398.

Doll, B., & Lyon, M. A. (1998). Risk and resilience: Implications for the delivery of educational and mental health services in schools. *School Psychology Review, 27,* 348–363.

Donnay, D. A. C., & Borgen, F. H. (1999). The incremental validity of vocational self-efficacy: An examination of interest, self-efficacy, and occupation. *Journal of Counseling Psychology, 46,* 432–447.

Dovidio, J. F., Allen, J. L., & Schroeder, D. A. (1990). The specificity of empathy-induced helping: Evidence for altruism motivation. *Journal of Personality and Social Psychology, 59,* 249–260.

Dovidio, J. F., Gaertner, S. L., & Johnson, J. D. (1999, October). *New directions in prejudice and prejudice reduction: The role of cognitive representations and affect.* Paper presented at the annual meeting of the Society of Experimental Social Psychology, St. Louis, MO.

Duncan, L. G., Coatsworth, J. D., & Greenberg, M. T. (2009). A model of mindful parenting: Implications for parent–child relationships and prevention research. *Clinical Child Family Psychology Review, 12,* 255–270. doi: 10.1007/s10567-009-0046-3

Durlak, J. A. (1995). *School-based prevention programs for children and adolescents.* Thousand Oaks, CA: Sage.

Durlak, J. A., & DuPre, E. P. (2008). Implementation matters: A review of research on the influence of implementation on program outcomes and the factors affecting implementation. *American Journal of Community Psychology, 41,* 327–350.

Durlak, J. A., & Wells, A. M. (1997). Primary prevention mental health programs for children and adolescents: A meta-analytic review. *American Journal of Community Psychology, 25,* 115–152.

Dweck, C. S. (1999). *Self theories: Their role in motivation, personality, and development.* Philadelphia: Psychology Press.

Easterbrook, J. A. (1959). The effects of emotion on cue utilization and the organization of behavior. *Psychological Review, 66,* 183–200.

Ebberwein, C. A., Krieshok, T. S., Ulven, J. S., & Prosser, E. C. (2004). Voices in transition:

Lessons on career adaptability. *Career Development Quarterly, 52,* 292–308.

Eckstein, M. P., Das, K., Pham, B. T., Peterson, M. F., Abbey, C. K., Sy, J. L., & Giesbrecht, B. (2012). Neural decoding of collective wisdom with multi-brain computing. *NeuroImage, 59,* 94–108.

Edmondson, R. (2012). Intergenerational relations in the West of Ireland and sociocultural approaches to wisdom. *Journal of Family Issues, 33,* 76–98.

Eichas, K., Albrecht, R. E., Garcia, A. J., Ritchie, R. A., Varela, A., Garcia, A., . . . Kurtines, W. M. (2010). Mediators of positive youth development intervention change: Promoting change in positive and problem outcomes? *Child & Youth Care Forum, 39,* 211–237.

Eisenberg, N., & Miller, P. (1987). Empathy and prosocial behavior. *Psychological Bulletin, 101,* 91–119.

Eisenberg, N., Miller, P. A., Shell, R., McNalley, S., & Shea, C. (1991). Prosocial development in adolescence: A longitudinal study. *Developmental Psychology, 27,* 849–857.

El Harbi, S., & Grolleau, G. (2012). Does self-employment contribute to national happiness? *Journal of Socio-Economics, 41,* 670–676.

Elias, M. J., Gara, M., Ubriaco, M., Rothbaum, P. A., Clabby, J. F., & Schuyler, T. (1986). Impact of a preventive social problem-solving intervention on children's coping with middle school stressors. *American Journal of Community Psychology, 14,* 259–275.

Ellison, C. G., & Levin, J. S. (1998). The religion–health connection: Evidence, theory, and future directions. *Health Education and Behavior, 25,* 700–726.

Ellison, C. G., & Sherkat, D. E. (1993). Obedience and autonomy: Religion and parenting values reconsidered. *Journal for the Scientific Study of Religion, 32,* 313–329.

Emmons, R. A. (1986). Personal strivings: An approach to personality and subjective well-being. *Journal of Personality and Social Psychology, 51,* 1058–1068.

Emmons, R. A. (1992). Abstract versus concrete goals: Personal striving level, physical illness, and psychological well-being. *Journal* of Personality and Social Psychology, 62, 292–300.

Emmons, R. A. (2004). *Cultivating gratitude: An interview with Robert Emmons.* Retrieved from http:www.todoinstitute.com/library/public/cultivating_gratitude_an_ inter view_with_robert_emmons_phd.php)

Emmons, R. A., Cheung, C., & Tehrani, K. (1998). Assessing spirituality through personal goals: Implications for research on religion and subjective well-being. *Social Indicators Research, 45,* 391–422.

Emmons, R. A., & Hill, J. (2001). *Words of gratitude for body, mind, and soul.* Radnor, PA: Templeton Foundation Press.

Emmons, R. A., & McCullough, M. E. (2003). Counting blessings versus burdens: Experimental studies of gratitude and subjective well-being. *Journal of Personality and Social Psychology, 84,* 377–389.

Emmons, R. A., & McCullough, M. E. (Eds.). (2004). *The psychology of gratitude.* New York: Oxford University Press.

Emmons, R. A., McCullough, M. E., & Tsang, J. (2003). The assessment of gratitude. In S. J. Lopez & C. R. Snyder (Eds.), *Positive psychological assessment: A handbook of models and measures* (pp. 327–342). Washington, DC: American Psychological Association.

Emmons, R. A., & Shelton, C. S. (2002). Gratitude and the science of positive psychology. In C. R. Snyder & S. J. Lopez (Eds.), *The handbook of positive psychology* (pp. 459–471). New York: Oxford University Press.

Endrighi, R., Hamer, M., & Steptoe, A. (2011). Associations of trait optimism with diurnal neuroendocrine activity, cortisol responses to mental stress, and subjective stress measures in healthy men and women. *Psychosomatic Medicine, 73,* 672–678.

Enright, R. D. (1996). Counseling within the forgiveness triad: On forgiving, receiving forgiveness, and self-forgiveness. *Counseling and Values, 40,* 107–126.

Enright, R. D. (2000). *Helping clients forgive: An empirical guide for resolving anger and restoring hope.* Washington, DC: American Psychological Association.

Enright, R. D., Freedman, S., & Rique, J. (1998). The psychology of interpersonal forgiveness. In R. D. Enright & J. North (Eds.), *Exploring forgiveness* (pp. 46–62). Madison: University of Wisconsin Press.

Enright, R. D., & Zell, R. L. (1989). Problems encountered when we forgive another. *Journal of Psychology and Christianity, 8,* 52–60.

Erickson, R. C., Post, R. D., & Paige, A. B. (1975). Hope as a psychiatric variable. *Journal of Clinical Psychology, 31,* 324–330.

Erikson, E. H. (1950). *Childhood and society.* New York: Norton.

Erikson, E. H. (1959). *Identity and the life cycle.* Madison, CT: International Universities Press.

Erikson, E. H. (1963). *Childhood and society* (2nd ed.). New York: Norton.

Erikson, E. H. (1964). *Insight and responsibility.* New York: Norton.

Erikson, E. H. (1982). *The life cycle completed: A review.* New York: Norton.

Ersner-Hershfield, H., Mikels, J. A., Sullivan, S. J., & Carstensen, L. L. (2008). Poignancy: Mixed emotional experience in the face of meaningful endings. *Journal of Personality and Social Psychology 94,* 158–167. doi: 10.1037/0022–3514.94.1.158

Estrada, C. A., Isen, A. M., & Young, M. J. (1997). Positive affect facilitates integration of information and decreases anchoring in reasoning among physicians. *Organizational Behavior and Human Decision Processes, 72,* 117–135.

Euben, J. P., Wallach, J. R., & Ober, J. (1994). *Athenian political thought and the reconstruction of American democracy.* Ithaca, NY: Cornell University Press.

Evans, A. B., Banerjee, M., Meyer, R., Aldana, A., Foust, M., & Rowley, S. (2012). Racial socialization as a mechanism for positive development among African American youth. *Child Development Perspectives, 6,* 251–257.

Exline, J. J., & Baumeister, R. F. (2000). Expressing forgiveness and repentance: Benefits and barriers. In M. E. McCullough (Ed.), *Forgiveness: Theory, research, and practice* (pp. 133–155). New York: Guilford Press.

Ey, S., Hadley, W., Allen, D. N., Palmer, S., Klosky, J., Deptula, D., et al. (2004). A new measure of children's optimism and pessimism: The youth life orientation test. *Journal of Child Psychology and Psychiatry, 46,* 548–558.

Eysenck, H. J. (1952). The effects of psychotherapy. *Journal of Consulting and Clinical Psychology, 16,* 319–324.

Fagin-Jones, S., & Midlarsky, E. (2007). Courageous altruism: Personal and situational correlates of rescue during the Holocaust. *Journal of Positive Psychology 2,* 136–147. doi: 10.1080/174397 60701228979

Farah, C. E. (1968). *Islam: Beliefs and observances.* Woodbury, NY: Baron's Woodbury Press.

Farran, C. J., Herth, A. K., & Popovich, J. M. (1995). *Hope and hopelessness: Critical clinical constructs.* Thousand Oaks, CA: Sage.

Feeney, J., & Noller, P. (1996). *Adult attachment.* Thousand Oaks, CA: Sage.

Federal Bureau of Investigation. (2012). Hate crime statistics 2012. *FBI: Federal Bureau of Investigation.* Retrieved from http://www.fbi .gov/about-us/cjis/ucr/hate-crime/2012/topic-pages/victims/victims_final

Fefer, M. D. (2002, February 13). A lot of love in the lovemaking: Avoiding chaos, relationshipwise. *Seattle Weekly,* n.p.

Fehr, R., & Gelfand, M. J. (2010). When apologies work: How matching apology components to victims' self-construals facilitates forgiveness. *Organizational Behavior and Human Decision Processes, 113,* 37–50.

Feldman, D. B., Rand, K. L., & Kahle-Wrobleski, K. (2009). Hope and goal attachment: Testing a basic prediction of hope theory. *Journal of Social and Clinical Psychology, 28,* 479–497.

Feldman, D., & Snyder, C. R. (2005). Hope and meaning in life. *Journal of Social and Clinical Psychology, 24,* 401–421.

Fenwick, M., Costa, C., Sohal, A. S., & D'Netto, B. (2011). Cultural diversity management in Australian manufacturing organisations. *Asia Pacifica Journal of Human Resources, 49,* 494–507.

Fernandez-Ballesteros, R., Diez-Nicolas, J., Caprara, G. V., Barbaranelli, C., & Bandura, A. (2002). Determinants and structural relation of perceived personal efficacy to perceived collective efficacy. *Journal of Applied Psychology: An International Review, 51,* 107–125.

Fetchenhauer, D., Groothuis, T., & Pradel, J. (2010). Not only states but traits—Humans can identify permanent altruistic dispositions in 20s. *Evolution and Human Behavior, 31,* 80–86.

Fincham, F. (2000). Optimism and the family. In J. Gillham (Ed.), *The science of optimism and hope* (pp. 271–298). Philadelphia: Templeton Foundation Press.

Finfgeld, D. L. (1995). Becoming and being courageous in the chronically ill elderly. *Issues in Mental Health Nursing, 16,* 1–11.

Finfgeld, D. L. (1998). Courage in middle-aged adults with long-term health concerns. *Canadian Journal of Nursing Research, 30*(1), 153–169.

Fingerhut, A. W., & Maisel, N. C. (2010). Relationship formalization and individual and relationship well-being among same-sex couples. *Journal of Social and Personal Relationships, 27,* 956–969.

Fitzgerald, T. E., Tennen, H., Affleck, G., & Pransky, G. S. (1993). The relative importance of dispositional optimism and control appraisals in the quality of life after coronary artery bypass surgery. *Journal of Behavioral Medicine, 16,* 25–43.

Fontaine, K. R., Manstead, A. S. R., & Wagner, H. (1993). Optimism, perceived control over stress, and coping. *European Journal of Psychology, 7,* 267–281.

Fordyce, M. W. (1977). Development of a program to increase personal happiness. *Journal of Counseling Psychology, 24,* 511–520.

Fordyce, M. W. (1983). A program to increase happiness: Further studies. *Journal of Counseling Psychology, 30,* 483–498.

Forgas, J. P., Bower, G. H., & Moylan, S. J. (1990). Praise or blame? Affective influences on attributions for achievement. *Journal of Personality and Social Psychology, 59,* 809–819.

Forgeard, M. J. C., & Seligman, M. E. P. (2012). Seeing the glass half full: A review of the causes and consequences of optimism. *Pratiques Psychologiques, 18,* 107–120.

Forsyth, D. R. (1999). *Group dynamics* (3rd ed.). Pacific Grove, CA: Brooks/Cole.

Forsyth, D. R., & Corazzini, J. G. (2000). Groups as change agents. In C. R. Snyder & R. E. Ingram (Eds.), *Handbook of psychological change: Psychotherapy processes and practices for the 21st century* (pp. 309–336). New York: Wiley.

Forsyth, J., & Carter, R. T. (2012). The relationship between racial identity status attitudes, racism-related coping, and mental health among Black Americans. *Cultural Diversity and Ethnic Minority Psychology, 18,* 128–140

Fouad, N. A. (2002). Cross-cultural differences in vocational interests: Between-group differences on the Strong Interest Inventory. *Journal of Counseling Psychology, 49,* 282–289.

Franco, Z. E., Blau, K., & Zimbardo, P. G. (2011). Heroism: A conceptual analysis and differentiation between heroic action and altruism. *Review of General Psychology, 15,* 99–113.

Frank, J. D. (1968). The role of hope in psychotherapy. *International Journal of Psychiatry, 5,* 383–395.

Frank, J. D. (1973). *Persuasion and healing* (Rev. ed.). Baltimore: Johns Hopkins University Press.

Frank, J. D. (1975). The faith that heals. *Johns Hopkins Medical Journal, 137,* 127–131.

Frank, J. D., & Frank, J. B. (1991). *Persuasion and healing: A comparative study of psychotherapy* (3rd ed.). Baltimore, MD: Johns Hopkins University Press.

Frankl, V. (1959). *Man's search for meaning.* Boston: Beacon Press.

Frankl, V. (1966). What is meant by meaning? *Journal of Existentialism, 7,* 21–28.

Frankl, V. (1992). *Man's search for meaning: An introduction to logotherapy.* (I. Lasch, Trans.). Boston: Beacon Press.

Franz, C. E., McClelland, D. C., Weinberger, J., & Peterson, C. (1994). Parenting antecedents of adult adjustment: A longitudinal study. In C. Perris, W. A. Arrindell, & M. Eisemann (Eds.), *Parenting and psychopathology* (pp. 127–144). San Diego, CA: Academic Press.

Fredricks, J. A., & Simpkins, S. D. (2012). Promoting positive youth development through organized after-school activites: Taking a closer look at participation of ethnic minority youth. *Child Development Perspectives, 6,* 280–287.

Fredrickson, B. L. (1999). What good are positive emotions? *Review of General Psychology, 2,* 300–319.

Fredrickson, B. L. (2000). Cultivating positive emotions to optimize health and well-being. *Prevention and Treatment, 3.* Retrieved from http://journals.apa .org/prevention

Fredrickson, B. L. (2001). The role of positive emotions in positive psychology: The broaden-and-build theory of positive emotions. *American Psychologist, 56,* 218–226.

Fredrickson, B. L. (2002). Positive emotions. In C. R. Snyder & S. J. Lopez (Eds.), *The handbook of positive psychology* (pp. 120–134). New York: Oxford University Press.

Fredrickson, B. L. (2013, July 15). Updated thinking on positivity ratios. *American Psychologist.* Advance online publication. doi: 10.1037/a0033584

Fredrickson, B. L., & Joiner, T. (2002). Positive emotions trigger upward spirals toward emotional well-being. *Psychological Science, 13,* 172–175.

Fredrickson, B. L., & Losada, M. F. (2005). Positive affect and the complex dynamics of human flourishing. *American Psychologist, 60,* 678–686.

Fredrickson, B. L., Mancuso, R. A., Branigan, C., & Tugade, M. M. (2000). The undoing effects of positive emotions. *Motivation and Emotion, 24,* 237–258.

Freedman, J. L., & Doob, A. N. (1968). *Deviancy: The psychology of being different.* New York: Academic Press.

Freeman, M. A., & Bordia, P. (2001). Assessing alternative models of individualism and collectivism: A confirmatory factor analysis. *European Journal of Personality, 15,* 105–121.

Freud, S. (1936). *The problem of anxiety.* (H. A. Bunker, Trans.). New York: Norton. (Original work published 1926)

Freud, S. (1957). Instincts and their vicissitudes. In J. Strachey (Ed.), *Standard edition of the complete psychological works of Sigmund Freud* (pp. 111–142). London: Hogarth. (Original work published 1915)

Friedman, T. L. (2005). *The world is flat: A brief history of the 21st century.* New York: Farrar, Straus & Giroux.

Frijda, N. H. (1994). Emotions are functional, most of the time. In P. Ekman & R. Davidson (Eds.), *The nature of emotion: Fundamental questions* (pp. 112–122). New York: Oxford University Press.

Frijda, N. H. (1999). Emotions and hedonic experience. In D. Kahneman, E. Diener, & N. Schwartz (Eds.), *Well-being: The foundations of hedonic psychology* (pp. 190–210). New York: Russell Sage.

Frisch, M. B., Cornell, J., Villanueva, M., & Retzlaff, P. J. (1992). Clinical validation of the Quality of Life Inventory: A measure of life satisfaction for use in treatment planning and outcome assessment. *Psychological Assessment, 4,* 92–101.

Frise, N. R., & McMinn, M. R. (2010). Forgiviness and reconciliation: The differing perspectives of psychologists and Christian theologians. *Journal of Psychology and Theology, 38,* 83–90.

Fritzberg, G. J. (2001). Opportunities of substance: Reconceptualizing equality of educational opportunity. [First article in a two-part series]. *Journal of Thought, 36*(1), 43–54.

Fritzberg, G. J. (2002). Freedom that counts: The historic underpinnings of positive liberty and equality of educational opportunity. [Second article in a two-part series]. *Journal of Thought, 37*(2), 7–20.

Froh, J. J., & Bono, G. (2013). *Making grateful kids: A scientific approach to helping youth thrive.* West Conshohocken, PA: Templeton Press.

Froh, J. J., Bono, G., & Emmons, R. (2010). Being grateful is beyond good manners: Gratitude and motivation to contribute to society among early adolescents. *Motivation and Emotion, 34,* 144–157.

Froh, J. J., Fan, J., Emmons, R. A., Bono, G., Huebner, E. S., & Watkins, P. (2011). Measuring gratitude in youth: Assessing the psychometric properties of adult gratitude scales in children and adolescents. *Psychological Assessment, 23,* 311–324.

Froh, J. J., Kashdan, T. B., Ozimkowski, K. M., & Miller, N. (2009). Who benefits the most from a gratitude intervention in children and adolescents? Examining positive affects as a moderator. *Journal of Positive Psychology, 4,* 408–422. doi: 10.1080/17439760902992464

Froh, J. J., Sefick, W. J., & Emmons, R. A. (2008). Counting blessings in early adolescents: An experimental study of gratitude and subjective well-being. *Journal of School Psychology, 46,* 213–233. doi: 10.1016/j.jsp/2007.03.005

Fromm, E. (1955). *The sane society.* New York: Holt, Rinehart & Winston.

Frost, D. M. (2011). Stigma and intimacy in same-sex relationships: A narrative approach. *Journal of Family Psychology, 25,* 1–10.

Frude, N., & Killick, S. (2011). Family storytelling and the attachment relationship. *Psychodynamic Practice, 17,* 441–445.

Fuchs, C., Lee, J. K., Roemer, L., & Orsillo, S. M. (2013). Using mindfulness—and acceptance-based treatments with clients from nondominant cultural and/or maginalized backgrounds: clinical considerations, meta-analysis findings, and introduction to the special series. *Cognitive and Behavioral Practice, 20,* 1–12.

Fulcher, M., & Coyle, E. F. (2011). Breadwinner and caregiver: A cross-sectional analysis of children's and emerging adults' visions of their future family roles. *British Journal of Developmental Psychology, 29,* 330–346.

Fung, H. H., Isaacowitz, D. M., Lu, A. Y., Wadlinger, H. A., Goren, D., & Wilson, H. R. (2008). Age-related positivity enhancement is not universal: Older Chinese look away from positive stimuli. *Psychology and Aging, 23,* 440–446.

Gable, S. L., & Reis, H. T. (2001). Appetitive and aversive social interaction. In J. Harvey & A. Wenzel (Eds.), *Close romantic relationships: Maintenance and enhancement* (pp. 169–194). Mahwah, NJ: Lawrence Erlbaum.

Gable, S. L., Reis, H. T., & Elliot, A. J. (2003). Evidence for bivariate systems: An empirical test of appetition and aversion across domains. *Journal of Research in Personality, 37*(5), 349–372.

Gable, S. L., Reis, H. T., Impett, E. A., & Asher, E. R. (2004). What do you do when things go right? The intrapersonal and interpersonal benefits of sharing positive events. *Journal of Personality and Social Psychology, 87,* 228–245.

Gailliot, M. T. (2012). Happiness as surplus or freely available energy. *Psychology, 3,* 702–712.

Galen, L. W. (2012). Does religious belief promote prosociality? A critical examination. *Psychological Bulletin, 138,* 876–906.

Gallagher-Thompson, D., McKibbon, C., Koonce-Volwiler, D., Menendez, A., Stewart, D., & Thompson, L. W. (2000). Psychotherapy with older adults. In C. R. Snyder & R. E. Ingram (Eds.), *Handbook of psychological change: Psychotherapy processes and practices for the 21st century* (pp. 614–628). New York: Wiley.

Gallup, G. G. (1998). Self-awareness and the evolution of social intelligence. *Behavioral Processes, 42,* 238–247.

Gallup Organization. (1995). *Disciplining children in America: Survey of attitude and behavior of parents*. Project registration #104438. Princeton, NJ: Author.

Gallup Poll Monthly. (1996, November). Princeton, NJ: Gallup Organization.

Gambin, M., & Święcicka, M. (2012). Construction and validation of self-efficacy scale for early school-aged children. *European Journal of Developmental Psychology. 9,* 723–729.

Gao, G. (2001). Intimacy, passion, and commitment in Chinese and US American romantic relationships. *International Journal of Intercultural Relations, 25,* 329–342.

Garber, J., Clarke, G. N., Weersing V. R., Beardslee, W. R., Brent, D. A., Gladstone, T. R. G., . . . Iyengar, S. (2009). Prevention of depression in at-risk adolescents: A randomized controlled trial. *Journal of the American Medical Association, 301,* 2215–2224.

Garczynski, A. M., Waldrop, J. S., Rupprecht, E. A., & Grawitch, M. J. (2013). Differentiation between work and nonwork self-aspects as a predictor of presenteeism and engagement: Cross-cultural differences. *Journal of Occupational Health Psychology, 18,* 417–429.

Gardner, W. L., & Schermerhorn, J. R. (2004). Unleashing individual potential: Performance gains through positive organizational behavior and authentic leadership. *Organizational Dynamics, 33,* 270–281.

Gareis, E., & Wilkins, R. (2011). Love expression in the United States and Germany. *International Journal of Intercultural Relations, 35,* 391–411.

Garmezy, N. (1985). Stress-resistant children: The search for protective factors. In J. E. Stevenson (Ed.), *Recent research in developmental psychopathology: Journal of Child Psychology and Psychiatry Book Supplement 4* (pp. 213–233). Oxford, England: Pergamon Press.

Garmezy, N. (1993). Children in poverty: Resilience despite risk. *Psychiatry: Interpersonal and Biological Processes, 56,* 127–136.

Garmezy, N., Masten, A. S., & Tellegen, A. (1984). The study of stress and competence in children: A building block for developmental psychopathology. *Child Development, 55,* 97–111.

Garrett, M. T., Brubaker, M. D., Gregory, D. E., & Williams, C. R. (2012). Ayeli: A Native American–based group centering technique for college students. *Group Work and Outreach Plans for College Counselors,* 259–264.

Garrett, M. T., & Garrett, J. T. (2002). "Ayeli": Centering technique based on Cherokee spiritual traditions. *Counseling and Values, 46,* 149–158.

Gaylord-Harden, N. K. (2008). The influence of student perceptions and coping on achievement and classroom behavior among African American children. *Psychology in the Schools, 25,* 763–777. doi: 10.1002/pits

Geng, L., Zhang, L., & Zhang, D. (2011). Improving spatial abilities through mindfulness: Effects on the mental rotation task. *Cousciousness and Cognition: An International Journal, 20,* 801–806.

Gentile, D. A., & Walsh, D. A. (2002). A normative study of family media habits. *Applied Developmental Psychology, 23,* 157–178.

George, B. (2003). *Authentic leadership: Rediscovering the secrets to creating lasting value*. San Francisco: Jossey-Bass.

George, C., Kaplan, N., & Main, M. (1985). *The Adult Attachment Interview*. Unpublished protocol, Department of Psychology, University of California at Berkeley.

Gerber, M. K., Nadeem, L., Sakari Clough, P. J., Perry, J. L., Pühse, U., Elliott, CA., . . . Brand, S. (2013). Are adolescents with high mental toughness levels more resilient against stress? *Journal of the International Society for the Investigation of Stress, 29,* 164–171.

Gergen, K. J. (1985). The social constructionist movement in modern psychology. *American Psychologist, 40,* 266–275.

Gergen, M. M., & Gergen, K. J. (1998). The relational rebirthing of wisdom and courage. In S. Srivastva & D. L. Cooperrider (Eds.), *Organizational wisdom and executive courage* (pp. 134–153). San Francisco: New Lexington Press.

Getzels, J. W., & Csikszentmihalyi, M. (1976). *The creative vision*. New York: Wiley.

Ghaemmaghami, P., Allemand, M., & Martin, M. (2011). Forgiveness in younger, middle-aged, and older adults: Age and gender matters. *Journal of Adult Development, 18,* 192–203.

Giamo, L. S., Schmitt, M. T., & Outten, H. R. (2012). Perceived discrimination, group identification, and life satisfaction among multiracial people: A test of the rejection-identification model.

Cultural Diversity and Ethnic Minority Psychology, 18, 319–328.

Gibson, B., & Sanbonmatsu, D. M. (2004). Optimism, pessimism, and gambling: The downside of optimism. *Personality and Social Psychology Bulletin, 30,* 149–160.

Gilbert, P. P., McEwan, K. K., Gibbons, L. L., Chotai, S. S., Duarte, J. J., & Matos, M. M. (2012). Fears of compassion and happiness in relation to alexithymia, mindfulness, and self-criticism. *Psychology and Psychotherapy: Theory, Research, and Practice, 85,* 374–390.

Gillham, J. E. (Ed.) (2000). *The science of optimism and hope.* Philadelphia: Templeton Foundation Press.

Gillham, J. E., & Reivich, K. J. (2004). Cultivating optimism in childhood and adolescence. *The Annals of the American Academy of Political and Social Science, 591,* 146–153.

Gillham, J. E., Reivich, K. J., Jaycox, L. H., & Seligman, M. E. P. (1995). Prevention of depressive symptoms in school children: Two year follow-up. *Psychological Science, 6,* 343–351.

Gilligan, C. (1982). *In a different voice: Psychological theory and women's development.* Cambridge, MA: Harvard University Press.

Gilman, R., Huebner, S., & Buckman, M. (2008). Positive schooling. In S. J. Lopez (Ed.), *Positive psychology exploring the best in people.* Westport, CT: Greenwood Publishing Co.

Given, C. W., Stommel, M., Given, B., Osuch, J., Kurtz, M. E., & Kurtz, J. C. (1993). The influence of cancer patients' symptoms and functional states on patients' depression and family caregivers' reaction and depression. *Health Psychology, 12,* 277–285.

Gladwell, M. (2005). *Blink: The power of thinking without thinking.* New York: Little, Brown.

Glass, T. A., Seeman, T. E., Herzog, A. R., Kahn, R., & Berkman, L. F. (1995). Change in productive activity in late adulthood: MacArthur Studies of Successful Aging. *Journal of Gerontology, 50,* 65–76.

Glomb, T. M., Bhave, D. P., Miner, A. G., & Wall, M. (2011). Doing good, feeling good: Examining the role of organizational citizenship behaviors in changing mood. *Personnel Psychology, 64,* 191–223.

Glück, J., Bischof, B., & Siebenhüner, L. (2012). "Knows what is good and bad," "Can teach you things," "Does lots of crosswords": Children's knowledge about wisdom. *European Journal of Developmental Psychology, 9,* 582–598.

Glück, J., & Bluck, S. (2011). Laypeople's conceptions of wisdom and its development: Cognitive and integarative views. *The Journals of Gerontology: Series B: Psychological Sciences and Social Sciences, 66B,* 321–324.

Glück, J., Strasser, I., & Bluck, S. (2009). Gender differences in implicit theories of wisdom. *Research in Human Development, 6,* 27–44.

Godfrey, J. J. (1987). *A philosophy of human hope.* Dordrecht, Germany: Martinus Nijhoff.

Godfrey, K. F., Bonds, A. S., Kraus, M. E., Wiener, M. R., & Toch, C. S. (1990). Freedom from stress: A meta-analytic view of treatment and intervention programs. *Applied H. R. M. Research, 1,* 67–80.

Goffman, I. (1963). *Stigma: Notes on the management of spoiled identity.* Englewood Cliffs, NJ: Prentice Hall.

Goldstein, R. (2010, January 11). Miep Gies, protector of Anne Frank, dies at 100. *The New York Times.* Retrieved from http://www.nytimes.com/2010/01 /12/world/europe/12gies.html?pagewanted = all &_r = 0

Goleman, D. (1995). *Emotional intelligence: Why it can matter more than IQ.* New York: Bantam Books.

Goodman, E. (2005, April 7). Being busy not an end in itself. *Lawrence Journal-World: The Washington Post* Writers Group. Retrieved from http://www2.ljworld.com/news/2005/apr/07/ being_busy_not/?print

Gordon, A. K., Musher-Eizenman, D. R., Holub, S. C., & Dalrymple, J. (2004). What are children thankful for? An archival analysis of gratitude before and after the attacks of September 11. *Applied Developmental Psychology, 25,* 541–553. doi: 10.1016/j.appdev.2004.08 .004

Gordon, A. M., Impett, E. A., Kogan, A., Oveis, C., & Keltner, D. (2012). To have and to hold: Gratitude promotes relationship maintenance in intimate bonds. *Journal of Personality and Social Psychology, 103,* 257–274.

Gordon, C. L., Arnette, R. A. M., & Smith, R. E. (2011). Have you thanked your spouse today?: Felt and expressed gratitude among married couples. *Personality and Individual Differences, 50,* 339–343.

Gordon, K. C., & Baucom, D. H. (1998). Understanding betrayals in marriage: A synthesized model of forgiveness. *Family Process, 37,* 425–450.

Gordon, K. C., Baucom, D. H., & Snyder, D. K. (2004). An integrative intervention for promoting recovery from extramarital affairs. *Journal of Marital and Family Therapy, 30,* 213–231.

Gordon, K. C., Baucom, D. H., & Snyder, D. K. (2005). Forgiveness in couples: Divorce, infidelity, and couples therapy. In E. Worthington (Ed.), *Handbook of forgiveness* (pp. 407–422). New York: Routledge.

Gordon, K. C., Burton, S., & Porter, L. (2004). The intentions of women in domestic violence shelters to return to partners: Does forgiveness play a role? *Journal of Family Psychology, 18,* 331–338.

Gosselin, E., Lemyre, L., & Corneil, W. (2013). Presenteeism and absenteeism: Differentiated understanding of related phenomena. *Journal of Occupational Health Psychology, 18,* 75–86.

Gottman, J. M. (1994). *Why marriages succeed or fail and how you can make yours last.* New York: Simon & Schuster.

Gottman, J. M. (1999). *The seven principles for making marriage work.* New York: Crown.

Gottman, J. M., Driver, J., & Tabares, A. (2002). Building the sound marital house: An empirically derived couple therapy. In N. S. Jacobsen & A. S. Gurman (Eds.), *Clinical handbook of couple therapy* (3rd ed., pp. 373–399). New York: Guilford Press.

Gottman, J. M., Murray, J. D., Swanson, C., Tyson, R., & Swanson, K. R. (2003). *The mathematics of marriage: Dynamic nonlinear models.* Cambridge: MIT Press.

Gottschalk, L. (1974). A hope scale applicable to verbal samples. *Archives of General Psychiatry, 30,* 779–785.

Gouveia, M., Pais-Ribeiro, J., Marques, M., & Cavallio, C. M. (2012). Validitiy and reliability of the Portuguese version of the Dispositional Flow Scale-2 in exercise. *Revista de Psicología del Deporte, 21,* 81–88.

Govindji, R., & Linley, P. A. (2007). Strengths use, self-concordance and well-being: Implications for strengths, coaching, and coaching psychologists. *International Coaching Psychology Review, 2,* 143–153.

Gray, S. A., Emmons, R. A., & Morrison, A. (2001, August). *Distinguishing gratitude from indebtedness in affect and action tendencies.* Poster session presented at the annual meeting of the American Psychological Association, San Francisco.

Gray-Little, B., & Kaplan, D. (2000). Race and ethnicity in psychotherapy research. In C. R. Snyder & R. E. Ingram (Eds.), *Handbook of psychological change; Psychotherapy processes and practices for the 21st century* (pp. 591–613). New York: Wiley.

Greason, P. B., & Cashwell, C. S. (2009). Mindfulness and counseling self-efficacy: The mediating role of attention and empathy. *Counselor Education & Supervision, 49,* 2–19.

Green, D. P., Salovey, P., & Truax, K. M. (1999). Static, dynamic, and causative bipolarity of affect. *Journal of Personal and Social Psychology, 76,* 856–867.

Green, M., DeCourville, N., & Sadava, S. (2012). Positive affect, negative affect, stress, and social support as mediators of the forgiveness-health relationship. *The Journal of Social Psychology, 152,* 288–307.

Green, M. C., Strange, J. J., & Brock, T. C. (2002). *Narrative impact: Social and cognitive foundations.* Mahwah, NJ: Lawrence Erlbaum.

Greitemeyer, T., Osswald, S., Fischer, P., & Frey, D. (2007). Civil courage: Implicit theories, related concepts, and measurement. *Journal of Positive Psychology, 2,* 115–119. doi: 10.1080/17439760701228789

Grier-Reed, T., & Ganuza, Z. M. (2011). Constructivism and career decision self-efficacy for Asian Americans and African Americans. *Journal of Counseling & Development, 89,* 200–205.

Groopman, J. (2004). *The anatomy of hope: How people prevail in the face of illness.* New York: Random House.

Grossmann, I., Karasawa, M., Izumi, S., Na, J., Varnum, M. E. W., Kitayama, S., & Nisbett, R. E. (2012). Aging and wisdom: Culture matters. *Psychological Science, 23,* 1059–1066.

Gruenewald, T. L., Liao, D. H., & Seeman, T. E. (2012). Contributing to others, contributing to oneself: Perceptions of generativity and health in later life. *The Journal of Gerontology: Series B: Psychological Sciences and Social Sciences, 67,* 660–665.

Gudykunst, W. B. (Ed.). (1993). *Communication in Japan and the United States.* Albany: State University of New York Press.

Guignon, C. (2002). Hermeneutics, authenticity and the aims of psychology. *Journal of Theoretical & Philosophical Psychology, 22,* 83–102.

Gurung, R. A. R., Taylor, S. E., & Seeman, T. E. (2003). Accounting for changes in social support among married older adults: Insights from the MacArthur Studies of Successful Aging. *Psychology and Aging, 18,* 487–496.

Haase, C. M., Poulin, M. J., & Heckhausen, J. (2012). Happiness as a motivator: Positive affect predicts primary control striving for career and educational goals. *Personality and Social Psychology Bulletin, 38,* 1093–1104.

Haase, J. E. (1987). Components of courage in chronically ill adolescents: A phenomenological study. *Advances in Nursing Science, 9*(2), 64–80.

Haberman, D. L. (1998). Confucianism: The way of the sages. In L. Stevenson & D. L. Haberman, *Ten theories of human nature* (3rd ed., pp. 25–44). New York: Oxford University Press.

Hackman, J. R., & Oldham, G. R. (1980). *Work design.* Reading, MA: Addison-Wesley.

Haidt, J. (2000, January). *Awe and elevation.* Paper presented at the Akumal II: A Positive Psychology Summit, Akumal, Mexico.

Haidt, J. (2002). The positive emotion of elevation. In C. R. Snyder & S. J. Lopez (Eds.), *The handbook of positive psychology* (p. 753). New York: Oxford University Press.

Haigh, E. P., Moore, M. T., Kashdan, T. B., & Fresco, D. M. (2011). Examination of the factor structure and concurrent validity of the Langer Mindfulness/Mindlessness Scale. *Assessment, 18,* 11–26.

Haitch, R. (1995). How Tillich and Kohut find courage in faith. *Pastoral Psychology, 44,* 83–97.

Haley, J. (Producer), & Fleming, V. (Director). (1939). *The wizard of Oz* [Motion picture]. United States: MGM.

Hall, G. S. (1922). *Senescence: The last half of life.* New York: D. Appleton.

Hall, J. H., & Fincham, F. D. (2005). Self-forgiveness: The stepchild of forgiveness research. *Journal of Social and Clinical Psychology, 24,* 621–637.

Halperin, D., & Desrochers, S. (2005). Social psychology in the classroom: Applying what we teach as we teach it. *Journal of Social and Clinical Psychology, 24,* 51–61.

Hamer, D. (2004). *The God gene: How faith is hardwired into our genes.* New York: Doubleday.

Hamilton, D. L. (1981). *Cognitive processes in stereotyping and intergroup behavior.* Hillsdale, NJ: Lawrence Erlbaum.

Hamilton, E. (1969). *Mythology: Timeless tales of gods and heroes.* New York: Mentor.

Hannah, S. T., Sweeney, P. J., & Lester, P. B. (2007). Toward a courageous mindset: The subject act and experience of courage. *Journal of Positive Psychology, 2,* 129–135. doi: 10.1080/17439760701228854

Hannon, P. A., Finkel, E. J., Kumashiro, M., & Rusbult, C. E. (2012). The soothing effects of forgiveness on victims' and perpetrators' blood pressure. *Personal Relationships, 19,* 279–289.

Hanushek, E. A. (1994). *Making schools work: Improving performance and controlling costs.* Washington, DC: Brookings Institution.

Hanushek, E. A., Kain, J. F., O'Brien, D. M., & Rivkin, S. G. (2004). *The market for teacher quality* (Working paper # 11154). Washington, DC: National Bureau of Economic Research.

Hart, P. M. (1999). Predicting employee satisfaction: A coherent model of personality, work, and nonwork experiences, and domain satisfaction. *Journal of Applied Psychology, 84,* 564–584.

Harter, J. K., & Schmidt, F. L. (2002). Employee engagement and business-unit performance. *Psychologist-Manager Journal, 4,* 215–224.

Harter, J. K., Schmidt, F. L., & Hayes, T. L. (2002). Business-unit-level relationship between employee satisfaction, employee engagement, and business outcomes: A meta-analysis. *Journal of Applied Psychology, 87,* 268–279.

Harvey, I., & Cook, L. (2010). Exploring the role of spirituality in self-management practices among older African American and non-Hispanic White women with chronic conditions. *Chronic Illness, 6,* 111–124.

Harvey, J., & Delfabbro, P. H. (2004). Resilience in disadvantaged youth: A critical overview. *Australian Psychologist, 39,* 3–13.

Harvey, J. H., & Ormarzu, J. (1997). Minding the close relationship. *Personality and Social Psychology Review, 1,* 223–239.

Harvey, J. H., Pauwels, B. G., & Zicklund, S. (2001). Relationship connection: The role of minding in the enhancement of closeness. In C. R. Snyder & S. J. Lopez (Eds.), *The handbook of positive psychology* (pp. 423–433). New York: Oxford University Press.

Haski-Leventhal, D. (2009). Altruism and volunteerism: The perceptions of altruism in four disciplines and their impact on the study of volunteerism. *Journal for the Theory of Social Behavior, 39,* 271–299. doi: 10.1111/j.1468-5914 .2009.00405.x

Hass, M., & Graydon, K. (2009). Sources of resiliency among successful foster youth. *Children and Youth Services Review, 31,* 457–463. doi:10.10 16/j.childyouth.2008.10.001

Hatfield, E. (1988). Passionate and companionate love. In R. J. Sternberg & M. L. Barnes (Eds.), *The psychology of love* (pp. 191–217). New Haven, CT: Yale University Press.

Hatfield, E., & Rapson, R. L. (1996). *Love and sex: Cross-cultural perspectives.* Boston: Allyn & Bacon.

Havighurst, R. J. (1961). Successful aging. *The Gerontologist, 1*(1), 8–13.

Haworth, J. T. (1997). *Work, leisure and well-being.* London: Routledge.

Hayashi, A., Abe, N., Ueno, A., Shigemune, Y., Mori, E., Tashiro, M., & Fujii, T. (2010). Neural correlates of forgiveness for moral transgressions involving deception. *Brain Research, 1332,* 90–99.

Hayes, L., Bach, P. A., & Boyd, C. P. (2010). Psychological treatment for adolescent depression: Perspectives on the past, present, and future. *Behaviour Change, 27,* 1–18.

Hays, P. A. (2008). *Addressing cultural competencies in practice, second edition: Assessment, diagnosis, and therapy.* Washington, DC: American Psychological Association.

Hazan, C., & Shaver, P. (1987). Romantic love conceptualized as an attachment process. *Journal of Personality and Social Psychology, 52,* 511–524.

Hebl, J. H., & Enright, R. D. (1993). Forgiveness as a psychotherapeutic goal with elderly females. *Psychotherapy, 30,* 658–667.

Hecht, T. L., Marston, P. J., & Larkey, L. K. (1994). Love ways and relationship quality. *Journal of Social and Personal Relationships, 11,* 25–43.

Heine, C. (1996). *Flow and achievement in mathematics.* (Unpublished doctoral dissertation). University of Chicago.

Heinonen, K., Räikkönen, K., Scheier, M. F., Pesonen, A.-K., Keskivaara, P., Järvenpää, A.-L., & Strandberg, T. (2006). Parents' optimism is related to their ratings of their children's behavior. *European Journal of Psychology, 20,* 421–445.

Heitmann, D., Schmuhl, M., Reinisch, A., & Bauer, U. (2012). Primary prevention for children of mentally ill parents: The *Kanu*-program. *Journal of Public Health, 20,* 125–130.

Hektner, J. (1996). *Exploring optimal personality development: A longitudinal study of adolescents.* (Unpublished doctoral dissertation). University of Chicago.

Heller, K., Wyman, M. F., & Allen, S. M. (2000). Future directions for prevention science: From research to adoption. In C. R. Snyder & R. E. Ingram (Eds.), *Handbook of psychological change: Psychotherapy processes and practices for the 21st century* (pp. 660–680). New York: Wiley.

Heller, K. J. (1989). The return to community. *American Journal of Community Psychology, 17,* 1–16.

Helms, J. E., & Cook, D. A. (1999). *Using race and culture in counseling and psychotherapy: Theory and process.* Needham Heights, MA: Allyn & Bacon.

Helweg-Larsen, M., Harding, H. G., & Klein, W. P. (2011). Will I divorce or have a happy marriage?: Gender differences in comparative optimism and estimation of personal chances among U.S. college students. *Basic and Applied Social Psychology, 33,* 157–166.

Hendrick, C., & Hendrick, S. S. (2009). Love. In S. J. Lopez & C. R. Snyder (Eds.), *Oxford handbook of positive psychology* (pp. 447–454). New York: Oxford University Press.

Hendrick, S. S., & Hendrick, C. (1992). *Romantic love.* Newbury Park, CA: Sage.

Hendrick, S. S., & Hendrick, C. (1993). Lovers as friends. *Journal of Social and Personal Relationships, 10,* 459–466.

Henry, J. (2004). Positive and creative organization. In P. A. Linley & S. Joseph (Eds.), *Positive psychology in practice* (pp. 269–285). Hoboken, NJ: Wiley.

Herrbach, O. (2006). A matter of feeling? The affective tone of organizational commitment and identification. *Journal of Organizational Behavior, 27,* 629–643. doi: 10.1002/job.362

Herzberg, F. (1966). *Work and the nature of man.* Chicago: World Publishing.

Hill, G., & Swanson, H. L. (1985). Construct validity and reliability of the Ethical Behavior Rating Scale. *Educational and Psychological Measurement, 45,* 285–292.

Hill, P. C., Pargament, K. I., Hood, R. W., Jr., McCullough, M. E., Swyers, J. P., Larson, D. B., & Zinnbauer, B. J. (2000). Conceptualizing religion and spirituality: Points of commonality, points of departure. *Journal for the Theory of Social Behavior, 30,* 51–77.

Hill, P. L., Allemand, M., & Roberts, B. W. (2013). Examining the pathways between gratitude and self-rated physical health across adulthood. *Personality and Individual Differences, 54,* 92–96.

Hillemeier, M. M., Morgan, P. L., Farkas, G., & Maczuga, A. (2013). Quality disparities in child care for at-risk children: Comparing Head Start and non-Head Start settings. *Maternal Child Health Journal, 17,* 180–188.

Hilton, J. M., Gonzalez, C. A., Saleh, M., Maitoza, R., & Anngela-Cole, L. (2012). Perceptions of successful aging among older Latinos, in cross-cultural context. *Journal of Cross-Cultural Gerontology, 27,* 183–199.

Hirsch, J. K., Visser, P. L., Chang, E. C., & Jeglic, E. L. (2012). Race and ethnic differences in hope and hopelessness as moderators of the association between depressive symptoms and suicidal behavior. *Journal of American College Health, 60,* 115–125.

Hitlin, S. (2007). Doing good, feeling good: Values and the self's moral center. *Journal of Positive Psychology, 2,* 249–259. doi: 10.1080/17439760 701552352

Ho, M. K. (1987). *Family therapy with ethnic minorities.* Newbury Park, CA: Sage.

Ho, S. M. Y., Rochelle, T. L., Law, L. S. C., Duan, W., Bai, Y., & Shih, S. (2014). Methodological issues in positive psychology research with diverse populations: Exploring strengths among Chinese adults. In J. T. Pedrotti & L. M. Edwards (Eds.), *Perspectives on the intersection of multiculturalism and positive psychology.* New York: Springer Science + Business Media.

Hodges, T. D. (2003). *Results of the 2002 StrengthsFinder follow-up survey.* Princeton, NJ: Gallup Organization.

Hodges, T. D., & Clifton, D. O. (2004). Strengths-based development in practice. In P. A. Linley & S. Joseph (Eds.), *Positive psychology in practice* (pp. 256–268). Hoboken, NJ: Wiley.

Hodges, T. D., & Harter, J. K. (2005). A review of the theory and research underlying the StrengthsQuest Program for students. *Educational Horizons, 83,* 190–201.

Hofmann, D. A., & Tetrick, L. E. (Eds.). (2003). *Health and safety in organizations: A multilevel perspective.* San Francisco: Jossey-Bass.

Hofstede, G. (1980). *Culture's consequences.* Beverly Hills, CA: Sage.

Hogan, R., & Kaiser, R. B. (2005). What we know about leadership. *Review of General Psychology, 9,* 169–180.

Hoge, D. R. (1996). Religion in America: The demographics of belief and affiliation. *Religion and the clinical practice of psychology* (pp. 21–42). Washington, DC: American Psychological Association.

Holden, E. W., & Black, M. M. (1999). Theory and concepts of prevention sciences as applied to clinical psychology. *Clinical Psychology Review, 19,* 391–401.

Holland, K. (2009, January 25). Can volunteers be a lifeline for nonprofit groups? *The New York Times.* Retrieved from http://www.nytimes .com/2009/01/25/jobs/25mgmt.html?_r = 0

Holliday, S. G., & Chandler, M. J. (1986). *Wisdom: Explorations in adult competence.* Basel, Switzerland: Karger.

Hollon, S. D., & Beck, A. T. (1994). Cognitive and cognitive-behavioral therapies. In A. E. Bergin & S. L. Garfield (Eds.), *Handbook of psychotherapy and behavior change* (4th ed., pp. 428–466). New York: Wiley.

Holmberg, D., Blair, K. L., & Phillips, M. (2010). Women's sexual satisfaction as a predictor of well-being in same-sex versus mixed-sex relationships. *Journal of Sex Research, 47,* 1–11.

Holmgren, M. R. (2002). Forgiveness and self-forgiveness in psychotherapy. In S. Lamb & J. G. Murphy (Eds.), *Before giving: Cautionary views of forgiveness in psychotherapy* (pp. 112–135). New York: Oxford University Press.

Holt, C. L., Wang, M., Caplan, L., Schulz, E., Blake, V., & Southward, V. L. (2011). Role of religious involvement and spirituality in functioning among African Americans with cancer: Testing a meditational model. *Journal of Behavioral Medicine, 34,* 437–448.

Holton, R. (2000). Globalization's cultural consequences. *The Annals of the American Academy of Political and Social Science, 570,* 140–152.

Holtz, C. A., & Martinez, M. J. (2014). Positive psychological practices in multicultural school settings. In J. T. Pedrotti & L. M. Edwards (Eds.), *Perspectives on the intersection of multiculturalism and positive psychology.* New York: Springer Science + Business Media.

Hood, C. D., & Carruthers, C. (2007). Enhancing leisure experience and developing resources: The leisure and well-being model, part II. *Therapeutic Recreation Journal, 41,* 298–325.

Hook, J. N., Worthington, E. L., Jr., & Utsey, S. O. (2009). Collectivism, forgiveness, and social harmony. *The Counseling Psychologist, 37,* 821–847. doi: 10.1177/0011000008326546

Hook, J. N., Worthington, E. L., Jr., Utsey, S. O., Davis, D. E., & Burnette, J. L. (2012). Collectivistic self-construal and forgiveness. *Counseling and Values, 57,* 109–124.

Hooker, K., Monahan, D., Shifren, K., & Hutchinson, C. (1992). Mental and physical health of spouse caregivers: The role of personality. *Psychology and Aging, 7,* 367–375.

Hothersall, D. (1995). *History of psychology.* New York: McGraw-Hill.

Houser, R. E. (2002). The virtue of courage. In S. J. Pope (Ed.), *The ethics of Aquinas* (pp. 304–320). Washington, DC: Georgetown University Press.

Houston, B. K., & Snyder, C. R. (Eds.). (1988). *Type A behavior pattern: Current trends and future directions.* New York: Wiley-Interscience.

Howard, K., Martin, A., Berlin, L. J., & Brooks-Gunn, J. (2011). Early mother-child separation, parenting, and child well-being in Early Head Start families. *Attachment & Human Development, 13,* 5–26.

Howell, A. J., Dopko, R. L., Turowski, J. B., & Buro, K. (2011). The disposition to apologize. *Personality and Individual Differences, 51,* 509–514.

Howell, R. T., & Howell. C. J. (2008). The relation of economic status to subjective well-being in developing countries: A meta-analysis. *Psychological Bulletin, 134,* 536–560. doi: 10.1037/0033-2909.134.4.536

Hsu, C., Chang, K., & Chen, M. (2012). Flow experience and internet shopping behavior: Investigating the moderating effect of consumer characteristics. *Systems Research and Behavioral Science, 29,* 317–332.

Hsu, L. M., & Langer, E. J. (2013). Mindfulness and cultivating well-being in older adults. *The Oxford Handbook of Happiness* (pp. 1026–1036). New York: Oxford University Press.

Huang, C. (2013). Gender differences in academic self-efficacy: A meta-analysis. *European Journal of Psychology of Education, 28,* 1–35.

Huber, J. T., II, & MacDonald, D. A. (2012). An investigation of the relations between altruism, empathy, and spirituality. *Journal of Humanistic Psychology, 52,* 206–221.

Huber, S., Allemand, M., & Huber, O. W. (2011). Forgiveness by God and human forgiveness: The centrality of the religiosity makes the difference. *Psychology of Religions, 33,* 115–134.

Hudson, J. L., Flannery-Schroeder, E., & Kendall, P. C. (2004). Primary prevention of anxiety disorders. In D. J. A. Dozois & K. S. Dobson (Eds.), *The prevention of anxiety and depression* (pp. 101–130). Washington, DC: American Psychological Association.

Huffman, A., Whetten, J., & Huffman, W. H. (2013). Using technology in higher education: The influence of gender roles on technology self-efficacy. *Computers in Human Behavior, 29,* 1779–1786.

Hui, C. H. (1988). Measurement of individualism-collectivism. *Journal of Research in Personality, 22,* 17–36.

Hume, D. (1888). *A treatise of human nature.* Oxford, England: Clarendon Press.

Hummer, R. A., Rogers, R. G., Nam, C. B., & Ellison, C. G. (1999). Religious involvement and U.S. adult mortality. *Demography, 36,* 273–285.

Huntington, S. P. (1993). The clash of civilizations. *Foreign Affairs, 72,* 22–49.

Hurley, D. B., & Kwon, P. (2013). Savoring helps most when you have little: Interaction between savouring the moment and uplifts on positive affect and satisfaction with life. *Journal of Happiness Studies, 14,* 1261–1271.

Hurlock, E. B. (1925). An evaluation of certain incentives in school work. *Journal of Educational Psychology, 16,* 145–159.

Huxhold, O., Fiori, K. L., & Windsor, T. D. (2013). The dynamic interplay of social network characteristics, subjective well-being, and health: The costs and benefits of socio-emotional selectivity. *Psychology and Aging, 28,* 3–16.

Hyre, A. D., Benight, C. C., Tynes, L. L., Rice, J., DeSalvo, K. B., & Mutner, P. (2008). Psychometric properties of the hurricane coping self-efficacy measure following Hurricane Katrina. *Journal of Nervous and Mental Disease, 196,* 562–567.

Icard, L. (1996). Assessing the psychosocial well-being of African American gays: A multidimensional perspective. In J. F. Longres (Ed.), *Men of color: A context for service to homosexually active men* (pp. 25–49). New York: Haworth Press.

Ide, R. (1998). 'Sorry for your kindness': Japanese interactional ritual in public discourse. *Journal of Pragmatics, 29,* 509–529.

Ie, A., Haller, C. S., Langer, E. J., & Courvoisier, D. S. (2012). Mindful multitasking: The relationship between mindful flexibility and media multitasking. *Computers in Human Behavior, 28,* 1526–1532.

Ilardi, S. S. (2009). *The depression cure: The 6-step program to beat depression without drugs.* Cambridge, MA: Da Capo Press.

Ilardi, S. S., & Karwoski, L. (2005). *The depression cure.* Unpublished book-length manuscript, University of Kansas, Lawrence.

Inclan, J. (1985). Variations in value orientations in mental health work with Puerto Ricans. *Psychotherapy: Theory, Research, and Practice, 22,* 324–334.

Inghilleri, P. (1999). *From subjective experience to cultural change.* Cambridge, England: Cambridge University Press.

Ingram, R. E., Hayes, A., & Scott, W. (2000). Empirically supported treatments: A critical analysis. In C. R. Snyder & R. E. Ingram (Eds.), *Handbook of psychological change: Psychotherapy processes and practices for the 21st century* (pp. 40–60). New York: Wiley.

Ingram, R. E., Kendall, P. C., & Chen, A. H. (1991). Cognitive-behavioral interventions. In C. R. Snyder & D. R. Forsyth (Eds.), *Handbook of social and clinical psychology: The health perspective* (pp. 509–522). New York: Pergamon.

Ingram, R. E., & Wisnicki, K. S. (1988). Assessment of positive automatic cognition. *Journal of Consulting and Clinical Psychology, 56,* 898–902.

Irving, L. M., Cheavens, J., Snyder, C. R., Gravel, L., Hanke, J., Hilberg, P., & Nelson, N. (2004). The relationships between hope and outcome at pre-treatment, beginning, and later phases of psychotherapy. *Journal of Psychotherapy Integration, 14,* 419–443.

Isen, A. M. (1970). Success, failure, attention, and reaction to others: The warm glow of success. *Journal of Personality and Social Psychology, 17,* 107–112.

Isen, A. M. (1987). Positive affect, cognitive processes, and social behavior. *Advances in Experimental Social Psychology, 20,* 203–253.

Isen, A. M. (2000). Some perspectives on positive affect and self-regulation. *Psychological Inquiry, 11,* 184–187.

Isen, A. M., Daubman, K. A., & Nowicki, G. P. (1987). Positive affect facilitates creative problem solving. *Journal of Personality and Social Psychology, 21,* 384–388.

Isen, A. M., & Levin, P. F. (1972). The effect of feeling good on helping: Cookies and kindness. *Journal of Personality and Social Psychology, 17,* 107–112.

Ishimura, I., & Kodama, M. (2006). Flow experiences in everyday activities of Japanese college students: Autotelic people and time management. *Japanese Psychological Resarch, 51,* 47–54.

Israelashvili, M., & Socher, P. (2007). An examination of a counsellor self-efficacy scale (COSE) using an Israeli sample. *International Journal for the*

Advancement of Counselling. 29, 1–9. doi: 10.1007/s10447-006-9019-0

Ivey, A. E., & Ivey, M. B. (1998). Reframing *DSM-IV:* Positive strategies from developmental counseling and theory. *Journal of Counseling and Development, 76,* 334–350.

Ivey, A. E., & Ivey, M. B. (1999). Toward a developmental diagnostic and statistical manual: The vitality of a contextual framework. *Journal of Counseling and Development, 77,* 484–490.

Iwamasa, G. Y., & Iwasaki, M. (2011). A new multidimensional model of successful aging: Perceptions of Japanese American older adults. *Journal of Cross-Cultural Gerontology, 26,* 261–278.

Iwasaki, Y. (2007). Leisure and quality of life in an international and multicultural context: What are major pathways linking leisure to quality of life? *Social Indicators Research, 82,* 233–264. doi: 10.1007/s11205-006-9032-z

Izuma, K., & Adolphs, R. (2011). The brain's rose-colored glasses. *Nature Neuroscience, 14,* 1355–1356.

Jacinto, G. A., & Edwards, B. L. (2011). Therapeutic stages of forgiveness and self-forgiveness. *Journal of Human Behavior in the Social Environment, 21,* 423–437.

Jackson, S., & Csikszentmihalyi, M. (1999). *Flow in sports.* Champaign, IL: Human Kinetics.

Jahoda, M. (1958). *Current concepts of positive mental health.* New York: Basic Books.

James, W. (1890). *Principles of psychology* (Vol. 1). New York: Holt.

Jamieson, K. H. (Ed.). (2005). *Treating and preventing adolescent mental health disorders: What we know and what we don't know.* New York: Oxford University Press.

Jaycox, L. H., Reivich, K. J., Gillham, J., & Seligman, M. E. P. (1994). Prevention of depressive symptoms in school children. *Behavior Research and Therapy, 32,* 801–816.

Jemmott, J. B., Jemmott, L. S., & Fong, G. T. (1992). Reductions in HIV risk-associated sexual behaviors among black male adolescents: Effect of an AIDS prevention intervention. *American Journal of Public Health, 82,* 372–377.

Jerath, R., Barnes, V. A., Dillard-Wright, D., Jerath, S., & Hamilton, B. (2012). Dynamic change of awareness during meditation techniques: Neural and psychological correlates. *Frontiers in Human Neuroscience, 6,* 1–4.

Jerga, A. M., Shaver, P. R., & Wilkinson, R. B. (2011). Attachment insecurities and identification of at-risk individuals following the death of a loved one. *Journal of Social and Personal Relationships, 28,* 891–914.

Jeste, D. V., Ardelt, M., Blazer, D., Kraemer, H. C., Vaillant, G., & Meeks, T. W. (2010). Expert consensus on characteristics of wisdom: A Delphi method study. *The Gerontologist, 50,* 668–680.

Jeste, D. V., & Harris, J. C. (2010). Wisdom—A neuroscience perspective. *JAMA: Journal of the American Medical Association, 304,* 1602–1603.

Jimenez, D. E., Cook, B., Bartels, S. J., & Alegría, M. (2013). Disparities in mental health service use of racial and ethnic minority elderly adults. *Journal of the American Geriatrics Society, 61,* 18–25.

Jin, M. K., Jacobvitz, D., Hazen, N., Jung, S. H. (2012). Maternal sensitivity and infant attachment security in Korea: Cross-cultural validation of the Strange Situation. *Attachment & Human Development, 14,* 33–44.

Johnson, D. L. (1988). Primary prevention of behavior problems in young children: The Houston Parent–Child Development Center. In R. H. Price, E. Cowen, R. Lorion, & J. Ramos-McKay (Eds.), *Fourteen ounces of prevention: A casebook for practitioners* (pp. 44–52). Washington, DC: American Psychological Association.

Johnson, F. (1988). Encounter group therapy. In S. Long (Ed.), *Six group therapies* (pp. 115–158). New York: Plenum.

Jose, P. E., Lim, B. T., & Bryant, F. B. (2012). Does savouring increase happiness? A daily diary study. *Journal of Positive Psychology, 7,* 176–187.

Judge, T. A., Thoresen, C. J., Bono, J. E., & Patton, G. K. (2001). The job-satisfaction performance relationship: A qualitative and quantitative review. *Psychological Bulletin, 127,* 376–407.

Judge, T. A., & Watanabe, S. (1993). Another look at the job satisfaction–life satisfaction relationship. *Journal of Applied Psychology, 78,* 939–948.

Jung, C. (1953). *Two essays on analytical psychology.* New York: Pantheon Books.

Kabat-Zinn, J. (1982). An outpatient program in behavioral medicine for chronic pain patients based on the practice of mindfulness meditation: Theoretical considerations and preliminary results. *General Hospital Psychiatry, 4,* 33–47.

Kabat-Zinn, J. (1990). *Full catastrophe living.* New York: Delacorte Press.

Kabat-Zinn, J. (2005). *Coming to our senses.* London, England: Piatkus Books.

Kabat-Zinn, J., & Skillings, A. (1989, March). *Sense of coherence and stress hardiness as predictors and measure of outcome of a stress reduction program.* Poster presented at the Society of Behavioral Medicine Conference, San Francisco.

Kabat-Zinn, J., & Skillings, A. (1992). *Sense of coherence and stress hardiness as outcome measures of a mindfulness-based stress reduction program: Three-year follow-up.* Unpublished raw data. University of Massachusetts Medical Center, Boston.

Kadiangandu, J. K., Gauché, M., Vinsonneau, G., & Mullet, E. (2007). Conceptualizations of forgiveness: Collectivist–Congolese versus individualist–French viewpoints. *Journal of Cross-Cultural Psychology, 38,* 432–437.

Kagitcibasi, C. (1994). A critical appraisal of individualism and collectivism: Toward a new formulation. In U. Kim, H. C. Triandis, C. Kagitcibasi, S.-C. Choi, & G. Yoon (Eds.), *Individualism and collectivism: Theory, method, and applications* (pp. 52–65). Thousand Oaks, CA: Sage.

Kahneman, D., Diener, E., & Schwartz, N. (1999). *Well-being: The foundations of hedonic psychology.* New York: Russell Sage.

Kalberg, J., Lane, K., & Menzies, H. (2010). Using systematic screening procedures to identify students who are nonresponsive to primary prevention efforts: Integrating academic and behavioral measures. *Education & Treatment of Children, 33,* 561–584.

Kaluza, G. (1997). Evaluation of stress management interventions in primary prevention—A meta-analysis of (quasi) experimental studies. *Zeitschrift für Gesundheitspsychologie, 5,* 149–169.

Kamen, C., Burns, M., & Beach S. R. H. (2011). Minority stress in same-sex male relationships: When does it impact relationship satisfaction? *Journal of Homosexuality, 58,* 1372–1390.

Kanekar, S., & Merchant, S. M. (1982). Aggression, retaliation, and religious affiliation. *Journal of Social Psychology, 117,* 295–296.

Kanfer, F. H. (1970). Self-regulation: Research, issues, and speculations. In C. Neuringer & J. L. Michael (Eds.), *Behavior modification in clinical psychology* (pp. 178–220). New York: Appleton-Century-Crofts.

Kaplan, J. S., & Sue, S. (1997). Ethnic psychology in the United States. In D. F. Halpern & A. E. Voiskounsky (Eds.), *States of mind: American and post-Soviet perspectives on contemporary issues in psychotherapy* (pp. 349–369). New York: Oxford University Press.

Kaplan, R. M. (2000). Two pathways to prevention. *American Psychologist, 55,* 382–396.

Kaplan, R. M., Alcaraz, J. E., Anderson, J. P., & Weisman, M. (1996). Quality-adjusted life years lost to arthritis: Effects of gender, race, and social class. *Arthritis Care and Research, 9,* 473–482.

Kaplan, R. M., & Anderson, J. P. (1996). The general health policy model: An integrated approach. In B. Spilker (Ed.), *Quality of life and pharmacoeconomics in clinical trials* (pp. 309–322). New York: Raven.

Kardiner, A., & Ovesey, L. (1951). *The mark of oppression: A psychological study of the American Negro.* New York: Norton.

Karreman, A., & Vingerhoets, Ad. J. J. M. (2012). Attachment and well-being: The mediating role of emotion regulation and resilience. *Personality and Individual Differences, 53,* 821–826.

Karremans, J. C., Regalia, C., Paleari, F. G., Fincham, F. D., Cui, M., Takada, N., ...Uskul, A. K. (2011). Maintaining harmony across the globe: The cross-cultural association between closeness and interpersonal forgiveness. *Social Psychological and Personality Science, 2,* 443–451.

Kaslow, N. J., Tanenbaum, R. L., & Seligman, M. E. P. (1978). *The KASTAN-R: A children's attributional style questionnaire (KASTAN-R-CASQ).* Unpublished manuscript, University of Pennsylvania.

Kastenmüller, A., Greitemeyer, T., Fischer, P., & Frey, D. (2007). The Munich civil courage instrument (MüZI): Development and validation. *Diagnostica, 53,* 205–217. doi: 10.1026/001219 24.53.4.205

Kayser, D. N., Greitemeyer, T., Fisher, P., & Frey, D. (2009). Why mood affects help giving, but not moral courage: Comparing two types of prosocial behaviour. *European Journal of Social Psychology, 40,* 1136–1157.

Kazdin, A. E. (1979). Imagery elaboration and self-efficacy in the covert modeling treatment of unassertive behavior. *Journal of Consulting and Clinical Psychology, 47,* 725–733.

Kazdin, A. E. (2008). Evidence-based treatment and practice: New opportunities to bridge clinical research and practice, enhance the knowledge base, and improve patient care. *American Psychologist, 63,* 146–159.

Kazdin, A. E., Siegel, T. C., & Bass, D. (1990). Drawing on clinical practice to inform research on child and adolescent psychotherapy: Survey of practitioners. *Professional Psychology: Research and Practice, 21,* 189–198.

Keller, A. C., & Semmer, N. K. (2013). Changes in situational and dispositional factors as predictors of job satisfaction. *Journal of Vocational Behavior, 83,* 88–98.

Kelloway, E. K., & Barling, J. (1991). Job characteristics, role stress, and mental health. *Journal of Occupational Psychology, 64,* 291–304.

Keng, S., Smoski, M. J., & Robins, C. J. (2011). Effects of mindfulness on psychological health: A review of empirical studies. *Clinical Psychology Review, 31,* 1041–1056.

Kennedy, J. F. (1956). *Profiles in courage.* New York: Harper.

Kennedy, Q., Fung, H. H., & Carstensen, L. L. (2001). Aging, time estimation, and emotion. In R. C. Atchley & S. H. McFadden (Eds.), *Aging and the meaning of time: A multidisciplinary exploration* (pp. 51–73). New York: Springer.

Kennedy, R. F. (1968, March 18). Address. University of Kansas, Lawrence.

Kenyon, D., & Hanson, J. D. (2012). Incorporating traditional culture into positive youth development programs with American Indian/Alaska native youth. *Child Development Perspectives, 6,* 272–279.

Keohane, R. O. (1993). Sovereignty, interdependence and international institutions. In L. Miller & M. Smith (Eds.), *Ideas and ideals: Essays on politics in honor of Stanley Hoffman* (pp. 91–107). Boulder, CO: Westview.

Keough, K. A., Zimbardo, P. G., & Boyd, J. N. (1999). Who's smoking, drinking, and using drugs? Time perspective as a predictor of substance abuse. *Basic and Applied Social Psychology, 21,* 149–164.

Keyes, C. L. M. (1998). Social well-being. *Social Psychology Quarterly, 61,* 121–140.

Keyes, C. L. M. (2009). Toward a science of mental health. In S. J. Lopez & C. R. Snyder (Eds.). *Oxford handbook of positive psychology* (pp. 89–95). New York: Oxford University Press.

Keyes, C. L. M., & Haidt, J. (Eds.). (2003). *Flourishing: Positive psychology and a life well lived.* Washington, DC: American Psychological Association.

Keyes, C. L. M., & Lopez, S. J. (2002). Toward a science of mental health: Positive directions in diagnosis and treatment. In C. R. Snyder & S. J. Lopez (Eds.), *The handbook of positive psychology* (pp. 45–59). New York: Oxford University Press.

Keyes, C. L. M., & Magyar-Moe, J. L. (2003). The measurement and utility of adult subjective well-being. *Positive psychological assessment: A handbook of models and measures* (pp. 411–426). Washington, DC: American Psychological Association.

Keyes, C. L. M., & Ryff, C. D. (2000). Subjective change and mental health: A self-concept theory. *Social Psychology Quarterly, 63,* 264–279.

Keyes, C., Shmotkin, D., & Ryff, C. (2000). Optimizing well-being: The empirical encounter of two traditions. *Journal of Personality and Social Psychology, 82,* 1007–1022.

Khan, S., Haynes, L., Armstrong, A., & Rohner, R. P. (2010). Perceived teacher acceptance, parental acceptance, academic achievement, and school conduct of middle school students in the Mississippi Delta region of the United States. *Cross-Cultural Research: The Journal of Comparative Social Sceince, 44,* 283–294.

Kihlstrom, J. F., & Cantor, N. (2000). Social intelligence. In R. J. Sternberg (Ed.), *Handbook of intelligence.* (pp. 359–379). New York: Cambridge University Press.

Kim, M., & Markus, H. R. (1999). Deviance or uniqueness, harmony or conformity? A cultural analysis. *Journal of Personality and Social Psychology, 77,* 785–800.

Kim, M., Sharkey, W. F., & Singelis, T. M. (1994). Relationship between individuals' self-construals and perceived importance of interactive constraints. *International Journal of Intercultural Relations, 18,* 117–140.

Kim, U. (1994). Individualism and collectivism: Conceptual clarification and elaboration. In U. Kim, H. C. Triandis, C. Kagitcibasi, S.-C. Choi, & G. Yoon (Eds.), *Individualism and collectivism: Theory, method, and applications* (pp. 19–40). Thousand Oaks, CA: Sage.

Kim, U., Triandis, H. C., Kagitcibasi, C., Choi, S.-C., & Yoon, G. (1994). *Individualism and collectivism: Theory, method, and applications.* Thousand Oaks, CA: Sage.

Kim, U., & Park, Y-S. (2006). Indigenous psychological analysis of academic achievement in Korea: The influence of self-efficacy, parents, and culture. *International Journal of Psychology, 41,* 11–26.

Kim, Y., & Glassman, M. (2013). Beyond search and communicaton: Development and validation of the Internet Self-Efficacy Scale (ISS). *Computers in Human Behavior, 29,* 1421–1429.

King, L. A., Eells, J. E., & Burton, C. M. (2004). The good life, broadly and narrowly considered. In P. A. Linley & S. Joseph (Eds.), *Positive psychology in practice* (pp. 25–52). Hoboken, NJ: Wiley.

King, L. A., & Napa, C. K. (1998). What makes a good life? *Journal of Personality and Social Psychology, 75,* 156–165.

King, M. L., Jr. (1968). *The peaceful warrior.* New York: Pocket Books.

Kirmayer, L. J. (2012). Cultural competence and evidence-based practice in mental health: Epistemic communities and the politics of pluralism. *Social Sciences & Medicine, 75,* 249–256.

Kitayama, S., & Markus, H. R. (2000). Culture, emotion, and well-being: Good feelings in Japan and in the United States. *Cognition and Emotion, 14,* 99–124.

Kitayama, S., Markus, H. R., Matsumoto, H., & Norasakkunkit, V. (1997). Individual and collective process in the construction of the self: Self-enhancement in the United States and self-criticism in Japan. *Journal of Personality and Social Psychology, 72,* 1245–1267.

Kitchener, K. S., & Brenner, H. G. (1990). Wisdom and reflective judgment: Knowing the face of uncertainty. In R. J. Sternberg (Ed.), *Wisdom: Its nature, origins, and development* (pp. 212–229). New York: Cambridge University Press.

Klassen, R. M., Bong, M., Usher, E. L., Chong, W. H., Huan, V. S., Wong, I. Y. F., & Georgiou, T. (2009). Exploring the validity of a teachers' self-efficacy scale in five countries. *Contemporary Educational Psychology. 34,* 67–76. doi: 10.101 6/j.cedpsych.2008.08.001

Klausner, E., Snyder, C. R., & Cheavens, J. (2000). A hope-based group treatment for depressed older adult outpatients. In G. M. Williamson, D. R. Shaffer, & P. A. Parmelee (Eds.), *Physical illness and depression in older adults: A handbook of theory, research, and practice* (pp. 295–310). New York: Plenum.

Klausner, E. J., Clarkin, J. F., Spielman, L., Pupo, C., Abrams, R., & Alexopoulos, G. S. (1998). Late-life depression and functional disability: The role of goal-focused group psychotherapy. *International Journal of Geriatric Psychiatry, 13,* 707–716.

Klerman, G., Weissman, M. M., Rounsaville, B. J., & Chevron, E. S. (1984). *Interpersonal psychotherapy of depression.* Northvale, NJ: Jason Aronson.

Kobasa, S. C. O. (1990). Stress-resistant personality. In R. Ornstein & C. Swencionis (Eds.), *The healing brain: A scientific reader* (pp. 219–230). New York: Guilford Press.

Koenig, H. G. (Ed.). (1998). *Handbook of religion and mental health.* San Diego, CA: Academic Press.

Koerner, S., Shirai, Y., & Pedroza, R. (2013). Role of religious/spiritual beliefs and practices among Latino family caregivers of Mexican descent. *Journal of Latina/o Psychology, 1,* 95–111.

Kohlberg, L. (1983). *The psychology of moral development.* New York: Harper & Row.

Kohn, M. L. (1969). *Class and conformity.* Homewood, IL: Dorsey Press.

Kohut, H. (1979). *Self-psychology and the humanities: Reflections on a new psychoanalytic approach.* New York: Norton.

Koltko-Rivera, M. E. (2004). The psychology of worldviews. *Review of General Psychology, 8,* 3–58.

Komorita, S. S., Hilty, J. A., & Parks, C. D. (1991). Reciprocity and cooperation in social dilemmas. *Journal of Conflict Resolution, 35,* 494–518.

Konrath, S., Fuhrel-Forbis, A., Lou, A., & Brown, S. (2012). Motives for volunteering are associated with mortality risk in older adults. *Health Psychology, 31,* 87–96.

Koydemir, S., Şimşek, Ö., Schütz, A., & Tipandjan, A. (2013). Differences in how trait emotional intelligence predicts life satisfaction: The role of affect balance versus social support in India and Germany. *Journal of Happiness Studies, 14,* 51–66.

Krause, N. (2012). Feelings of gratitude toward God among older whites, older African Americans, and older Mexican Americans. *Research on Aging, 34,* 156–173.

Krauss, H. H., & Krauss, B. J. (1968). Cross-cultural study of the thwarting-disorientation theory of suicide. *Journal of Abnormal Psychology, 73,* 352–357.

Krech, G. (2001). *Naikan: Gratitude, grace, and the Japanese art of self-reflection.* Berkeley, CA: Stone Bridge Press.

Kross, E., & Grossmann, I. (2012). Boosting wisdom: Distance from the self enhances wise reasoning, attitudes, and behavior. *Journal of Experimental Psychology: General, 141,* 43–48.

Kruglanski, A. W., & Webster, D. M. (1996). Motivated closing of the mind: "Seizing" and "freezing." *Psychological Review, 103,* 263–283.

Kwon, P. (2013). Resilience in lesbian, gay, and bisexual individuals. *Personality and Social Psychology Review, 17,* 371–383.

LaBouff, J. P., Rowatt, W. C., Johnson, M. K., Tsang, J., & Willerton, G. M. (2012). Humble persons are more helpful than less humble persons: Evidence from three studies. *The Journal of Positive Psychology, 7,* 16–29.

Labouvie-Vief, G. (1990). Wisdom as integrated thought: Historical and developmental perspectives. In R. J. Sternberg (Ed.), *Wisdom: Its nature, origins, and development* (pp. 52–83). New York: Cambridge University Press.

Laird, S. P., Snyder, C. R., Rapoff, M. A., & Green, S. (2004). Measuring private prayer: The development and validation of the Multidimensional Prayer Inventory. *International Journal for the Psychology of Religion, 14,* 251–272.

Lambert, M. J. (Ed.). (2013). *Bergin and Garfield's handbook of psychotherapy and behavior change* (6th ed.). New York: Wiley.

Lambert, N. M., Clark, M. S., Durtschi, J., Fincham, F. D., & Graham, S. M. (2010). Benefits of expressing gratitude: Expressing gratitude to a partner changes one's view of the relationship. *Psychological Science, 21,* 574–580.

Lambert, N. M., Fincham, F. D., & Stillman, T. F. (2012). Gratitude and depressive symptoms: The role of positive reframing and positive emotion. *Cognition and Emotion, 26,* 615–633.

Lamond, A. J., Depp, C. A., Allison, M., Langer, R., Reichstadt, J., Moore, D. J., & Jeste, D. V. (2009). Measurement and predictors of resilience among community-dwelling older women. *Journal of Psychiatric Research, 43,* 148–154. doi: 10.1016/j.jpsychires.2008.03.007

Landis, D., & O'Shea W. A., III. (2000). Cross-cultural aspects of passionate love: An individual differences analysis. *Journal of Cross-Cultural Psychology, 31,* 752–777. doi: 10.1177/0022002 2100031006005

Landman, J. T., & Dawes, R. M. (1982). Psychotherapy outcome: Smith and Glass' conclusions stand up under scrutiny. *American Psychologist, 37,* 504–516.

Lane, R. D., Reiman, E. M., Bradley, M. M., Lang, P. J., Ahern, G. L., Davidson, R. J., et al. (1997). Neuroanatomical correlates of pleasant and unpleasant emotion. *Neuropsychologia, 35,* 1437–1444.

Langer, E. (1989). *Mindfulness.* Reading, MA: Addison-Wesley.

Langer, E. (1997). *The power of mindful learning.* Reading, MA: Addison-Wesley.

Langer, E. (2009a). Mindfulness versus positive evaluation. In S. J. Lopez & C. R. Snyder (Eds.), *Oxford handbook of positive psychology* (pp. 279–294). New York: Oxford University Press.

Langer, E. (2009b). *Clockwise: Mindful health and the power of possibility.* New York: Random House.

Langer, E., Blank, A., & Chanowitz, B. (1978). The mindlessness of ostensibly thoughtful action: The role of placebic information on interpersonal interaction. *Journal of Personality and Social Psychology, 36,* 635–642.

Langer, E. J., Cohen, M., & Djikic, M. (2012). Mindfulness as a psychological attractor: The effect on children. *Journal of Applied Social Psychology, 42,* 1114–1122.

Langer, E. J., & Rodin, J. (1976). The effects of enhanced personal responsibility for the aged: A field experiment in an institutional setting. *Journal of Personality and Social Psychology, 34,* 191–198.

Langston, C. A. (1994). Capitalizing on and coping with daily-life events: Expressive responses to positive events. *Journal of Personality and Social Psychology, 67,* 1112–1125.

Lao-Tzu. (1994). *Tao Te Ching.* (D. C. Lau, Trans.). New York: Knopf.

Larsen, K. S., & Giles, H. (1976). Survival or courage as human motivation: Development of an attitude scale. *Psychological Reports, 39,* 299–302.

Latane, B., & Darley, J. M. (1970). *The unresponsive bystander: Why doesn't he help?* New York: Appleton-Century-Crofts.

Lauring, J. (2013). International diversity management: Global ideas and local responses. *British Journal of Management, 24,* 211–224.

Lawson, W. (2004, January/February). Praise: Encouraging signs. *Psychology Today.* Retrieved from http:// www.psychologytoday.com/arti cles/pto-20040209-000003.html

Layous, K. L., Lee, H., Choi, I., & Lyubormirsky, S. (2013). Culture matters when designing a successful happiness-increasing activity: A comparison of the United States and South Korea. *Journal of Cross-Cultural Psychology, 44,* 1294–1303.

Le, T. N. (2011). Life satisfaction, openness value, self-transcendence, and wisdom. *Journal of Happiness Studies, 12,* 171–182.

Le, T. N., Lai, M. H., & Wallen, J. (2009). Multiculturalism and subjective happiness as mediated by cultural and relational variables. *Cultural Diversity and Ethnic Minority Psychology, 15,* 303–313.

Leach, M. M., Baker, A., & Zeigler-Hill, V. (2011). The influence of Black racial identity on the forgiveness of Whites. *Journal of Black Psychology, 37,* 185–209.

Leadbetter, B. J., Gladstone, E., Yeung Thompson, R. S., Sukhawathanakul, P., & Desjardins, T. (2012). Getting started: Assimilatory processes of uptake of mental health promotion and primary prevention programmes in elementary schools. *Advances in School Mental Health Promotion, 5,* 258–276.

Leary, M. R., Tchividjian, L. R., & Kraxberger, B. E. (1994). Self-presentation can be hazardous to your health: Impression management and health risk. *Health Psychology, 13,* 461–470.

LeDoux, J. E. (1996). *The emotional brain: The mysterious underpinnings of emotional life.* New York: Simon & Schuster.

Lee, B.-O. (2013). Ambivalence over emotional expression and symptom attribution are associated with self-reported somatic symptoms in Singaporean school adolescents. *Asian Journal of Social Psychology, 16,* 169–180.

Lee, G. R., Seccombe, K., & Shehan, C. L. (1991). Marital status and personal happiness: An analysis of trend data. *Journal of Marriage and the Family, 53,* 839–844.

Lee, H. E., & Park, H. S. (2011). Why Koreans are more likely to favor "apology" while Americans are more likely to favour "thank you." *Human Communication Research, 37,* 125–146.

Lee, J. (2009). Universals and specifics of math self-concept, math self-efficacy, and math anxiety across 41 PISA 2003 participating countries. *Learning and Individual Differences, 19,* 355–365.

Lee, L., Kuo, Y., Fanaw, D., Perng, S., & Juang, I. (2012). The effect of an intervention combining self-efficacy theory and pedometers on promoting physical activity among adolescents. *Journal of Clinical Nursing, 21,* 914–922.

Lee, Y.-T., & Seligman, M. E. P. (1997). Are Americans more optimistic than the Chinese? *Personality and Social Psychology Bulletin, 23,* 32–40.

Leitner, L. M. (2003). *Honoring suffering, tragedy, and reverence: The fully human is more than positive.* Paper presented at the American Psychological Association Annual Convention, Toronto, Canada.

Lemola, S., Räikkönen, K., Matthews, K. A., Scheier, M. F., Heinonen, K., Pesonen, A., & Lahti, J. (2010). A new measure for dispositional optimism and pessimism in young children. *European Journal of Personality, 24,* 71–84.

Lent, R. (2004). Toward a unifying theoretical and practical perspective on well-being and psychosocial adjustment. *Journal of Counseling Psychology, 51,* 482–509.

Leong, F. T. L., & Wong, P. T. P. (2003). Optimal human functioning from cross-cultural perspectives:

Cultural competence as an organizing framework. In W. B. Walsh (Ed.), *Counseling psychology and optimal human functioning* (pp. 123–150). Mahwah, NJ: Lawrence Erlbaum.

Lerner, M. (1996). *The politics of meaning*. Reading, MA: Addison-Wesley.

Lerner, R. M., von Eye, A., Lerner, J. V., Lewin-Bizan, S., & Bowers, E. P. (2010). Special issue introduction: The meaning and measurement of thriving: A view of the issues. *Journal of Youth and Adolescence, 39,* 707–719.

Leu, J., Wang, J., & Koo, K. (2011). Are positive emotions just as "positive" across cultures? *Emotion, 11,* 994–999.

Levenson, M. R. (2009). Gender and wisdom: The roles of compassion and moral development. *Research in Human Development, 6,* 45–59.

Lewandowski, G. W., & Bizzoco, N. M. (2007). Addition through subtraction: Growth following the dissolution of a low quality relationship. *Journal of Positive Psychology, 2,* 40–54. doi: 10.1080/17439760601069234

Lewin, K. (1951). *Field theory in social science*. New York: Harper & Row.

Lewis, R. K. (2011). Promoting positive youth development by understanding social contexts. *Journal of Prevention & Intervention in the Community, 39,* 273–276.

Li, C. (2012). Validation of the Chinese version of the Life Orientation Test with a robust weighted least squares approach. *Psychological Assessment, 24,* 770–776.

Lightman, E. S. (1982). Technique bias in measuring acts of altruism: The case of voluntary blood donation. *Social Science & Medicine, 16,* 1627–1633.

Linley, P. A., & Harrington, S. (2006). Playing to your strengths. *The Psychologist, 19,* 85–89.

Linley, P. A., & Joseph, S. (Eds.). (in press). *Positive psychology in practice*. Hoboken, NJ: Wiley.

Lippmann, S. (2008). Rethinking risk in the new economy: Age and cohort effects on unemployment and re-employment. *Human Relations, 61,* 1259–1292. doi: 10.1177/001872670804912

Little, B. L., & Madigan, R. M. (1997). The relationship between collective self-efficacy and performance in manufacturing work teams. *Small Group Research, 28,* 517–534.

Liu, W. T. (1986). Culture and social support. *Research on Aging, 8,* 57–83.

Locke, E. A. (1976). The nature and causes of job satisfaction. In M. D. Dunnette (Ed.), *Handbook of industrial and organizational psychology* (pp. 1297–1347). Chicago: Rand McNally.

Locke, E., & Latham, G. P. (2002). Building a practically useful theory of goal setting and task motivation: A 35-year odyssey. *American Psychologist, 57,* 705–717.

Locke, T. F., & Newcomb, M. D. (2004). Adolescent predictors of young adult and adult alcohol involvement and dysphoria in a prospective community sample of women. *Prevention Science, 5,* 151–168. doi: 10.1023/B:PREV.0000037639.78352.3c

Long, B. C. (1993). Coping strategies of male managers: A prospective analysis of predictors of psychosomatic symptoms and job satisfaction. *Journal of Vocational Behavior, 42,* 184–199.

Long, C. (2010). Apology in Japanese gratitude situations: The negotiation of interlocutor role-relations. *Journal of Pragmatics, 42,* 1060–1075.

Lopes, P. N., Brackett, M. A., Nezlek, J. B., Schutz, A., Sellin, I., & Salovey, P. (2004). Emotional intelligence and social interaction. *Personality and Social Psychology Bulletin, 30,* 1018–1034.

Lopes, P. N., Salovey, P., Cote, S., Beers, M., & Petty, R. E. (2005). Emotion regulation abilities and the quality of social interaction. *Emotion, 5,* 113–118.

Lopes, P. N., Salovey, P., & Straus, R. (2004). Emotional intelligence, personality, and the perceived quality of social relationships. *Personality and Individual Differences, 35,* 641–658.

Lopez, F. G. (2003). The assessment of adult attachment security. In S. J. Lopez & C. R. Snyder (Eds.), *Positive psychological assessment: A handbook of models and measures* (pp. 285–299). Washington, DC: American Psychological Association.

Lopez, F. G., & Brennan, K. A. (2000). Dynamic processes underlying adult attachment organization: Toward an attachment-theoretical perspective on the healthy and effective self. *Journal of Counseling Psychology, 47,* 283–300.

Lopez, S. J. (2000). *Positive psychology in the schools: Identifying and strengthening our hidden resources*. Unpublished manuscript, University of Kansas, Lawrence.

Lopez, S. J. (2005). *Head, heart, holy test of hope*. Unpublished document. University of Kansas, Lawrence.

Lopez, S. J. (2013). *Making hope happen*. New York: Atria.

Lopez, S. J., Edwards, L. M., Magyar-Moe, J. L., Pedrotti, J. T., & Ryder, J. A. (2003). Fulfilling its promise: Counseling psychology's efforts to understand and promote optimal human functioning. In B. Walsh (Ed.), *Optimal human functioning* (pp. 297–308). Mahwah, NJ: Lawrence Erlbaum.

Lopez, S. J., Edwards, L. M., Pedrotti, J. T., Prosser, E. C., Walton, S. L., Spalitto, S. V., & Ulven, J. C. (2006). Beyond the DSM: Assumptions, alternatives, and alterations. *Journal of Counseling & Development, 84,* 259–267.

Lopez, S. J., Floyd, R. K., Ulven, J. C., & Snyder, C. R. (2000). Hope therapy: Helping clients build a house of hope. In C. R. Snyder (Ed.), *Handbook of hope: Theory, measures, and applications* (pp. 123–150). San Diego, CA: Academic Press.

Lopez, S. J., Harter, J. K, Juszkiewicz, P. J., & Carr, J. A. (2007). *Clifton Youth StrengthsExplore™ technical report: Development and validation*. Omaha, NE: Gallup Organization.

Lopez, S. J., Hodges, T. D., & Harter, J. K. (2005). *Clifton StrengthsFinder technical report: Development and validation*. Omaha, NE: Gallup Organization.

Lopez, S. J., Janowski, K. M., & Quinn, R. (2004). *KU Strengths Cardsort for Children*. Unpublished manuscript, University of Kansas, Lawrence.

Lopez, S. J., Janowski, K. M., & Wells, K. J. (2005). *Developing strengths in college students: Exploring programs, contents, theories, and research*. Unpublished manuscript, University of Kansas, Lawrence.

Lopez, S. J., & McKnight, C. (2002). Moving in a positive direction: Toward increasing the utility of positive youth development efforts. *Prevention and Treatment, 5*. Retrieved from http://journals.apa.org/prevention/volume5/pre0050019c.html

Lopez, S. J., & Snyder, C. R. (2003). *Positive psychological assessment: A handbook of models and measures*. Washington, DC: American Psychological Association.

Lopez, S. J., & Snyder, C. R. (2009). *Oxford handbook of positive psychology*. New York: Oxford University Press.

Lopez, S. J., Snyder, C. R., Magyar-Moe, J. L., Edwards, L. M., Pedrotti, J. T., Janowski, K.,…Pressgrove, C. (2004). Strategies for accentuating hope. In P. A. Linley & S. Joseph (Eds.), *Positive psychology in practice* (pp. 388–404). Hoboken, NJ: Wiley.

Lopez, S. J., Snyder, C. R., & Rasmussen, H. N. (2003). Striking a vital balance: Developing a complementary focus on human weakness and strength through Positive Psychological Assessment. *Positive psychological assessment: A handbook of models and measures* (pp. 3–20). Washington, DC: American Psychological Association.

Lowe, N. K. (1993). Maternal confidence for labour: Development of the childbirth self-efficacy inventory. *Research in Nursing & Health, 16,* 141–149.

Lowman, J. (1995). *Mastering the techniques of teaching* (2nd ed.). San Francisco: Jossey-Bass.

Lu, L., & Gilmour, R. (2004). Culture and conceptions of happiness: Individual oriented and social oriented swb. *Journal of Happiness Studies, 5,* 269–291.

Lu, L., Lin, H. Y., & Cooper, C. L. (2013). Unhealthy and present: Motives and consequences of the act of presenteeism among Taiwanese employees. *Journal of Occupational Health Psychology, 18,* 406–416.

Lucas, R. E., Diener, E., & Suh, E. (1996). Discriminant validity of well-being measures. *Journal of Personality and Social Psychology, 71,* 616–628.

Lucas, R. E., & Fujita, F. (2000). Factors influencing the relations between extraversion and pleasant affect. *Journal of Personality and Social Psychology, 79,* 1039–1056.

Luke, M. A., Sedikides, C., & Carnelley, K. (2012). Your love lifts me higher! The energizing quality of secure relationships. *Personality and Social Psychology Bulletin, 38,* 721–733.

Lukes, S. (1973). *Individualism*. Oxford, England: Basil Blackwell.

Luthans, F., & Avolio, B. (2003). Authentic leadership: A positive development approach. In K. S. Cameron, J. E. Dutton, & R. E. Quinn (Eds.), *Positive organizational scholarship* (pp. 241–258). San Francisco: Berrett-Koehler.

Luthans, F., Avolio, B. J., Walumbwa, F. O, & Li, W. (2005). The psychological capital of Chinese workers: Exploring the relationship with performance. *Management and Organization Review, 1,* 818–827.

Luthans, F., Luthans, K. W., & Luthans, B. C. (2004). Positive psychological capital: Beyond human and social capital. *Business Horizons, 47,* 45–50.

Luthans, F., & Youssef, C. M. (2004). Investing in people for competitive advantage. *Organizational Dynamics, 33,* 143–160.

Luthar, S. S., Cicchetti, D., & Becker, B. (2000). The construct of resilience: A critical evaluation and guidelines for future work. *Child Development, 71,* 543–562.

Lutsky, N. (1999, August). *Not on the exam: Teaching, psychology and the examined life.* Paper presented at the annual convention of the American Psychological Association, Boston, MA.

Lutz, S. (2000). Mapping the wellsprings of a positive life: The importance of measure to the movement. *Gallup Review, 3,* 8–11.

Lykken, D. (1999). *Happiness: The nature and nurture of joy and contentment.* New York: St. Martin's Press.

Lynn, M., & Snyder, C. R. (2002). Uniqueness. In C. R. Snyder & S. J. Lopez (Eds.), *The handbook of positive psychology* (pp. 395–410). New York: Oxford University Press.

Lyubomirsky, S., Dickerhoof, R., Boehm, J. K., & Sheldon, K. M. (2011). Becoming happier takes both a will and a proper way: An experimental longitudinal intervention to boost well-being. *Emotion, 11,* 391–402.

Lyubomirsky, S., King, L., & Diener E. (2005). The benefits of frequent positive affect: Does happiness lead to success? *Psychological Bulletin, 131,* 803–855. doi: 10.1037/0033-2909.131.6.803

Lyubomirsky, S., & Layous, K. (2013). How do simple positive activities increase well-being? *Current Directions in Psychological Science, 22,* 57–62.

Lyubomirsky, S., Sheldon, K. M., & Schkade, D. (2005). Pursuing happiness: The architecture of sustainable change. *Review of General Psychology, 9,* 111–131.

Maccani, M. A., Delahanty, D. L., Nugent, N. R., & Berkowitz, S. J. (2012). Pharmacological secondary prevention of PTSD in youth: Challenges and opportunities for advancement. *Journal of Traumatic Stress, 25,* 543–550.

Madera, J. M. (2013). Best practices in diversity management in customer service organizations: An investigation of top companies cited by Diversity, Inc. *Cornell Hospitality Quarterly, 54,* 124–135.

Madhusoodanan, S., Ibrahim, F. A., & Malik, A. (2010). Primary prevention in geriatric psychiatry. *Annals of Clinical Psychiatry, 22,* 249–261.

Maddux, J. E. (1991). Self-efficacy. In C. R. Snyder & D. R. Forsyth (Eds.), *Handbook of social and clinical psychology: The health perspective* (pp. 57–58). New York: Pergamon.

Maddux, J. E. (Ed.). (1995). *Self-efficacy, adaptation, and adjustment: Theory, research, and application.* New York: Plenum.

Maddux, J. E. (2009a). Self-efficacy: The power of believing you can. In S. J. Lopez & C. R. Snyder (Eds.), *Oxford handbook of positive psychology* (pp. 335–343). New York: Oxford University Press.

Maddux, J. E. (2009b). Stopping the "madness": Positive psychology and deconstructing the illness ideology and the DSM. In S. J. Lopez & C. R. Snyder (Eds.), *Oxford handbook of positive psychology.* (pp. 61–69). New York: Oxford University Press.

Maddux, J. E., Brawley, L., & Boykin, A. (1995). Self-efficacy and healthy decision making: Protection, promotion, and detection. In J. E. Maddux (Ed.), *Self-efficacy, adaptation, and adjustment: Theory, research, and application* (pp. 173–202). New York: Plenum.

Maddux, J. E., & Lewis, J. (1995). Self-efficacy and adjustment: Basic principles and issues. In J. E. Maddux (Ed.), *Self-efficacy, adaptation, and adjustment: Theory, research, and application* (pp. 37–68). New York: Plenum.

Maddux, J. E., & Mundell, C. E. (1999). Disorders of personality: Diseases or individual differences? In V. J. Derlega, B. A. Winstead, & W. H. Jones (Eds.), *Personality: Contemporary theory and research* (pp. 541–571). Chicago: Nelson-Hall.

Maddux, J. E., Snyder, C. R., & Lopez, S. (2004). Toward a positive clinical psychology: Deconstructing the illness ideology and constructing an ideology of happiness and human strengths. In P. A. Linley & S. Joseph (Eds.), *Positive psychology in practice* (pp. 320–334). Hoboken, NJ: Wiley.

Maeran, R., & Cangiano, F. (2013). Flow experience and job characteristics: Analyzing the role of flow in job satisfaction. *TPM-Testing, Psychometrics, Methodology in Applied Psychology, 20,* 13–26.

Magnuson, C. D., & Barnett, L. A. (2013). The playful advantage: How playfulness enhances coping with stress. *Leisure Sciences, 35,* 129–144.

Magyar-Moe, J. L. (2014). Infusing multicutluralism and positive psychology in psychotherapy. In J. T. Pedrotti, & L. M. Edwards (Eds.) *Perspectives on the intersection of multicutluralism and positive psychology* (pp. 235-249). New York: Springer Science + Business Media.

Mahan, B. B., Garrard, W. M., Lewis, S. E., & Newbrough, J. R. (2002). Sense of community in a university setting. In A. T. Fisher, C. C. Sonn, & B. J. Bishop (Eds.), *Psychological sense of community: Research, applications, and implications* (pp. 123–140). New York: Kluwer/Plenum.

Mahoney, A., Pargament, K. I., Cole, B., Jewell, T., Magyar, G. M., Tarakeshwar, N., et al. (2005). A higher purpose: The sanctification of strivings in a community sample. *International Journal for the Psychology of Religion, 15,* 239–262.

Mahoney, A., Pargament, K. I., Jewell, T., Swank, A. B., Scott, E., Emery, E., et al. (1999). Marriage and the spiritual realm: The role of proximal and distal religious constructs in marital functioning. *Journal of Family Psychology, 13,* 321–338.

Mahoney, J. L., Cairns, B. D., & Farmer, T. W. (2003). Promoting interpersonal competence and educational success through extracurricular activity participation. *Journal of Education Psychology, 95,* 409–418. doi: 10.1037/0022-0663.95.2.409

Maier, S. F., Laudenslager, M. L., & Ryan, S. M. (1985). Stressor controllability, immune function, and endogenous opiates. In F. R. Brush & J. B. Overmier (Eds.), *Affect, conditioning, and cognition: Essays on the determinants of behavior* (pp. 183–201). Hillsdale, NJ: Lawrence Erlbaum.

Main, M., & Goldwyn, R. (1984). *Adult attachment scoring and classification system.* Unpublished manuscript, University of California at Berkeley.

Main, M., & Goldwyn, R. (1998). *Adult attachment interview scoring and classification system.* Unpublished manuscript, University of California at Berkeley.

Malgady, R. G., Rogler, L. H., & Costantino, G. (1990). Culturally sensitive psychotherapy for Puerto Rican children and adolescents: A program of treatment outcome research. *Journal of Consulting and Clinical Psychology, 58,* 704–712.

Mandler, G. (1975). *Mind and emotion.* New York: Wiley.

Mansbridge, J. J. (Ed.). (1990). *Beyond self-interest.* Chicago: University of Chicago Press.

Mares, M., Braun, M. T., & Hernandez, P. (2012). Pessimism and anxiety: Effects of tween sitcoms on expectations and feelings about peer relationships in school. *Media Psychology, 15,* 121–147.

Marjoribanks, K. (1991). Sex composition of family sibships and family learning environments. *Psychological Reports, 69,* 97–98.

Markus, H. R., & Kitayama, S. (1991). Culture and self: Implications for cognition, emotion and motivation. *Psychological Review, 98,* 224–253.

Marques, S. C., Lopez, S. J., & Mitchell, J. (2013). The role of hope, spirituality, and religious practice in adolescents' life satisfaction: Longitudinal findings. *Journal of Happiness Studies, 14,* 251–261.

Marques, S. C., Pais-Ribeiro, J. L., & Lopez, S. J. (2009). Validation of a Portuguese version of the Children's Hope Scale. *School Psychology International, 30,* 538–551.

Marston, P. J., Hecht, M. L., & Robers, T. (1987). "True love ways": The subjective experience and communication of romantic love. *Journal of Social and Personal Relationships, 4,* 387–407.

Martin, A. J. (2011). Courage in the classroom: Exploring a new framework predicting academic performance and engagement. *School Psychology Quarterly, 26,* 145–160.

Martin, R. (2004, May 21). Wisdom difficult to define, attain. *Lawrence Journal-World*. Retrieved from http://www.news.ku.edu/ archive

Maslach, C. (1982). *Burnout—The cost of caring*. Englewood Cliffs, NJ: Prentice Hall.

Maslach, C., & Jackson, S. E. (1981). The measurement of experienced burnout. *Journal of Occupational Behavior, 2*, 99–113.

Maslow, A. (1954). *Motivation and personality*. New York: Harper.

Maslow, A. (1970). *Motivation and personality*. New York: Harper & Row.

Massimini, F., & Carli, M. (1988). The systematic assessment of flow in daily experience. In M. Csikszentmihalyi & I. Csikszentmihalyi (Eds.), *Optimal experience* (pp. 266–287). Cambridge, England: Cambridge University Press.

Massimini, F., Csikszentmihalyi, M., & Carli, M. (1987). The monitoring of optimal experience: A tool for psychiatric rehabilitation. *Journal of Nervous and Mental Disease, 175*(9), 545–549.

Masten, A. S. (1999). Resilience comes of age: Reflections on the past and outlook for the next generation of research. In M. D. Glantz, J. Johnson, & L. Huffman (Eds.), *Resilience and development: Positive life adaptations* (pp. 282–296). New York: Plenum.

Masten, A. S. (2001). Ordinary magic: Resilience process in development. *American Psychologist, 56*, 227–239.

Masten, A. S., Cutuli, J. J., Herbers, J. E., & Reed, M. J. (2009). Resilience in development. In S. J. Lopez & C. R. Snyder (Eds.), *Oxford handbook of positive psychology* (pp. 117–131). New York: Oxford University Press.

Masten, A. S., & Garmezy, N. (1985). Risk, vulnerability, and protective factors in the developmental psychopathology. In B. B. Lahey & A. E. Kazdin (Eds.), *Advances in clinical child psychology*. (Vol. 8, pp. 1–51). New York: Plenum.

Masterson, J. (1981). *The narcissistic and borderline disorders*. New York: Brunner/Mazel.

Mathers, C. D., & Schofield, D. J. (1998). The health consequences of unemployment: The evidence. *Medical Journal of Australia, 168*, 178–182.

Matsumoto, D., Kudoh, T., & Takeuchi, S. (1996). Changing patterns of individualism and collectivism in the United States and Japan. *Culture and Psychology, 2*, 77–107.

Matsushita, M., Adachi, H., Arakida, M., Namura, I., Takahashi, Y., Miyata, M.,…Sugita, Y. (2011). Presenteeism in college students: Reliability and validity of the Presenteeism Scale for Students. *Quality of Life Research: An International Journal of Quality of Life Aspects of Treatment, Care, & Rehabilitation, 20*, 439–446.

Matthews, K. A., Batson, C. D., Horn, J., & Rosenman, R. H. (1981). "Principles in his nature which interest him in the fortune of others . . .": The heritability of empathic concern for others. *Journal of Personality, 49*, 237–247.

Mayer, J. (2005). *Who is emotionally intelligent—And does it matter?* Retrieved from http://www.unh.edu/emotional_ intelligence/

Mayer, J. D., DiPaolo, M. T., & Salovey, P. (1990). Perceiving affective content of ambiguous visual stimuli: A component of emotional intelligence. *Journal of Personality Assessment, 54*, 772–781.

Mayer, J. D., & Salovey, P. (1997). What is emotional intelligence? In P. Salovey & D. Sluyter (Eds.), *Emotional development and emotional intelligence: Implications for educators* (pp. 3–31). New York: Basic Books.

Mayer, J. D., Salovey, P., & Caruso, D. (2001). *The Mayer-Salovey-Caruso Emotional Intelligence Test (MSCEIT)*. Toronto, Ontario: Multi-Health Systems, Inc.

Mayer, J. D., Salovey, P., & Caruso, D. (2002). *The Mayer-Salovey-Caruso Emotional Intelligence Test (MSCEIT), 2.0*. Toronto, Ontario: Multi-Health Systems, Inc.

Mayer, J. D., Salovey, P., & Caruso, D. (2004). Emotional intelligence: Theory, findings, and implications. *Psychological Inquiry, 15*, 197–215.

Mayne, T. J., & Bonanno, G. A. (Eds.). (2001). *Emotions: Current issues and future directions*. New York: Guilford Press.

McCarthy, G., & Maughan, B. (2010). Negative childhood experiences and adult love relationships: The role of internal working models of attachment. *Attachment & Human Development, 12*, 445–461.

McClelland, D. C., Atkinson, J. W., Clark, R. W., & Lowell, E. L. (1953). *The achievement motive*. New York: Appleton-Century-Crofts.

McCrae, R. R., & Costa, P. T. (1987). Validation of the five-factor model of personality across instruments and observers. *Journal of Personality and Social Psychology, 52,* 81–90.

McCraty, R. (2002). Influence of cardiac afferent input on heart-brain synchronization and cognitive performance. *International Journal of Psychophysiology, 45,* 72–73.

McCraty, R., & Atkinson, M. (2003). *Psychophysiological coherence.* Boulder Creek, CA: HeartMath Research Center, Institute of HeartMath, Publication No. 03–016.

McCraty, R., & Childre, D. (2004). The grateful heart: The psychophysiology of appreciation. In R. A. Emmons & M. E. McCullough (Eds.), *The psychology of gratitude* (pp. 230–255). New York: Oxford University Press.

McCullough, M. E. (2000). Forgiveness as a human strength: Theory, measurement, and links to well-being. *Journal of Social and Clinical Psychology, 19,* 43–55.

McCullough, M. E., Emmons, R. A., & Tsang, J. (2002). The grateful disposition: A conceptual and empirical topography. *Journal of Personality and Social Psychology, 82,* 112–127.

McCullough, M. E., Kilpatrick, S., Emmons, R. A., & Larson, D. (2001). Is gratitude a moral affect? *Psychological Bulletin, 127,* 249–266.

McCullough, M. E., Pargament, K. I., & Thoresen, C. E. (Eds.). (2000a). *Forgiveness: Theory, research, and practice.* New York: Guilford Press.

McCullough, M. E., Pargament, K. I., & Thoresen, C. E. (2000b). The psychology of forgiveness: History, conceptual issues, and overview. In M. E. McCullough, K. I. Pargament, & C. E. Thoresen (Eds.), *Forgiveness: Theory, research, and practice* (pp. 1–14). New York: Guilford Press.

McCullough, M. E., Rachal, K. C., Sandage, S. J., Worthington, E. L., Jr., Brown, S. W., & Hight, T. L. (1998). Interpersonal forgiving in close relationships: II. Theoretical elaboration and measurement. *Journal of Personality and Social Psychology, 75,* 1586–1603.

McCullough, M. E., Tsang, J., & Emmons, R. A. (2004). Gratitude in intermediate affective terrain: Links of grateful moods to individual differences and daily emotional experience. *Journal of Personality and Social Psychology, 86,* 295–309.

McCullough, M. E., Worthington, E. L., Jr., & Rachal, K. C. (1997). Interpersonal forgiving in close relationships. *Journal of Personality and Social Psychology, 73,* 321–336.

McDermott, D., Hastings, S., Gariglietti, K. P., Gingerich, K., Callahan, B., & Diamond, K. (1996, April). *Fostering hope in the classroom.* Paper presented at the meeting of the Kansas Counseling Association, Salina, KS.

McDermott, D., & Snyder, C. R. (1999). *Making hope happen: A workbook for turning possibilities into realities.* Oakland, CA: New Harbinger.

McDermott, D., & Snyder, C. R. (2000). *The great big book of hope.* Oakland, CA: New Harbinger.

McDermott, P. A. (1980). Congruence and typology of diagnoses in school psychology: An empirical study. *Psychology in the Schools, 17,* 12–24.

McDougall, D., & Granby, C. (1996). How expectation of questioning method affects undergraduates' preparation for class. *Journal of Experimental Education, 65,* 43–54.

McFarland, M. J., Smith, C. A., Toussaint, L., & Thomas, P. A. (2012). Forgiveness of others and health: Do race and neighborhood matter? *The Journals of Gerontology: Series B: Psychological Sciences and Social Sciences, 67B,* 66–75.

McGorry, P. (2012). Early intervention in the Asian century. *Asian Journal of Psychiatry, 5,* 106–107.

McKay, J., & Greengrass, M. (2003). People. *Monitor, 34,* 87.

McKeachie, W. J. (2002). Ebbs, flows, and progress in the teaching of psychology. In S. F. Davis & W. Buskist (Eds.), *The teaching of psychology: Essays in honor of Wilbert J. McKeachie and Charles L. Brewer* (pp. 487–498). Mahwah, NJ: Lawrence Erlbaum.

McKiernan, P., Cloud, R., Patterson, D. A., Golder, S., & Besel, K. (2011). Development of a brief abstinence self-efficacy measure. *Journal of Social Work Practice in the Addictions, 11,* 245–253.

McMillan, D. W., & Chavis, D. M. (1986). Sense of community: A definition and theory. *Journal of Community Psychology, 14,* 6–23.

McMillan, L. H. W., O'Driscoll, M. P., Marsh, N. V., & Brady, E. C. (2001). Understanding workaholism: Data synthesis, theoretical critique, and future design strategies. *International Journal of Stress Management, 8,* 69–91.

McNeal, R. E. (1998). Pre- and post-treatment hope in children and adolescents in residential treatment: A further analysis of the effects of the teaching family model. *Dissertation Abstracts International, 59*(5-B), 2425.

McNeely, C. A., & Barber, B. (2010). How do parents make adolescents feel loved? Perspectives on supportive parenting from adolescents in 12 cultures. *Journal of Adolescent Research, 25,* 601–631.

McNulty, J. K. (2011). The dark side of forgiveness: The tendency to forgive predicts continued psycholcial and physical aggression in marriage. *Personality and Social Psychology Bulletin, 37,* 770–783.

Meehl, P. (1975). Hedonic capacity: Some conjectures. *Bulletin of the Menninger Clinic, 39,* 295–307.

Meichenbaum, D. H. (1977). *Cognitive-behavior modification: An integrative approach.* New York: Plenum.

Mendoza, N. S., Walitzer, K. S., & Connors, G. J. (2012). Use of treatment strategies in a moderated drinking program for women. *Addictive Behaviors, 37,* 1054–1057.

Menninger, K., Mayman, M., & Pruyser, P. W. (1963). *The vital balance.* New York: Viking Press.

Merrill, R. M., Aldana, S. G., Pope, J. E., Anderson, D. R., Coberley, C. R., & Whitmer, R. W. (2012). Presenteeism according to healthy behaviors, physical health, and work environment. *Population Health Management, 15,* 293–301.

Metalsky, G. I., Halberstadt, J., & Abramson, L. Y. (1987). Vulnerability to depressive mood reactions: Toward a more powerful test of the diathesis-stress and causal mediation components of the reformulated theory of depression. *Journal of Personality and Social Psychology, 52,* 386–393.

Metheny, J., & McWhirter, E. H. (2013). Contributions of social status and family support to college students' career decision self-efficacy and outcome expectations. *Journal of Career Assessment, 21,* 378–394.

Michael, S. T., & Snyder, C. R. (2005). Getting unstuck: The rules of hope, finding meaning, and rumination in adjustment to bereavement among college students. *Journal of Death Studies, 29,* 435–458.

Miller, A. J., & Worthington, E. L., Jr. (2010). Sex differences in forgiveness and mental health in recently married couples. *The Journal of Positive Psychology, 5,* 12–23.

Miller, D. N., Nickerson, A. B., & Jimerson, S. R. (2009). Positive psychology and school-based interventions. In R. Gilman, E. S. Huebner, & M. J. Furlong (Eds.), *Handbook of positive psychology in schools* (pp. 293–304). New York: Routledge/Taylor & Francis Group.

Miller, D. R. (1963). The study of social relationships: Situation, identity, and social interaction. In S. Koch (Ed.), *Psychology: A study of science* (Vol. 5, pp. 639–737). New York: McGraw-Hill.

Miller, D. T. (1999). The norm of self-interest. *American Psychologist, 54,* 1053–1060.

Miller, J. G. (1994). Cultural diversity in the morality of caring: Individually oriented versus duty-oriented interpersonal scales. *Cross-Cultural Research, 28,* 3–39.

Miller, M. J., Yang, M., Farrell, J. A., & Lin, L. (2011). Racial and cultural factors affecting the mental health of Asian Americans. *American Journal of Orthopsychiatry, 81,* 489–497.

Miller, N. E. (1944). Experimental studies of conflict. In J. M. Hunt (Ed.), *Personality and behavior disorders* (Vol. 1, pp. 431–465). New York: Ronald Press.

Miller, T. (1995). *How to want what you have: Discovering the magic and grandeur of ordinary existence.* New York: Avon Books.

Mio, J. S., Barker, L. A., & Tumambing, J. (2009). *Multicultural psychology: Understanding our diverse communities.* New York: McGraw-Hill.

Miranda, J., Bernal, G., Lau, A., Kohn, L., Hwang, W. C., & LaFromboise, T. (2005). State of the science on psychosocial interventions for ethnic minorities. *Annual Review of Clinical Psychology, 1,* 113–142.

Mischel, W. (1979). On the interface of cognition and personality: Beyond the person–situation debate. *American Psychologist, 34,* 740–754.

Mitchell, N. (2003). Interview with Nobel Laureate Daniel Kahneman: Toward a science of well-being. Retrieved from http://www.abc.net.au/rn/science/mind/s923773.htm

Miyake, K., Chen, S. J., & Campos, J. J. (1985). Infant temperament, mother's mode of interaction, and attachment in Japan: An interim report. In

I. Bretherton & E. Waters (Eds.), Growing points of attachment theory and research. *Monographs of the Society for Research in Child Development, 50*, 276–297.

Mohr, S., Perroud, N., Gillieron, C., Brandt, P. Y., Rieben, I., Borras, L., & Huguelet, P. (2011). Spirituality and religiousness as predictive factors of outcome in schizophrenia and schizo-affective disorders. *Psychiatry Resarch, 186*, 177–182.

Moneta, G. B. (2004a). The flow experience across cultures. *Journal of Happiness Studies, 5*, 115–121.

Moneta, G. B. (2004b). The flow model of intrinsic motivation in Chinese: Cultural and personal moderators. *Journal of Happiness Studies, 5*, 181–217.

Moorhead, H. J. H., Gill, C., Minton, C. A. B., & Myers, J. E. (2012). Forgive and forget? Forgiveness, personality, and wellness among counselors-in-training. *Counseling and Values, 57*, 81–95.

Moraitou, D., & Efklides, A. (2012). The Wise Thinking and Acting Questionnaire: The cognitive facet of wisdom and its relation with memory, affect, and hope. *Journal of Happiness Studies, 13*, 849–873.

Morimoto, T., Matsuyama, K., Ichihara-Takeda, S., Murakami, R., & Ikeda, N. (2012). Influence of self-efficacy on the interpersonal behaviour of schizophrenia patients undergoing rehabilitation in psychiatric day-care services. *Psychiatry and Clinical Neurosciences, 66*, 203–209.

Morris, M. W., & Peng, K. (1994). Culture and cause: American and Chinese attributions for social and physical events. *Journal of Personality and Social Psychology, 67*, 949–971.

Motl, R. W., McAuley, E., Wynn, D., Sandroff, B., & Suh, Y. (2013). Physical activity, self-efficacy, and health-related quality of life in persons with multiple sclerosis: Analysis of associations between individual-level changes over one year. *Quality of Life Research: An International Journal of Quality of Life Aspects of Treatment, Care, & Rehabilitation, 22*, 253–261.

Mowrer, O. H. (1960). *Learning theory and behavior*. New York: Wiley.

Mrazek, P. J., & Haggerty, R. J. (1994). *Reducing risks for mental disorders: Frontiers for preventive intervention research*. Washington, DC: National Academy Press.

Mundy, L. (2012). *The richer sex: How the new majority of female breadwinners is transforming sex, love, and family*. New York: Simon & Schuster.

Munoz, R. F., & Mendelson, T. (2004). Prevention of mental disorders. In W. E. Craighead & C. B. Neroff (Eds.), *The Corsini concise encyclopedia of psychology and behavioral science* (pp. 724–725). New York: Wiley.

Murata, A., Moser, J. S., & Kitayama, S. (2013). Culture shapes electrocortical responses during emotion suppression. *Social Cognitive and Affective Neuroscience, 8*, 595–601.

Muris, P., Mayer, B., & Schubert, T. (2010). "You might belong in Gryffindor": Children's courage and its relationships to anxiety symptoms, Big Five personality traits, and sex roles. *Child Psychiatry and Human Development, 41*, 204–213.

Murnane, R. J., & Steele, J. L. (2007). What is the problem? The challenge of providing effective teachers for all children. *The Future of Children, 17*, 15–43.

Mutrie, N., & Faulkner, G. (2004). Physical activity: Positive psychology in motion. In P. A. Linley & S. Joseph (Eds.), *Positive psychology in practice* (pp. 146–164). Hoboken, NJ: Wiley.

Myers, D. (1993). *The pursuit of happiness*. New York: Avon Books.

Myers, D. G. (1992). *The pursuit of happiness*. New York: Morrow.

Myers, D. G. (1993). *The pursuit of happiness*. New York: HarperCollins.

Myers, D. G. (2000). The funds, friends, and faith of happy people. *American Psychologist, 55*, 56–67.

Myers, D. G. (2004). Human connections and the good life: Balancing individuality and community in public policy. In P. A. Linley & S. Joseph (Eds.), *Positive psychology in practice* (pp. 641–657). Hoboken, NJ: Wiley.

Myers, D. G. (2012). Reflections on religious belief and prosociality: Comment on Galen (2012). *Psychological Bulletin, 138*, 913–917.

Nakamura, J., & Csikszentmihalyi, M. (2009). Flow theory and research. In S. J. Lopez & C. R. Snyder

(Eds.), *Oxford handbook of positive psychology* (pp. 195–206). New York: Oxford University Press.

Napolitano, C. M., Bowers, E. P., Gestsdottir, S., Depping, M., von Eye, A., Chase, P., & Lerner, J. V. (2011). The role of parenting and goal selection in positive youth development: A person-centered approach. *Journal of Adolescence, 34,* 1137–1149.

National Organization for Women. (2012). Violence against women in the United States: Statistics. *National Organization for Women.* Retrieved from https://www.now.org/issues/violence/stats .html

Nebelkopf, E., King, J., Wright, S., Schweigman, K., Lucero, E., Habte-Michael, T., & Cervantes, T. (2011). Growing roots: Native American evidence-based practices. *Journal of Psychoactive Drugs, 43,* 263–268.

Negy, C., Shreve, T. L., Jensen, B. J., & Uddin, N. (2003). Ethnic identity, self-esteem, and ethnocentrism: A study of social identity versus multicultural theory of development. *Cultural Diversity and Ethnic Minority Psychology, 9,* 333–344.

Nelson, K., & Tom, N. (2011). Evaluation of substance abuse, HIV and hepatitis prevention initiative for urban Native Americans: The Native Voices Program. *Journal of Psychoactive Drugs, 43,* 349–354.

Newberg, A. B., d'Aquili, E. G., Newberg, S. K., & deMarici, V. (2000). The neuropsychological correlates of forgiveness. In M. E. McCullough, K. I. Pargament, & C. E. Thoresen (Eds.), *Forgiveness: Theory, research, and practice* (pp. 91–110). New York: Guilford Press.

Newbrough, J. R. (1995). Toward community: A third position. *American Journal of Community Psychology, 23,* 9–31.

Newton, N. A., Brauer, D., Gutmann, D. L., & Grunes, J. (1986). Psychodynamic therapy with the aged: A review. *Clinical Gerontologist, 5,* 205–229.

Nickell, G. S. (1998, August). *The Helping Attitude Scale.* Paper presented at the American Psychological Association Convention, San Francisco.

Niederhoffer, K. G., & Pennebaker, J. W. (2002). Sharing one's story: On the benefits of writing or talking about emotional experience. In C. R. Snyder & S. J. Lopez (Eds.), *The handbook of positive psychology* (pp. 573–583). New York: Oxford University Press.

Nisbett, R. E. (2003). *The geography of thought: How Asians and Westerners think differently . . . and why.* New York: Free Press.

Nisbett, R. E., Caputo, C., Legant, P., & Maracek, J. (1973). Behavior as seen by the actor and as seen by the observer. *Journal of Personality and Social Psychology, 27,* 154–164.

Nolen-Hoeksema, S. (1987). Sex differences in depression: Theory and evidence. *Psychological Bulletin, 101,* 259–282.

Nolen-Hoeksema, S. (2000). Growth and resilience among bereaved people. In J. Gillham (Ed.), *The science of optimism and hope* (pp. 107–127). Philadelphia: Templeton Foundation Press.

Norcross, J. C., & Prochaska, J. O. (1986). The psychological distress and self-change of psychologists, counselors, and laypersons. *Psychotherapy, 23,* 102–114.

Noricks, J. S., Atgler, L. H., Bartholomew, M., Howard-Smith, S., Martin, D., Pyles, S., & Shapiro, W. (1987). Age, abstract thinking, and the American concept of person. *American Anthropologist, 89,* 667–675.

Norton, P. J., & Weiss, B. J. (2009). The role of courage on behavioral approach in a fear-eliciting situation: A proof-of-concept pilot study. *Journal of Anxiety Disorders, 23,* 212–217. doi: 10.1016/j .janxdis.2008.07.002

Nussbaum, M. (2001). *Upheavals of thought: The intelligence of emotions.* London: Cambridge University Press.

Oatley, K., & Jenkins, J. M. (1992). Human emotion: Function and dysfunction. *Annual Review of Psychology, 43,* 55–86.

Obama, B. (2004, July 27). Keynote speech. Democratic National Convention. Retrieved from http://www.2004dnc.com/barackoba maspeech/

Obeysekere, G. (1995). Depression, Buddhism, and the work of culture in Sri Lanka. In A. Kleinman & B. Good (Eds.), *Culture and depression: Studies in the anthropology and cross-cultural psychiatry of affect and behavior* (pp. 134–152). Berkeley: University of California Press.

O'Brien, K. M. (2003). Measuring career self-efficacy: Promoting confidence and happiness at work. In S. J. Lopez & C. R. Snyder (Eds.), *Positive psychological assessment: A handbook of models and measures* (pp. 109–126). Washington, DC: American Psychological Association.

O'Brien, K. M., Heppner, M. J., Flores, L. Y., & Bikos, L. H. (1997). The Career Counseling Self-Efficacy Scale: Instrument development and training applications. *Journal of Counseling Psychology, 44,* 20–31.

O'Byrne, K. K., Lopez, S. J., & Petersen, S. (2000, August). *Building a theory of courage: A precursor to change?* Paper presented at the 108th Annual Convention of the American Psychological Association, Washington, DC.

O'Connor, R., Hallam, R., & Rachman, S. (1985). Fearlessness and courage: A replication experiment. *British Journal of Psychology, 76,* 187–197.

Oda, R., Hiraishi, K., Fukukawa, Y., & Matsumoto-Oda, A. (2011). Human prosociality in altruism niche. *Journal of Evolutionary Psychology, 9,* 283–293.

Odom, E. C., & Vernon-Feagans, L. (2010). Buffers of racial discrimination: Links with depression among rural African American mothers. *Journal of Marriage and Family, 72,* 346–359.

Office of the Governor. (2009, July 28). *Gov. Schwarzenegger highlights increased volunteerism in the golden state.* Retrieved from http://gov.ca.gov/press-release/12905/

Ojeda, L., Piña-Watson, B., Castillo, L. G., Castillo, R., Khan, N., & Leigh, J. (2012). Acculturation, enculturation, ethnic identity, and conscientiousness as predictors of Latino boys' and girls' career decision self-efficacy. *Journal of Career Development, 39,* 208–228.

Okano, K.-I. (1994). Shame and social phobia: A transcultural viewpoint. *Bulletin of the Menninger Clinic, 58,* 323–338.

Oldham, J. M., & Morris, L. B. (1995). *New personality self-portrait: Why you think, work, love, and act the way you do.* New York: Bantam Books.

O'Leary, A., & Brown, S. (1995). Self-efficacy and the physiological stress response. In J. E. Maddux (Ed.), *Self-efficacy, adaptation, and adjustment: Theory, research, and application* (pp. 227–248). New York: Plenum.

Olson, S. L., Sameroff, A. J., Landsford, J. E., Sexton, H., Davis-Kean, P., Bates, J. E.,…Pettit, G. S. (2013). Deconstructing the externalizing spectrum: Growth patterns of overt aggression, covert aggression, oppositional behavior, impulsivity/inattention, and emotion dysregulation between school entry and early adolescence. *Development and Psychopathology, 25,* 817–842.

Ong, A. D., & van Dulmen, M. H. M. (2007). *Oxford handbook of methods in positive psychology.* New York: Oxford University Press.

Ong, A. D., & Zautra, A. J. (2009). Modeling positive human health: From covariance structures to dynamic systems. In S. J. Lopez & C. R. Snyder (Eds.), *Oxford handbook of positive psychology* (pp. 97–104). New York: Oxford University Press.

Opler, M., Sodhi, D., Zaveri, D., & Madhusoodanan, S. (2010). Primary psychiatric prevention in children and adolescents. *Annals of Clinical Psychiatry, 22,* 220–234.

Ortony, A., Clore, G. L., & Collins, A. (1988). *The cognitive structure of emotions.* New York: Cambridge University Press.

Orwoll, L. (1989). Wisdom in later adulthood: Personality and life history correlates. *Dissertation Abstracts International, 49,* 5054.

Orwoll, L., & Achenbaum, W. A. (1993). Gender and the development of wisdom. *Human Development, 36,* 274–296.

Ory, M. G., & Cox, M. (1994). Forging ahead: Linking health and behavior to improve quality of life in older people. *Social Indicator Research, 33,* 89–120.

Outten, R. H., Schmitt, M. T., Garcia, D. M., & Branscombe N. R. (2009). Coding options: Missing links between minority group identification and psychological well-being. *Applied Psychology: An International Review, 58,* 146–170. doi: 10.1111/j.1464–0597.2008.00386.x

Ouweneel, E., Le Blanc, P. M., & Schaufeli, W. B. (2013). Do-it-yourself: An online positive psychology intervention to promote positive emotions, self-efficacy, and engagement at work. *The Career Development International, 18,* 173–195.

Oyama, H., Sakashita, T., Hojo, K., Ono, Y., Watanabe, N., Takizawa, T.,…Tanaka, E. (2010). A community-based survery screening for depression in the elderly: The short-term effect on suicide risk in Japan. *Crisis: The Journal of Crisis Intervention and Suicide Prevention, 31,* 100–108.

Oyserman, D., Coon, H. M., & Kemmelmeier, M. (2002). Rethinking individualism and collectivism: Evaluation of theoretical assumptions and meta-analyses. *Psychological Bulletin, 128,* 3–72.

Paez, D., Velasco, C., & Gonzales, J. L. (1999). Expressive writing and the role of alexithymia as a dispositional deficit in self-disclosure and psychological health. *Journal of Personality and Social Psychology, 77,* 630–641.

Palmer, A. (2003, November). In brief: Positive emotion styles linked to the common cold. *The Monitor in Psychology, 34*(10), 16.

Palmer, S. (1970). *Deviance and conformity: Roles, situations, and reciprocity.* New Haven, CT: College and University Press.

Panter-Brick, C., Rowley-Conwy, P., & Layton, R. H. (Eds.). (2001). *Hunter-gatherers: An interdisciplinary perspective.* New York: Cambridge University Press.

Pargament, K. I. (1997). *The psychology of religion and coping: Theory, research, practice.* New York: Guilford Press.

Pargament, K. I., & Mahoney, A. (2009). Spirituality: The search for the sacred. In S. J. Lopez & C. R. Snyder (Eds.), *Oxford handbook of positive psychology* (pp. 611–620). New York: Oxford University Press.

Parham, T. A., White, J. L., & Ajamu, A. (1999). *The psychology of Blacks: An African centered perspective* (3rd ed.). Englewood Cliffs, NJ: Prentice Hall.

Park, H. S., & Lee, H. E. (2012). Cultural differences in 'thank you.' *Journal of Language and Social Psychology, 31,* 138–156.

Park, N., Peterson, C., & Seligman, M. E. P. (2006). Character strengths in fifty-four nations and the fifty US states. *Journal of Positive Psychology, 1,* 118–129. doi: 10.1080/17439760600619567

Parker, D. (1929, November). Interview with Ernest Hemingway. *The New Yorker, 30,* n.p.

Pascual-Leone, J. (1990). An essay on wisdom: Toward organismic processes that make it possible. In R. J. Sternberg (Ed.), *Wisdom: Its nature, origins, and development* (pp. 244–278). New York: Cambridge University Press.

Pasupathi, M., Staudinger, U., & Baltes, P. B. (1999). *The emergence of wisdom-related knowledge and judgment during adolescence.* Berlin, Germany: Max Planck Institute for Human Development.

Pavot, W., & Diener, E. (2008). The satisfaction with life scale and the emerging construct of life satisfaction. *Journal of Positive Psychology, 3,* 137–152. doi: 10.1080/17439760701756946

Payne, B. P. (1977). The older volunteer: Social role continuity and development. *The Gerontologist, 29,* 710–711.

Paz, R., Neto, F., & Mullet, E. (2008). Forgiveness: A China-Western Europe comparison. *Journal of Psychology, 142,* 147–157.

Pedrotti, J. T. (2012). Broadening perspectives: Strategies to infuse multiculturalism into a positive psychology course. *Journal of Positive Psychology, 6,* 506–513.

Pedrotti, J. T. (2013a). Positive psychology, social class, and counseling. In W. M. Liu (Ed.) *Handbook of social class* (pp. 131–143). New York: Oxford University Press.

Pedrotti, J. T. (2013b). Culture and identity: Integrating an understanding of cultural context into a discussion of positive traits. In J. J. Froh & A. C. Parks (Eds.), *Activities for teaching positive psychology: A guide for instructors* (pp. 41–44). Washington, DC: American Psychological Association.

Pedrotti, J. T. (2014, January). Shifting the lens: Including culture in discussions of positive psychology. Keynote address presented at the meeting of the Asian Pacific Conference on Applied Positive Psychology, Hong Kong.

Pedrotti, J. T. (2014) Taking culture into account with psychological interventions. In A. C. Parks (Ed.), *The Wiley-Blackwell handbook of positive psychological interventions.* West Sussex, London: Wiley Blackwell Publishing.

Pedrotti, J. T., & Edwards, L. M. (2009). The intersection of positive psychology and multiculturalism in counseling. In J. G. Ponterotto, J. M. Casas, L. A. Suzuki, & C. M. Alexander (Eds.), *Handbook of multicultural counseling* (3rd ed., pp. 165–174). Thousand Oaks, CA: Sage.

Pedrotti, J. T., & Edwards, L. M. (2010). The intersection of positive psychology and multiculturalism in counseling. In J. G. Ponterotto, J. M. Casas, L. A. Suzuki, & C. M. Alexander (Eds.), *Handbook of multicultural counseling* (3rd ed., pp. 165–174). Thousand Oaks, CA: Sage.

Pedrotti, J. T., & Edwards, L. M. (Eds.). (2014). *Perspectives on the intersection of multiculturalism and positive psychology.* New York: Springer Science + Business Media.

Pedrotti, J. T., Edwards, L. M., & Lopez, S. J. (2009). Positive psychology within a cultural context. In S. J. Lopez & C. R. Snyder (Eds.), *Oxford handbook of positive psychology* (pp. 49–57). New York: Oxford University Press.

Pedrotti, J. T., & Sweatt, L. I. (2007, August). *Effects of a multicultural course on undergraduate students.* Poster session presented at the annual meeting of the American Psychological Association, San Francisco, CA.

Pennebaker, J. W. (1989). Confession, inhibition, and disease. In L. Berkowitz (Ed.), *Advances in experimental social psychology* (Vol. 22, pp. 211–244). New York: Academic Press.

Pennebaker, J. W. (1997). *Opening up: The healing power of expressing emotions* (Rev. ed.). New York: Guilford Press.

Perrone, K. M., Wright, S. L., & Jackson, Z. V. (2009). Traditional and nontraditional gender roles and work–family interface for men and women. *Journal of Career Develoment, 36,* 8–24.

Perry, S. K. (1999). *Writing in flow.* Cincinnati, OH: Writer's Digest Books.

Peters, R. M. (2006). The relationship of racism, chronic stress emotions, and blood pressure. *Journal of Nursing Scholarship, 38,* 234–340.

Peterson, C. (2000). Optimistic explanatory style and health. In J. Gillham (Ed.), *The science of optimism and hope* (pp. 145–162). Philadelphia: Templeton Foundation Press.

Peterson, C., & Barrett, L. (1987). Explanatory style and academic performance among university freshmen. *Journal of Personality and Social Psychology, 53,* 603–607.

Peterson, C., Bettes, B. A., & Seligman, M. E. P. (1985). Depressive symptoms and unprompted causal attributions: Content analysis. *Behavior Research and Therapy, 23,* 379–382.

Peterson, C., Maier, S. F., & Seligman, M. E. P. (1993). *Learned helplessness: A theory for the age of personal control.* New York: Oxford University Press.

Peterson, C., & Park, N. (2003, March). *Assessment of character strengths among youth: Progress report on the Values in Action Inventory for Youth.* Paper presented at the Child Trends Conference on Indicators of Positive Youth Development, Washington, DC.

Peterson, C., Schulman, P., Castellon, C., & Seligman, M. (1992). CAVE: Content Analysis of Verbal Explanations. In C. Smith (Ed.), *Motivation and personality: Handbook of thematic content analysis* (pp. 383–392). New York: Cambridge University Press.

Peterson, C., & Seligman, M. E. P. (2004). *Character strengths and virtues: A handbook and classification.* Washington, DC: American Psychological Association.

Peterson, C., Seligman, M. E. P., Yurko, K. H., Martin, L. R., & Friedman, H. S. (1998). Catastrophizing and untimely death. *Psychological Science, 9,* 127–130.

Peterson, C., Semmel, A., von Baeyer, C., Abramson, L. Y., Metalsky, G. I., & Seligman, M. E. P. (1982). The Attributional Style Questionnaire. *Cognitive Therapy and Research, 6,* 287–299.

Peterson, C., & Steen, T. A. (2002). Optimistic explanatory style. In C. R. Snyder & S. J. Lopez (Eds.), *The handbook of positive psychology* (pp. 244–256). New York: Oxford University Press.

Peterson, C., & Villanova, P. (1988). An expanded attributional style questionnaire. *Journal of Abnormal Psychology, 97,* 87–89.

Peterson, P. E., & West, M. R. (Eds.). (2003). *No child left behind? The politics and practice of accountability.* Washington, DC: Brookings Institution.

Phillips, V. (1998/2011). *Empowering discipline: An approach that works with at-risk students.* Carmel Valley, CA: Personal Development Publishing.

Piaget, J. (1932). *The moral judgment of the child.* London: Routledge and Kegan Paul.

Piccard, B. (1999). Around at last! *National Geographic, 196*(3), 30–51.

Pickering, A., & Gray, J. (1999). The neuroscience of personality. In L. Pervin & O. John (Eds.),

Handbook of personality (2nd ed., pp. 277–299). New York: Guilford Press.

Pickett, K., Yardley, L., & Kenderick, T. (2012). Physical activity and depression: A multiple mediation analysis. *Mental Health and Physical Activity, 5,* 125–134.

Piedmont, R. (2004, November). *Spirituality predicts psychosocial outcomes: A cross-cultural analysis.* International Society for Quality of Life Studies Conference, Philadelphia.

Pieper, J. (1966). *The four cardinal virtues.* Notre Dame, IN: Notre Dame Press.

Piet, J., Hougaard, E., Hecksher, M. S., & Rosenberg, N. K. (2010). A randomized pilot study of mindfulness-based cognitive therapy and group cognitive-behavioral therapy for young adults with social phobia. *Scandinavian Journal of Psychology, 51,* 403–410.

Pieterse, A. L., & Carter, R. T. (2010). The role of racial identity in perceived racism and psychological stress among Black American adults: Exploring traditional and alternative approaches. *Journal of Applied Social Psychology, 40,* 1028–1053.

Piliavin, J. A., & Charng, H.-W. (1990). Altruism: A review of recent theory and research. *American Sociological Review, 16,* 27–65.

Pines, A. M., Aronson, E., & Kafry, D. (1981). *Burnout: From tedium to personal growth.* New York: Free Press.

Pinker, S. (1997). *How the mind works.* New York: Norton.

Piper, W. (1989). *The little engine that could.* New York: Platt and Monk. (Original work published 1930)

Pipher, M. B. (1995). *Reviving Ophelia: Saving the selves of adolescent girls.* New York: Ballantine Books.

Pipher, M. B. (2003). *Letters to a young therapist.* New York: Basic Books.

Pittman, K. J., & Fleming, W. E. (1991). *A new vision: Promoting youth development.* Washington, DC: Center for Youth Development and Policy Research.

Pitts, D. (2009). Diversity management, job satisfaction, and performance: Evidence from U.S. federal agencies. *Public Administration Review, 69,* 328–338.

Plante, T. G. (2005). *Contemporary clinical psychology* (2nd ed.). New York: Wiley.

Plato. (1953). *The dialogues of Plato, Volume 1: Laches.* (B. Jowett, Trans.). New York: Modern Library.

Plomin, R., Scheier, M. F., Bergeman, C. S., Pederson, N. L., Nesselroade, J. R., & McClearn, G. E. (1992). Optimism, pessimism, and mental health: A twin/adoption analysis. *Personality and Individual Differences, 13,* 921–930.

Ponterotto, J., Costa-Wofford, C., Brobst, K., Spelliscy, D., Kacanski, J., Scheinholtz, J., & Martines, D. (2007). Multicultural personality dispositions and psychological well-being. *Journal of Social Psychology, 147,* 119–135.

Ponterotto, J., Mendelowitz, D., & Collabolletta, E. (2008). Promoting multicultural personality development: A strengths-based, positive psychology worldview for schools. *Professional School Counseling, 12,* 93–99.

Pool, L., & Qualter, P. (2012). The dimensional structure of the Emotional Self-Efficacy Scale (ESES). *Australian Journal of Psychology, 64,* 147–154.

Pretzer, J. L., & Walsh, C. A. (2001). Optimism, pessimism, and psychotherapy: Implications for clinical practice. In E. C. Chang (Ed.), *Optimism & pessimism: Implications for theory, research, and practice* (pp. 321–346). Washington, DC: American Psychological Association.

Prigatano, G. P. (1992). Disordered mind, wounded soul: The emerging role of psychotherapy in rehabilitation after brain injury. *Journal of Head Trauma and Rehabilitation, 6,* 1–10.

Procci, K., Singer, A. R., Levy, K. R., & Bowers, C. (2012). Measuring the flow experience of gamers: An evaluation of the DFS-2. *Computers in Huamn Behavior, 28,* 2306–2312.

Proctor, C., Maltby, J., & Linley, P. (2011). Strengths use as a predictor of well-being and health-related quality of life. *Journal of Happiness Studies, 12,* 153–169.

Proyer, R. T. (2012). Examining playfulness in adults: Testing its correlates with personality, positive psychological functioning, goal aspirations, and multi-methodically assessed ingenuity. *Psychological Test and Assessment Modeling, 54,* 103–127.

Proyer, R. T., & Ruch, W. (2011). The virtuousness of adult playfulness: The relation of playfulness with strengths of character. *Psychology of Well-Being: Theory, Research and Practice, 1,* 4–12.

Pruyser, P. W. (1976). *The minister as diagnostician: Personal problems in pastoral perspective.* Philadelphia: Westminster Press.

Pury, C. L. S., Kowalski, R. M., & Spearman, J. (2007). Distinctions between general and personal courage. *Journal of Positive Psychology, 2,* 99–114. doi: 10.1080/17439760701237962

Pury, C. L. S., & Lopez, S. J. (2009). Courage. In S. J. Lopez & C. R. Snyder (Eds.). *Oxford handbook of positive psychology* (pp. 375–382). New York: Oxford University Press.

Pusker, K. R., Bernardo, L., Ren, D., Haley, T. M., Tark, K., Switala, J., & Siemon, L. (2010). Self-esteem and optimism in rural youth: Gender differences. *Contemporary Nurse, 34,* 190–198.

Putman, D. (1997). Psychological courage. *Philosophy, Psychiatry and Psychology, 4*(1), 1–11.

Pyone, J. S., & Isen, A. M. (2011). Positive affect, intertemporal choice, and levels of thinking: Increasing consumers' willingness to wait. *Journal of Marketing Research, 48,* 532–543.

Quinn, R. (2004). *Development and initial validation of the KU Strengths Cardsort for Adolescents.* (Unpublished master's thesis). University of Kansas, Lawrence.

Rachman, S. J. (1978). Human fears: A three-systems analysis. *Scandinavian Journal of Behaviour Therapy, 7,* 237–245.

Rachman, S. J. (1984). Fear and courage. *Behavior Therapy, 15,* 109–120.

Ramey, C. T., & Ramey, S. L. (1998). Early intervention and early experience. *American Psychologist, 53,* 109–120.

Ramírez-Esparza, N., & Pennebaker, J. W. (2006). Do good stories produce good health?: Exploring words, language, and culture. *Narrative Inquiry, 16,* 211–219.

Ramírez-Maestre, C., Esteve, R., & López, A. E. (2012). The role of optimism and pessimism in chronic pain patients' adjustment. *The Spanish Journal of Psychology, 15,* 286–294.

Rashid, T. (2006). *Promoting well-being through character strengths.* Unpublished manuscript, University of Pennsylvania.

Raskin, J. D., & Lewandowski, A. M. (2000). The construction of disorder as human enterprise. In R. A. Neimeyer & J. D. Raskin (Eds.), *Constructions of disorder: Meaning-making frameworks for psychotherapy* (pp. 15–40). Washington, DC: American Psychological Association.

Rath, T. (2002). *Measuring the impact of Gallup's strengths-based development program for students.* Princeton, NJ: Gallup Organization.

Rath, T. (2006). *Vital friends: The people you can't afford to live without.* Washington, DC: Gallup Organization.

Rath, T. (2007). *StrengthsFinder 2.0.* New York: Gallup.

Rath, T., & Clifton, D. O. (2004). *How full is your bucket? Positive strategies for work and life.* New York: Gallup Organization.

Reddy, L. A., Newman, E., De Thomas, C. A., & Chun, V. (2009). Effectiveness of school-based prevention and intervention programs for children and adolescents with emotional disturbance: A meta-analysis. *Journal of School Psychology, 47,* 77–99. doi: 10.1016/j.jsp2008.11.001

Reed, A. E., & Carstensen, L. L. (2012). The theory behind the age-related positivity effect. *Frontiers in Psychology, 3,* 1–9.

Regan, P. C., Lakhanpal, S., & Anguiano, C. (2012). Relationship outcomes in Indian-American love-based and arranged marriages. *Psychological Reports, 110,* 915–924.

Reis, H. T., & Gable, S. L. (2003). Toward a positive psychology of relationships. In C. L. M. Keyes & J. Haidt (Eds.), *Flourishing: Positive psychology and the life well lived* (pp. 129–159). Washington, DC: American Psychological Association.

Reyes, J. A., & Elias, M. J. (2011). Fostering social-emotional resilience among Latino youth. *Psychology in the Schools, 48,* 723–737.

Reykowski, J. (1994). Collectivism and individualism as dimensions of social change. In U. Kim, H. C. Triandis, C. Kagitcibasi, S.-C. Choi, & G. Yoon (Eds.), *Individualism and collectivism: Theory, method, and applications* (pp. 276–292). Newbury Park, CA: Sage.

Ribeiro, J., Pedro, L., & Marques, S. (2012). Dispositional optimism is unidimensional or bidimensional? The Portuguese revised Life Orientation Test. *The Spanish Journal of Psychology, 15,* 1259–1271.

Rice, E. F. (1958). *The Renaissance idea of wisdom.* Cambridge, MA: Harvard University Press.

Rice, J. K. (2003). *Teacher quality: Understanding the effectiveness of teacher attributes.* Washington, DC: Economic Policy Institute.

Riegel, K. F. (1973). Dialectical operations: The final period of cognitive development. *Human Development, 16,* 346–370.

Rigazio-DiGilio, S. A. (2000). Reconstructing psychological distress from a relational perspective: A systemic coconstructive-developmental framework. In R. A. Neimeyer & J. D. Raskin (Eds.), *Constructions of disorder: Meaning-making frameworks for psychotherapy* (pp. 309–332). Washington, DC: American Psychological Association.

Rigsby, L. C. (1994). The Americanization of resilience: Deconstructing research practice. In M. Wang & E. Gordon (Eds.), *Educational resilience in inner-city America: Challenges and prospects* (pp. 85–94). Hillsdale, NJ: Lawrence Erlbaum.

Rime, B. (1995). Mental rumination, social sharing, and the recovery from emotional exposure. In J. W. Pennebaker (Ed.), *Emotion, disclosure, and health* (pp. 271–291). Washington, DC: American Psychological Association.

Rios, D., Stewart, A. J., & Winter, D. G. (2010). Thinking she could be the next president: Why identifying with the curriculum matters. *Psychology of Women Quarterly, 34,* 328–338.

Ripley, J. S., & Worthington, E. L., Jr. (2002). Hope-focused and forgiveness-based group interventions to promote marital enrichment. *Journal of Counseling and Development, 80,* 452–472.

Riskind, J. H., Sarampote, C. S., & Mercier, M. A. (1996). For every malady a sovereign cure: Optimism training. *Journal of Cognitive Psychotherapy: An International Quarterly, 10,* 105–117.

Ritschel, L. (2005). Lessons in teaching hope: An interview with C. R. Snyder. *Teaching of Psychology, 32,* 74–78.

Roberts, B. W., Caspi, A., & Moffitt, T. E. (2003). Work experiences and personality development in young adulthood. *Journal of Personality and Social Psychology, 84,* 582–593. doi: 10.1037/0 0223514.84.3.582

Roberts, M., Vernberg, E., & Jackson, Y. (2000). Psychotherapy with children and families. In C. R. Snyder & R. E. Ingram (Eds.), *Handbook of psychological change: Psychotherapy processes and practices for the 21st century* (pp. 500–519). New York: Wiley.

Robey, D., Khoo, H. M., & Powers, C. (2000). Situated learning in cross-functional virtual teams. *Professional Communication,* March, 51–61.

Robinson, C., & Rose, S. (2010). Predictive, construct, and convergent validity of general and domain-specific measures of hope for college student academic achievement. *Research in the Schools, 17,* 38–52.

Robinson, D. N. (1990). Wisdom through the ages. In R. J. Sternberg (Ed.), *Wisdom: Its nature, origins, and development* (pp. 13–24). New York: Cambridge University Press.

Rodin, J., & Langer, E. J. (1977). Long-term effects of a control-relevant intervention among the institutionalized aged. *Journal of Personality and Social Psychology, 35,* 275–282.

Rodriguez-Hanley, A., & Snyder, C. R. (2000). The demise of hope: On losing positive thinking. In C. R. Snyder (Ed.), *Handbook of hope: Theory, measures, and applications* (pp. 39–54). San Diego, CA: Academic Press.

Rogers, R. W., & Prentice-Dunn, S. (1997). Protection motivation theory. In D. Gochman (Ed.), *Handbook of health behavior research 1: Personal and social determinants* (pp. 113–132). New York: Plenum.

Rokke, P. D., & Rehm, L. P. (2001). Management therapies. In K. S. Dobson (Ed.), *Handbook of cognitive-behavioral therapies* (pp. 173–210). New York: Guilford Press.

Root, B. L., & Exline, J. J. (2011). Gender differences in response to experimental forgiveness prompts: Do men show stronger responses than women? *Basic and Applied Social Psychology, 33,* 182–193.

Rorty, A. O. (1988). *Mind in action: Essays in the philosophy of mind.* Boston: Beacon Press.

Rosen, H. S., & Sims, S. T. (2011). Altruistic behaviour and habit formation. *Nonprofit Management and Leadership, 21,* 235–253.

Rosmarin, D. H., Pirutinsky, S., Cohen, A. B., Galler, Y., & Krumrei, E. J. (2011). Grateful to God or just plain grateful? A comparison of religious and general gratitude. *The Journal of Positive Psychology, 6,* 389–396.

Ross, K. L. (2003). *Confucius.* Retrieved from http://friesian.com/confuci.htm

Roth, A., & Fonagy, P. (Eds.). (2005). *What works for whom? A critical review of psychotherapy research.* New York: Guilford Press.

Roth, A., Fonagy, P., & Parry, G. (1996). Psychotherapy research, funding, and evidence-based practice. In A. Roth & P. Fonagy (Eds.), *What works for whom? A critical review of psychotherapy research* (pp. 37–56). New York: Guilford Press.

Rothbaum, F., Weisz, J., Pott, M., Miyake, K., & Morelli, G. (2000). Attachment and culture: Security in the United States and Japan. *American Psychologist, 55,* 1093–1104.

Rothblum, E. D., Balsam, K. F., & Solomon, S. E. (2011). The longest "legal" U.S. same-sex couples reflect on their relationships. *Journal of Social Issues, 67,* 302–315.

Rotter, J. B. (1966). Generalized expectancies for internal versus external control of reinforcement. *Psychological Monographs, 80*(1), 1–28.

Rowe, J. W., & Kahn, R. L. (1998). *Successful aging.* New York: Pantheon Books.

Rowles, J., & Duan, C. (2012). Perceived racism and encouragement among African American adults. *Journal of Multicultural Counseling and Development, 40,* 11–23.

Royal, M. A., & Rossi, R. J. (1996). Individual-level correlates of sense of community: Findings from the workplace and school. *Journal of Community Psychology, 24,* 395–416.

Ruch, W., Proyer, R. T., Harzer, C., Park, N., Peterson, C., & Seligman, M. P. (2010). Values in Action Inventory of Strengths (VIA-IS): Adaptation and validation of the German version and the development of a peer-rating form. *Journal of Individual Differences, 31,* 138–149.

Rue, L. (1994). *By the grace of guile: The role of deception in natural history and human affairs.* New York: Oxford University Press.

Ruehlman, L. S., & Wolchik, S. A. (1988). Personal goals and interpersonal support and hindrance as factors in psychological distress and well-being. *Journal of Personality and Social Psychology, 55,* 293–301.

Rushton, J. P., Chrisjohn, R. D., & Fekken, G. C. (1981). The altruistic personality and the Self-Report Altruism Scale. *Personality and Individual Differences, 2,* 293–302.

Rushton, J. P., Fulker, D. W., Neale, M. C., Nias, D. K., & Eysenck, H. J. (1986). Altruism and aggression: The heritability of individual differences. *Journal of Personality and Social Psychology, 50,* 1192–1198.

Ruthig, J. C., Hanson, B. L., Pedersen, H., Weber, A., & Chipperfield, J. G. (2011). Later life health optimism, pessimism and realism: Psychological contributors and health correlates. *Psychology & Health, 26,* 835–853.

Rutter, M. (1985). Resilience in the face of adversity: Protective factors and resistance to psychiatric disorder. *British Journal of Psychiatry, 147,* 598–611.

Ryan, R. M., & Deci, E. L. (2001). On happiness and human potentials: A review of research on hedonic and eudaemonic well-being. *Annual Review of Psychology, 52,* 141–166.

Ryff, C. D. (1989). Happiness is everything, or is it? Explorations on the meaning of psychological well-being. *Journal of Personality and Social Psychology, 57,* 1069–1081.

Ryff, C. D., & Keyes, C. L. M. (1995). The structure of psychological well-being revisited. *Journal of Personality and Social Psychology, 57,* 1069–1081.

Saccuzzo, D. P., & Ingram, R. E. (1993). *Growth through choice: The psychology of personal adjustment.* New York: Harcourt Brace Jovanovich.

Sahraian, A., Gholami, A., Javadpour, A., & Omidvar, B. (2013). Association between religiosity and happiness among a group of Muslim undergraduate students. *Journal of Religion and Health, 52,* 450–453.

Sajatovic, M., Sanders, R., Alexeenko, L., & Madhusoodanan, S. (2010). Primary prevention of psychiatric illness in special populations. *Annals of Clinical Psychiatry, 22,* 262–273.

Sakade, F. (1958). Momotaro. In F. Sakade (Ed.), *Japanese children's favorite stories.* Rutland, VT: Tuttle.

Salkind, N., (2004). *An introduction to theories of human development.* Thousand Oaks, CA: SAGE.

Salovey, P., & Mayer, J. D. (1990). Emotional intelligence. *Imagination, Cognition, and Personality, 9,* 185–211.

Salovey, P., Mayer, J. D., & Caruso, D. (2002). The positive psychology of emotional intelligence. In C. R. Snyder & S. J. Lopez (Eds.), *The handbook of positive psychology* (pp. 159–171). New York: Oxford University Press.

Sameroff, A. J., Lewis, M., & Miller, S. M. (2000). *Handbook of developmental psychopathology.* New York: Plenum.

Sandage, S., Hill, P. C., & Vang, H. C. (2003). Toward a multicultural positive psychology: Indigenous forgiveness and Hmong culture. *The Counseling Psychologist, 31,* 564–592.

Sandage, S. J., Hill, P. C., & Vaubel, D. C. (2011). Generativity, relational spirituality, gratitude, and mental health: Relationships and pathways. *International Journal for the Psychology of Religion, 21,* 1–16.

Sanders, M. R., Markie-Dadds, C., & Turner, K. M. T. (2003). Theoretical, scientific and clinical foundations of the Triple P-Positive Parenting Program: A population approach to the promotion of parenting competence. *Parenting Research and Practice, 1,* 1–21.

Sanders, M. R., Mazzucchelli, T. G., & Studman, L. (2004). Stepping Stones Triple P—An evidence-based positive parenting program for families with a child who has a disability: Its theoretical basis and development. *Journal of Intellectual and Developmental Disability, 29,* 1–19.

Sanders, M. R., & Turner, K. M. T. (2005). Reflections on the challenges of effective dissemination of behavioural family intervention: Our experience with the Triple P-Positive Parenting Program. *Child and Adolescent Mental Health, 10,* 158–169.

Sangharakshita. (1991). *The three jewels: An introduction to Buddhism.* Glasgow, UK: Windhorse.

Santiago, C. D., Kaltman, S., & Miranda, J. (2013). Poverty and mental health: How do low-income adults and children fare in psychotherapy?. *Journal of Clinical Psychology, 69,* 115–126.

Saphire-Bernstein, S., Way, B. M., Kim, H. S., Sherman, D. K, & Taylor, S. E. (2013). Oxytocin receptor gene (OXTR) is related to psychological resources. *PNAS: Proceedings of the National Academy of Sciences of the United States of America, 108,* 15118–15122.

Sarafino, E. (2002). *Health psychology* (4th ed.). New York: Wiley.

Sarason, S. B. (1974). *The psychological sense of community: Prospects for a community psychology.* San Francisco: Jossey-Bass.

Saroglou, V. (2012). Is religion not prosocial at all? Comment on Galen (2012). *Psychological Bulletin, 138,* 907–912.

Saroglou, V., Buxant, C., & Tilquin, J. (2008). Positive emotions as leading to religion and spirituality. *Journal of Positive Psychology, 3,* 165–173. doi: 10.1080/17439760801998737

Satterfield, J. (2000). Optimism, culture, and history: The roles of explanatory style, integrative complexity, and pessimistic rumination. In J. Gillham (Ed.), *The science of optimism and hope* (pp. 349–378). Philadelphia: Templeton Foundation Press.

Saulsberry, A., Corden, M. E., Taylor-Crawford, K., Crawford, T. J., Johnson, M., Froemel, J.,…Van Voorhees, B. W. (2013). Chicago Urban Resiliency Building (CURB): An internet-based depression-prevention intervention for urban African American and Latino adolescents. *Journal of Child and Family Studies, 22,* 150–160.

Sawtelle, V., Brewe, E., & Kramer, L. H. (2012). Exploring the relationship between self-efficacy and retention in introductory physics. *Journal of Research in Science Teaching, 49,* 1096–1121.

Sayle, M. (1998). Japan's social crisis. *Atlantic Monthly, 281,* 84–94.

Schachter, S. (1951). Deviation, rejection, and communication. *Journal of Abnormal and Social Psychology, 46,* 190–207.

Schauber, A. C. (2001). Effecting extension organizational change toward cultural diversity: A conceptual framework. *Journal of Extension, 39,* 12–15.

Scheibe, S., Freund, A. M., & Baltes, P. B. (2007). Toward a developmental psychology of *Sehnsucht* (life longings): The optimal (utopian) life. *Developmental Psychology, 43,* 778–795.

Scheibe, S., Kunzmann, U., & Baltes, P. B. (2009). New territories of positive life-span development: Wisdom and life longings. In S. J. Lopez & C. R. Snyder (Eds.), *Oxford handbook of positive psychology* (pp. 171–183). New York: Oxford University Press.

Scheier, M. F., & Carver, C. S. (1985). Optimism, coping, and health: Assessment and implications of generalized outcome expectancies. *Health Psychology, 4,* 219–247.

Scheier, M. F., & Carver, C. S. (2001). Adapting to cancer: The importance of hope and purpose. In A. Baum & B. L. Anderson (Eds.), *Psychosocial interventions for cancer* (pp. 15–36). Washington, DC: American Psychological Association.

Scheier, M. F., Carver, C. S., & Bridges, M. W. (1994). Distinguishing optimism from neuroticism (and trait anxiety, self-mastery, and self-esteem): A reevaluation of the Life Orientation Test. *Journal of Personality and Social Psychology, 67,* 1063–1078.

Scheier, M. F., Carver, C. S., & Bridges, M. W. (2001). Optimism, pessimism, and psychological well-being. In E. C. Chang (Ed.), *Optimism & pessimism: Implications for theory, research, and practice* (pp. 189–216). Washington, DC: American Psychological Association.

Scheier, M. F., Weintraub, J. K., & Carver, C. S. (1986). Coping with stress: Divergent strategies of optimists and pessimists. *Journal of Personality and Social Psychology, 51,* 1257–1264.

Schimmel, S. (2000). Vices, virtues, and sources of human strength in historical perspective. *Journal of Social and Clinical Psychology, 19,* 137–150.

Schleien, S., Ross, H., & Ross, M. (2010). Young children's apologies to their siblings. *Social Development, 19,* 170–186.

Schmidt, F. L., & Rader, M. (1999). Exploring the boundary conditions for interview validity: Meta-analytic findings for a new interview type. *Personnel Psychology, 52,* 445–464.

Schmidt, N. B., & Koselka, M. (2000). Gender differences in patients with panic disorder: Evaluating cognitive mediation of phobic avoidance. *Cognitive Therapy and Research, 24,* 531–548.

Schmitt, D. P., Youn, G., Bond, B., Brooks, S., Frye, H., Johnson, S., . . . Stoka, C. (2009). When will I feel love? The effects of culture, personality, and gender on the psychological tendency to love. *Journal of Research in Personality, 43,* 830–846. doi: 10.1016/j.jrp.2009.05.008

Schneider, S. L. (2001). In search of realistic optimism: Meaning, knowledge, and warm fuzziness. *American Psychologist, 56,* 250–263.

Schneiderman, I., Zilberstein-Kra, Y., Leckman, J. F., & Feldman, R. (2011). Love alters autonomic reactivity to emotions. *Emotion, 11,* 1314–1321.

Schor, J. B. (1991). *The overworked American: The unexpected decline of leisure.* New York: Basic Books.

Schore, A. N. (1994). *Affect regulation and the origin of the self: The neurobiology of emotional development.* Hillsdale, NJ: Lawrence Erlbaum.

Schore, A. N. (2003). *Affect regulation and the repair of the self.* New York: Norton.

Schulman, P., Keith, D., & Seligman, M. E. P. (1993). Is optimism heritable? A study of twins. *Behaviour Research and Therapy, 31,* 569–574.

Schumann, H. W. (1974). *Buddhism.* Wheaton, IL: Theosophical.

Schur, E. M. (1969). Reactions to deviance: A critical assessment. *American Journal of Sociology, 75,* 309–322.

Schure, M. B., Christopher, J., & Christopher, S. (2008). Mind–body medicine and the art of self-care: Teaching mindfulness to counseling students through yoga, meditation, and qigong. *Journal of Counseling & Development, 86,* 47–56.

Schutte, N. S., Malouff, J. M., Hall, L. E., Haggerty, D. J., Copper, J. T., Golden, C. J., & Domheim, L. (1998). Development and validation of emotional intelligence. *Personality and Individual Differences, 25,* 167–177.

Schwartz, S. H. (1994). Beyond individualism and collectivism: New cultural dimensions of values. In U. Kim, H. C. Triandis, C. Kagitcibasi, S.-C. Choi, & G. Yoon (Eds.), *Individualism and collectivism: Theory, method, and applications* (pp. 85–122). Thousand Oaks, CA: Sage.

Schwarzer, R., & Renner, B. (2000). Social-cognitive predictors of health behavior: Action self-efficacy and coping self-efficacy. *Health Psychology, 19,* 487–495.

Schweizer, K., & Koch, W. (2001). The assessment of components of optimism by POSO-E. *Personality and Individualism, 31,* 563–574.

Seeman, T. E. (1996). Social ties and health: The benefits of social integration. *Annals of Epidemiology, 6,* 442–451.

Segal, Z. V., Williams, J. M. G., & Teasdale, J. D. (2002). *Mindfulness-based cognitive therapy for depression: A new approach to preventing relapse.* New York: Guilford Press.

Segerstrom, S. C. (2006). How does optimism suppress immunity? Evaluation of three affective pathways. *Health Psychology, 25,* 653–657. doi: 10.1037/0278-6133.25.5.653

Segerstrom, S. C., & Sephton, S. E. (2010). Optimistic expectancies and cell-mediated immunity: The role of positive affect. *Psychological Science, 21,* 448–455.

Seligman, M. E. P. (1991). *Learned optimism.* New York: Knopf.

Seligman, M. E. P. (1994). *What you can change and what you can't.* New York: Knopf.

Seligman, M. E. P. (1995). The effectiveness of psychotherapy: The *Consumer Reports* study. *American Psychologist, 50,* 965–974.

Seligman, M. E. P. (1998a). Building human strength: Psychology's forgotten mission. *APA Monitor, 29*(1), 2.

Seligman, M. E. P. (1998b/2006). *Learned optimism: How to change your mind and your life* (2nd ed.). New York: Pocket Books.

Seligman, M. E. P. (1998c). Positive social science. *APA Monitor, 29*(4), 2, 5.

Seligman, M. E. P. (1998d). The gifted and the extraordinary. *APA Monitor, 29*(11), 2–3.

Seligman, M. E. P. (1998e). Work, love, and play. *APA Monitor, 29,* 2. Retrieved from www.apa.org/monitor/aug98/pc.html

Seligman, M. E. P. (2002). *Authentic happiness: Using the new positive psychology to realize your potential for lasting fulfillment.* New York: Free Press.

Seligman, M. E. P., Abramson, L. Y., Semmel, A., & von Baeyer, C. (1979). Depressive attributional style. *Journal of Abnormal Psychology, 88,* 242–247.

Seligman, M. E. P., & Csikszentmihalyi, M. (2000). Positive psychology: An introduction. *American Psychologist, 55,* 5–14.

Seligman, M. E. P., Kaslow, N. J., Alloy, L. B., Peterson, C., Tanenbaum, R., & Abramson, L. Y. (1984). Attributional style and depressive symptoms among children. *Journal of Abnormal Psychology, 93,* 235–238.

Seligman, M. E. P., Nolen-Hoeksema, S., Thornton, N., & Thornton, K. M. (1990). Explanatory style as a mechanism of disappointing athletic performance. *Psychological Science, 1,* 143–146.

Seligman, M. E. P., Reivich, K., Jaycox, L., & Gillham, J. (1995). *The optimistic child.* New York: Houghton Mifflin.

Seligman, M. E. P., & Schulman, P. (1986). Explanatory style as a predictor of performance as a life insurance agent. *Journal of Personality and Social Psychology, 50,* 832–838.

Seligman, M. E. P., Steen, T. A., Park, N., & Peterson, C. (2005). Positive psychology progress: Empirical validation of interventions. *American Psychologist, 60,* 410–421.

Sellers, R. M., Copeland-Linder, N., Martin, P. P., & Lewis, R. L. (2006). Racial identity matters: The relationship between racial discrimination and psychological functioning in African American adolescents. *Journal of Research on Adolescence, 16,* 187–216.

Selye, H. (1936). A syndrome produced by diverse nocuous agents. *Nature, 138,* 32.

Sengupta, N. K., Osborne, D., Houkamau, C. A., Hoverd, W., Wilson, M., Halliday, L. M., . . . Sibley, C. G. (2012). How much happiness does money buy? Income and subjective well-being in New Zealand. *New Zealand Journal of Psychology, 41,* 21–34.

Seuss, Dr. (1961). *Sneetches and other stories.* New York: Random House Books for Young Readers.

Shafranske, E. P., & Malony, H. N. (1990). Clinical psychologists' religious and spiritual orientations and their practices of psychotherapy. *Psychotherapy: Theory, Research, Practice, Training, 27,* 72–78.

Shah, P. (2012). Toward a neurobiology of unrealistic optimism. *Frontiers in Psychology, 3,* 344.

Shapiro, D. A., & Shapiro, D. (1982). Meta-analysis of comparative therapy outcome studies. *Psychological Bulletin, 92,* 581–604.

Shapiro, D. H. (1980). *Meditation: Self-regulation strategy and altered state of consciousness.* New York: Aldine.

Shapiro, S. L. (2009). The integration of mindfulness and psychology. *Journal of Clinical Psychology, 65,* 555–560.

Shapiro, S. L., & Schwartz, G. E. (2000). The role of intention in self-regulation: Toward intentional systemic mindfulness. In M. Boekaerts, P. R. Pintrich, & M. Zeidner (Eds.), *Handbook of self-regulation* (pp. 253–273). New York: Academic Press.

Shapiro, S. L., Schwartz, G. E. R., & Bonner, G. (1998). The effects of mindfulness-based stress reduction on medical and pre-medical students. *Journal of Behavioral Medicine, 21,* 581–599.

Shapiro, S. L., Schwartz, G. E. R., & Santerre, C. (2002). Meditation and positive psychology. In C. R. Snyder & S. J. Lopez (Eds.), *The handbook of positive psychology* (pp. 632–645). New York: Oxford University Press.

Sharma, S., Biswal, R., Deller, J., & Mandal, M. K. (2009). Emotional intelligence: Factorial structure and construct validity across cultures. *International Journal of Cross Cultural Management, 9,* 217–236.

Sharot, T., Korn, C. W., & Dolan, R. J. (2011). How unrealistic optimism is maintained in the face of reality. *Nature Neuroscience, 14,* 1475–1479.

Shaver, P., Hazan, C., & Bradshaw, D. (1988). Love as attachment. In R. J. Sternberg & M. L. Barnes (Eds.), *The psychology of love* (pp. 68–99). New Haven, CT: Yale University Press.

Shaver, P. R., & Mikulincer, M. (2006). Attachment theory, individual psychodynamics, and relationship functioning. In A. L. Vangelisti & D. Perlman (Eds.), *The Cambridge handbook of personal relationships* (pp. 251–271). Cambridge, England: Cambridge University Press.

Shaw, W. S., Patterson, T. L., Semple, S. J., Grant, I., Yu, E. S. H., Zhang, M. Y.,...Wu, W. Y. (1997). A cross-cultural validation of coping strategies and their associations with caregiving distress. *The Gerontologist, 37,* 490–504.

Sheldon, K. M., & Lyubomirsky, S. (2004). Achieving sustainable new happiness: Prospects, practices, and prescriptions. In P. A. Linley & S. Joseph (Eds.), *Positive psychology in practice* (pp. 127–145). Hoboken, NJ: Wiley.

Shelp, E. E. (1984). Courage: A neglected virtue in the patient–physician relationship. *Social Science and Medicine, 18*(4), 351–360.

Sherer, M., Maddux, J. E., Mercandante, B., Prentice-Dunn, S., Jacobs, B., & Rogers, R. (1982). The self-efficacy scale: Construction and validation. *Psychological Reports, 51,* 663–671.

Sherry, J. L. (2004). Flow and media enjoyment. *Communication Theory, 14,* 328–347.

Sheu H.-B. (2014). Affective well-being viewed through a lens of race and ethnicity. In J. T. Pedrotti & L. M. Edwards (Eds.), *Perspectives on the intersection of multiculturalism and positive psychology*. New York: Springer Science + Business Media.

Shin, Y., & Kelly, K. R. (2013). Cross-cultural comparison of the effects of optimism, intrinsic motivation, and family relations on vocational identity. *The Career Department Quarterly, 61,* 141–160.

Shiota, M. N., Campos, B., Gonzaga, G. C., Keltner, D., & Peng, K. (2010). I love you but...: Cultural differences in complexity of emotional experiences during interaction with a romantic partner. *Cognition and Emotion, 24,* 786–799.

Shiota, M. N., Keltner, D., & John, O. P. (2006). Positive emotion dispositions differentially associated with Big Five personality and attachment style. *Journal of Positive Psychology. 1,* 61–71. doi: 10.1080/17439760 500510833

Shmotkin, D. (1998). Declarative and differential aspects of subjective well-being and implications for mental health in later life. In J. Lomranz (Ed.), *Handbook of aging and mental health: An integrative approach* (pp. 15–43). New York: Plenum.

Shmotkin, D. (2005). Happiness in the face of adversity: Reformulating the dynamic and modular bases of subjective well-being. *General Psychology Review, 9,* 291–325.

Shorey, H. S., Snyder, C. R., Yang, X., & Lewin, M. R. (2003). The role of hope as a mediator in recollecting parenting, adult attachment, and mental health. *Journal of Social and Clinical Psychology, 22,* 685–715.

Shure, M. B. (1974). Training children to solve interpersonal problems: A preventive mental health program. In R. F. Munoz, L. R. Snowden, & J. G. Kelly (Eds.), *Social and psychological research in community settings* (pp. 30–68). San Francisco: Jossey-Bass.

Shure, M. B., & Spivak, G. (1988). Interpersonal cognitive problem solving. In R. H. Price, E. L. Cowen, R. P. Lorion, & J. Ramos-McKay (Eds.), *Fourteen ounces of prevention: A casebook for practitioners* (pp. 69–82). Washington, DC: American Psychological Association.

Siegel, D. J. (1999). *The developing mind: Toward a neurobiology of interpersonal experience.* New York: Guilford Press.

Silberman, S. W. (1995). The relationship among love, marital satisfaction, and duration of marriage. *Dissertation Abstracts, 56,* 2341.

Simmel, G. (1950). *The sociology of Georg Simmel.* Glencoe, IL: Free Press.

Simonton, D. K., & Baumeister, R. F. (2005). Positive psychology at the summit. *Review of General Psychology, 9,* 99–102.

Sin, N. L., & Lyubomirsky, S. (2009). Enhancing well-being and alleviating depressive symptoms with positive psychology interventions: A practice-friendly meta-analysis. *Journal of Clinical Psychology, 65,* 467–487.

Singer, I. (1984a). *The nature of love: Vol. 1. Plato to Luther* (2nd ed.). Chicago: University of Chicago Press.

Singer, I. (1984b). *The nature of love: Vol. 2. Courtly and romantic.* Chicago: University of Chicago Press.

Singer, I. (1987). *The nature of love: Vol. 3. The modern world.* Chicago: University of Chicago Press.

Singh, K., & Choubiasa, R. (2010). Empirical Validation in Action-Inventory of Strengths (VIA-IS) in Indian context. *Psychological Studies, 55,* 151–158.

Skinner, E. A. (1995). *Perceived control, motivation, and coping.* Thousand Oaks, CA: Sage.

Skog, J. (2003, March 3). Beach man named nation's happiest. *The Virginian-Pilot,* p. A1.

Smith, A. (1976). *The theory of moral sentiments* (6th ed.). Oxford, England: Clarendon Press. (Original work published 1790)

Smith, B., & Rutigliano, T. (2003). *Discover your sales strengths: How the world's greatest salespeople develop winning careers.* New York: Warner Books.

Smith, C. A. (1991). The self, appraisal, and coping. In C. R. Snyder & D. R. Forsyth (Eds.), *Handbook of social and clinical psychology: The health*

perspective (pp. 116–137). New York: Pergamon Press.

Smith, J., & Baltes, P. B. (1990). Wisdom-related knowledge: Age/cohort in response to life planning problems. *Developmental Psychology, 26,* 494–505.

Smith, J., Staudinger, U., & Baltes, P. B. (1994). Occupational settings facilitating wisdom-related knowledge: The sample case of clinical psychologists. *Journal of Consulting and Clinical Psychology, 66,* 989–999.

Smith, K. D., Türk-Smith, S., & Christopher, J. C. (1998, August). *Prototypes of the ideal person in seven cultures.* Paper presented at the International Congress of the International Association for Cross-Cultural Psychologists, Bellingham, WA.

Smith, M. L., Glass, G. V., & Miller, T. I. (1980). *The benefits of psychotherapy.* Baltimore: Johns Hopkins University Press.

Smith, R. (1987). *Unemployment and health: A disaster and a challenge.* Oxford, England: Oxford University Press.

Smith, T. W., Pope, M. K., Rhodewalt, F., & Poulton, J. L. (1989). Optimism, neuroticism, coping, and symptom reports: An alternative interpretation of the Life Orientation Test. *Journal of Personality and Social Psychology, 56,* 640–648.

Snyder, C. R. (1989). Reality negotiation: From excuses to hope and beyond. *Journal of Social and Clinical Psychology, 8,* 130–157.

Snyder, C. R. (1992). Product scarcity by need for uniqueness interaction: A consumer catch-22? *Basic and Applied Social Psychology, 13,* 9–24.

Snyder, C. R. (1994/2000). *The psychology of hope: You can get there from here.* New York: Free Press.

Snyder, C. R. (1997). Unique invulnerability: A classroom demonstration in estimating personal mortality. *Teaching of Psychology, 24,* 197–199.

Snyder, C. R. (2000a). Genesis: The birth and growth of hope. In C. R. Snyder (Ed.), *Handbook of hope: Theory, measures, and applications* (pp. 25–38). San Diego, CA: Academic Press.

Snyder, C. R. (Ed.). (2000b). *Handbook of hope: Theory, measures, and applications.* San Diego, CA: Academic Press.

Snyder, C. R. (2000c). The past and the possible futures of hope. *Journal of Social and Clinical Psychology, 19,* 11–28.

Snyder, C. R. (2002a). Hope theory: Rainbows of the mind. *Psychological Inquiry, 13,* 249–275.

Snyder, C. R. (2002b). Part 2—The application, interview, and negotiation stages of obtaining a position in clinical psychology. *The Clinical Psychologist, 56,* 19–25.

Snyder, C. R. (2003, November). *Forgiveness and hope.* Paper presented at the International Campaign for Forgiveness Conference, Atlanta, GA.

Snyder, C. R. (2004a). *Measuring hope in American businesses.* Unpublished manuscript, University of Kansas, Lawrence.

Snyder, C. R. (2004b, November). *Hope and spirituality.* International Society for Quality of Life Studies Conference, Philadelphia.

Snyder, C. R. (2004c, December 17). Graceful attitude eases adversity. *Lawrence Journal-World,* p. D4.

Snyder, C. R. (2005a). Teaching: The lessons of hope. *Journal of Social and Clinical Psychology, 24,* 72–83.

Snyder, C. R. (2005b). Closing thoughts on teaching and teachers: Our roles in presenting self-referential course content to students. *Journal of Social and Clinical Psychology, 24,* 123–128.

Snyder, C. R., & Elliott, T. R. (2005). 21st-century graduate education in clinical psychology: A four-level matrix model. *Journal of Clinical Psychology, 61,* 1033–1054.

Snyder, C. R., & Feldman, D. (2000). Hope for the many: An empowering social agenda. In C. R. Snyder (Ed.), *Handbook of hope: Theory, measures, and applications* (pp. 389–412). San Diego, CA: Academic Press.

Snyder, C. R., Feldman, D. B., Taylor, J. D., Schroeder, L. L., & Adams, V., III (2000). The roles of hopeful thinking in preventing problems and promoting strengths. *Applied & Preventive Psychology: Current Scientific Perspectives, 15,* 262–295.

Snyder, C. R., & Fromkin, H. L. (1977). Abnormality as a positive characteristic: The development and validation of a scale measuring need for uniqueness. *Journal of Abnormal Psychology, 86*(5), 518–527.

Snyder, C. R., & Fromkin, H. L. (1980). *Uniqueness: The human pursuit of difference.* New York: Plenum.

Snyder, C. R., Harris, C., Anderson, J. R., Holleran, S. A., Irving, L. M., Sigmon, S. T., . . . Wu, W. Y. (1991). The will and the ways: Development and validation of an individual-differences measure of hope. *Journal of Personality and Social Psychology, 60,* 570–585.

Snyder, C. R., & Higgins, R. L. (1997). Reality negotiation: Governing one's self and being governed by others. *General Psychology Review, 4,* 336–350.

Snyder, C. R., Higgins, R. L., & Stucky, R. J. (1983/2005). *Excuses: Masquerades in search of grace.* New York: Wiley Interscience. Republished 2005 by Percheron Press, Clinton Corners, NY.

Snyder, C. R., Hoza, B., Pelham, W. E., Rapoff, M., Ware, L., Danovsky, M., . . . Stahl, K. J. (1997). The development and validation of the Children's Hope Scale. *Journal of Pediatric Psychology, 22,* 399–421.

Snyder, C. R., Ilardi, S. S., Cheavens, J., Michael, S. T., Yamhure, L., & Sympson, S. (2000). The role of hope in cognitive behavior therapies. *Cognitive Therapy and Research, 24,* 747–762.

Snyder, C. R., Ilardi, S., Michael, S., & Cheavens, J. (2000). Hope theory: Updating a common process for psychological change. In C. R. Snyder & R. E. Ingram (Eds.), *Handbook of psychological change: Psychotherapy processes and practices for the 21st century* (pp. 128–153). New York: Wiley.

Snyder, C. R., & Ingram, R. E. (1983). "Company motivates the miserable": The impact of consensus upon help-seeking for psychological problems. *Journal of Personality and Social Psychology, 45,* 1118–1126.

Snyder, C. R., & Ingram, R. E. (Eds.). (2000a). *Handbook of psychological change: Psychotherapy processes and practices for the 21st century.* New York: Wiley.

Snyder, C. R., & Ingram, R. E. (2000b). Psychotherapy: Questions for an evolving field. In C. R. Snyder & R. E. Ingram (Eds.), *Handbook of psychological change: Psychotherapy processes and practices for the 21st century* (pp. 707–726). New York: Wiley.

Snyder, C. R., LaPointe, A. B., Crowson, J. J., Jr., & Early, S. (1998). Preferences of high-and low-hope people for self-referential input. *Cognition & Emotion, 12,* 807–823.

Snyder, C. R., & Lopez, S. J. (Eds.). (2002). *The handbook of positive psychology.* New York: Oxford University Press.

Snyder, C. R., Lopez, S. J., Edwards, L. M., Pedrotti, J. T., Prosser, E. C., Larue-Walton, S., . . . Ulven, J. C. (2003). *Measuring and labeling the positive and the negative. Positive psychological assessment: A handbook of models and measures* (pp. 21–40). Washington, DC: American Psychological Association.

Snyder, C. R., McDermott, D., Cook, W., & Rapoff, M. (2002). *Hope for the journey: Helping children through the good times and the bad* (Rev. ed.). Clinton Corners, NY: Percheron Press.

Snyder, C. R., Omens, A. E., & Bloom, L. J. (1977, April). *Signature size and personality: Some truth in graphology?* Paper presented at the Southwestern Psychological Association Convention, Dallas, TX.

Snyder, C. R., Parenteau, S., Shorey, H. S., Kahle, K. E., & Berg, C. (2002). Hope as the underlying process in Gestalt and other psychotherapy approaches. *International Gestalt Therapy Journal, 25,* 11–29.

Snyder, C. R., & Pulvers, K. (2001). Dr. Seuss, the coping machine, and "Oh, the places you will go." In Snyder, C. R. (Ed.), *Coping and copers: Adaptive processes and people* (pp. 3–19). New York: Oxford University Press.

Snyder, C. R., Rand, K., King, E., Feldman, D., & Taylor, J. (2002). "False" hope. *Journal of Clinical Psychology, 58,* 1003–1022.

Snyder, C. R., Ritschel, L. A., Rand, K. L., & Berg, C. J. (2006). Balancing psychological assessments: Including strengths and hope in client reports. *Journal of Clinical Psychology, 62,* 33–46.

Snyder, C. R., & Shorey, H. (2002). Hope in the classroom: The role of positive psychology in academic achievement and psychology curriculum. *Psychology Teacher Network, 12,* 1–9.

Snyder, C. R., & Shorey, H. (2004). Hope and leadership. In G. Goethals, G. J. Sorenson, & J. M. Burns (Eds.), *Encyclopedia of leadership* (pp. 673–675). Thousand Oaks, CA: Sage.

Snyder, C. R., Shorey, H., Cheavens, J., Pulvers, K. M., Adams, V. H., III, & Wiklund, C. (2002). Hope and academic success in college. *Journal of Educational Psychology, 94,* 820–826.

Snyder, C. R., Sympson, S. C., Ybasco, F. C., Borders, T. F., Babyak, M. A., & Higgins, R. L. (1996). Development and validation of the State Hope Scale. *Journal of Personality and Social Psychology, 2,* 321–335.

Snyder, C. R., Tennen, H., Affleck, G., & Cheavens, J. (2000). Social, personality, clinical, and health psychology tributaries: The merging of a scholarly "river of dreams." *Personality and Social Psychology Review, 4,* 16–29.

Snyder, C. R., Thompson, L. Y., & Heinze, L. (2003). The hopeful ones. In G. Keinan (Ed.), *Between stress and hope* (pp. 57–80). Westport, CT: Greenwood.

Sobczak, L. R., & West, L. M. (2013). Clinical considerations in using mindfulness- and acceptance-based approaches with diverse populations: Addressing challenges in service delivery in diverse community settings. *Cognitive and Behavioral Practice, 20,* 13–22.

Sohl, S. J., Moyer, A., Lukin, K., & Knapp-Oliver, S. K. (2011). Why are optimists optimistic? *Individual Differences Research, 9,* 1–11.

Soldier, L. L. (1992). *Working with Native American children.* Unpublished manuscript, College of Education, Texas Tech University, Lubbock (National Association for the Education of Young Children at http://www.enc.org/features/ focus/ archive/multi/document.shtm? input = ACQ-111 362–1362).

Solberg Nes, L., & Segerstrom, S. C. (2006). Dispositional optimism and coping: A meta-analytic review. *Personality and Social Psychology Review, 10,* 235–251.

Solomon, L. D. (2006). *From Athens to America: Virtues and formulation of public policy.* New York: Lexington.

Soothill, W. E. (1968). *The analects of Confucius.* New York: Paragon.

Spears-Brown, C., & Chu, H. (2012). Discrimination, ethnic identity, and academic outcomes of Mexican immigrant children: The importance of school context. *Child Development, 83,* 1477–1485.

Spencer-Rodgers, J., Peng, K., & Wang, L. (2010). Dialecticism and the co-occurrence of positive and negative emotions across cultures. *Journal of Cross-Cultural Psychology, 41,* 109–115.

Spivak, G., & Shure, M. B. (1974). *Social adjustment of young children*. San Francisco: Jossey-Bass.

Sprecher, S., & Fehr, B. (2010). Dispositional attachment and relationship-specific attachment as predictors of compassionate love for a partner. *Journal of Social and Personal Relationships, 28,* 558–574.

Staats, S. R. (1989). Hope: A comparison of two self-report measures for adults. *Journal of Personality Assessment, 53,* 366–375.

Stahl, J. M. (2005). Research is for everyone: Perspectives from teaching at historically Black colleges and universities. *Journal of Social and Clinical Psychology, 24,* 84–95.

Stajkovic, A. D., & Luthans, F. (1998). Self-efficacy and work-related performance: A meta-analysis. *Psychological Bulletin, 124,* 240–261.

Stanton, A. L., Danoff-Burg, S., Cameron, C. L., Bishop, M., Collins, C. A., Kirk, S. B., . . . Twillman, R. (2000). Emotionally expressive coping predicts psychological and physical adjustment to breast cancer. *Journal of Consulting and Clinical Psychology, 68*(5), 875–882.

Stanton, A. L., Danoff-Burg, S., Cameron, C. L., & Ellis, A. P. (1994). Coping through emotional approach: Problems of conceptualization and confounding. *Journal of Personality and Social Psychology, 66*(2), 350–362.

Stanton, A. L., Danoff-Burg, S., & Huggins, M. E. (2002). The first year after breast cancer diagnosis: Hope and coping strategies as predictors of adjustment. *Psycho Oncology, 11*(2), 93–102.

Stanton, A. L., Kirk, S. B., Cameron, C. L., & Danoff-Burg, S. (2000). Coping through emotional approach: Scale construction and validation. *Journal of Personality and Social Psychology, 78*(6), 1150–1169.

Stanton, A. L., Parsa, A., & Austenfeld, J. L. (2002). The adaptive potential of coping through emotional approach. In C. R. Snyder & S. J. Lopez (Eds.), *The handbook of positive psychology* (pp. 148–158). New York: Oxford University Press.

Stanton, A. L., Sullivan, S. J., & Austenfeld, J. L. (2009). Coping through emotional approach: Emerging evidence for the utility of processing and expressing emotions in responding to stressors. In S. J. Lopez & C. R. Snyder (Eds.), *Oxford handbook of positive psychology*. (pp. 225–235). New York: Oxford University Press.

Staudinger, U. (1999). Older and wiser? Integrating results from a psychological approach to study of wisdom. *International Journal of Behavioral Development, 23,* 641–664.

Staudinger, U., & Baltes, P. B. (1994). Psychology of wisdom. In R. J. Sternberg (Ed.), *Encyclopedia of human intelligence* (Vol. 2, pp. 143–152). New York: Macmillan.

Staudinger, U., & Baltes, P. B. (1996). Interactive minds: A facilitative setting for wisdom-related performance? *Journal of Personality and Social Psychology, 71,* 746–762.

Staudinger, U., & Leipold, B. (2003). The assessment of wisdom-related performance. In S. J. Lopez & C. R. Snyder (Eds.), *Positive psychological assessment: A handbook of models and measures* (pp. 171–184). Washington, DC: American Psychological Association.

Staudinger, U., Smith, J., & Baltes, P. B. (1992). Wisdom-related knowledge in a life-review task: Age differences and the role of professional specialization. *Psychology and Aging, 7,* 271–281.

Stavrova, O., Fetchenhauer, D., & Schlösser, T. (2013). Why are religious people happy? The effect of the social norm of religiosity across countries. *Social Science Research, 42,* 90–105.

Steffen, P. R. (2012). Approaching religiosity/spirituality and health from the Eudaimonic perspective. *Social and Personality Psychology Compass, 6,* 70–82.

Steger, M. F., & Kashdan, T. B. (2013). The unbearable lightness of meaning: Well-being and unstable meaning in life. *Journal of Positive Psychology, 8,* 103–115.

Stein, M. (1989). Gratitude and attitude: A note on emotional welfare. *Social Psychology Quarterly, 52,* 242–248.

Steiner, M., Allemand, M., & McCullough, M. E. (2011). Age differences in forgivingness: The role of transgression frequency and intensity. *Journal of Research in Personality, 45,* 670–678.

Steiner, M., Allemand, M., & McCullough, M. E. (2012). Do agreeableness and neuroticism explain age differences in the tendency to forgive others?

Personality and Social Psychology Bulletin, 38, 441–453.

Sternberg, R. (1985). Implicit theories of intelligence, creativity, and wisdom. *Journal of Personality and Social Psychology, 49,* 607–627.

Sternberg, R. (1990). *Wisdom: Its nature, origins, and development.* New York: Cambridge University Press.

Sternberg, R. (1998). A balance theory of wisdom. *Review of General Psychology, 2,* 347–365.

Sternberg, R. J. (1986). A triangular theory of love. *Psychological Review, 93,* 119–135.

Sternberg, R. J. (1998). *Love is a story: A new theory of relationships.* New York: Oxford University Press.

Sternberg, R. J. (2012). Intelligence in its cultural context. In M. J. Gelfand, C. Ciu, & Y. Hong (Eds.), *Advances in culture and psychology* (pp. 205–248). New York: Oxford University Press.

Sternberg, R. J., & Hojjat, M. (1997). *Satisfaction in close relationships.* New York: Guilford Press.

Stevens, V., Hornbrook, M., Wingfield, D., Hollis, J., Greenlick, M., & Ory, M. (1992). Design and implementation of a falls prevention intervention for community-dwelling older persons. *Behavior, Health and Aging, 2,* 57–73.

Stevenson, L., & Haberman, D. L. (1998). *Ten theories of human nature.* New York: Oxford University Press.

Stewart, E. C. (1972). *American cultural patterns: A cross-cultural perspective.* Yarmouth, ME: Intercultural Press.

Stickney, L. T. (2010). Who benefits from Pennebaker's expressive writing? More research recommendations: A commentary on Range and Jenkins. *Sex Roles, 63,* 165–172.

Stocks, E. L., Lishner, D. A., & Decker, S. K. (2009). Altruism or psychological escape: Why does empathy promote prosocial behavior? *European Journal of Social Psychology, 39,* 649–665. doi: 10.1002/ejsp.561

Stotland, E. (1969). *The psychology of hope.* San Francisco: Jossey-Bass.

Strecher, V. J., Champion, V. L., & Rosenstock, I. M. (1997). The health belief model and health behavior. In D. Gochman (Ed.), *Handbook of health behavior research 1: Personal and social determinants* (pp. 71–92). New York: Plenum.

Strelan, P. (2007). Who forgives others, themselves, and situations? The roles of narcissism, guilt, self-esteem, and agreeableness. *Personality and Individual Differences, 42,* 259–269.

Strom, S. (2009, August 27). Volunteering waning in recession, report says. *The New York Times.* Retrieved from http://www.nytimes.com/2009/08/27/us/27volunteer.html?_r = 0

Strupp, H. H. (1964). *A bibliography of research in psychotherapy.* Private Circulation.

Stumblingbear-Riddle, G., & Romans, J. C. (2012). Resilience among urban American Indian adolescents: Exploration into the role of culture, self-esteem, subjective well-being, and social support. *American Indian and Alaska Native Mental Health Research, 19,* 1–19.

Stuss, D. T., & Benson, D. S. (1984). Neuropsychological studies of frontal lobes. *Psychological Bulletin, 95,* 3–28.

Subkoviak, M. J., Enright, R. D., Wu, C. R., Gassin, E. A., Freedman, S., Olson, L. M., & Sarinopoulos, I. (1995). Measuring interpersonal forgiveness in late adolescence and middle childhood. *Journal of Adolescence, 18,* 641–655.

Sue, D. W., & Constantine, M. G. (2003). Optimal human functioning in people of color in the United States. In W. B. Walsh (Ed.), *Counseling psychology and optimal human functioning* (pp. 151–169). Mahwah, NJ: Lawrence Erlbaum.

Sue, D. W., & Sue, D. (2003). *Counseling the culturally diverse: Theory and practice* (4th ed.). New York: Wiley.

Sue, D. W., & Sue, D. (2012). *Counseling the culturally diverse: Theory and practice* (6th ed.). New York: Wiley.

Sue, S. (1998). In search of cultural competence in psychotherapy and counseling. *American Psychologist, 53,* 440–448.

Suh, E. M., & Koo, J. (2008). Comparing subjective well-being across cultures and nations: The "what" and "why" questions. In M. Eid & R. J. Larsen (Eds.), *The science of subjective well-being* (pp. 414–427). New York: Guilford Press.

Super, D. E., & Knasel, E. G. (1981). Career development in adulthood: Some theoretical problems and a possible solution. *British Journal of Guidance and Counselling, 9,* 194–201.

Swanson, J. L., & Gore, P. A., Jr. (2000). Advances in vocational psychology theory and research. In S. D. Brown & R. W. Lent (Eds.), *Handbook of counseling psychology* (3rd ed., pp. 233–269). New York: Wiley.

Szagun, G. (1992). Age-related changes in children's understanding of courage. *Journal of Genetic Psychology, 153,* 405–420.

Szagun, G., & Schauble, M. (1997). Children's and adults' understanding of the feeling experience of courage. *Cognition and Emotion, 11*(3), 291–306.

Szapocznik, J., Scopetta, M. A., & King, O. E. (1978). Theory and practice in matching treatment to the special characteristics and problems of Cuban immigrants. *Journal of Community Psychology, 6,* 112–122.

Szcześniak, M., & Soares, E. (2011). Are proneness to forgive, optimism, and gratitude associated with life satisfaction? *Polish Psychological Bulletin, 42,* 20–23.

Szendre, E. N., & Jose, J. E. (1996). Telephone support by elderly volunteers to inner-city children. *Journal of Community Psychology, 24,* 87–96.

Tabak, B. A., McCullough, M. E., Luna, L. R., Bono, G., & Berry, J. W. (2012). Conciliatory gestures facilitate forgiveness and feelings of friendship by making transgressors appear more agreeable. *Journal of Personality, 80,* 503–536.

Takahashi, M. (2000). Toward a culturally inclusive understanding of wisdom: Historical roots in the east and west. *International Journal of Aging and Human Development, 51,* 217–230.

Takahashi, M., & Overton, W. F. (2005). Cultural foundations of wisdom: An integrated developmental approach. In R. J. Sternberg & J. Jordan (Eds.), *A handbook of wisdom: Psychological perspectives* (pp. 32–60). New York: Cambridge University Press.

Takaku, S. (2001). The effects of apology and perspective taking on interpersonal forgiveness: A dissonance–attribution model of interpersonal forgiveness. *The Journal of Social Psychology, 141,* 494–508.

Tang, Y., & Posner, M. I. (2013). Tools of the trade: Theory and method in mindfulness neuroscience. *Social Cognitive and Affective Neuroscience, 8,* 118–120.

Tangney, J. P., Boone, A. L., & Dearing, R. (2005). Forgiving the self: Conceptual issues and empirical findings. In E. Worthington (Ed.), *Handbook of forgiveness* (pp. 143–158). New York: Routledge.

Tangney, J. P., Fee, R., Reinsmith, C., Boone, A. L., & Lee, N. (1999, August). *Assessing individual differences in the propensity to forgive.* Paper presented at the American Psychological Association Convention, Boston.

Tatar, M. (2002). *The annotated classic fairy tales.* New York: W. W. Norton.

Tatli, A. (2011). A multi-layered exploration of the diversity management field: Diversity discourses, practices, and practitioners in the UK. *British Journal of Management, 22,* 238–253.

Tauber, M. (2010, January 25). She saved Anne Frank's words. *People,* 111.

Taylor, R. D., Budescu, M., & McGill, R. (2011). Demanding kin relations and depressive symptoms among low-income African American women: Mediating effects of self-esteem and optimism. *Cultural Diversity and Ethnic Minority Psychology, 17,* 303–308.

Taylor, S. E., Dickerson, S. S., & Klein, L. C. (2002). Toward a biology of social support. In C. R. Snyder & S. J. Lopez (Eds.), *The handbook of positive psychology* (pp. 556–572). New York: Oxford University Press.

Taylor, S. E., Kemeny, M. E., Aspinwall, L. G., Schneider, S. G., Rodriguez, R., & Herbert, M. (1992). Optimism, coping, psychological distress, and high-risk sexual behavior among men at risk for acquired immunodeficiency syndrome (AIDS). *Journal of Personality and Social Psychology, 63,* 460–473.

Taylor, Z. E., Larsen-Rife, D., Conger, R. D., Widaman, K. F., & Cutrona, C. E. (2010). Life stress, maternal optimism, and adolescent competence in single mother, African American families. *Journal of Family Psychology, 24,* 468–477.

Teasdale, J. D., Segal, Z. V., Williams, J. M. G., Ridgeway, V. A., Soulsby, J. M., & Lau, M. A. (2000). Prevention of relapse/recurrence in major depression by mindfulness-based cognitive therapy. *Journal of Consulting and Clinical Psychology, 68,* 615–623.

Tellegen, A., Lykken, D. T., Bouchard, T. J., Wilcox, K. J., Segal, N. L., & Rich, S. (1988). Personality similarity in twins reared apart and together. *Journal of Personality and Social Psychology, 54,* 1031–1039.

Teresa, J. S. (1991). *Increasing self-efficacy for careers in young adults from migrant farmworker backgrounds.* (Unpublished doctoral dissertation). Washington State University, Pullman.

Terman, L. M., & Oden, M. H. (1947). *The gifted child grows up: Twenty five years' follow-up of a superior group.* Stanford, CA: Stanford University Press.

Tetrick, L. E., & Peiró, J. M. (2012). Occupational safety and health. In S. W. J. Kozlowski (Ed.), *The Oxford handbook of organizational psychology* (Vol. 2, pp. 1228–1244). New York: Oxford University Press.

Thatcher, A., Wretschko, G., & Fridjhon, P. (2008). Online flow experiences, problematic internet use and internet procrastination. *Computers in Human Behavior, 24,* 2236–2254.

Thomas, D. C. (2006). Domain and development of cultural intelligence. *Group & Organizational Management, 31,* 78–99. doi: 10.1177/1059 601105275266

Thomas, J. L., Britt, T. W., Odle-Dusseau, H., & Bliese, P. D. (2011). Dispositional optimism buffers combat veterans from the negative effects of warzone stress on mental health symptoms and work impairment. *Journal of Clinical Psychology, 67,* 866–880.

Thomas, R. R. (1990). From affirmative action to affirming diversity. *Harvard Business Review, 68,* 107–117.

Thompson, L. W. (1996). Cognitive–behavioral therapy and treatment for late-life depression. *Journal of Clinical Psychiatry, 57*(Suppl. 5), 29–37.

Thompson, L. W., Gallagher, D., & Lovett, S. (1992). Increasing life satisfaction: Class leaders' and participant manuals (rev.). Palo Alto, CA: Dept. of Veterans Affairs Medical Center and Stanford University.

Thompson, L. Y., Snyder, C. R., Hoffman, L., Michael, S. T., Rasmussen, H. N., Billings, L. S., . . . Roberts, D. E. (2005). Dispositional forgiveness of self, others, and situations: The Heartland Forgiveness Scale. *Journal of Personality, 73,* 313–359.

Thompson, M. G., & Heller, K. (1990). Facets of support related to well-being: Quantitative social isolation and perceived family support in a sample of elderly women. *Psychology and Aging, 5,* 535–544.

Thoresen, C. E., Harris, A. H. S., & Oman, D. (2001). Spirituality, religion, and health: Evidence, issues, and concerns. In T. G. Plante & A. C. Sherman (Eds.), *Faith and health: Psychological perspectives* (pp. 15–52). New York: Guilford Press.

Tierney, J. P., & Grossman, J. B. (2000). *Making a difference: An impact study of Big Brothers/Big Sisters.* Philadelphia: Public/Private Ventures.

Tiller, W. A., McCraty, R., & Atkinson, M. (1996). Cardiac coherence: A new, noninvasive measure of autonomic nervous system order. *Alternative Therapies in Health and Medicine, 2,* 52–65.

Tillich, P. (1980). *The courage to be.* New Haven & London: Yale University Press.

Ting-Toomey, S. (1994). Managing intercultural conflict in intercultural personal relationships. In D. D. Cahn (Ed.), *Intimate conflict in personal relationships* (pp. 47–77). Hillsdale, NJ: Lawrence Erlbaum.

Tipton, R. M., & Worthington, E. L. (1984). The measurement of generalized self-efficacy: A study of construct validity. *Journal of Personality Assessment, 48,* 545–548.

Toepfer, S. M., Cichy, K., & Peters, P. (2012). Letters of gratitude: Further evidence for author benefits. *Journal of Happiness Studies, 13,* 187–201.

Tomlinson, J. M., & Aron, A. (2013). The positive psychology of romantic love. In M. Hojjat & D. Cramer (Eds.), *Positive psychology of love* (pp. 3–15). New York: Oxford University Press.

Tong, E. W., Fredrickson, B. L., Chang, W., & Lim, Z. (2010). Re-examining hope: The roles of agency thinking and pathways thinking. *Cognition and Emotion, 24,* 1207–1215.

Toussaint, L. L., Owen, A. D., & Cheadle, A. (2012). Forgive to live: Forgiveness, health, and longevity. *Journal of Behavioral Medicine, 35,* 375–386.

Triandis, H. C. (1988). Collectivism v. individualism: A reconceptualization of a basic concept in cross-cultural social psychology. In G. K. Verma

& C. Bagley (Eds.), *Cross-cultural studies of personality, attitudes and cognition* (pp. 6–95). London: MacMillan.

Triandis, H. C. (1990). Cross-cultural studies of individualism and collectivism. In J. Berman (Ed.), *Nebraska Symposium on Motivation* (pp. 41–133). Lincoln: University of Nebraska Press.

Triandis, H. C. (1995). *Individualism and collectivism.* Boulder, CO: Westview Press.

Triandis, H. C., Brislin, R., & Hui, C. H. (1988). Cross-cultural training across the individualism–collectivism divide. *International Journal of Intercultural Relations, 12,* 269–289.

Trimble, J. E. (1976). Value differences among American Indians: Concerns for the concerned counselor. In P. Pederson, W. J. Lonner, & J. G. Graguns (Eds.), *Counseling across cultures* (pp. 65–81). Honolulu: University of Hawaii Press.

Trivers, R. L. (1971). The evolution of reciprocal altruism. *Quarterly Review of Biology, 46,* 35–57.

Trump, M. R. (1997). The impact of hopeful narratives on state hope, state self-esteem, and state positive and negative affect for adult female survivors of incest. *Dissertation Abstracts International, 58*(4A), 1211.

Tsang, J.-A., Schulwitz, A., & Carlisle, R. D. (2012). An experimental test of the relationship between religion and gratitude. *Psychology of Religion and Spirituality, 4,* 40–55.

Twenge, J., & King, L. A. (2003). *A good life is a good personal life: Relationship fulfillment and work fulfillment in judgments of life quality.* Unpublished manuscript, University of Missouri, Columbia.

Uchida, Y., Norasakkunkit, V., & Kitayama, S. (2004). Cultural considerations of happiness: Theory and empirical evidence. *Journal of Happiness Studies, 5,* 223–239.

Unger, J. B., McAvay, G., Bruce, M. L., Berkman, L., & Seeman, T. (1999). Variation in the impact of social network characteristics on physical functioning in elderly persons: MacArthur Studies of Successful Aging. *Journals of Gerontology, 54,* 245–251.

Urry, H. L., Nitschke, J. B., Dolski, I., Jackson, D. C., Dalton, K. M., Mueller, C. J.,...Davidson, R. J. (2004). Making a life worth living: Neural correlates of well-being. *Psychological Science, 15,* 367–372.

USA Today. (2009, July 10). Four-day workweek creates new volunteers in Utah. *USA Today.* Retrieved from http://usatoday30.usatoday.com/news/nation/2009-07-10-utah-volunteers_N.htm?csp=15

U.S. Bureau of Labor Statistics. (2012). Employment status of mothers with own children under 3 years old by single year of age of youngest child and marital status, 2011–2012 annual averages. Retrieved from http://www.bls.gov/news.release/famee.t06.htm

U.S. Census Board. (2010). Overview of race and Hispanic origin: 2010. Retrieved from http://www.census.gov/prod/cen2010/briefs/c2010br-02.pdf

U.S. Department of Education. (2011). Our future, our teachers: The Obama administration's plan for teacher education reform and improvement. Retrieved from http://www.ed.gov/sites/default/files/our-future-our-teachers.pdf

U.S. Department of Health and Human Services. (1998). *Suicide: A report of the surgeon general.* Rockville, MD: Author.

U.S. Department of Health and Human Services. (1999). *Mental health: A report of the surgeon general.* Rockville, MD: Author.

U.S. Department of Health and Human Services. (2001). *Mental health: Culture, race, ethnicity,* supplement to *Mental health: Report of the surgeon general* (Inventory number SMA 01–3613). Rockville, MD: Author.

U.S. Department of Health and Human Services. (2013). *Key features of the Affordable Care Act.* Retrieved from http://www.hhs.gov/healthcare/facts/timeline/index.html

Utsey, S., Hook, J., Fischer, N., & Belvet, B. (2008). Cultural orientation, ego resilience, and optimism as predictors of subjective well-being in African Americans. *Journal of Positive Psychology, 3,* 202–210. doi: 10.1080/17439760801999610

Vaillant, G. (1994). "Successful aging" and psychosocial well-being: Evidence from a 45-year study. In E. H. Thompson (Ed.), *Older men's lives: Research on men and masculinities series* (pp. 22–41). Thousand Oaks, CA: Sage.

Vaillant, G. E. (1977). *Adaptation to life*. New York: Little, Brown.

Vaillant, G. E. (2002). *Aging well: Surprising guideposts to a happier life from the landmark Harvard Study of Adult Development*. New York: Little, Brown.

Vandello, J. A., & Cohen, D. (1999). Patterns of individualism and collectivism across the United States. *Journal of Personality and Social Psychology, 77*, 279–292.

Van der Zee, K. I., & Van Oudenhoven, J. R. (2000). The Multicultural Personality Questionnaire: A multidimensional instrument of multicultural effectiveness. *European Journal of Personality, 14*, 291–309.

Vargas, J. H., & Kemmelmeier, M. (2013). Ethnicity and contemporary American culture: A meta-analytic investigation of horizontal–vertical individualism–collectivism. *Journal of Cross-Cultural Psychology, 44*, 195–222.

Vassar, M., & Bradley, G. (2010). A reliability generalization study of coefficient alpha for the Life Orientation Test. *Journal of Personality Assessment, 92*, 362–370.

Veroff, J. B., Douvan, E., & Kulka, R. A. (1981). *The inner American: A self-portrait from 1957 to 1976*. New York: Basic Books.

Versey, S. H., & Newton, N. J. (2013). Generativity and productive pursuits: Pathways to successful aging in late midlife African American and White women. *Journal of Adult Development, 20*(4), 185–196.

Vessey, G. N. A. (1967). Volition. In P. Edwards (Ed.), *Encyclopedia of philosophy* (Vol. 8). New York: Macmillan.

Vessey, J. T., & Howard, K. I. (1993). Who seeks psychotherapy? *Psychotherapy, 30*, 546–553.

Vignoles, V. L. (2009). The motive for distinctiveness: A universal, but flexible human need. In S. J. Lopez & C. R. Snyder (Eds.), *Oxford handbook of positive psychology*. (pp. 491–499). New York: Oxford University Press.

Visser, M. R., & Roelofs, M. R. (2011). Heterogeneous preferences for altruism: Gender and personality, social status, giving and taking. *Experimental Economics, 14*, 490–506.

Visser, P. L., Loess, P., Jeglic, E. L., & Hirsch, J. K. (2013). Hope as a moderator of negative life events and depressive symptoms in a diverse sample. *Stress and Health: Journal of the International Society for the Investigation of Stress, 29*, 82–88.

Voiskounsky, A. E. (2010). Internet addiction in the context of positive psychology. *Psychology in Russia: State of the Art, 35*, 541–549.

Voss, M., Nylen, L., Floderus, B., Diderichsen, F., & Terry, P. (2004). Unemployment and early cause-specific mortality: A study based on the Swedish twin registry. *American Journal of Public Health, 94*, 2155–2161.

Wade, N. G. (2010). Introduction to the special issue on forgiveness in therapy. *Journal of Mental Health Counseling, 32*, 1–4.

Walker, L. J., & Hennig, K. H. (2004). Differing conceptions of moral exemplarity: Just, brave, and caring. *Journal of Personality and Social Psychology, 86*, 629–647.

Walker, L. J., & Pitts, R. C. (1998). Naturalistic conceptions of moral maturity. *Developmental Psychology, 34*, 403–419.

Wallach, M. A., & Wallach, L. (1983). *Psychology's sanction for selfishness: The error of egoism in theory and therapy*. San Francisco: Freeman.

Walsh, R. (2012). Wisdom: An integral view. *Journal of Integral Theory and Practice, 7*, 1–21.

Walsh, R. N. (1983). Meditation practice and research. *Journal of Humanistic Psychology, 23*, 18–50.

Wampold, B. E. (2011). Psychotherapy is effective and here's why. *APA Monitor, 42*, 14.

Wampold, B. E. (2013). The good, the bad, and the ugly: A 50-year perspective on the outcome problem. *Psychotherapy, 50*, 16–24.

Wang, M., & Gordon, E. (Eds.). (1994). *Risk and resilience in inner-city America: Challenges and prospects*. Hillsdale, NJ: Lawrence Erlbaum.

Wang, Y., Davidson, M. M., Yakushko, O. F., Savoy, H. B., Tan, J. A., & Bleier, J. K. (2003). The scale of ethnocultural empathy: Development, validation, and reliability. *Journal of Counseling Psychology, 50*, 221–234.

Wang, M., & Wong, M. C. S. (2013, February). Happiness and leisure across countries: Evidence from international survey data. *Journal of Happiness Studies, 15*(1), 85–118.

Wang, Y., Xin, T., Liu, X., Zhang, Y., Lu, H., & Zhai, Y. (2012). Mindfulness can reduce automatic responding: Evidences from Stroop task and prospective memory task. *Acta Psychologica Sinica, 44,* 1180–1188.

Warr, P. (1999). Well-being and the workplace. In D. Kahneman, E. Diener, & N. Schwartz (Eds.), *Well-being: The foundations of hedonic psychology* (pp. 393–412). New York: Russell Sage.

Waterman, A. S. (1993). Two conceptions of happiness: Contrasts of personal expressiveness (eudaemonia) and hedonic enjoyment. *Journal of Personality and Social Psychology, 64,* 678–691.

Watkins, D. A., Hui, E. K. P., Luo, W., Regmi, M., Worthington, E. L., Jr., Hook, J. N., & Davis, D. E. (2011). Forgiveness and interpersonal relationships: A Nepalese investigation. *The Journal of Social Psychology, 151,* 150–161.

Watkins, P. C., Cruz, L., Holben, H., & Kolts, R. L. (2008). Taking care of business? Grateful processing of unpleasant memories. *Journal of Positive Psychology, 3,* 87–99. doi: 10.1080/17 439760701760567

Watkins, P. C., Grimm, D. L., & Hailu, L. (1998, June). *Counting your blessings: Grateful individuals recall more positive memories.* Paper presented at the American Psychological Society Convention, Denver, CO.

Watson, D. (1988). The vicissitudes of mood measurement: Effects of varying descriptors, time frames, and response formats on measures of positive and negative affect. *Journal of Personality and Social Psychology, 55,* 128–141.

Watson, D. (2000). *Mood and temperament.* New York: Guilford Press.

Watson, D. (2002). Positive affectivity: The disposition to experience pleasurable emotional states. In C. R. Snyder & S. J. Lopez (Eds.), *The handbook of positive psychology* (pp. 106–119). New York: Oxford University Press.

Watson, D., & Clark, L. A. (1994). *The PANAS-X: Manual for the Positive and Negative Affect Schedule-Expanded Form.* Unpublished manuscript, University of Iowa, Iowa City.

Watson, D., Clark, L., & Tellegen, A. (1988). Development and validation of brief measures of positive and negative affect: The PANAS scales. *Journal of Personality and Social Psychology, 54,* 1063–1070.

Watson, M., & Ecken, L. (2003). *Learning to trust: Transforming difficult elementary classrooms through developmental discipline.* San Francisco: Jossey-Bass.

Watson, M., & Naragon, K. (2009). Positive affectivity: The disposition to experience positive emotional states. In S. J. Lopez & C. R. Snyder (Eds.), *Oxford handbook of positive psychology* (pp. 207–215). New York: Oxford University Press.

Webster, J. D. (2010). Wisdom and positive psychological values in young adulthood. *Journal of Adult Development, 17,* 70–80.

Weir, K., & Duveen, G. (1981). Further development and validation of the Prosocial Behavior Questionnaire for use by teachers. *Journal of Child Psychology and Psychiatry, 22,* 357–374.

Weissberg, R. P., Barton, H. A., & Shriver, T. P. (1997). The social-competence promotion program for young adolescents. In G. W. Albee & T. P. Gullotta (Eds.), *Primary prevention works* (pp. 268–290). Thousand Oaks, CA: Sage.

Weisz, J. R., Rothbaum, R. M., & Blackburn, T. C. (1984). Standing out and standing in: The psychology of control in America and Japan. *American Psychologist, 39,* 955–969.

Weisz, J. R., Weiss, B., Alicke, M. D., & Klotz, M. L. (1987). Effectiveness of psychotherapy with children and adolescents: Meta-analytic findings for clinicians. *Journal of Consulting and Clinical Psychology, 55,* 542–549.

Wenar, C., & Kerig, P. (1999). *Developmental psychopathology.* New York: McGraw-Hill.

Werner, E. E., & Smith, R. S. (1982). *Vulnerable but invincible: A study of resilient children.* New York: McGraw-Hill.

Werner, E. E., & Smith, R. S. (1992). *Overcoming the odds: High-risk children from birth to adulthood.* Ithaca, NY: Cornell University Press.

Westburg, N. G. (2001). Hope in older women: The importance of past and current relationships. *Journal of Social and Clinical Psychology, 20,* 354–365.

Western Reform Taoism. (2003). *Our beliefs.* Retrieved from http://wrt.org

Whalen, S. (1999). Challenging play and the cultivation of talent: Lessons from the Key School's flow activities room. In N. Colangelo

& S. Assouline (Eds.), *Talent development III* (pp. 409–411). Scottsdale, AZ: Gifted Psychology Press.

Whaley, A. L., & Davis, K. E. (2007). Cultural competence and evidence-based practice in mental health services: A complementary perspective. *American Psychologist, 62,* 563–574. doi: 10.10 1037/0003-066x.62.6.563

Whelan, R., & Garavan, H. (2013, June). When optimism hurts: Inflated predictions in psychiatric neuroimaging. *Biological Psychiatry.*

White, R. W. (1959). Motivation reconsidered: The concept of competence. *Psychological Review, 66,* 297–333.

Williams, J. M. G., Russell, I., & Russell, D. (2008). Mindfulness-based cognitive therapy: Further issues in current evidence and future research. *Journal of Consulting and Clinical Psychology, 76,* 524–529.

Williams, O. F., & Houck, J. W. (1982). *The Judeo-Christian vision and the modern corporation.* Notre Dame, IN: University of Notre Dame Press.

Williams, S. L. (1995). Self-efficacy, anxiety, and phobic disorders. In J. E. Maddux (Ed.), *Self-efficacy, adaptation, and adjustment: Theory, research, and application* (pp. 69–107). New York: Plenum.

Williamson, G. M., & Christie, J. (2009). Aging well in the 21st century: Challenges and opportunities. In S. J. Lopez & C. R. Snyder (Eds.), *Oxford handbook of positive psychology* (pp. 165–169). New York: Oxford.

Williamson, G. M., Shaffer, D. R., & Parmalee, P. A. (Eds.). (2000). *Physical illness and depression in older adults: A handbook of theory, research, and practice.* New York: Plenum.

Wills, T. A., & DePaulo, B. M. (1991). Interpersonal analyses of the help-seeking process. In C. R. Snyder & D. R. Forsyth (Eds.), *Handbook of social and clinical psychology: The health perspective* (pp. 350–375). Elmsford, NY: Pergamon.

Winerman, L. (2005). Mirror neurons: The mind's mirror. *Monitor, 36,* 49–50.

Winseman, A. L., Clifton, D. O., & Liesveld, C. (2003). *Living your strengths: Discover your God-given talents, and inspire your congregation and community.* Washington, DC: Gallup Organization.

Wohl, M. J. A., & Thompson, A. (2011). A dark side to self-forgiveness: Forgiving the self and its association with chronic unhealthy behaviour. *British Journal of Social Psychology, 50,* 354–364.

Woodard, C. (2004). *Hardiness and the concept of courage.* Unpublished manuscript, The Groden Center, Providence, RI.

Woodard, C. R., & Pury, C. L. S. (2007). The construct of courage: Categorization and measurement. *Consulting Psychology Journal: Practice and Research 59,* 135–147. doi: 10.1037/10659293 .59.2.135.

Wood, A. M., Brown, G. D. A., & Maltby, J. (2011). Thanks, but I'm used to better: A relative rank model of gratitude. *Emotion, 11,* 175–180.

Wood, M. D., Britt, T. W., Wright, K. M., Thomas, J. L., & Bliese, P. D. (2012). Benefit finding at war: A matter of time. *Journal of Traumatic Stress, 25,* 307–314.

Woods, R., & Roth, A. (1996). Effectiveness of psychological interventions with older people. In A. Roth & P. Fonagy (Eds.), *What works for whom? A critical review of psychotherapy research* (pp. 321–340). New York: Guilford Press.

Woolfolk, R. L. (2002). The power of negative thinking: Truth, melancholia, and the tragic sense of life. *Journal of Theoretical & Philosophical Psychology, 22,* 19–27.

World Health Organization. (1992). *ICD 10: International statistical classification of diseases and related health problems.* Washington, DC: American Psychiatric Association.

Worrell, F. C. (2007). Ethnic identity, academic achievement, and global self-concept in four groups of academically talented adolescents. *Gifted Child Quarterly, 51,* 23–38.

Worthington, E. L., Jr. (1998). An empathy-humility-commitment model of forgiveness applied within family dyads. *Journal of Family Therapy, 20,* 59–71.

Worthington, E. L., Jr. (Ed.). (2005). *Handbook of forgiveness.* New York: Routledge.

Worthington, E. L., Jr., & Drinkard, D. T. (2000). Promoting reconciliation through psychoeducational and therapeutic interventions. *Journal of Marital and Family Therapy, 26,* 93–101.

Worthington, E. L., Jr., Hight, T. L., Ripley, J. S., Perrone, K. M., Kurusu, T. A., & Jones, D. R.

(1997). Strategic hope-focused relationship-enrichment counseling with individuals. *Journal of Counseling Psychology, 44,* 381–389.

Wright, B. A. (1988). Attitudes and fundamental negative bias. In H. E. Yuker (Ed.), *Attitudes toward persons with disabilities* (pp. 3–21). New York: Springer.

Wright, B. A. (1991). Labeling: The need for greater person–environment individuation. In C. R. Snyder & D. R. Forsyth (Eds.), *The handbook of social and clinical psychology: A health perspective* (pp. 469–487). New York: Pergamon.

Wright, B. A., & Lopez, S. J. (2002). Widening the diagnostic focus: A case for including human strengths and environmental resources. In C. R. Snyder & S. J. Lopez (Eds.), *The handbook of positive psychology* (pp. 71–87). New York: Oxford University Press.

Wright, R. (1994). *The moral animal: The new sciences of evolutionary psychology.* New York: Pantheon.

Wrzesniewski, A., McCauley, C. R., Rozin, P., & Schwartz, B. (1997). Jobs, careers, and callings: People's relations to their work. *Journal of Research in Personality, 31,* 21–33.

Wrzesniewski, A., Rozin, P., & Bennett, G. (2001). Working, playing, and eating: Making the most of most moments. In C. Keyes & J. Haidt (Eds.), *Flourishing: The positive person and the good life* (pp. 185–204). Washington, DC: American Psychological Association.

Wu, C. (2009). Factor analysis of the general self-efficacy scale and its relationship with individualism/collectivism among twenty-five countries: Application of multilevel confirmatory factor analysis. *Personality and Individual Differences. 46,* 699–703. doi: 10.1016/j.paid.2009.01.025

Wyatt-Nichol, H., & Antwi-Boasiako, K. B. (2012). Diversity management: Development, practices, and perceptions among state and local government agencies. *Public Personnel Management, 41,* 749–772.

Xing, C., & Sun, J.-M. (2013). The role of psychological resilience and positive affect in risky decision-making. *International Journal of Psychology, 48,* 935–943.

Yamaguchi, S., Kuhlman, D. M., & Sugimori, S. (1995). Personality correlates of allocentric tendencies in individualist and collectivist cultures. *Journal of Cross-Cultural Psychology, 26,* 658–672.

Yang, S. (2001). Conceptions of wisdom among Taiwanese Chinese. *Journal of Cross-Cultural Psychology, 32,* 662–680.

Yang, S. (2008). Real-life contextual manifestations of wisdom. *International Journal of Aging and Human Development, 67,* 273–303.

Yang, M.-J., & Chen, M.-H. (2011). Effect of altruism on the regulation of negative emotion. *Bulletin of Educational Psychology, 42,* 701–718.

Yoshikawa, H. (1994). Prevention as cumulative protection: Effects of early family support and education on chronic delinquency and its risks. *Psychological Bulletin, 115,* 28–54.

Young Kaelber, K. A., & Schwartz, R. C. (2014, January). Empathy and emotional intelligence among eastern and western counsellor trainees: A preliminary study. *International Journal for the Advancement of Counselling,* Online first publication.

Youssef-Morgan, C. M., & Hardy, J. (2014). A positive approach to multiculturalism and diversity management in the workplace. In J. T. Pedrotti & L. M. Edwards (Eds.), *Perspectives on the intersection of multiculturalism and positive psychology.* New York: Springer Science + Business Media.

Zahn-Wexler, C., Robinson, J., & Emde, R. N. (1992). The development of empathy in twins. *Developmental Psychology, 28,* 1038–1047.

Zalaquett, C. P., Chatters, S. J., & Ivey, A. E. (2013). Psychotherapy integration: Using a diversity-sensitive developmental model in the initial interview. *Journal of Contemporary Psychotherapy, 34,* 53–62.

Zalaquett, C. P., Fuerth, K. M., Stein, C., Ivey, A. E., & Ivey, M. B. (2008). Reframing the DSM-IV-TR from a multicultural/social justice perspective. *Journal of Counseling & Development, 86,* 364–371.

Zautra, A. J., Potter, P. T., & Reich, J. W. (1997). The independence of affect is context dependent: An integrative model of the relationship between positive and negative affect. In K. W. Schaie & M. P. Lawton (Eds.), *Annual review of gerontology and geriatrics* (Vol. 17, pp. 75–103). New York: Springer.

Zeidner, M., & Hammer, A. L. (1992). Coping with missile attack: Resources, strategies, and outcomes. *Journal of Personality, 60,* 184–199.

Zelazo, P., & Lyons, K. E. (2012). The potential benefits of mindfulness training in early childhood: A developmental social cognitive neuroscience perspective. *Child Development Perspectives, 6,* 154–160.

Zettler, I., Hilbig, B. E., & Haubrich, J. (2011). Altruism at the ballots: Predicting political attitudes and behavior. *Journal of Research in Personality, 45,* 130–133.

Zhang, X., & Cao, Q. (2010). For whom can money buy subjective well-being? The role of face consciousness. *Journal of Social and Clinical Psychology, 29,* 322–346.

Zillman, D. (1979). *Hostility and aggression.* Hillsdale, NJ: Lawrence Erlbaum.

Zimbardo, P. G. (2007). *The Lucifer Effect: Understanding how good people turn evil.* New York: Random House.

Zimbardo, P. G. (2005). Optimizing the power and magic of teaching. *Journal of Social and Clinical Psychology, 24,* 11–21.

Zimbardo, P. G., & Boyd, J. N. (1999). Putting time in perspective: A valid, reliable individual-differences metric. *Journal of Personality and Social Psychology, 77,* 1271–1288.

Zimmerman, F. J., Glew, G. M., Christakis, D. A., & Katon, W. (2005). Early cognitive stimulation, emotional support, and television watching as predictors of subsequent bullying among grade-school children. *Archives of Pediatric Adolescent Medicine, 159,* 384–388.

Zinnbauer, G. J., Pargament, K. I., Cole, B. C., Rye, M. S., Butter, E. M., Belavich, T. G., . . . Hipp, K. M. (1997). Religion and spirituality: Unfuzzying the fuzzy. *Journal for the Scientific Study of Religion, 36,* 549–564.

Zullig, K. J., Teoli, D. A., & Valois, R. F. (2011). Evaluating a brief measure of social self-efficacy among U.S. adolescents. *Psychological Reports, 109,* 907–920.

Author Index

Papierno, P. B., 30
Parenteau, S., 385
Pargament, K. I., 281, 282, 304, 305
Parham, T. A., 89
Park, H.S., 298, 299
Park, N., 65, 69, 195, 396, 397
Park, Y-S., 185
Parker, D., 238
Parks, C. D., 312
Parry, G., 383
Parsa, A., 158
Pascual-Leone, J., 229
Pasupathi, M., 121, 169, 234
Patnoe, S., 417
Patterson, D. A., 187
Patterson, T. L., 97
Patton, G. K., 426
Paulson, R. M., 171
Pauwels, B. G., 326, 338, 339, 340, 341
Pavot, W., 144
Payne, B. P., 381
Paz, R., 307
Pedersen, H., 199
Pederson, N. L., 197
Pedro, L., 198
Pedrotti, J. T., 31, 69, 88, 92, 93, 97, 99, 100, 197,
    254, 292, 310, 315, 366, 370, 373, 374
Peiró, J. M., 432
Pelham, W. E., 207
Peng, K., 30, 135, 174, 326
Pennebaker, J. W., 171, 173
Perng, S., 188
Perroud, N., 282
Perry, J. L., 401
Perry, S. K., 278
Pesonen, A.-K., 197, 198
Peters, P., 301
Peters, R. M., 159, 160
Petersen, S., 238, 239, 240, 246, 259, 260
Peterson, C., 19, 21, 23, 25, 43, 54, 62, 64, 65,
    69, 94, 120, 192, 193, 194, 195, 236, 240,
    252, 281, 282, 378, 396, 397
Peterson, M. F., 233
Peterson, P. E., 413
Pettit, G. S., 361
Petty, R. E., 165
Pham, B. T., 233
Phillips, M., 335

Phillips, V., 415
Piaget, J., 228, 232, 361
Piccard, B., 212, 395
Pickering, A., 206
Pickett, K., 188
Piedmont, R., 393
Pieper, C., 426
Pieper, J., 224
Piet, J., 269
Pieta, M. A. M., 313
Pieterse, A. L., 367
Piliavin, J. A., 291
Pines, A. M., 440
Pingel, E., 336
Pinker, S., 392
Piotrowski, N. A., 188
Piper, W., 183
Pipher, M., 235
Pirutinsky, S., 299
Pittman, K. J., 113, 117
Pitts, D., 432
Pitts, R. C., 94
Plante, T. G., 387
Plato, 237
Plomin, R., 197
Pokorny, J. J., 312
Pollack, J. M., 426
Polycarpou, M. P., 314, 315
Ponterotto, J., 99, 100, 102
Pool, L., 187
Pope, J. E., 430
Pope, K. S., 384
Pope, M. K., 198
Popovich, J. M., 203
Porter, L., 311
Posner, M. I., 270
Post, R. D., 218
Pott, M., 328
Potter, P. T., 134
Poulin, M. J., 428
Poulin de Courval, L., 382
Poulton, J. L., 198
Powers, C., 48
Pozo, C., 199
Pradel, J., 291
Pransky, G. S., 199
Prentice-Dunn, S., 187, 188
Pressgrove, C., 310

Scheier, M. F., 158, 196, 197, 198, 199, 201, 222, 402
Scheinholtz, J., 100
Scheller, V. K., 396
Schermerhorn, J. R., 434
Schimmel, S., 19
Schkade, D., 149, 150
Schleien, S., 307
Schlösser, T., 393
Schmid, K. L., 117
Schmidt, F. L., 56, 58, 426, 429, 432, 450
Schmidt, N. B., 251
Schmitt, M. T., 159, 160
Schneider, B., 415
Schneider, S. L., 365
Schneiderman, I., 347
Schofield, D. J., 379
Schor, J. B., 430
Schore, A. N., 346, 347, 348
Schroeder, D. A., 291
Schroeder, L. L., 204, 377
Schubert, C. M., 269
Schubert, T., 252, 253
Schulman, P., 193, 194, 195
Schulwitz, A., 299
Schumann, H. W., 24
Schur, E. M., 40
Schure, M. B., 271
Schutte, N. S., 162
Schutz, A., 165
Schütz, A., 165
Schuyler, T., 381
Schwartz, B., 263, 422, 429, 448
Schwartz, G. E., 266, 267, 269, 270, 394
Schwartz, N., 392
Schwartz, R. C., 165
Schwartz, S. H., 27
Schwarzer, R., 187
Schweizer, K., 198
Scollon, C. N., 144
Scopetta, M. A., 216
Scott, W., 384
Search Institute, 66, 68
Seccombe, K., 146
Sedikides, C., 333
Seeley, M. S., 381
Seeman, T. E., 121, 124, 347
Sefick, W. J., 313
Segal, N. L., 144

Segal, Z. V., 269
Segerstrom, S. C., 199, 200
Selby, E. A., 313
Seligman, M. E. P., 3, 4–5, 8, 14, 19, 21, 23, 25, 43, 54, 62, 64, 65, 69, 79, 88, 93, 94, 120, 147, 192, 193, 194, 195, 196, 200, 236, 239, 240, 252, 281, 282, 378, 381, 384, 387, 390, 392, 393, 396, 397, 418, 438, 447, 448
Sellers, R. M., 114
Sellin, I., 165
Selye, H., 133
Semmel, A., 194
Semmer, N. K., 426
Semple, S. J., 97
Sengupta, N. K., 397
Sephton, S. E., 199, 200
Serretti, A., 270, 271
Servátka, M., 292
Seuss, Dr., 369
Sexton, H., 361
Seyforth, R., 28
Shah, P., 202
Shapiro, D., 384
Shapiro, D. A., 384
Shapiro, S., 264, 265, 266, 267, 269
Shapiro, S. L., 269, 270, 394
Shapiro, W., 31
Sharkey, W. F., 28
Sharma, S., 165
Sharot, T., 194, 202
Sharp, K. L., 396
Shaver, P. R., 328, 332, 333
Shaw, W. S., 97
Shea, C., 317
Sheeber, L. B., 381
Shehan, C. L., 146
Sheldon, K. M., 143, 144, 149, 150, 151, 299, 313
Shell, R., 317
Shelp, E. E., 237, 239, 242, 245
Shelton, C. S., 300
Sherer, M., 187
Sherman, D. K., 202
Sherry, J. L., 279
Sheu, H.-B., 150
Shifren, K., 199
Shigemune, Y., 312
Shih, S., 70, 99
Shin, Y., 199

Shiota, M. N., 144, 326
Shmotkin, D., 75, 392
Shoham, V., 384
Shorey, H. S., 206, 208, 385, 415, 419,
    428, 433, 434
Shreve, T. L., 114
Shure, M. B., 381
Sibley, C. G., 397
Siebenhüner, L., 227
Siegel, D. J., 347
Siegel, T. C., 384
Siemon, L., 201
Sigmon, S. T., 92, 132, 203, 207, 209, 447
Sikes, J., 417
Sikorski, J. F., 410, 415, 419, 420, 422, 423
Silberman, S. W., 335
Simmel, G., 317, 318
Simon, T., 414
Simonton, D. K., 3
Simpkins, S. D., 114
Sims, S. T., 295
Şimşek, Ö., 165
Sin, N. L., 143
Singelis, T. M., 28
Singer, A. R., 279
Singer, I., 334
Singh, K., 70
Skillings, A., 269
Skinner, E. A., 184
Skog, J., 148, 149
Smenner, P. C., 302
Smith, A., 317
Smith, B., 436
Smith, C. A., 308
Smith, H., 75, 137
Smith, J., 226, 228, 229, 233, 234, 235
Smith, K. D., 94
Smith, M., 392
Smith, M. L., 384
Smith, R., 379
Smith, R. E., 315
Smith, R. S., 107, 108, 119
Smith, T. W., 198
Smollan, D., 330
Smoski, M. J., 264, 269
Smuts, B., 28
Snapp, M., 417
Snowdon, D. A., 125

Snyder, C. R., 7, 9, 19, 37, 40, 41, 45, 48, 92, 98,
    132, 143, 184, 194, 203, 204, 206, 207, 208,
    209, 210, 239, 262, 282, 295, 302, 305, 310,
    311, 314, 318, 322, 341, 358, 360, 369, 374,
    377, 378, 382, 383, 384, 385, 386, 387, 388,
    390, 393, 398, 399, 401, 402, 410, 415, 419,
    420, 428, 433, 434, 438, 440, 447
Snyder, D. K., 308, 309
Soares, E., 195, 313
Sobczak, L. R., 270
Socher, P., 188
Sohal, A. S., 432
Sohl, S. J., 197
Sokal, A. D., 142
Solberg Nes, L., 199
Soldier, L. L., 216
Solomon, L. D., 20, 21
Solomon, S. E., 146, 349, 350
Somerfield, M. R., 199
Song, F., 292
Sonn, C. C., 28
Soothill, W. E., 23
Soulsby, J. M., 269
Spalitto, S. V., 373
Spearman, J., 246
Spears-Brown, C., 114
Spelliscy, D., 100
Spencer-Rodgers, J., 135, 174
Spielman, L., 388
Spivak, G., 381
Sprecher, S., 327, 332, 334
Spreitzer, G. M., 451
Srivastava, K., 201
Staats, S. R., 217, 218
Stahl, J., 417
Stahl, K. J., 207
Stanton, A. L., 158, 160, 171
Staudinger, U. M., 19, 43, 125, 224, 226, 228,
    229, 230, 232, 233, 234, 235, 236, 259
Stavrova, O., 393
Stayton, D. J., 326
Steele, J. L., 414
Steen, T. A., 194, 195, 396, 397
Steffen, P. R., 282
Steger, M. F., 398
Stein, C., 366, 367
Stein, M., 302
Stein, M. B., 125

Subject Index